Wilma Jo Bush &
Kenneth W. Waugh
West Texas State University

DIAGNOSING
LEARNING PROBLEMS

Third Edition

Charles E. Merrill Publishing Company
A Bell & Howell Company
Columbus   Toronto   London   Sydney

Published by
Charles E. Merrill Publishing Company
A Bell & Howell Company
Columbus, Ohio 43216

International Standard Book Number: 0-675-09822-X
Library of Congress Catalog Card Number: 81-84795

1 2 3 4 5 6 7 8 9 10—88 87 86 85 84 83 82

Printed in the United States of America

Table of Contents

Part I. Informal Assessment

Part II. Formal Assessment

Part III. Special Education Assessment

Appendixes

Glossaries

Figures

Illustrations

Tables

Preface

All educators share a common problem: how to ensure that students learn. When students have learning problems, the challenge of effective teaching becomes even more critical. Procedures that work with the normal child fail with the handicapped learner. Thus, for learning to take place, diagnosis/assessment must pinpoint specific strengths and weaknesses to show the teacher where to begin instruction.

Diagnosing Students With Learning Problems, third edition, is written for people who will work closely with youngsters with learning problems. Specifically, it's written for the teacher, school psychologist, and counselor. It may prove a useful book for the special services personnel involved in planning educational programs for students.

This book has been designed to:
1. help identify the major learning problems
2. show how to use data in diagnosing for remediation
3. improve the understanding of the school psychologist and teacher regarding the student's learning and behavior problems
4. use case studies to show how to translate test scores and profiles into effective teaching for the child

The case studies provide examples for making diagnostic decisions and interpreting test data for a given child. The teacher should consider each of these studies carefully and how it might fit with a prescriptive teaching strategy.

Our chief change in this edition has been to include *all* handicaps: learning disabilities, mental retardation, visual and learning impairment, multiple and physical handicaps. This edition has added a manual that contains an outline of each chapter and multiple-choice questions which we have found useful in examinations of the contents.

We salute all those consultants striving to produce appropriate evaluations of the handicapped student. We also salute those teachers who have worked so diligently and patiently with handicapped children and who have made special efforts to understand these children and their problems. We hope our book will be of value to both teachers and consultants as they work to better the lives of these children.

Wilma Jo Bush
Kenneth W. Waugh

Acknowledgments

Very special thanks are extended to

Our editors who were so diplomatic and patient: Vicki Knight and Marianne Taflinger

Our typist: Mary Stephenson

Professionals who shared their ideas and works with us: Dr. Alan Kaufman, Dr. Michael Wiebe, Richard Piotrowski, and Dr. Jim Gilliam.

Colleagues and friends who supported our efforts with suggestions and encouragement: "The Firths"—Louise and Frank Rapstine; Dr. John and Millie Roberts; Claud and Inell Zevely; and Avaril Wedemeyer and Dr. Jan Lambert Koci.

Our contributing writer friends: Dr. Louis Fairchild, Dr. Louise Murphy, Claud "R" Zevely, and Jane Norris.

Our students who helped in writing the manual: Jean DiNuccio and Marilyn Mize.

Our families: Guy E. Bush; Dwight, Jo Betsy and Jason Huber; Jean Waugh; Mike, Celinda, and Denae Waugh; and Patti, Sam, and Kenny Jim Steen.

Part I

Informal Assessment

A teacher or diagnostician must become familiar with all terminology used in testing and appraisal if proficiency is to be accomplished in using techniques to determine how a child functions. Where the stage of function requires less training, this is designated as informal assessment. Part I covers these specific areas of information: (1) terminology common to all appraisal, (2) content appraisal known as criterion-referenced testing, and (3) task appraisal.

Chapter 1

Foundations of Testing

After you have studied this chapter you should be able to do the following:
1. *Identify the kinds of scores used in test interpretation and understand their meaning*
2. *Explain how a test is standardized*
3. *Understand the relationship between the norm group and the individuals being tested*
4. *Use measurement data to assist in selecting appropriate test instruments*
5. *Distinguish between validity and reliability*
6. *Develop and/or use guidelines to make test selection and interpretation more valid*

Introduction

Tests are of little value unless the results are appropriate for the purpose intended and, furthermore, the test user can make a valid interpretation of the obtained scores. Selecting an appropriate test involves much more than searching for an instrument whose name suggests it measures the skill or characteristic one desires to measure. The name of the test may be misleading and the test may not measure what it purports to measure at all. The test may be appropriately named but the scores obtained may not apply to the intended group because there is little or no similarity between the group on which it was normed and the students or clients being tested. Unless the students being tested are very similar to the students included in the norming in all important characteristics, valid inferences cannot be made.

The score obtained on a test does not interpret itself. The consultant has to make inferences from the data. How sure can one be that the score is a valid score? How well does it predict? How much can we expect it to vary from the true score? We must have answers to these questions and many others before we can make valid use of the data. The manual should provide answers to questions such as these. In addition, the test user must understand certain statistical concepts before being able to adequately interpret the data obtained from the test.

This chapter will provide information that a test user can use to interpret the factual data provided in the test manual. Formulas for figuring statistical concepts such as standard deviation and coefficient correlations will not be provided. The purpose is to provide the information that will assist in understanding and applying the concepts to test selection and interpretation; it is not to demonstrate the mathematical calculations by which they are obtained. A test user may desire this knowledge and, if so, should consult one of the hundreds of books that provide information on statistical calculations. There will be one exception, however: the authors will demonstrate how to find the standard error of measurement. Sometimes a test publisher will not provide this very important information but will provide other data from which it can be calculated. It is important that a test user be able to calculate the standard error of measurement if it is not provided and to understand its application to test interpretation.

Test users should study in detail test manuals and research data provided by the publishers. Most publishers will indicate how the test was standardized; the characteristics of the norm group; data on reliability and validity studies, standard deviation, standard error of measurement; and other data to assist in test selection and test interpretation. If a test publisher does not provide such information, there may be many reasons. It may be that little research has been done on the instrument, so little can be reported. Perhaps the research that has been done does not support the test and the publishers elect not to provide the data. There may be other reasons. A general guideline that test users may apply is, "Be cautious about using a test on which publishers have provided only limited information on standardization, norm statistics, and research data on reliability and validity." Such tests may, however, be used for research studies, since such studies may confirm that they are, in fact, good instruments.

Standardization of Tests

Standardization of tests involves a systematic procedure of test development and the subsequent administration to a defined sample of the population. This process results in a standardized procedure for administering and scoring the test and for the development of norms that are used in the interpretation of raw scores. The norms give a standard by which we can determine if a person being tested has an ability or characteristic to a greater, equal, or lesser extent than the individuals representing the population in the standardization sample. A raw score without a reference or standard for measurement is of no value. Knowing that a person scored 57 on an arithmetic test does not provide helpful information until it is compared to a norm or standard. Once we can do this we can determine the person's relative standing to individuals in the selected population.

Tests that are given to a large number of persons to determine how typical persons in the sample perform are referred to as *norm-referenced tests*. The norm provides the reference for interpretation. The norms may be stated in terms of age or grade relationships, percentiles, or various types of standard or derived scores. Each has advantages and some have some very serious limitations. Each test user must be aware of these limitations. The advantages and limitations of each type of score will be reported in the section describing the scores.

To arrive at a table of norms, the test must first be administered to a selected group of individuals who, it is thought, represent the total population of the group being studied. If it is an achievement test, it may involve thousands of students representing various geographical areas, socioeconomic levels, races, educational experiences, etc.

For other tests the numbers may be significantly less and the selection process may be much different.

The norms indicate the typical score of persons in the sample. If it is determined that normal 12-year-old females obtain a score of 57 out of 72 items, then the 12-year-old norm for females for that test is a score of 57. Other types of tests would use a similar procedure to find scores that are typical for individuals in the sample. Persons taking the test later can be referenced to the data found in the standardization.

The norm, therefore, is a scale for measurement. As such it is appropriate only for the characteristics for which it was developed. A ruler is designed to measure length and it is inappropriate to attempt to use it to measure weight. Although this is absurd, some tests and test norms have been used in equally inappropriate ways. To compare an individual to a test norm can only be valid if the individual is similar to the group used in establishing the norm. It is imperative, then, that one know precisely the population on whom the test was standardized. Suppose the norms on a verbal-ability test were obtained by testing college-bound students and your students were mentally retarded. It might be a good test to determine the verbal ability of bright students but would be of no value to measure the verbal ability of your mentally retarded students. Or suppose a social studies test were normed on culturally and experientially deprived inner-city children. One could not use the norms to measure the grade-level placement of children from an affluent neighborhood accurately. In this case all the students might exceed their regular grade placement on this test; yet on an appropriately normed test, most would probably score within the grade level where they were presently placed. It is impossible to overstress the importance of using only those tests that utilize a norm sample similar to the students or clients one wishes to test.

Norms may also be misused because of a misunderstanding of what they really mean. This is often the case with tests that use grade-equivalent norm tables. The Psychological Corporation (Test Service Notebook 34) in a question-and-answer format entitled *Some Things Parents Should Know About Testing* addresses some of the questions and concerns arising from grade-level norms:

Q. *But we usually hear about grade equivalents. What are they?*

A. A grade equivalent indicates the grade level, in years and months, for which a given score was the average or middle score in the standardization sample. For example, a score of 25 with the grade equivalent of 4.6 means that, in the norm group, 25 was the average score of pupils in the sixth month of the fourth grade. If, after the test has been standardized, another pupil in the sixth month of the fourth grade were to take the same fourth-grade test and score 25 correct, his performance would be "at grade level" or average for his grade placement. If he were to get 30 right or a grade equivalent of 5.3, he would have done as well as the typical fifth grader in the third month on that test. This does not mean that the fourth grader can do all fifth grade work. There are many things a fifth grader has learned that are not measured on a fourth-grade test. Similarly, a 3.3 grade equivalent for a third grader would mean that he is performing, on the fourth-grade test, the way the average pupil in the third month of third grade would perform on that same test. It does not suggest that he has learned only third grade material.

Although grade equivalents may sound like a simple idea, they can be easily misunderstood. For this reason, schools are increasingly coming to rely on percentile ranks and stanines as more useful ways to interpret scores in relation to a norm group. In fact, some publishers recommend that grade equivalents not be used to report to teachers, parents, pupils, or the general public.

Q. *Newspapers sometimes write about "scoring at or above the norm." What does scoring at the norm mean?*

A. Whereas the word norms is used to describe the full range of scores the norm group obtained, the term the norm refers only to the mid-point in that range. People sometimes refer to the norm as the acceptable or desirable score. This is inaccurate. On a norm-referenced test, the norm is the average score obtained by the pupils who took the test during its standardization. The norm only indicates what is average; it does not describe how good that performance is in absolute terms. Suppose a reading test were given to a large, representative, national norm group and the average score for the group was 25. The norm for that group then is 25. It must be remembered, however, that of all the pupils in the national norm group, half scored above 25 and half scored at or below 25!

When the norm is expressed as a grade equivalent, it is still describing the middle score in the norm group. If the norm group was tested in the sixth month of grade 4, the average score for the group would convert to the grade equivalent of 4.6. But note that even in that norm group, fully half of all pupils actually in the sixth month of fourth grade scored at or below that norm or "grade level." If the same test is then given to another group, it would not be surprising to find many pupils scoring "below the norm." Remember, half of the norm group itself scored at or below the norm; that's the meaning of the word.

Q. *But if a child's reading is "below the norm," that means he is a poor reader, doesn't it?*

A. Not necessarily. It probably means he is not reading as well as the average American child in his grade, assuming that the test was well standardized. But it doesn't tell you how well the average child reads. If most of the children in the norm group read "well," the norm or average represents good reading. If most children read poorly, the norm would represent "poor" reading. Whether the norm group reads well or poorly is a judgment the test cannot make. Such decisions must be made by school and parents.

Q. *But wouldn't it be worthwhile to try to teach all children to read at or above the norm?*

A. Suppose that to score at the norm on a fourth-grade test, a pupil must answer 25 questions out of 40 correctly. Then, suppose we improve the teaching of reading so that all fourth-grade children in the nation score at least 25 and many score much higher than 25. Now all children are reading "at or above the norm," right? Wrong! As the scores have changed, so has their average — the norm. If you were to standardize the test again, you might find that the middle or average score for the national norm group is now 31 out of 40. So, the norm now is 31, not 25, and half the pupils are still reading at or below the norm and half are reading above the norm. In other words, if everybody is above average, it's not the average anymore! This is the reason that the norm is not an absolute goal for everyone to attain. It is simply a statement of fact about the average of a group. If they all read better, then the norm moves higher. You've done something worthwhile, indeed, but it didn't bring everyone "up to the norm"!

The purpose of test norms is not to determine whether the student or client meets some standard or level of performance as much as it is to determine how characteristic that performance is in relation to other similar examinees. To determine the population on which the test is standardized and whether the norms provided make the test appropriate for use in specific situations, one must depend on the information provided in the manual. Some publishers provide detailed information regarding the standardization population, methods of sampling, ethnic mix, socioeconomic levels and other data to help the user make a valid decision regarding choice and use of the test. Others provide very sketchy information. The user should study the information provided in the manual very carefully before selecting a test. The *Standards for Educational and Psychological Tests and Manuals* (APA et al., 1974) provide some specific recommendations for what information should be available in the manual regarding test norms. The user should use these standards as a guide when analyzing tests and manuals for potential use.   *guidelines:*

   . . . Norms presented in the test manual should refer to defined and clearly described populations. These populations should be the groups with whom users of the test will ordinarily wish to compare the persons tested.

   . . . The test manual should report the method of sampling from the population of examinees and should discuss any probable bias in this sampling procedure.

   . . . Norms reported in any test manual should be based on well-planned samplings rather than on data collected primarily because it is readily available. Any deviations from the plan should be reported along with descriptions of actions taken or not taken with respect to them.

   . . . The description of the norms group in the test manual should be complete enough so that the user can judge its appropriateness for his use. The description should include number of cases, classified by one or more of such relevant variables as ethnic mix, socioeconomic level, age, sex, locale, and educational status. If cluster sampling is employed, the description of the norms group should state the number of separate groups tested.

   . . . The populations upon which the psychometric properties of a test were determined and for which normative data are available should be *clearly and prominently described* in the manual. Any accompanying report forms should provide space for identifying the normative groups used in interpreting the scores.

   . . . Norms on students or groups of test items should be reported in the test manual only if the validity and reliability of such subtests or groups of items are also indicated.

   . . . The significant aspects of conditions under which normative data were obtained should be reported in the test manual.

   . . . In reporting norms, test manuals should use percentiles for one or more appropriate reference groups or standard scores for which the basis is clearly set forth; any exceptional type of score or unit should be explained and justified. Measures of central tendency and variability always should be reported. . . .*

---

*From *Standards for Educational and Psychological Tests.* Copyright © 1974 by the American Psychological Association. Reprinted by permission.

Standardization involves more than the selection of appropriate test items and a representative sample for norming purposes. It also includes uniform procedures for administration and scoring of the test. Unless a test user adheres strictly to these established procedures, no valid comparison can be made between the scores obtained and the norms. Some test users may be tempted to overlook some minor deviation or to try to make some adjustment in the score to compensate for the error in administration. Neither procedure should be used. Adding information to the standardized directions will provide assistance to a student that was not available to the group that provided the standard for measurement. It is similar to adding an inch to a 12-inch measure and expecting to get valid measurements. Some may elect to mark an answer right because it is close or because they "know" what the student meant. This procedure will produce invalid scores that cannot be validated by using a standard measure. It is somewhat comparable to attempting to measure the surface of rippling water with a straight-edge ruler. Trying to adjust a score when there is a mistake in timing a test is impossible. No amount of tinkering with the invalid data is going to validate them or the score. It is still invalid.   *Timing a test is impt.*

Normal Curve and Measures of Central Tendency and Measures of Dispersion

Norm-referenced tests provide a means of comparison when a particular score is in reference to some norm or standard. The normal curve with its known characteristics is central to making this possible. An understanding of these characteristics is necessary if one is to become skilled in test interpretation.

We are not always interested in where a score falls, but, rather, where the scores tend to cluster. At other times we want to know how the scores spread, or disperse. The mean and median are statistics that tell us where scores tend to cluster; the standard deviation provides a measure that explains how they spread from the clusters or central tendencies. It is, therefore, a measure of dispersion.

Normal Curve

Whenever human characteristics, whether mental or physical, are assessed in some fashion for a large number of people, we find the characteristics to be distributed so they fit the pattern of a normal curve. A large number of people will possess the characteristic to a similar degree and very few will possess it to a much greater or lesser degree. The cases will concentrate near the mean and will decrease in frequency according to a precise mathematical formula.

Figure 1 shows a normal curve with the percentage of cases to be found at various distances from the mean. An understanding of the normal curve distribution is necessary for understanding tests and the statistical manipulations of test data for interpretation.

In the normal probability curve:
1. The curve is bilaterally symmetrical; i.e., the left and right halves are mirror images of each other.
2. The curve is highest in the middle of the distribution.
3. The limits of the curve are plus and minus infinity. (Therefore, the tails of the curve will never quite touch the baseline.)

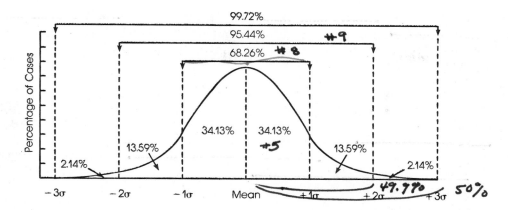

Figure 1. Percentage Distribution of Cases in a Normal Curve

4. The shape of the curve changes from convex to concave at points one standard deviation above and one below the mean.
5. 34.3 percent, or about 34 percent, of the total area under the curve lies between the mean and a point one standard deviation away. (Since area represents number of cases, about 34 percent of the examinees have scores that fall between the mean and a point one standard deviation away.)
6. 47.72 percent, or nearly 48 percent, of the area (or cases) lies between the mean and a point two standard deviations away.
7. 49.87 percent, or nearly 49.9 percent, of the area (or cases) lies between the mean and a point three standard deviations away.
8. About 68 percent of the area lies within one standard deviation (plus and minus) of the mean.
9. About 95 percent of the cases lie within two standard deviations on either side of the mean and only about one quarter of 1 percent of the cases lie beyond three standard deviations on either side of the mean.

Important concepts in test interpretation include standard deviation, standard score, and standard error of measurement. Each of these is based on the normal curve. These are discussed later in this chapter and one may desire to refer to the above characteristics of the normal curve to assist in understanding each of these concepts.

Measures of Central Tendency
Quite often it is important to use one number to characterize a set of scores or the central tendency of the distribution. The common ones used in testing are the median and the mean.

The *median* is a point that divides a distribution or a set of scores into two halves, so that one half of the scores are below the point and one half are above the point or position. The size of a score is not important, except as it places a score above or below the score next to it. As a consequence, a very high or low score has little effect on the median. It is, therefore, a good measure to use to describe the central tendency of a distribution when there are a few very high or very low scores present.

The *mean* is the arithmetic average. It is the sum of all the scores divided by the number of scores. It is an interval statistic, as compared to a position or rank statistic such as the median. The distance between scores or their values has an effect on the mean. It is the most common measure of central tendency used in standardized testing.

Measures of Dispersion

Whereas measures of central tendency provide a single most typical or representative score to characterize the performance of the entire group, measures of dispersion indicate the *variability*, or the extent of individual differences, around the central tendency. The most common measure is the *standard deviation* (S. D. or σ). It measures the dispersion of each score from the mean. In a normal curve there is an exact relationship between the standard deviation and the percentage of cases to be found, in terms of score units distances from the mean (Figure 1). Approximately two-thirds of the scores will be between plus and minus one standard deviation from the mean. It can also be observed from Figure 1 that about 95.5 percent of the scores will be ±2 standard deviations from the mean. If the mean of the test scores is 84 and the S.D. is 6, then two-thirds of the scores will be between 78 and 90 (84±6), and 95 percent will be between 72 and 96 (84±12). We can think of the S.D. as a distance along the baseline of a normal-curve graph and representing the original raw-score units.

Sometimes we want to know the percent of cases represented by a fractional part of a standard deviation. With the help of Table 1 we can do this. First note that Table 1 identifies the percent of the normal curve area for various z scores. The standard deviations along the baseline in Figure 1 can be converted to z scores by simply using the same integers with their proper signs, since standard deviations and z scores occupy identical positions along the base of the normal curve. For example +2σ has a z score of +2.0 and −1σ has a z score of −1.0.

Now suppose we desire to find the percentile rank of a z score of +1.65 (S.D. of +1.65). The percentile rank would be the percentage of cases or scores below 1.65. In Table 1 we would locate 1.60 in the z column and go across to the column headed by .05. The reading is .4505. The areas identified in Table 1 represent the total area under the normal curve bounded by the mean and the z score. Since +1.65 is to the right of the mean, we must add .4505 to .50, or the 50 percent of the cases below the mean. The sum is .95, or 95 percent. This indicates that approximately 95 percent of the scores in a normal distribution will fall below a z score or standard deviation of +1.65. The percent below a −z score can be figured similarly from the table. In this case one must subtract the value found from .50. The percent of cases below a z score of −1.2 is .50−.3849, or .1151, or 11.5 percent.

Since the S.D. measures dispersion of each score from the mean, knowing the mean and standard deviation of tests assists one in knowing something about the score intervals to expect on a test. Figure 2 indicates two distributions with the same mean but different standard deviations. The distribution with wider individual differences will yield a larger standard deviation than the one with narrower individual differences.

Scores

The raw score on any test is meaningless except as it can be related to other data for interpretation. It does not indicate one's standing within a group nor does it indicate one's ability or accomplishment on a test. It shows how many items were answered

2-scores   ## Table 1.   Normal Curve Areas

z	.00	.01	.02	.03	.04	.05	.06	.07	.08	.09
0.0	.0000	.0040	.0080	.0120	.0160	.0199	.0239	.0279	.0319	.0359
0.1	.0398	.0438	.0478	.0517	.0557	.0596	.0636	.0675	.0714	.0753
0.2	.0793	.0832	.0871	.0910	.0948	.0987	.1026	.1064	.1103	.1141
0.3	.1179	.1217	.1255	.1293	.1331	.1368	.1406	.1443	.1480	.1517
0.4	.1554	.1591	.1628	.1664	.1700	.1736	.1772	.1808	.1844	.1879
0.5	.1915	.1950	.1985	.2019	.2054	.2088	.2123	.2157	.2190	.2224
0.6	.2257	.2291	.2324	.2357	.2389	.2422	.2454	.2486	.2517	.2549
0.7	.2580	.2611	.2642	.2673	.2704	.2734	.2764	.2794	.2823	.2852
0.8	.2881	.2910	.2939	.2967	.2995	.3023	.3051	.3078	.3106	.3133
0.9	.3159	.3186	.3212	.3238	.3264	.3289	.3315	.3340	.3365	.3389
1.0	.3413	.3438	.3461	.3485	.3508	.3531	.3554	.3577	.3599	.3621
1.1	.3643	.3665	.3686	.3708	.3729	.3749	.3770	.3790	.3810	.3830
1.2	.3849	.3869	.3888	.3907	.3925	.3944	.3962	.3980	.3997	.4015
1.3	.4032	.4049	.4066	.4082	.4099	.4115	.4131	.4147	.4162	.4177
1.4	.4192	.4207	.4222	.4236	.4251	.4265	.4279	.4292	.4306	.4319
1.5	.4332	.4345	.4357	.4370	.4382	.4394	.4406	.4418	.4429	.4441
1.6	.4452	.4463	.4474	.4484	.4495	.4505	.4515	.4525	.4535	.4545
1.7	.4554	.4564	.4573	.4582	.4591	.4599	.4608	.4616	.4625	.4633
1.8	.4641	.4649	.4656	.4664	.4671	.4678	.4686	.4693	.4699	.4706
1.9	.4713	.4719	.4726	.4732	.4738	.4744	.4750	.4756	.4761	.4767
2.0	.4772	.4778	.4783	.4788	.4793	.4798	.4803	.4808	.4812	.4817
2.1	.4821	.4826	.4830	.4834	.4838	.4842	.4846	.4850	.4854	.4857
2.2	.4861	.4864	.4868	.4871	.4875	.4878	.4881	.4884	.4887	.4890
2.3	.4893	.4896	.4898	.4901	.4904	.4906	.4909	.4911	.4913	.4916
2.4	.4918	.4920	.4922	.4925	.4927	.4929	.4931	.4932	.4934	.4936
2.5	.4938	.4940	.4941	.4943	.4945	.4946	.4948	.4949	.4951	.4952
2.6	.4953	.4955	.4956	.4957	.4959	.4960	.4961	.4962	.4963	.4964
2.7	.4965	.4966	.4967	.4968	.4969	.4970	.4971	.4972	.4973	.4974
2.8	.4974	.4975	.4976	.4977	.4977	.4978	.4979	.4979	.4980	.4981
2.9	.4981	.4982	.4982	.4983	.4984	.4984	.4985	.4985	.4986	.4986
3.0	.4987	.4987	.4987	.4988	.4988	.4989	.4989	.4989	.4990	.4990

This table is reprinted by permission. From Billy L. Turner and George P. Robb, *Simplified Statistics for Education and Psychology: A Worktext With Feedback* (New York: Harper & Row Publishers, 1968).

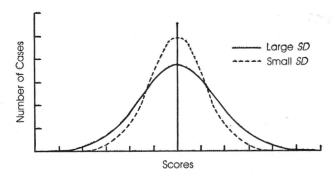

Figure 2. Frequency Distributions with the Same Mean but Different Variability

correctly; but without any idea of the difficulty of the test or how others have done on it we cannot make an adequate interpretation. The raw score must be converted into a derived score. Generally the raw score is converted to age scores, percentiles, or standard scores. Achievement tests may use grade norms, since they are used in a school setting. These derived scores will represent the test performance of the group included in the standardization of the test.

Mental Age

The *mental age* is an age-score concept originally introduced in the 1908 revision of the Binet-Simon scales. To arrive at a mental-age standard, items were administered to children at each age level. The items passed by a majority of the children at their age level became the age-level norm. A person who passed the item at the 10-year-old level, had a mental age of 10 regardless of the person's chronological age. Since an individual will pass some items that are not typical for one's age and will also fail some, a scoring procedure has to be utilized that recognizes this fact. The general procedure is to establish a *basal age level*, an age level at which all items are answered correctly; as items are passed at higher age levels, additional months of credit are added to the basal age.

An example of the use of M.A. (mental age) would be in drawing a picture of a person. If a child of 6 years and no months (chronological age or C.A. 6.0) were to draw a person, the drawing would be compared with drawings of other children of 6 years and no months. If the drawing had the same amount of detail and comparable skill to the norm, then the child would have a M.A. of 6 years and no months. If the drawing demonstrated more or less detail or more or less skill when compared to other children of 6 years and no months, the child would have a mental age above or below the age group. In summary, mental age may be thought of as the average age of individuals making an average score on the test.

There is a serious drawback to the use of the mental age, since intellectual growth does not increase in a straight-linear growth projection with age. It is very rapid at an early age and slows as one reaches adolescence and moves toward maturity. Also, other characteristics may cause the score to be misleading; e.g., a mentally defective adult with a M.A. of 6 is not equal to an average child with an M.A. of 6. To provide a more uniform interpretation the IQ, which provided a ratio of mental age to chronological age $\left(\dfrac{MA}{CA}\right)$, was introduced. The ratio was first used with the 1916 form of the Stanford-Binet. Even the ratio IQ presents problems for adequate interpretation. Unless the variability (SD) is the same at the various age levels, one cannot compare the IQs directly at the various ages. The 1937 edition of the Stanford-Binet met this requirement fairly well, but not completely. The limitations of the mental-age concept caused its replacement in the 1960 revision of the Stanford-Binet with a deviation IQ.

The age norm is not applicable where there is not a constant change with age in the characteristic being measured. When it is used, the test user must verify that the standard deviations are the same throughout the age span of the subjects covered before he can compare the results at all the age levels.

Percentiles

Percentiles are derived scores that are very popular because they can be readily understood and are applicable to any type of test and to persons of any age. Although they can be readily understood, they are sometimes confused with *percent* and, therefore, are misunderstood and misused.

A percentile has nothing to do with the percent of correct answers an examinee makes on a test. It is one of the 99 points that divide a frequency distribution into 100 groups. The scores are ranked from lowest to highest and the points on the ranking scale indicate the percent of scores or cases that fall below that point. It is commonly referred to as *percentile rank*.

A percentile of 47 indicates that the individual has a score equal to or greater than 47 percent of the students tested. One may recall that the median is the point in a score distribution indicating that 50 percent of the scores fall at or below that point. The median is, therefore, the same as the 50th percentile.

The largest single drawback to the use of the percentile in interpreting test results is the tendency to overemphasize the differences in scores near the median and to underemphasize differences near the extremes. It must be remembered that they do not show the amount of difference between scores, but just relative rank.

If we measured the height of a thousand males we would find most near the mean and median. There would be little difference in the height of those males near the median, but each is counted as one in the rank order, as are those at the extremes. At the extremes we may find differences of 3 or 4 inches between those at the 80th percentile and those at the 90th percentile but maybe only a fraction of an inch difference between the 45th and 55th percentiles. If we translate this analogy to test scores, we will realize there may be little difference in the number of right answers between individuals with percentiles of 40 and 50 but a much larger difference in the number of right answers of those between the 85th and 95th percentiles.

If we will note the distances covered by the different percentages on the baseline of Figure 3, we can easily observe that the difference between percentiles of 10 and 20, or 80 and 90, is more than the difference of percentile ranks of 40 and 50. This is always more pronounced as one moves away from the mean of a distribution. Perhaps it will help if one always remembers that the baseline represents the dispersion of the actual scores.

Grade Norms

Grade norms are traditionally used with achievement tests to describe a student's achievement level. Raw scores correspond to the typical score made by students in

Figure 3. Percentile Ranks in a Normal Distribution

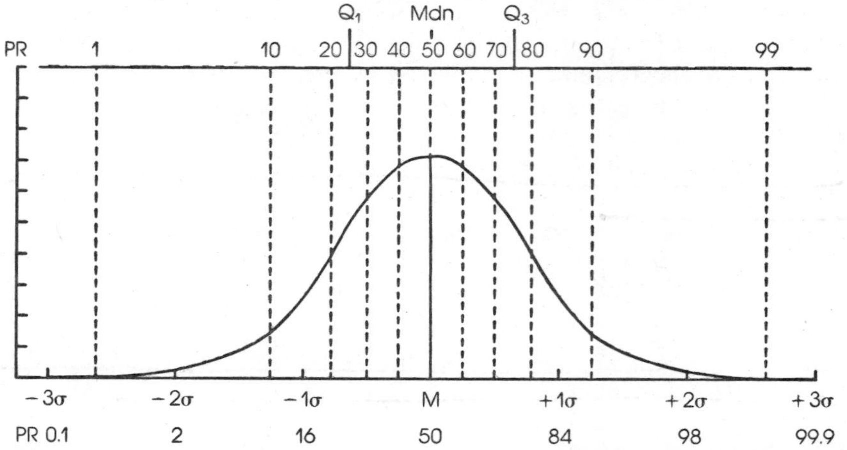

From Anne Anastasi, *Psychological Testing,* 3rd edition (New York: Macmillan, 1968), p. 59. Copyright © 1968 by Anne Anastasi.

each grade. Since there is a common core of subjects taught in the elementary school, grade norms can be applied at this level. They are inappropriate for use at the high-school level since there is not a common core of subjects taken by every student. Even when a subject such as math is required, one student may take business math and another advanced algebra to meet the requirements, so that there is not really a core common for all students.

Grade norms appear to be easy to interpret but it is their so-called simplicity that causes most problems with interpretation. An assumption is made that placement of content in each grade is consistent in every school. This, of course, is a false assumption. The tests may have content validity for one school and not another. The time certain material is taught in a grade will affect the students' test results. If particular skills and concepts are included on a fourth-grade test but are taught after the test has been administered, the children will receive a grade placement below what they would have had had the material been presented earlier in the year.

Another problem that represents a serious drawback to grade-level norms is the need to extrapolate grade levels above and below the grade level at which the test was normed. If, for example, the test is administered to fourth-grade students, the average scores for the grade are found and plotted as in Figure 4. The line is extended to show the above-average and below-average in the fourth grade. The line has to extend above 4.9 and below 4.0, because these will represent the scores of the average students. The test does not measure the skills and concepts taught in the fifth, sixth, or seventh grade, nor what the individual would have actually done if tested on the materials at these levels. Yet the extrapolation will show a fifth, sixth, or seventh grade placement. If given a test normed on sixth-grade students, the child would probably score significantly below the sixth-grade level. Parents, many teachers, and some consultants continue to give credence to the extrapolated grade placement.

One may infer that the student with an extrapolated sixth-grade-equivalent level is one who may do much better than his classmates; i.e., be able to perform the tasks more accurately, with more understanding, with more speed, etc. It is possible the individual could learn the content at a higher level but has not done so at this time. A

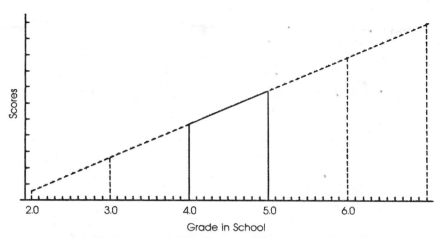

Figure 4. Fourth-Grade Grade Placements With Extrapolated Scores for Other Grades

much better reporting norm would be the percentile rank. Test users must remember the grade equivalent has less meaning the farther it varies from the student's actual grade placement.

A third significant problem with grade equivalents is the belief that all students should be at grade level. This belief fails to take into consideration the fact that to establish the norm, one-half of the students, by definition of the norm, have to fall below the grade-level norm.

A fourth problem with grade norms applies to achievement batteries. Unless the test maker has established equal or very similar standard deviations for each of the tests in the battery, the grade placement scores on the various tests are not comparable. That is, if the standard deviations are different, one cannot assume that a student with a grade placement of 4.9 in arithmetic and 5.4 in English is really a half-grade better in English. Test users should also check to see if there are similar standard deviations from age to age within the same test. Unless there is, it is not possible to make valid comparisons of students at the several age levels of the tests.

Since there seems little likelihood that misunderstandings regarding the grade-placement norm will change, we as test users should consider eliminating it as a norm measure.

Standard Scores

Standard scores provide a means of translating raw scores into derived scores, so that score differences at any place on the scale are equal to score differences at any other place on the scale. As indicated previously, percentiles do not meet this standard and, therefore, may be misinterpreted. Also, standard scores retain the same relative weight as the original scores and, therefore, can be used in calculations, as can the original scores. Percentiles are rankings and cannot be averaged or used in arithmetical calculations. Standard scores, therefore, are very important in any test research and interpretation because they represent equal units of measurement and can be manipulated mathematically.

Various terms may be used to express the standard score. It may be expressed as z score, Z score, T score, stanine, or some other standard score, as desired by the test designer. The key factors used to distinguish the various standard scores are the mean and standard deviation assigned. Do not confuse the mean of the raw-score units with the mean of the standard-score units. The standard score is a derived score based on an assumed normal curve. The base standard score from which all others come is referred to as *z score*. It is defined as a deviation from the mean expressed in terms of the standard deviation of the distribution. The formula is

$$z = \frac{\text{raw score} - \text{mean of the scores}}{\text{standard deviation}}.$$ A distribution of z scores will have a mean

of zero and a standard deviation of 1. It is simple to find the z score for any raw score by substituting in this formula. Suppose a student scored 56 on a test that had a mean for the group of 44 and a standard deviation of 10. Her z or standard score would be

$$\frac{56-44}{10} = \frac{12}{10} = 1.2.$$

Standard scores (z) have the same range as standard deviations. That is, they extend from -3 to $+3$. The negative numbers make calculations more difficult, so test makers may desire to convert the z scores to other standard scores that will not have this limitation. A popular derived standard score is the Z score. This is accomplished by multiplying the z score by 10 and adding 50. The mean of this distribution would be 50 and the standard deviation 10. The range of scores would be 20 [50−(10×3)] to 80 [50+(10×3)].

A T score has the same mean and standard deviation as a Z score. It is used when the distribution of raw scores does not fit the normal curve and the statistician desires to normalize the distribution of standard scores. This is a relatively easy procedure and persons desiring to know the process will find it explained in a measurement or statistics book.

The stanine scale has become a popular scale with test makers. The scale provides for a range of 1–9, with a mean of 5 and a S.D. of 2. The CEEB scale is representative of a standard-score scale with a much larger S.D. It has a mean of 500 and a S.D. of 100. There is less likelihood of attaching significance to an insignificant difference in scores when using a scale such as the stanine, as compared to the CEEB.

Test users may desire to set up a stanine scale when the manual does not have such a table. One can convert to stanines by assigning stanines according to percentages for each stanine, as indicated in Table 2. Percentiles 1–4 would be assigned a stanine score of 1, 5–11 as stanines of 2, and on until percentile ranks of 97–100 would be assigned a stanine of 9.

The deviation IQ is actually a standard-score scale. It is appropriate to call them IQs if they are calculated so that their mean is 100 and their standard deviation is 16 or very near to that. The IQ was first used with the Stanford-Binet and the mean on that test was 100 with a standard deviation of 16. The Wechsler scales first employed the deviation IQ. They were designed with an IQ of 100 and a S.D. of 15. Other tests of intelligence have designed scales with their mean and S.D. similar to the Stanford-Binet so their IQs

Table 2. Normal Curve Percentages for Use in Stanine Conversion

Percentage	4	7	12	17	20	17	12	7	4
Stanine	1	2	3	4	5	6	7	8	9

Table 3. Percentage of Cases at Each IQ Interval in Normal Distributions with Mean of 100 and Given Standard Deviations

IQ Interval	Percentage Frequency			
	SD = 12	SD = 14	SD = 16	SD = 18
130 and above	0.7	1.6	3.1	5.1
120–129	4.3	6.3	7.5	8.5
110–119	15.2	16.0	15.8	15.4
100–109	29.8 } 59.6	26.1 } 52.2	23.6 } 47.2	21.0 } 42.0
90–99	29.8	26.1	23.6	21.0
80–89	15.2	16.0	15.8	15.4
70–79	4.3	6.3	7.5	8.5
Below 70	0.7	1.6	3.1	5.1
Total	100.0	100.0	100.0	100.0

in terms of %'s.

Courtesy Test Department, Harcourt Brace Jovanovich, Inc.

Illustrates importance of knowing the S.D. of tests.

will be similar to the Stanford-Binet. As you recall, the 1960 revision of the Stanford-Binet changed from a ratio IQ to a deviation IQ.

Test users should check to see if the S.D. remains constant throughout the age ranges of the test. If they aren't, then IQs may vary from age to age and certain types of interpretation may be difficult. The Otis is an example of a test that failed to control the standard deviation throughout the age ranges and thereby limited its use for certain situations, since IQs are not exactly comparable at different ages.

Table 3 shows the percentage of cases at each IQ interval in a normal distribution, with a mean held constant at 100 and various standard deviations. With a S.D. of 18, over 5 percent of the students would register IQs of below 70 and over 130; with an S.D. of 12, less than 0.7 percent would obtain IQs at these two extremes. This illustrates the importance of knowing the S.D. of tests.

Various standard scores, as well as percentiles, applied to a standard distribution are identified and compared in Figure 5.

Figure 5 provides a graphic illustration of the relationship among types of test scores in a normal distribution. The standard score (z) occupies the same position on the normal curve as the standard deviation (σ). They also have the same numeric values. Likewise, one can see that standard scores may have different means and standard deviations, but they occupy the same relative positions on the normal curve. Therefore, knowing the mean and standard deviation makes it possible to compare the relative position of scores on one test with those on another. One should also note that the measure on standard scores shows equal units of measurement from the highest to the lowest, so that a similar difference in standard scores near the mean represents the same difference at the extremes of the scores. The percentile-rank measure, on the other hand, does not represent equal units of measurement. The distance between the 40th percentile and the 50th percentile is much less than the distance between the 1st and 10th percentiles. Not only can one not compare differences in whatever characteristics the test measures at different percentile ranks, but the scores cannot be used in

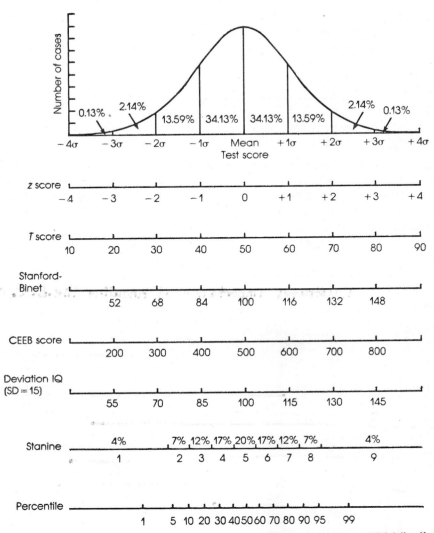

Figure 5. Relationships Among Types of Test Scores in a Normal Distribution.

mathematical analysis because they do not represent equal units. To do this, one must revert percentile scores to the raw-score units or convert them to some standard-score measure.

Correlation

One of the most useful tools for use in standardized testing is the *correlation coefficient*. It describes the degree of relationship between scores or sets of scores, or scores and some other variable. Although it describes a relationship, it does not necessarily demonstrate a casual relationship. A correlation may show that two variables have something in common but it does not establish the reason that they do. It just explains that they are related in some way.

If one can predict without error what will happen to one variable based on information on the other, there is said to be a perfect correlation, which would be expressed as a correlation of +1.0 or −1.0. It is a positive correlation if an increase in one results in an increase in the other or if a decrease in one accompanies a decrease in the other. There is a negative correlation when there is an inverse relationship: when there is a decrease in one variable there is an increase in the other or when an increase in one is accompanied by a decrease in the other.

If a prediction of one variable from another is no better than chance, the coefficient of correlation is 0.0. Rarely would we expect to obtain a coefficient of correlation of exactly +1.0, −1.0, or 0.0.

Because correlation coefficients are expressed as decimals, there is a tendency for some people to interpret them as percents. Frank B. Womer (1968) has stated:

> It is not correct to interpret a +.60 as meaning that 60 percent of the two variables are the same, or that the two variables overlap by 60 percent, or that they have 60 percent of anything in common. If one wants to interpret the relationship of two variables as a percentage overlap, as the percentage of variability that two sets of scores have in common, one can square the correlation coefficient. Thus a correlation of .60 may be interpreted as representing a 36 percent overlap between two variables, or one may say that 36 percent of the variation in one variable may be explained by the other variable. One must be cautious, however, not to take out the word "explained" and insert the word "caused".... Suppose that the correlation between a reading test and an arithmetic problem solving test is +.50. We then could say that the two tests overlapped 25 percent, that 25 percent of what goes into success on that reading test also goes into success on the arithmetic problem solving test. It might be that reading proficiency is the common element, or it might be that general intelligence is the common element, or it might be that some combination of reading proficiency and general intelligence and motivation etc. is the *cause* of the overlap."

It is difficult to determine how high a coefficient of correlation should be since it varies with circumstances. A rough guide that is generally accepted by authorities to describe the amount of relationship is as follows:

.80–1.00	very high correlation
.60– .79	substantial correlation
.40– .59	moderate correlation
.20– .39	slight correlation
0– .19	negligible correlation

A different use of correlation is in making predictions regarding one variable when the other variable is known. An example of this would be to use test data to predict school grades. A question that one may ask is "How much does a particular coefficient of correlation improve our *accuracy of prediction over chance alone?*" Table 4 provides information to help answer this question.

Table 4. Relationships of Coefficients of Correlation to Prediction

Coefficient of Correlation	Increase Prediction over Chance
.20	2%
.40	8%
.60	20%
.80	40%
.866	50%
.90	56%

Although this may seem to present a discouraging picture, one must remember this involves making predictions about an individual. Anything better than chance is an improvement. However, it does suggest that although the prediction is better than chance, one must be aware that predicting for an individual from one variable alone (e.g., one test) may be subject to much error.

Coefficients of correlation are used in reporting the reliability of tests. They are also used in reporting their validity. As will be explained later, the coefficient correlations for reliability must be much higher than for validity.

Test users should be aware of certain factors that can affect the correlation between two tests or sets of scores. In general, the greater the range of scores, the higher the correlation coefficient. That is, the more heterogeneous the group, the more chance that as one score varies the corresponding score will vary the same way. Conversely, the more the group is similar, the less the correlation coefficient. This is easily seen if we compare age and height of males. Generally, the older a boy is the taller he is, so if we correlated this relationship for boys in grade 1–6, this relationship would generally hold. If, however, we selected only one grade, say the fifth, there would be little variation in age or height and we could be less sure that this relationship existed, since two months' difference in age might not result in a consistent increase in height. If we test a very homogeneous group in ability and experiences, the test scores will cluster close together. A change of 3 or 4 raw-score points may cause the student rank to change by 20 or more percentile points. Since correlation is concerned with accuracy of rank, the farther apart the scores, the less chance for reversals in rank.

Reliability and Validity

Two terms that immediately come to mind when one is describing a test are *reliability* and *validity*. They are not the same and should not be confused. Correlation coefficients may be used to measure each, but not always. Some types of validity do not lend themselves to coefficients-of-correlation measurement. Reliability can be determined by four methods, all of which are not equally valid for every type of test. The test users must understand the ways reliability and validity are measured and the appropriateness of each method for various types of tests. Likewise, they must be cognizant of acceptable levels of reliability and validity for different uses.

Reliability

Reliability refers to the consistency of scores obtained by the same individuals when reexamined on the same test or on an equivalent form of the same test. Other terms that are frequently used to explain test reliability are "dependable", "stable", "trustworthy".

No tests will produce perfect reliability, but a test user must know the level of confidence that can be put on the test to produce the same score if it had been given at another time. This can be expressed as a coefficient of correlation, since test reliability is concerned with the degree of consistency of the relationship between two independently derived sets of scores.

Sometimes test manuals or articles reporting on research will report the significance of the correlation in terms of levels of confidence. For example, if a statement is made that the correlation is significant at the .01 or .05 level, it means that the chances are no greater than one or five out of 100 that the correlation is zero. It provides the indicated level of confidence that the reliability found did not happen by chance.

The reliability of a test that is really its correlation with itself sets a limit on anything else that it can predict. In other words, it cannot predict anything else better than it can predict itself. A test cannot, therefore, be valid unless it is first reliable. It may, on the other hand, be reliable but not valid.

These are four methods of determining reliability. As will be seen, some are more appropriate procedures under certain circumstances than others.

a. Test-retest reliability
This involves the repeating of the same test on a second occasion.

b. Split-half reliability
The test is divided into comparable halves. The usual procedure is to find separate scores for the odd and even items.

c. Alternate-form reliability
This involves developing comparable forms of the same test and administering the two separate forms to the same individuals. Alternate forms are most often developed with achievement tests.

d. Single administration and use of Kuder-Richardson formula reliability
It is based on the consistency of the subjects' responses to all items on the test.

A significant factor affecting reliability when using the test-retest procedure is the interval between the two administrations of the test. One would expect the reliability to be higher if the test interval were short, since the subjects might recall many of their former responses. Intervening practice or learning may also affect the results of the second test and, therefore, the reliability coefficient. For a number of tests the test-retest procedure is a poor procedure to establish reliability. It is a good method to use with interest tests to determine the stability of interval patterns over a period of time. It is also appropriate for sensory-discrimination and motor tests and others where time and additional learning will have minimal effects.

It is important for the manual to state the time interval between the administration of the test and any factors that may have affected the scores on the second administration.

Many tests have been developed with two or more comparable forms. Since no two forms will be prepared with exactly the same level of difficulty, for any one individual the reliability will be affected by the test items selected for each form. The reliability coefficient will be a little less than in other methods of determining the coefficient of correlation. The time difference in the two administrations may also affect the reliability. The manual should state the time interval between the two test administrations and any experiences that might affect the result of the second test and, therefore, the reliability of the test.

Temporal stability is not a factor when the split-half procedure is used, since there is only one test used and only one administration of the test. This procedure indicates the internal consistency of the test. If the manual reports use of the Spearman-Brown formula it can generally be assumed reliability was determined by the split-half method.

The Kuder-Richardson method of determining reliability involves a single administration of a test and, therefore, temporal stability is not a factor. Rather than dividing the test in some way to get two half-test scores, the Kuder-Richardson technique is based on an examination of performance on each item. If the items making up the test are highly homogeneous, the coefficient obtained by this method will be lower than with the split-half technique.

Any single administration to determine the reliability of a test, whether odd-even or the Kuder-Richardson technique, is not applicable to speed tests. This is because speed tests are designed so that individuals taking the tests will not finish them. The items not completed are equally divided between the two sections on which the correlation is figured and they correlate perfectly. To the extent that individual differences in test scores depend on speed of performance, the reliability coefficients will be spuriously high when found by a single administration of the test.

Coefficients of reliability are affected by many things besides the items on the tests. The test user should be aware of these, since the method chosen to determine the reliability may produce a higher or lower coefficient than another method.

1. Other things being equal, a longer test will be more reliable than a shorter test.
2. The more heterogeneous a group being tested, the higher the correlation.
3. A split-half method of establishing reliability will be spuriously high for a test in which speed is a factor.
4. A comparable form test will produce a lower coefficient than a single administration of either form.

The test user must not only understand what a reliability coefficient is and the factors that may affect it, but has to make the decision ultimately whether it is stable enough to use. The decision is difficult to make and two people given the same information on reliability may make different decisions. Womer (1968) uses the following informal guideline for judging reliability coefficients.

> For split-half coefficients, from a single test administration one should be skeptical of reliability coefficients lower than .85 and one should hope for .90 or above. Comparable-form reliability coefficients tend to run at least .04 to .06 points lower and sometimes more. Thus, one can "accept" any reliability above .80, while hoping for coefficients in the high .80's. These suggestions must not be taken to imply a .79 is poor while .80 is good.

He further indicated that some may feel those suggestions are too rigorous and others think them not rigorous enough.

A committee of members of the American Psychological Association, the American Educational Research Association, and the National Council on Measurement in Education has prepared a set of standards for test development (APA et al., 1974). Some of their recommendations on reliability are:

> ... The test manual or research report should present evidence of reliability, including estimates of the standard error of measurement, that permits the reader to judge whether scores are sufficiently dependable for the intended uses of the test. If any of the necessary evidence has not been collected, the absence of such information should be noted.
> ... The procedures and samples used to determine reliability coefficients or standard errors of measurement should be described sufficiently to permit a user to judge the applicability of the data reported to the individuals or groups with which he is concerned.
> ... When a test is recommended or ordinarily employed in homogeneous

subsamples, the reliability and standard error of measurement should be independently investigated within each subsample and reported in the test manual.

... Reports of reliability studies should ordinarily be expressed in the test manual in terms of variances of error components, standard errors of measurement, or product-moment reliability coefficients. Unfamiliar expressions of data should be clearly described, with references to their development.

... If two or more forms of a test are published for use with the same examinees, information on means, variances, and characteristics of items in the forms should be reported in the test manual along with the coefficients of correlation among their scores. If necessary evidence is not provided, the test manual should warn the reader against assuming equivalence of scores.

... The test manual should indicate to what extent test scores are stable, that is, how nearly constant the scores are likely to be if a parallel form of a test is administered after time has elapsed. The manual should also describe the effect of any such variation on the usefulness of the test. The time interval to be considered depends on the nature of the test and on what interpretation of the test scores is recommended.*

Validity

The name of a test is no guarantee that it does in fact test what the name implies. What the test really measures can be determined only by the performance on the test and one or more independently observable facts about the characteristic being measured.

When we speak of *validity* we are concerned with what the test measures and how well it does it. We use it to measure a characteristic or to predict future behavior and we want to know if it is likely to do the job we desire. A test may be valid for one purpose but not valid for another. Therefore, when we speak of validity we must identify the specific purpose for which the test is to be used.

We have many purposes for use of test results. The various purposes call for different kinds of validity evidence. Validity is classified as content or curricular validity, criterion-related validity, and construct validity. The approach to validation differs with each.

Content validity is concerned with whether the content of the test covers all major aspects of the behavior domain (knowledge, skills, etc.) and in the correct proportion. Content validity is commonly used in evaluating achievement tests. It is best evidenced by a comparison of the test content with courses of study, instructional materials, and statements of educational goals, and often by analysis of the processes required in making correct responses to the items.

The manual should include information on how the content to be included in the test was determined. This should include information on how the proportional allocation of skills and knowledge was derived.

Content validity is not appropriate for aptitude or personality tests, since these are not based on a specific course of instruction. These tests require empirical evidence for validation. Content validity is determined by how well it covers the content and, therefore, how appropriate it is for one's use. There will be no coefficient of correlation reported for content validity.

2. *Criterion-related validity* is determined by checking the performance on the test against some criterion. For example, an aptitude test is measured against predictive success in some fields. A scholastic aptitude test is checked against predictive success in academic pursuits. These are examples of predictive ability related to some future criterion measure of success. Criterion-related validity may also involve *concurrent validity*. That is, there are not significant time-interval lapses between administration of the test being validated and of the criterion measure. The test may be compared to a test generally accepted or known to be valid, or other criterion data already known. A new intelligence test may use the Stanford-Binet as the criterion by which it is determined that it is a valid IQ test. Personality tests may attempt to gain their validation by use of contrasted groups. Ratings by experts may also be used to define the criterion.

Since there is an outside criterion, the test should report a validity coefficient, which will ordinarily range from +.40 to .70. The subjectivity and inadequacies in many outside criteria such as teacher ratings tend to lower coefficients of correlation. However, if an outside criterion is a test of established validity such as the Stanford-Binet, the correlation coefficient should be above .80.

3 *Construct validity* is the extent to which a test measures some relatively abstract psychological trait or construct, such as anxiety. Any data that provide information on the trait or that may influence its development or manifestations may be appropriate to help validate the test. Tests of personality, mechanical aptitude, critical thinking, etc. are validated in terms of their construct and the relation of their scores to pertinent external data.

Test developers may show that the trait being tested is not affected by some other factor. If a test also correlates highly with a reading test, then reading ability may adversely affect the results of the test. Test manuals will quite often report low validities in such a situation to show that the trait being measured is not influenced by reading ability, or intelligence, or some other factor that tests users might suspect would influence the test. Test users should be alert to checking for low correlations to verify that the test is indeed measuring the trait itself, and not a combination of the trait and other factors.

Care must be taken when evaluating validity coefficients in older tests. Although the tests may have had good validity when first produced, the standards may have changed over the years to make the test a less valid instrument now.

It is difficult to set a minimum coefficient of validity for a test; .60 is very high and is rarely achieved, except when validated against another like test. The problem may be in the test, the criterion, multiple factors affecting the result, etc. If prediction is the purpose, even low correlations may have some value if they improve the prediction over chance alone. One must not expect the high coefficients of correlation that one needs and is able to achieve on reliability to be achievable with validity. One should try to get the most valid test possible, because without validity one has nothing.

The booklet *Standards for Educational and Psychological Tests* (APA et al., 1974) includes a number of recommendations concerning test validity. Some of the major recommendations are indicated below.

> . . . A manual or research report should present the evidence of validity for each type of inference for which use of the test is recommended. If validity for some

suggested interpretation has not been investigated, that fact should be made clear.

... All measures of criteria should be described completely and accurately. The manual or research report should comment on the adequacy of a criterion. Whenever feasible, it should draw attention to significant aspects of performance that the criterion measure does not reflect and to irrelevant factors likely to affect it.

... The criterion score should be determined independently of test scores. The manual should describe precautions taken to avoid contamination of the criterion or should warn the reader of possible contamination.

... A test manual should report evidence of validity for each type of criterion about which a recommendation is made. If validity for some recommended interpretation has not been tested, that fact should be made clear.

... The sample employed in a validity study and the conditions under which testing is done should be consistent with recommended test use and should be described sufficiently for the reader to judge its pertinence to his situation.

... A report of criterion-related validity should give full information about the statistical analysis and should ordinarily include, in addition to such basic descriptive statistics as means and standard deviations, one or more of the following: (a) one or more correlation coefficients of a familiar type, (b) descriptions of the efficiency with which the test separates criterion groups, (c) expectancy tables, or (d) charts that graphically illustrate the relationship between test and criterion.

... If test performance is to be interpreted as a representative sample of performance in a universe of situations, the test manual should give a clear definition of the universe represented and describe the procedures followed in the sampling from it.

... If the author proposes to interpret scores on a test as measuring a theoretical variable (ability trait, or attitude), his proposed interpretation should be fully stated. His theoretical construct should be distinguished from interpretations arising on the basis of other theories.*

A final word needs to be said to test users regarding use of tests. A validity coefficient may be evaluated in terms of how much additional information it will give. If one already has valid information, a test that correlates very well with the test already given may not be justified. It may be better to find a test that will provide something new to understanding the individual.

Standard Error of Measurement

The reliability of a test may be expressed in terms of the standard error of the score or the standard error of measurement. We know that the score received on a test is not necessarily the person's true score. If the test had been taken on another day, the person would probably have received a different score. Which one is the true score?

---

*From *Standards for Educational and Psychological Tests.* Copyright © 1974 by the American Psychological Association. Reprinted by permission.

We do not know. We do know that if he took the test a number of times, the results would vary around the mean of that person's score to approximate a normal distribution. If we assume the mean is the true score, then 68 percent of the scores would be between plus or minus one standard deviation from the mean. Since we cannot give the test to the same individual many times to determine the true score, we need a way to tell us how close we are with the score we have. The reliability coefficient indicates how consistent the test is when it is applied to a group, but it does not help in this situation, because we are dealing with an individual score. The standard error of measurement does provide the information we want.

The *standard error of measurement* is derived from a formula using the standard deviation and the reliability coefficient. The *reliability coefficient* indicates the stability of scores and the *standard deviation* indicates the dispersion according to the normal curve. The result is information that tells us how much we can expect the obtained score to vary within certain probability limits. The formula is standard error of measurement = standard deviation $\sqrt{1}$-reliability coefficient. If the standard deviation of a deviation IQ is 15 and the reliability coefficient is .89, then the standard error of measurement $=15\sqrt{1-.89}=15\sqrt{.11}=15\times.33=5.$ If a student obtains an IQ of 107, we can conclude that the chances are 2:1 (68:32) that the true score will be within the limits of ±5 of the obtained score, or 102–112. That is, the true score will be within bounds of plus or minus the standard error of measurement 68 percent of the time. If we desire a higher level of confidence in our prediction, we can move to ±2 standard error of measurement. In the above example, we would be 95 percent sure the true score was between 97 and 117. Another way of stating the latter example is: the chances are 19:1 that the true score was within ±2 standard error of the score or between 97 and 117. By recalling the percentages under the normal curve for the various standard deviations, one can figure it out for any standard error. To change from a percent to chances, subtract the percent under the curve from 100 and set up the ratio,

(2 S.D. = 95% certain, 95–100 = 5% uncertain), ($\frac{5}{95}$ = $\frac{1}{19}$, 19:1 certain)

(1 S.D. = 68% certain, 68–100 = 32% uncertain), ($\frac{32}{68}$ = $\frac{1}{2}$, 2:1 certain).

Test scores must not be interpreted as precise, exact measures of the skill or characteristic one is measuring, because they are not. The standard error of measurement provides a reasonable and logical way to present and interpret test scores.

Summary

Tests are administered for the purpose of obtaining information to measure what a person has learned, to assist in instruction or therapy, or to aid in the diagnosis of some specific problem. The test must be appropriate for its use and provide valid information. An understanding of the standardization process and the procedure for establishing norms is the first step in the test-selection process. One must investigate such things as the reliability and validity of the test in order to determine if, in fact, the test meets criteria for stability or consistency and usefulness.

Tests do not provide for automatic interpretation. The test user must know many things about the tests and characteristics about the scores and their distribution. A test user must understand the derived scores, such as age and grade scores, percentiles, and standard scores. Age and grade norms have many limitations. Percentiles are very useful but must not be confused with percent of right answers. The most useful derived scores are standard scores. They retain the intervals between raw scores and can be used in mathematical calculations. They also provide for a comparison of scores. The most common standard scores are z, Z, T, and stanine.

The fact that measures of human characteristics tend to distribute themselves into a normal curve distribution makes it possible to make projections and inferences about test-score distribution. For example, approximately 68 percent of the scores will lie within one standard deviation on each side of the mean and that 95 percent will lie 1.96 S.D. on each side of the mean. By means of a normal curve table, it is possible to determine the percent of scores within any plus or minus standard deviation and, thereby, establish percentile tables for a distribution of scores.

Finally, the standard error of measurement makes it possible for test users to apply test results to individuals with specific degrees of confidence. Although one does not know a person's true score for the test result, but only an estimate, by applying the standard error of measurement one can ascertain how likely the true score will be to lie between two scores. The chances are 2 to 1 that the true score will lie within ±1 standard error of measurement of the obtained score.

Testing is not an exact science. One must understand the problems involved in test selection and score use and minimize the possibility of misuse of tests. By understanding measurement procedures and using this information, individuals with responsibilities to help students and clients will find tests to be a great asset.

Student Assignments

1. *Select two or more achievement tests designed for administration to elementary-age students. Study the information provided in the manuals and determine the appropriateness of each test for a particular elementary population you select.*
2. *Select three or more test manuals and critique the manuals regarding norms, reliability, and validity, using the standards identified in the Standards for Education and Psychological Tests and Manuals.*
3. *If any manuals used in exercises 1 or 2 do not report a standard error of measurement, determine what it is by using the formula for determining the standard error of measurement.*

Discussion Questions

1. *What are the hazards involved in reporting and using grade norms?*
2. *Why is it inappropriate to expect validity coefficients of correlation to be as high as reliability coefficients of correlation?*
3. *No test can be perfectly reliable, because of factors involved in the construction of the test and the testing environment. The standard error of measurement provides a means of reporting the results with certain degrees of certainty. Explain what is meant by this.*
4. *What are the advantages and disadvantages of the following means of reporting test scores: age norms, grade norms, percentiles, standard scores?*

REFERENCES

American Psychological Association, American Educational Research Association, & National Council on Measurement in Education. *Standards for educational and psychological tests and manuals.* Washington, D.C.: Authors, 1974.

Anastasi, A. *Psychological testing* (3rd ed.). New York: Macmillan Publishing Company, Inc., 1968.

Cronbach, L. J. *Essentials of psychological testing* (3rd ed.). New York: Harper & Row Publishers, Inc., 1970.

Downie, N. M. Types of test scores. In Stone, S. C., & Shertzer, B. (Eds.), *Guidance monograph series, Series III testing.* Boston: Houghton Mifflin Company, 1968.

Guilford, J. P. *Fundamental statistics in psychology and education.* New York: McGraw-Hill Book Company, 1950.

Lyman, H. *Test scores and what they mean.* Englewood Cliffs, N. J.: Prentice-Hall, 1963.

Miller, R. B. *Tests and the selection process.* Chicago: Science Research Associates, 1966.

Turney, B. L., & Robb, G. P. *Simplified statistics for education and psychology.* Scranton, Pa.: International Textbook Company, 1968.

Womer, F. B. Basic concepts in testing. In Stone, S. C., & Shertzer, B. (Eds.), *Guidance monograph series, Series III testing.* Boston: Houghton Mifflin Company, 1968.

Chapter 2

Criterion-Referenced Testing

After you have studied this chapter, you should be able to do the following:

1. *Understand criterion-referenced testing*
2. *Understand the differences between norm-referenced tests and criterion-referenced tests*
3. *Know the value and the limitations of criterion-referenced testing*
4. *Identify a sample group of criterion-referenced tests*
5. *Understand principles of criterion-referenced tests*
6. *Understand the general procedure in making criterion-referenced tests*

Introduction

An innovative "shift" in student evaluation methods is criterion-referenced tests, which are not dependent on norm references. Rather, they evaluate skills through specific objectives, or criteria: a student's strengths and weaknesses are measured by the number of objectives achieved. The objectives are referenced to content in specific texts or other teaching materials. No assumptions or generalizations are made. Instead the tests measure only what is stated in the objectives. The test results show what students can do relative to the stated criteria, rather than in comparison to other students. Since criterion-referenced tests evaluate what a student knows or does not know, they provide the basis for instructional procedures appropriate to meet individual needs. The results can be organized so that appropriate instructional groups can be identified; if comparisons are desired, the results may be evaluated by comparing records from other schools. Such comparisons are not the purpose of criterion-referenced testing, but when curriculum specialists wish to evaluate the effectiveness of their curriculum with that of other schools, criterion-referenced information may be used.

Differences Between Norm-Referenced and Criterion-Referenced Tests

The major difference between criterion-referenced (CRT) and norm-referenced (NRT) tests is that the former identify *what information* is known or *what skill* has been mastered (without reference to the developmental age related to or normal for this learning), whereas the norm-referenced tests are concerned with *levels* of ability or mastery of any skill. These levels may be representative of either age (generally cited by year or month) or grade. The grade norms may also include month levels. For example, a child achieving in reading at grade 3.3 is said to be reading at the third grade and third month of that nine-month school session.

Some norm-referenced tests will include subcategories of knowledge and skill under general headings. For instance, reading sections on individual norm-referenced achievement tests may measure more than just reading recognition and reading comprehension, measures typical of most reading achievement tests. They may also provide measures that are more typical of criterion-referenced tests such as listening skills and vocabulary. Group achievement norm-referenced tests are known to have a greater variety of such measures. The Stanford Diagnostic Reading Test, Level I, for instance, includes the following categories: reading comprehension, vocabulary, auditory discrimination, syllabication, beginning and ending sounds, blending, and sound discrimination. The main point is that some norm-referenced tests do measure subskills typical of criterion-referenced tests. Second, they do emphasize the age and grade level, which are not emphasized by criterion-referenced tests.

Whereas norm-referenced tests are of two types, point scales and age scales, as reported by Salvia and Ysseldyke (1978), the criterion-referenced tests do not have this differentiation. An example of the construction of the two types of norm-referenced tests helps to highlight their differences from the criterion-referenced tests, which have a different construction approach.

The 1937 Revision of the Stanford-Binet Test of Intelligence is the first well-known example of an age-scale test. In the standardization procedure, a mass of test items was assembled and critically examined, and the materials that seemed most promising were selected by the authors, Terman and Merrill, for the experimental trial. Curves of percents passing at successive mental ages were plotted and the steepness of these curves afforded a graphic indication of the validity of the tests. In the final tryout, each test was given a provisional age location at the level where the proportion of passes was approximately 50 percent. That is, if 50 percent of a four-year-old group passed a test chosen for the four-year level, this test was placed in the group of tests for that year measurement.

An example of a point-scale norm-referenced test is the WISC-R (Wechsler Intelligence Scale for Children—Revised). Wechsler (1974) called his point scale score a "deviation IQ," which was obtained by comparing each subject's test performance not with a composite age group, but exclusively with the scores earned by individuals in the subject's own single-age group. A four-months' age grouping—as 7 years, 4 months, and 0 days to 7 years, 7 months, and 30 days—constitutes a single age group. The deviation IQ from the WISC-R is dependent on the normal distribution of the test scores; and the standard deviation, as well as the mean IQ of all age groups, are identical.

By comparison, criterion-referenced testing, rather than determining how a student compares with another student of the same age and grade placement, seeks to provide measurements that reveal the information the child needs to know and the skills the child needs to accomplish. These tests may be teacher-made or they may be commercially made. Their authors, of necessity, must know what the objectives of each grade in public school will be. It is on these objectives that the tests are built. They must determine that children in grade three, for example, should learn division and fractions in addition to reinforcement of the multiplication, addition, and subtraction skills learned in the first and second grades. Such information is not difficult to find; one may look at any third-grade arithmetic text on the market and find what third-grade children are studying. The material found therein has been developed through the years by professionals working directly with students, who understand growth patterns and expectations of abilities. The significant feature of a criterion-referenced test is that each task involved with any one function is included: that is, addition involves simple addition with no carrying, addition with carrying in the ones column, in the tens column, and on to more complicated carrying with larger numbers. All of these steps are implemented by problems that, when solved, measure what a child has or has not mastered in the process of learning how to add. The addition example is representative of the minute process followed in each single learning area, whether it is math, reading, or the language arts.

Criterion-referenced tests use the same basic approach to content validity as do standardized tests. A difference is that the content of the criterion-referenced test is based on a specified set of objectives instead of general curriculum content. The objectives, which are developed by professionals in each academic field, provide a comprehensive approach to content validity.

Advantages and Disadvantages

Criterion-referenced tests are particularly useful as guidelines for assisting the teacher in making individual plans for children. Since they are geared more specifically toward the academic material taught in the classroom, the teacher can learn which skill or which set of knowledge is lacking in a child's achievement. It is with such information that the teacher may direct appropriate plans, rather than burdening the child with materials and skills already satisfactorily mastered.

In one case study regarding a gifted child,* Tom S., it was found that a criterion-referenced test was very advantageous in helping parents make a decision about allowing their son to skip the first grade. He had had no *formal* training in kindergarten or from his parents and he had missed entrance into the first grade the year before by only 19 days. The kindergarten teacher had informed his family that he was ready for the second grade and that he was capable of functioning far above his peers. The parents were concerned, however, that Tom might not have mastered the necessary skills to become successful in the second grade. A psychological and educational evaluation was administered, followed by a criterion-referenced test—in this case, the Brigance, a test that is described in this chapter.

The following evaluation demonstrates that Tom was found to be normally adjusted socially and emotionally and that he was reading at the beginning fifth-grade level with comprehension at that same level. The reading skills learned through his own initiative

---

*Criterion-referenced tests should be used with children at any level of intelligence.

and desire were mastered at a higher level than his math and spelling, which were found to be at grade 2.5 and 1.8, respectively (see section V, Educational Factors). This was understandable since he had had no formal help in any subject but did have exposure to reading material in the form of library books. Because of this lack of formal training, Tom's parents were not convinced that the grade levels he had attained provided enough information to assure them that Tom would be successful in second grade. It was the criterion-referenced data that helped them make this determination. These data are found in the evaluation, in section VI, Learning Competencies.

A summer session was planned, during which Tom was taught the material that had not been mastered, as indicated by the criterion-referenced test. As expected, he was able to pick up the loose ends and was at the top of his class in the second grade. In reading, of course, he was allowed to read at his own pace, though his placement was in the second grade. The psychometric summary of his skills and the evaluation follow.

PSYCHOLOGICAL EVALUATION

Name: Tom K   Examined:
Born: Examiner: _____
                                                 C. A.: 6–8

I. Language Factors
   English is the language spoken in the home.

II. Physiological Factors
   A. Fine-motor skills are above average. Tom is printing his name and many words with no problems noted. He is right-handed.
   B. Gross-motor skills are normal. He was agile in movements and there was no evidence of any irregularity.
   C. Health was reported by mother to be normal.
   D. Appearance: Tom is an attractive six-year, eight-month child who appears to be normal in physiological features. While within normal limits for size, he was on the small side of the scale, but not significantly so. He has light brown hair and he was dressed in good casual school clothes.

III. Emotional/Behavioral Factors
   There was no evidence of any emotional problem. Tom is a well-adjusted six-year-old. He was quiet and reserved but responsive and he appeared to enjoy the tasks. He readily admitted it when he did not know answers and this admission did not appear to bother him. Several questions were challenging to him and he sat thoughtfully as if he were weighing every point before answering. When I asked him what a lecturer was, he took his time and finally answered, "It's someone who sits or stands behind a desk and a bunch of people are sitting out front listening to him." His responses were all this thorough. It was as if he were trying to be exact in his remarks.

IV. Intellectual Factors
   Tom was examined and found to be functioning in the high gifted range of intellectual ability. His Stanford Binet, Form L-M, IQ was found

to be 154 and his Peabody Picture Vocabulary IQ was found to be above 144, which number was the top of the norms. Tom's score was above the score equivalent for 144 IQ.

Tom's responses were all of high quality. His first failure, a marginal one at the eight-year level, was a verbal reasoning task, yet at both year 9 and year 12, he easily passed the same kind of verbal reasoning subtest. Therefore verbal reasoning is not felt to be his major weakness. His first "true" weakness was at the nine-year level where he failed to solve three math problems. His greatest strength was found to be memory for sentences at the thirteen-year level.

V. Educational Factors

Tom was found to be achieving in reading recognition at grade 5 and in reading comprehension at the same level. His math was found to be at grade 2.5 and spelling at grade 1.8. He has had no formal training. What he achieved has been what he has picked up through his own maneuvers except for kindergarten play activities. He received no first grade training in kindergarten.

VI. Learning Competencies

It is obvious that Tom is having no learning problems. His language, memory, conceptual thinking, verbal reasoning, numerical reasoning, and social intelligence were found to be in the gifted range. His visual-motor skills were found to be above average.

His reading skills apparently have been developed by a "whole word" method. It was obvious, also, that his word attack skills were based on contextual clues. When he reached his ceiling in reading and he did not know all the words, he still made guesses after reading the words he knew, but he did not make haphazard guesses. He made the word fit the sense of the sentence.

From the criterion-referenced test it was found that Tom needed an introduction to the different symbols used in computation, such as minus, plus and equal. He also needed to know that some problems were written out in vertical fashion with the answer written underneath a short line, and that some were written in horizontal fashion with answers following the equal sign. He did not know the approaches to adding with carrying, but he figured answers to math problems by his own means, another skill without formal training.

Tom needs to be introduced to the concept of spelling and to become aware of how letters are aligned in words. He prints well but he does need to learn to print on lined paper and to learn the difference between capital and lower case letters and their positions on the lines.

VII. Summary

Tom is a six-year, eight-month child who has high gifted intelligence. His reading was found to be his highest achievement but there are some basic first grade facts which he needs to learn. It is recommended that he enter public schools in the second grade, but prior to this action he should be taught first grade math and spelling procedures during the summer months and should be introduced to conventional reading approaches. Tom is as near in age to the second grade children as he is to the first grade children. This is an important factor, but the most important is that first grade will have little to offer him, except a few approaches toward learning which he can be taught during the summer and during the first grade review provided by teachers of beginning second grade children.

Even in the second grade, it is expected that it will be necessary for him to read at his own pace since he is so far above the second graders in reading. It is very important that we not allow gifted children to become bored. Tom must be challenged with new materials and information and continue to believe that learning is a privilege and a pleasure.

_____

Reporting Psychologist

This case study highlights advantages in the case of a gifted child. The same advantages can be seen if criterion-referenced tests are used in the case of the learning disabled, mentally retarded, or emotionally disturbed children. In each situation, regardless of level of intelligence or type of handicapping condition, the information from the criterion-referenced testing can provide the beginning position for training/remediation.

In contrast on the advantages, there are some reasons for criticism of dependence on CRT for curriculum planning. A major concern of many professionals is that the curriculum may be limited to the number of specific objectives outlined in the criterion-referenced test. Some teachers or commercial specialists may not design CRTs that cover a broad enough perspective and, as a consequence, the content of the curriculum may not form a basis necessary for all developmental tasks. In addition, some commercially planned content, if followed rigidly, might not involve basic points and materials needed at specific local levels. Also, where only commercially or teacher-made criterion-referenced tests are administered, information regarding how a person processes information may be a major missing feature in planning ways and means of approaches to remediation for the materials/skills not learned. Other tests, such as language or perceptual tests, could provide such information.

In spite of the limitations of criterion-referenced testing, the logic behind a plan that involves assessment of what a person can and cannot do, for use in prescribing remediation or developmental help seems worthwhile. If the objectives chosen deal with basic skills and if the whole curriculum is not restricted to a set of limited objectives, the individualized prescription would probably not limit the learning opportunities for the student.

Criterion-Referenced Tests

Basic School Skills Inventory (BSSI)
An inventory that measures learning and behavior difficulties in young children has been designed by Goodman and Hammill (1975). It is a criterion-referenced test that

makes it easy to translate the findings of the evaluation into instructional practice. The BSSI consists of 84 items, representing seven areas of school performance:

Basic information
Self-help
Handwriting
Oral communication
Reading readiness
Number readiness
Classroom behavior

Each of the 84 items is stated in question form, and inquires about the child's school-related performance. Each item indicates a desired outcome. An example follows:

53. Can the child recognize which of the following pairs of words rhyme: dog—hog, star—pen, blow—slow?
Since rhyming exercises are included in most readiness training programs, you will probably already know the children who do well or poorly on such activities. The example is to be used when you have some doubt about a child's ability in this area. The child must answer all three pairs to pass this item. (Goodman & Hammill, p. 7)

To each item the teacher responds, "Yes, the child can do this," or "No, the child cannot do this." All items are followed by an explanation that clarifies the expected outcome.

At the beginning of the subscales of the inventory are lists of materials needed to complete the various assessment areas. Pupil record sheets are provided to record individual performances.

The inventory does not encompass a total preschool readiness curriculum. It is recommended that the BSSI be used as a *supplement*. Goodman and Hammill describe their test as follows:

1. BSSI was constructed with professional opinions from teachers. . . . It is unfortunate that teachers have had so little input into the development of the construct called "school readiness"; they, more than any other professional group, are most cognizant of the characteristics, skills, and behaviors that contribute to school success. BSSI reflects teachers' judgments of what is educationally important in a child's behavior and performance.

2. BSSI embodies a behavioral orientation. All the inventory items are presented as behavioral statements of desired learning objectives. The items represent important entrance skills that children who are beginning academic work will need; therefore, they are the terminal behaviors toward which kindergarten and first grade teachers should direct an appreciable amount of their efforts. Presentation of the times as behavioral objectives also increases the specificity, objectivity, and measurability of the instrument. . . . Each item is either directly teachable or represents a behavior that is subject to modification through training.

3. BSSI is both a norm-reference and a criteria-reference instrument. In the interpretation of the inventory results, you are likely to be concerned with two

basic questions: 1.) How does the youngster compare with other children of his age? and 2.) what are the child's specific and educational deficits? The first question, which involves a comparison of the child's performance with the performance of others in his age group requires essentially a norm-referenced interpretation. The second, the child's mastery of the subject content entails a criterion-referenced interpretation. The inventory has been designed to accommodate either type of evaluation.

4. BSSI bridges the gap between assessment and training. Having administered the inventory, you can determine some of the performance areas in which the child is having difficulty and can plan a daily program that emphasizes those specific skills which are absent from his repertoire. One of the advantages of this criterion-based approach is that there is no difference between the inventory assessment items and the prescribed training tasks—they are identical. With this kind of consistency, no time is wasted in translating the test results into classroom action.*

Individual Criterion-Referenced Test (ICRT)

The ICRT was developed by Educational Progress, a division of the Educational Development Corporation of Tulsa, Oklahoma. The test includes math and reading sections with the objectives referenced to as many as five different instructional programs. Two of the programs are distributed by Educational Progress, but the school district can designate three basal tests or reading series for prescriptive references.

A partial printout, Figure 6 indicates skills the student was able to demonstrate and notes skills to review and learn. The company provides printouts that prescribe materials to match the diagnosis.

Prescriptive Reading Inventory (PRI) and Prescriptive Math Inventory (PMI) (Grades 1.5–6)

The PRI and PMI are criterion-referenced tests distributed by the California Test Bureau of the McGraw-Hill Publishing Company. Since these are referenced to basal tests or series, a school district must specify which series they are using. The printouts will reference the objectives to the pages in the correct series for that school district. (See Appendix R for sample printouts of these tests.)

Behavioral Characteristics Progression (BCP)

A criterion-referenced test for the very young and for the retarded is the Behavioral Characteristics Progression (BCP). The instrument is arranged as a matrix of behaviorally stated developmental objectives. Its central element is the behavioral objectives, which allows clients to be assessed on a given trait. There are 59 behavioral areas (strands), each containing up to 50 behavioral steps (characteristic traits). They progress from virtually no abilities in an area to what is considered adult behavior in that area. Examples of two strands identified as "Feeding and Eating" (No. 3) and Math (No. 35) are as follows:

*From Libby Goodman and Donald Hammill, Manual for *Basic School Skills Inventory* (1975) p. 7.

Figure 6. Individualized Criterion-Referenced Test Report

You Were Able To

Find the difference of a vertical subtraction problem
Find the sum of a horizontal addition problem (to 9)
Find the difference of a horizontal subtraction problem
Match like shapes
Find the figure that represents the fraction ½
Measure an object to the nearest inch
Find the sum of a pictured word problem (to 9)
Identify a subset of a set of 10 members
Identify appropriate symbols to complete a number sentence
Identify the equation for an addition problem
Identify the sum of three addends
Identify the missing addend in an incomplete addition problem
Identify the total value of a set
Identify the number of hundreds, tens, and ones in a number

Should be called list of objectives.

You Need To Review How To

Find the difference of a pictured word problem (minuend to 9)
Find the product of two three-digit factors
Identify the perimeter of a rectangle

You Need To Learn How To

Find the product of a two-digit factor and a four-digit factor
Solve a multiplication word problem (one-digit and two-digit factors)
Solve a word problem using basic operation on money
Solve a multiplication/subtraction word problem
Find the missing factor of a counting number

IDENTIFYING BEHAVIORS: (No. 3, Feeding and Eating) 1–50 Behaviors
□ Eats only blended or strained foods □ Thrusts food out of mouth with tongue □ Gags on foods · □ Sucks food instead of chewing it □ Bites down on spoon when inserted into mouth □ Chews food only partially before swallowing □ Swallows foods without chewing them □ Chews in other than rotary motion □ Takes large pieces of food into mouth without biting □ Eats with fingers □ Crumbles food in hand when finger feeding □ Drools while eating □ Spits out food □ Holds spoon/fork in fist rather than fingers

1.0 Opens mouth when physically stimulated by spoon held by another
2.0 Opens mouth voluntarily at the sight of food
3.0 Removes semi-liquid food from spoon with mouth when being fed—some rejection
5.0 Allows spoon to be removed from mouth
13.0 Grasps finger foods offered by adult and carries them to mouth
17.0 Carries finger foods to mouth and bites off smaller pieces
49.0 Serves self in cafeteria
50.0 Manages to eat different types of foods: liquids, crisp foods, slippery foods.

Identifying behaviors (No. 35, Math) 1–50 Behaviors

☐ Does not add or subtract correctly   ☐ Does not multiply or divide correctly   ☐ Has difficulty solving word problems   ☐ Forgets sequence of steps in long division   ☐ Carries and/or borrows from wrong direction in addition, subtraction

1.0 Sorts according to shape, size and length.

2.0 Locates big and little, large and small in groups of two objects.

3.0 Arranges objects in order of size from smallest to largest.

10.0 Counts orally to three.

15.0 Locates front and back, left and right.

20.0 Identifies what number comes before and after a given number or between two numbers (up to 10).

23.0 Reads and writes numerals to 19.

50.0 Multiplies and divides fractions and decimals. Computes simple percentages.

KeyMath Diagnostic Arithmetic Test

An individualized test of arithmetic skills is the KeyMath Diagnostic Arithmetic Test, by Connolly, Nathman, and Pritchett (1971). A description of this test is found in Chapter 7. It may be used as both criterion-referenced and norm-referenced objectives are provided for each item.

The Brigance Diagnostic Inventory of Early Development, Brigance (1978)

The Inventory includes 98 skill sequences, from birth through the developmental age of 6 years for the following areas: psychomotor, self-help, speech and language, general knowledge and comprehension, and early academic skills. The inventory is based on observable functions, sequenced by task analysis, correlated with child development and curriculum objectives, and can be applied directly to observable functions, sequenced by task analysis, correlated with child development and curriculum objectives, and can be applied directly to individualizing instruction.

In addition to being criterion-referenced, the Inventory is also norm-referenced. All skills of a developmental nature are given developmental ages, indicating the age range of each skill in the usual developmental sequence. In establishing and validating the skill sequences and developmental ages, many professional materials have been examined and are cited in the Bibliography and Appendix P of the Manual.

The format is easy to follow. When the inventory is opened to an assessment procedure, the printed material for the examiner is in correct position for reading and the visual material is facing the child. The instrument does not require specialized training in testing. The procedures are simplified. Complex statistical procedures are not required for deriving and interpreting the results. Many of the assessment procedures can be done by a paraprofessional with professional supervision.

The Inventory was designed to meet P.L. 94-142 requirements. It identifies the present level of performance, yields results easily interpreted to parents, and lists objectives for individual education planning. A sample Developmental Record is shown in Figure 7.

Brigance Diagnostic Inventory of Basic Skills, Brigance (1977)

This test commonly called "The Brigance" is a criterion-referenced test designed for use with students whose achievement is between kindergarten and sixth-grade level.

Syntax:

"N Ac" = Not Achieved   "DNA" = Did Not Administer

1. One word.
2. Three words other than "mama" or "dada."
3. Abbreviated sentences.
4. Names object shown.
5. Noun phrases with adjectives.
6. Subject-predicate phrases.
7. Uses plurals.
8. Noun phrase with article.
9. Refers to self by name.
10. Three word phrases.
11. Possesive noun
12. Three word sentences.
13. Uses pronoun to refer to others.
14. Asks simple questions.
15. Refers to self by pronoun.
16. Adds "ing."
17. Uses past tense.
18. Uses negative phrases other than "no."
19. Uses plurals other than by adding "s," (e.g., "foot, feet").
20. Asks questions about persons and things.
21. Relates experiences with some understanding of sequence and closure.
22. Asks definition of words.

F-1   122-4
F-1C

Developmental Age: 0-10
Notes: _Speech syntax more fluid - good improvement_

Length of Sentences:

Average number of words used in sentences:
Developmental Age: 2-0
Notes: _no improvement noted_

F-2   125
F-2

Personal Data Response:

1. First name
2. Full name
3. Age
4. Sex
5. Siblings
6. Town/city
7. Parent name
8. Birthday
9. Phone number
10. Street address
11. Complete address

F-3   126-7
F-3

Developmental Age: 2-0
Notes: _Confident of information_

Social Speech:

1. Expresses wants and needs.
2. Responds to simple "yes or no" questions.
3. Calls at least one person by name.
4. Asks for food at table.
5. Vocalizes toilet needs.
6. Responds appropriately to questions involving choices.
7. Says "thank you" and "please."
8. Delivers simple message.
9. Shows an interest in conversation of others.
10. Responds and makes verbal greetings.
11. Acknowledges compliments/service.
12. Says "excuse me" to interrupt politely.
13. Participates in a conversation without monopolizing it.
14. Answers phone and summons person requested.
15. Delivers two-part message orally.
16. Answers phone, takes simple message, delivers it.

F-4   128-30
F-4C

Developmental Age: 1-0
Notes: _Not very cooperative - not interested in conversation_

Figure 7. "Typical" Developmental Record

When an individual scores at or above grade level in a given skill, he or she should be able to advance and perform successfully at the next grade level. The inventory provides an additional aid for the teacher who wants to develop an individual program for junior-high and secondary students who need special instruction in basic skills at the elementary level.

The format and assessment procedures are simplified, so that no specialized training in testing is required; paraprofessionals can be involved readily in its use. It should be noted, however, that the teacher should be the one to decide whether the student has mastered a skill adequately, or whether additional instruction will be needed. This will be dependent on the particular program in the grade in which the child is placed.

The purpose of the inventory is:
—to assess basic readiness and academic skills in key subject areas from kindergarten to sixth-grade levels;
—to provide a systematic performance record, expressed in grade-level terms, for diagnosis and evaluation;
—to define instructional objectives in precise terms in order to measure a student's performance in a given subject area effectively;
—to determine the student's level of achievement, readiness to advance or need for reinforcement;
—to serve as a guide to the teacher in the design of an instructional program to meet the specific needs of the student.

Each skill area is arranged in a developmental and sequential hierarchy, and one may use the entire inventory or select individual skills to be tested.

The author suggests that principals and curriculum specialists would use the inventory primarily as a resource to recommend to teachers who need assistance in assessment procedures and instructional planning. The administrator and specialist would find their personal copies to be a usable reference or resource for making a quick assessment of new students to determine the most appropriate placement. The grade-level notations, scope, and sequence of the Student Record Book serve as quick, solid reference in performing curriculum-development leadership responsibilities.

The psychologist and diagnostician should find that the comprehensiveness and compactness of the inventory may eliminate the need for a collection of separate assessment instruments. This is particularly true for academic assessment, since the inventory contains procedures for assessing skills in readiness, reading, language arts, and math. The coverage is of sufficient scope to perform a comprehensive assessment of the abovementioned basic-skills areas. The information can be easily communicated to parents and other school personnel, since it provides references to specific skills taught in the classroom.

Brigance further suggests that the special-help teacher and evaluation team will use the total inventory more often than other school personnel because of the individualized nature of the program, where in-depth assessment is usually needed or required. He also states that the paraprofessional (personnel instructional aide) who helps the teacher will need only a minimal amount of training and supervision in administering the test but that the interpretation should be the responsibility of the teacher/professional staff.

The time required for assessing is determined by (a) the assessment data needed, (b) the skill range of the student, and (c) the method of assessment. Grade-level assessment may be made in about 15 minutes. Skill range will depend on the grade level of the student, i.e., a sixth grader will need more time than a second grader. The test may be administered to a group or an individual. Adaptation will, of necessity, have to be made for a group.

The major areas listed in Figure 8 are taken from the contents pages of the Brigance, so that the reader may know of the comprehensiveness of the test and understand that it can serve as a good curriculum guide. Part of an evaluation on a student is shown on pages 32–34. In the case study presented, the reader will note that other information is included that involves tests that are described in other chapters of this text. Please note specifically the sections on educational- and learning-competency factors for information from the Brigance.

Guidelines for Making Criterion-Referenced Tests

It has been stated at the beginning of this chapter that items for criterion-referenced tests are not difficult to find. It should be emphasized, however, that consideration should be given to some basic principles before choosing these items. Garvin (1971) states that arbitrary standards of performance specified by an instructor are not always a criterion. He notes that an instructor for purposes of his own may require, e.g., that his students diagram four out of five sentences correctly or recite all the capitals of Europe in alphabetical order in one minute. The explanation is that these could be criteria, but they are not necessarily meaningful criteria and may not be within the capabilities of those available to perform the task involved.

Four points emphasized by Garvin, in Popham (1971), are identified as follows: (1) to be classified as criterion-referenced material, a minimum of one instructional objective of a unit must envision a task that must subsequently be performed; (2) licensing standards of any profession involved, medical arts, finance, applied sciences or engineering, should be followed to insure that only those qualified to perform the tasks may be involved within such specific-learning situations; (3) criterion-referenced material should be used to control entry into any instructional sequence where the content is inherently cumulative and the rigors progressively greater. Where sequences are more irregular, norm-referenced materials may be used for placements—examples are math, physical and biological sciences in the secondary grades, and reading in the elementary grades; (4) each person need not meet each criterion in certain content areas. Required subjects (which everyone is expected to try to learn *but does not*) such as home economics and physical education at the secondary level serve as examples. At the college level, these become professions, and criteria must be met.

In point number three above, Garvin's suggestion that reading is an example of a domain at the elementary level better suited for norm-referenced material appears to oppose the views of some authors of criterion-referenced tests in popular use. It is true that the majority of criterion-referenced tests that include elementary reading do reference their content to the elementary stages of reading, as is seen in the skills involving phonics.* Beyond that, references to higher elementary-reading skills (beyond third grade) are generally not seen.

Popham (1971) also makes points concerning CRTs for consideration by those making their own criterion-referenced materials. He suggests that (1) variability is

---

*There are other methods such as language, linguistic or whole word approaches.

Figure 8. Table of Contents

Table of Contents

III. LANGUAGE ARTS

IV. MATH

From Brigance® *Diagnostic Inventory of Basic Skills*, © 1977 Curriculum Associates, Inc., Billerica, Mass.

irrelevant; meaning of scores is not dependent on comparison with other scores; meaning comes from the connection between the item and the criterion; (2) the item must be an accurate reflection of the criterion behavior: if one wishes to determine whether a child hears the sound *wh*, the *wh* sound must be present within the item; (3) CRTs are validated primarily in terms of the adequacy with which they represent the criterion (judgment should be made on the relevance of the behaviors inferable from those delimited by the criteria); (5) criteria for the number of allowable errors should be decided in the beginning of each section of a CRT. This latter allows for simple careless error, such as those made when working math problems in a hurry. Popham states further that in making decisions about treatment, it is not bad to find the proportion of a group mastering the tasks. It could, then, be said that performance is 92–80, meaning that 92 percent of the group had achieved 80 percent or better in the test.

The items that appear on a criterion-referenced test should be parts of a domain providing information regarding whether such kinds of performance can or cannot be demonstrated. In the domain of math, one criterion could be simple addition, single column as in $\dfrac{+1}{1}$ or $\dfrac{+3}{2}$. It is apparent that one should consider all basic calculations in

math to determine exactly what a student has mastered in the developmental sequence of learning mathematical calculation.

To be thorough in a domain, one should start with the most elemental steps. The test designer and the teacher who administers the test should have knowledge of children's competency expectancies in the various domains—such as reading, math, or language—and administer those competency items representing appropriate levels for the individual or individuals being tested.

Should the reader decide to compose a criterion-referenced test, the first step should be to review expectancies for grade levels for the subject chosen. For example, if the subject is reading at first-grade level, one should review materials to determine the skills expected of children at that level. A sample outline would cover the following:

1. Discrimination of sounds—vowels, consonants, blends and digraphs
2. Discrimination of shapes and of letters of the alphabet
3. Reading of simple (a) two-, three-, and four-letter words—action words and nouns, (b) direction words, (c) abbreviations, (d) contractions, (e) meaningful words with more than four letters, such as mother, father, teacher, etc.
4. Comprehension of content found in first-grade primers and readers

From such an outline, the reader would then proceed to choose the content representative of each of the categories. The second step would be to review the outline and the content of the test with a first-grade teacher. Step three would be to determine the number of children in the first grade (end of the year) who could master the test, or a major percentage of the test. This last step would provide information to serve as a guideline as to whether the local first-grade children are competing well with the standards set up in general commercial materials.

The following test is presented as an example of teacher-made CRT for math at the fourth-grade level.

Criterion-Referenced Test for Math Calculation Grade 4
A group of math problems is presented in Figure 9. They are representative of the level and kinds of problems children should be able to master within the fourth grade. The second part lists the process involved in each problem. From this list the teacher may determine the specific processes with which the child is having trouble. These processes should be the criterion for special help for this child before entry into the fifth grade. There is no time limit; however, the teacher should note the time required for specific students and make allowances in planning requirements for those who are slow or unusually fast. The important point is, however, that it must be determined that the student understands the process involved in one task before proceeding to a related and more difficult task.

Figure 9. Criterion-Referenced Test for Math Calculation—Grade 4

Addition

1. 250	2. 135	3. 425	4. 113	5. 5253
101	201	16	590	4376
+ 20	142	+ 127	+ 671	+ 2416
	+ 111			

Subtraction

6. 758	7. 8942	8. 849	9. $8.92	10. 96
− 427	− 4520	− 293	− 6.50	− 39

11. 437	12. 8736	13. 960	14. 6403
− 182	− 6958	− 259	− 3294

Multiplication

15. 5	16. 33	17. 502	18. 330	19. 276
× 2	× 2	× 4	× 6	× 2

20. 128	21. 33	22. 327	23. 23	24. 805
× 8	× 16	× 48	× 78	× 37

Division

25. $4\overline{)84}$ 26. $9\overline{)720}$ 27. $7\overline{)60}$ 28. $8\overline{)809}$

29. $62\overline{)930}$ 30. $15\overline{)890}$

Fractions

31. $\dfrac{15}{17} - \dfrac{9}{17} =$ 32. $\dfrac{1}{6} \times \dfrac{5}{6} =$ 33. $\dfrac{2}{10} + \dfrac{5}{10} =$

Rename these fractions:

34. $\dfrac{2}{6} =$ 35. $\dfrac{3}{9} =$ 36. $\dfrac{4}{12} =$ 37. $\dfrac{2}{12} =$ 38. $\dfrac{5}{10} =$

Figure 9. (Continued)

Math Processes Involved in Sample Criterion-Referenced Test:

1. Addition, no carrying involved
2. Addition, no carrying involved
3. Addition, carrying involved in one's column
4. Addition, carrying involved in ten's column
5. Addition, carrying involved in one hundred's column
6. Subtraction, no borrowing involved
7. Subtraction, no borrowing involved
8. Subtraction, no borrowing involved
9. Subtraction, no borrowing involved
10. Subtraction, borrowing in one's column
11. Subtraction, borrowing in ten's column
12. Subtraction, borrowing in all columns
13. Subtraction, zeroes in one's column
14. Subtraction, zeroes in ten's column
15. Multiplication, (one digit) simple basic facts
16. Multiplication, (one digit) no carrying
17. Multiplication, (one digit) no carrying, zeroes in ten's place
18. Multiplication, (one digit) carrying in ten's place
19. Multiplication, (one digit) carrying in one's and ten's place
20. Multiplication, (one digit) carrying in one's and ten's place
21. Multiplication, (two digits) two places
22. Multiplication, (two digits) three places
23. Multiplication, (two digits) two places
24. Multiplication, (two digits) three places, zero included
25. Division, simple one digit, no remainder
26. Division, simple one digit, division doesn't go into first number, no remainder
27. Division, simple one digit, remainder
28. Division, simple one digit, remainder
29. Division, two digits, no remainder
30. Division, two digits, remainder
31. Fraction, subtraction with answer being a proper fraction
32. Fraction, multiplication with answer being a proper fraction
33. Fraction, addition with answer being a proper fraction
34–38. Reduction of fractions

Summary

Criterion-referenced tests bridge the gap that often exists between diagnosis and remediation. The specific objectives make for definitive diagnosis of skills and identification of those behaviors that need remediation or are not yet learned. Since the objectives are referenced to specific texts or other teaching materials, the tests provide a basis for individualizing instruction.

Criterion-referenced tests differ from other standardized tests in that they are not normed on a specific population. They are similar to diagnostic tests, which may be norm-referenced, however. Designers of criterion-referenced tests should know expectancies for individuals at various age and/or grade levels, to provide questions that are fair and within the capability range of those being tested.

Discussion Questions

1. *Discuss the differences between norm-referenced and criterion-referenced tests.*
2. *How do these differences relate to the classroom curriculum?*
3. *Describe the two types of norm-referenced tests.*
4. *Defend criterion-referenced tests for use over norm-referenced.*
5. *How would one go about making one's own criterion-referenced test?*
6. *Discuss principles suggested by Garvin and Popham.*

Student Assignment

Make a criterion-referenced test of the area in which you are most interested, math, reading, or language arts. Consider the comprehensive coverage of each area.

REFERENCES

Behavioral characteristic progression. Santa Cruz, Calif.: Santa Cruz County Office of Education, 1973.

Brigance, A. H. *Brigance diagnostic inventory of basic skills.* Woburn, Mass.: Curriculum Associates, 1977.

Goodman, L., & Hammill, D. *Basic school skills inventory.* Chicago: Follett Publishing Company, 1975.

Garvin, A. D. The applicability of criterion-referenced measurement by content area and level. In Popham, W. J. (Ed.), *Criterion-referenced measurement.* Englewood Cliffs, N. J.: Prentice-Hall, 1971, pp. 55–63.

Individual criterion-referenced tests. Tulsa, Okla.: Educational Development Corporation, 1973.

KeyMath diagnostic arithmetic test. Circle Pines, Minn.: American Guidance Service Inc., 1971.

Popham, W. J., & Husek, T. R. Implications of criterion-referenced measurement. In Popham, W. J. (Ed.), *Criterion-referenced measurement.* Englewood Cliffs, N. J.: Prentice-Hall, 1971, pp. 17–37.

Prescriptive reading inventory. Monterey, Calif.: California Testing Bureau/McGraw-Hill Book Company, 1973.

Salvia, J., & Yssledyke, J. E. *Assessment in special education.* Boston: Houghton Mifflin Company, 1978.

Stanford achievement test series. New York: Harcourt Brace Jovanovich, Inc., 1973.

Terman, L. M., & Merrill, M. A. *Measuring intelligence.* Boston: Houghton Mifflin Company, 1937.

Chapter 3

Task Analysis

After you have studied this chapter, you should be able to do the following:
1. *Understand task-analysis procedure*
2. *Differentiate the approaches to task analysis*
3. *Discuss the value of using task analysis in diagnosis and remediation*
4. *Relate task analysis to other analytic procedures*
5. *Understand a process of adapting task analysis to a different style of learning*
6. *Demonstrate a task analysis of some academic skill*

Introduction

The ultimate purpose of diagnosis is to provide the proper educational program for the child who is experiencing difficulty in learning. To meet this goal, the diagnostician has a responsibility beyond the task of making a global diagnosis of the learning problem. Whereas identification of the problem is the first step, it must be followed by a plan to implement remediation procedures. If proper remediation is to be prescribed, it is important to know all the steps required in the learning of a task and to pinpoint where in this process a breakdown occurred. Therefore, to the data collected through standardized tests and teacher observation, a new approach to assessment is added—task analysis, i.e., determining the demands of a task to know which approach to use in presenting the material to be learned. (See continuum shown in Figure 10).

Figure 10. Continuum Line for Learning a Task

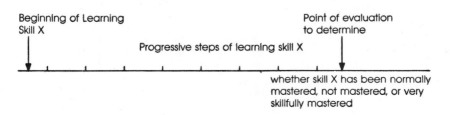

Beginning of Learning
Skill X

Point of evaluation
to determine

Progressive steps of learning skill X

whether skill X has been normally
mastered, not mastered, or very
skillfully mastered

Task analysis must not be equated with remediation per se. To place it in proper perspective, we may say that the process of task analysis is essentially the analysis of the behaviors required to reach a goal. These behaviors may designate how instruction should be carried out as in what to remediate and when to remediate. Thus, task analysis becomes another diagnostic procedure, but one examining the task rather than the subject. Once the demands of the task are determined then one may look at the subject's capacities to formulate how the materials and/or the training for the skills should be presented.

The use of task analysis has wide coverage. Industry has for many years examined tasks and experimented with different approaches to determine in what ways individuals can increase their hourly production. King et al. (1978) and Frederickson (1978) analyzed skills required of secretaries. They used task-analysis procedures as a foundation for the development of a career-relevant instruction for both secretaries and stenographers. Thomas (1978) suggests the use of task analysis to develop a procedure for needs-assessment-implementation process. Different tasks are identified and systemized for use of needs assessment in the community school context.

There are others who have examined the concept of task analysis and have provided background theory and suggestions for procedures to follow when analyzing tasks. They believe that there is a systematic procedure involved in developing skills. Resnick (1973) states that learning occurs in small, carefully guided steps, except when the child has developed generalized competencies such as learning how to learn or problem-solving skills. Gagne (1962) proposed the thesis that intellectual tasks are organized hierarchically. This means that the high-level skills in structures have subskills that must first be attained before performing the high-level skills. Each subskill has immediate descendants, prerequisite to the one in question. Such a concept, as a guide to instruction, suggests that the lowest-level skills should be mastered before moving to the one above, and that this process should continue until the top-level skill is accomplished. Later in 1968, Gagne stated that verbalized knowledge and retrieval of specified facts do not form a hierarchy (Cotton et al., 1977). Therefore some curricula, as in most social-science subject matter units, would not be applicable for the above rationale concerning subskill learning. Cotton et al. (1977) state further that exceptions to hierarchical ordering are frequent enough to merit consideration of an assumption that skill on an item may simply transfer to the next higher item rather than being fully prerequisite to it.

There is some evidence to show that the arbitrary arrangement of sequential steps in learning a task may not always be in accordance with statistical findings for that task. Walker (1978) used a scaleogram analysis to determine whether a hierarchical sequence existed. The hypothesized sequence did not meet the criterion for a developmental sequence. However, a computer-generated sequence in which the order of the first and second task was reversed did meet the criterion.

Another concern is that the difficulty of the task, and particularly of the list materials employed, may underlie a number of findings at variance with the strict scanning interpretation. For example, Schmitt and Scheirer (1977) found that probes of lettersets that form words are responded to faster than those of nonwords, irrespective of the number of list items. Another influence noted was that of practice, search strategies for items in a categorized list changed from hierarchical structure to associative. Miller and Bigi (1977) also found that the nature of the stimuli affects performance on a task, while Wellman (1977) found that more items, distractions, and interference make a task harder. In addition and relative to practice, Wellman found that more time to study makes memorization more certain. We can assume from these studies that the hierarchical steps, when they are identified and validated, may need consideration concerning the difficulty of the task and the time needed for practice. Though steps may be sequenced in learning, e.g., a list of words, the difficulty of the individual words may make a difference in the time schedule for completion of the task.

Relationship to Criterion-Referenced Testing

There is a relationship between task analysis and criterion-referenced testing. The goal of task analysis is to examine where in the task the individual is failing or succeeding; the goal of criterion-referenced testing is to determine what task the child is failing or passing. Task analysis is an intra-analytic function and criterion-referenced testing is an inter-analytic function. For example, in Section II, Reading A, on the Brigance Inventory of Basic Skills (Brigance, 1977), information is provided to show in what area of reading a child is having difficulty. The specific areas are: word recognition, basic sight vocabulary, direction words (action verbs), abbreviations, contractions, and common signs. Inter-analysis is made within this portion of the reading section to show what kinds of tasks or which specific tasks have been accomplished. The intra-analysis, identified with the procedure in task analysis, deals with the act of determining what is involved in learning any one single task. After the weak area has been determined, as in direction words, for example, one would examine the steps necessary for an individual to learn direction words. A direction word might be *draw*. The analysis of the important skills needed to learn that word would include such questions as: does the child see the word?; does the child hear the sounds within the word?; does the child know the meaning of the word?; and can the child repeat the word, sounding it out or saying it? It can be seen that in criterion-referenced tests, we are looking at the task areas with which one is having difficulty; in task analysis we are looking at the procedure involved in helping that individual learn the specific task, or looking at what is involved in learning such a task. Task analysis, thus, can be said to be a step following criterion-referenced assessment.

The following discussion examines the relationship between task analysis and test analysis. The example is provided to show how a battery of tests on one child may be analyzed.

Task Analysis vs. Test Analysis

The term *diagnosis* was first identified and used in the field of medicine. It was associated with determining the nature of a disease (Dorland, 1965). One definition from Webster (1967) adds a broader view: "analysis of the cause or condition, situation or problem". Using that concept, psychologists and educators gradually adopted the term *diagnosis* and by this means analyzed the differences within the body of a standardized test and also the differences between the standardized tests that had been administered as a battery of tests. One has the choice (for educational-planning purposes but not category-identification purposes) to diagnose with either test analysis or task analysis or with both.

Historically speaking, educational/psychological diagnosis has been performed through the use of measurements, namely: intelligence, achievement, aptitude, and personality. These instruments dealing with the skills and abilities of individuals have not included, in any formal way, consideration for the developmental aspects of learning the task being measured. Within the last decade, the concept of analyzing a task has been seen in the writings of a number of concerned authorities: Johnson and Kress (1971), Chalfant and Scheffelin (1969), Gagne (1970), Siegel (1972), Resnick (1973), and Glasser (1973). While this concept was being introduced, clinicians in informal ways were examining the tasks required as they analyzed the test-data responses of a child. No concise plan was followed. It was simply the habit of the clinician to use common logic based on educational training. This logic included a review of not only differences in children's own performances, but also the demands of certain tasks that might not be possible for them.

Some authors accept both test analysis and task analysis: Bush and Waugh (1976), Smead (1977), Bannatyne (1968), and Blackman (1963). Ewing and Brecht (1977) contend that neither test-analysis nor task-analysis procedures have been validated. They do agree that environmental variables (such as teacher, motivation, etc.) have an impact on the teacher-directed learning process and, therefore, any useful assessment-remediation model would need to include processes environmentally oriented. Ysseldyke and Sabatino (1973), who appear to prefer task analysis, accept the test-analysis (diagnostic/prescriptive) model only if a significant interaction between learner aptitude and differential treatment can be demonstrated.

The entire issue emanates from the source of controversy concerning remediation that has been established on constructs such as perceptual-motor, psycholinguistic and/or other.* There are two different issues involved, but the diagnostic issue (test vs. task) probably would not exist if causal relationships could be established conclusively between processing skills (measured by tests) and remediation, which is established on these processing skills. The immediate issue in this chapter, however, deals with the development of the differences between task and test analysis. A brief review of the development of test analysis follows.

The prototype for the test analysis procedure is the work of the psychologists of the late forties and early fifties. A review of the development shows that it became the prominent practice not to use only one major test such as the Stanford Binet** or one of the Wechsler scales**. Instead, several tests were used in the attempt to understand the nature of children's underachievement. The training for clinicians involved analysis of the differences among subtests, as well as analysis of different performances on several tests, such as vocabulary IQ tests and vocabulary subtests on the Stanford Binet or a Wechsler scale. In addition, visual-motor, auditory discrimination, and achievement tests became a part of a battery used in psychological evaluation.

Following the statistical guidelines of Wechsler (1944, 1958), a "convenient cut-off point of two or more scaled scores from the mean" as an abnormal deviation was generally accepted for analysis of the scatter of scores among the subtests. However, at the 15-percent level, F. B. Davis (Wechsler, 1944) found differences of significance

---

*For information on the issues regarding remediation, please read from Hammill and Larsen (1974), Newcomer and Hammill (1976), and Sowell, Larsen, and Parker (1975) for opponents of psycholinguistic and/or other teaching. Read from Kirk (1966), McCarthy, James (1964), McCarthy, Jeanne (1967), Karnes (1968, 1972), Mcleod (1976), Bush (1976), Minskoff (1976), and Lund et al. (1978) for advocates of psycholinguistics.

**These scales are described in Chapter 6.

between pairs of scaled scores on the WAIS to range between 2 and 4 points. This was reported by Wechsler (1958) in the same context of the suggested 2-point cut-off. (It is significant that Wechsler did not say that the 2-point cut-off made a significant difference. He identified this difference as being abnormal and he did say that the magnitude of difference used would depend on the level of significance the examiner wished to set.) Recognition that as much as 4 points' difference would be needed to show some significant differences at the low level of .15 caused many clinicians to be very careful about assuming true significance unless there were a greater magnitude in the difference score. When Glasser and Zimmerman (1967) reported the work of Hopkins and Michael to show that 5 or more points' difference might be needed on the WISC to show significance, this became more widely accepted than differences beginning at 3 scaled points. They showed, for example, that when the Coding score was compared with Information, Comprehension, Arithmetic, Similarities, Vocabulary, or Block Design, a difference of 5 or more points would be needed. A score of 6 or more points would be needed if Coding were compared with Digit Span, Picture Completion, Picture Arrangement, or Object Assembly.

Eventually analysis using the tests mentioned in the preceding paragraphs and the subtest differences reported by Glasser and Zimmerman became the standard procedure. Other tests—as the Illinois Test of Psycholinguistic Abilities, the Frostig Test of Visual Perception, the Wepman Auditory Discrimination and/or the Detroit Test of Learning Apitude—were included, to complete a battery that formed the background data used to determine intelligence levels, process deficits, and achievement levels. Diagnosticians made cross-check comparisons between mental ages and chronological ages on these measures, as well as between differences seen in the processing skills. In this manner, the test analysis was made and prescriptions for remediation were planned from the information obtained.

The issue with the procedure of diagnosis (test analysis) and prescription involves the question of whether inter-test (between tests) and intra-test (within tests) differences can truly represent differences upon which appropriate educational plans for children with learning problems can be established. No longer is it accepted by many authorities that one may assume strengths and weaknesses unless certain stringent statistical analyses are made. In 1976 Piotrowski and Grubbs very ably presented the concept that the worth of inter-test and intra-test analysis has yet to be empirically demonstrated. They cite the work of Littell (1960) and the work of Zimmerman and Woo-Sam (1972) as showing the difficulty of predicting on the basis of individual subtest scores and as showing that subtest patterns have not been established. Bush and Waugh (1976) presented several WISC patterns to show the difficulty of diagnosing for specific categories such as learning disabled, nonreaders, adolescent sociopaths, and dyslexics. Of a more recent data, Salvia and Ysseldyke (1978), who project task analysis as having greater validity than most test analyses, state their concern regarding test patterns. They believe that it is possible to make complex interpretations of underlying pathology in a pupil's profile but they do not believe that school personnel typically have the training and experience necessary to interpret intra-individual differences as indicative of underlying pathology appropriately.* The significant point is that they do

---

*There is probably no controversy that pathological conditions should be diagnosed only by scientist/psychologists who have had specific training under neuropsychologists.

believe that individual differences may be seen in test analysis. They, however, also believe that the vast majority of norm-referenced ability measures lack the necessary reliability and validity to be used in designing educational programs for children, and that hypothesized constructs have not been reliably and validly assessed and, thus, have questionable relevance to instruction. They say that ability (test analysis) trainers see children as demonstrating "figure-ground" difficulties, "visual-motor" difficulties, and "visual-sequencing memory" deficits on the basis of their performance on ability measures with limited reliability. In contrast, they say that "task analysts do not have to demonstrate that their measures reliably and validly assess some hypothetical construct; they need only demonstrate that at least two people can agree on a description of the behavior to be assessed" (Salvia and Ysseldyke, 1978, p.448). All ability trainers, of course, do not make critical decisions on the basis of only one test, but it is recognized that some may, and that some of the tests used may have limited reliability. It is, however, overlooked by many writers that decisions regarding weaknesses are discussed in the placement committee (a multidisciplinary team that makes decisions concerning special-education placement) and input comes not only from the test-ability analysts, but also from the teacher and parent (and sometimes from the supervisors). Empirical evidence is presented to help validate the true weakness. Regarding the reliability of the task analysts' decisions, one task analyst must not defer to another, an act that could occur as often as the use of unreliable tests. In both cases, the integrity of the diagnostician is involved, and caution concerning such critical decisions should be exercised. Whereas Salvia and Ysseldyke do show a negative side to test-analysis procedure, they do provide a means for a psychologist/educational diagnostician to find significant differences within and between the major tests used in test analysis. They provide examples to show true significant differences between subtests on the WISC-R (45 steps are required) and they also provide examples to show significant differences between the WISC-R and other measures, namely, the PIAT and the ITPA.

Piotrowski and Grubbs (1976), who earlier pointed to the need to be cautious concerning subtest differences, considered the fact that the Wechsler table of significant subtest differences is computed using the average subtest standard error of measurement for all eleven age groups. To avoid the error that could arise from the subtest reliability and, thus, from the subtest standard error of measurement for different age levels, they have used the standard error at each age level obtained from Table 10 of the WISC-R Manual (Wechsler, 1974) and have established norms for significant subtest differences at each of these age levels. The standard error of the difference for each comparison was multiplied by 1.96 and 2.58, the z scores corresponding to the .05 and the .01 levels of confidence. The established norms are found in Chapter 6. To secure significant differences between subtests on the WISC-R, diagnosticians may use Piotrowski-Grubbs norms with confidence. *One must, however, go beyond the step of finding significant differences.* Once this difference is established, one must seek to understand the source of the difference. Strengths and weaknesses may be due to many sources; unless these are known, remediation techniques based on such a foundation are certainly questionable. Weaknesses and strengths may be due to a number of factors. Most subtests on the WISC-R have been factored to measure more than one skill. For example, memory is needed when responding to the requirements of subtests of Information, Digit Span, and Arithmetic. A low score in Coding, as pointed out by Piotrowski and Grubbs, may result from poor memory, poor fine-motor skills, poor visual discrimination, anxiety, lack of motivation, lack of experience with paper-and-pencil tasks, or the inability to follow directions. Consideration of the source of the significant difference may be a significant factor in establishing a relationship between ability and performance after training.

We can understand that diagnosticians must determine significant weaknesses if they are to "prove" these weaknesses about a child's ability. However, doing so will not insure that the child can be remediated, nor that a relationship will exist between the remediation and learner aptitude, particularly if the remediation is measured by group performance. While most research is involved with fractionated teaching of one technique to a group of children, perhaps there is only one child in a group who will truly benefit from such a treatment. Keogh (1977) says, "Although few diagnostic or remedial interventions have data to support their claims, almost all interventionists can point to individual cases of strikingly effective 'cures'."

A fact that appears to be completely overlooked by opponents of test analysis is that over the nation there are many children in remediation making their first satisfactory gains in learning the basic skills. These children have been placed in resource rooms, and their educational plans have been established on test analysis. Huber (1979) reports that out of 22 children in a resource room, only four were not making satisfactory progress. Somewhere within the diagnosis established on (ability) test analysis, the findings were correct enough to provide the information on which effective remediation could be planned for 18 children. Research should be generated to determine the influential factors related to success of the majority of children in resource rooms. Could it be the Hawthorne effect, could it be the evidence found in the test analysis on which remediation is planned, or could it be both? Where group research is controversial regarding significant gains in treatment established on test-analysis procedures, perhaps examination of programs for children on an individual basis rather than from means of a group of children warrants greater consideration. It is not likely that we will ever have a cookbook approach for teaching any subject or for diagnosing every child, from task analysis or from test analysis. While we may surely have homogeneous groups for practical purposes of funding and placement, there will likely never be two learning-disabled children who learn exactly alike; never be two children with the same attitude toward learning the same material; nor ever be two who have the same environmental background for learning like material. The efforts to find perfect solutions for groups may be worthy if we attend to the variances within the studies, but such efforts to establish Towers of Babel will lead, no doubt, to more and more individual differences, providing information valuable for working with individual cases.

The challenge is to learn to examine a syndrome such as (1) failure, (2) specific individual differences from test analysis, (3) a child's approach to academic tasks, (4) attitudes of the child toward his work, and (5) environmental influences, both within the school and without. Consideration should be given to every one of these to enhance the chances for success for the child.

Henry Dyer (1962) has said that we do not get rid of yardsticks because they do not measure the distance from here to the moon—they're very mundane items to have around the house. Neither, he says, do we get rid of IQ tests because they do not measure "pure" intelligence; they help us, both school professionals and parents, to understand and predict how children will compete in school! While this is said of IQ tests only and in reference to nonuse of such instruments, it could be said of test analysis—that it does provide a means of help. As in the game of golf, there must be a tee-off position. Information from test analysis provides the teacher with general information about a child. The teacher in turn can consider this with the information obtained from criterion-referenced test information showing the specific content that has not been mastered by the child. From this position, an evaluation can be made of the type of task being failed and of the demands required of the child to perform this task. The teacher, thus, has more information to make a decision concerning how this task will be presented. Let us use the hypothetical case of Mary, who was found to have normal mental age on the Peabody Picture Vocabulary Test (a pictorial presentation) and average ability to *understand the meaning* of words, as shown on the Auditory Reception subtest on the Illinois Test of Psycholinguistic Abilities. However, her ability to *express the meaning* of words, as found on the WISC-R Vocabulary subtest, was found to be below average and significantly different from her other abilities on the same test. It is obvious that the problem at the time of testing dealt with her ability to *express* the meaning of words—the knowledge was intact but not the skill/ability to retrieve and/or express this knowledge. Further evaluation is necessary. In the committee meeting where plans are made for placement and educational treatment, it should be ascertained whether Mary (1) is shy with strangers, adults, and/or friends; (2) has difficulty retrieving ideas in general conversation; (3) has a general memory deficit; (4) has a cooperative or rebellious attitude; (5) is failing only tasks on certain subjects; and (6) whether there is any evidence to show a relationship between her failure and the ability to express ideas. It can be seen that information from every source would be helpful in making the proper decisions concerning both remediation treatment and the evaluation of Mary's performance.

The authors believe that both task analysis and test analysis are valuable in planning for individual differences in children, but they also believe that self-concept, attitudes, and outside pressures must be considered before effective educational prescriptions can be made. Smead (1977) suggests that rejecting either model, task analysis or test analysis, seems unwarranted. Instead, both should be extended to allow adequate coverage of the teaching-learning situation. And finally, she says, the complementary use of both models should not preclude a continuing investigation of different approaches to diagnostic teaching—the process of model building around these issues is just beginning, not concluding.

Case Samples

The following example is the case of Daniel, a child who was not diagnosed as being a special-education candidate. Nonetheless, he was referred as having problems in school. It was decided to make separate test analysis and task analysis on the assessment information. The test analysis was made first, without reference to the criterion-referenced information, except from the observations made while Daniel was taking the norm-referenced tests. Following this and on a different day, the criterion-referenced test was evaluated; an example of a task analysis of one of the failed tasks is shown.

Test-Analysis Procedure of Daniel's Scores

Initial Steps

1. Daniel functions within the normal range of intelligence.
2. IQ scores are on the low side of the mean of 100.
3. The score of 5 on the Information test is 4.33 scaled scores below the mean of his verbal score. (This suggests an uneven skill development in comparison with the majority of his other skills. Achievement in reading has been below average according to the teacher. Information subtest is known to measure memory, cultural milieu, and education experiences. Parents report Daniel never reads and this low score could be caused by lack of reading experiences. Reading and/or broad education experiences would be needed to provide him with general information.)
4. The second lowest score is on the Coding subtest. This score, 6, is 3.22 scores below the mean of his Performance scores. (The time factor and/or visual discrimination could have depressed this score, since other pencil-manipulation tasks with no time limits were accurate enough to place this function in the normal range. Visual Motor Integration age is 8-7 and the Memory for Designs test score is within normal limits. The geometric designs are all drawn without precision but this is at expectancy for his age group and intelligence.)
5. There is some evidence that Daniel may have a figure-ground problem. He drew the diamond on the MFD test (design # 7) with the inside design first. This same procedure was noted on design # 11, where he drew the inside design first and then drew the outside, not completing the total figure around. The teacher reports very poor handwriting skills. This provides other evidence for mild visual-motor problems, along with the fact that his spelling words were written very unevenly.
6. Though his achievement standard scores on the WRAT and the PIAT Reading Comprehension tests were commensurate with the IQ range, there were some features that bear examination. He tended not to try to sound out new words. Instead he said, "I don't know that one." On the Wepman test, there was evidence of an auditory-discrimination problem. Specifically, he had trouble with beginning and ending sounds—*vow* and *thou, clothe* and *clove.* Daniel was easily distracted—attention could be an influence.
7. On the Detroit Test of Learning Ability, where he was required to remember spoken sentences and to remember visual objects and letters, he was slow but within normal limits. However, when required to remember unrelated words, his response was similar to that of a four-year-old. (Whether attention was the basic problem or whether lack of auditory discrimination caused him to fail to remember is not known. The two possibilities should be considered seriously and a program should include both practice in auditory discrimination and activities to help him to *attend at will.* Teacher specifically needs to keep this in mind in the classroom.)
8. Daniel's spelling was approached with a correct beginning sound but not completed correctly, e.g., *cue* for *cook, dres* for *dress,* and *liet* for *light.* (This suggests that he needs help in visual memory of words.)

9. Math-achievement performance showed that Daniel does not attend carefully to math symbols. He added when he should have subtracted and also added when he should have divided. Had he not made these simple errors, he would have made nearer the third-grade level. (Again, attention to detail should be emphasized, also training for perception of the total gestalt instead of the figure against the ground, which appears to be an approach that he uses. It would be wise to present his arithmetic problems with greater spaces in between or teach him to use a marker to occlude other problems as he works.

This first rough draft in making a test analysis shows that one can consider the approach the child makes toward the task, as well as examining the inter-test and intra-test scatter of scores that represent ability and achievement functions.

The battery of tests presented to Daniel included a criterion-referenced test, the Brigance Inventory of Basic Skills. Examination of Daniel's scores on the Brigance reveals that he is behind his age group in the following tasks:

1. Basic vocabulary words and abbreviations
   (Specifically he needs help with the *c* and *k* sounds. He could not identify the beginning sound of *city* as being *c*. He identified *candy*, *can*, and *cat* as beginning with the letter *k*. He also could not identify the letter for the beginning sound of *quart*, *quit*, and *quick*. When Daniel was asked to give the sound of two letters together that would form the first sound of a word, as in *motel*, he kept sounding out the two letters as being separate—*mmm o*. When told to say *mo*, he kept saying *mmm o*, and for *ho* he kept saying *huh o*. He needs to develop skills to recognize configurations as one unit. In addition, he needs help with initial blends and digraphs—*sl, gl, bl, cl, tr, cr, ch,* and *sc*. These should be given particular emphasis, but a review of all seems in order.

2. Language Skills
   (In the language area, Daniel has a need to improve his writing skills. In the math area he was working simple problems, but he added 8 and 3 when he should have subtracted 3 from 8. He could add $12+2$ but he could not subtract 6 from 12 or 9 from 15.

Daniel was found to be achieving at the second-grade level in math, reading, and spelling on the Brigance. (This is the same level found on the WRAT and the PIAT.) With the above information, we have an idea with what content Daniel is having difficulty. The next step is to determine the tasks prerequisite for the completion of each task with which he is shown to be having difficulty. An example of the procedure to follow in only *one task* failed is as follows. Let us take the problem of $12-6=$____. The hierarchical steps begin and follow the assumptions as listed below:

1. Student must pay attention to the requested task.
2. Student must be able to count from 1 to 12.
3. Student must be able to recognize the numerals 1 to 12.
4. Student must be able to identify the set values of the numbers 1 to 12.
5. Student must be able to identify the set values of the numbers 1 and 12.
6. Student must understand the concept of taking away numbers from other numbers.
7. Student must be able to identify the number left after a certain number has been removed.

8. Student must be able to recognize minus symbol.
9. Student must be able to write the answer on the paper unless the problem is stated to request a verbal response.

Should one question the hierarchical position of step two before step three, it is chosen because most children learn to rote count before recognizing the numerals. However, this does not mean that they absolutely must learn to count before recognizing numerals.

In this task-analysis procedure, one can find the "what-to-work-on" information. However, one must follow with step two and find where within the failed task the individual is having difficulty. After this is determined, a flow chart could be made to highlight where to begin with remediation. An example is seen in Figure 11.

It may not be necessary for the teacher to make a flow chart for each weakness. The teacher does need to know where within the task the child is unable to perform in order to plan remediation. In most cases, a well-trained teacher will be able to determine what the child understands by careful observation.

The task-analysis procedure is concerned only with the task and not with the methodology to use to train the child at any point along a scale. The same may be said of the

Figure 11. Flow Chart: Task Analysis and Beginning Remediation

	Question		Remediation
1.	Does student pay attention?	If no →	Plan activities to get attention.
	If yes ↓		
2.	Does student count from 1 to 12?	If no →	Train for rote counting.
	If yes ↓		
3.	Does student recognize numerals 1–12?	If no →	Train for recognition of numerals.
	If yes ↓		
4.	Does student recognize set values, 1–12?	If no →	Train for recognition of set values.
	If yes ↓		
5.	Does student understand concept of take away?	If no →	Train for take-away concept.
	If yes ↓		
6.	Does student recognize minus symbol?	If no →	Train for recognition of minus symbol.
	If yes ↓		
7.	Does student understand and identify the numbers left?	If no →	Train for identification of numbers left.
	If yes ↓		
8.	Can child write the answer on the page?	If no →	Train for writing skills.

test-analysis procedure, with the exception that in the test-analysis procedure, more clues may be found to suggest the direction for remediation. In both the materials the child must learn in the classroom must also be the material involved in the remediation, regardless of the procedure used.

After analysis has been made, an evaluation, as seen in the following example, may be written and placed in the child's folder.

PSYCHOMETRIC DATA

Name: Daniel   *Examined:*
Birthdate: *Age:* 8-2 *Examiner:*
State I: Physical, Mental, Sociological, and Emotional Conditions

Wechsler Scales		*Verbal*		*Performance*	
Verbal IQ:	94	*Information:*	5	*Picture Completion:*	8
Perfor. IQ:	93	*Similarities:*	11	*Picture Arrangement:*	9
Full Sc.:	92	*Arithmetic:*	10	*Block Design:*	12
		Vocabulary:	9	*Object Assembly:*	11
		Comprehension:	10	*Coding:*	6
		Digit Sp.:	(11)	*Mazes:*	

Other Intelligence Tests:

PPVT	*Basal Age:*	—	*Mental Age:*	10-4
	Ceiling:	—		
	Chrono. Age:	—	*IQ:*	120

Other Data:

Brigance Basic Inventory:
Needs help with: c and k sounds, recognition of combinations as units of sounds, writing skills, and practice in very simple addition and subtraction.

					Highest	
State II: Educational Performance Levels					Wechsler	
Achievement Levels	Grade	%	SS	Level	IQ	IQ-SS Discrepancy
WRAT and PIAT Reading Recog.	2.5		91		94	3
Reading Comp.	2.1		89		94	5
Spelling	2.9		96		94	2 (above IQ)
Arithmetic	2.4		90		94	4
General Inf.						
Total						
Reading Cluster						
Math Cluster						
Written Lang. Cl.						
Knowledge Cluster:						

Stage III: Learning Competencies:
Language and Learning Test Data:* Test/s used: DTLA   MA

Visual Attention for Objects	7-4
Visual Attention for Letters	7-6
Auditory Attention for Words	4-5
Auditory Attention for Syllables	7-0

Visual and/or Motor Tests* VMI & MFD   Auditory Tests: Wepman

Mental Age: 8-7   Mental Age: ____   x = 8/30
Comments: Functions within normal   Comments: Daniel has
  limits, but figure ground difficulty.   difficulty discriminating.

PSYCHO-EDUCATIONAL EVALUATION

Name: Daniel   *Examined:*
Birthdate: *Examiner:*
                                        C. A.: 8-2

I. Language Factor

English is the language spoken in the home.

II. Physiological Factors

a. Gross-motor functions are normal.

b. Fine-motor skills are within normal limits, with two exceptions. His psychomotor speed is slow and he has a tendency to make many erasures before completing a drawing. There, also, is evidence of figure-ground problems.

c. Health is normal.

d. *Appearance:* Daniel is a wholesome-looking child with freckles sprinkled about his face. He was dressed in casual clothes and was clean and neat.

III. Emotional/Behavioral Factors

Daniel was quiet and somewhat shy at the outset of the testing. As we moved on into the session, he appeared more relaxed. He responded positively to the performance tasks but responded in a more reserved manner to the verbal tasks. There was no evidence of emotional problems, yet he did show some test apprehension by his questioning facial expression and by his concern about the time.

IV. Intellectual Factors

The evaluation showed that Daniel is functioning in the normal range of intellectual ability, with strengths at the high-average level and weaknesses at the dull-normal level. The total IQ was found to be 92 on the WISC-R. In contrast, and a significant difference, was the IQ of 120 on a picture-vocabulary test. This latter reflected one of his strengths. He appears to recognize objects with much greater skill than his ability to describe them.

V. Educational Factors

Daniel was found to be achieving in reading recognition at grade 2.5, in spelling at grade 2.9, and in arithmetic at grade 2.4. His reading comprehension was found to be at grade 2.1. This general second-grade level was found on the WRAT, the PIAT, and the Brigance. It is commensurate with his total WISC-R IQ of 92, but not with his strengths found in the inter-test scatter. He has difficulty remembering when to attach the *k* sound to *c*, and in seeing letter configurations as having one sound. Writing skills are below par for his years and his attention to math symbols is not consistent.

VI. Learning-Competency Factors

Daniel's responses show that his psychomotor speed is slow and that he is slow to discriminate essential from nonessential detail. In addition, he did not remember general information normally remembered by his peers. There is evidence to indicate that he has difficulty in concentrating/attending to tasks, that he has a mild figure-ground problem, and that he has an auditory-discrimination problem. None of these is critically low, but the degree of severity could make it difficult for Daniel to compete satisfactorily with his peers in academics.

VII. Summary

Daniel is a child who functions within the normal range of intelligence, but one who has some mild problems that could be interfering with his learning. It is recommended that he be provided some remediation help through kinesthetic techniques, to aid his spatial and motor skills and his memory for words. Words and information he is to be held accountable for in the schoolroom should be used when planning the remediation procedure. The neurological-impress method is recommended to help develop his recognition of words during the reading process.

Reporting Psychologist

The case above shows that one may move from test analysis into task analysis of specific problems.

In the field of special education, the teacher-planners will be more concerned with task analyses made on the basic skills. They may choose to run a task analysis (1) on any task in a lesson assignment, (2) on any learning skill, or (3) on any subtest; but they must accede to the demands of the proper procedure to follow in setting up a task analysis. The following discussion on the analyses of lesson assignments, on subtests, and on developmental tasks provides examples to follow in setting up hierarchical steps.

Task Analysis on Lesson Assignments

Let us begin with a reading assignment as an example. Chalfant and Scheffelin (1969) offer as examples two representative approaches to beginning reading. The steps necessary to accomplish the task of reading are analyzed. These are shown in Figures 12* and 13*.

Figure 12 shows the task analysis of a whole-word system of reading. The first step, or subtask, requires the reader to attend to the "word"; the next step is to identify it as a

---

*Figures 12 and 13 from James C. Chalfant and M. A. Scheffelin, "Central Processing Dysfunctions in Children," *NINDS Monograph No. 9*, H.E.W. (Washington, D.C., 1969).

Figure 12. A Whole-Word System of Reading: A Task Analysis

1. Attends to visual stimulus   CAT
2. Identifies visual stimulus as graphic word unit   CAT
3. Retrieves auditory language signal for
   graphic word unit   CAT → (/KAET/)
4. Responds by saying /KAET/   /KAET/
   Terminal behavior—Given a graphic word unit such as "CAT," the reader says the word name "/KAET/" within five seconds

Legend:

CAT	Visual stimulus
CAT	Graphic word unit perceived as a whole visual image
→	Association in the direction indicated
(/KAET/)	Recalled auditory language signal
/KAET/	Spoken word or auditory language signal

Figure 13. A Sound-Symbol System of Reading: A Task Analysis

1. Attends to visual stimulus   CAT
2. Recognizes stimulus as graphic
   word unit   CAT
3. Identifies stimulus as sequence of
   discreet letters   1st=C, 2nd=A, 3rd=T
4. Retrieves phoneme for   C → (/K/)
   each grapheme   A → (/AE/)
                                T → (/T/)
5. Recalls phonemes in temporal
   sequence corresponding to graphic
   sequence in step 3

$$\frac{\text{1st}}{(/K/)} + \frac{\text{2nd}}{(/AE/)} + \frac{\text{3rd}}{(/T/)}$$

6. Blends phonemes into familiar
   auditory language signal   (/KAET/)
7. Responds by saying /KAET/   /KAET/
   Terminal behavior—Given a graphic word unit such as "CAT," the reader says the word name /KAET/ within five seconds

Legend:

CAT	Visual stimulus
C—A—T	Discrete letters in sequence (graphemes)
(/K/)	Recalled auditory sound signal (phoneme)
→	Association or correspondence in the direction indicated
(/KAET/)	Discrete sounds blended into word
/KAET/	Spoken word or auditory language signal

graphic word unit. Following this procedure, the reader must then be able to retrieve the auditory-language signal for the graphic word unit and finally say the word name.

Figure 13 shows an analysis of a sound-symbol system of reading. The first step in this analysis requires the reader to *attend* rather than observe, as in *look at*. (This means to look *at* something rather than to observe and comprehend.) Second, the graphic word unit (visual stimulus) is identified as discrete letters in a sequence. The reader must retrieve (recall and comprehend) a phoneme for each grapheme and place these in a temporal sequence. Finally, the reader must blend the phonemes into a familiar auditory language signal and *say* the "word name". Once the task is analyzed, the appropriate approach to the child's style of learning, whether it deals with a physiological or a psychological problem, may be determined. If child A is a nonverbal-learning child, then the way to start remediation would be to use the whole-word system of reading, which does not demand as much auditory-vocal response. Perhaps child B is also a nonverbal learner, but is, in addition, an uncooperative learner. In order to make a proper remediation plan for child B's styles of learning, counseling and group or play therapy should be considered in addition to use of whole-word system. The therapy may include contingency management, as in behavior modification, or it may involve structuring the reading material around what the child likes to read and is able to read.

Johnson (1968) recommends a different task-analysis approach, citing spelling as an example. Two cases are discussed. An eight-year-old child with dyslexia and severe visual-memory deficiencies made only three errors on an oral-spelling test, but missed more than half of the words when they were dictated, because of being unable to revisualize letters. The child was able to associate the spoken letters, *j a m* with the sweet substance put on bread, but could not associate the printed word with the object. A high-school sophomore had a different type of spelling disability. On a multiple-choice spelling test, the student earned a B, but earned a D on a dictated test. Examine the nature of the task. The first was purely visual and required recognition of the correct spelling. The second called for the conversion of an auditory stimulus to a visual-motor pattern. Because this student was unable to tranduce information from the auditory to the visual modality, it was not possible to write words from dictation. In contrast, some can write but are unable to spell orally because they cannot reauditorize letter names. Throughout the diagnostic study and daily teaching, this type of task analysis is invaluable.

A list of functions to be examined in task analysis is provided by Johnson as follows (the definitions are those of the authors):

Intrasensory—discrimination between two sounds with eyes closed
Intersensory—association of picture or letter that goes with a sound, the integration of two modalities
Sensory modality related—visual, auditory, or haptic task
(a) Verbal—written materials to read and interpret and vocal expression to be interpreted
(b) Nonverbal—pictorial and concrete instructions with a minimum of verbal directions, whether written or vocal

Johnson, also, suggests that a level of the task should be identified after the functions are analyzed. She designates these levels as follows:

Perception—to be known and identified
Memory—to be recalled
Symbolization or conceptualization—to be generalized and categorized

The use of a procedure that analyzes the suggested functions according to Johnson involves a study of the modality and the *type* of response rather than the developmental aspects required in the process of learning the task.* Both are good procedures and could be used in the planning stages of teacher evaluation.

---

*Chalfant and Scheffelin approach task analysis through developmental aspects.

A last suggestion in terms of analysis is for teachers to decide how they expect the subject to respond—through pointing, gesturing, speaking, or writing. This points out the need for modifying assignments in the classroom. Some children have learning styles different enough to handicap their progress unless consideration is given to the most appropriate means of response (for example, oral spelling instead of written spelling) in individual cases. Not only must alternative presentations be chosen for learning-disabled children, but allowances for different means of expressive communication must also be made.

It has been mentioned in the introduction to this chapter that the theorist Gagne (1970) believes some academic skills, verbalizing knowledge and retrieving specified facts, do not form hierarchies. Palmatier, Franzen, Marshman, and Price (1977), recognizing that a teaching comprehension skill demands knowledge of prerequisite competencies, have approached this difficult task of helping students in the learning of basic comprehension skills, which might require (when measured on an achievement test) verbalizing of knowledge and retrieval of specified facts. The following (Figure 14) task analysis is an example of the methodology they applied to teaching the specific comprehension skill of delineating sequence of events in a reading selection. They present it as a sample of one manner in which instruction in this skill area may be approached.

To teach seq. of events

Figure 14. Methodology of Applying Task Analysis*

Entry Behavior
After reading a selection students are unable to sequence the events of the story into the correct order by numbering the sentences.

Final Goal
Given a list of the events from a reading selection students will be able to number the main events in sequential order.

Prerequisites
Reading selections are at the student's independent reading level. Concepts presented within the materials have been previously developed. Other comprehension skills essential to sequencing, such as locating details, have been previously mastered at the student's reading level.

Successive Goal Behaviors
1. *Objective:* Given an 11″ × 18″ piece of drawing paper divided by lines into three parts the students will draw and properly sequence illustrations of a three step activity described by the teacher.
    Procedure:
    1. Teacher prepares drawing paper by marking lines to divide the paper into three 11″ × 6″ sections.
    2. Teacher distributes paper and drawing materials.
    3. Teacher explains that students will draw a picture in each box to illustrate a step in a familiar activity sequence (i.e. leaving room for a fire drill).
    4. Teacher describes the activity sequence to be illustrated being sure to include only three major steps.
    5. Students draw illustrations for each step.
    6. Students compare illustrations with teacher providing guidance in determining accuracy of each student's illustration of the activity.
    7. Students failing to present the activities in proper order will cut their papers and reassemble sections into proper order.

*By the permission of the authors.

Figure 14 (Continued)

8. Activity is repeated with other familiar sequences until all students can illustrate activities in correct order.
9. More complex sequences could be illustrated once three step activities are mastered by dividing the paper into four, five, and then six sections.

II. *Objective:* Given three separate frames of a cartoon depicting a sequence with an explicit beginning middle and ending the students will sequence the frames in logical order.
Procedure:
1. Teacher demonstrates the technique of examining the individual frames of a cut-up cartoon and placing them in sequential order.
2. Students examine individual frames of a cut-up cartoon and place them in sequential order.
3. Students retell the events in order.
4. Repeat steps 1–3 using cartoons of 4, 5 and 6 frames in length.

III. *Objective:* Given teacher-made strips, each stating an occurrence in student's daily routine, the student will sequence the strips in the correct order.
Procedure:
1. Students dictate, in a language experience format, activities from a small portion of the daily class routine in order of occurrence.
2. Teacher uses dictation results to list each event on separate strips of paper for each student's use the next day.
3. Teacher scrambles the strips.
4. Students rearrange strips into correct order.
5. Students check accuracy against chart of original dictation.
6. Repeat steps 1–5 using a larger portion of daily routine.

IV. *Objective:* Given teacher-made strips, each stating one event from a taped selection, students will sequence the strips in the correct order.
Procedure:
1. Students listen to short taped selection at an easy listening level.
2. Students receive scrambled strips each containing a separate event from the taped selection.
3. Students arrange strips into correct order.
4. Students check accuracy, using recording (step 1).
5. Repeat steps 1–5 using longer selections.

V. *Objective:* Given a biography, students will arrange the events into life-stage categories.
Procedure:
1. Students dictate biographies to teacher or on tape for later transcription.
2. Student reads transcribed biography.
3. Teacher, using events from his own biography, demonstrates ordering of events into life-stage categories (i.e., childhood, adolescence, adulthood).
4. Students place the events from their own biographies into life-stage categories.
5. Repeat step 4 using the biography of an individual of interest to students.

VI. *Objective:* Given student-made strips, each stating a major event from a short selection, the student will sequence the strips in the correct order.
Procedure:
1. Students read short selection containing three major events.
2. Students list each major event on a separate strip of paper, referring (if necessary) to the selection.

Figure 14 (Continued)

3. Students scramble the strips.
4. Students rearrange strips into correct order.
5. Student checks accuracy, referring to selection.
6. Repeat steps 3, 4, and 5 with each student having exchanged strips with a class-mate.
7. Repeat steps 1–5, using selections with 4, 5, and 6 main events.

VII. *Objective*: Given student-made strips and teacher-made strips each stating a main event from a short selection, students will match the corresponding strips and arrange and number the strips in the correct sequence.
Procedure:
1. Students read a short selection containing four or five major events.
2. Students list each event on a separate strip of paper, referring (if necessary) to the selection.
3. Students match each student-made strip with the corresponding teacher-made strip.
4. Teacher checks accuracy of matching activity. (Discussion and practice are provided when necessary.)
5. Students number pairs of strips corresponding with the order of events in the selection.
6. Students check accuracy, referring to a key.
7. Repeat steps 1–6, using selections with six to ten main events.

VIII. *Objective*: Given teacher-prepared strips, each stating a major event from a short selection, students will arrange and number the strips in the correct sequence.
Procedure:
1. Students read a short selection containing five major events.
2. Students arrange teacher-prepared strips in correct sequence.
3. Students number each strip corresponding with the order of events in the selection.
4. Students check accuracy, referring to a key.
5. Repeat steps 1–4 using selections with six to ten main events.

IX. *Objective*: Given a teacher-prepared worksheet listing the main events of a short selection, students will be able to number the events in the correct order of occurrence.
Procedure:
1. Students read short selection containing five major events.
2. Students read the list of events presented on the worksheet.
3. Students number the events on the worksheet in the correct order of occurrence.
4. Students check accuracy, referring to a key.
5. Repeat steps 1–4, using selections with six to ten major events.

The authors of this task-analysis format agree that not all skills need to be taught in such small steps, nor that all instructional plans require such detailed delineation; however, it is offered to show one way that assures student mastery at each step.

Task Analysis of Classifications of Developmental Tasks

Figures 15 through 19 show the task-analysis procedure, which may be applied to various classifications (Chalfant and Scheffelin, 1969).

According to the construct in Figure 15, the learner must initially attend the vocal-sound units and then must discriminate between the sounds made. Step three includes a reciprocal association formed between the sound unit and an experience. This association allows the learner to interpret the vocal sound as a meaningful language signal, which is stored until retrieved when needed. In the fourth step, analysis of more complex signals occurs. This allows for greater refinement of interpretation, and subse-

Figure 15. Acquiring Auditory Receptive Language: A Task Analysis

1. *Attention*. Attend to vocally produced auditory sound units; i.e., noises, speech sounds, words, phrases, sentences
2. *Discrimination*. Discriminate between auditory-vocal sound units
3. *Establishing correspondences*. Establish reciprocal association between the auditory-vocal sound units and objects or events
    (a) Store and identify auditory-vocal sound units as meaningful auditory-language signals—substitute auditory-language signals for actual objects and/or events.
    (b) Establish word order sequences and sentence patterns
4. *Automatic auditory-vocal decoding*
    (a) Improve interpretation by analyzing increasingly more complex auditory-language signals
    (b) Increase the speed and accuracy of the reception of auditory-language signals through variation, practice, and repetition to the point of automatic interpretation
    (c) Shift attention from the auditory-language signals to the total meaning that is carried by the signal sequence
5. *Terminal behavior*. Respond appropriately to verbal commands, instructions, explanations, questions, and statements.

quently, through practice, it encourages automatic interpretation. Following this, the emphasis shifts from the mechanics of sequencing the language, or the making of sentences, to the meaning to be conveyed. In the last step appropriate response occurs.

Figure 17 deals with the acquisition of expressive auditory language, which begins with *intention* instead of *attention*. First, the learner must have a need to communicate through vocal speech. In step two the message is retrieved and the appropriate vocal-language signals are sequenced. Next the vocal-motor sequence is organized. Automatic encoding follows, in which the learner combines simple vocal-language

Figure 16. Acquiring Expressive Auditory Language: A Task Analysis

1. *Intention*
    (a) Possess the need to communicate
    (b) Decide to send message vocally
2. *Formulate message*. Retrieve and sequence the appropriate vocal-language signals
3. *Organize the vocal-motor sequence*
    (a) Retrieve the vocal-motor sequence for producing the selected vocal-language signals
    (b) Execute the vocal-motor sequence for producing the vocal-language signal
4. *Automatic vocal encoding*
    (a) Combine simple vocal-language signals to form more complex vocal-language signal sequences
    (b) Increase the rate, accuracy, length, total number, and types of vocal-language signal sequences to the point of automatic production
    (c) Shift attention from the mechanics of producing vocal-language signal sequences to the contents of the message to be sent
5. *Terminal behavior*. To produce appropriate verbal instructions, commands, explanations, descriptions, and questions

Figure 17. Acquiring Vocal-Motor Production: A Task Analysis

1. *Motion.* Random movements of the vocal-motor apparatus produce random vocal-sound units
2. *Attention*
   (a) Attends to kinesthetic stimuli produced by movement of the child's own vocal-motor apparatus
   (b) Attends to vocal-sound units produced by self and others
3. *Repetition.* Begins to repeat vocal-motor movements which result in the repetition of vocal-sound units
4. *Discrimination.* Discriminate between different vocal-sound units and between different motor movements
5. *Establishing correspondences*
   (a) Establish a reciprocal association between a vocal-sound unit and the motor movement which produces that sound unit
   (b) Store and retrieve vocal-sound units and motor movements
6. *Automatic vocal production.* Increase the speed and accuracy of vocal-sound production through variation, practice, and repetition, to the point of automatic reproduction
7. *Terminal behavior.* To deliberately reproduce the appropriate vocal-sound unit

signals to form more complex vocal-language signal sequences. The speed, accuracy, length, total number, and types of signal sequences become more automatic through practice. Soon attention is shifted from the mechanics of communication to the meaningfulness of the message. The terminal behavior in step five is to produce appropriate verbal vocalizations.

Three other task analyses are provided by Chalfant and Scheffelin and are shown here in Figures 17, 18, and 19.

Task Analysis of Subtests

In the process of diagnosis, it is often found that students are capable of mastering some processing skills and primary mental abilities, but not others. For example, a student may show high scores in subtests measuring comprehension but not in subtests dealing

Figure 18. Encoding Graphic-Language Symbols: A Task Analysis

1. *Intention*
   (a) Possess the need to communicate
   (b) Decide to send the message in graphic form
2. *Formulate the message*
   (a) Sequence the general content of the message
   (b) Retrieve the appropriate auditory-language symbols which best express the intent of the communication
3. *Retrieve* the graphic-language symbols which correspond to the selected auditory-language signals
4. *Organize the graphic-motor sequence*
   (a) Retrieve the appropriate graphic-motor sequence
   (b) Execute the graphic-motor sequence for producing the graphic-language symbols

Figure 19. Developmental Hierarchy of Writing Tasks

1. *Scribbling*
2. *Tracing*
    (a) Connected letters or figures
    (b) Disconnected letters or figures
3. *Copying*
    (a) From a model
    (b) From memory
    (c) Symbolic and nonsymbolic
4. *Completion tasks*
    (a) Figure
    (b) Word completion—supply missing letters
        (1) Multiple choice
        (2) Recall
    (c) Sentence completion—supply missing word
5. *Writing from dictation*
    (a) Writing letters as they are spoken
    (b) Writing words and sentences
    (c) Supply missing word
    (d) Supply missing sentence
6. *Propositional writing*

*Figures 15 through 19 from James C. Chalfant and M.A. Scheffelin, "Central Processing Dysfunctions in Children," *NINDS Monograph No. 9,* H.E.W. (Washington, D.C., 1969).

with association; i.e., the individual has difficulty relating what is understood about one situation to other events. In such cases, one may wish to analyze what is required of one task that is not required of another. For this reason, one may wish to task analyze subtests to illuminate possible weaknesses that may be interfering with any specific task.

We have analyzed the auditory-association subtest from the ITPA to describe how subtest analyses may be adapted from the Chalfant and Scheffelin guides. Further, to show use of such analyses in a concrete situation, an example using the demonstrator item from the same subtest on the ITPA is provided. These are found in Figures 20 and 21.

To make practical use of subtest analysis, one may move to a remediation procedure that involves examining a child at each step within a task. By use of the example in Figure 22, a flow chart for remediation is shown in Figure 22.

One is reminded that task analysis does not tell one *how* to remediate; in the flow chart above if the child has mastered all steps up to making the association, then the problem is to begin a series of experiences to help develop skills in relating one object/event to another. If the child has not mastered the initial steps, remediation at the last step will be more difficult.

Figure 20. Auditory Association Process: Task Analysis of a Subtest From the ITPA

1. *Attention.* Attention to vocally produced auditory sound units (i.e., noises, speech sounds, words, phrases, sentences)
2. *Discrimination.* Discriminate between auditory-vocal sounds units found in two sets of sentences or phrases
3. *Establishing correspondences.* Establish reciprocal associations between the auditory-vocal sound units and objects or events
   (a) Retrieve and identify auditory-vocal sound units as meaningful auditory-language signals. Substitute auditory language signals of the two sets
   (b) Establish word order sequences and sentence patterns of the two sets
4. *Automatic auditory-vocal decoding.*
   (a) Shift attention from the auditory-language signals to the total meaning that is carried by the signal sequences
   (b) Retrieve a common denominator term (aud-vocal symbol) that makes association between the two sets
   (c) Retrieve the auditory-vocal symbol that stands for the common denominator to fit set two
5. *Terminal behavior.* Respond with appropriate auditory-vocal symbol to complete set two

Figure 21. Application of Task Analysis to Auditory Association Task

"Grass is green—sugar is _____"

1. *Attention* to vocally produced words and phrases "Grass is green, sugar is _____"
2. *Discriminate* sound units of *grass, is, green, sugar*
3. *Establish correspondence*
   Associate object (*grass*) with color (*green*) and object (*sugar*)
   (a) Retrieve and identify *grass* and *green* and *sugar* as meaningful auditory language signals. Substitute auditory language signals for actual objects and events
   (b) Establish word sequences and sentence patterns of "Grass is green, sugar is _____"
4. *Automatic auditory-vocal decoding*
   (a) Shift attention from auditory language signals to the total meaning that is carried by the sequence "Grass is green, sugar is _____"
   (b) Retrieve a common denominator term (auditory-vocal signal) which makes association between the two sets of signal sequences—*"color"*
   (c) Retrieve the auditory-vocal symbol that stands for the common denominator to fit the second set—*"white"*
5. *Terminal behavior.* Respond with appropriate auditory-vocal symbol to complete second set—*"white"*

Another means of analyses of subtests is that reported by Hakim (1974–75)*, whose purpose is to delineate the critical skills necessary for tasks in the academic areas of reading, writing, and arithmetic. He suggests four dimensions: (1) input, (2) output, (3) cognition, and (4) memory.

*Hakim's concepts are from Junkala (1972, 1973a, 1973b).

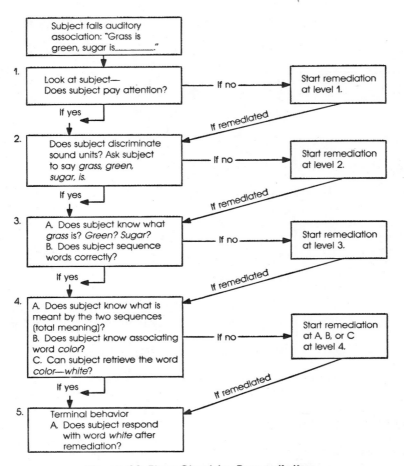

Figure 22. Flow Chart for Remediation

Input. Input is the receiving of information and the beginning of the learning process through sensory modalities. Both verbal and nonverbal experiences are included. The sensory modalities to be utilized are auditory and visual.

Input

	Verbal	Nonverbal
Auditory		
Visual		

If the task includes the teacher's giving verbal information, the input would be auditory-verbal because the child must hear the stimulus, and verbal because words are involved.

Output. Output is the expression of information through vocalization or motor expression. The stimulus may be either verbal or nonverbal.

Output

	Verbal	Nonverbal
Vocal		
Motor		

If the teacher asks a student to write a word, the output is motor-verbal because the child is writing (motor) a word (verbal).

Cognition. The act of knowing involves perceptual, coding, and conceptual levels.

Cognition

Perception	
Coding	
Conceptual	

Hakim identifies the perceptual as the level of differentiation among stimuli, as between *feather* and *father*.

The conceptual level involves classifying and categorizing experiences; whereas, the coding level deals with letters that will graphically record the sound of their names.

Memory. The memory dimension incorporates the level of awareness, recognition, and recall.

Memory

Awareness	
Recognition	
Recall	

At the awareness level, a person has a model to copy or reproduce. Clues are present to assist in the solution of the problem at the recognition level; at the recall level no concrete clues are available to aid the person.

Hakim presents the following model to illustrate his approach to task analysis.

Task. The student is required to write the word that the teacher says on a piece of paper (spelling quiz).

1. *Input*—Auditory-verbal (auditory because the student must hear the word and verbal because a word is used)

2. *Output*—motor-verbal (motor because the student must write, and verbal because a word is being written)

3. *Cognition*—coding (because letter sounds are being transformed into the graphic representation)

4. *Memory*—recall (because no clues are present—we are asking the student to re-visualize the word)

The educational diagnostician needs to analyze the tasks involved in the various tests used in the diagnostic process. With this information, the diagnostician can pinpoint more precisely the strengths and weaknesses of the student. One example of the use of this task-analysis procedure applied to tests has been identified by Hakim.

On subtest 9 of the Detroit Test of Learning Aptitudes, visual attention span for objects, the examiner shows the child a card, removes the card, and asks the child what he or she saw. The analysis can be

1. Input—visual-nonverbal
2. Output—vocal, verbal
3. Cognition—perceptual
4. Memory—recall

It can quickly be determined that this task requires visual input skills with initial nonverbal demands. Then the requirements change. They become vocal-verbal when the student must state through cognition (perceptual) what is recalled (memory).

Such an analysis helps the examiner analyze the data. If the child does not respond to an item, the examiner may, through the process of checks and counterchecks with other analyzed responses, begin to eliminate the dimensions that tend to be true or to hold when compared with other subtests. Continued analysis can finally highlight which dimensions are being failed most often—visual or auditory input, motor or vocal expression, perception, conceptualization, coding, or the various levels of memory.

The reader may choose, after having read the many possible approaches to task analysis, to modify any of these to meet a particular need. Figures and charts graphically portray the information needed to determine the demands of the task, making it easier to match the cognitive style of learning peculiar to any one student.

Summary

This chapter introduces some relatively new approaches to task analysis, and a description of how to begin and plan a task analysis is explained. Three specific areas are covered: (1) task analysis of lesson assignments, (2) task analysis of classification, and (3) task analysis of subtests. In addition, the controversy between task analysis and test analysis is discussed.

The classification analysis from Chalfant and Scheffelin (1969) deals with developmental demands for learning, as they relate to basic language skills. They are explicit, offering steps to help determine some possible areas where the breakdown in learning may have occurred.

The Johnson (1968) approach to task analysis offers a framework in which to examine academic tasks like intersensory and intrasensory modal tasks. The Palatier et al. model describes a step-by-step procedure for teaching comprehension skills. Two flow charts show the procedure to follow in using task analysis in remediation. Junkala's model for task analyzing a subtest is described according to Hakim (1974–75).

Student Assignments

Student will make a task analysis on the learning of two words, was *and* saw.

Student will make a task analysis on the learning of a simple problem in division.

Student will make a task analysis on the development of any primary mental ability.

Student will make a task analysis on a failed subtest response as in the following:

"*A table is made of wood, a typewriter is made of ____.*"

Student will make a flow chart for remediation on the failed subtest.

Student will use a hypothetical position, such as inattention, as the cause for failure to discriminate sounds, and then make a series of objectives for remediation.

Discussion Questions

Where no significant differences between erratic subtest scores on the WISC-R are found and one says that this simply means uneven skill development, what could be the difference between the two?

Discuss the practicality of making task analysis on all basic skills learned in the public schools.

In determining strengths and weaknesses within tests and test batteries, is it enough to show that there are significant differences?

If a student does not discriminate between auditory-vocal sound units, what would be the logical steps to follow in analyzing the failure of this task?

REFERENCES

Bannatyne, A. Diagnosing learning disabilities and writing remedial prescriptions. *Journal of Learning Disabilities*, 1968, *1*: 242–249.

Biggee, M. L., & Hunt, M. P. *Psychological foundations of education: An introduction to human development and learning.* New York: Harper and Row, 1958.

Blackman, L. S. Research needs in the special education of the mentally retarded. *Exceptional Children*, 1963, *29*, 377–384.

Brigance, A. H. *Brigance diagnostic inventory of basic skills.* Woburn, Mass.: Curriculum Associates, 1977.

Bush, W. J., & Waugh, K. W. *Diagnosing learning disabilities* (2nd ed.). Columbus, Ohio: Charles E. Merrill, 1976.

Bush, W. J. Psycholinguistic remediation in the schools. In Newcomer, P., & Hammill, D. *Psycholinguistics in the schools.* Columbus, Ohio: Charles E. Merrill, 1976.

Chalfant, J., & Scheffelin, M.A. *Central processing dysfunctions in children.* NINDS Monograph No. 9. Washington, D.C.: U.S. Department of Health Education and Welfare, 1969.

Cotton, J., Gallagher, J. P., & Marshall, S. P. Identification and decomposition of hierarchical tasks. *American Educational Research Journal,* Summer 1977, *14*: 189–212.

Dorland's Medical Dictionary (24th ed.). Philadelphia: W. B. Saunders Co., 1965.

Dyer, H., An interview with Dr. Henry S. Dyer (Jeanne Shea, Interviewer). New York: J. Walter Thompson Co., February 1962.

Ewing, N., & Brecht, R. Diagnostic/prescriptive instruction: A reconsideration of some issues. *Journal of Special Education*, Fall 1977, *11*: 323–327.

Frederickson, E. Task analysis of secretaries in the Washington D.C. area. *Delta Pi Epsilon Journal*, January 1978, *20*, no. 1: 26–31.

Gagné, R. M. Learning hierarchies. *Educational Psychologist*, 1968, *6*: 1–9.

Gagné, R. M. The acquisition of knowledge. *Psychological Review,* 1962, *69*: 355–365.

Gagné, R. M. *The conditions of learning* (2nd ed.). New York: Holt, Rinehart and Winston, 1970.

Glasser, A. J., & Zimmerman, I. L. *Clinical interpretation of the Wechsler intelligence scale for children.* New York: Grune and Stratton, 1967.

Glasser, R. Hierarchies in children's learning: a symposium (L. B. Resnick, Ed.). *Instructional Science,* 1973, *2,* no. 3: 353–357.

Hakim, C. S. Task analysis: One alternative. *Academic Therapy*, 1974–1975, *X*, no. 2.

Hammill, D., & Larsen, S. The effectiveness of psycholinguistic training. *Exceptional Children*, 1974, *41*: 5–14.

Johnson, D., Educational principle for children with learning disabilities. In *Minimal brain dysfunction.* Chicago: Society for Crippled Children and Adults, 1968.

Johnson, D. J., & Myklebust, H. B. *Learning disabilities: Educational principles and practices.* New York: Grune and Stratton, 1967.

Johnson, M. S., & Kress, R. A., Task analysis for criterion-referenced tests. *The Reading Teacher*, 1971, *24*, no. 4: 355–359.

Junkala, J. Task analysis and instructional alternatives. *Academic Therapy*, Fall 1972: 36.

Junkala, J. Task analysis: Part I. *Teacher Guide for Exceptional Children*, June 1973a: 10.

Junkala, J. Task analysis: The processing dimension. *Academic Therapy,* Summer 1973b: 401–409.

Karnes, M. B., *Helping young children develop language skills.* Arlington, Va.: Council for Exceptional Children, 1968.

Karnes, M. B. *Goal program: Language development.* Springfield, Mass.: Milton Bradley, 1972.

Keogh, B. K. Attentional analysis of learning problems. *Claremont Reading Conference Yearbook*, 1977, 41: 121–124. Also, Working together: A new direction. *Journal of Learning,* October 1977, 10: 478–82.

King, P. H., Lee, D. W., & Dale, O. J. Development of a catalogue of performance objectives for secretarial, stenographic, typing and related occupations. *Delta Pi Epsilon Journal.* January 1978, 20, no. 1: 32–40.

Kirk, S. *Diagnosis and remediation of psycholinguistic abilities.* Urbana, Ill.: University of Illinois, 1966.

Littell, W. M. The WISC—A review of a decade of research. *Psychological Bulletin*, 1960, 57: 132–162.

Lund, K., Foster, G. E., McCall-Perez, F. The effectiveness of psycholinguistic training: a reevaluation. *Exceptional Children,* Fall 1978, 44: 310–319.

McCarthy, J. How to teach the hard to reach. *Grade Teacher,* May–June 1967: 97–101.

McCarthy, J. J. The importance of linguistic ability in the mentally retarded. *Mental Retardation*, 1964, 2: 90.

McLeod, J. Psycholinguistic training today. In Newcomer, P., & Hammill, D., *Psycholinguistics in the schools.* Columbus, Ohio: Charles E. Merrill, 1976.

Miller, P. H., & Bigi, L. Children's understanding of how stimulus dimensions affect performance. *Child Development*, December 1977, 48: 1712–1715.

Minskoff, E. H. Research on the efficacy of remediating psycholinguistic disabilities; critique and recommendations. In Newcomer, P., & Hammill, D., *Psycholinguistics in the schools.* Columbus, Ohio: Charles E. Merrill, 1976.

Newcomer, P., & Hammill, D. *Psycholinguistics in the schools.* Columbus, Ohio: Charles E. Merrill, 1976.

Palmatier, R. A., Franzen, A. M., Marshman, K., & Price, A. Detailed task analysis and planning for insuring student learning of basic comprehension skills. *Reading Improvement*, Winter 1977, 14, no. 4: 275–279.

Piotrowski, R. J.; & Grubb, R. D. Significant subtest score differences on the WISC-R. *Journal of School Psychology*, 1976, 14, no. 3.

Resnick, L. B. Hierarchies in children's learning: A symposium. *Instructional Science*, 1973, 2, no. 3: 311–349.

Salvia, J., & Ysseldyke, J. E. *Assessment in special and remedial education.* Boston: Houghton Mifflin Company, 1978, p. 448.

Schmitt, J. C., & Scheirer, C. J. Task difficulty as a mediator of subject strategy in memory scanning. *American Journal of Psychology*, December 1977, 90, no. 4: 565–575.

Seigel, E. Task analysis and effective teaching. *Journal of Learning Disabilities*, 1972, 5: 519–532.

Smead, V. Ability training and task analysis in diagnostic/prescriptive teaching. *Journal of Special Education*, Spring 1977, *11*: 113–125.

Sowell, V., Larsen, S., & Parker, R. The efficacy of psycholinguistic training through the MWM program. (Unpublished manuscript) Austin, Texas: University of Texas, 1975.

Thomas, D. F. From needs assessment to implementation; a planning and action guide. *Educational Technology*, July 1978, *18*: 5–9.

Walker, A. A. Developmental sequence of skills leading to conservation. *Journal of Genetic Psychology*, June 1978, *132*: 313–14.

Webster's seventh new collegiate dictionary. Springfield, Mass.: G. and C. Merriam Company, 1967.

Wechsler, D. *Measurement of adult intelligence* (3rd ed.). Baltimore: Williams and Wilkins, 1944.

Wechsler, D. *The measurement and appraisal of adult intelligence.* (4th ed.). Baltimore: Williams and Wilkins, 1958.

Wechsler, D. *Manual, Wechsler intelligence test for children—revised.* New York: Psychological Corp., 1974.

Wellman, H. M. Preschoolers' understanding of memory-relevant variables. *Child Development*, December 1977, *48*: 1720–1723.

Zimmerman, I. L., & Woo-Sam, J. Research with the Wechsler intelligence scale for children: 1960–1970. *Journal of Clinical Psychology Monograph Supplement*, 1972, no. 33.

Part II

Formal Assessment

Part II of this text discusses tests used in more formal diagnosis. Chapter 4, which deals with observation and screening, could be considered to cover quasi-formal procedures; however, it is felt that formal diagnosis should be preceded by a study of the kinds of academic problems to be measured and the processing deficits that may be related. Specific emphasis concerning the identification of the emotionally disturbed is discussed in a paper by Louis Fairchild, Ph.D., Head of the Department of Psychology at West Texas State University and a member of the Texas Board of Psychological Examiners. In this paper, the teacher/diagnostician is made aware of the research on identifying the child who is emotionally/behaviorally disturbed and of the discrete differences that characterize these children. The other three chapters are presented to introduce the kinds of tests that are used to measure skills and behaviors described in Chapter 4. These tests are specifically concerned with perceptual-motor, intelligence, adaptive, achievement, and language/learning measures.

Chapter 4

Observational and Screening Assessment

After completing this chapter, the student should have the ability to do the following:

1. *Have knowledge of the processing problems learning-disabled children may experience*
2. *Have knowledge of the academic problems children encounter*
3. *Have knowledge of screening instruments to be used in initial assessment procedures*
4. *Know how to organize information to improve observation*
5. *Understand the differences between symptoms and signs in medical diagnosis*
6. *Understand the function of diagnosis*
7. *Understand the problem of defining emotional disturbance*
8. *Be able to discuss the problem of teacher identification of the emotionally disturbed*
9. *Know the importance of the school's responsibility in identification of emotional disturbance*
10. *Be aware of the criteria for classifying problem behavior*
11. *Know the principles involved in determining aberrant behavior*
12. *Know categories and classification systems to follow in identification of the emotionally disturbed*
13. *Justify reasons for caution in identifying behavioral disorders*

Introduction

Diagnosis of learning and/or behavior problems has been the responsibility of clinical experts, psychologists, counselors, and educational diagnosticians. A major move today is to prepare teachers to handle a part of this duty of assessment. Check lists covering the varieties of observable behavior among children in special education are not only available commercially, but are also being devised within local school systems. Even as early as 1957, Slingerland had a checklist survey for language disabilities. More recently Meier, Cazier, and Giles (1971), Goodman and Hammill (1976), and Myklebust (1971) have authored screening instruments designed specifically for student evaluation by teachers. In 1966, Clements identified the characteristics of the minimally brain injured, which provided some clues in determining channels and styles of learning as well as perception, discrimination, conceptual, motor, and academic problems. Whereas these characteristics are not to be used to qualify placement of children in special education, they continue to be important for consideration in determining how material may be presented to a child or whether the child has difficulty learning in the regular classroom. For example, a child who cannot attend or is hyperactive may need one-to-one teaching rather than training within a group. If the child has a perceptual and/or discrimination problem, it may be necessary to learn letters/words by tracing them or by viewing them in different sizes or colors. Also, if there is a psycholinguistic problem, the child may need a very special language program to facilitate communication.

This chapter covers (1) the kinds of problems to observe, both academic and processing, and (2) the kinds of screening instruments that may be used by the teacher to collect important data to be added to the evaluation procedure. Teacher observation and clinical testing together comprise a thorough approach to evaluation from the standpoint of the school's responsibility. However, to make the evaluation complete, it is often necessary to have some social and medical information from other sources. The teacher may need to make referrals outside of the school and, in such cases, will need to develop the skills of knowing what to look for in observation and screening. Having these skills will build adeptness in the evaluation procedure.

The first part of this chapter pertains to the kinds of behavior to be observed.* These behaviors are presented under the headings of specific processing functions that have been identified by authorities in the various academic and special-education fields. Each authority has arranged the problems in language or learning from a different hierarchy of experiences. These categories may be used as frameworks for instructional planning.

Academic Processing Skills

Identification of Sensory and Perceptual Disturbances in Reading

Children who have problems in reading may be having difficulty in perception. If the child is reading and miscalls words in a sentence, as in "The boy ran *there* (through) the house," the inference is that the child has a form-perceptual problem. Particularly is this inferred if the sentence is immediately corrected and the child reads *through* instead of *there*. The logic of the understood action aids the student in making the change, even though the visual form of the word is not recognized. If the error is not corrected, it can be inferred that the child has a perceptual and a comprehension problem.

One of the difficulties in observation is knowing what to look for and/or how to identify what one is observing. Examination of what the authorities in reading and

---

*See page 86 for an example in the use of Task Analysis to extend the possible behaviors to be observed.

special education say shows that they have identified specific processing functions that help us in this observation procedure.

Let us look first at Gray's frequently used definition of reading (Cheek and Cheek, 1980, p. 5). It is identified as a four-step process as follows:

1. Word Perception: The printed word is perceived.
2. Comprehension: The meaning of the printed word is understood.
3. Reaction: Feelings and past experiences of the reader influence the ideas about the word.
4. Integration: A person's own personal perspective of the word is integrated with ideas and applied to daily activities.

Second, we may examine the processes needed to develop comprehension and oral reading (a product), as arranged by Burns and Roe (1980) and Aukerman and Aukerman (1981).

Burns and Roe (p. 3) organize aspects of the reading process as follows:*

Sensory: The reading process begins with a sensory impression. The reader perceives the printed symbol visually if not blind. The blind person uses the tactile sense. The auditory sense is that of associating the printed word/letters with spoken words/sounds.

Perceptual: The perceptual process involves interpretation of the sensory impressions.

Sequential: The printed data written in English generally appear from left to right, and from top to bottom. The reader's eyes must follow the sequence.

Experiential: Meaning of the printed word is derived from the reader's background of experiences. Children will find it easier to read words that they know.

Thinking: The reader uses the printed word as information from which he makes inferences and draws conclusions.

Learning: The reader may use his skill in reading to learn other information.

Association: Associations may be made between the written word and pictures, objects or events. When phonics is being taught, associations are made between the written symbols (graphemes) and the sounds (phonemes).

Affective: Interest, attitudes, and self-concepts influence the efforts put forth to learn to read. Children with a positive regard for reading will put forth more effort than those with negative regard.

Aukerman and Aukerman (1981, p. 5) divide the "very complicated psychological process" (reading) into four major categories:

1. Perceptual learning (or perceptual discrimination)
2. Association learning (or stimulus-response association)
3. Cognitive learning
4. Affective learning

They also state that sensory modalities, visual, hearing, touching, and feeling are at the origin of perception.

From the reading theorist's organizations, we move to the special educator's hierarchical steps in learning and see that there are similarities in the analyses of the learning

---

*The first five aspects are at task analysis of the reading process.

process. For example, Johnson and Myklebust (1967) provide the following processing steps: Sensation, Perceptual, Imagery, Symbolization, Conceptualization, Inner Language, Receptive Language and Expressive Language. Chalfant and Scheffelin analyze three broad categories: (1) Analysis of Sensory Information, (2) Synthesis of Sensory Information, and (3) Symbolic Operations. Mary Meeker (1973, 1974) has identified from the Guilford Structure of Intellect several functions that are needed for a child to learn to read: Cognition of Figural Units (CFU—Auditory and Visual), Evaluation of Figural Units (EFU—Auditory and Visual), and Memory for Figural Units (MFU—Auditory and Visual). For advanced reading, other triads are needed: Cognition of Semantic Relations (CMR), Evaluation of Semantic Relations (EMR), and Convergent Production of Semantic Relations (NMR).

In all of the above categories of steps, *perception* appears to be a common term identified as a beginning process. One can see use of this term by the following discussion. Johnson and Myklebust (1967) identify a *perceptual dysfunction* as a dysfunction in the reaction to patterns. They quote from Young (p. 33) that the neurological deficiency may consist of inadequate converting of sensations into electrical impulses. When this occurs, the child may not be able to discriminate among letters, words, or sounds, or perceive differences in texture, taste, or smell. They consider this function to be second in the hierarchical steps in learning, feeling that it "by reciprocation disturbs all the levels of experience that fall above it."

Chalfant and Scheffelin (1969) infer perceptual processing skills in task analyzing sensory functions, including auditory, visual, and haptic processing. *Auditory processing dysfunction*, they say, causes difficulty in (1) identifying the source of sounds, (2) the discrimination between sounds or words, (3) discrimination of pitch, rhythm, and melody, (4) discriminating significant from insignificant stimuli; and (4) combining speech sounds into words and/or understanding the meaning of environmental sounds in general. They consider the *visual processing* dysfunction to cause difficulty in (1) visually examining the individual details of an object; (2) determining the dominant visual cues; (3) integrating individual visual stimuli into simultaneous groups and obtaining meaning; (4) classifying objects into visual categories; and (5) making comparisons of the visual hypothesis with the actual object as it is perceived. *Haptic processing* dysfunction causes difficulty in obtaining information from the cutaneous and kinesthetic systems as they operate independently and simultaneously. Although their analysis goes before and beyond what is commonly known as perception, elements of the term, perception, can be seen in their use of such expressions as understanding and obtaining meaning.

Perception inferences from the Structure of Intellect categories identified by Meeker are seen in the first triad, Cognition of Figural Units, meaning the act or process of knowing, including awareness and judgment of figural units (forms without specific meaning in the SOI construct). Whereas perception can be identified as impression of an object obtained by use of the senses; or direct or intuitive cognition; or attainment of awareness or understanding (Webster, 1967), one can see that cognition (Meeker categories) and determining dominant cues (Chalfant and Scheffelin categories) are related to Webster's definition of perception.

The observer can be safe in trying to detect specific errors by using steps/categories from authorities to furnish clues to observe. Looking for processing function is not now needed for placement of children in special-education training. Processing functions, however, are used in the PL 94–142 definition to identify learning disabilities and are, thus, considered important for the teacher to understand *if* appropriate plans are to be made for remediation. Studying such processing steps is actually task analyzing the reading process; from such analysis, the observer may detect where in this process the reader is having difficulty, and/or whether one modality is preferred over another for learning.

To aid the observer in looking for problems at the sensory level, the following clues are listed from Burns and Roe (1980, pp. 4–5). For visual problems, they suggest looking for: squinting, scowling, closing or covering one eye, rubbing the eyes frequently, holding work too close or too far away, frequently losing place, red or inflamed eyes, frequent blinking, moving head excessively, or frequent errors in copying board work. For auditory problems, they suggest: inattentiveness in class, turning the head so that a particular ear always faces the speaker, requests for repetition of directions and other verbal information, frowning when trying to listen, frequent rubbing of ears, frequent earaches, and dizziness.

To aid the observer in looking for problems at the perceptual level, the following behavior clues are suggested:

1. Stumbling on words
2. Calling words incorrectly but using contextual cues to make the sentence complete
3. Laboriously trying to sound out words
4. Interchanging the letter position in words, as in perceiving the word *stop* as *tops*, or *saw* as *was*.

Identification of Comprehension Disturbances in Reading

When children correct errors into meaningful language usage, it can be inferred that they understand what they read, even though they cannot perceive the words correctly. Understanding what one reads is called *reading comprehension* by both reading and the special-education specialists. Many of these authorities analyze the process of comprehension in the same way that they analyze perception. Most agree that this process is dependent to a large degree on the child's background and that it is difficult for children to be proficient in comprehension if they have not been exposed to the language patterns used by the teacher. There are other aspects than cultural difference, as important as this is, that should aid the observer in detecting comprehension problems in children. Dauzat and Dauzat (1981) identify three levels of comprehension:

Literal comprehension. This is the easiest level which requires recall of details and fact specifically mentioned in the passage read. Both knowledge and comprehension are involved. Knowledge signifies fact and detail and comprehension signifies an understanding about the facts and details.

Inferential comprehension. This is based on literal comprehension. The reader uses the information in the passage in combination with personal background experiences to make meaning that is not directly stated but is implied. The reader, thus, "reads between the lines."

Critical comprehension. This is the most complex level of reading comprehension. The literal meanings and the inferential meanings in a passage must be utilized and related to concepts beyond what is written in the passage. This level requires divergent or evaluative thinking. Critical comprehension relates to the

Guilford triad of EMR, Evaluation of Semantic Relations, which is identified by Meeker as being necessary for advanced reading.

The critical observer may use this information as an aid to determining comprehension skills. It can be determined whether (1) the child identifies facts and details; (2) identifies relationships, inferences, and characterization and traits implied; and/or (3) predicts outcomes, separates fiction from fact, identifies moods, tones or purposes, or forms conclusions.

Identification of Sensory, Perceptual, and Concept Problems in Mathematics

A student in a math class may be observed to rub his eyes, squint and/or look closely at the assignment on the desk. This behavior, as in reading, may indicate a sensory-deprivation problem. This child may have difficulty in seeing the print and should be referred for a visual-acuity examination. In contrast, a child may be observed to write the number I⌐ when the teacher has asked the child to write I7. This behavior may indicate another category of difficulty, a perceptual problem, and one would need to examine further how the child perceives numbers. Does the child have a clear distinction about the order of numerals as they are spoken, or does he reverse numbers as he might do letters in the reading process? Problems in developing mathematics skills may be examined somewhat in the light of the approach made in examining problems in reading. However, mathematics theorists do not generally use such processing terms as *sensory*, *perception*, or *comprehension* in their study analysis of children's lack of proficiency in math. They do recognize that mathematics is a language; they do recognize that space and symbolism are involved; and it is not unusual for them to identify quantitative thinking problems as *dyscalculia*. The School Mathematics Study Group (1965–1966) identifies math as:

> Mathematics is a language. It provides a precise means of communicating such ideas as number and space. It has special terms, expressions, and symbolism which, if understood, facilitate its use as a language, and which, if not understood, inhibit its use as a language.

The concept of *perception* in mathematics is found in the early work of the Gestalt psychologists who emphasized that the number concept is rooted in the perception of objects in space and grows from the organism's inherent ability to organize (Strauss, 1947, p. 148). Strauss says that at first there is the concrete perceptual element of the number concept, which eventually fades somewhat and yields to the gradual development of a scheme of visual spatial relationships, which, in turn, becomes the essential base for operations on an abstract level. In Piaget's writings on the growth and development of intelligence (Piaget, 1967), he uses the terms *sensori-motor space* or *perceptual space* and *haptic space*. In another source (Piaget, 1965), he says that quantity is no more than the asymmetrical relations between qualities—i.e., "more" or "less", "it's higher", "not so wide"—and that these relations depend on perception. Math practitioners do identify problems in math as involving lack of verbal concepts as in *up* and *down*, *in* and *out*, and *more than* or *less than*. Such concepts are generally included in their approach to analyzing developmental steps in learning math and are considered to be basic to the skills of problem solving. The importance of recognizing these terms in the observation and identification of problems in math skills lies in the ultimate plans for remediation. For example, if a child has a perceptual problem of not knowing numbers or of not being able to perceive any one object as being *one*, or any two objects as being *two*, then the apparent proper training should involve a perceptual-motor type of training, as in tracing numbers while saying them and seeing them, and as in working with concrete objects to establish one-to-one relationships. That is, we would need to go back to developmental stages of function to try to facilitate a learning pattern that has not developed.

In the field of learning disabilities, Johnson and Myklebust (1967) suggest that there are inner, receptive and expressive aspects of mathematical language, just as there are with other forms of symbolic behavior (p. 245). To aid in making math dysfunctions more meaningful, they suggest that arithmetic can be related to auditory reception*, to auditory memory, to reading and to writing disorders. They define these as follows:

1. Auditory Receptive Language Disorders and Arithmetic—These are disorders in understanding the meaning of spoken words that vary in meaning. Many words such as *sets*, *times*, and *base*, for instance, are very difficult for a "receptive aphasic" to understand, because of being unable to shift meaning from one context to another. The problem is not one of quantitative thinking, but of word meaning. This individual may do well in computation but poorly in reasoning and arithmetic vocabulary. In this context, it can be said that the child's problem in math is due to auditory comprehension.

2. Auditory Memory and Arithmetic—Two types of auditory memory are identified as interfering with mathematical performance. First is a reauditorization problem that prevents the child from quickly recalling numbers. The child recognizes the number on hearing it, but cannot remember how to say it. Second is a disability in listening to story problems presented orally. The individual cannot keep the facts in mind or in sequential order and, thus, cannot work the problems.

3. Disorders of Reading and Arithmetic—These disorders involve the lack of ability to sound out the words as *two* or *three*, and, therefore, this disorder will cause a child to be unable to solve problems in which the written word rather than the numerical symbol is used. Visual-perceptual disturbances resulting in confusion of letters, such as *b* and *d*, usually also affect number work as well as reading. For example, a child may confuse numerals 6 and 9, or 3 and 8.

4. Disorders of Writing and Arithmetic—This is a disorder in learning the motor patterns for writing either letters or numbers. When this problem exists, the child cannot write the numbers in the problem even when able to work the problem mentally.

Medical and psychological studies provide another dimension in the observation and identification of math deficits. Luria (1973, p. 40) reports that a lesion in the parietal-

---

*If the difficulty is auditory reception, the observer may look for other behaviors by making a task analysis of any word used in the problem. Let us use the word *sets* as an example. The observer may set up a task analysis as follows:

Problem: The task at hand requires understanding the word *sets* in terms of mathematical meaning.
To understand the word, the simplified requirements in the task are:
Prerequisites: the student must have vision and hearing.
1. The student must pay attention.
2. The student must discriminate the sound symbols *sets* as a unit.
3. The student must be able to verbalize what sets are in terms of math, or point to the sets in a visual presentation.

By using the means of task analysis, the observer will find extended behaviors to examine.

occipital lobe region of the left hemisphere has an effect on the spatial organization of perception and movement. Patients with this problem cannot interpret the position of the hands of a clock or find their bearings on a map. They cannot solve even relatively simple arithmetical problems and they are confused when faced with the problem of subtracting from a number of two digits requiring carrying over from the tens column. When subtracting 7 from 31, for instance, they do the first stage of this operation, but they do not know whether the odd 1 should be added or subtracted. Luria also reports (p. 337) that lesions in the left temporal region disturb audio-verbal memory and, naturally, create a difficulty in the retention of the conditions of a problem. Patients with such brain dysfunction find it difficult to remember such simple problems as, "There were eighteen books on two shelves, but they were not equally divided; there were twice as many books on one shelf. How many books were there on each shelf?" A patient with a lesion in another area, the frontal lobe of the cortex, could remember most of the wording of the problem above, but the patient would not perceive it as a problem. The individual would respond with a statement of two facts, "There are eighteen books on two shelves. And on the second shelf there were eighteen books." In the first case, we see a memory problem and in the second case we see a verbal disturbance in auditory association.

Strauss (1947, pp. 150–152) in his study of difficulties encountered by the brain-injured child in his acquisition of number concept, observed that brain-injured children who had great difficulty in drawing geometric designs tended to be inferior in math skills. He cites this as being a visual-perception problem but does not consider it to be the sole factor causing arithmetic difficulties. From this study he did offer principles to follow in planning arithmetic instruction. They are summarized as follows:

1. Organized perceptual experiences form the base for *number concept*, which depends upon the relationships of objects in space and the resulting development of a number scheme.
2. A number scheme is the outgrowth of ability to organize and is a semiabstract structure evolved from the understanding of relationships of parts and of parts to the whole.
3. A number scheme is a visuospatial scheme abstracted from its perceptual concrete origins when relationships and meanings are understood. (Strauss remarks that this implies the need for concrete and semiconcrete experiences until such organization occurs.)
4. It may often be necessary to develop special material and techniques of instruction that are based on any of the above disturbances.

From the foregoing discussion and from Myklebust and Johnson (1967, p. 248), we list a number of dysfunctions common to a dyscalculic. Children who can understand and use spoken language, who can read and write, but who cannot learn to calculate are said to have *dyscalculia.* The following dysfunctions may be helpful to the observer in the screening process.

1. Dysfunction in Visual-Spatial organization
   a. If counting objects seen, the child may skip one or more objects.
   b. There may be a difficulty in determining distance and in making judgment about sizes.

c. When working number problems on a page, subtraction problems may be added instead of subtracted.

d. There may be an imagery problem in organizing numerical data.

e. There may be difficulty with abstract concepts.

f. The child may not be able to recognize numbers in groups.

2. Dysfunctions in Memory

a. The child may not know the multiplication tables, even though he is of the age and grade to learn them.

b. The child may not remember all the parts of a stated problem.

3. Dysfunction in Verbal Aspects

a. There may be a difficulty naming amounts or numbers of things.

b. There may be difficulty with word meaning and reasoning.

c. There will likely be a poor arithmetic vocabulary.

d. The child may know that $1 + 3 = 4$, but may not understand that $3 + 1 = 4$.

4. Dysfunctions in Reading and Writing Numbers

a. The child may have difficulty in writing or reading numbers.

b. Unless a zero is called a zero in a number, difficulty may be seen in writing the number from dictation.

There are many deficits to consider when planning the beginning and ongoing procedure of evaluating a child who has a problem in learning math. The reader may, from the above discussion, make a list or use the four dysfunctions with the itemized behaviors.

Identification of Disturbances in Oral Expression

A child may be observed to recognize in a picture book a normal amount of objects for the age level, yet when asked to describe them orally, may have great difficulty in responding with adequate definitions. The inability to use such spoken language as a means of communication is usually categorized as an expressive language disorder (Wallace and McLoughlin, 1979). Johnson and Myklebust (1967) identify this language deficit as being expressive aphasia. They explain that these children may be able to follow instructions and perform successfully until they are required to speak. They may point or mark to identify objects, but when asked to name them, they are unable to do so.

Johnson and Myklebust list expressive language as the third major facet of symbolization, following inner and receptive language. They then identify three dysfunctions that may be observed in children with expressive language problems:

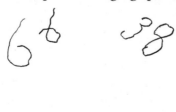

(69)   (38)

Illustration 1. Difficulty in Writing Numbers by a 12-Year-Old Boy

(1) Reauditorization and word selection dysfunction: a problem in retrieving words spontaneously even though the words are recognized and understood.

(2) Dysfunction in the execution of motor patterns of speech even though speech is understood and reauditorized.

(3) Defective syntax: an inability to formulate words into expressions of complete thought, while the ability to use single words and short phrases is intact.

Most writers discuss oral-expressive problems in accordance with the Johnson and Myklebust format; e.g., Gearhart (1973) differentiates expressive auditory (expressive aphasia) language as *apraxias*, the lack of ability to execute motor patterns when the motor system is intact. Wallace and McLoughlin (1979) report the same three categor· ies as Johnson and Myklebust, but list them as problems in (1) expressing speech sounds, (2) formulating words and sentences, and (3) word selection or inability to retrieve words. Rutherford (1977) describes the term *dysnomia*, a specific word-finding difficulty, and in the same frame of reference as reauditorization and/or word selection. He reports that a child with this problem will often settle for words that are available at the moment, though they may not reflect thought content accurately. The child may say, "I knew the answer, but I just couldn't say it."

From the field of medicine and psychology Strauss (1947) and Luria (1973) both speak of the findings of Broca in 1861 that provided proof that when a lesion was located in a very particular area of the brain (the third frontal gyrus) the expressive phase of language or motor speech was destroyed. Since then, Luria, in his study of focal lesions in the cortex, has differentiated several speech-behavior problems related to these lesions. Among these are audio-verbal memory, amnestic aphasia, paraphasia, and difficulty in formulating the linear scheme of a sentence. A person with amnestic aphasia (from lesion in the occipito-parietal area) has difficulty in remembering names. This person may immediately recall the forgotten word and pronounce it without any acoustical-verbal difficulty if he is prompted with the first sound or the first syllable.

In his discussion, Luria cites the work of Tsevtkova in 1972, who found the difficulty in finding names to be concentrated mainly on the naming of objects—the use of verbs and adjectives is remembered much more easily than the naming of concrete objects (Luria, 1973, p. 158).

A person with acoustico-verbal memory difficulties (lesion in the left temporal lobe) shows a particular difficulty with remembering a short series of words. The first or last word may be remembered after a time but the other words he cannot remember and "prompting is of little help" (Luria, 1965). A person with paraphasia speech problems will add irrelevant words into the conversation. These irrelevant words will resemble the required word in either its (1) morphology, (2) meaning, or (3) phonetic composition. Examples are: (1) *horse* for *house*, (2) *red carpet* for *hospital* (coming through a chain of *hospital*, *Red Cross*, to *red carpet*) and (3) *riddle* for *little*. A person who has difficulty in formulating the "linear scheme of a sentence" (related to the inferior post-frontal zones of the left hemisphere) may easily name objects, but will not be able to give a description of a thematic picture. These individuals are able to speak in simple sentences if the content is found within a question such as "Did you go to town?" An answer from such a patient could be "Yes, I went to town", but if the question were asked differently as "Where have you been?" then the individual would have difficulty in expressing a complete thought. Kirk (1966a) called this an *ideational fluency problem.*

In this information from the field of medicine and psychology, we can see the categories of Johnson and Myklebust and others. These categories are identified by different terms, yet with the same behaviors, i.e., inability to retrieve or name objects, inability to perform motor patterns of speech, and inability to formulate words into sentences. Since expressive language is a part of the most important accomplishments of the human race and because it is so necessary in communication, it is very important that any deficits in this regard be identified as early as possible. Rutherford (1977) does caution that judgments regarding the severity of a child's dysnomia should not be based on test results obtained in a single day. The degree of word-finding difficulty fluctuates from mild to moderately severe over a period ranging from three days to to two weeks. We agree that observing and collecting data should extend over a period of time and that this same procedure should be followed in observing and screening for other language problems.

Children who are found to have expressive-language problems need much practice in using words and in formulating sentences. If the teacher is trained in observations and screening skills, it may be possible to detect the kind of language deficit and make appropriate remedial and/or referral plans. Characteristics to look for could be: omission of words, addition of inappropriate words, incorrect use of grammar, distortion of the order of words and phrases, communication with only one or two words, and difficulty in remembering words. For activities to use in remediation, the reader is referred to Lerner (1981), Johnson and Myklebust (1967), Wiig and Semel (1976), Bush and Giles (1976), Hammell and Barten (1978), and Kirk (1966).

Identification of Perceptual and Sensory Disturbances in Written Expression

A child may be observed to have difficulty staying within the lines when writing. A child may sit with pencil in hand as if trying to remember how to write some specific word, or be observed to make so many gross errors in writing that it is a simple matter to recognize that a writing problem exists. Such problems in written expression may be examined by similar approaches made to problems in other academic skills. We may ask, "Does the child remember what to write? Is there a perceptual problem or is there a physiological disability that interferes with the motor act of writing?" If the observer can determine such information, the approach to the problem of remediation is likely to be more appropriate. For example, if a child has a perceptual problem, the teacher will need to make a plan different from the one made for a child with a memory problem. Such techniques as helping the child in spacing and staying within the lines would be necessary when the problem is largely poor visual organization; tracing and much copy work would be needed if it were determined that a child could not remember the letters or words to write. Authorities in handwriting problems provide us with many clues from which we may develop our skills of screening and remediation of written-expression problems.

Difficulty in handwriting is often called *dysgraphia*, which Dorland's Medical Dictionary identifies as "—the inability to write properly because of ataxis, tremor, or motor neurosis". Whereas this definition does include handwriting problems due to the motor act per se, and to interference due to neuroses, it does not include perceptual base causes, which are considered to be one of the main problems by many handwriting theorists. Otto, McMenemy, and Smith (1973) have found that most handwriting problems are caused much more often by perceptual and personality factors than by physiological and motor factors.

Furner (1970) emphasizes the necessity to build perception of letters and their formation as a guide for motor practice, rather than emphasizing only the motor aspect. She lists three major steps: (1) the accurate perception of letter forms, (2) the general features of handwriting, and (3) appropriate procedures to permit the pupil to compare his writing to models of desired writing in order to make plans for improvement.

Lerner (1981, p. 333) reports that handwriting problems may be due to many other deficits than dysgraphia, all characterized by the inability to transfer the input of the visual information to the output of fine-motor movement or the inability to make motor and spatial judgments. She also cites the work of Hildreth, who identifies the writing act as a thinking process, entailing activities of the cortical nerve areas and requiring accurate perception of the symbol patterns rather than a mechanical, lower-level reflex response.

Johnson and Myklebust (1967) consider written language to be the highest forms of language and "the last to be learned." They list three main types of problems in learning written language:

(1) A disorder in visual-motor integration: the child may be able to speak and read but unable to perform the motor act of writing numbers, letters, or words. This is identified as dysgraphia.

(2) A deficit in revisualization: the child may recognize words and, hence, can read, but cannot revisualize letters or words, thereby being unable to write spontaneously. The visual image is not evoked to allow the patterns to be written.

(3) A deficiency in formulation and syntax: the child may be able to read, to speak (communicate orally), to spell, and to revisualize words to write, but unable to organize thoughts into the proper form for written communication.

From the field of psychology and medicine, Luria (1973) lists disturbance of phonemic hearing as cause of the loss of the ability to write. If there is a lesion in the left temporal lobe, the individual may not be able to distinguish the acoustic content of a word. A patient with such lesions confuses similar-sounding phonemes and can no longer analyze complex combinations of sounds. Writing is an attempt to find required sounds and letters composing the words. This person may be able to write familiar words such as one's name, which have become a stable motor stereotype, but will not be able to analyze the acoustic content of words that have not been clearly established for automatic motor responses. An example of the writing would be *kagle* for *table*. If a lesion occurs in the parieto-occipital region of the cortex, Luria (p. 150) has found that an individual has great difficulty in drawing letters. The individual may distinguish the sound or phoneme, but will have the inability to retain the required spatial positions of

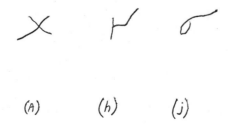

(A)   (h)   (j)

Illustration 2. A Revisualization Problem

A 12-year-old boy could copy letters, but when they were dictated, he could not revisualize them.

the lines forming the letters. Or the individual may write a *B* in this fashion,ɱ\. Luria associates one other distinct writing behavior to a lesion in the cortex, the Broca Area (in the frontal lobe). A lesion in this area is reported not only to cause an expressive-speech problem, but to cause a writing problem in addition, i.e., if the lesion is in the lower zones of the left premotor region. The order of the elements is lost and the smooth transition from one component of a word to another and the retention of the required sequence are not possible.

From a brief review of the writing disturbance, we itemize some writing behaviors for the observer to use as clues to look for specific writing problems. They are:

	Dysfunction	Observable Behavioral Deficit
Johnson and Myklebust	Visual-motor integration (can speak and read)	Cannot execute motor patterns (form letters)
	Revisualization (can read and speak)	Cannot evoke visual symbols to write (can copy from board but not from dictation)
	Formulation and Syntax (can read and speak)	Cannot organize thought to write words in proper grammatical order
Lerner	Motor-spatial dysfunction	Has difficulty making spatial judgment when writing
	Perception	Does not perceive the symbol pattern well enough to write
	Auditory difficulty	Cannot determine acoustic content of words
Luria	Spatial	Cannot form words in accordance with proper spacing
	Memory	Cannot retain the sequence of the words

Identification of Perceptual and Sensory Disorders in Spelling

In a written spelling lesson, a child may be observed to add extra letters to words. A child may write or spell a word phonetically, yet the spelling will be incorrect. Such errors as *boye* for *boy*, or *uncal* for *uncle* are common among children who are underachieving in spelling, and it is not difficult for a teacher to recognize inferior performance in this particular skill. It is necessary to isolate the child's basic deficit to begin remediation. One may begin this study through differentiating the types of errors and through analysis of the perceptual functions in the act of spelling.

Spelling is an encoding skill that moves from sound to symbol. In comparison, reading is a decoding skill that moves from symbol to sound. It is not unusual for dyslectic children to be poor spellers as well as poor readers, according to Johnson and

Myklebust (1967, p. 153). They attribute this fact to the requirement of simultaneous ability to revisualize and to reauditorize letters. If either of these perceptual skills is deficient, the result will be disorders in both reading and spelling. A child who cannot reauditorize a word cannot determine the sounds needed to begin and finish the spelling. If one cannot revisualize the word, it cannot be determined how the symbols (letters) are associated with the sound, the individual cannot write the word. Some children who cannot revisualize a word to write it, can reauditorize the word and can spell it orally. Many parents report that children have correctly spelled words orally the night before a test, then failed the test the following day because of their inability to write the same words from dictation.

The teacher, in analyzing the spelling function to determine the basic deficit, could observe the results of spelling through three different means of evaluation. First, the teacher could dictate the spelling words for the child to spell orally (reauditorization). Second, the teacher could dictate the spelling words for the child to write (revisualization); third, the teacher could present the words in four different spellings with only one correct spelling. The child should choose the one that is correct. In this approach, we are examining how the child responds. In another approach, looking at the *words* to determine the more difficult ones, one may divide them according to whether they are in accordance with standard rules in spelling or whether they cannot be spelled according to the rules. The teacher may then observe whether the child responds successfully with one group of words (rule-governed) or with the other group (those that cannot be spelled by rules).

While many judgments concerning academic behavior are based on clinical impressions, Kinsbourne (1977) provides the observer with a classification built on a systematic quantitative analysis. His study was designed to determine whether different children exhibit different patterns or error types. The original study was made with adults with focal cerebral disease. There were four groups: (1) patients with Gerstmann's syndrome (finger agnosia, right-left disorientation, a spelling difficulty, and an arithmetic difficulty); (2) aphasic patients; (3) patients with right-hemisphere damage; and (4) patients with lesions located elsewhere than in the brain (controls). Each patient was presented with a standard spelling list. The error-pattern scores were derived from the first ten misspelled words yielded by each patient, i.e., the easiest words on which the individual manifested his spelling difficulty. It was from this work that the following classification of error types was made.

(1) Extraneous letter errors—letters that do not normally occur in the word
(2) Order errors—the mislocation of the letter within the word
(3) Vowel substitutions—the substitution of one vowel for another
(4) Omissions—letters left out of the word
(5) Reduplications

In later studies they found that patterns similar to the adults' patterns were obtained for two types of children, "language problem cases" and "Gerstmann cases". The language cases made a disproportionate number of extraneous-letter errors and the Gerstmann cases showed a greater-than-expected incidence of order errors.

A teacher who is competent in the teaching of spelling should find it easy to make the observations necessary for the teacher's input in a multidisciplinary team committee meeting. This will not only provide valuable information for the decisions made by the

I. What is it
  a. revesal bd 69
      Saw was
      Right Lifted

II. my expruns in Elamety
  a Could not Right
  B Teacher did not know what
      was rong, stad back
      First Grad. did not do any
      Good
  C. Ritardes clas
      do not do any good
  D. Todor

III Put resos room
      Math
      English
      Sicens
  always Puade us cut
      off neaager thining
  Trobla get out of school for Toutar

III Higschool
  Stell manstringmeing
  Don't not Learn much
      Tourtor did most

V My oppeun How to handl
  a. Exspet the child to do
      His work.
  b. one to one bass is good
  c. Dica plin
  d. Growming
  E. The room be in Ordly form
  f. Lct Parents Know
      Prest mabey well Help

Illustration 3. Written Notes of a Dyslexic 20-Year-Old

Notes written for a presentation to a parent-teacher group.

committee, but also will provide information to use for planning remediation. The foregoing discussion may be used as a guide from which to develop an organization for the observation procedure.

Observation Procedures

Observation of individuals, both in the school and out of the school, is historically the oldest technique in the act of gathering information concerning the behavior of students. In spite of its years of use, it still remains one of the most effective tools available for school personnel when data are needed for the evaluation of children*. If the information is properly gathered, recorded, and interpreted, the procedure becomes a practical and a scientific means. When the observation does not follow a systematic plan, the results obtained often are not truly representative of the general behavior of the children involved. Some teachers inadvertently may draw conclusions from only one behavioral incident. For this reason, school personnel need guidelines to follow. Such guidelines are seen in the next section.

Creative Classroom Observation

The standard procedure of observation reported by Prescott (1957) has had years of success. It involves the observation of a student in the classroom, on the playground, and elsewhere in and around the school. The observer writes descriptive anecdotes about routine bits of behavior, as well as more significant or revealing episodes. Cumulative records at the school are studied and pertinent data are transferred to the observer's record. The date, the place, and the situation in which the action occurred are also recorded. Specific details as to what one person said to another are carefully noted, and then at the end of a designated period, the data are examined and conclusions are drawn. If sensory and academic skill dimensions are added to Prescott's time-sampling technique, the teacher can consider, for instance, whether content and/ or energy depletion could be influential factors, along with visual or auditory perceptual problems. Figure 23 suggests the procedure to follow. A similar checklist of behaviors common to learning-disability problems should be completed daily for each child who is failing and shows need for individual diagnosis. At the end of a week, a tally should be made, including such things as the times of day the child appeared most disturbed, the classes in which the problem behaviors occurred, the conditions surrounding the problem, and the teacher's behavior just prior to each atypical performance. If teachers use this anecdotal-observation procedure and some of the following assessments described, they should have selective information from which individualized planning can be pursued. This procedure also serves as a way of getting a *base line* (number of observations in a specified time) for use with operant conditioning techniques.

It is expected that the teacher will become creative in the use of any observation sheet and devise other codes of reporting. O-X (oral expression) and W-X (written expression) are easy codes to remember. The subcodes may be more difficult to remember, and the teacher may prefer to write the description of the entire behavior

---

*These evaluations should, however, be used only as reference points for more complete diagnoses if critical education decisions are to be made.

observed. Consistency of reporting is of much greater importance than use of a specified code. Coding devices make tallying the number of times certain behaviors occur easier, and for this reason the teacher may wish to code the behavior only after a complete week of observation. It is important to emphasize that the *situation surrounding the eventful behavior* must also be recorded and this, of course, includes the teacher's actions at the time.

Teaching-Testing Techniques and Screening Instruments

There are many good teacher-oriented assessment instruments that may be used in addition to the daily observation. Only a few of these are described here.

Instruments Related to Modal Learning

Test for Three Types of Learners (Baster; 1972*)

Baster has designed a test to determine whether a person is a visual learner, an auditory learner, or a kinesthetic learner. It is a test that can be administered in about 15 minutes and should not be given to more than four students at one time because of the difficulty of observing more than that number at once. Three reactions should be observed by the teacher, each related to a specific area of learning. There are three simple presentations. In one the teacher writes a list of words on the board and the students reproduce them from memory after they have been erased. In the second presentation, the teacher dictates the list orally and asks the students who wish to repeat orally. In the third presentation, the students write down words that are dictated orally. They are then rewritten by copying and then from memory. The instructions for interpretations are easy, and the teacher can quickly determine a mode for planning remediation for a child.

VADS (Koppitz, 1970)

Koppitz has designed a test dealing only with digit span, as on the Stanford-Binet and the Wechsler scales. The uniqueness of her test lies in the variety of presentations and responses required. The following four learning modes are measured:

Aural intake
Visual intake
Oral expression
Written expression

In the aural-oral test; the teacher dictates a list of digits, and the child repeats the same digits in the same order. In the visual-oral test, the teacher shows a series of digits on a stimulus card to a child and asks the child to say as many as possible in the same order after the card has been removed. The child writes the series of digits heard in the aural-written test and writes the series of digits seen in the visual-written test.

This short test has been normed to identify learning problems among those with IQs of 70—89 and a group with IQs of 90 and above. It is an easy test to give and should be a very good supplement to provide information concerning input and output styles of learning.

---

*For information concerning this informal test contact Claud "R" Zevely, WTSU, Canyon, TX, 79016.

Figure 23. Teacher Observation Tally Sheet

Weekly Teacher Observation
Talley Sheet

	Mon.	Tues.	Wed.	Thurs.	Fri.
8–9 Class Behavior*					
9–10 Class Behavior*					
10–12 Class Behavior*					
12–1 Class Behavior*					
1–2 Class Behavior*					
2–3 Class Behavior*					
3–4 Class Behavior*					

*See code

Code for Behavior

Child Behavior	Code	Observed Behavior
	O-X	1. Oral-expression problems
	sow	Stumbles on words
	wos	Words out of sequence
		Poverty of expression
	poe	(Can't tell story from pictures)
	art	Articulation problem
	W-X	2. Written-expression problems
	poe	Poverty of expression
	uwa	Unfinished written assignments
	eo	Erases often
	M-X	3. Gross-motor expression problems
	cig	Cannot imitate in gestures
	A-P	4. Auditory-perception problems
	ar	Asks to repeat
	lop	Looks at others' papers
	dnl	Does not listen
		or
	occ	Observes closely for clues
	V-P	5. Visual-perception problems
	cr	Cannot read well
	sow	Stumbles on words
	bro	Bumps into room objects
	pbe	Places books on edge of table or desk
	Mot	6. Motor problems
	aw	Awkward walk
	b	Balance
	csl	Can't stay in line

Figure 23 (continued)

Child Behavior	Code	Observed Behavior
	cwl	Can't write within lines
	ppg	Poor pencil grasp

Teacher Behavior	T-GD	1. Giving directions
Prior to Overt	T-WD	2. Writing directions on board
Actions of Child	T-AQ	3. Asking questions
	T-R	4. Reprimanding

A Diagnostic Screening Procedure Based on Styles of Learning

Boder Reading and Spelling Patterns* (Boder, 1969)

This screening procedure is based on reading and spelling patterns. Boder has categorized three kinds of problems seen in the daily work of children with academic problems. Group I is by far the largest of the three groups, and it includes dysphonetic problems, which indicate dysfunction in the auditory channel. Children in this group read globally, responding to whole words as gestalten or configurations. Lacking phonetic skills, they are unable to decipher words that are not yet in their sight vocabulary, and they consistently spell nonphonetically. Their most striking errors are "semantic-substitution errors"—words that are related conceptually, but not phonetically, are confused, so that these children might substitute *funny* for *laugh, human* for *person, quack* for *duck*, or the name of their own city for the word *city*.

In Group II are dyseidetic problems. Children with these problems reflect a deficiency in the function of the visual channel. Their reading-spelling pattern shows an inability to perceive whole words as configurations. When reading, these children sound out every word as if it had been seen before. They spell phonetically, and the words are intelligible. Examples of spellings are: *sed* for *said, litl* for *little, lisn* for *listen, sos* for *sauce*, and *onkle* for *uncle*.

Group III includes dysphonetic and dyseidetic problems. These indicate patterns of deficiencies in both the visual and the auditory channels. Children with this problem spell nonphonetically, as in Group I, but their spelling is even more bizarre, and they neither perceive configurations nor are able to sound out words. The prognosis for this group is guarded and if there has not been intensive training at early grade levels, children with these problems remain nonreaders, even at the high-school level.

Boder's reading and spelling patterns provide the following diagnostic screening format of learning-disabled children:

1. The visual learner (auditory deficit or dysphonetic)

Sees	Says
laugh	funny
person	human
ask	answer
duck	quack
train	airplane
city	hometown
father	daddy
home	house

*This test also may be used to identify modal learning styles.

(a) Spells nonphonetically
(b) Misspellings unintelligible
(c) Is dependent on words learned by sight

2. The auditory learner (visual deficit or dyseidetic)
   Spells

said	as	sed
little		letl
listen		lisn
sauce		sos
right		rit
business		bisnis
uncle		onkle or uncal

(a) Reads phonetically
(b) Sounds out each word as if seen for the first time
(c) Does not recognize words by sight

3. The learner with both auditory and visual deficit, dysphonetic and dyseidetic
   Spells

pamaset	for	picture
pamlhe		front
pame		court
came		frame
phasene		scene
bamthe		person

(a) Spelling is nonphonetic—usually an unintelligible jumble
(b) Remains nonreader even at high-school level

Screening Instruments

Slingerland Screening Tests for Identifying Children with Specific Learning Disabilities (Slingerland, revised 1970)

Description and Administration

The Slingerland Screening Instrument contains three forms to cover items for children from grade one through grade four: Form A, grades 1 and 2; Form B, grades 2 and 3; and Form C, grades 3 and 4. Each of the three forms contains nine subtests, eight of which are designed for group administration. The tests show relative strengths and weaknesses in perceptual-motor, visual, auditory, and kinesthetic functions, and they reveal deficits that may exist in receptive- and expressive-language performance.

Administration of the Slingerland may be executed by the classroom teacher, reading specialist, supervisor, school psychologist, diagnostician, or principal. The test may be administered to a group of as many as 30 if there is an assistant. It is recommended, however, that the class be divided into smaller groups of 10 or 15. Each form of the test takes about an hour to an hour and a half to complete.

Specific instructions are that children are to be placed so that another's work is not in view; that all pencils used in the test should have no erasers; and that no child should be more than 20 feet from both the examiner and the charts to be copied. When the children are provided booklets, they are told to wait until the specific directions are given for the individual subtests. Each subtest is described as follows:

Tests 1 and 2: These tests require copying from far point and near point. Discrimination of shape and sequence of symbols is involved in both the act of visual perception and in the motor responses of writing. In the first subtest the children copy from a wall-chart, and in the second, from a page.

Test 3: This is a test of visual perception-memory of words, letters and numbers seen in a brief exposure, one at a time, on a card. After the model is withdrawn, distraction and delay are used to test memory. The item recalled is matched to one of a group printed on the test page.

Test 4: This test is a matching-words test which requires discrimination of symbols and sequences within words and the ability to perceive similarities and differences.

Test 5: This is a test of visual perception and memory linked with kinesthetic- motor performance. After exposure to phrases, letter and number groups, and geometric forms, distraction and delay occur. Then without a model the child is to write or draw the items from memory.

Test 6: This is a test of auditory perception and memory linked with a visual-kinesthetic motor association. Groups of letters, numbers and words are dictated to be written on the test pages after a brief period of distraction and delay.

Test 7: This test with the auditory-visual-kinesthetic linkage adds the requirement of making auditory discrimination of single sounds within the sequence of sounds in whole words. For example, the child must discriminate the initial phoneme and, after a slight distraction and delay, write it in the test booklet.

Test 8: This is a test of auditory-visual performance. Dictation of a word or letter or number group is followed by a brief distraction and delay before it is located among a group printed on the test page.

Individual Auditory Tests: Children who have exhibited difficulty in the last three subtests are administered this section on an individual basis. Words and phrases spoken by the examiner are echoed by the child, sentences are completed orally, and the child is asked to retell a brief story immediately after hearing it.

Interpretation and Use

The Slingerland Screening Instrument is so designed that at each grade level involved, Grades 1, 2, 3, and 4, relative strengths or weaknesses that may exist in visual, auditory, and kinesthetic functioning may be identified. Both a Quick Analysis Form and a Detailed Analysis Form are provided for the evaluations. The Quick Analysis scale sheet shows the total errors for all the subtests, the self-correction, and the poor formations. The Detailed Analysis score sheet shows the type of errors made. They are identified as:

Right or wrong	Letter Forms
Recall	Number Formations
Substitutions	Geometric Forms
Insertions	Mixed Cursive and Manuscript
Reversals	Mixed Capitals and Lowercase
Inversions	Omissions
Transpositions	Incompletions
Number Reversals	Spelling Errors
	Spatial Organization
	Circle Formation
	Kinesthetic-Motor Performance

The information above can be used as a source (1) for referrals for complete diagnostic evaluations, or (2) for planning remediation programs. After reviewing prior observation data with the data from this screening instrument, the teacher should have a significantly greater understanding regarding a student's academic successes and failures.

The Jansky Screening Index (Jansky, 1972)

Jansky demonstrated in her study that three out of four failing readers can be identified at preschool level. Her purpose for the instrument, which is a revision of earlier work with de Hirsch (1966), is that of prevention of reading problems rather than remediation after the child has experienced failure. Her index uses scores from a screening index and from the teacher's predictions. It adapts norms, or cutting points, to the academic expectations of a given school.

The screening index includes the following:

1. Bender Motor Gestalt: Cards A, 1, 2, 4, 6, 8
2. Gates Words Matching Subtest from Bates Reading Readiness Battery (selected exercises)
3. Letter naming: six index cards on which letters are printed in capital letters with black ink
4. Picture naming: 22 pictures of line drawings of common items
5. Binet Sentence Memory Test: list of sentences read to the child by the examiner

According to Jansky, the procedure for developing cutting-point data in a given school is as follows:

Procedure to follow for prediction

1. In the spring, a kindergarten teacher ranks students' potential for reading.
2. The teacher divides the list into four categories, one for students who are likely to do well, one for those who will probably do average work, one for those who will probably fall in the "doubtful range", and one for those who are likely to fail.
3. In the late spring the school psychologist, kindergarten teacher Y, a first grade teacher, or a paraprofessional administers the screen index to the children of teacher X.
4. This tester ranks the children according to their scores on the predictive screening index.
5. The school psychologist or the principal determines the school's expected reading failure rate.
6. This failure rate, inflated by a 10% safety factor is then used to designate the kindergarten children to be considered high risks.
7. The tester and kindergarten teacher X then compare lists to settle on a final high-risk group.

Teachers, psychologists, diagnosticians, or paraprofessionals may be trained in a simple, short session to administer the tests. The testing time per child is only about 20 minutes. When Jansky's procedure is followed and the norms are established for the high-risk group, the school will have a good predictor screening instrument that should be a significant factor in the prevention of reading failure, if the high-risk children are placed in remediation programs at the beginning of the first grade.

Screening for Emotional Problems

This text is concerned with the assessment and diagnosis of learning problems in children in special education. Among these we find behavior problems that overlap with other handicapping conditions, compounding the problem and making remediation more difficult. One of these is emotional disturbance, which often results from learning problems in combination with environmental problems.

Classes for the emotionally disturbed have been recently established throughout the nation. Many of the children in these programs are known to experience academic failures, and they need individualized instruction. Conversely, some learning-disabled children are known to have emotional problems, and they need to be referred for management programs, as well as for individualized instruction.

The preceding data have covered systematic means of observation and screening. The following paper is presented to make the teacher cognizant of the complex problems involving identification and classification of the emotionally disturbed child.

Recognizing Psychological Disorders in Children
by Louis Fairchild, Ph.D.

In *Les Miserables*, Victor Hugo observes that "children at once accept joy and happiness with quick familiarity, being themselves naturally all happiness and joy" (Hugo, 1862, p. 369). Hugo, however, is apparently prepared to acknowledge that nature can go wrong, for in the Preface to the same classic he states, "So long as there shall exist, by reason of law and custom, a social condemnation which artificially creates hells on earth . . . and the dwarfing of childhood by physical and spiritual night . . . so long as ignorance and misery remain on earth, books like this cannot be useless."

Obviously, most children experience their share of happiness and joy, but such is not inevitable. Many know firsthand the "dwarfing of childhood by physical and spiritual night," and they may respond through a range of disturbed behaviors. Some of these disturbances may be typical for an age group while other may be more profound. Most, however, are disorders of behavior (Shaw and Lucas, 1970).

Harvey and Bordley (1972) discuss two categories of clinical data used in medical diagnosis: symptoms and signs. Symptoms are personal, subjective sensations or observations that the patient describes to the physician. Signs are abnormalities directly observed by the physician in an examination. These more objective manifestations may also be observed by the patient, as well as by acquaintances and relatives. The behavioral and emotional disturbances in children are more akin to the latter category, signs. Children openly express through their behavior that something is wrong, and this expression may be vivid and dramatic for "no one mourns like a child, not even a lover (Doctorow, 1975)."

The recognition of psychological disorders in the classroom is important for at least two reasons. First, a disturbed child may be a distraction to the teacher and other children and, thereby, interfere with the learning processes of a whole class. The child may create an extended learning disability. Second, the child's own learning may be disrupted by this psychological status. The individual's emotions and behavior can make learning and schooling twin "hells on earth . . . and spiritual night." In this sense, learning difficulties are secondary to other problems, and these problems must be recognized and receive some attempt at understanding if impaired learning is to be corrected.

The attempt to understand this disturbance in children is the function of diagnosis. In its more literal, medical sense, *diagnosis* means to know thoroughly the nature of a diseased condition. This knowledge is achieved through two procedures: (1) collection of the facts, and (2) analysis of the facts (Harvey and Bordley, 1972). While diagnosis is more technically a medical procedure, in its broader application the term has been used to refer to the identification and understanding of problems in everything from automobiles to pot plants.

The identification of "diseased conditions" in human behavior, however, is not always an easy task. "One of the psychiatric dilemmas of our time is the decision as to what is normal and what is abnormal in human behavior" (Lapouse and Monk, 1959, p. 803, as quoted in Anthony, 1970). Despite the most careful scrutiny and investigation, this determination is often elusive.

Studies have demonstrated the difficulty in achieving agreement between trained professionals called upon to place adult psychiatric patients in diagnostic categories. Reliability between psychiatrists as to the most appropriate category is far from perfect when a great number of specific categories are used, but tends to improve substantially with reduction to a few major categories. In other medical specialities, elaborate laboratory procedures are available to follow up on a diagnosis. Treatment itself can be a source of confirmation. In the diagnosis of disordered behavior, however, objective and infallible techniques for supporting or refuting a diagnosis are not readily available.

If the above is true with respect to adults, the problem becomes even more pressing with children. While there are arguments to suggest the discernment of normal and abnormal in adults is more confusing, many authorities would agree that the tasks of teasing out what is abnormal in the lives of children is uniquely difficult. In writing about diagnostic procedures with children, Zubin (1967) says that the state is even more disjointed at this level than in the adult. "It has been demonstrated that the problem pupil in one classroom may even be on the 'good-citizen list' in another" (Long, Morse, and Newman, 1965, p. 113). Clarizio and McCoy (1976) report that a review of the literature indicates the effort to describe and classify children's disorders has resulted in the proposal of more than 24 classification systems. Even the child categories in the American Psychiatric Association's recent *Diagnostic and Statistical Manual of Mental Disorders (DSM III)* (1980) have been assailed (Foltz, 1980). Trippe suggests that it is no secret about who the disturbed children are, yet universally accepted criteria of identification are not available. There is no official definition. In writing about the nature of psychopathology, Knopf (1979) acknowledges that it "may be easier to recognize than to define" (p. 27). Reinert (1976) points out that the term "emotionally disturbed," as applied to children, first appeared in the literature 75 years ago without adequate definition. Kauffman (1977) observes that the problem of definition is compounded by the range of behaviors characterizing disturbed children. They are distinguished both by excesses and deficiencies. Kauffman maintains that the "primary distinguishing feature of most categories of handicapped children is clearly either a behavioral deficiency *or* an excess, whereas in the case of disturbed children the problem may be defined as both excesses and deficiencies." (p. 18).

The variability of behaviors among normal children is impressive, indeed, and any number of studies have pointed out the similarities between clinic and nonclinic populations of children.

For a number of years the American Psychiatric Association recognized the temporary and circumstantial nature of some emotional problems by categorizing them as "Transient Situational Disorders." Underscoring the prevalence of temporary disorders in younger ages, three of the five subcategories in this division were related to youthful periods of development: infancy, childhood, and adolescence. Children and adolescents are in such a state of flux and developmental immaturity, that in probing life they are bound to encounter their share of difficulties. Studies of diagnostic practices in clinics have found that some 40–70 percent of the children brought to these clinics were classified as having a transient problem (Rosen, Bahn, and Kramer, 1964).

In light of the above, what hope is there for the layperson or teacher to be very successful in recognizing levels of childhood disturbances and making appropriate response to such? It is very important that the layperson have some measure of recognition skill because it is at this level that the diagnostic process has its beginning. Parents, teachers, and an array of community members other than mental-health professionals are going to be the first to recognize that a child has a problem suggesting attention. Ross (1980) reminds us that while it may not be too important to be able to classify a child's problem or problems, it is important that problems be recognized.

Teachers are especially important in this process. While the child may drop out of public view between birth and formal education, once the child enters school the teacher becomes the primary evaluator of behavior. Teachers are in an excellent position to evaluate adjustment and note disturbances in children. Ross (1980) maintains that the data used for classifying the psychological disorders of children should come from the observations of those who have daily contact with the child, such as parents and teachers.

Reinert (1976) recognizes the teacher as the primary person, in a screening program to identify high-risk children likely to experience failure and conflict. While some authorities and some research may question the teacher's role and effectiveness in this process, there is abundant evidence in support of teachers as effective detectors of childhood disturbances.

Engel (1972) reported that teachers, psychologists, and psychiatrists have a range of agreement of 70–80 percent when a comparison is made of their judgments about maladjusted children. Gropper, Kress, Hughes, and Pekich (1968) found that teachers could be effectively trained both to recognize and manage behavioral problems in the classroom. In a test consisting of ten case studies, teachers were able to identify 3.6 of the problem cases before training and 7.0 in a posttraining trial. This was an improvement of 34 percent.

Reinert (1976) continues by pointing out the factors contributing to the teacher's effectiveness as an observer. The teacher has had some level of training in the personality development of children. The classroom provides a spectrum of normal behaviors on which teachers can base their impressions. Teachers interact several hours a day over extended periods of time; finally, there is the opportunity to observe children in both individual and group activities, as well as in structured and unstructured circumstances.

There are at least two reasons for the importance for teachers to recognize disturbed behavior in their pupils. First, the teacher may be able to intervene and directly modify the child's behavior. The Report of the Joint Commission on Mental Health of Children (1970) recognized that schools are in a unique position to enhance mental health, prevent serious disorders from further development, and improve the condition of those children already having problems.

A second reason for teacher recognition of problem behavior is for purposes of consultation or referral. It is important for teachers to be sensitive to their own limited resources for working with some children unassisted. When this occurs, the teacher must be prepared to seek consultation or to refer. If consultation or referral is effective, the contribution of the teacher is now at a premium, because that teacher serves as an invaluable resource person. As noted above, the teacher has a privileged vantage point from which to observe classroom behavior, and these observations are indispensable to the professional now entering the case. While there has been repeated criticism of the diagnostic workup and equal criticism of the validity of classification systems, nevertheless, many, if not a majority of, mental-health professionals spend a large portion of their time in this very activity. The teacher should be prepared to contribute to this effort.

To what should the teacher be prepared to attend? Gropper, Kress, Hughes, and Pekich (1968) offered a program for training teachers in what to look for in making judgments about the seriousness of children's problems. They maintain that teachers are expected to recognize problem behaviors at three progressive levels of seriousness: normal, problem, and referable. *Normal* problems are those occasionally seen in a generally well-adjusted child. These may be problems inherent in a given age range, characteristic of many children this age, and more temporary in nature. These problems are generally not damaging to the child or to those around the child. At the *problem* level, the difficulties tend to have more of a disruptive effect on the child. They last longer and have a more damaging impact on others. However, at both of these levels, normal and problem, the difficulties are not ordinarily of sufficient severity to require professional help. The teacher can manage both levels but, obviously, will have to devote more time and be more resourceful with those children whose behaviors are at the problem level. When problems reach the *referable* level, they go beyond the teacher's independent competence and warrant intervention by professional mental-health practitioners and facilities. Table 5 summarizes criteria proposed by Gropper et al. (1968) for classifying problem behavior.

Rutter (1975) takes the position that the assessment of severity of a disorder involves two different elements: abnormality and impairment. The first issue is whether or not the child's behavior, in terms of pattern or frequency, is abnormal in statistical terms. The second issue is, granted there is abnormality, does it lead to any degree of handicap in the child's functioning.

Criteria employed by Rutter to assess the possible abnormality of any behavior include the following:

(1) *Age and sex appropriateness.* Many behaviors are appropriate at one age but not at another, and while many behaviors are shared by boys and girls alike, it would be rare for a child to show all or most of the behaviors generally associated with the opposite sex.

(2) *Persistence.* At any point in time many children will show various kinds of troublesome behavior, but it is not common for their behaviors to persist over a long period of time.

(3) *Life circumstances.* A child's behavior will often fluctuate as a function of environmental circumstances and the influence of these circumstances must be taken into consideration.

(4) *Sociocultural setting.* Assessment must evaluate a child's behavior in context of the norms of his culture or subculture.

Table 5. Summary of Criteria for Classifying Problem Behavior

Description of Criteria	Normal	Problem	Referable
A. Intensity How disruptive of the child's other activities is the problem behavior?	NON-DISRUPTIVE Behavior does *not* interfere with the child's other activities	DISRUPTIVE Behavior interferes with the child's other activities	EXTREMELY DISRUPTIVE Behavior completely disrupts child's other activities
B. Appropriateness is the behavior a reasonable response to the situation?	REASONABLE Response is acceptable or expected for the situation	INAPPROPRIATE Response is undesirable for the situation	EXCESSIVE Response is out of proportion to the situation
C. Duration How long does the behavior episode last?	SHORT-LIVED Episode lasts only a short time (short time within a class period)	MODERATELY LONG Episode extends over a longer period (some carry-over from one class to the next)	LONG-LASTING Episodes are long-lasting (greater part of a day)
D. Frequency How often does the behavior occur?	INFREQUENT Behavior usually is not repeated (rarely repeated in a day; rarely repeated on other days)	FREQUENT Behavior is repeated (may be repeated several times a day, may be repeated on several days)	HABITUAL Behavior happens all the time (repeated often during day; repeated on many days)
E. Specificity/ Generality In how many types of situations does the behavior occur?	OCCURS IN SPECIFIC SITUATION Behavior occurs in specific type of situation	OCCURS IN SEVERAL SITUATIONS Behavior occurs in more than one type of situation	OCCURS IN MANY SITUATIONS Behavior occurs in many types of situations

Table 5 (Continued)

Description of Criteria	Normal	Problem	Referable
F. Manageability How easily does the behavior respond to management efforts?	EASILY MANAGED Responds readily to management efforts	DIFFICULT TO MANAGE Inconsistent or slow response to management efforts	CANNOT BE MANAGED Does not respond to management efforts
G. Assessability of Circumstances How easily can the circumstances that produced the behavior be identified?	EASILY ASSESSED Easy to identify situation of condition producing behavior	DIFFICULT TO ASSESS Situation or condition producing behavior difficult to identify	CANNOT BE ASSESSED Cannot identify situation or condition producing behavior
H. Comparison with Maturity Level of Class How close to the norm of the class is the problem behavior?	NO DEVIATION FROM LEVEL OF CLASS Behavior is par for the group	BELOW LEVEL OF CLASS Behavior is below the group level	CONSIDERABLY BELOW LEVEL OF CLASS Behavior is considerably below the group level
I. Number of Problem Behaviors Exhibited	Rarely more than one	Usually more than one	Usually many and varied
J. Acceptance by Peers Does the child have difficulty being accepted by peers?	ACCEPTED Is accepted by peers	HAS DIFFICULTY GETTING ALONG May have difficulty with particular Individuals	NOT ACCEPTED Unaccepted by group

Table 5 (Continued)

Description of Criteria	Normal	Problem	Referable
K. Recovery Time How quickly is the situation leading to the episode forgotten?	RAPID Gets over episode quickly	SLOW Gets over episode more slowly	DELAYED Does not get over episode
L. Contagion 1. Does the behavior disrupt the activities of others? 2. Do others copy the problem behavior?	LITTLE OR NO EFFECT ON OTHERS Behavior does not disturb or does not serve as a model for others	CONSIDERABLE EFFECT ON OTHERS Behavior disturbs immediate neighbors or neighbors copy behavior	EXCESSIVE EFFECT ON OTHERS Behavior disturbs whole class or whole class copies behavior
M. Degree of Contact with Reality Does the behavior represent a loss of contact with reality?	NO CONFUSION BETWEEN REAL/UNREAL	SOME CONFUSION BETWEEN REAL/UNREAL	CONFUSES REAL/UNREAL
N. Response to Learning Opportunities How readily does the child respond when learning opportunities are provided?	RESPONDS POSITIVELY TO ENRICHMENT/ REMEDIAL WORK	RESPONDS SLOWLY OR WEAKLY TO ENRICHMENT/ REMEDIAL WORK	DOES NOT RESPOND TO ENRICHMENT/ REMEDIAL WORK

Note: Reprinted from G. L. Gropper, G. C. Kress, R. Hughes, and J. Pekich, Training teachers to recognize and manage social and emotional problems in the classroom, *The Journal of Teacher Education*, Winter 1968, *19*, no. 4: 481.

(5) *Extent of disturbance.* An isolated symptom will generally not merit the concern that would be generated by many displays of emotional or behavioral disturbance.

(6) *Type of symptom.* By their very nature some symptoms are more likely to be associated with more serious disturbance than are others, e.g. nail-biting versus disturbed peer relationships.

(7) *Severity and frequency of symptoms.* Mild difficulties are of much less concern than those that are severe and frequent.

(8) *Change in behavior.* Attention should be paid to an unexpected change in a child's behavior, especially if it is not in keeping with the child's level of maturation.

(9) *Situation-specificity.* Problems which are manifest in all settings probably reflect more disturbance than if limited to only one situation.

It is also necessary to question whether the behavior is causing any harm for the child. Is it impairing the child? Rutter offers four criteria of impairment.

(1) *Suffering.* Does a symptom cause a child to experience psychological pain and discomfort. Is the child miserable?

(2) *Social restriction.* Does a symptom interfere with a child doing what he wants to do?

(3) *Interference with development.* Some problem behaviors will impede the normal progression of personal and social development.

(4) *Effects on others.* Some behaviors alienate others and prevent appropriate relationships and interactions.

This fourth pattern is emphasized by Evans and Nelson (1977). One of the very best predictors of adult maladjustment is a tendency for a child to be disliked by his peers.

Looking more directly at the classroom, Bower and Lamberth (1965) see emotionally disturbed children as experiencing a reduction of behavioral freedom, and this reduction interferes with learning and relationships with others. They note that this disturbance may manifest itself in the classroom by one or more of the following patterns:

(1) Difficulties in learning that cannot be explained by intellectual or physical factors

(2) Difficulties in establishing and maintaining relationships with peers and teachers

(3) Inappropriateness or immaturity in behaviors or feelings under normal circumstances

(4) Continued unhappiness or depression

(5) The development of physical symptoms, speech disorders, reported pains, or fears associated with personal or school problems

Bower and Lamberth's fourth pattern merits additional comment because until recently it was thought that children did not suffer from serious depressive conditions. This may have been due to the fact that clinicians rarely see psychotic depression in children and younger adolescents (Conger, 1977). Cytryn and McKnew (1972), however, identify three types of depression to be found in children:

(1) Chronic depressive reactions frequently found in children whose lives have been disrupted by separation from a loved one, an unstable series of attachments, a history of poor adjustment, and, often, a disturbed mother;

(2) acute depressive reactions to a traumatic loss; and

(3) masked depressive reactions characterized by behavior problems such as truancy, agitation, hyperactivity, and temper tantrums.

The authors report that the most common type is the third, masked depression, and to an observer would frequently not appear to be depression at all.

It is obvious that there are everyday, routine disturbances to which the teacher cannot and should not attend in detail. Guidelines for discriminating behavior deserving of more careful attention have been spelled out by Buhler, Smitter, and Richardson (1965). They suggested that all repetitious disturbances should be investigated. Repetitious behavior is more than release of simple tension but may imply problems more serious and chronic in nature. A second guideline is that a single, serious disturbance is more ominous. Some disturbances are more than a deviation from or exaggeration of more normal behavior. They have a qualitative and intrinsic difference. Goldstein (1954) wrote about the "catastrophic reaction". An unusually juvenile temper tantrum, an uncontrollable fit of tears, or a flagrant act of violence may serve as examples. A third guideline is a succession of different disturbances. While the behaviors may appear unrelated, each may be in some way related to the same core problem. Quay and Werry (1972) observed that the "quantitative" approach to categorizing disorders conceives of the disorder as a collection of symptoms. The intensity of the disorder is a function of the number of symptoms present.

Buhler et al. (1965) proceed to mention several general principles to help teachers evaluate the problems of their children. First, do not assume that a child's difficulty can be attributed to a single cause. Second, explanations should not be embraced without consideration of the individual child's situation. Third, do not rely on explanations that may not be borne out by the facts. Fourth, weigh symptom behaviors and take into consideration their proportionate relationship to the known or assumed causes. The authors acknowledge that this is the most difficult skill to achieve.

In the final analysis, when making judgments about children's behavior, two baseline principles derived from Ross (1980) must be kept in mind. First, judgments must derive from directly "observable behaviors". The discrete, overt behavior of the child provides the data for determining where that behavior falls on a normal-abnormal continuum. Observable behavior can be communicated to others, and they, in turn, can repeat the observations. "Objectivity, communicability, and repeatability are the requisites of a science, and the data gathered by a behavioral approach thus permit the development of scientific knowledge about psychological phenomena" (p. 6). A second important principle is that the final determination or judgment made about an observable behavior will be a function of the observer's background in a given social environment. It will be influenced by the cultural, historical, and social setting in which the behavior occurs. If a child deviates from the prevailing norms that child will be judged deviant. Every society has its own expectations about what is appropriate behavior for a child, and these expectations will vary, depending on such characteristics as the child's age and sex, as well as a host of other variables. The child who departs from these expectations will, in time, come to the attention of certain authority figures.

The teacher must be prepared to answer a number of questions about the behavior of any child in the classroom. Is the child's behavior basically normal or is it a problem? If the answer suggests disturbance, then the potential for impairment must be considered. Low potential may suggest that the teacher first attempt to deal with the behavior in the classroom. Should impairment be noticeable or loom as a distinct possibility, then the advisability of referral increases. It should be noted that consultation might be beneficial at any level, even at the primary point of deciding whether a child's behavior is normal or not.

Following an attempt to resolve the above questions, there is benefit to the teacher's being able to describe or place the behavior within some general framework or classification scheme. Communication between educators, mental-health professionals, and members of other disciplines may be improved by a common vocabulary and classification network. As mentioned earlier, however, even professionals have difficulty when many narrow categories are used, but they are much more likely to agree within a few broad categories. Quay (1972) recognizes the merit of a "common framework for communication about the treatment of behavioral deviance..." (p. 25). But what is a satisfactory, manageable framework? As noted earlier, classification systems for locating childhood symptomology abound. Dissatisfaction with these classification systems also abounds, and, as Kauffman (1977) points out, "Educators are even more disappointed by current classifications than psychologists and psychiatrists" (p. 27).

The most official and authoritative classification system in current use is that of the American Psychiatric Association, *Diagnostic and Statistical Manual of Mental Disorders* (DSM-III), revised in 1980. This edition has a major category for classifying disorders usually arising in childhood and adolescence, and within this category are to be found nine subcategories:

(1) Mental retardation,
(2) Attention deficit disorders, with or without hyperactivity,
(3) Conduct disorders,
(4) Anxiety disorders,
(5) Other disorders including attachment disorder of infancy, schizoid behavior, elective mutism, oppositional behavior, and identity disorder,
(6) Eating disorders,
(7) Stereotyped movement disorders,
(8) Other disorders with physical manifestations including stuttering, enuresis, encopresis, sleep walking, and sleep terror, and
(9) Pervasive developmental disorders.

Given the fact that some children have problems and are classifiable, there must be, nevertheless, caution in labeling a child as a behavioral problem or for placing him in an even more restricted category of disturbance. A child might function normally in his own environment or social setting but be stigmatized in school with a label based on limited assessment. The diagnosis of mental retardation, for example, is not simply a function of an IQ score but must take into consideration the total adjustment of the individual. A label may encompass only a small portion of a child's total behavior. Another risk in labeling is the potential for limiting a child's opportunities. These opportunities may be educational or vocational and, in turn, alter his social options to a considerable degree. The expectations and responses of others may be seriously prejudiced. Achenbach and Edelbrock (1978) observe that experts generally agree that "most current labels for exceptional children are not only of little use but may be harmful because of the stigmata they confer and the categorical nature of services they dictate" (p. 1276). Another reason for caution is the permanency of labels. Once a child has been pegged, it may be difficult for the child to extricate himself from the label. The author recalls early in his career the experience of diagnosing a young child as schizophrenic following psychological testing. When the senior psychiatrist was questioned as to why he had chosen other terms, he replied that a diagnosis of schizophrenia might dog the boy for many years and probably more time was justified before coming to such an ominous conclusion. A host of additional criticisms of labeling have been proffered: it emphasizes the negative, it ignores individual differences, it can expose the child to unnecessary and potentially harmful treatment, and it implies that the problem is solely that of the child. One last source of caution, however, is worth mentioning: the possibility of creating a self-fulfilling prophecy. The child's self-expectations and self-esteem may be affected and the child may develop the assumptions of a particular label. A vicious circle is perpetuated in which disordered behavior leads to a diagnostic label, which in turn intensifies the behavioral disturbance. A mother in one of the author's classes responded to this point with the following written observation of her own daughter:

Mickie is a "normal," healthy teenager and wishes to be treated as such. She loves clothes, record albums and can talk for hours to her girlfriends on the phone about boys and such.

She is generally a happy, easygoing type of person. She has one problem though and that is she cannot read or write at a level with her own age group. An ophthalmologist diagnosed her as having a neurodysfunction connected to the eye. Her EEG, read by a neurologist, diagnosed her as having an abnormal brain wave and showed a tendency toward epilepsy.

In spite of her handicap she manages very well in society. She has friends and is more independent than a lot of girls her age because she wants to prove that she is capable in other areas besides reading and writing. She can sew some although cutting patterns is difficult, but she still tries hard. She can cook and do simple baking and accepts responsibility well.

She feels very strongly about being accepted by her peer group and is proud of her friends who all have decided not to smoke because it is "dumb," and she feels her group is one of the best in the school.

She recently became concerned about a girl who is going with the wrong crowd. We had a long talk about it and how that decisions that she and her friends make now could influence their future either for good or bad.

In the past, after the school would call me in to try to convince me to sign the necessary papers for Special Education, she would stop doing her homework, her bedroom would be in shambles and she'd start losing keys, money, etc. She'd say, "If they think I am retarded then I must be retarded." She would begin to mistrust me and I'd have to reassure her that I hadn't signed the papers.

The Special Education Counselor at the Junior High School said that a child should not have any right to decide whether or not they belong in Special Education. He felt that I should sign the papers regardless of Mickie's feelings.

Mickie feels that if she is labeled "special," she'll lose her friends and everyone will treat her like they do the other students who are in special classes. She doesn't care if kids call her dumb, or stupid because she knows she can't compete scholastically but to be called an "EMR" to her is devastating.

It is my hope that someday children like Mickie will be able to learn in an atmosphere of acceptance by educators and not be labeled in such a way that they are made to feel that they are so different from the norm that they can never find their place in society.

To return to a beginning theme, "of all the uncertainties regarding the disturbed child, the matter of identification is one of the most vexing" (Long *et al.,* 1965, p. 113). We do know, however that in the final analysis, judgment will be the result of human decision making, and, while not perfect, this process is to be desired over a policy of arbitrary and impervious formulas. "If policy is iron-clad, why not let a machine make the decisions? Policy isn't thinking, it's a reflex" (Vonnegut, 1952, p. 79).

Summary

There is a need for teachers to develop diagnostic skills by using observation, screening instruments, check lists, and other assessments. A combination of information obtained through teacher observations and normative data collected by trained diagnosticians sets the optimum situation at the school level for diagnosing learning problems. Physical, social, intellectual, academic, learning styles and emotional data are needed to give a total picture of the individual. Before such information can be provided, the teacher must have adequate understanding and knowledge of the categories related to the learning process. For this purpose, academic, language, and learning functions as identified by Aukerman and Aukerman, Burns and Roe, Dauzat and Dauzat, Myklebust and Johnson, Luria, Strauss, Kirk, Lerner, Chalfant and Scheffelin, and Meeker are included.

To aid the teacher and diagnostician in screening for behavior and learning disabilities, formal and informal screening instruments should be used. The informal ones are check lists devised to simplify observation procedures. Formal screening instruments such as the Slingerland tests are reviewed. Some discriminate between three modes of learning; others cut across several dimensions of behavior and learning disabilities. The Jansky Screening Index for kindergarten children also provides a means of developing local norms, and is presented as an aid to the development of preventive techniques at the beginning of first grade. Because of the overlapping of emotional problems with learning disabilities, teachers are urged to use their most sensitive observations to check for emotional symptoms. We have included a paper by Louis Fairchild, which covers the research on identification of the child who is emotionally/behaviorally disturbed and also describes the discrete differences that characterize these children.

Student Assignments

1. The student will choose one screening instrument and evaluate a child.
2. The student will observe a child in a classroom, using a schedule. The observation should be in at least two sessions in the same situation and at least four sessions in other situations. Evaluation will be made at the end of the observation periods.
3. The students will discuss specific problems children in special education experience.
4. The student will observe in a room for the emotionally disturbed and discuss with the teacher the characteristics that identify the children as having emotional problems.

Discussion Questions

Compare the Aukerman and Aukerman organization of the reading process with that of Burns and Roe.

How do sensory and perceptual problems differ?

Discuss the auditory-receptive problems in reading and the auditory-receptive problems in math.

Explain the speech problems of a person with paraphasia. In what way do these problems compare to a deficiency in formulation and syntax?

Discuss the limitations of observation and screening instruments in the evaluation process.

What is the importance of the teacher in identifying the emotionally disturbed?

REFERENCES

Achenbach, T., & Edelbrock, C. The classification of child psychopathology; a review and analysis of empirical efforts. *Psychological Bulletin,* 1978, *85*: 1275–1301.

Anthony, E. J. The behavior disorders of childhood. In Mussen, P. (Ed.), *Charmichael's manual of child psychology*; vol. 2. New York: Wiley, 1970.

American Psychiatric Association. *Diagnostic and statistical manual of mental disorders* (3rd ed.). Washington, D. C.: Author, 1980.

Aukerman, R. C., & Aukerman, L. R. *How do I teach reading?* New York: John Wiley and Sons, 1981.

Baxter, W. Pasadena, Calif.: (unpublished screening instrument) Veritas Publications, 1972.

Boder, E. Developmental dyslexia: a diagnostic screening procedure based on reading and spelling patterns. *Academic Therapy,* 1969, *IV,* no. 4: 285–287.

Bower, E., & Lamberth, N. In-school screening of children with emotional handicaps. In Long, N., Morse, W., and Newman, R. (Eds.). *Conflict in the classroom.* Belmont, Calif.: Wadsworth, 1965.

Buhler, C., Smitter, F., & Richardson, S. What is a problem? In Long, N., Morse, W., & Newman, R. (Eds.), *Conflict in the classroom.* Belmont, Calif.: Wadsworth, 1968.

Brown, J. Modified Joseph Hill model for cognitive mapping. An unpublished model used at Alvin Community College, Alvin, Texas.

Burns, P. C., & Roe, B. D. *Teaching reading in today's elementary schools.* Chicago: Rand McNally Company, 1968.

Bush, W. J., & Giles, M. T. *Aids to psycholinguistic teaching.* Columbus, Ohio: Charles E. Merrill Publishing Company, 1976.

Chalfant, J., & Scheffelin, M. A. *Central processing dysfunctions in children.* NINDS Monograph no. 9. Washington, D. C.: U.S. Department of Health, Education and Welfare, 1969.

Clarizio, H., & McCoy, G. *Behavior disorders in children.* New York: Crowell, 1976.

Clements, S. D. *Minimal brain dysfunction in children.* Washington, D. C.: Department of Health, Education and Welfare, 1966.

Conger, J. *Adolescence and Youth.* New York: Harper & Row, 1977.

Cytryn, L., & McKnew, Jr., D. Proposed classification of childhood depression. *American Journal of Psychiatry*, 1972, *129*: 149–154.

Dauzat, J. A., & Dauzat, S. V. *Reading: The teacher and the learner.* New York: John Wiley and Sons, 1981.

de Hirsch, K., Jansky, J. J., & Langford, W. S. *Predicting reading failure: a preliminary study of reading, writing and spelling disabilities in pre-school children.* New York: Harper and Row, 1966.

Doctorow, E. L. *Ragtime.* New York: Random House, 1975.

Engle, M. *Psychopathology in childhood.* New York: Harcourt Brace Jovanovich, Inc., 1972.

Fernald, G. *Remedial techniques in basic school subjects.* New York: McGraw-Hill, 1942.

Foltz, D. Judgment withheld on DSM III, new child classification pushed. *APA Monitor,* 1980, *11,* no. 1: 33.

Furner, B. A. An analysis of the effectiveness of a program of instruction emphasizing the perceptual-motor nature of learning in handwriting. *Elementary English,* January 1970, 47: 61–69.

Gates, A. I. *The improvement of reading: A program of diagnostic and remedial methods.* (Rev. ed.). New York: Macmillan Publishing Company, 1935.

Gearhart, B. R. *Learning disabilities: educational strategies.* St. Louis: C. V. Mosby, 1973.

George, J. *Project child.* Austin, Texas: Texas Education Agency, 1974.

Gersten, J., Langner, T., Eisenberg, J., Simcha-Fagan, O., & McCarthy, E. Stability and change in types of behavioral disturbance in children and adolescents. *Journal of Abnormal Child Psychology,* 1976, 4: 111–127.

Glass, G. G. Perceptual conditioning for decoding: rationale and method. In Bateman, B. *Learning disorders,* vol. 4. Seattle: Special Child Publications, 1971.

Goldstein, K. The brain-injured child. In Michael-Smith, H. (Ed.), *Pediatric problems in clinical practice.* New York: Grune and Stratton, 1954.

Goodman, K. S. Dialect barriers to reading comprehension. In Goodman, G., and Hammill, D. *Basic school skills inventory.* Chicago: Follett Publishing Company, 1976, pp. 122–130.

Goodman, L., & Hammill, D. *Basic school skills inventory.* Chicago: Follett Publishing Company, 1976.

Gropper, G., Kress, G., Hughes, R., & Pekich, J. Training teachers to recognize and manage social and emotional problems in the classroom. *The Journal of Teacher Education,* 1969, *19*: 477–485.

Group for the Advancement of Psychiatry. *Psychopathological disorders of childhood: Theoretical considerations and a proposed classification,* June 1966, vol. VI.

Harris, A. J., and Sipay, E. R. *How to teach reading.* New York: Longman, Inc., 1979.

Harvey, A. M., & Bordley III, J. *Differential diagnosis.* Philadelphia: Saunders, 1972.

Hugo, V. *Les miserables.* New York: The Modern Library, 1862.

Jansky, J., & de Hirsch, K. *Preventing reading failure.* New York: Harper & Row, 1972.

Jansky, J. *The Jansky screening index.* New York: Author, 1972.

Johnson, D. J. & Myklebust, H. R. *Learning disabilities: Educational principles and practices.* New York: Grune and Stratton, 1967.

Jones. C. (unpublished paper), Texas Technological University, Lubbock, Texas: 1974.

Kauffman, J. *Characteristics of children's behavior disorders.* Columbus, Ohio: Charles E. Merrill Publishing Company, 1977.

Kinsbourne, M. Selected difficulties in learning to read, write and calculate. In Millichap, J. G. (Ed.), *Learning disabilities and related disorders.* Chicago: Year Book Medical Publishers, Inc., 1977, pp. 79–92.

Kirk, S. A. *The diagnosis and remediation of psycholinguistic abilities.* Urbana, Ill.: University of Illinois Press, 1966.

Koppitz, E. Bender Gestalt test, visual aural digit span test and reading achievement. *Journal of Learning Disabilities,* March 1975, 8: 154–157.

Knopf, I. *Childhood psychopathology.* Englewood Cliffs, N.J.: Prentice-Hall, 1979.

Krantz, L. O. (Ed.). *The author's word list for the primary grades.* Minneapolis: Curriculum Research Co., 1945.

Lapouse, R., & Monk, M. Fears and worries in a representative sample of children. *American Journal of Orthopsychiatry,* 1959, *29*: 803–818.

Lerner, J. *Learning disabilities.* Boston: Houghton Miffllin Co., 1981.

Long, N., Morse, W., & Newman, R. *Conflict in the classroom.* Belmont, Calif.: Wadsworth, 1965.

Luria, A. R. *The working brain.* New York: Basic Books, 1973.

Luria, A. R. Neuropsychological analysis of focal brain lesions. In Wolman, B. J. (Ed.), *Handbook of clinical psychology.* New York: McGraw-Hill, 1965, p. 722.

McLoughlin, J. A., & Lewis, R. B. *Assessing special students.* Columbus, Ohio: Charles E. Merrill, 1981.

Meeker, M., and Cromwell, *Meeker-Cromwell behavior rating scale,* Calif.: SOI Institute, El Segundo, Calif.

Meeker, M. N. Unpublished research, El Segundo, Calif.: Institute for Applied SOI Studies, 1973, 1974.

Meeker, M. N. *The structure of intellect.* Columbus, Ohio: Charles E. Merrill, 1969.

Meier, J. H., Cazier, V. O., & Giles, M. T. *Individual learning disabilities classroom screening instrument.* Evergreen, Colo.: Learning Pathways, Inc., 1971.

Mills, R. E. *The teaching of word recognition and the learning methods test* rev. ed. Fort Lauderdale, Fla.: The Mills School, Inc., 1964.

Myklebust, H. R. *The development of disorders of written language.* New York: Grune and Stratton, 1965.

Myklebust, H. R., & Boshes, B. *Minimal brain dysfunction in children: Final report contract 108-45-142 neurological and disease control program.* Washington, D.C.: U.S. Department of Health, Education and Welfare, 1969.

Otto, W., McMenemy, R. A., and Smith, R. J. *Corrective and remedial teaching.* Boston: Houghton Miffllin Co., 1973.

Piaget, J. *The child's conception of physical causality.* Totawa, N.J.: Littlefield, Adams and Co., 1966.

Piaget, J. *The child's conception of space.* New York: W. W. Norton and Co., 1967.

Piaget, J. *The child's conception of number.* New York: W. W. Norton and Co., 1965.

Prescott, D. A. *The child in the educative process.* New York: McGraw-Hill, 1957.

Quay, H. Patterns of aggression, withdrawal, and immaturity. In Quay, H., and Werry, J. (Eds.), *Psychopathological disorders of childhood.* New York: Wiley, 1972.

Reinert, H. *Children in conflict.* St. Louis: C. V. Mosby, 1976.

Report of the Joint Commission on Mental Health of Children. *Crises in child mental health: Challenge for the 1970's.* New York: Harper, 1970.

Rosen, B., Bahn, A., & Kramer, M. Demographic and diagnostic characteristics of psychiatric outpatient clinics in the United States; 1961. *American Journal of Orthopsychiatry,* 1964, *34*: 455–468.

Ross, A. *Psychological disorders of children.* New York: McGraw-Hill, 1980.

Rutherford, D. Speech and language disorders and MBD. In Millichap, J. G. (Ed.), *Learning disabilities and related disorders.* Chicago: Year Book Medical Publishers, 1977, p. 49.

Rutter, M. *Helping troubled children.* New York: Plenum Press, 1975.

Salvia, J., & Ysseldyke, J. E. *Assessment in special and remedial education.* Boston: Houghton Mifflin Co., 1981.

School Mathematics Study Group. *Studies in mathematics*, vol. XIII. Palo Alto, Calif.: Board of Trustees of the Leland Stanford University, 1966.

Shaw, C., & Lucas, A. *The psychiatric disorders of childhood.* New York: Appleton-Century-Crofts, 1970.

Slingerland, B. H. *Slingerland screening tests for identifying children with specific language disability* (rev. ed.). Cambridge, Mass.: Educator's Publishing Service, Inc., 1970.

Smith, E. B., Goodman, K. S., & Meredith, R. The reading process: A psycholinguistic view. In Ruddell, R. B., Ahern, E. J., Hartson, E. K., & Taylor, J. (Eds.), *Resources in reading-language instruction.* Englewood Cliffs, N.J.: Prentice-Hall, 1974, pp. 85–100.

Strauss, A. A., & Lehtinen, L. E. *Psychopathology and education of the brain-injured child.* New York: Grune and Stratton, 1947, p. 13.

Thomas, A., Chess, S., & Birch, H. *Temperament and behavior disorders in children.* New York: New York University Press, 1968.

Trippe, M. Education dimensions of emotional disturbance—Past and forecast. In Knobloch, P. (Ed.) *Intervention approaches in educating emotionally disturbed children.* Syracuse, N.Y.: Syracuse University Press, 1966.

Vonnegut, Jr., K. *Player piano.* New York: Dell, 1952.

Wallace, G., & McLoughlin, J. A. *Learning disabilities.* Columbus, Ohio: Charles E. Merrill, 1979.

Werry, J., & Quay, H. The prevalence of behavior symptoms in younger elementary school children. *American Journal of Orthopsychiatry,* 1971, *41*: 136–143.

Zubin, J. Classification of the behavior disorders. In Farnsworth, P., McNeman, O., & McNeman, Q. (Eds.) *Annual review of psychology.* Palo Alto, Calif.: Annual Reviews, Inc., 1967.

Chapter 5

Perceptual-Motor Assessment

After you have studied this chapter, you should be able to do the following:
1. *Understand the theoretical concepts underlying perceptual-motor assessment*
2. *Identify the major contributions/authorities who emphasize perceptual-motor assessment*
3. *Discuss the perceptual-motor tests most commonly used*
4. *Differentiate between fine- and gross-motor tests*

Introduction

Perceptual-motor assessment and training has been a significant part of special-education programs for several decades and the perceptual-motor activities have been heralded by some authorities to be necessary for developing academic skills. Within the last decade, however, the use of perceptual-motor training has been under fire because it has not been shown conclusively that these activities will significantly increase academic gains among school-age children.

The writers present this chapter to provide information concerning (1) the background theory behind this training, (2) the classifications involved, (3) assessment instruments used, and (4) the issues regarding the use of perceptual-motor assessment and training. The philosophy herein is that perceptual-motor activities are a natural and integral part of growing up—important for the general health of any child/youth. However, as a structured program specifically for handicapped students, its use is a relative matter and for remediation purposes should be used only for perceptually handicapped children to develop perceptual-motor skills. As research becomes more refined, perhaps the relationship between perceptual-motor training to over-all growth and development and academic skills will be better understood. The theories underlying the use of perceptual-motor programs are discussed in the following paragraphs.

Background Information

The first two years of a child's life, according to Piaget (Phillips, 1969), is the sensorimotor period, a period involving sensorimotor function, which is also identified as the first phase of intellectual functioning. Piaget and Inhelder (1967, p. 3), in speaking of sensorimotor space, state, "... it is perfectly true that a sensorimotor space begins to evolve right from the child's birth, and together with perception and motor activity it undergoes considerable development up until the appearance of speech and symbolic images, i.e., the symbolic functions in general." In all of the Piagetian writings, one can find evidence of the beginning stages of all perception during this period of life. While Piaget examined the nature of intelligence and perception as having its beginning in this sensorimotor stage, the Gestalt psychologists, as early as 1912, studied the principles and properties of perception (Hilgard and Atkinson, 1967), both of which deal with the basics of perceptual-motor functioning.

The work of Piaget and the Gestalt psychologists provide information concerning normal perceptual-motor growth, but the prototype for the learning-disorder syndrome is brain damage (Kephart, 1968). Goldstein's (1939) early work with the adult brain-injured individuals found perseveration, figure-background confusion, meticulosity, forced responsiveness to stimuli, and catastrophic reaction to be characteristic behaviors of this group. Werner and Strauss (1939) became interested in whether the same characteristics would be evidenced in children with brain injury. Their clinical and classroom observation revealed that some children showed behavior that was comparable to that of the brain-injured adults. Further observation revealed that children who showed these peculiar characteristics showed also a history of some damage to the brain. They sought further to objectify their data: (1) with a marble-board test and with a picture test, a test of pure visual perception, they were able to show that brain-injured children do exhibit the characteristics of forced responsiveness; (2) with a tactual-motor test, consisting of two sets of boards, they found that brain-injured children do have figure-ground problems; (3) through the use of twelve rhythmic tone patterns and cards of line drawings, the brain-injured children were shown to make a significantly greater number of perseverations than did the nonbrain-injured children; and (4) through an experiment in auditory perception, they concluded that the disturbances of brain-injured children belong to a characteristic perceptual-motor syndrome that can be observed to exist in the visual, tactual, and the auditory fields. Within the work of the Gestalt experimentalists, the Piagetian studies on growth and development, and those specifically interested in the brain pathology observed in brain-injured individuals, e.g., Strauss and Werner (1939) and Goldstein (1939), can be seen the source of the theories and the practices in perceptual-motor assessment and training found in the public schools today.

Kephart (1960), Cruickshank (1958), Barsch (1965), and Frostig et al. (1964) were among those responsible for creating specific interest among special educators regarding the relationships between perception, perceptual-motor growth patterns, and academic learning. Kephart's work, e.g., with Strauss (1947), and his interest in the Piagetian concept of the growth of intelligence prompted his writings and studies on the perceptually handicapped child. He reasoned that balance, posture, and body image formed an important base for learning. Since the written page is fixed in time and space and since there is a rhythm to the structure of this written work, a child must be aware of body position in relation to the fixed stimuli with which he is confronted. Kephart, also, believed that the perception of the fixed stimuli could be influenced by muscle tonus. If the body were tense *(hyperkinetic),* a baby kinesthetically perceived (felt) the foreground figure to be extended farther from the background that it actually was. This kinesthetic perception influenced the *visual perception* of the same figure to be distorted in the same manner; i.e., the figure would be perceived to stand out from the background at a higher level than normally seen by others. Later in life, this hyperkinetic state could influence the visual perception of the printed word, causing it to stand out unrealistically *and* with a group of other words create one giant word. Spaces between the words would be overlooked. If the muscle tonus were *hypokinetic,* the kinesthetic perception also would be distorted and the figure foreground would be farther away than normally perceived, i.e., fading somewhat into the background, and also later creating a faulty perception of the printed word. Many special educators accepted concepts such as the preceding example and began to include perceptual-motor training as a means of helping the learning-disabled child, albeit, many also overlooked the fact that perceptual-motor skill is a multi-faceted skill and general perceptual-motor training was not recommended for every specific kind of deficit.

In order to understand what is to be measured in perceptual-motor assessment, classifications according to several authorities are presented in the following section.

Perceptual Motor Classifications

Kephart Categories

Kephart, as noted above, was among the first to relate motor functions to the slow learning (Kephart, 1960). He does not make a *specific* list of perceptual-motor functions, but he lists motor bases for achievement and emphasizes the importance of other correlates of learning, such as figure-ground discrimination, space discrimination, and the time dimensions that occur in the course of development. Eight of the perceptual-motor functions are considered here to be less overlapping with the language classifications than the others, and they are also considered to be related to learning when there is underachievement.* These eight are listed as perceptual-motor functions, yet it is impossible to separate all perceptual-motor aspects from language functions. Most writers, whether emphasizing motor problems or language problems, include both, giving primary emphasis to one or the other. For example, Kephart, who emphasizes motor training, speaks of the total perceptual process including auditory, visual, and memory functions, all of which are included by writers like Myklebust (1968) and Kirk (1966), who emphasize the language aspects. This list does not include all of the related perceptual-motor functions, but it does include those commonly used in perceptual-motor evaluations and those that appear to be amenable to remediation in the classroom. The eight perceptual-motor functions to be considered are as follows:

Posture
Laterality
Directionality

---

*Some children are fortunately able to compensate for their deficiencies and achieve in spite of them; i.e., some children may have perceptual-motor problems and with no special remediation find success in the academic process. Others may have these same problems, but do not achieve until they have engaged in perceptual-motor remediation activities.

Body image
Form perception
Figure-ground discrimination
Space discrimination
Time discrimination

Posture Problems.   This problem deals with the inability of the body muscles to become innervated in a pattern so that the position of the body with reference to its center of gravity will be maintained (Kephart, 1971). Posture is the basic movement pattern from which all other movement patterns develop. If posture is not maintained in a consistent manner, a person cannot maintain a consistent orientation and will lose efficiency of both gross- and fine-motor movements.

Laterality Problems.   A child who is unaware of the different sides of the body has a problem in laterality. This is not the same as recognizing right or left; rather, it is the ability to differentiate sides of the body, as in *inner-being awareness.* The importance of this awareness is that it is the first step in learning directions of right, left, up, down, before, behind, etc. The human body is anatomically and neurologically designed to be bilaterally symmetrical. There are two relatively independent systems, one for the right and one for the left. "All the nerve systems, for example, innervating the left side of the body are kept distinct, pass up through the spinal cord, cross in the brain stem, and enter the right hemisphere of the cortex" (Kephart, 1971, p. 86). If these two systems are functioning adequately, the basis for learning *where one is in time and space* is intact, and there is no problem in this area.

Directionality Problem.   This is the inability to project directional concepts into external space whether up, down, in front of, in back of, right, or left. Movement patterns experienced are not directed to objects and/or individuals. Such a problem makes it difficult for children to relate to fixed objects in a room or to materials on their desks. It can also affect the child's ability to follow directions. If the teacher tells the child to start reading at the top of the page or on the left side of the page, the child is unable to comply. The child hears the directions and understands the words the teacher is using but lacks a basic reference point from which to proceed and complete the task.

Body-Image Problem.   Body-image problems result from the lack of a point of reference around which relative impressions can be organized. When there is a poor body image, objects and persons cannot be referred to one's body, and, thus, cannot be oriented in space with reference to it. The importance of a sound body image is that it provides a reference point from which to estimate direction and amplitude of movement. Those who have written on concepts of the body image are L. Bender (1956), Goldstein (1939), and Schilder (1935).

Discussion

There is a distinct relationship among the motor problems of posture, laterality, directionality, and body image. When children do not experience a sound motor base, it is very likely they will have difficulty with fine-motor tasks such as writing, drawing, keeping up with the place in reading, catching a ball, picking up a book, or innervating movement from the teacher's directions. The difficulty experienced will depend on the degree of the impairment, compensatory factors (not easily identified), and the teacher's awareness of the problem.

Figure-Ground Relationship Problems.   Figure-ground relationship disturbance is the inability to discriminate foreground stimulus from background stimulus or background stimulus from foreground stimulus. This causes letters in words and words in sentences to become fused or separated in erratic ways. In faulty auditory figure-ground relationships, sounds may not be heard from their points of origin, or they may not be discriminated properly, causing a person to separate words and syllables incorrectly. The phonemes and morphemes become less meaningful, or stated another way, the groupings of sounds within the spoken sentence become like nonsense syllables. Kephart has cited an auditory figure-ground problem situation of a child who heard "I pledge allegiance to the flag" and interpreted it as "Yipes led alley chintz tooth lag." An example of a visual figure-ground problem is that of a child who sees "Tim batted the ball" and interprets it as "Timbat tedtheball."

Form-Perception Problems.   Form-perception disturbance is the inability to perceive objects, sounds, texture, odors, and taste correctly and in a manner common to the mode of perception utilized. Veridical discrimination and interpretation are involved. A child may see all the points around a square (that is, each side) but may not perceive the sides arranged in such a manner that four 90-degree angles are fitted into the organization of the lines. This child sees the four sides but may not see any angles. People with a "sound-form perceptual" problem may not perceive the sound form of words in the same manner as they are perceived by people who have no auditory-perceptual problems. A child may perceive a door as being slanted rather than upright or a banana as having a rough texture rather than a smooth one. In the case of form-perception problems, the form of the stimulus is always perceived incorrectly.

Space-Discrimination Problems.   Space-discrimination problems deal with the location of objects in space. The child who has difficulty perceiving spatial relations will have difficulty dealing with grouping phenomena in arithmetic and forming abstract concepts. This child will have difficulty making associations of events seen or heard. Vision is considered to be one of the most efficient senses to indicate the relationship of objects in space (Kephart, 1971); but sound, smell, taste, and vibrations are also indicators. Those who have written about the importance of space discrimination in the learning process are Strauss and Lehtinen (1947), Stern (1949), Piaget and Inhelder (1956), Vinacke (1952), Welch (1947), and Barsch (1965 and 1967).

Time-Dimension Problems.   Time-dimension problems deal with inability to perceive the meanings of time as related to tomorrow, yesterday, last week, next month, and "pretty soon." Children with this problem do not have the temporal dimension to help them locate events in terms of the future or the past. The child may not be able to skip, jump rope, or even jump in a simple pattern without getting one foot out of step. Kephart relates this problem to reading: "Many children read along, moving from one fixation to another until, at a given fixation, they do not pick up the clue or clues vital to the recognition of the word. At this point their eyes glue to the page" (1971, p. 179). The temporal activity of the visual process is disrupted. This type of performance is typical of the child with a reading problem. In order to develop fluency in reading, it is necessary for a child to develop temporal-spatial skills.

Discussion

The problems in figure-ground relationship, form perception, space discrimination, and temporal dimension are closely related and may affect each other. For example, figure-ground problems could create problems in form perception, space discrimination, and time discrimination. Further, there is a relationship between perception and muscle tension. Kephart (1972) explains that hypokinetic and hyperkinetic states become the origin for the discrimination of foreground and background. The theory is that hyperkinetic conditions in the body in the early stages of development cause children to feel more foreground (become aware of more foreground), and this influences the sensations of seeing or hearing. The figure stands out unrealistically against a background and catches the attention without reference to background visual or auditory stimuli.

The hypokinetic condition in the child (lack of muscle tonus) is said to cause awareness of less foreground. The child is, therefore, perceptually fixated on background without reference to the foreground.

Barsch Categories

Barsch (1967), another writer who espouses motor theories, does not identify specific perceptual-motor functions, but, like Kephart, he identifies functions that he relates to learning and establishes these as components of movement efficiency. He identifies the following components of movement efficiency:

Muscular strength
Dynamic balance
Body awareness
Spatial awareness
Temporal awareness

Muscular-Strength Problems.

If there is a breakdown in the muscular strength of a person, the first dimension of movement efficiency is disturbed. The thrust-counterthrust operation in a moving body is disrupted, and the person does not have control. The implications for academic learning are specifically noted in both fine-motor coordination tasks and gross-motor coordination tasks. For example, with a fine-motor task such as *holding a pencil,* the grasp may be insufficient to propel the pencil back and forth.

Dynamic-Balance Problems.

Balance problems relate to the state of instability resulting from failure to establish an equal distribution of weight on each side of the vertical axis. Lowman and Young (1960) indicate that when the body segments are aligned in a state of equilibrium with a minimum amount of energy and a minimum amount of fatigue upon any particular muscle or muscle group, a person can be described as being *in balance* (Barsch, 1967). The importance of body balance in the learning process appears to be related to the proper development of physical growth, which in turn contributes to the body self-image each person holds.

Body-Awareness Problems.   Body-awareness problems include the inability to have a coordinated and coherent understanding of one's own body image. A child with this problem does not realize that there is meaning to the relationship of the several parts of the body. Body awareness is associated with the lack of foundation needed for the development of number concepts, the building of a system of spatial relationships, and finally the act of reading.

Spatial-Awareness Problems.   A person with this problem is unable to physically relate to objects and other people. The problem appears to relate physically to objects and other people. The problem appears to be related to laterality and right-and-left orientation, and spatial awareness is believed to be a part of the foundation for the learning process.

Temporal-Awareness Problems.   A child with a temporal-awareness problem will have difficulty understanding time concepts and will be unable to accelerate or decelerate his or her own actions according to the demands of the environment. This specifically may result in problems in punctuality, tardiness, "saving for the future," and travel time from place to place (Barsch, 1967). A student with temporal-awareness problems will have difficulty completing work on a time schedule and learning time concepts.

Frostig Visual-Perceptual Categories
Among the first to identify categories of visual perception was Frostig (1966). Her classification includes the following categories:

Eye-hand coordination
Figure-ground
Form constancy
Position in space
Spatial relations

Eye-Hand Coordination Dysfunction.   This is the inability to accurately reproduce visual symbols through the media of writing, drawing, and printing.

Figure-Ground Perception Dysfunction.   This is the inability to identify relevant visual stimuli from distracting backgrounds. The ability is needed in such activities as using a dictionary, finding specific items in a table of contents or an index, reading the printed word in a paragraph or sentence, and solving word problems in arithmetic.

Form-Constancy Dysfunction.   This is the inability to identify forms, regardless of differences in size, color, position, or angle of viewing. This skill is needed in the recognition of a word, regardless of whether it is in a different print or in any unfamiliar context.

Position-in-Space Dysfunction.   This causes an inability to recognize the formation and directionality of figures and characters. This ability is needed in reading and writing skills, for example, to distinguish *3* from *E* and *was* from *saw*.

Spatial-Relationship Dysfunction.   This is the inability to perceive positional relationships between various objects or points of reference, as in the order of letters in a word or of digits in a number. This skill is needed in reading and in computation.

(The Frostig visual-perception categories cannot be purely separated from the language categories that follow, but they are included with the perceptual-motor classification because they show greater similarity to that area.)

Ayres Categories

Jean Ayres's (1975) approach to the study of learning disabilities includes five perceptual-motor classifications, which provide a base from which to examine problems in children. She calls these the *sensory integrative dysfunctions,* and they include:

Generalized dysfunctions
Postural and bilateral integrative deficit
Apraxia
Problems in the left cerebral hemisphere
Problems in the right cerebral hemisphere

Generalized Dysfunction.   These are "across-the-board" dysfunctions involving sensory-integrative deficiencies in most sensory channels and not falling into a recognizable pattern.

Postural- and Bilateral-Integrative Dysfunction.   This is a disorder of the vestibular system that results in inadequate interhemisphere communication and a subsequent poor lateralization of language in the hemispheres, as shown on dichotic listening tests.

Apraxia.   Apraxia is a disorder of motor planning resulting from poor sensory integrative processes. The tactile and vestibular systems are usually involved; kinesthesia occurs occasionally.

Problems in the Left Cerebral Hemisphere.   These cause problems in verbal learning and sometimes poor auditory perception.

Problems in the Right Cerebral Hemisphere.   These are harder to ascertain and the symptoms are more varied than in the left hemisphere. One symptom is the tendency to disregard the left side of self and space. The interference with academic work often is not severe until about the third grade.

Cratty Categories

Another leader in the field of perceptual-motor education is Cratty, whose classifications show similarity to those of Kephart and Barsch. His pragmatic approach regarding activity has grown out of his research with handicapped children. He considers the following sequence to be of importance in planning a program of motor abilities (Cratty, 1967):

Perceptions of the body and its position in space
Balance
Locomotion

Ability
Strength, endurance, flexibility
Catching and throwing
Moving and thinking

Cratty relates his sequences, most of which have been described under some of the previous classifications, to the social and emotional aspects of development. He also theorizes that figure recognition, serial-memory ability, and similar perceptual attributes may be enhanced by the proper kinds of motor tasks (Cratty, 1967, p. 205). He says that intellectually applied motor tasks aid in formation of basic perceptions necessary to reading and writing. Motor tasks help people to think in a more organized fashion and improve their general self-concept (Cratty, 1969, p. 87).

Issues: Perceptual-Motor Training and Perceptual-Motor Tests

Most reports cite the review of Hammill and Larsen (1974) and Larson and Hammill (1975) from which it is concluded that experimental training based on improving perception and perceptual-motor development does not facilitate academic achievement. Though the Hammill and Larson conclusions have been negative regarding the effects of perceptual and/or motor training, publications in both special education and reading continue to give as much attention to this training as is given any other programs used in the remediation of learning problems, albeit, the controversy is emphasized with consensus among most that perceptual and/or motor training cannot be recommended.

Two of the later studies that show positive relationships are those of White (1979), who found that early training in sensory-integrative therapy does affect a change in poor-risk readers and Fuchs (1979), who found that reading and perceptual-motor training may help perceptual-motor skills. The Fuchs study shows a reversed relationship; i.e., reading and perceptual-motor training may help perceptual-motor skills instead of perceptual-motor training's helping reading.

Whereas the bulk of empirical evidence favors the lack of relationship between perceptual-motor training and reading improvement, an earlier study by Marion Faustman (1968) reported by Ekwall (1973) seems worthy of note. Faustman's study involved children in fourteen experimental kindergarten classes who were given perceptual training. Fourteen other kindergarten classes served as controls. After a year of perceptual training, the pupils were mixed in with many other first-grade children. The first-grade teachers were not told which children had had perceptual training. At the end of the first grade year, the children who had been in the experimental groups scored significantly higher (.01 level) in the Gates Word Recognition Test than did the control group. This study involved ideas from Strauss, Frostig, Kephart, and Faustman; and, as Ekwall says, this combination of perceptual-motor programs may produce more positive results than any single program has done so far. The main point is that many perceptual-motor training programs include cognitive-related activities, as in classification of objects, sizes, color, and verbal instructions, and this may be the reason for significant differences found, but they are still perceptual-motor activities.

A significant point made by Ekwall highlights an often overlooked fact. He explains that Kephart was interested in the diagnosis and treatment of children on an *individual* basis and that in his clinic he was quite successful in attacking perceptual problems from that standpoint. Then in his discussion of one "Kephart Study" (Roach, 1967), where nonsignificant results were found, he says that in all fairness to Kephart, it should be reported that the group in the Roach study received their training for *only* eight weeks, and that the ones of the group who continued their training on an individual basis, not only made better scores on the Purdue Perceptual-Motor Survey, but they also scored significantly higher (.05 level) on the Gates-McKillop Reading Diagnostic Test than did a control group who continued to receive group training.

There appear to be many misconceptions concerning perceptual-motor skill training and its relationship to other learning skills. Even a decade ago, Ames (1969), in her critique of the Bibace and Hancock study (1969), agreed with them on many points but pointed to their incorrect assumption that the authorities claim *mastery* of lower processes as being necessary to the higher cognitive processes. Denhoff (1969), who also made a critique of this study, explains that except for Shedd none of the perceptual-motor advocates states or implies that the connection between the two variables is "necessarily prior" or indicates that "mastery" is essential. Denhoff cites (1) Hurst as saying that it (perceptual-motor function) "is a basis"; (2) Ajuriaguerra as saying "it modified other systems evolving with it"; (3) Kephart as indicating that "it will affect" and Mehrabian as saying that "it facilitates". He suggests further that the authors had raised a straw man to do battle within their assumption that perceptual-motor authorities adhere to a rigid one-to-one causal relationship. In his final discussion, Denhoff emphasizes two significant points, both of which could have significant bearing on research:

> First, perceptual-motor skill and scholastic achievement are not unitary variables. Even a cursory look at the Kephart, Frostig and Ayres tests indicates there are components to perceptual-motor skill: including perceptual awareness and focusing, ocular tracking, visual matching of form and spatial relationships, sequencing and memory of perceptual and motor elements, eye-hand coordination, fine finger skills, awareness of spatial coordinates, etc. Scholastic achievement is undoubtedly even more complex. In trying to relate these two complex variables at a general level, the best that one could hope for would be a modest correlation coefficient indicating a general trend of relationship. There would always be some cases showing results neutral or opposite to the main trend.
>
> Second, the individual child is also complex and children vary in the way they approach learning. For instance, if one views learning to read as an information processing skill, there are several modalities (visual, auditory, and kinesthetic) which can be involved in the input of information to be learned, and many factors which may facilitate or impede the integration and output of the learning (memory, conceptual skill, freedom from distractibility, oral language facility, pencil control, etc.) . . . .
>
> Because of these two considerations, it seems only reasonable to conclude that different components of perceptual motor-skills likely facilitate and hamper academic achievement in various academic subjects for different types of children taught by various educational methods.

Another problem regarding perceptual-motor research deals with the tests available for measuring specific perceptual-motor skills. Hudgins (1977) has found (what professionals have known for many years) support for the existence of semiautonomous visual, motor, and integrative components in a visual-motor integrative test, the Bender Visual-Motor Gestalt Test. No doubt the interrelationship of these semiautonomous functions gives cause to question some of the results of the research findings of the past, since the individuality of each function was not considered separately.

A major factor regarding available tests is that many tests lack the reliability and validity to be used in different kinds of decision making. It would be difficult to devise tests that are perfectly reliable. Where research is concerned, reliability coefficients may be as low as .50, particularly where group performance is the issue (Remmers, Gage and Rummel, 1965). Noll (1957) quotes higher figures with coefficients of .95 desirable for good standardized tests and .75 for tests used in studying groups. Downie and Heath (1970) quote .90 for good standardized tests, but they add that reliability is a relative thing and there are certain areas and certain techniques where reliability coefficients fall well below this .90, and the techniques are still used and found to be useful.

The teacher/diagnostician/researcher should seek standardized tests whose reliability is as high as possible, but the reliability must be interpreted in light of the group on which it is based, the variability of the group, and the method of estimating reliability. Unless the investigators are competent statisticians, it would be difficult for them to make proper decisions concerning test data, e.g., with a reliability coefficient of below .90.

Where a reliability coefficient on tests available is not sufficiently high, the investigator making a decision concerning their uses, e.g., in planning remediation, has three alternatives: (1) use the test with the highest reliability; (2) depend on teacher wisdom concerning psychological traits; or (3) use both the test with the highest reliability and information from the teacher. Rich (1978) has shown that teachers' perception of motor activity falls short of being accurate; however, if test data are used as suggested with the teacher information, the proper choice of a remediation technique should be increased substantially.

Review of the reliability and validity of the perceptual-motor tests described in this chapter does not show adequate statistical levels on all the tests and, therefore, the diagnostician should not use them without question. Each subtest reliability and validity coefficient should be examined and compared to the total reliability and validity coefficients when possible. Except for the Bruininks-Oseretsky (new edition of the Lincoln-Oseretsky), these tests have had many years of use, and it is suggested that if and when any has been used singly to make decisions there has been a great chance for error involved in the decision making. Where several tests have been administered as in a battery and where careful evaluation has been made of the differences found and then compared to observations of teachers and parents, there will have been less likelihood of error. One means of determining the effectiveness of the decisions made is to examine the gains made by children who are in remediation classes. These gains should then be compared to the growth made by these children prior to testing and remediation. In a school world of imperfection, there will of necessity be much trial and error; however, judicious use of tests and techniques available, coupled with the honest efforts of teachers, should diminish much of the useless trial and error and lead more adroitly toward better results.

Discussion

Review of the controversial issues regarding perception and perceptual-motor programs reveals no evidence to suggest that perceptual-motor problems do not exist. Specifically, the evidence does question the relationship between these problems and the learning skills required in academics. Many researchers continue their studies, although their own research results have varied between positive and negative findings from experiment to experiment (Thomas and Chissom, 1972), (Thomas, Chissom, et al., 1974a, 1974b), (Thomas, 1975), (Ismail and Gruber, 1967), (Gruber and Kirkendall, 1969, 1971) (Gruber, 1975), (Gruber and Noland, 1977).

Research on perceptual-motor skills has not been confined to comparisons with academic achievement. Much of the research has also involved comparisons with behavior, self-concept, and with different socioeconomic groups (Leithwood, 1971), (Doubros and Mascarenhas, 1969), (Mann and others, 1973), (Rubin, 1968), (Kirkendall and Gruber, 1970), (Gruber and Noland, 1977), (Richmond and Aliotti, 1977), and (Cobb, Chissom and Davis, 1975). A review of these studies also shows conflicting data ranging from significant relationships to nonsignificant relationships between one aspect of academic achievement/self-concept/attitude/socioeconomic status, and perceptual-motor training. In most cases, motor skills have been helped. Since the number of cases, ages of children, socioeconomic status, specific research design, choice of perceptual-motor activity, and length of experimentation were different in each study, it would be meaningless to try to group these as equal. One can only say that there is a question as to the efficacy of using certain training techniques at certain times with certain groups of children involved in the studies.

Hallahan and Kauffman (1978), who state that there is very little research to support the notion that perceptual and perceptual-motor training will automatically lead to academic gains, also add, "The most that can be said, and the research is equivocal even on this, is that perceptual training may increase perceptual skills that can then serve as the basis for academic remediation." The writers recognize that the research has not shown conclusively that "perceptual-motor activities" positively influence academic gains. However, since some research has shown significant academic gains after treatment with these activities, we hold that their use has a place in the curriculum for some learning-disabled children who have perceptual-motor problems. If one studies the literature, one will find that most authorities have recommended these activities for this specific purpose, regardless of whether they had hopeful expectations that they might benefit academic skills.

There are many individual cases where children's academic skills have been helped after perceptual-motor training. In one case, which we use as an example, the writers saw a child change from writing upside down and backwards to writing manuscript letters in the correct direction and right side up after two months of training, using the Frostig program for visual perception. The teacher, who had been a skeptic, decided to find out if such training would actually help a child with such a visual-motor problem. She devoted thirty minutes of specific training daily after school and the child was not allowed to move from an activity until it had been completely mastered. We do not question that this was the appropriate program for this child. We believe remediation to be a matter of individual consideration. No single perceptually impaired child will likely learn just like another. Stating this in another way—there is no homogeneity among perceptually impaired children and youth. This can account for the fact that some children benefit from supplemental perceptual-motor training and others do not. We believe, further, that perceptual-motor activities should be used specifically to benefit perceptual-motor skills and, as Wallace and McLoughlin (1979) say, they should not be considered as *alternate* activities for academics. If reading is to be remediated, of course, the child must read, and walking a balance beam should not be an alternative.

However, if perceptual-motor activities are cognitively related, as in *tracing* words and letters, they should be used; for when cognitive components are the same as other (perceptual-motor) components, they reinforce the learning process. A final implication of the matter of related components is made by Husak and McGill (1979). They say that if there is any substantial relationship between the motor and cognitive domains and if self-concept is an intervening variable, then it would appear that alternative approaches to the investigation of these interrelationships must be developed. A last point is that the use of perceptual-motor activities should not be dependent on proof that they will help every child, but on whether they will help some children. Research to date has not shown that perceptual-motor activities will *not* help some children.

Assessment Instruments for Fine Motor Skills

Bender Visual-Motor Gestalt Test (Bender, 1938)

Description and Administration

The Bender Visual-Motor Gestalt Test (BVMGT) is a maturational test in visual-motor gestalt functions. It is a test made up of nine 4 x 6 inch cards* with one geometric design on each card. The first card is Figure A, which has been popularly used as the demonstrator design card. With many scoring systems, however, it is scored along with the other designs listed numerically from Figure 1 to Figure 8.

Standard administration requires that the subject be given a white, unlined sheet of paper, 8½ x 11 inches. One of the 4 x 6 stimulus designs is presented and the subject copies the design. The cards are presented, one after the other, until all are completed. Memory is not a factor in this test—the subject copies the design while viewing it. After the designs have been copied, the diagnostician has a graphic record of the individual's test performance. The reproductions are evaluated on the basis of distortion of shape, rotation, integration, and perseveration of each design.

There have been many scoring systems devised for use with the Bender design cards (see Table 6). The majority of these systems have been normed on children between the ages of 4 and 11 years. Most use the same directions for administration. Hain (1964) varies his approach slightly, in that the 8½ x 11 sheet of white paper is placed vertically on the table and the stimulus card is placed directly above the paper. No rotation of the card or movement of the paper is allowed. Another system by Canter (1963) provides a background interference paper (BIP)** over which the subject draws the designs *after* having drawn them on the white paper. The BIP paper is placed over a carbon sheet, which, in turn, is placed over another white sheet of paper. The carbon copy (copy #2) may be compared with the first drawing to determine whether BIP paper has influence on the subject's performance.

---

*The nine designs used in the Bender Test are adapted from those used for perceptual experiments by Wertheimer (1923).

**The BIP paper is a sheet of paper on which there are large swirling black lines. Canter (1963) devised the BIP paper for the purpose of studying drawings of brain-injured individuals on both white and BIP paper.

Table 6. Some Popular BV-MGT Scoring Systems

Author	Year	For Age/Grade Levels	Norm/Nonnormed data
Bender	1938	4 through adulthood	Clinical evaluation Maturational data
Pascal and Suttell	1951	15 hrs. to 50 yrs.	Z score norms
Hutt and Briskin	1960	Adults	Clinical observation
Keogh and Smith	1961	Kdg. and 1st grade	Error score for mental ages
Quast	1961		Clinical (brain injury)
Clawson	1962		Clinical evaluation
Canter	1963	Adults and older children	Clinical (brain injury)
Koppitz	1963	5-0 through 10-11	Error score for mental ages
Hain	1964	Adults	Error score for brain injury
Mogin	1966	Primary grade children	Clinical evaluation (emotionally disturbed)
Flint	1966	10-11 and young adults	Clinical evaluation (brain injury)
Weiner	1966	8 to 10 yrs.	Clinical (MBD)
Watkins	1976	5 through 14 yrs.	Error score (L/LD)

Interpretation and Use

The BVMGT is useful in exploring retardation, regression, loss of function, and organic brain defects in children and adults. However, this kind of diagnostic exploration should be left to the professional diagnostician. Its use relative to learning disorders should be confined to visual-motor aspects. This point cannot be overemphasized. The role of medicine is to diagnose medical problems, but the role of education is to diagnose academic problems. The Visual-Motor Gestalt Test has application to school-related functions. Bender (1938) has stated, "It appears . . . that the visual motor gestalt function is a fundamental function associated with language ability and closely associated with various functions of intelligence—such as visual perception, manual motor ability, memory, temporal and spatial concepts, and organization or representation."

Bender (1965) prefers to evaluate the reproductions by means of a "clinical inspec-tion", to determine atypical performances. For example, the test protocol of a subject may be compared with the performances typical of individuals with handicapping conditions such as emotional disturbance, mental illness, or brain injury. Koppitz (1975), in support of *formalized* scoring systems, points out that only well-trained and highly skilled clinicians can derive much meaningful insight from Bender Test records when using only clinical inspection. A great many psychologists/diagnosticians are not as skilled or experienced as others and prefer scoring systems that provide age-level norms, where total-error scores are compared with "normal" scores for a specific age group.

One of the most popularly used scoring systems was completed by Koppitz in 1963. It was standardized for children age 5 years, 0 months to 10 years, 11 months, and is known as the Developmental Bender Test Scoring System. Beyond the age of 10 it cannot be regarded as a developmental test for normal children. After the maturation of the visual-motor function in children, their copied designs tend to be very adequate and no problem is observed. Therefore, the test does not discriminate between average and above-average performance, and Koppitz does not recommend the system for groups of normal teenagers. Koppitz also cautions about its use with very immature children or for those with minimal brain dysfunction, whose mental age is below the 5-year level. Last, she emphasizes that great pains were taken to exclude from the Developmental Scoring System all signs or scoring items that were not related to maturation in visual-motor perception and to achievement in the first and second grade (Koppitz, 1975, p. 14).

Standardization Information

The "Bender" was standardized on 800 school- and nursery-age children 3–11 years of age, inclusive (Bender 1938). The standardization was based on the work of Gesell, who had standardized the drawing ability of young children and found that by age 11, all normal children could reproduce the designs. Below age 11, the data show what percent of children at various ages are able to copy the designs or the type of designs they produce. It is the Koppitz Scoring System (1963), however, that has been used widely with school-age children between the ages of 5 and 11. Koppitz renormed the test in 1974 on 975 children. The largest group was from the northeast (83 percent) and the smallest group from the south (2 percent). Interscorer reliabilities ranged between .79 and .99. Reliability coefficients (test-retest) ranged between .50 and .90.

The preferred geographic range with sampling from each section of the United States was not attained and some of the studies reported on reliability were not high enough to establish the reliability needed to make major decisions. Koppitz herself (1975) cautions that (1) a diagnosis of MBD should not be made solely on the basis of a single Bender Test record (p. 81); (2) it is not possible to make a differential diagnosis between neurotic, psychotic, and brain-damaged on the basis of emotional indicators (p. 92); (3) the Developmental Bender Test Scores by themselves are only moderately effective as screening instruments for school beginners (p. 108); (4) the Bender Test should be combined with a verbal test if used in screening children for intellectual function (p. 47). Research findings (Koppitz, 1975, p. 126) do indicate (1) that Bender Test scores of primary-grade and young clinic patients are significantly related to

Frostig's Developmental Test of Visual Perception (not with 9- and 10-year-olds) and (2) that there is a significant relationship with scores on the Beery Developmental Test of Visual-Motor Integration, Raven's Progressive Matrices, and to Beeker's Visual Discrimination Test of Words.

Watkins (1976) has standardized a scoring system (WBSS) using 1046 learning-disabled children and 3,355 normal children. The ages ranged from 5 years through 14 years for both normal and learning-disabled groups. In the normal group, approximately 70 percent of the children were tested by group administration; whereas, approximately 50 percent of the LD children were tested in groups. Subjects were chosen from 42 school districts in the following states: North Carolina, Tennessee, Mississippi, Texas, Oklahoma, New Jersey, and California. Eighty-five percent of the group were Anglo, ten percent were Black, three percent were Hispanic and two percent were "Other" (Japanese, Chinese, Cuban, Puerto Rican, and American Indian). Socioeconomic status, occupation, education, and income data were obtained on only 60 percent of the parents; therefore, it was not possible to control for these variables.

The correlation between IQ and the Total Error Score was found to be statistically significant, but low, at each age level. This indicates that the Bender Visual-Motor Gestalt is really not an instrument to measure intelligence, but a measure of the development of the neural-visual perceptual system (Watkins, 1976, p. 10).

The norms designate whether the error score indicates a mild, moderate, or severe visual-perceptual problem. The reliability coefficients for the normal subjects are: Age 5, $r = .72$; Age 6, $r = .86$; Age 8, $r = .92$; and age 12, $r = .95$. For the learning-disabled group, reliability coefficients are: Age 5, $r = .66$; Age 6, $r = .75$; Age 8, $r = .85$; and Age 12, $r = .95$. Between scorers A and B, A and C, and B and C, the range of reliability coefficients was .80 to .97. To determine validity as to whether the WBSS would discriminate between normal subjects and children with learning disabilities, the Bender Test was given to the 1,046 children with learning disabilities between the ages of 5 and 14, and then scored according to the WBSS and compared with the normal group. The tests for the significance of the difference between the LD group and the normal subjects was found to be significant at each level. Though the WBSS was not standardized on a complete geographic cross-section, the reliability coefficients obtained appear to justify its use for the purpose described by Watkins.

The BV-MGT has remained one of the most used visual-motor integration tests and much research (both positive and negative) is available to relate scores to developmental levels of visual-motor maturation, brain injury, emotional disturbance, and visual-motor integration. The test may be considered of value as a maturational screening test of performance in the visual-motor gestalt function between the ages of 4 and 11.

The Southern California Sensory Integration Tests (Ayers, 1972)

Description and Administration

The Southern California Sensory Integration Test battery includes a series of separate tests. These tests produce separate scores, some of which are rarely included in other tests. The age limits include children 4–10 years, but each test has its own upper limit, e.g., the Motor Accuracy test has norms that extend only to 7 years, 11 months. The tests with the functions the scores identify are indicated in Figure 24.

Figure 24. Southern California Sensory Integration Test Battery

Test	Functions
The Ayers Space Test A Formboard Test, 10–20 minutes	Space visualization
Southern California Figure-Ground Visual Perception Uses figure ground designs 20–30 minutes	Figure-Ground Perception
Southern California Kinesthesia and Tactile Perception Tests 15–20 minutes	Kinesthesia Manual Form Perception Finger Identification Graphesthesia Localization of Tactile Stimuli Double Tactile Stimuli Perception
Southern California Perceptual-Motor Tests 20 minutes	Motor Accuracy Imitation of Posture Crossing Midline of Body Bilateral Motor Coordination Right-Left Discrimination Standing Balance with eyes open Standing Balance with eyes closed
Southern California Motor Accuracy Test	Degree and changes in sensorimotor integration of upper extremities of individuals with nervous system dysfunction
Positions for Inhibition of the Neck Reflex Uses diagrams for 11 positions	Tonic Neck Reflex Inhibition
Southern California Postrotary Nystagmus Test 5 minutes	Duration of nystagmus following rota- tion—Indicators of disorders in the Vestibular System

Standardization Information

The tests were normed on youngsters residing in the metropolitan area of Los Angeles. There is no indication the sample is comparable for each test in the battery and, therefore, that the results from the various tests can be compared directly. The number in the standardization samples varied, with 280 being included in the Motor Accuracy

Test sample, 1,164 in the Figure-Ground Visual Perception Test, 226 in the Postrotary Nystagmus Test, 953 in the Kinesthetic and Tactile Test, and 1,000 in the Perceptual-Motor Tests. The consultant should note the variance in the norms when using this battery.

The manuals for each test report the reliability for that test. Correlations were reported for the Figure-Ground Visual Perception Test, using a test-retest design, with an interval of one week, of .37 to .52. Three hundred and one children, classified into seven age groups, were used in this correlation study. The range of correlations for the individual tests in the Kinesthesia and Tactile Perception Tests ranged from .01 to .75, with a test-retest procedure. The reliability of the Motor Accuracy Test is high, with coefficients of from .91 to .92 reported from a test-retest study.

Validity studies that relate directly to child achievement are not reported. Some tests such as Motor Accuracy have face validity for school tasks using eye-hand coordination. This test also distinguishes between children with suspected perceptual deficits and those with no known deficits. A study of mean scores of the two groups in the 6- and 7-year-old range yielded a difference at the .01 level of significance.

The Marianne Frostig Test of Visual-Motor Perception (Frostig, Maslow, Lefever, and Whittlesey, 1964)

Description and Administration

The Developmental Test of Visual-Motor Perception (DTVP) is designed to measure five specific areas of visual perception:

(1) Eye-Motor Coordination—a test of eye-hand coordination involving the drawing of continuous straight, curved, or angled lines between boundaries of various widths, or from point to point without guidelines.

(2) Figure-Ground—a test involving shifts in perception of figures against increasingly complex grounds. Intersecting and "hidden" geometric forms are used.

(3) Constancy of Shape—a test involving the recognition of certain geometric figures presented in a variety of sizes, shadings, textures, and positions in space, and their discrimination from similar geometric figures. Squares, circles, rectangles, ellipses and parallelograms are used.

(4) Position in Space—a test involving the discrimination of reversals and rotations of figures presented in series. Schematic drawings representing common objects are used.

(5) Spatial Relationships—a test involving the analysis of simple forms and patterns. These consist of lines of various lengths and angles which the child is required to copy, using dots as guide points.

The administration procedure requires that the child be given an expendable booklet with sixteen pages of different designs. The child is given specific instructions regarding what to do with the designs, e.g., "With a pencil draw a line from one position to another," or "Trace over a specific design" (a design that may be superimposed over another). The test may be group-administered; however, it should not be attempted at the nursery-school, kindergarten, or first-grade levels until the students have been in the classroom for at least two weeks. This is to avoid the acute stress of a new school situation that the child may be experiencing. Time element for administration is approximately one hour.

Interpretation and Use

The DTVP, as described by its authors, is intended "to explore the relationship of visual-perceptual disabilities to problems of school learning and adjustment, brain damage and other handicaps" (Frostig et al., 1964, p. 5). While this is the intention as stated, the authors caution, and advisedly so, that this test does not presume to measure organic dysfunctions. Any nonmedical diagnostician should not, for that matter, diagnose brain damage under any conditions and certainly not from any paper-and-pencil tests. Such diagnosis is for the medical profession and not within the jurisdiction of psychology and/or education. Though relationships between writing/drawing patterns and cerebral dysfunction may be established, this does not prove cause.

This test is a visual perception test and should be used for that purpose. Determining whether a child is able to stay "within the lines" while writing or is able to differentiate designs in various positions are school-related tasks, regardless of what they are called or whether they may be differentiated. We have found that the DTVP is useful in determining visual-perceptual skills, such as keeping children with spatial problems when writing and in establishing control when writing letters and other designs. One of the DTVP major values is that developmental work sheets are established on the five measurements, and are available to provide visual perceptual training. Though there are norms for each perceptual skill, the test may be criterion-referenced to the work sheets. When a child is slow in visual-motor development, daily practice may be very helpful in improving these skills. Frostig's well-planned remediation program, thus, may be useful in helping the consultant prescribe remediation for visual-perception problems.

Regarding other school-related tasks the DTVP has only moderate predictive ability when discriminating poor readers from good ones at grade 1. The correlations range from .40 to .50. Frostig emphasizes that the test should not stand alone, but be part of a total evaluation. Kephart (1972) has emphasized that a child who scores low on the DTVP is likely to have trouble in school, but that it is possible for a child to score high and have trouble because of other deficits.

Standardization Information

The instrument was normed on 2,116 children in Southern California. The sample was primarily "middle class". The lack of representation of minority groups and children from low socioeconomic levels indicates the problem of making direct application of data to these groups.

The subtest reliability coefficients range from .42 to .80. Using the test-retest procedure with a two-week interval, a reliability coefficient of .80 was found for the perceptual quotient. This was raised to .98 with individual administration to a sample of learning-disabled children. Other studies have shown that subtests #2 and #5 have adequate internal consistency. The range is from .90 + for test #2 to between .65 to .85 for test #5. Coefficients for tests #1, #3, and #4 range from .35 to the upper .70s.

Memory-for-Designs Test (Graham and Kendall, 1946–60)

Description and Administration

The *Memory-for-Designs Test* (MFD) involves the reproduction of single geometric designs from memory. In the 1920s, the inability to perform such tasks was associated with "organic" impairment, and the MFD was developed to accompany the test battery for the clinical study of possible brain-damaged patients. It is one of the most popular psychological tests presently used to assess brain damage in children and adults. The minimum age for this test is 8.5 years, and the time required is five to ten minutes.

The test is composed of 15 cardboard squares, with a single black design printed on each. The subject views a card for five seconds and must reproduce the design from memory on a sheet of white 8½X11-inch paper. The higher the score received, the poorer the performance. When tabulated from the raw score, the difference score gives an approximate rating of normal, borderline, or critical (possible brain damage).

Interpretation and Use

Interpretation of this test is simply that of determining (after the scoring procedure) whether an individual's performance does or does not compare to the performance of a group of individuals who have been diagnosed as being brain-injured. However, from the standpoint of education and psychology, if a student's drawings compare with drawings from a group with brain injury, the suggestion is that this student should be referred for neurological evaluation if it is to be determined that a brain injury truly exists.

Where brain injury is inferred, practical implications could be that the teacher might realize that, indeed, a student could have a physiological cause for an inability to remember information, and that this student might not be malingering in his academic performance. The teacher might also anticipate difficulties in his learning to read. Some studies do show a relationship between MFD reproductions and reading (Payne, 1972) (Bruininks, 1969). Payne (1972) also suggests that the MFD score might enable the psychologist to uncover a previously unsuspected pattern of associated psychological abnormalities that might have implications for the adjustment of the individual.

We have found that the MFD may be used to compare a student's performance on a memory test with performance on an eye-hand coordination test such as the Bender Visual-Motor Gestalt or the Visual-Motor Integration Test. If, for example, the student does better on the MFD, it may be inferred that this student may have difficulty when having to move his eyes from a design to the motor act of copying the design, and has less difficulty if allowed to study the design and then concentrate only on drawing from memory. If the student should do better on the Bender, as another example, it could be that he cannot remember the design seen, and that there obviously is no problem when asked to perform a motor act in copying a design. A teacher may use such information in the first case by minimizing work to be copied from board or actually teaching the child to examine the copy work carefully and then to make the copy from memory. In the opposite case, the teacher should minimize work dependent on memory where motor performance is concerned and evaluate the student through multiple-choice questions and/or oral means when appropriate.

Standardization Information

The MFD was standardized on 535 normal subjects, 243 brain-injured subjects, and 47 subjects who had idiopathic epilepsy. The subjects, aged eight years to seventy years, were all from the St. Louis area.

Kendall and Graham (1960) reported that the coefficient of reliability using the split-half method was .92 for a population of 140 patients. Using the test-retest approach, a reliability of .77 was found with a mental defective population.

Various studies are reported in the manual that show that the test differentiates between those with brain damage and those identified as non–brain damaged. The significance level of the mean scores was reported at better than the .01 level. Validity is claimed on the basis of the above information, even though the significant relationship between scores from normal and brain-injured individuals does not prove cause. The MFD test is a good test to use to determine a student's skill in drawing designs from memory.

The Developmental Test of Visual Motor Integration (VMI) (Beery, 1967)

Description and Administration
The Developmental Test of Visual-Motor Integration is a series of 24 geometric forms to be copied using pencil and paper. Normal A. Buktenica is credited with the design of several of the geometric forms and much of the data collection (Beery, 1967). The test can be administered to children between 2 and 15 years old, but it was designed primarily for the preschool and the early primary grades. The manual provides instructions for group and individual administration and scoring criteria for the geometric drawings. The scoring is either pass or fail when compared to samples of actual reproductions by children.

The child is presented a booklet with three designs to a page and told not to open the booklet until told. Thereafter, the individual is told to copy what is shown at the top of the page. The test continues until three consecutive failures occur.

Interpretation and Use
The VMI is basically a tool for educational assessment to measure the degree to which visual perception and motor behavior are integrated in young children. VMI age equivalents for both boys and girls are established between ages 2-10 to 15-11 (Female norms stop at 15-9). Beery (p. 68) outlines the procedure to use in assessment and teaching strategies. If the failure is at a higher level, the child should be given simpler visual-motor tasks to determine the source of difficulty. In contrast, teaching begins with the simple tasks at the first level. The levels are as follows: Level I, Motor Proficiency; Level II, Factual-Kinesthetic Sense; Level III, Tracing; Level IV, Visual Perception; Level V, Visual-Motor Integration.

In addition to the procedure that Beery describes fully at each level, sample practice designs to be used for remediation are shown for each level. These remediation techniques using ten basic forms are recommended for the improvement of visual-motor integration skills and add to the value and use of this test.

Standardization Information
The VMI was standardized using 1,039 children residing in the state of Illinois. Fifty-seven percent were from suburban schools, seventeen percent from rural areas, and twenty-six percent from schools in urban areas.

The technical manual reports an internal consistency reliability of .93. The developmental sequence of the items is evidenced by a correlation of .89 between the scores on the VMI and chronological age of the students (evidence reported for validity). Separate reliability is reported for suburban and rural children. The internal consistency reliability of a population from suburban schools was reported as .93 and a test-retest reliability over a two-week period was .83 for boys and .87 for girls from rural areas.

Predictive studies using an outside criterion are limited. Bateman (Berry, 1967) obtained correlations of .70 and .73, respectively, between the VMI and the visual-motor association and visual-sequencing subtests of the ITPA. A correlation of the VMI with the Frostig PTVP was reported as being .80. Beery concludes that the VMI is a measure of visual-motor integrative function, but that the presumption that improved visual-motor performance will lead to improved academic performance has not been demonstrated statistically.

Raven's Coloured Progressive Matrices Test, Sets A, Ab, and B (Raven, 1956, Revised Order)

Description and Administration

The Raven's Progressive Matrices test* is described by its author as a test of "innate educative ability". Two forms of the test are available, a form-board edition and a booklet edition. The booklet edition consists of a set of designs printed on a brightly colored background. Each design has a blank space within, where a portion has been removed. Below each design smaller designs are shown. One of the smaller designs is the portion taken from the larger pattern. Simple directions are that the child is to choose from among the small designs the appropriate one to fit into the blank space. The child is told, "Point to the piece which came out of this pattern." Prior to these specific instructions, the child is encouraged to examine all of the six smaller designs before deciding which one fits into the larger design.

Interpretation and Use

Raven (1956) interprets the scale as a "test of observation and clear thinking." Each problem presented is considered the "mother" or course of a system of thought. The order in which the problems are presented provides the standard training in the method of working. From this, the name "Progressive Matrices" is derived. It is not considered as an intelligence test, but is explained as a test that can assess the chief cognitive processes of which children under 11 years of age are usually capable. Raven recommends that a vocabulary test be given with this test for the advantage of assessing "separately a person's present capacity for intellectual activity, irrespective of his acquired knowledge, and at the same time the fund of verbal information he has acquired in the past, with as little present intellectual activity as possible" (p. 3).

Information is provided in the manual to show the degree to which children of different ages respond to the three sets. Other information reveals that a high-grade intellectually defective person (in his life time) is not capable of solving the more difficult problems of Set B, but is usually able to solve many of the problems in Set Ab; a person who is seriously defective intellectually fails to solve the problems in Set Ab successfully, even with practice. The emotionally disturbed are described as finding the test to be of interest and will respond to the form-board version when they will not respond to another type of test. The Coloured Progressive Matrices Test appears to be useful to use with non–English speaking children, or ones with physical disabilities,

---

*The first form of this test is known as Progressive Matrices and consists of Sets A, B, C, D, and E. The one most often used in the United States is the Coloured Progressive Matrices described.

with aphasia, cerebral palsy, or deafness, as well as with those who are intellectually subnormal or have deteriorated. Corman and Budoff (1974) found in their research with Spanish- and English-speaking children support for Raven's belief that ability to solve the puzzles on this test is independent of previously developed verbal skills.

The scores provided for Sets A, Ab, and B are the raw scores. From these a percentile score may be found in the appropriate table. An approximate mental-age score may be derived by locating at the 50th percentile the subject's raw score and reading up the vertical column to obtain an *approximate mental age.*

Standardization Information

Raven (1956) reports a test-retest reliability (three administrations, three months apart) to range between .86 and .90 with normal children (ages 6½–12½) and between .92 and .96 with emotionally disturbed children (ages 6½–12½). The tentative percentile norms were established on 608 children ages 5 to 11.5 residing in Dumfries, Scotland.

The validity is not reported as established. Correlation with the Crighton Vocabulary Scale ranges between .84 and .90 for normal children and between .63 and .66 for emotionally disturbed children. In general, it can be seen that the coloured PM Test could be used as a good screening instrument for children to determine a child's capacity for observation and clear thinking.

Assessment Instrument for Gross-Motor Skills

The Purdue Perceptual Motor Survey (Roach and Kephart, 1966)

Description and Administration

The Purdue Perceptual-Motor Survey (PMS) by Eugene G. Roach and Newell C. Kephart (1966) is not a test. It is a survey that enables one to observe a broad spectrum of behavior within a structured, but not stereotyped, set of circumstances. The framework originated in Kephart's *The Slow Learner in the Classroom* (1960) and is designed primarily to detect rather than to diagnose perceptual-motor behavior in a series of behavioral performances. The consultant will find it easy to administer and will need little or no equipment.

Consisting of 22 scorable items, the survey is divided into 11 subtests, each measuring some aspect of the child's perceptual-motor development. Basically, these subtests are concerned with laterality, directionality, and the skills of perceptual-motor matching.

The 11 subtests with their major areas of perceptual motor development are as follows:

Major Areas	Subtests
Balance and Posture	Walking Board
	Forward
	Backward
	Sidewise
	Jumping

Major Areas	Subtests
Body Image and Differentiation	Identification of Body Parts
	Imitation of Movement
	Obstacle Course
	Over
	Under
	Between
	Kraus-Weber
	Angels-in-the-snow
Rhythmic Writing	Rhythm
	Reproduction
	Orientation
Ocular Pursuits	Both Eyes
	Right Eye
	Left Eye
	Convergence
Visual-Achievement Program	Form
	Organization

Specific instructions and the equipment needed are given for each individual test in the PPM Survey. The equipment is to be obtained at the local level. An example of one test, the Walking Board test, and the materials needed are as follows: a section of a 2 x 4 board measuring 8–12 feet long is to be provided by the examiner. It should be placed on brackets, so that the board is at least 6 inches off the floor. The 4-inch side of the 2 x 4 is the surface on which the child is to walk. Instructions request that the child walk forward, backward, and sidewise. The child is assigned a rating on each of the three tasks. A score of four is the highest rating and is given if the child walks easily and maintains body balance throughout. The efforts are graded on the basis of a decreasing performance, and finally a score of one may be given if the child has more than one-fourth of his performance out of balance.

The only other large equipment needed is a chalk board. Most of the tests need no equipment beyond paper and pencil. The activities deal largely with functions such as imitation of body parts, balance, or body-movement skills.

Interpretation and Use

The Purdue Perceptual-Motor Survey should not be used for children who have specific defects such as blindness, paralysis, or known motor problems. Although designed for children in grades two through four, the survey can also be used with older children who are retarded. The normative scores were determined by using children between the ages of six and ten. One should note, however, that one test is designated for children 8 years and older, and one is for children 5 years of age and older.

The PPM Survey is designed primarily to detect errors in perceptual-motor development. It is considered a qualitative scale that designates areas for remediation of perceptual-motor problems. Roach and Kephart (1966, p. 11) point out that the test should be regarded merely as an instrument that allows the examiner to observe a series of perceptual-motor behaviors and to isolate areas that may need further study.

Standardization Information

Two hundred students, chosen from grades one through four in the Klondike School, Lafayette, Indiana, were used to develop the normative data for the PPM Survey. The children were reported to be achieving within their assigned grade levels. They represented a group coming from a wide range of socioeconomic levels and from both rural and urban environments.

A test-retest reliability of .95 was obtained using 30 students who were tested one week apart. A concurrent-validity study using teacher rating of overall academic performance and Kephart's original scale produced a coefficient of correlation of .65.

Bruininks-Oseretsky Test of Motor Proficiency (BOTMP) (Bruininks, 1972)

Description and Administration

The Bruininks-Oseretsky Test of Motor Proficiency is an individually administered test that assesses the motor functioning of children 4½–14½ years of age. The complete battery of eight subtests, which is comprised of 46 separate items, provides a comprehensive index of motor proficiency, as well as separate measures of both gross- and fine-motor skills. The Short Form—4 items from the Complete Battery—provides a brief survey of general motor proficiency.

The work on the test was begun in 1972 and is an adaptation of the Oseretsky Tests of Motor Proficiency (Doll, 1946). There is some similarity between the items in the two tests, but the Bruininks adaptation reflects advances in content, structure, and technical qualities.

The purpose of the Bruininks-Oseretsky Test is to provide useful information in assessing the motor skills of individual students. Normative data based on the performance of a carefully selected sample of subjects tested in the standardization program include standard scores for each age group, percentile ranks, and stanines. Age equivalents are also provided for each of the eight subtests, four of which measure gross-motor skills, three measure fine-motor skills, and one measures both gross- and fine-motor skills. The differentiated measurement of gross- and fine-motor skills makes it possible to obtain meaningful comparisons of performance in the two areas.

The eight subtests are:

Subtest 1: *Running Speed and Agility (one item):* This subtest measures running speed during a shuttle run.

Subtest 2: *Balance (eight items):* Three items assess static balance by requiring the subject to maintain balance while standing on one leg. Five items assess performance balance by requiring the subject to maintain balance while executing various walking movements.

Subtest 3: *Bilateral Coordination (eight items):* Seven items assess sequential and simultaneous coordination of the upper limbs with the lower limbs. One item assesses coordination of upper limbs only.

Subtest 4: *Strength (three items):* This subtest assesses arm and shoulder strength, abdominal strength, and leg strength.

Subtest 5: *Upper-Limb Coordination (nine items):* Six items assess coordination of visual tracking with movements of the arms and hands. Three items assess precise movement of arms, hands, or fingers.

Subtest 6: *Response speed (one item):* This subtest measures the ability to respond quickly to a moving visual stimulus.

Subtest 7: *Visual-Motor Control (eight items):* This subtest measures the ability to coordinate precise hand and visual movements.

Subtest 8: *Upper-Limb Speed and Dexterity (eight items):* This subtest measures hand and finger dexterity, hand speed and arm speed.

Structure of Test:

Gross-Motor Skills	Fine-Motor Skills
Subtest 1 Running Speed and Agility	Subtest 6 Response Speed
Subtest 2 Balance	Subtest 7 Visual-Motor Control
Subtest 3 Bilateral Coordination	Subtest 8 Upper-Limb Speed and Dexterity
Subtest 4 Strengths	

Subtest 5
Upper-Limb Coordination

Administration of the Complete Battery requires 45–60 minutes; the Short Form requires 15–20 minutes. Examiners need not have special training, but must become thoroughly familiar with the directions for administering the test and practice giving it in simulated situations before actual administration.

Interpretation and Use

The Bruininks-Oseretsky Test may be used to examine the motor proficiency of children and youth. One of its unique features is to differentiate between the fine-motor and gross-motor skills. The Individual Record Form is so designed as to make analysis of the differences easy. The examiner can quickly see where the strengths and weaknesses lie. A case* in point is shown in Table 7, where a seven-year and seven-month male child (Carl) is seen to have weaknesses in fine-motor functions, and two specific strengths in gross-motor functions.

Carl had been referred because of poor writing skills, lack of attention to directions, and a habit of never completing his assignments.

Remediation should include tasks that are considered as quasi-gross-motor, i.e., activities such as throwing and catching a large ball, throwing large bean bags, and handling large objects. Specific fine-motor tasks should be minimized. For training in writing, Carl should practice at the blackboard in making large figures, then move to paper and pencil after it is established that he has better fine-motor control. Normal gross-motor activities should be continued on a daily basis. The fact that he has some specific gross-motor strengths should help keep his self-concept at an appropriate level and provide wholesome exercises.

*Information provided by Kathryn McBride, Teacher, Amarillo, Texas ISD.

Table 7. Profile for Carl

Subtest	Percentile Rank	Stanine	Age Equivalent
Gross-Motor			
1. Running Speed and Agility			15-11
2. Balance			7-5
3. Bilateral Coordination			15-11
4. Strength:			8-8
Gross Motor Composite	50	5	14-1
5. Upper-Limb Coordination			5-11
6. Response Speed			6-2
7. Visual-Motor Speed			5-5
8. Upper-Limb Speed and Dexterity:			5-5
Fine Motor Composite	16	3	5-7
Battery Composite	42	5	9-10

Standardization Information

The standardization sample for the BOTMP included 765 subjects, of which 386 were girls and 379 were boys. The multi-stage stratified sampling procedure was based on the 1970 U.S. census. There were 80 subjects in each of eight age groups ranging from four years, six months to fourteen years, six months. Eighty-eight-point-three percent of the sample were white, 6.9 percent black, and 4.8 percent were of other races. Both urban and rural populations were involved in four geographic regions: North, Central, South and West. Eighty-nine subjects from Canada were included, since no subjects from the Northeast were available. No students with severe physical impairments were included.

Test-retest reliability was established on all subtests with a sample of 63 second graders and 63 sixth graders who took the Bruininks-Oseretsky Test twice within a 7- to 12-day period. One sixth grader was enrolled in a special-education program for mildly retarded children and four of the second-graders were enrolled in programs for the retarded or learning-disabled. For both grade groups, test-retest coefficients for the separate subtests ranged from .58 to .89 for Grade 2 and from .29 to .89 for Grade 6. It is pointed out that interpretation of scores on the separate subtests for individual subjects must be made with caution, but that low reliabilities on some subtests may be due largely to the fact that many older subjects achieve maximum or near-maximum point scores. On Subtest 5: Upper-Limb Coordination, for example, the test-retest correlation coefficient of .29 for Grade 6 occurred because these subjects had mastered the skills assessed by this subtest, and, therefore, obtained point scores at or near the maximum (Bruininks, 1972).

Bruininks reports that the validity of the Bruininks-Oseretsky test is based on its ability to assess the construct of motor development or proficiency. The evidence of construct validity is offered to be: (1) the relationship of test content to significant aspects of motor development cited in research studies; (2) the relevant statistical properties of the test; and (3) the functioning of the test with contrasting groups of handicapped and normal children. He concludes that the evidence seen in this standardization sample should be viewed as necessarily incomplete, since additional studies are needed to delineate further the usefulness of the test with children having different types of handicaps.

Summary

This chapter has briefly introduced the history of the use of perceptual-motor activities, a use that had its theoretical source in the work of Piaget on the development of intelligence and in the work of the Gestalt psychologists on the principles of perception. It is explained that the actual protocol for the use of these activities for children in special education is found in the work of Strauss, Werner, and Goldstein with brain-injured children. Special-education authorities such as Kephart, Barsch, Cruickshank and Frostig were among the first to make application of these earlier theories and principles. The categories of both earlier and later advocates are described, as well as the major tests used to measure perceptual-motor skills. Of the latter, more coverage is given to the Bruininks-Oseretsky, since it is the most recently devised edition and does provide much information on its standardization. It is noted that many of the tests described are not shown to be satisfactorily reliable or valid in all cases. Last, the discussion of the issues relates that there has been confusion concerning the recommendation of the perceptual-motor authorities and that the research to date has not shown *conclusively* that they benefit the academic skills of learning-disabled children.

Discussion Questions

1. *Should we use any activity in a remediation procedure (not just perceptual motor) that has not been proved to be successful through research? Justify your reasoning, whether positive or negative.*
2. *Should we use any perceptual-motor tests that do not show adequate statistical reliability or validity? Justify your reasoning.*
3. *Is the term "Perceptual-Motor Activities" generic in the sense that all activities could be said to be similar?*
4. *What differences do you find between fine-motor functions and gross-motor functions?*
5. *Should reading, writing, spelling, and arithmetic be left completely out of the domain of perceptual-motor functions?*
6. *Relate question #5 to the Gestalt concept that the whole is different from the sum of the parts.*

Student Assignments

Choose various academic subjects and identify any perceptual-motor components related in any way to these subjects.

REFERENCES

Ames, L. B. Critique to Bibace and Hancock study, Relationships between perceptual and conceptual processes. *Journal of Learning Disabilities*, January 1969, *2*, no. 1: 25–26.

Ayers, J. *Southern California, sensory integration tests.* Los Angeles: Western Psychological Services, 1972.

Barsch, R. H. *A movigenic curriculum* (bulletin no. 25). Madison, Wisc.: Department of Public Instruction, Bureau for the Handicapped, 1965.

Barsch, R. H. *Achieving perceptual motor efficiency.* Seattle, Wash.: Special Child Publications, 1967.

Bender, L. *Psychopathology of children with organic brain disorders.* Springfield, Ill.: Charles C Thomas, 1956.

Bender, L. On the proper use of the Bender Gestalt test. *Perceptual motor skills,* 20 (189190), 1965.

Beery, K. E., & Buktenica, N. *Developmental test of visual-motor integration.* Chicago: Follett Publishing Company, 1967.

Bibace, R., & Hancock, K. Relationships between perceptual and conceptual processes. *Journal of Learning Disabilities,* January 1969, *2*, no. 1: 17–31.

Bruininks, R. H. Auditory and visual perceptual skills related to the reading performance of disadvantaged boys. *Perceptual and Motor Skills,* 1969, *29,* no. 1: 179–186.

Bruininks, R. H. *Examiner's manual, Bruininks-Oseretsky test of motor proficiency.* Circle Pines, Minn.: American Guidance Service, 1978.

Canter, A. A background interference procedure for graphmotor tests in the study of deficit. *Perceptual and Motor Skills,* 1963, *16:* 914.

Cobb, P. R., Chissom, B. S., & Davis, M. W. Relationships among perceptual-motor, self concept, and academic measures for preschool and early elementary school children. *Perceptual and Motor Skills,* 1975, *41:* 539–546.

Corman and Budoff. Factor structures of Spanish-speaking and non-Spanish speaking children on Raven's progressive matrices. *Educational and Psychological Measurement,* 1974, *34:* 972–981.

Cratty, B. J. *Developmental sequences of perceptual-motor tasks.* Freeport, N.Y.: Educational Activities, 1967.

Cratty, B. J. *Perceptual motor behavior and educational processes.* Springfield, Ill.: Charles C Thomas, 1969.

Cratty, B. J. *Psychology and physical activity.* Englewood Cliffs, NJ: Prentice-Hall, 1968.

Cruickshank, W. M., & Johnson, G. O. (Eds.), *Education of exceptional children and youth.* Englewood Cliffs, NJ: Prentice-Hall, 1958.

Denhoff, E. Critique to Bibace and Hancock study, Relationship between perceptual and conceptual processes. *Journal of Learning Disabilities,* January 1969, *2,* no. 1: 26–28.

Doll, E. A. (Ed.), *The Oseretsky tests of motor proficiency.* Translation from the Portuguese adaptation. Circle Pines, Minn.: American Guidance Service, 1946.

Doubros, S., & Mascarenhas, J. Relations among Wechsler full-scale scores, organicity-sensitivity subtest scores and Bender Gestalt error scores. *Perceptual and Motor Skills.* December 1969, *29:* 719–22.

Downie, N. M., & Heath, R. W. *Basic statistical methods.* New York: Harper and Row, 1970.

Ekwall, E. E. *Psychological factors in the teaching of reading.* Columbus, Ohio: Charles E. Merrill Publishing Company, 1973.

Faustman, N. M. Some effects of perception training in kindergarten on first grade reading. In Smith, H. K. (Ed.), *Perception and reading.* Proceedings of the Twelfth Annual Convention of the International Reading Association. Newark, Del.: International Reading Association, 1968.

Flint, F. S. A validation and developmental study of some interpretations of the Bender Gestalt test. Ph.D. Dissertation, New York: New York University, 1966.

Frostig, M., & Horne, D. *The Frostig program for the development of visual perception.* Chicago: Follett Publishing Company, 1964.

Fuchs, D. Reading and perceptual-motor performance: can we strengthen them simultaneously? *Journal of Special Education,* Fall 1979, *13:* 265–273.

Goldstein, K. The modification of behavior consequent to cerebral lesions. *Psychiatric Quarterly,* 1963, *10:* 586–610.

Goldstein, K. *The organism.* New York: American Book, 1939.

Graham, F., and Kendall, B. S. Memory for designs test: revised general manual. *Perceptual and Motor Skills,* 1960, *11:* 147–188.

Gruber, J. J., & Kirkendall, D. R. Review of data processing techniques needed to interpret mental-motor relationships in culturally deprived high school students. In *Foundations and practices in perceptual-motor learning–quest for understanding.* Washington, D.C.: American Association for Health, Physical Education and Recreation, 1971.

Gruber, J. J. Exercise and mental performance. *International Journal of Sport Psychology,* Spring 1975, *6:* 28–40.

Gruber, J. J., & Kirkendall, D. R. Interrelationships among mental, motor, personality and social variables in low achieving high school students with high intelligence. In *Proceedings of the seventy-third annual meeting of the national college physical education association for men.* Chicago: The National College Physical Education Association, 1969.

Gruber, J. J., & Noland, M. Perceptual-motor and scholastic achievement relationships in emotionally disturbed elementary school children. *Research Quarterly,* March 1977, *48,* 1: 68–73.

Hain, J. D. A scoring method for identifying brain damage. *Journal of Consulting Psychology,* 1964, *28:* 34–40.

Hallahan, D. P. & Kauffman, J. M. *Exceptional children.* Englewood Cliffs, NJ: Prentice-Hall, 1978.

Hammill, D. D., & Larsen, S. C. The relationship of selected auditory perceptual skills and reading ability. *Journal of Learning Disabilities,* 1974, *1:* 429–436.

Hilgard, E. R., & Atkinson, R. C. *Introduction to psychology.* New York: Harcourt, Brace and World, Inc., 1967.

Hudgins, A. L. Assessment of visual-motor disabilities in young children: Toward differential diagnosis. *Psychology in the Schools*, July 1977, *14*, no. 3: 252–259.

Husak, W. S., & Magill, R. A. Correlations among perceptual-motor ability, self-concept and reading achievement in early elementary grades. *Perceptual and Motor Skills*, 1979, *49*: 447–450.

Hutt, M. & Briskin, G. J. *The clinical use of the revised Bender.* (Gestalt test). New York: Grune and Stratton, 1960.

Ismail, A. H., & Gruber, J. J. *Integrated development: motor aptitude and intellectual performance.* Columbus, Ohio: Charles E. Merrill Publishing Company, 1967.

Keogh, B., Smith, C. E. Group techniques and proposed scoring system for the Bender Gestalt test with children. *Journal of School Psychology*, 1961, *17*: 172–175.

Kephart, N. C. *Learning disability: an educational adventure.* West Lafayette, Ind.: Kappa Delta Pi Press, 1968.

Kephart, N. C. *The slow learner in the classroom.* Columbus, Ohio: Charles E. Merrill Publishing Company, 1960, 1971.

Kephart, N. C. Review of Developmental test of visual-motor perception. In Buros, O. K. (Ed.), *Seventh annual mental measurements yearbook*, vol. II. Highland Park, N.J.: The Gryphon Press, 1972, p. 871.

Kirk, S. A. *The diagnosis and remediation of psycholinguistic disabilities.* Urbana, Ill.: University of Illinois Press, 1966.

Kirkendall, D. R., & Gruber, J. J. Canonical relationships between the motor and intellectual achievement domains in culturally deprived high school pupils. *Research Quarterly*, December 1970, *41*: 496–502.

Koppitz, E. M. *The Bender-Gestalt test for young children.* New York: Grune and Stratton, 1964.

Koppitz, E. M. *The Bender-Gestalt test for young children.* Vol. II, Research and application, 1963–1973. New York: Grune and Stratton, 1975.

Larsen, S. C., and Hammill, D. D. The relationship of selected visual skills to school learning. *Journal of Special Education*, 1975, *9*: 85–91.

Leithwood, K. A. Motor, cognitive and affective relationships among advantaged preschool children. *Research Quarterly*, March 1971, *42*: 47–53.

Lowman, C., & Young, C. *Postural fitness.* Philadelphia: Lea and Febiger, 1960.

Mann, L., et al. Final report on the research project: a comparison of three methods of physical education programming for emotionally disturbed children. *U.S. educational resources information center.* Doc. Ed 083776, March 1973.

Mogin, L. S. Administration and objective scoring of the Bender Gestalt test in group screening of primary grade children for emotional maladjustment. Rutgers, NJ: Ph.D. dissertation. Rutgers State University, 1966.

Myklebust, H. R. Definition and overview. In Myklebust, H. (Ed.), *Progress in learning disabilities*, vol. 1. New York: Grune and Stratton, 1968, pp. 1–15.

Noll, V. H. *Educational measurement.* Boston: Houghton Mifflin Co., 1957.

Payne, R. W., Buros, O. K. *The seventh mental measurement yearbook*, vol. 1. Highland Park, NJ: The Gryphon Press, 1972.

Phillips, J. L. Jr. *The origins of intellect: Piaget's theory.* San Francisco: W. H. Freeman, 1969.

Piaget, J., & Inhelder, B. *The child's conception of space.* New York: W. W. Norton and Co., 1967, 2. Permission to reprint was granted by Humanities Press Inc., New York, holder of U.S. rights, and Koutledge and Kegan Paul Ltd., holder of world rights.

Quast, W. The Bender Gestalt: A clinical study of children's records. *Journal of Consulting Psychology,* 1961, *25:* 405–408.

Remmers, H. H., Gage, N. O., & Rummel, J. B. *A practical introduction to measurement and evaluation.* New York: Harper and Row, 1965.

Rich, H. L. Teachers' perceptions of motor activity and related behaviors. *Exceptional Children,* November 1978: 210–211.

Richmond, B. O., & Aliotti, N. C. Developmental skills of advantaged and disadvantaged children on perceptual tasks. *Psychology in the Schools,* October 1977, *14,* no. 4: 461–465.

Roach, E. G. Evaluation of an experimental program of perceptual motor training with slow readers. In Figurel, J. A. (Ed.), *Vistas in reading.* Proceedings of the Eleventh Annual Convention of the International Reading Association. Newark, Del.: International Reading Association, 1967.

Roach, E. G., and Kephart, N. C. *The Purdue perceptual-motor survey,* Columbus, Ohio: Charles E. Merrill Publishing Company, 1966.

Rubin, E. Z., et al. An investigation of an evaluation method and retraining procedures for emotionally handicapped children with cognitive-motor deficits. *U.S. Educational Resources Information Center,* Doc. ED 024204, June, 1968.

Schilder, P. *The image and appearance of the human body.* New York: International University Press, 1935.

Stern, C. *Children discover arithmetic.* New York: Harper and Brothers, 1949.

Strauss, A. A., and Kephart, N. C. *Psychopathology and education of the brain-injured child,* vol. II. New York: Grune and Stratton, 1955.

Strauss, A. A., and Lehtinen, L. E. *Psychopathology and education of the brain-injured child,* vol. I. New York: Grune and Stratton, 1947.

Thomas, J. R., & Chissom, B. S. Relationships as assessed by canonical correlation between perceptual-motor and intellectual abilities for pre-school and early elementary age children. *Journal of Motor Behavior,* March 1972, *4:* 23–29.

Thomas, J. R., & Chissom, B. S. Prediction of first grade academic performance from perceptual-motor data. *Research Quarterly,* May 1974, *45:* 148–153.

Thomas, J. R., Chissom, B. S., & Booker, L. Perceptual-motor and academic relationships for disadvantaged children classified as learning disabled and normal. *American Corrective Therapy Journal,* May–June 1974, *28:* 95–99.

Thomas, J. R., et al. Effects of perceptual-motor training on preschool children. *Research Quarterly,* December 1975, *46:* 505–513.

Vinacke, W. E. *The psychology of thinking.* New York: McGraw-Hill Book Company, 1952.

Wallace, G. & McLoughlin, J. A. *Learning disabilities.* Columbus, Ohio: Charles E. Merrill Publishing Company, 1979.

Watkins, E. D. *The Watkins Bender Gestalt scoring system.* San Rafael, Calif.: Academic Therapy Publications, 1976.

Weiner, G. The Bender Gestalt test as a predictor of minimal neurological deficit in children eight to ten years of age. *Journal of Nerve and Mental Diseases.* 1966, 143: 275–280.

Welch, L. The transition from simple to complex forms of learning. *Journal of Genetic Psychology,* 1947, 71: 223–251.

Werner, H., & Strauss, A. A. Types of visual-motor activity in their relationship to low and high performance ages. *Proceedings from the American Association on Mental Deficiency,* 1939a, *XLIV:* 163–168.

Werner, H., & Strauss, A. A. Problems and methods of functional analysis in mentally deficient children. *Journal of Abnormal Psychology*, January 1939b, *34:* 37–67.

Wertheimer, M. Studies in the theory of Gestalt psychology. *Psychological Forsch.*, 1923, *4:* 300.

Wechsler, D. *Measure of adult intelligence.* Baltimore: Williams and Wilkins, 1939.

Wechsler, D. *The measure and appraisal of adult intelligence,* 4th ed. Baltimore: Williams and Wilkins, 1958.

Wechsler, D. *Manual for the Wechsler preprimary scale of intelligence.* New York: Psychological Corporation, 1967.

Wechsler, D. *Manual for the Wechsler intelligence scale for children, revised.* New York: Psychological Corporation, 1974.

White, M. A first-grade intervention program for children at risk for reading failure. *Journal of Learning Disabilities,* April 1979, *12,* no. 4: 26–32.

Wiebe, R. Unpublished work sheet on the WISC-R, Denton, Texas: Texas Woman's University, 1979.

Wiebe, R. Unpublished work sheet analysis on the McCarthy scales of children's abilities. Denton, Texas: Texas Woman's University, 1980.

Wiebe, R., & Watkins, E. Factor analysis of the McCarthy scales of children's abilities on preschool children. *Journal of School Psychology,* 1980, *18,* no. 2.

Chapter 6

Intelligence and Social Adaptive Tests

After you have studied this chapter, you should:
1. *Be familiar with intelligence tests and the cognitive processes involved*
2. *Have specific knowledge of the Wechsler Scales and the Stanford Binet*
3. *Know the difference between verbal and performance scales*
4. *Have knowledge of the strategy of using pattern analysis to help in determining strengths and weaknesses*
5. *Have knowledge of some commonly used teacher administered intelligence tests.*
6. *Have knowledge of scales used to measure adaptive behavior.*
7. *Have a reading reference source for the reliability and validity of tests described herein.*

Introduction

The fact that individuals do differ in intellectual and other psychological/educational characteristics has been apparent for over 100 years. As early as 1870, Galton, an English scientist, wrote concerning the extensiveness of individual differences. Other investigators of individual difference are Kraepelin, Oehrn, and Munsterberg from Germany; Esquirol, Sequin, and Binet from France; and Thorndike, Woodrow, and Thurstone from the United States (Guilford, 1967). All of these concerned experimentalists were interested in how children and youth function mentally; but the major thrust of testing for intellectual differences can be attributed to Binet, whose first scale was used to determine whether children in France could benefit by formal schooling.

In the United States, Terman and Merrill (1937) were responsible for expanding the practice of testing by their revisions of the Binet scale. Other kinds of psychological tests became popular—achievement, social/adaptive, and specific aptitude—but the prototype for all measurement today is the measurement of intelligence, the major purpose of which is assessing problem-solving and thinking abilities in people. These purposes have continued to be appropriate in the assessment process but other specific purposes have subsequently followed. Because of the greater awareness of individual differences, special education in the public schools has accelerated and legislation regarding differentiation of educational services for exceptional children has been passed. In order to have such legislation enacted, differences in handicapping conditions have had to be carefully identified. Intelligence tests have been the major identifying instruments used to determine these differences dealing with mental-ability levels. Children are placed in classes for the mentally retarded and for the gifted on the basis of qualifying intelligence test data. The learning-disabled children must be shown to have intelligence within normal or above-normal limits before qualifying for special services. Thus, we can see that intelligence testing is important in the placement of the mentally retarded, the gifted, and the learning-disabled child. Where mental retardation is considered, the tests are also used for determining the specific level of retardation, severe, moderate, or mild, for in each case a different placement and curriculum may be needed. In the assessment of the emotionally disturbed, intelligence tests are also administered for purposes of examining whether emotional disturbances in children are influencing intellectual functions.

Intelligence testing has not always been without opposition. It has often met claims that the tests discriminate against various cultural groups and also are not complete enough to cover all aspects of intellectual function. There is no question that children who have experiences different from those of the culture in which a test is standardized will have greater difficulty with the test than those raised in that specific culture. Yet, as Dyer (1962) relates, tests do not discriminate; they point out where the different environments have discriminated. Regarding the second criticism, it is understood that IQ tests do not cover all mental functions, albeit they remain the best instruments for revealing intellectual-functioning levels of individuals, and they are very good predictors of academic achievement (Kaufman, 1979). While intelligence tests may be used for practical purposes, diagnosticians should never conclude that an IQ reflects the total of one's ability. They should know that an IQ may be used as (1) a *guide* for determining range of intelligence, (2) a *help* in curriculum planning, and (3) an *aid* in determining proper placement of children in the public schools.

Adaptive scales, which also are discussed in this chapter, are social-ability measures that can be used to help predict how a child or youth may function in the social world. The information from these scales can be identified as social intelligence. It is a good practice to administer social-maturity scales to detect differences within a group of social skills and, also, to compare with mental functions that deal with language and numerical problem-solving skills. This provides information that affords a more global evaluation of a person's competence.

This chapter is designed to describe tests that are commonly used measurements for the purpose of predicting an individual's responses in academic and social competition with school mates. It is further designed to provide some strategies to use when using these tests in the evaluation process. The tests are described as follows under headings of Intelligence Tests and Social Maturity Scales.

Intelligence Tests

Stanford Binet, Form L-M (Terman and Merrill, 1960)*

Description and Administration Procedure

The 1937 Forms, L and M, of the Stanford Binet were used until 1960, when the authors made a revision incorporating in a single scale the best subtests from the earlier two forms (Terman and Merrill, 1972). The design of the 1960 form,** identified as Form L-M, has the original format; i.e., it is a test designed for subjects between the ages of two years and adulthood with specific tasks required at each level. The series of subtests at the different levels are representative of tasks commonly performed by individuals at these designated ages. For example, at the three-year level (III) the subtests involve: copying a circle, copying a block pattern, stringing beads, and recognizing pictures of items such as airplane, telephone, and hat. At an adult level the subtests require such tasks as verbal description of vocabulary words, knowledge of differences between abstract words, arithmetical reasoning, and ability to comprehend meanings of proverbs.

The general procedure in administration is to begin testing at the year just below the age of the subject. When the subject has passed all tests at one age level, this is said to be the *basal age*, the level at which it can be assumed that all items answered below that point would be correct. Testing is to continue until the subject has failed all subtests at one age level. This level is said to be the ceiling, a point beyond which all items are assumed to be too difficult for the person and would be answered incorrectly.

The Stanford Binet test requires approximately one to one and one-half hours to administer. The length of the administration time is dependent on the age, the motivation of client to verbalize, and on the skill of the examiner. If the client is younger and less inclined to talk, the time for administration will be shortened.

The administration of the Stanford Binet requires training, and only those individuals who have completed a course in mental testing and a supervised practicum should give the test. The tester needs to develop skill in (1) establishing rapport with the subject; (2) following standard procedure, a part of which is knowing when to question in order to obtain clarification of the subject's responses; and (3) scoring the test correctly, which requires practice in differentiating between concrete, functional, and abstract responses, each of which merits a different credit point. In addition, the tester must avoid the "halo" effect, an effect that assumes the subject has earned credit not on the basis of a correct response but on the basis of what the tester believes the subject knows.

Interpretation and Use of the Stanford Binet

The Stanford Binet Test provides both a mental age and an IQ. The original aim of the test was to provide a measure of general intelligence; it was not meant to be diagnostic or to measure various separate aspects of mentality. It does not provide a profile

---

*The senior author, Terman, was deceased before the revision was completed.

**A new set of norms was established in 1972 by Robert L. Thorndike and the 1960 revision is now under restandardization procedure.

showing individual mental abilities as do many other tests, but psychologists and diagnosticians through the years have analyzed the strengths and weaknesses within clients' tests and have not found the Stanford Binet difficult to use in diagnosis.

Sattler (1974) is one who has provided help in expanding the usefulness of the Stanford Binet in the diagnostic procedure. He has factor-analyzed the subtests and has found that they are loaded in favor of the following areas: language, memory, conceptual thinking, reasoning, numerical reasoning, visual-motor, and social intelligence. His model is presented as one of the strategies to aid in the analysis of the test responses. Following the model in Table 8 we have listed learning components of each subtest, along with the abbreviations that identify Sattler's classification.

Sattler's model. Sattler's model, to be used with the Stanford Binet, affords a profile for purposes of analysis (Sattler, 1965, pp. 74–75). By analyzing the subtests and classifying them under factors or kinds of abilities, one can easily identify a subject's strengths and weaknesses. The model is as follows:

Sattler's Model

(L)		Language
(M)		Memory
	(mM)	Meaningful memory
	(nmM)	Nonmeaningful memory
	(vM)	Visual memory
(CT)		Conceptual thinking
(R)		Reasoning
	(vR)	Verbal reasoning
	(nvR)	Nonverbal reasoning
(NR)		Numerical reasoning
(VM)		Visual motor
(SI)		Social Intelligence

The general abilities measured and identified by Sattler can be examined in terms common to the study of learning disability. Adjacent to and more descriptive of each general factor, in accordance with this framework, is a specific learning component. These clues are commonly used in other tests and aid in identifying problems. This is necessary for purposes of remediation. For example, the measurement of language in Test 1, Year II-6, can be identified as auditory comprehension or auditory reception. Or in Test 5, Year II, the measurement of language can be identified as both visual reception and expressive language. This profile analysis of the test data is a good diagnostic tool, since the learning mode, such as auditory or visual, is also noted. The factors and their locations in the test are indicated at each age level by the subtest number.

Figure 25, on page 161, may provide additional assistance for a profile analysis of the Stanford Binet. The Sattler model is placed to the left of the graph worksheet. The test numbers representing specific factors are placed opposite the factors and under the age levels on the test where they are found. For example, at the II-year level on the Stanford Binet, tests 3, 4, 5, and A are all language tests and are placed opposite the factor Language on the graph. The diagnostician may cross out or

Table 8. Year Levels of the Stanford Binet with Learning Components for Each Subtest*

learning components of each subtest. (handwritten)

To aid in analysis of test responses. (handwritten)

Test	Factor	Learning Components (Abilities)
		Year II 2
1	VM	Visual discrimination
2	nmM	Visual imagery
3	L	Visual discrimination
4	VM	Depth perception
5	L	Visual reception and expressive language
6	L	Word fluency
A	L	Expressive language
		Year II-6
1	L	Auditory reception
2	L	Visual discrimination
3	L	Visual perception
4	L	Visual reception and expressive language
5	nmM	Auditory sequencing
6	SI	Auditory reception
A	VM	Visual discrimination
		Year III
1	VM	Eye-hand coordination and perceptual motor
2	L	Visual reception and expressive language
3	VM	Depth perception
4	vM	Perceptual memory
5	VM	Eye-hand coordination and perceptual motor
6	VM	Eye-hand coordination and perceptual motor
A	nmM	Auditory sequencing
		Year III-6
1	nvR	Perceptual discrimination
2	nvR	Spatial relationship
3	nvR	Visual discrimination
4	SI	Verbal expression and visual reception
5	nvR	Color discrimination
6	SI	Auditory reception
A	nvR	Visual discrimination
		Year IV
1	L	Visual reception and expressive language
2	mM	Visual memory
3	CT	Auditory association
4	L	Auditory discrimination and visual reception
5	nvR	Visual discrimination
6	SI	Auditory reception
A	mM	Auditory memory

*The abbreviations for the adult levels that follow Year XIV are AA for average adult and SA for superior adult.

Table 8 (continued)

Test	Factor	Learning Components
		Year IV-6
1	SI	Visual reception and visual discrimination
2	CT	Auditory association
3	nvR	Visual association and visual discrimination
4	SI	Auditory reception
5	mM	Auditory memory and sequence
6	SI	Auditory reception
A	L	Auditory discrimination and visual perception
		Year V
1	VM	Perceptual motor
2	VM	Spatial and perceptual motor
3	L	Auditory reception
4	VM	Perceptual motor
5	nvR	Visual association and visual discrimination
6	nvR	Spatial relationship and perceptual motor
A	VM	Perceptual motor
		Year VI
1	L	Auditory reception and expressive language
2	CT	Meaningful auditory discrimination
3	nvR	Spatial discrimination
4	NR	Problem solving
5	CT	Auditory association
6	VM	Perceptual motor
A	SI	Expressive language and visual reception
		Year VII
1	SI	Visual reception
2	CT	Auditory association
3	VM	Perceptual motor
4	SI	Auditory reception
5	CT	Auditory association
6	nmM	Auditory memory and sequencing
A	nmM	Auditory memory for patterns and sequencing
		Year VIII
1	L	Auditory reception and expressive language
2	mM	Auditory memory and sequencing
3	vR	Auditory reception and expressive language
4	CT	Auditory association
5	SI	Auditory reception
6	SI	Auditory sequencing
A	SI	Auditory reception
		Year IX
1	VM	Perceptual motor and spatial reasoning
2	vR	Auditory reception
3	vM	Perceptual motor

Table 8 (continued)

Test	Factor	Learning Components
4	L	Auditory and memory association
5	NR	Problem solving
6	nmM	Auditory sequencing and pattern memory
A	L	Auditory association

Year X

Test	Factor	Learning Components
1	L	Auditory reception and expressive language
2	NR	Visual-spatial reasoning
3	L	Auditory reception and expressive language
4	SI	Reasoning and verbal expression
5	L	Word fluency and memory
6	nmM	Auditory sequencing
A	vR	Auditory reception

Year XI

Test	Factor	Learning Components
1	vM	Memory and perceptual motor
2	vR	Auditory reception and expressive language
3	L	Auditory reception and expressive language
4	mM	Auditory memory
5	SI	Verbal expression
6	CT	Auditory association
A	SI	Auditory reception and expressive language

Year XII

Test	Factor	Learning Components
1	L	Auditory reception and expressive language
2	vR	Auditory reception
3	SI	Visual reception
4	nmM	Sequencing
5	L	Auditory reception and expressive language
6	L	Memory and visual association
A	vM	Memory and perceptual motor

Year XIII

Test	Factor	Learning Components
1	nvR	Spatial reasoning
2	L	Auditory reception and expressive language
3	mM	Auditory memory
4	vR	Auditory reception and expressive language
5	L	Visual reception and visual relation
6	vM	Visual memory for patterns and perceptual motor
A	VM	Spatial reasoning

Year XIV

Test	Factor	Learning Components
1	L	Auditory reception and expressive language
2	NR	Spatial reasoning
3	vR	Auditory reception
4	NR	Auditory reception
5	nvR	Position in space and spatial reasoning
6	CT	Auditory association
A	NR	Auditory reception

→

Table 8 (continued)

Test	Factor	Learning Components
		Year AA
1	L	Auditory reception and verbal comprehension
2	NR	Problem solving
3	L	Auditory association
4	NR	Problem solving
5	CT	Verbal comprehension
6	nvR	Position in space
7	CT	Auditory association
8	L	Expressive language and auditory reception
A	VM	Spatial reasoning
		Year SAI
1	L	Expressive language and auditory reception
2	NR	Problem solving
3	L	Memory and visual association
4	nmM	Memory for patterns
5	L	Verbal expression and auditory reception
6	CT	Auditory association
A	CT	Auditory association
		Year SAII
1	L	Expressive language
2	vR	Expressive langauge and auditory reception
3	CT	Auditory association
4	NR	Auditory reception
5	CT	Auditory association
6	mM	Auditory memory
A	vR	Auditory reception
		Year SAIII
1	L	Expressive language and verbal comprehension
2	CT	Auditory association
3	CT	Auditory association
4	nvR	Position in space
5	vR	Problem solving
6	mM	Auditory memory
A	CT	Auditory association

black out the language tests that are passed at a specific age level and can readily detect the language development level measured by the Stanford Binet. All other factors may be graphed in the same manner.

An example of the use of this model and the learning components is that case of an eleven-year-old who has passed all subtests through age nine years. At the ten-year level, subtests 3 and 5 are failed and at the eleven-year level, subtests 3 and 2 are failed. All subtests are failed at the twelve-year level. (See following draft, Table 9.) At year X, the analysis of these failures and passes shows that this individual's first failures are in the language area, dealing with auditory reception (understanding what the questions are, in these cases) and being able to express the answers correctly. Numerical reason-

Figure 25. Stanford Binet Worksheet

Ceiling _____
Base _____

CA _____
MA _____
I.Q. _____

STANFORD BINET WORKSHEET
FOR
DIAGNOSING LEARNING DISABILITIES

Year of Tests	2	2-6	3	3-6	4	4-6	5	6	7	8	9	10	11	12	13	14	AA	SAI	SA =	SA ≡
Language	3,5, 6,A	1,2, 3,4	2		1,4	A	3	1		1	4,A	1,3, 5	3	1,5, 6	2,5	1	1,3, 8	1,3, 5	1	1
Meaningful					2A	5				2			4	4	3				6	6
Nonmeaningful		5	A						6,A		6	6		4				4		
Visual			4								3		1	A	6					
Conceptual Thinking					3	2		2,5	2,5	4			6			6	5,7	6,A	3,5	2,3, A
Verbal										3	2	A	2	2	4	3			2,A	5
Nonverbal	2			1,2, 3,5,A	5	3	5,6	3							1	5	6			4
Numerical								4			5	2				2,4 A	2,4,	2	4	
Visual-Motor	1,4	A	1,3, 5,6				1,2, 4,A	6	3		1				A		A			
Social Intelligence		6		4,6	6	1,4, 6		A	1,4	5,6, A		4	5,A	3						

Factors

additional information for a profile analysis of the Stanford – ~~analysis~~ Binet.

Table 9. Draft of Passes and Failures of an Eleven-Year-Old

Subtests Failed:		
Year X	Sattler Classification	Learning Components
1 Vocabulary	Language (L)	Auditory reception expressive language
3 Abstract Words	Language (L)	Auditory reception expressive language
5 Word Naming	Language (L)	Word fluency and memory

Subtests Passed:		
Year X		
2 Block Counting	Numerical reasoning (NR)	Visual-spatial reasoning
4 Finding Reasons	Social intelligence (SI)	Auditory reception expressive language
6 Repeating 6 Digits	Nonmeaningful memory (nmM)	Auditory-sequencing memory

Subtests Failed:		
Year XI		
2 Verbal Absurdities	Verbal reasoning (vR)	Auditory receptive expressive language
3 Abstract Words	Language (L)	Auditory receptive expressive language

Subtests Passed:		
Year XI		
1 Memory for Designs	Visual memory (vM)	Memory and perceptual motor
4 Memory for Sentences	Meaningful memory (mM)	Auditory memory
5 Problem Situation II	Social intelligence (SI)	Comprehension and verbal expression
6 Similarities	Conceptual thinking (CT)	Auditory association

ing involving visual-spatial skills, nonmeaningful memory (auditory-sequencing memory of six digits), and social intelligence, which also deals with auditory reception and expressive language, were found to be adequate. Since there were *three failures* dealing with auditory-receptive and expressive language and *one success* involving these processes, an examination of the content was made. This revealed that the subtest failures involved language dealing with a higher level of abstraction and use of words than did the subtest passed. The subtest passed dealt more specifically with understanding social procedures. Analysis at year XI shows a language subtest (abstract words) and a verbal-reasoning (verbal absurdities) test that requires an understanding of words and ideas and the ability to express them. The subtests passed involved visual memory of designs, auditory memory of sentences spoken, conceptual thinking (auditory association), and social intelligence. It appears that the language weaknesses of this individual lie in the lack of vocabulary skills—typical of a tenth grader. Words dealing with social skills are understood and handled adequately.

Standardization Information

Anastasi (1968) has criticized the 1960 edition because it was not a restandardization, the end result of which is that an IQ of 100 represents the population mean as of 1937. She emphasizes that with cultural changes and educational results obtained with other tests over the 30-year interval, it is to be expected that the mean IQ on the test would be above 100. This expectancy was verified by Fischman, Proger, and Duffey (1976) in a study comparing the 1960 norms with the 1972 norms. They have shown that hypothetical subjects taking both the 1960 test and the 1972 test and rendering the exact same responses will make a lower IQ score on the 1972 than on the 1960 edition. Their conclusion was that any test interpretation based upon 1960 norms must be to a large extent invalid if carried out after 1972 and, in many cases, even before that date.

The 1972 edition of the Stanford Binet has the same structure in terms of content, design, and directions. The purpose of its publication was to update the norms for the 1960 revision. It was renormed on approximately 2,100 subjects, 100 subjects at each Stanford Binet age level. The stratifying variable was test scores obtained from a large population of students, who participated in a 1970 national standardization of the publisher's group mental-ability test known as the Cognitive Abilities Test. This test has been standardized on students in grades 3–12. In order to get samplings of children at younger ages and adults older than 17 years, siblings of individuals tested in the large-scale group test norming were tested. The mean IQ for this normed edition is 100 with a standard deviation of 16. The reliability of both the 1960 and the 1972 editions is based on the performances of individuals in the 1937 standardization. The 1972 normed edition is said to be valid because the earlier editions* were valid; however, there are no data regarding reliability and validity in the manual for the 1972 norms.

The Stanford Binet has been a prestigious test for over four decades. The 1960 and 1972 editions have been accepted at face value on the basis of the 1937 standardization and its success through the years. This acceptance, however, has not been without recognition that a new standardization was needed. It is readily apparent that as times and experiences change, so should any measurements be changed to be in keeping with current trends. The 1972 edition, when used, should be reported judiciously, recognizing that (1) the 1972 version is a new edition and not a restandardized test; (2) intelligence tests measure present abilities and not innate intelligence; (3) intelligence tests are influenced by the subject's personality and emotional state; and (4) that when making critical educational decisions, IQs should not be the sole determining factors.

Itemized facts on the Stanford Binet are listed below:

1. The 1972 edition has a mean of 100 and standard deviation of 16.
2. Reliability of both 1960 and 1972 is based on the reliability established on the 1937 edition.
3. Validity is said to exist because the earlier editions were valid.
4. The 1972 edition was renormed on 2,100 subjects, 100 at each age level.
5. All editions of the test are highly verbal in nature, especially at the upper levels.
6. The test measures somewhat different mental abilities at difference age levels.

---

*The mean biserial correlations between the subtests and the total for the 1960 scale is .66, as compared with a mean of .61 for all tests in both forms of the 1937 edition.

The Wechsler Scales (Wechsler, 1949, 1963, 1974)

Description and Administration Procedures

David Wechsler developed his first scale in 1939—The Wechsler Bellevue Scale. He was at that time a clinical psychologist at the Bellevue Hospital in the city of New York and he prepared this edition to provide clinical information about the patients in the hospital. The Stanford Binet, according to Wechsler, had both improper norms and some tasks too childish for adults. He, also, did not agree with the authors of the Stanford Binet on the use of the traditional mental-age IQ. Instead, he used a deviation IQ, obtained by comparing each subject's test performance with scores earned by individuals in a single age group. The population in which this first test was standardized was within the environs of New York City. The revisions following this first scale were standardized on a population living in four major geographic regions in the United States.

The WISC (1949), Wechsler Intelligence Scale for Children, for ages 5-0 through 15-11, was the first revision. Then in 1955 the WAIS*, Wechsler Adult Intelligence Scale, for ages 16 through adulthood was published. The WPPSI, the Wechsler Pre-school and Primary Scale of Intelligence, for ages 4–6½ was completed and published in 1963. The WISC-R, a revision of the WISC of 1949, was completed in 1974 and is standardized to be used with subjects between the ages of 6–16 years.

The Wechsler Scales are considered to be serial tests, in that each ability subtest within each scale is offered at one time. The vocabulary test, for example, is offered only once. Clients may continue responding to this subtest until five consecutive failures occur. Rules for administration are different for each subtest, but each one is administered only once, and each person, regardless of age, has an opportunity to be measured by each specific ability measured in the test. This differs from the Stanford Binet, in that tests of all specific abilities covered by the test are not offered at each age level.

Only trained personnel should be allowed to administer and interpret the Wechsler Scales. Specific skill must be developed in (1) discriminating values regarding different verbal responses; (2) learning when to question for added information or clarification; (3) figuring the correct chronological ages; and (4) following the procedure in all clerical aspects. Intelligence quotients may be easily miscalculated from errors made in any of these four functions.

The subtests in all three Scales are subgrouped under Verbal and Performance areas. The understanding is that some subtests deal more specifically with language and some deal more specifically with nonlanguage skills. The greatest difference among the presently used Scales is the age-level appropriateness. Since the subtests remain essentially the same from test to test, the behaviors measured by each are described as follows in one group listing. Notations are made where a subtest is found in only one of the Scales.

The *Information Test* measures the limits of a child's general information. The extent of one's general information has long been thought to be closely related to total IQ.

---

*A revision of the WAIS is now available.

The *Comprehension Test* can be called a test of common sense, since achievement on it seems to depend upon a certain amount of practical information and a general ability to evaluate past experience. It is frequently valuable in detecting emotional instability, and almost invariably it reveals something about a person's social and cultural background.

The *Arithmetic Test* tests ability to solve arithmetic problems. Since mathematical aptitude is often indicative of mental alertness, children who do poorly on this test often have difficulty with other subjects. Thus, this subtest can be valuable in the evaluation of educational abilities, especially when supplemented by the results of the Information Test. The combined scores of these two tests frequently furnish an accurate estimate of the child's scholastic achievement.

The *Similarities Test* measures a kind of general intelligence in which the responses reveal the logical character of the thinking processes. In this subtest, the individual is required to identify similarities between two objects or ideas.

The *Vocabulary Test* is an excellent measure of general intelligence. It assesses learning ability, verbal resources, and general range of ideas through the number and kinds of words comprehended. The individual is required to define through verbal expression the meaning of words.

The *Digit Span Test*, as pointed out in the test manual, is perhaps one of the least effective tests of general intelligence. It is a good test for rote memory for digits, but is not an integral part of global intelligence. Rappaport (1945) identifies this test as measuring passive attention, rather than attention requiring active concentration, as the arithmetic test does.

The *Sentence Test* (WPPSI only) assesses an ability to repeat sentences exactly as heard—an auditory attentive ability.

The *Picture Completion Test* requires the subject to discover and identify the missing part of an incompletely drawn picture. The test is particularly good for determining intelligence at the lower levels. Most conspicuously it measures the individual's basic perceptual and conceptual abilities, insofar as these are involved in the visual recognition and identification of familiar objects and forms. In a broader sense, however, the test measures the ability of the individual to differentiate between essential and nonessential details. It has been found to have the highest "general intelligence" loading of any of the performance tests.

The *Picture Arrangement Test* consists of a series of pictures which, when placed in the right sequence, tell a little story. This test measures ability to comprehend sequence and to reconstruct situations—abilities some theorists have referred to as "social intelligence." Those who do fairly well on this test are rarely mentally deficient, even though they may score poorly on other tests.

The *Block Design Test* measures ability to perceive and analyze forms and to perceive pattern. An excellent test of general intelligence, the Block Design Test is good for qualitative analysis. How the subject approaches a task in this test can help define if and why there is a problem. Patients suffering from mental deterioration, senility, and brain disease have particular difficulty in managing this test, and often, even with repeated efforts, they cannot complete the simplest design.

The *Object Assembly Test*, which requires the assembling of puzzle pieces, correlates less with general intelligence than any other of the Wechsler subtests (except Digit Span). It does, however, contribute something to the total score. The best features of this test are its qualitative merits. Various examiners have praised it because it tells them something about the thinking and working habits of the subject. When object assembly is analyzed in terms of Guilford's structure of intellect (1959), three factors emerge: spatial orientation, visualization, and figural selection.

The *Coding Test* (WISC-R) and the Digit Symbol Test (WAIS) are tests that show their most consistent loadings in nonverbal organization and memory. On both tests, the subject is required to associate certain symbols with certain other symbols, and the speed and accuracy with which the association is completed measure intellectual ability. Reading-disabled children may be handicapped because they read slowly, and unstable people generally may do poorly on this test.

The *Animal House Test* (WPPSI only) requires the child to associate sign with symbol and may be considered as a measure of learning ability. Memory is a basic factor, but attention span, goal awareness, and ability to concentrate may also be involved.

The *Geometric Design Test* (WPPSI only) assesses perceptual and visual-motor organization and is relatively free of the limitations inherent in verbal tests.

The *Mazes Test* (WPPSI and WISC-R only) provides information on how well a child can trace through mazes that become progressively more difficult. It is an eye-hand coordination task.

The subtests on all three scales are shown in Table 10.

These subtests have been defined by Glasser and Zimmerman (1967) to measure other abilities, according to the research of Guilford (1965). The factors described by Wechsler, however, are often the same as the Guilford factors identified by Glasser and Zimmerman. For example, the information subtest is said by both to measure verbal comprehension and memory, but the Guilford research extends the concept of mem-

Table 10. Subtests on the WPPSI, WISC-R, and WAIS

	WPPSI	WISC-R	WAIS
Verbal subtests			
Information	X	X	X
Comprehension	X	X	X
Similarities	X	X	X
Arithmetic	X	X	X
Vocabulary	X	X	X
Digit Span		X	X
Sentences	X		
Performance subtests			
Picture Completion	X	X	X
Picture Arrangement		X	X
Block Design	X	X	X
Object Assembly		X	X
Coding		X	
Digit Symbol			X
Animal House	X		
Mazes	X	X	
Geometric Design	X		
Animal House Retest	X		

ory to include associational memory, memory for ideas, and semantic-relation selection (answers made on the basis of meaningful relations). Such added data broaden the meaning of the responses made and help the interpreter identify strengths and weaknesses of the person taking the test. The factors for each subtest are listed in Table 11.

Table 11. Wechsler and Guilford Factors

WISC	Wechsler's Factors	Guilford's Factors
Subtest scores Information	Range of information picked up through the years, memory (cultural milieu inferred), verbal comprehension	Memory for ideas, verbal comprehension, associational memory, semantic-relation selection
Comprehension	Verbal comprehension, judgment, understanding	Judgment, verbal comprehension, sensitivity to problems
Arithmetic	Arithmetical reasoning, concentration, memory, numerical fluency	General reasoning, symbol facility
Similarities	Concept formation, abstract thinking vs. functional and concrete, verbal comprehension	Associational fluency, semantic relations, expressional fluency
Vocabulary	Vocabulary, word meaning (cultural milieu inferred), verbal comprehension	Verbal comprehension (all items)
Digit span	Memory—attention (automatic factor)	Memory span (forward), memory for symbol patterns (backward)
Picture completion	Discrimination between essential and nonessential detail, memory	Visual or auditory cognition, perceptual foresight, figural-relation selection (lack of evidence as yet)
Picture arrangement	Social alertness, common sense, planning and anticipating, sequencing, ability to synthesize	Convergent production, evaluation
Block design	Perception, analysis, synthesis, reproduction of abstract designs (logic and reasoning applied to space relationships)	Figural relations, figural redefining, figural selection

Table 11 (continued)

WISC	Wechsler's Factors	Guilford's Factors
Object assembly	Perception, visual-motor coordination, visual imagery, synthesis of concrete forms, flexibility of working toward a goal, spatial relationships	Spatial orientation, visualization, figural selection
Coding	Psychomotor speed, eye-hand coordination, pencil manipulation	Symbolic possibilities, symbolic facility
Mazes	Ability to plan in a new situation (problem solving), ability to delay action, visual-motor coordination	Perceptual foresight

Use and Interpretation of the WISC-R

Subtest Differences

For the purpose of differentiating differences in abilities, as suggested by differences in subtest scores on the Wechsler Intelligence Scale for Children Revised, Wechsler (1974) provides a table of significant subtest-score differences based on the average values for all eleven age groups included in the standardization sample. The level of significance used was only the .15 level and, as a result, only 2.35 to 3.45 scaled score points between subtests are needed to show significance. This level is not the preferred standard and is not considered to be realistic in showing valid individual differences. Kaufman (1976) reports that rather large differences between subtest scores are typical (not the exception to the rule) and Piotrowski (1978) points to the error of such differences. Using the .05 and the .01 levels of significance, Piotrowski and Grubbs* (1976) provide significant differences between the subtest scores at each age level and between verbal and performance scaled scores. These are found in Tables 12 and 13. The diagnostician may turn to the age of the client and determine whether the score differences found between specific subtests are not by chance. Through the use of these difference scores, more realistic strengths and weaknesses may be found.

Another use of the Wechsler scales has been the establishment of patterns for purposes of differentiating handicapping conditions. The results of such efforts have not been shown to discriminate discrete contrasts among the groups. Bush and Waugh (1976) point to the problem by showing the similarity of the score levels established for different categories. Their discussion is repeated here and one can see that *unlike* handicapping conditions show *like* patterns.

*By permission of authors.

Table 12. Significant Verbal-Performance Discrepancy at the .05 and .01 Levels

	.05	.01
6½	12	16
7½	12	16
8½	12	15
9½	11	15
10½	12	15
11½	11	14
12½	11	14
13½	12	16
14½	11	15
15½	12	15
16½	11	15

Note: Reprinted by permission of the author.

Table 13. Significant Subtest Scaled-Score Differences on the WISC-R at the .05 and .01 Levels*

Children 6½ Years of Age

	I	S	A	V	C	DS	PC	PA	BD	OA	CD
S	4/5										
A	4/5	3/5									
V	4/6	4/5	4/5								
C	5/6	4/5	4/5	4/6							
DS	4/6	4/5	4/5	4/6	4/6						
PC	4/5	3/4	4/5	4/5	4/5	4/5					
PA	4/6	4/5	4/5	4/6	4/6	4/6	4/5				
BD	4/6	4/5	4/5	4/5	4/5	4/5	4/5	4/5			
OA	5/6	4/5	4/5	4/6	4/6	4/6	4/5	4/6	4/5		
CD	5/7	4/6	5/6	5/6	5/6	5/6	4/6	5/6	5/6	5/6	
M	4/5	3/4	4/5	4/5	4/5	4/5	3/5	4/5	4/5	4/5	4/6

Children 7½ Years of Age

	Infor.	Similarities	Arithmetic	Vocabulary	Comprehension	DS digit span	PC picture completion	PA picture arrangement	BD block design	OA object assembly	CD Coding
S	4/5										
A	4/5	4/5									
V	4/5	4/5	4/5								
C	4/5	4/5	4/6	4/6							
DS	3/5	3/5	4/5	4/5	4/5						
PC	4/5	4/5	4/5	4/5	4/5	3/4					
PA	4/6	4/6	4/6	5/6	5/6	4/5	4/5				
BD	4/5	4/5	4/5	4/5	4/5	3/4	3/5	4/5			
OA	4/6	4/5	4/6	4/6	5/6	4/5	4/5	5/6	4/5		
CD	4/6	4/6	5/6	5/6	5/6	4/6	4/6	5/6	4/6	5/6	
Mazes	4/5	4/5	4/5	4/5	4/5	4/5	4/5	4/6	4/5	4/6	4/6

*Code: The first number designates difference at the .05 level. The second number designates difference at the .01 level.

Reprinted by personal permission from Richard Piotrowski.

Table 13 (continued)

Children 8½ Years of Age

	I	S	A	V	C	DS	PC	PA	BD	OA	CD
S	4/5										
A	4/5	4/5									
V	3/5	4/5	4/5								
C	4/5	4/5	4/5	4/5							
DS	3/4	4/5	4/5	3/4	4/5						
PC	3/4	4/5	4/5	3/4	4/5	3/4					
PA	4/5	4/6	4/6	4/5	4/6	4/5	4/5				
BD	3/4	4/5	4/5	3/4	4/5	3/4	3/4	4/5			
OA	4/5	4/6	4/6	4/5	4/6	4/5	4/5	5/6	4/5		
CD	4/5	4/5	4/5	4/5	4/5	4/5	4/5	4/6	4/5	4/6	
M	4/5	4/5	4/5	4/5	4/5	4/5	4/5	4/6	4/5	4/6	4/5

Children 9½ Years of Age

	I	S	A	V	C	DS	PC	PA	BD	OA	CD
S	4/5										
A	4/5	4/5									
V	4/5	4/5	3/5								
C	4/5	4/5	4/5	4/5							
DS	4/5	4/6	4/5	4/5	4/6						
PC	4/5	4/5	4/5	4/5	4/5	4/5					
PA	4/5	4/5	4/5	4/5	4/5	4/6	4/5				
BD	4/5	4/5	4/5	3/5	4/5	4/5	4/5	4/5			
OA	4/5	4/6	4/5	4/5	4/5	4/6	4/5	4/6	4/5		
CD	4/5	4/5	4/5	4/5	4/5	4/6	4/5	4/5	4/5	4/6	
M	4/5	4/6	4/5	4/5	4/6	5/6	4/5	4/6	4/5	4/6	4/6

Children 10½ Years of Age

	I	S	A	V	C	DS	PC	PA	BD	OA	CD
S	4/5										
A	3/5	4/5									
V	3/4	4/5	4/5								
C	4/5	4/5	4/5	4/5							
DS	4/5	4/6	4/6	4/5	4/6						
PC	4/5	4/6	4/5	4/5	4/6	4/6					
PA	4/5	4/6	4/5	4/5	4/5	4/6	4/6				
BD	3/4	4/5	3/5	3/4	4/5	4/5	4/5	4/5			
OA	4/5	4/6	4/6	4/5	4/6	5/6	5/6	5/6	4/5		
CD	4/5	4/5	4/5	4/5	4/5	4/6	4/6	4/5	4/5	4/6	
M	4/5	5/6	4/6	4/6	5/6	5/6	5/6	5/6	4/5	5/6	5/6

Children 11½ Years of Age

	I	S	A	V	C	DS	PC	PA	BD	OA	CD
S	3/4										
A	3/4	4/5									
V	3/4	4/5	3/5								
C	3/4	4/5	3/5	3/4							
DS	4/5	4/5	4/5	4/5	4/5						
PC	3/4	4/5	4/5	4/5	4/5	4/5					

Table 13 (continued)

Children 11½ Years of Age (continued)

	I	S	A	V	C	DS	PC	PA	BD	OA	CD
PA	4/5	4/5	4/5	4/5	4/5	4/5	4/5				
BD	3/4	3/4	3/4	3/4	3/4	4/5	3/4	4/5			
OA	4/5	4/6	4/5	4/5	4/5	4/6	4/6	4/6	4/5		
CD	3/4	4/5	4/5	4/5	4/5	4/5	4/5	4/5	3/5	4/6	
M	4/5	4/5	4/5	4/5	4/5	4/6	4/5	4/6	4/5	5/6	4/5

Children 12½ Years of Age

	I	S	A	V	C	DS	PC	PA	BD	OA	CD
S	3/4										
A	3/4	4/5									
V	3/4	3/4	3/4								
C	3/4	3/4	3/5	3/4							
DS	4/5	4/5	4/5	4/5	4/5						
PC	4/5	4/5	4/5	4/5	4/5	4/5					
PA	4/5	4/5	4/5	4/5	4/5	4/5	4/5				
BD	3/4	3/4	3/5	3/4	3/4	4/5	4/5	4/5			
OA	4/5	4/6	5/6	4/5	4/5	5/6	5/6	5/6	4/6		
CD	3/4	4/5	4/5	3/4	3/5	4/5	4/5	4/5	3/5	5/6	
M	4/6	5/6	5/6	4/5	4/6	5/6	5/6	5/6	4/6	5/7	5/6

Children 13½ Years of Age

	I	S	A	V	C	DS	PC	PA	BD	OA	CD
S	3/5										
A	3/4	4/5									
V	3/4	3/4	3/4								
C	3/4	4/5	4/5	3/4							
DS	4/5	4/5	4/5	3/5	4/5						
PC	4/5	4/5	4/5	4/5	4/5	4/6					
PA	4/5	4/5	4/5	4/5	4/5	4/5	4/6				
BD	3/4	3/5	3/4	3/4	3/4	4/5	4/5	4/5			
OA	4/5	4/6	4/6	4/5	4/5	4/6	5/6	5/6	4/5		
CD	4/5	4/6	4/6	4/5	5/6	4/6	5/6	5/6	4/5	5/6	
M	4/6	5/6	5/6	4/6	5/6	5/6	5/7	5/7	4/6	5/7	5/7

Children 14½ Years of Age

	I	S	A	V	C	DS	PC	PA	BD	OA	CD
S	3/4										
A	4/5	4/5									
V	3/4	3/4	3/4								
C	3/4	4/5	4/5	3/4							
DS	3/5	4/5	4/5	3/4	4/5						
PC	4/5	4/5	4/5	4/5	4/5	4/5					
PA	4/5	4/5	4/5	4/5	4/5	4/5	4/6				
BD	3/4	3/5	4/5	3/4	3/4	4/5	4/5	4/5			
OA	4/5	4/6	4/6	4/5	4/5	4/6	4/6	4/6	4/5		
CD	4/5	4/6	5/6	4/5	4/6	4/6	5/6	4/6	4/5	5/6	
M	4/5	4/6	4/6	4/5	4/5	4/6	4/6	4/6	4/5	5/6	5/6

Table 13 (continued)
Children 15½ Years of Age

	I	S	A	V	C	DS	PC	PA	BD	OA	CD
S	3/5										
A	3/4	4/5									
V	3/3	3/5	3/4								
C	3/5	4/6	4/5	3/5							
DS	3/4	4/5	4/5	3/4	4/5						
PC	4/5	5/6	4/6	4/5	5/6	5/6					
PA	4/5	4/6	4/5	4/5	4/6	4/5	5/6				
BD	3/4	4/5	3/4	3/4	4/5	3/5	4/6	4/5			
OA	4/5	5/6	4/6	4/5	5/6	5/6	5/7	5/6	4/5		
CD	3/4	4/5	4/5	3/4	4/5	4/5	5/6	4/5	4/5	5/6	
M	4/5	4/6	4/6	4/5	5/6	5/6	5/7	5/6	4/5	5/7	5/6

Children 16½ Years of Age

	I	S	A	V	C	DS	PC	PA	BD	OA	CD
S	3/4										
A	4/5	4/5									
V	3/4	3/4	4/5								
C	4/5	4/5	4/6	3/4							
DS	4/5	4/5	4/5	3/4	4/5						
PC	4/5	4/5	4/6	3/4	4/5	4/5					
PA	4/5	4/5	4/6	4/5	4/6	4/6	4/6				
BD	3/4	3/4	4/5	3/3	4/5	3/4	4/5	4/5			
OA	4/5	4/6	5/6	4/5	5/6	4/6	5/6	5/6	4/5		
CD	4/5	4/5	4/6	3/4	4/5	4/5	4/5	4/6	3/5	4/6	
M	5/6	5/6	5/7	4/6	5/7	5/6	5/7	5/7	5/6	5/7	5/7

Problems of Identification of Categories By Profile Patterns

The following sections include test patterns that are similar in design but different in their category designations. The difficulty in using test patterns for diagnosis is shown in the studies made by Graham, Wechsler, McGlannan, and Clements. Graham (1952, p. 270) found that some nonreaders have performance IQs higher than their verbal IQs and that other nonreaders have verbal IQs higher than their performance IQs. He also found a similarity between the higher-performance IQ group and the Wechsler pattern of the adolescent sociopath (Table 14). Figure 26 shows a graph of Graham's nonreader pattern superimposed on Wechsler's pattern.

Clements found three patterns typical of MBI children (Clements, 1966, pp. 47–48). In Graham's and Wechsler's studies, the patterns of the nonreader and the sociopath (representing different categories) are similar (Figure 26 and Table 14). To further complicate the situation, McGlannan (1968) designates two patterns for dyslexic children, which she calls *specific dyslexia* and *complex dyslexia*, and both show scores that fall into patterns much like the others. Figure 27 shows the relative positions of these six patterns.

In 1974 McCarthy and Elkins completed studies made in five states to determine homogeneous clusters among language-disabled and learning-disabled children. Twenty-two subscores from the WISC and the ITPA were used. The authors sought to determine whether there were clusters of subtest scores that could accurately identify specific-learning disabilities.

Table 14. Mean Scale Scores of Sociopaths and Nonreaders

	Wechsler Adolescent Sociopath Mean-Scaled Scores	Graham's Nonreader (High Performance) Mean-Scaled Scores
Information	9.0	8.0
Comprehension	9.5	10.5
Arithmetic	9.0	7.0
Similarities	10.0	12.0
Vocabulary	10.0	8.5
Digit span	9.0	9.0
Picture completion	11.0	12.2
Picture arrangements	13.0	11.0
Block design	11.0	11.6
Object assembly	13.0	11.5
Coding	9.0	9.5

represents different categories

The results of their study suggested "that psychiatrists, psychologists, and psychoeducational diagnosticians need to be very cautious about the entire profile literature in which profiles of specific strengths and weaknesses on the WISC and ITPA are said to be indicative of problems in academic achievement." They found no pattern on the WISC typical of learning-disabled children. Evidence showed that patterns on the WISC may vary among locales. Significantly, children who fail in a linguistic reading program may have different patterns from those who fail in phonetic reading. The patterns McCarthy and Elkins found on the WISC among the learning-disabled children were similar to those found by Clements among minimally brain-injured children. Children who are learning disabled or have a minimal brain injury may exhibit a number of patterns on the WISC.

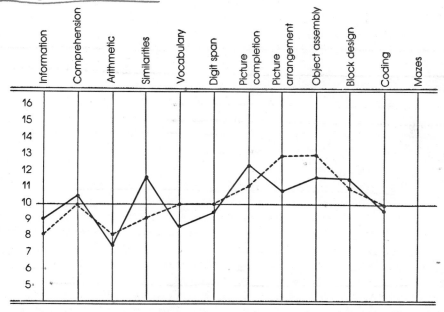

Figure 26. Comparison of Nonreader and Adolescent Sociopath Test Patterns

Figure 27. Similarity of Test Patterns Identifying Six Behaviors

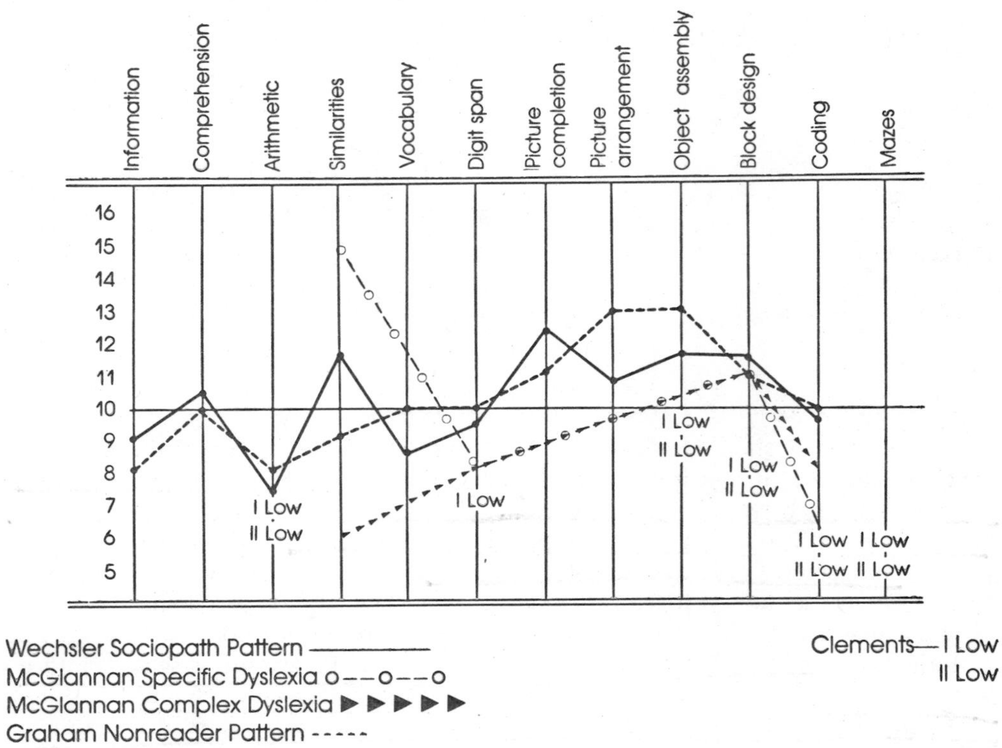

Wechsler Sociopath Pattern ——————
McGlannan Specific Dyslexia o——o——o
McGlannan Complex Dyslexia ▶▶▶▶▶
Graham Nonreader Pattern - - - - -

Clements— I Low
II Low

The following variety of patterns was found on the WISC by McCarthy and Elkins:

1. A profile showing few discrepancies between scaled scores or between verbal and performance scores with above-average scores.
2. A profile of low-verbal, high-performance scores
3. A profile of high-verbal, low-performance scores
4. A profile showing extreme discrepancies on both scales, but little difference between verbal and performance scores
5. Low scores on all subtests

Bush and Mattson (1973) report their findings on WISC underachiever patterns at two levels of intelligence, the normal level and the bright and gifted level. Figure 28 shows the scaled-score differences between achievers and underachievers with normal intelligence. Figure 29 shows the scaled-score differences between achievers and underachievers with bright and gifted intelligence. As was hypothesized, some significant differences were found in both cases. In the normal-intellect group, underachievers tended to show significantly less aptitude on the following subtests: information, arithmetic, vocabulary, digit span, and picture arrangement. In the bright and gifted group underachievers showed significantly less aptitude on arithmetic, digit span, and block-design subtests.

Figure 28. A Comparison of WISC Scaled Scores of Achievers and Underachievers With Normal Intelligence

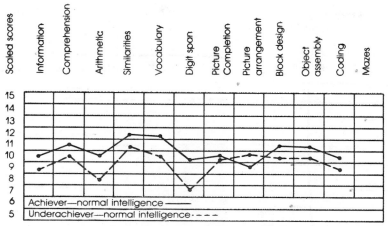

Figure 29. A Comparison of WISC Scaled Scores of Bright/Gifted Underachievers and Bright/Gifted Achievers

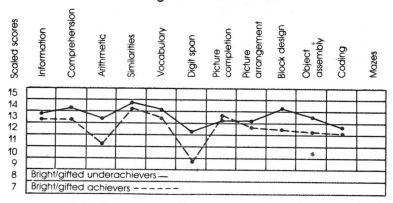

A Wilcoxson Rank-Sum Test was made between the deviations of the subtests in the underachievers at the various levels of intelligence. The only significant difference was found to be on the deviations of the information subtests. Where normal-level underachievers showed negative deviations from the mean of their group, the bright and gifted underachievers showed positive deviations from the mean of their group.

Most other subtests tended to deviate from their means in the same directions. When there was a difference among the others, it was not significant. A plausible inference was made for the deviation of the information subtest. Among underachievers who do not read extensively and do not store as much information from that source as their achieving peers, it would appear logical that the bright and gifted underachiever with higher intelligence would have more "going for him" and, therefore, would retain more than would the underachiever with normal intelligence. It can be seen from these studies that special-education categories cannot be established on a single test—in this case, the Wechsler Scales.

Though it is difficult to find patterns on tests that define specific handicapped groups, it can be helpful in a diagnosis to analyze patterns within the profiles to better discern strengths and weaknesses. Different subtest groupings under different factors are seen in the following discussion.

WISC-R Subtest Patterns for Analyses

Since the organization of the Wechsler Scales by Rappaport (1945–1946) and Cohen (Money, 1962) other combinations have been analyzed by Bannatyne (1968, 1974) and by Kaufman (1979). These regroupings of subtests afford an evaluation of differences from various vantage points. Kaufman (1979), who supports the use of such groupings, suggests that this type of psychological sophistication and flexibility of profile analysis, coupled with awareness of the tests' limitations, is essential for breaking an examiner's overdependency on the obtained scores. Bannatyne's groupings are shown below with an example of how they may be used.

Groupings by Bannatyne:

1. Spatial abilities can be determined from the results of the picture-completion, block-design, and object-assembly subtests. Add the three scaled scores and divide by 3.

Picture completion	6
Block design	8
Object assembly	6
	20

$$20 \div 3 = 6.7$$

2. Conceptual abilities can be determined from the results of the comprehension, similarities, and vocabulary subtests. Add the three scaled scores and divide by 3.

Comprehension	11
Similarities	12
Vocabulary	9
	32

$$32 \div 3 = 10.6$$

3. Sequencing abilities can be determined from the results of the digit-span, coding (digit symbol), and picture-arrangement subtests. Add the three scaled scores and divide by 3.

Digit span	7
Coding	5
Picture arrangement	9
	21

$$21 \div 3 = 7$$

4. Acquired knowledge can be determined from the results of the information, vocabulary, and arithmetic subtest scores. Add the three scaled scores and divide by 3.

Information	10
Vocabulary	9
Arithmetic	9
	28

$$28 \div 3 = 9.3$$

A quick comparison of the averaged subtest scores shows that sequencing abilities and spatial abilities indicate tendencies toward weakness in those abilities. The diagnostician is, thus, advised to examine this possibility by other detective work (other related test scores, teachers' and parents' comments).

Other groupings are listed below:

Groupings by Cohen:

Perceptual organization	Verbal comprehension	Freedom from distractibility
Block design	Information	Arithmetic
Object assembly	Comprehension	Digit span
	Similarities	
	Vocabulary	

Groupings by Kaufman:

Verbal comprehension	Perceptual organization	Freedom from distractibility
Information	Picture completion	Arithmetic
Similarities	Picture arrangement	Digit span
Vocabulary	Block design	Coding
Comprehension	Object assembly	
	Mazes	

Kaufman (1979) reports that these factors yielded striking consistency for all children and youth within six-to-sixteen-year-age groups—blacks, whites, and both sexes. He, also, reports other studies showing the emerging of the three factors among the mentally retarded, those with learning or behavioral disorders, adolescent psychiatric patients, and Chicanos. The value of these groupings, as identified by Kaufman, aid in recognizing the culturally disadvantaged by the fluctuating pattern within the verbal area, i.e., if the acquired-knowledge grouping (Bannatyne, 1974) scores are the very lowest scores. Studies show that highly distractible children evidence marked weaknesses in arithmetic, digit span, and coding. Poor scores on coding and picture arrangement may reflect sequencing problems, according to Bannatyne, and also convergent-production abilities, according to Guilford (Meeker, 1969).

Other groupings suggested by Kaufman are:

Reasoning	Recall	Long stimuli*	Brief stimuli
Similarities	Information	Information	Similarities
Arithmetic	Vocabulary	Arithmetic	Vocabulary
Comprehension	Digit span	Comprehension	Digit span

Much expression* required	Little expression required	Least dependent on culture
Similarities	Information	Picture completion
Vocabulary	Arithmetic	Block design
Comprehension	Digit span	Object assembly

*Each item in the three tasks with long stimuli requires the individual to respond to a lengthy question. Each item in the brief-stimuli grouping requires children to respond to brief stimuli.

Simultaneous*	Successive
Picture completion	Picture arrangement
Block design	Coding
Object assembly	Mazes

Meaningful stimuli	Abstract stimuli
Picture completion	Coding
Picture arrangement	Block design
Object assembly	

Visual organization	Visual-motor coordination	
Picture completion	Block design	From Lutey (1977,
Picture arrangement	Object assembly	p. 170) in Kaufman
	Coding	(1979)
	Mazes	

Left-brain processing	Right-brain processing	Integrative function
Vocabulary	Object assembly	Picture arrangement
similarities	Picture completion	Block design
		Coding
		Mazes

Cognition	Convergent Production	
Picture completion	Picture arrangement	Guilford—From Operation
Block design	Coding	Function on SOI
Object assembly		(Kaufman, 1979)
Mazes		

These groupings may be arranged in graph form for ease of handling. The following adaptation (Figure 30) from Wiebe's (1979) work sheet on the WISC-R provides a visual format for quickly viewing the strengths or weaknesses of the individual according to the pattern analyses described by Kaufman and others. After the WISC-R has been scored, the scaled scores may be placed in the appropriate blank spaces. One may accomplish this very speedily by putting, e.g., the information scaled score all across the chart in each appropriate spot, then following with the other scaled scores completing each line of the chart at one time. An average should be taken of the total of each group and placed below each designated pattern. One may compare all average scores with the score *10* (the mean subtest score on the WISC-R). Relative strengths and weaknesses according to the group patterns may be noted. For example, if the

*From Das and colleagues (Kaufman, 1979, p. 163). The two modes of processing, successive and simultaneous, involve *serial* and *serial* and *temporal* handling of information and visual-spatial ability, respectively.

Figure 30. WISC-R Subtest Groupings: Scanning Sheet

	Ver. comp.	Per. orga.	Free. dist.	Acq. knowl.	Recall	Reas.	Much expr.	Lit'l. expr.	Long stim.	Brief stim.	Right brain	Left brain	Inte. func.	Simul-tan.	Success.	Meaning	Abs. stimu-	Vis. org.	Vis.-motor coor.	Spat.	Cog.	Con. prod.	
Inf.	10																						Inf.
Sim.	14																						Sim.
Ar.																							Ar.
Voc.	10																						Voc.
Com.	12																						Com.
D.S.																							D.S.
P.C.																							P.C.
P.A.																							P.A.
B.D.		8																					B.D.
O.A.		7																					O.A.
Cod.																							Cod.
Maz.																							Maz.
Total	46	15																					
Ave. Scores	11.5	7.5																					

(needs help here:)

*Groupings from Cohen, Banatyne, Kaufman, Lutey and Guilford
Adapted from M. J. Wiebe's WorkSheet on the WISC-R (1979) by Wilma Jo Bush, West Texas State University, Canyon, Texas.

compare w/ 10

scaled scores from the group Verbal comprehension are Information: 10, Similarities: 14, Vocabulary: 10, and Comprehension: 12, the average would be 11.5; if the scaled scores from the Perceptual-organization group are Block design: 8, and Object assembly 7, the average would be 7.5. One could conclude that at the time of the testing this client's verbal comprehension was certainly better than the child's ability to perceptually organize visual materials. All averages may be compared and varying dimensional views may provide areas of specific abilities or disabilities that may not have been observed otherwise.

Standardization Information
The three editions of the Wechsler Scales, WAIS, WPPSI and WISC-R, were standardized on a population of whites and nonwhites from the north central, southern, and western regions in the United States. The standardization samples included 100 to 200 subjects in each age group.

Reliability for WPPSI and WISC-R
The reliability coefficients of the individual tests and of the Verbal, Performance, and Full Scale IQs for the WPPSI and WISC-R were obtained by the split-half technique, except for Digit Span and Coding (WISC-R) and Animal House (WPPSI). The reliability coefficients for these tests were established from test-retest technique. The reliability coefficient for the Verbal, Performance, and Full Scale IQs were obtained as follows: WPPSI estimations were obtained from the formula for the correlation between two sums of equally weighted scores according to Kelly (Wechsler, 1963); WISC-R estimations were obtained from a formula for computing the reliability of a composite group of tests according to Guilford (Wechsler, 1974). The reliability averages for each subtest from the WISC-R and WPPSI are shown in Table 15.

Validity for the WPPSI and WISC-R
The validity for the WPPSI was obtained by comparing IQs on the WPPSI with IQs from three tests, the Stanford Binet, the Peabody Picture Vocabulary Test and the Pictorial Test of Intelligence. The correlations are shown in Table 16.

The validity for the WISC-R was obtained by studying the relationship between the WISC-R and three other individually administered intelligence tests: the Wechsler Preschool and Primary Scale of Intelligence (WPPSI), the Wechsler Adult Intelligence Scale (WAIS), and the Stanford Binet, Form L-M, 1972 norms. The coefficients of correlation for these comparisons are shown in Tables 17 and 18. Coefficients of correlation of scaled scores and IQs on the WISC-R with the Stanford Binet were obtained for four groups of normal children, aged 6, 9½, 12½, and 16½. The correlations for the IQs only are shown in Table 18.

Itemized Facts.

1. The WPPSI is designed for ages 4 through 6.
2. The WISC-R is designed for ages 6 through 16.
3. The WAIS is designed for ages 16 through adulthood.
4. All Wechsler Scales provide a profile showing ability measures within both the verbal and performance areas. The supplementary tests are provided for the verbal and performance scales on the WPPSI and WISC-R.

Table 15. Average Reliability Coefficients for the WPPSI and the WISC-R

	WPPSI	WISC-R
Verbal IQ	.94	.94
Performance IQ	.93	.90
Full Scale IQ	.96	.96
Verbal Subtests		
Information	.81	.85
Vocabulary	.84	.86
Arithmetic	.82	.77
Similarities	.83	.81
Comprehension	.81	.77
Sentences	.85	
Digit Span		.78
Performance Subtests		
Animal House	.77	
Picture Completion	.83	.77
Mazes	.87	.72
Geometric Design	.82	
Block Design	.82	.85
Picture Arrangement		.73
Object Assembly		.70
Coding		.72

Average coefficients are for 11 ages on the WISC-R and for 6 ages on the WPPSI

Table 16. Coefficients of Correlation of IQs on the WPPSI and Three Other Intelligence Tests for 98 Children Between 5 and 6 Years of Age

WPPSI	Stan.-Binet IQ	PPVT IQ	PTI IQ
Verbal IQ	.76	.57	.53
Performance IQ	.56	.44	.60
Full Scale IQ	.75	.58	.64

Table 17. Coefficients of Correlation of IQs on the WISC-R With IQs on the WPPSI and the WAIS

WISC-R	WPPSI IQs* Verbal	Perform.	F.S.	WAIS IQs** Verbal	Perform.	FS.
Verbal IQ	.80	.56	.73	.96	.74	.94
Performance IQ	.63	.80	.78	.68	.83	.79
Full Scale IQ	.78	.74	.82	.91	.85	.95

*Subjects were 50 children aged 6 years, 0 months (± 8 weeks), tested within a 3-week interval.

**Subjects were 40 individuals aged 16 years, 11 months (± 8 weeks), tested within a 3-week interval.

Table 18. Coefficients of Correlation of IQs on the WISC-R With IQs on the Stanford-Binet at Ages 6, 9½, 12½, 16½*

WISC-R IQs	Stanford-Binet IQs			
	Age 6	Age 9½	Age 12½	Age 16½
Verbal	.77	.64	.66	.73
Performance	.74	.57	.51	.51
Full Scale	.82	.69	.63	.74

*29 to 33 children were tested at each age level.

5. The mean of the Wechsler Scales is 100 with a standard deviation of 15.
6. The mean scaled score for all of the Wechsler subtests is 10, with range of possible scores between 0 and 19.

McCarthy Scales of Children's Abilities (MSCA)

Description and Administration

A test that is very popular among diagnosticians is the *McCarthy Scales of Children's Abilities.* It is used with young children and provides a scale index for the following areas: verbal (V), perceptual-performance (P), quantitative (Q), memory (Mem), and motor (Mot). From the verbal, perceptual-performance, and quantitative scales, a general cognitive index (GC) can be derived. A position for evaluation of laterality is also provided.

The measurements obtained in this test afford the diagnostician a valuable tool for examining individual differences in psychological processes. The provision of such descriptive indices in the profile make this a very good test for the novice diagnostician. Since this test is for young children, ages 2½–8½, it helps to meet the assessment needs of kindergarten children, which is growing because of the extension of services provided this age child in the public schools. There are 18 subtests, which are listed as follows:

1. Block Building, a subtest measuring perception of spatial relations
2. Puzzle Solving, a subtest measuring perceptual and motor skills
3. Pictorial Memory, a subtest measuring short-term memory and verbal ability
4. Word Knowledge, a subtest, made up of two parts, measuring both receptive- and oral-vocabulary ability
5. Number Questions, a subtest measuring both number ability and numerical reasoning
6. Tapping Sequence, a subtest measuring memory, perceptual-motor coordination, and general cognition
7. Verbal memory, a two-part subtest measuring ability to remember words and paragraph meaning
8. Right-Left Orientation, a subtest measuring orientation ability (not administered to children under 5 years)
9. Leg Coordination, a subtest measuring maturation of leg coordination
10. Arm Coordination, a subtest measuring maturation of arm coordination
11. Imitation Action, a subtest measuring eye performance
12. Draw-a-Design, a subtest measuring eye-hand coordination

13. Draw-a-Child, a subtest measuring eye-hand coordination and imagery visualization

14. Numerical Memory, a subtest measuring memory for digits (both forward and backward)

15. Verbal Fluency, a subtest measuring ability to classify

16. Counting and Sorting, a subtest measuring ability of both counting and quantitative similarities

17. Opposite Analogies, a subtest measuring auditory association

18. Conceptual Grouping, a subtest measuring concept formation

Interpretation and Use of the MSCA

It has been a popular procedure to analyze the MSCA profile to determine strengths and weaknesses. Research has shown that the MSCA measures the same abilities of intelligence as the leading intelligence tests, the WISC-R, the WPPSI and the Stanford Binet (Davis, 1975), (Davis and Rowland, 1974), (Kaufman and Dicuio, 1975). Kaufman (1975) examined the profiles of Scale Indexes for each of the 1,032 children in the standardization sample of the MSCA. He found that 7-point deviations were significant for the Verbal, Perceptual-Performance, and Quantitative Scales, and 8-point deviations were significant for Memory and Motor. The diagnostician may use these data as a means of determining differences for individual lesson plans. However, the fact that in a later study Kaufman found that the majority of children have one or more significant deviations from their mean Indexes, makes another step necessary before determining strengths and weaknesses. One must consider the basal-scatter levels. Kaufman found that:

38 percent had no significant deviations from their mean
30 percent had one significant deviation
23 percent had two significant deviations
9 percent had three or more deviations

If 53 percent have one or two deviations from their means, it would be safer for the diagnostician not to determine strengths or weaknesses on the basis of two deviations of 7 points each, unless this were substantiated by other tests of the same nature.

Wiebe has devised a means of using mental ages with two-year deviations before determining strengths or weaknesses. His analysis sheet with instructions is presented in Figure 31.

Instructions for McCarthy Analysis Form

The McCarthy Scales of Children's Abilities (MSCA) use both *T* and normal IQ means along with standard deviations for summary statistics. However, for comparative purposes, an age score may be more appropriate. Thus, this analysis form is proposed.

1. Using the form provided (Figure 31) record a mental age (MA) score for each of the MSCA's subtests. The mental age is an estimate derived from the raw score (Table 19) of each subtest achieved by the standardization group on the table.

2. Transfer each subtest MA into the spaces provided in the right portions of the form.

3. For each of the MSCA scales (Verbal, Perc/Perf, etc.) add the MAs indicated in that column. Record the age total in the space provided at the bottom of each column.

4. Divide the age total for each scale or factor by the number of subtests in that scale.

Figure 31. McCarthy Analysis Form

MSCA SUBTEST:	MA	Verbal	Perc/Perf	Quant.	Memory	Motor
1. Block Building						
2. Puzzle Solving						
3. Pictorial Memory						
4. Word Knowledge						
5. Number Questions						
6. Tapping Sequence						
7. Verbal Memory I						
Verbal Memory II						
8. Right-Left Orient.						
9. Leg Coordination						
10. Arm Coordination						
11. Imitative Action						
12. Draw-A-Design						
13. Draw-A-Child						
14. Numerical Memory I						
Numerical Memory II						
15. Verbal Fluency						
16. Counting and Sorting						
17. Opposite Analogies						
18. Conceptual Grouping						

Age Totals:
Mean MAs:

GCI Age Totals:
GCI Mean MA:

Difference from MA:
Difference from CA:

5. The GCI age totals are determined by adding the mean MAs of the Verbal, Perc/Perf, and Quant. scales together. This sum is then divided by 3 to determine the GCI mean MA.   ART 22
6. To complete the "Difference" section of the form, each of the five MSCA factors or scales will be compared to either the child's CA or "GCI Mean MA," whichever is lower.
7. The difference between the scale or factor Mean MAs and the child's CA or MA can be used to interpret individual strengths or weaknesses. Once again, the rule of 2 years' or more difference is used to determine if a "true difference" exists for a child.

Standardization Information

One hundred children at each age level were involved in the standardization, wherein father's occupation, urban-rural residence, geographic region, and sex and age of the children were stratified in accordance with the 1970 U.S. Census information. The reliability data vary according to the subtest. Coefficients for the scales are as follows:

Table 19. McCarthy Raw Scores

RAW SCORES OF SUBTESTS

Mean Age of Standardization	Block Bldg.	Puzzle Solv.	Pict. Memory	Word Know.	Number Quest.	Tapping Seq.	Verbal Mem. I	Verbal Mem. II	Right-Left Orient.	Leg Coord.	Arm Coord.	Imitative Act.	Draw-A-Design	Draw-A-Child	Num. Memory I	Num. Memory II	Verbal Fluency	Cntg. and Sorting	Opp. Analogies	Conc. Grouping
*2-6	4	1	1	7	1	1	4	—	X	4	2	2	1	0	2	0	3	1	0	2
2-9	(5)	—	—	(8-9)	—	—	(5-8)	—	X	(5)	—	—	—	—	—	—	(4)	—	—	—
*3-0	6	2	2	10	2	—	9	1	X	6	(3)	3	2	1	3	0	5	2	1	3
3-3	—	(3)	—	—	—	—	(10-11)	—	X	—	—	—	—	—	—	—	—	—	—	—
*3-6	7	4	—	11	—	—	12	2	X	7	4	3	3	2	4	0	6	3	2	4
3-9	—	—	—	(12)	—	—	(13-16)	—	X	(8)	—	—	—	(3-4)	—	—	(7-8)	—	—	—
*4-0	(8)	5	3	13	3	2	17	3	X	9	5	3	4	5	4	0	9	4	3	5
4-3	—	(6)	—	(14)	—	—	(18-19)	(4)	X	—	(6)	—	(5)	(6)	—	—	(10)	—	—	—
*4-6	9	7	—	15	—	3	20	—	X	10	7	3	6	7	5	0	11	5	4	6
4-9	—	—	—	—	—	—	(21)	—	X	—	—	—	—	(8)	—	—	(12)	—	—	—
*5-0	—	11	—	16	—	—	22	5	6	11	8	4	7	9	6	1	13	6	5	7
*5-6	10	12	—	17	—	4	24	6	—	—	10	4	8	10	—	2	15	7	5	8
6-0	—	(14)	—	(18)	—	—	(25)	—	—	—	—	—	(9-10)	—	—	—	(16-19)	(8)	—	—
*6-6	—	16	4	19	6	5	26	7	7	12	13	4	11	11	7	3	18	9	6	9
7-0	—	(17)	—	(20)	—	—	—	—	—	—	—	—	(12-13)	—	—	—	(19-20)	—	—	—
*7-6	—	18	—	21	8	—	27	8	9	13	17	4	14	14	8	4	22	9	7	10
8-0	—	(19-20)	—	(22)	(9)	—	—	—	—	—	(18-19)	—	—	—	—	—	(23)	—	—	—
*8-6	—	21	5	23	10	6	28	8	10	13	20	4	15	15	8	4	24	9	8	10

*From MSCA Manual, Table 17, pp 204–205 (parentheses indicate extrapolated ages)

Verbal Scale range .84–.92; Perceptual-Performance, .75–.90; Quantitative, .77–.86; General Cognitive, .90–.96; Memory, .72–.84 and Motor, .60–.84. The validity was established by comparing the McCarthy scores with the scores on the Metropolitan Achievement Tests, Correlations were adequate to high for all subtests except Verbal, Memory, and Motor. Concurrent validity information was obtained through the comparison of the performance on the McCarthy Scale with the performance on the Stanford Binet and the WPPSI. In both cases, concurrent validity of the MSCA appears to be adequate, but there are some limitations. McCarthy states that the results at the lower levels, e.g., scores in the mentally retarded range, should be interpreted with caution because of the small size of the sample in the standardization process.

A general cognitive index, scale indexes, mental ages, and percentile ranks are available measures for this test. The general cognitive index has a scaled-score mean of 100 and a standard deviation of 16; the other scales have a mean of 50 and a standard deviation of 10.

This test appears to be well-liked because of its appeal to children and because it forms a nice bridge between the WPPSI and the WISC-R. The test overlaps the upper end of the WPPSI and the lower end of the WISC-R, both of which positions often yield truncated basal and ceiling levels for those children who are 5–6 years of age.

Slosson Intelligence Test for Children and Adults

Description and Administration Procedure

The Slosson Intelligence Test for Children and Adults (SIT), by Richard L. Slosson (1963), is an individual-screening instrument made for use by the whole range of school professionals. The items used in this short screening test are similar in nature to the Stanford Binet tasks, and the estimated time for administering and scoring varies from 10 to 30 minutes.

The SIT has an infant and early-childhood section that contains items taken directly or adapted from the Gesell Developmental Schedules.* These items cover tasks typical of babies' and children's responses from age two weeks up to four years. Each single response up through the fourth year represents a mental-age growth of one month. Beginning with age five and continuing through age fifteen, each response represents a mental-age growth of two months; thereafter, each response represents a mental-age growth of three months. For the questions the client is able to answer correctly, credit is earned and the client's total months are added after the completion of the testing.

The age at which the testing begins is determined by the examiner. If the person is considered to be average in intelligence, the procedure is to start at one year below the chronological age. If the person is thought to be dull or retarded, two to three years below the chronological age is recommended. For the very bright individual, it is acceptable to start at or a little above the chronological age. The testing is discontinued when the client has failed ten responses consecutively. Very complete instructions for determining chronological age, mental age, basal age, and ceiling level are provided. In addition, a very handy "I.Q. Finder" is attached to the back of the manual. Scoring is done by checking responses with a plus or minus on the scoring sheet.

---

*Published by The Psychological Corporation, 757 Third Ave., New York, N.Y. 10017.

Standardization Information

The Slosson, for validation purposes, followed the procedures used in the Stanford Binet (L-M Form). Thus, it has "all the advantages of the 'deviation I.Q.'" (Slosson, 1963). To obtain comparative results between the SIT and the Stanford Binet, the author administered a large number of both tests in alternate manner. The author tested a group of individuals on the Stanford Binet and a teacher, principal, guidance counselor, social worker, or nurse tested this group on the SIT.

The children and adults used in obtaining comparative results resided in both urban and rural districts in the state of New York. No specific numbers are identified as coming from the variety of locations or cultural classes mentioned. Many of the individuals were identified as being disturbed, negativistic, withdrawn, and having difficulty in reading, but again only general data are reported.

Reliability and Validity.   The author reports a high reliability coefficient of .97 (test-retest interval within a period of 2 months). These data were obtained on 139 individuals, ages 4–50 years. The Mean IQs of the initial tests and of the retests were 99.0 and 101.3. The Standard Deviations were 24.7 and 25.1. For ages below 4 years, no retesting was administered. It is cautioned that IQs on children .5 months–3.9 years be considered tentative.

Slosson reports validity correlations at each age level between 4 and 17, and for age level 18 and above. These coefficients of correlation between the Stanford Binet and the SIT range between .99 and .98. The items on the two tests are similar and, therefore, this high correlation would be expected; but both the *means* and the *standard deviations* on the SIT *vary* so much at each age level, it would be unwise to use the test as a means of establishing any strengths and weaknesses and of making any critical educational decisions on the basis of any IQ established.

Itemized facts.

1. The SIT is a quick test for *screening* purposes. Time required for administration is 10–30 minutes.
2. The IQ is figured on the basis of mental age. An "I.Q. Finder" is provided for convenience.
3. Ages for the SIT range between .5 month and 27 years.
4. The standard deviations at various ages range between 24.7 and 25.1. The mean IQs range between 99.0 and 101.3. The Standard Error of measurement is 4.5. (These data do not include means and standard deviations for ages below 4 years.)
5. No reading is required by the examinee.
6. The SIT is not considered appropriate for those unfamiliar with the English language.
7. IQs on individuals below 4 years should be considered as tentative.

Pictorial Test of Intelligence

Description and Administration Procedure

The *Pictorial Test of Intelligence* (PTI) (French, 1964) is another test that may be used with young children, ages 3–8. It is a Binet-type instrument that allows the subject to respond in a multiple choice fashion—no verbal responses are required. The instructions are simple and the subject responds by pointing to one of four pictures on a test card. The examiner records the position of the choice on an answer sheet. The total number of correct items, the raw score, is converted by table to mental-age units and to deviation IQs.

There are six subtests arranged in order of difficulty, and there is no base or ceiling to be obtained. All items are administered (with a few exceptions), regardless of the successes or failures of the subject. The subtests are described as follows:

1. Picture vocabulary subtest requires the child to identify the picture that best represents the meaning of a stimulus word read by the diagnostician. Verbal comprehension is the primary ability measured.
2. Form discrimination subtest requires the child to match stimulus drawings that become increasingly more difficult, to one of four response drawings. Perceptual organization is the primary ability measured.
3. Information and Comprehension subtest requires the child to point to pictures in response to verbal statements read by the diagnostician. Range of information, general understanding, and verbal comprehension are the primary abilities measured.
4. Similarities subtest requires the child to identify which of four pictures does not belong in the same category as the other three. Visual perception and concept formation are the primary abilities measured.
5. Size and Number subtest requires the child to demonstrate knowledge of quantitative skills by pointing to the correct answer (out of four) to a problem presented by the diagnostician. Basic skills in number ability and numerical reasoning are the primary abilities measured.
6. Immediate recall subtest requires the child to examine a stimulus card for 5 seconds and to choose the same stimulus on a 4-choice card *after* the first stimulus card has been removed. Memory for perceptions of size, space, and form relationships are the primary abilities measured.

Standardization Information

There were 1,830 children between the ages of 3 and 8-11 years used in the standardization population. The stratification of the population was on the basis of sex, community size, occupational status of household head, and geographic region. Experienced psychologists tested the children in the sample used.

Reliability for internal consistency is reported to range between .87 and .93 for all of the age levels. French (1964) reports five studies investigating the test-retest reliability. These studies report correlations between .69 and .94. Only the .69 correlation in one study fell below the higher levels of .90 and above for all the other four correlations. Himelstein (1972) reports that the test is least reliable at the 8-year level.

Concurrent validity of the PTI was established by correlating it with three other tests, the Stanford Binet ($r = .72$), Columbia Mental Maturity ($r = .53$), and the WISC ($r = .65$). Sattler (1974) reports the work of Elliott, who made a predictive-validity study of the PTI with the Wide Range Achievement Test. He found .68 correlation with Spelling, .56 with Reading, and .79 with Arithmetic. The PTI (with a mean IQ of 100 and standardization of 16) has a reputable standardization and is considered a very good test to be used in evaluating children with language, speech, and motor handicaps. Particularly it is recommended for children ages of 3–6 as a test of learning aptitude (Newland, 1971).

Itemized Points.

1. The PTI is a very good test of intelligence for children with language, speech, and motor handicaps.
2. The PTI is to be used with children ages three to eight years, eleven months.
3. The mean of the PTI is 100 and the standard deviation is 16.
4. All children take all the items of the test.
5. A short form is available for children of ages three and four.
6. No verbal responses are needed for the PTI.

Columbia Mental Maturity Scale

Description and Administration Procedure

Baurgemeister, Blum, and Lorge in 1972 made the third revision* of the Columbia Mental Maturity Scale. It is a test to be used with children 3 years, 6 months to 9 years, 11 months. There are 92 cards, 6 x 19 inches, on which there are drawings, and among these drawings there is one that is perceptually different in some manner. Perceptual discriminations regarding color, size, shape, function, number, missing parts, and symbolic matter are required of the child. Administration is simple, for the instructions are to ask the child to point to the one that does not belong. The first three cards are training items and the test takes 15–20 minutes.

Standardization Information

The standardization population involved 2,600 children, who resided in 25 states.

The authors report split-half reliability coefficients ranging between .85 and .91, with a median coefficient of .88. Test-retest reliabilities for three groups are reported between .84 and .86. The validity was established by comparing the performance on the CMMS with the performance on the Stanford Binet ($r = .67$), the Otis-Lennon Mental Ability Test ($r = .69$), the Stanford Achievement Test (range of $r = .31$ to $.61$), and the 1959 CMMS edition ($r = .84$). The mean IQ of the test is 100 and the Standard Deviation is 16.

The 1972 edition appears to be a valid test to measure discrimination and classification abilities, as well as some general reasoning ability where symbolic materials are involved. Since it can be given in 15–20 minutes, it is a good test to be used in a battery of tests for handicapped children.

Itemized Points.

1. A quick test to measure IQs based on discrimination and classification
2. Time of administration is 15–20 minutes.
3. The mean IQ is 100 and the standard deviation is 16.
4. A good test to be used for the deaf and the speech-handicapped because verbal expression is not required.

---

*Doubt has been expressed about how well the first and second editions were fulfilling their objectives. For further information please read from Bligh (1959), Hirschenfang, Jaramillo, and Benton (1966), Rosenberg and Stroud (1966), Sattler (1974), and Salvia and Ysseldyke (1978).

Leiter International Performance Scale (1969)

Description and Administration Procedure

The Leiter International Performance Scale was originally published in 1929 for the purpose of measuring the intellectual function of children who could not respond to such verbal tests as the Stanford Binet. A revision in 1948 (LIPS, the fifth revision of the first experimental edition) was adapted by Grace Arthur in 1949 and published in 1950.

The Grace Arthur edition (AALIPS) is an untimed test for children 2–12 years. The 1948 LIPS may be used for individuals 2–18 years. Both the LIPS and the AALIPS consist of a series of wooden frames into which the child must insert small blocks with pictures and symbols into the appropriate sections of the frames. These small blocks are to be matched with colors, designs, and categories, and used for completing patterns in the frames. The illustrations for instruction in the manual are in black and white, while some of the items in the test are in color. This is difficult for the examiner but the verbal instructions applied in the administration are simple. If the child seems not to understand directions, the examiner instructs her or him to put the block where she/he thinks it ought to go.

An MA and a ratio IQ may be obtained on the AALIPS. A basal position is noted by the level at which a child answers all items correctly. A ceiling is attained when the child fails all items at two consecutive year levels. Sattler (1974) cites Werner's view of the scale as having certain characteristics: uneven item-dificulty levels; certain outdated pictures; undetermined culture-free qualities; unclear measures of the scale; and too few tests at each level. Correct answers (arrangements of blocks) to test questions are not included in the AALIPS manual. Ysseldyke and Salvia (1979) suggest that examiners obtain the consensus of others, particularly very bright persons, about the correctness of the responses, and that they then mark the blocks using a coding system to avoid scoring errors.

Standardization Information

Leiter (1959) reports evidence for the reliability and validity of the Leiter scales. His manuals for the various editions have not provided adequate information regarding standardization. No reliability data are published in the manual for the AALIPS. Validity determined from a number of studies on the AALIPS and reported by Arthur show correlations with the Stanford Binet for 4-, 5-, 7-, and 8-year-old children to range between .60 to .93. In 1969 an edition of the test was published and the reported mean IQ was cited as being 95 with a standard deviation of 16. A group of graduate students administered the tests to 158 Headstart children and found the mean IQ to be 86.02 with a standard deviation of 15.9. Since this group would be expected to be children without the "normal" experiences of children in higher socioeconomic levels, the mean IQ comes as no surprise for this group. Leiter (1969) explains that time did not permit him to adapt the tests at each year level so that the mean IQ would be 100. The alternative he offers is to add a constant, namely 5 points of IQ, to the first obtained IQ in the case where the test is administered to the children in the continental United States.

The AALIPS has merit in being considered a culture-free test, at least to a degree (even though this has not been clearly established). It could be used in testing handicapped children (2–12 years) who cannot be tested by the Stanford Binet, WISC, or

WPPSI (Arnold, 1953). However, only a trained diagnostician, who is thoroughly familiar with many tests and with appropriate standardization procedures, should administer
the AALIPS.

Itemized Points.

1. The Leiter tests, LIPS, and AALIPS are nonverbal tests to be used with individuals
   who are not skilled in the English language or are handicapped in expressing themselves verbally.
2. The LIPS may be used for ages 2–18 years.
3. The AALIPS may be used for ages 2–12 years.
4. Mean IQ for a group of Headstart children (158) is found to be 86.02 with standard
   deviation of 15.9.
5. One study (1969) shows a mean IQ of 95 and a standard deviation of 16.
6. Inadequate reliability and validity are reported in the manuals.

Peabody Picture Vocabulary Test-Revised

Description and Administration Procedure

The Peabody Picture Vocabulary Test-Revised (PPVT-R) by Dunn, L. L., and Dunn, L. M.
(1981) is the second edition of the PPVT (1959). It is made up of two forms, L and M.
Each form is in a separate easel book of 175 plates, and each plate contains four
pictures arranged in a multiple-choice format. The pictures are uncluttered, bold, line
drawings, which are easier for the partially blind to perceive. To administer the scale,
the examiner shows a plate and says the corresponding stimulus word. The subject
points to, or otherwise indicates, the picture that best illustrates the meaning of the
stimulus word. Since the plates (with pictures of objects and design) are arranged in
ascending order of difficulty, only the block of items of the difficulty level appropriate
for the individual are administered.

The time for administration and scoring ranges between 10 and 20 minutes, and the
age level covers a range of ages two and one-half to forty years.

The PPVT-R is a good test to use in screening for receptive vocabulary and a good
test to use in a battery of tests. However, this test, as any other IQ test established on
only one ability, should not be used singly to determine a "true IQ." When there is a
specific weakness or strength in receptive vocabulary, the child/adult will have a PPVT
IQ below or above an IQ obtained on a more comprehensive test such as the WISC-R or
the Stanford Binet. Sometimes these scores will be excessively deviant and the diagnostician must be cautious in making specific assumptions about intelligence. Where
the test is used in making comparisons between receptive and expressive vocabulary, it
can be useful in writing individual lesson plans. It also can be used as a very good
screening device in the hands of a capable and trained examiner.

Standardization Information

The norms for the PPVT-R were established from an equating study conducted to
equate the PPVT-R Form L and the PPVT Form A. A total of 1,849 children, aged 3–18
years, were tested. Construct Validity study was made by correlating the PPVT Form A
and PPVT-R Form L with the Short Form Test of Academic Aptitude. Correlations
between the total IQ on the SFTAA and the PPVT-L ranged from .57 to .78. Criterion-

Related Predictive Validity was established between California Achievement Test, Form C and the PPVT-R. The correlations ranged from .51 to .70 for grades 2, 4, 6, 8, and 10. The number of students in each grade ranged between 35 and 46. Both split-half and alternate form reliability were used. Split-half reliability coefficients for ages 2½–18 on Form L ranged between .67 and .88; for Form M, between .61 and .86. For ages 19 to 40 years, the split-half reliability coefficients (on Form L only) ranged between .80 and .83.

Alternate form reliabilities were established by both age and grade. For ages two and one-half to eighteen, average coefficients were between .73 and .91; for grades pre-school through grade 12, average coefficients were shown to be from .64 to .90. In both alternate-form studies, the testing was sequenced from Form L to Form M and then from Form M to Form L.

The test was nationally standardized in 1979 with children and adolescents selected to represent the geographic regions, community sizes, socioeconomic levels, and ethnic groups in the United States. Each person was individually tested. Also in 1979, 800 adults, ages 19–40, were tested. These adults were chosen from all four geographic regions to represent major occupational groups of employed persons in the United States. The norms were linked to the original PPVT by an equating study. The mean is 100 and the S.D. is 15.

Itemized Points.

1. The PPVT-R requires 10–20 minutes to administer and score.
2. It does not require oral responses.
3. It is a quick test to *screen* for giftedness and mental retardation.
4. The PPVT-R is for ages 2½–40 years.
5. The PPVT-R is a test to measure receptive vocabulary.
6. A mental age, IQ score, and percentile rank are provided.

Social-Maturity Scales

The need for measurements involving social competency skills has been widely known since Doll's concern with the diverse abilities seen among the retarded in the Vineland Training in Vineland, New Jersey during the 1940s. His work was inspired by the earlier work of Henry H. Goddard in the days "when the work of Binet, and research with the feeble-minded, were yielding a new orientation and a more profitable approach in the field of human development," (Doll, 1953, p vii). Prior to the time of the Vineland Social Maturity Scale (Doll's Scale), there was no specific assessment tool to help determine whether mentally retarded individuals could adapt to society, either in sheltered workshops or in independent job positions. At this time, Stanley D. Porteus was working independently on a similar work on industrial and social rating scales that eventually became his social-adjustment score card. The score card was completed in association with Lloyd N. Yepsen. Later Porteus, in association with Myra W. Kuenzel, constructed a scale of industrial virtues, which was followed by a work with Dr. Henry A. Cotton and known as a scale for measuring mental deterioration and recovery (Doll, 1953). It was Doll's work, however, that became the most widely known and most used as a social-maturity scale. He used the Binet and Simon model, but he sought to measure accustomed performance in mastered attainment, rather than innate capacity for problem-solving abilities. Concerning his scale, his postulates were that:

—Social competence may be defined as the functional ability of the individual for exercising personal independence and social responsibility.

—An individual's competence may be measured progressively in terms of maturation by sampling its genetic states by means of representative performances at successive life ages.

—Maturation may be taken as a practical measure of the changing organism as a whole.

—Individual status in social competence may be expressed in terms of numerical and descriptive deviation from established maturational norms and evaluated in terms of related variables.

The Vineland Social Maturity Scale (Doll, 1947) has been followed by the Adaptive Behavior Scales (Nihira, Foster, Shellhaas, and Leland, 1969, 1974, 1975, 1981) and published by the American Association on Mental Deficiency, The AAMD Adaptive Behavior Scale Public School Version (Lamberth, Windmiller, Cole, and Figueroa, 1975) and the ABIC, an adaptive scale within a system known as the SOMPA (Mercer, 1979). All of these measures are very important in examining the social skills of those who are found to be functioning in the retarded range of intelligence. Mercer's work has provided a new dimension, since the SOMPA includes more than an adaptive scale. It is a pluralistic system involving both a medical and a social-system model with consideration of different cultures. The Vineland Social Maturity Scale, The Public School Version of the AAMD Behavior Scale, and the ABIC (from the SOMPA) are described as follows. They are presented in order of their occurrence.

Vineland Social Maturity Scale* (VSMS)

Description and Administration Procedure

The Vineland Social Maturity Scale (Doll, 1947) is a scale to measure social competence from birth to adulthood. It includes behaviors, each of which can be identified as being Self-help General (SHG), Self-help Dressing (SHD), Self-help Eating (SHE), Communication (C), Self-direction (SD), Socialization (S), Locomotion (L) or Occupation (O).

Self-Help General (SHG)—Questions involve whether or not the client is capable of sitting, standing, avoiding hazards, or toileting.

Self-Help Dressing (SHD)—Questions involve whether or not an individual is capable of pulling off socks/coat, drying hands, putting on coats, washing face, and dressing self.

Self-Help Eating (SHE)—Questions involve whether the client is capable of drinking without help, using a spoon to eat, discriminating edible foods, or eating independently at the table.

Locomotion (L)—Questions involve whether the individual is mature enough to go about the yard, neighborhood, or town unguided.

Occupation (O)—Questions involving whether an individual is mature enough to participate in gainful employment. Items begin with handling chores in the home to performing skilled work.

---

*The VSMS is under restandardization by American Guidance Services, and will be available in 1982.

Communication (C)—Questions involving information regarding the capability of demonstrating comprehension of instructions, reading, or writing.

Self-Direction (SFD)—Questions involving whether the individual can be trusted with money for minor and major purchases, with going out independently both in the day and in the night, and with making plans for the future.

The scale is more heavily "loaded" at the early stages with behaviors per year. These behaviors "thin out" progressively toward the higher levels. Doll explains this by saying that the infant has a narrow spread of years over which the examination may be considered, and consequently the number of items must be increased in relation to the age interval in order to obtain reliability and representativeness for the measure. Toward the adult level the situation changes as year differences become less meaningful due to the "compression effect" of the ultimate ceiling of maturation.

The administration is that of an interview technique with a parent or someone who cares for the individual on whom the social competency measure is being done. Scores for each function are credited with a plus or a minus and consideration is given to functions where there has been no opportunity and to functions which are in a developmental process at the time of the interview.

Use and Interpretation of the VSMS

After the scale has been completed and a social age has been established, a graph may be drawn, as seen in Figure 32, to show the numbers of the passes and failures. The failures may be marked out and the tasks to be trained may be circled. By this means a criterion position is noted as to what developmental needs are major in the case of each client. The teacher may use this information to plan a curriculum. The graph shown covers ages 2 months to 15 years. For older individuals another graph may be drawn if needed.

Standardization Information

The Vineland Social Maturity Scale, the first major test of its kind, has had four and one-half decades of use. Its original standardization was on 650 white subjects, ten males and ten females at each age level from birth to thirty years of age. The subjects were from the city and environs of Vineland, New Jersey.

The *validity* of the test is principally established by evidence on studies with feeble-minded subjects. For all subjects, an estimation was made from the informant's estimation of the subject's state of social maturity in terms of social competence of persons in general of the same age and sex as the subject. This was the first approach toward establishing validity. The results for the normative subjects showed so little difference between estimated and obtained scores that the data did not seem to warrant statistical treatment. For the feeble-minded subjects, an initial analysis of 250 reexaminations yielded a coefficient of correlation of .85 between obtained and estimated social-age scores, with a median social-age difference of .2 years lower for estimated scores. The average range of deviations was within approximately plus or minus one year of social age. With another sample of 175 subjects, similar results were obtained—$r = .88$, mean difference .2 years lower for estimated social age. Other studies were made by Doll, each of which left no doubt that the test is a valid test.

Reliability was established by test-retest with 250 subjects from the normative standardization population. The test interval was 1.7–1.9 years, and the correlation between first and second social ages was .976. When social quotients between first and

Figure 32. Social Age

Category	(pre)	1	2	3	4	5	6	7	8	9	10	11	12	15
Self-Help General	2 3 5 6 8 9 13 15	23 26	35	41				66						
Self-Help Eating	11	16 20 25 28 30 33	38 39		51		62	67		75				
Self-Help Dressing		21	37	40 42 47 50	52 54		64 65	70	74				86	
Locomotion	12	16	29 32	45	53	61				77				92
Occupation	7	19 22 24	36	43	48	55 57			71 72		80	82	89	
Communication	1 10 17		31 34	44			58		73		78 79 81	84		90 91
Self-Direction							60			76		83	87	93 94 95
Socialization	4 14	27		46 49	56	59		68 69					85 88	

second testings were grouped at 10-point intervals, the r was .57. Evidence on the reliability of reexamination scores was obtained with respect to informants and examiners in a group of 123 feeble-minded subjects. Twelve subjects were reexamined by the same examiner, using the same informants; 68 subjects by the same examiners using different informants; 19 subjects by different examiners using the same informants; and 25 subjects by different examiners using different informants. The informants were adequately familiar with the subjects and the examiners were adequately skilled in the examination procedure. The correlation between social ages for the group as a whole was .92.

Itemized Points.

1. The VSMS is a test to determine how an individual is adapting to society in general.
2. The ages covered for this scale range between one month and adulthood.
3. The test was established principally on studies on the feeble-minded.
4. No mean or standard deviation for the test is provided in the statistical data.
5. The test is under revision by American Guidance Series.
6. This test is the "grandfather" of all adaptive scales.

The AAMD Adaptive Behavior Scale (Public School Version, 1974)

Description and Administration Procedure

The AAMD Adaptive Behavior Scale was standardized on 2,600 school children in the state of California during the 1972–73 school year. The 1975 (Lambert et al.) public-school version differs from the 1974 Revision of the AAMD Adaptive Behavior Scale (Nihira et al., 1974) and from earlier versions, in that items that do not pertain to school and behaviors that cannot necessarily be observed in school have been eliminated.

The purpose of the scale is to aid school personnel in obtaining a measure of a child's adaptive behavior, and secondarily, to suggest those areas of functioning where special recommendations for remediation may be applied. It is made up of two parts, one dealing with developmental skills and the other dealing with measures of maladaptive behavior related to personality and behavior disorders.

The format of the test is as follows:

Part One

I. Independent Functioning
   A. Eating
   B. Toilet Use
   C. Cleanliness
   D. Appearance
   E. Care of Clothing
   F. Dressing and Undressing
   G. Travel
   H. General Independent Functioning

II. Physical Development
   A. Sensory Development
   B. Motor Development

III. Economic Activity
   A. Money Handling and Budgeting
   B. Shopping Skills

IV. Language Development
   A. Expression
   B. Comprehension
   C. Social Language Development

V. Numbers and Time

VI. Domestic Activity (Not included in Public-School Version)
   A. Cleaning
   B. Kitchen Duties
   C. Other Domestic Activities

VII. Vocational Activity

VIII. Self-Direction
   A. Initiative
   B. Perseverance
   C. Leisure Time

IX. Responsibility

X. Socialization

Part Two
   I. Violent and Destructive Behavior

   II. Antisocial Behavior

   III. Rebellious Behavior

   IV. Untrustworthy Behavior

   V. Withdrawal

   VI. Stereotyped Behavior and Odd Mannerisms

   VII. Inappropriate Interpersonal Manners

   VIII. Unacceptable Vocal Habits

   IX. Unacceptable or Eccentric Habits

   X. Self-Abusive Behavior (Deleted from Public School Version)

   XI. Hyperactive Tendencies

   XII. Sexually Aberrant Behavior (Deleted from Public School Version)

   XIII. Psychological Disturbances

   XIV. Use of Medications

Use and Interpretation of the AAMD Adaptive Behavior Scale
To provide an easy means of evaluation, two profiles including all the domains measured in Part One and in Part Two are shown in Figures 33 and 34. By using different colors, more than one profile (on the same individual) taken from different norm

Deciles	Independent Functioning	Physical Development	Economic Activity	Language Development	Numbers and Time	Domestic Activity	Vocational Activity	Self-Direction	Responsibility	Socialization
D9 (90)										
D8 (80)										
D7 (70)										
D6 (60)										
D5 (50)										
D4 (40)										
D3 (30)										
D2 (20)										
D1 (10)										
Scores										

Figure 33. AAMD Adaptive Behavior Scale: Part One

groups may be plotted on one graph. The AAMD has norms on the educable mentally retarded, the trainable mentally retarded, the educable handicapped, and the regular child. Such a graphic portrayal readily shows the group with which the client could best compete. Also the use of the profiles shows the major developmental needs on which individual lesson plans for social training may be made. For example, if the client is compared with EMR group of comparable age and the percentile rank Language Development is at the 65th percentile level, this means that that individual will be able to perform in language skills as well as 65 percent of the children in an EMR classroom.

Standardization Information

For the purposes of sample selection, the school population of the state of California was defined on the basis of six school and demographic variables. These were class placement (Regular, EMR, TMR and EH), sex, population density of residence,

Figure 34. AAMD Adaptive Behavior Scale: Part Two

Name: _____ Examined: _____

Birthdate: _____ Examiner: _____

Profile 2
AAMD Adaptive Behavior Scale: *Part Two*

Deciles	Violent and Destructive Behavior	Antisocial Behavior	Rebellious Behavior	Untrustworthy Behavior	Withdrawal	Stereo. Behavior and Odd Mannerisms	Inappropriate Inter-personal Manners	Unacceptable Vocal Habits	Unacceptable or Eccentric Habits	Self-Abusive Behavior	Hyperactive Tendencies	Sexually Aberrant Behavior	Psych. Disturbances	Use of Medications
D9 (90)														
D8 (80)														
D7 (70)														
D6 (60)														
D5 (50)														
D4 (40)														
D3 (30)														
D2 (20)														
D1 (10)														
Scores														

Figures 33 and 34 were adapted from the profiles in the test booklets.

socioeconomic status (census-tract data on both percent of unemployment and average education level), ethnic status (Black, Spanish, Asian, and White), and age (children enrolled in 2nd, 3rd, 4th, 5th and 6th grade). The master sampling plan listed the required number of subjects from regular, educable mentally retarded, trainable mentally retarded, and educationally handicapped classes from each ethnic group by socioeconomic status and population density, with provisions for sampling equal numbers of boys and girls. A final population of 2,600 subjects resulted.

To determine validity of the domain scores, a comparison was made between class placement (EMR and regular subjects) and domain scores, with controls for ethnic status and sex. On Part One, the only correlations that were not significant were several of those within the 12-3 to 13-2 age group. Regarding this age group, the authors state that they did not know how long the EMR subjects had been in a special-education program and did not know whether the nonsignificance was a reflection of the effect of the program experience. They point out that in evaluating the results of the analyses for Part Two, one must keep in mind that the domains assess the extent of behaviors that are incompatible with school attendance. The only age level at which class placement was not significantly related to the domain scores was again in the age range 12-3 to 13-2. According to their thinking, one can infer from these results that by age 13, or at the end of the elementary-school program, six of eleven Part Two domain scores of EMR pupils are not significantly different from regular-class pupils of the same age.

For Part Two, after analysis of the data, it was decided to produce an additional set of norms by ethnic-status group and an additional set of norms by sex, because of the number of significant relationships between ethnic status and because of the possibility of an ethnic-status and sex interaction.

No reliability studies were made with the public-school version. The authors accepted the reliability data reported in the manual for the 1974 revision. The range of reliability coefficients for Part One domains is from .71 to .93, with a mean reliability coefficient of .86. For Part Two domains, the Manual reports the reliabilities to range from .44 to .77, with a mean reliability of .57.

Itemized Points.

1. The AAMD Adaptive Behavior Scale is a scale to measure a child's ability to adapt to a social system.
2. The Public School Version is designed for ages 7 years, three months to 13 years (The 1969 and 1974 edition cover ages 3 years to adulthood).
3. Norms are established on EMR, TMR, EH, and regular children.
4. Norms are presented as percentiles.
5. The lower the scores in Part One, the more severe are the problems.
6. The higher the scores in Part Two, the more severe are the problems.
7. The AAMD Scales are very helpful in developing individualized programs.

System of Multicultural Pluralistic Assessment (SOMPA) (Mercer, 1979)

The SOMPA (Mercer, 1979) is a system of testing devised to measure adaptive behavior, intelligence, and physical dexterity. In addition, health history and sensory skills are assessed. It is based on three conceptual models: the medical model, the social-system model, and the pluralistic model, each of which is different in characteristics and based on a different set of assumptions.

The Medical Model involves scales that provide information from: Physical Dexterity Tasks, Bender Visual Motor Gestalt Test, Weight by Height, Visual Acuity, Auditory Acuity, and Health History Inventories. The Adaptive Model is described below.

Adaptive Behavior Inventory for Children (ABIC) (Mercer, 1979)

Description and Administration Procedure

The ABIC is an adaptive scale and part of the SOMPA social-system model, the other part of which is the Wechsler Intelligence Scale for Children-Revised. These two measures provide evidence regarding whether the child meets the expectations of the social systems in which he or she is participating. A low cutoff for labeling behavior as deviant is used, i.e., two or more standard deviations below the mean, or the lowest 2.5 percent of the population.

The ABIC measures the child's role performance in the family, peer group, and community. Role performance in nonacademic school activities, earner/consumer activities, and self-maintenance activities are also measured.

The data are obtained through parent interview. The questions are found in the Parent Interview Manual. From the 242 questions, only those questions appropriate for the child's age are asked. Mercer and Lewis (1977) suggest that the interviewer should wear simple clothing, similar to that worn by persons belonging to the social class of the parent. They also warn against wearing badges, pins, or uniforms that signify membership in any political, religious, or social group. Interviewers should be trained by experienced social workers, psychologists, or other professionals who have thoroughly familiarized themselves with the Inventory.

Both English and Spanish versions of the questions are available and the interviewer uses the version preferred by the respondent. The interview is held with the parent or other adult who knows the most about the child's health history and who has the best opportunity to observe the child's activities outside the school.

Interpretation and Use of the ABIC

A profile to interpret the ABIC is available in a stiff paper folder that includes space to record the data from all of the models within the SOMPA system. Most diagnosticians using only the ABIC find it convenient to use this profile form, but use only the spaces provided for the ABIC. When the quantitative data are plotted, it can be seen whether the scores signify that the child falls within the "at risk" range in terms of educational placement. For convenience, the writer has combined positions for all the systems on a *single* profile sheet, as seen in Figure 35. This is suitable for making copies and will take up less space in a folder that must contain more information than the ABIC data. When only the adaptive-behavior scale is to be used, the diagnostician need only fill in the blanks beginning with Adaptive Behavior. If school placement is the purpose of the evaluation, the WISC-R is used and the information derived from the WISC-R and the ABIC may be translated, by following the directions in the Manual, to meaningful scores designated as estimated learning potential, ELP.

Mercer & Lewis point out that in interpreting estimated learning potentials (ELP) several cautions should be borne in mind. The meanings of ELPs and school-functioning levels (SFL) are different. The ELPs signify whether the child will be likely to benefit from an educational program that takes account of the individual's sociocultural background. The SFL (WISC-R IQs) predicts the extent to which a child is likely to succeed in mainstream public school. Mercer also points out that the ELPs reflect the California samples used in the standardization, and that a difference of 15 points between the ELP and SFL indicates that the estimated potential is greater than what the WISC-R IQs signify (Mercer and Lewis, 1978).

Figure 35. Psychometric Data

SOMPA Summary	Scaled Scores	Percentile	At Risk
Physical Dexterity			
Ambulation			
Equilibrium			
Placement			
Fine motor sequencing			
Finger-tongue dexterity			
Involuntary movement			
Average			
Bender visual Gestalt			
Weight by height			

	Visual acuity					
Uncorrected R/L eye	(R) 20/			(L) 20/		
Corrected R/L eye	(R) 20/			(L) 20/		

Auditory acuity	CPS:	250	500	1000	2000	4000		
Uncorrected R/L ear	db							
Corrected R/L ear	db							

	Scores		Percentiles	At Risk
Health-History	DK	Raw		
Prenatal/postnatal				
Trauma				
Disease and illness				
Vision				
Hearing				

Adaptive Behavior	Scaled Scores		
Family			
Community			
Peer relations			
Nonacademic school roles			
Earner/consumer			
Self maintenance			
Average			
School Functioning			
WISC-R verbal IQ			
Performance IQ			
Full scale IQ			
Estimated learning potential			
Verbal			
Performance			
Full scale			
Sociocultural Scales			
Family size			
Family structure			
Socioeconomic status			
Urban acculturation			
Ethnic group_____			

In any profile when the scores are found to be within the "at risk" range, it is self-evident that the child needs help in that behavior measured. A curriculum that includes remediation techniques for the weaknesses shown may be planned. However, in making short-term objectives, one will need to look beyond the general behaviors, such as Family, Community, and others. One will need to examine the questions in the inventory to find the behaviors that determine how a child relates to family or community. For this reason, curriculum planning may be slower when using the SOMPA, but one will find that the test provides a very easy means of determining retardation for placement purposes when using the ABIC.

The standardization of the ABIC is described in the following section within the standardization procedure for the entire system.

Standardization Information

The total system was standardized on 2,085 California public-school children between the ages of five and eleven years. There were three independently selected samples: 700 Blacks, 700 Hispanics, and 700 Whites.

Split-half technique to determine reliability was used for each age level on all physical-dexterity tasks. The coefficients ranged from a low of .61 to a high of .94. The mean coefficients for tasks—Ambulation, Equilibrium, Placement, Fine Motor Sequencing, Finger-Tongue Dexterity and Involuntary Movement—at the different age levels are listed as follows: Age 5, .82; Age 6, .78; Age 7, .79; Age 8, .77; Age 9, .80; Age 11, .72. The correlations between the Physical Dexterity Tasks (PDT) and the Sociocultural Scales were found to be low; however, they were statistically significant. Mercer concluded that sociocultural factors are of minimal significance in accounting for differences in children's performance on the PDT and that the battery meets the sociocultural assumptions of the medical model. She does state, however, that the small but reliable relationships between performance on the PDT and the Sociocultural Scales, especially Socioeconomic Status, warrant further exploration.

Split-half reliability for the Bender Visual-Motor Test revealed a range between .65 and .74 for the total sample. The range was .54 to .70 for the Blacks, .63 to .67 for the Hispanics, and .54 to .72 for Whites. The pattern of raw-score means across ethnic group at each level shows Black children making more errors than Hispanic children, who, in turn, are making more errors than White children.

Although the raw score differences are statistically significant one must be cognizant of the effect different child-rearing practices may have on the development of children. Mercer cites Koppitz (1975), who states that indeed the rate of development in visual motor perception varies among ethnic groups and that this may be influenced by different child-rearing practices. These differences were not considered to be influential enough to keep the Bender out of the medical model. Mercer does warn that when interpreting the Bender scores, persons should be careful not to over-interpret low scores, particularly if the Bender score is the only "At Risk" score in the medical model. In case of questionable situations, Koppitz provides a table that presents the mean scores for each ethnic group. All of the correlations between the Bender and the PDT were found to be significant beyond the .01 level of probability.

Sociocultural correlates of vision and weight by height were found to be very small and were found to fit within the assumptions of the medical model. Correlations of vision and weight by height with the PDT and the Bender were also found to be small but in the hypothesized directions.

There were no significant differences among the three ethnic groups in mean raw scores for 26 of the 45 questions in the Health History Inventories. White mothers were more likely to report operations and hospitalizations for various reasons than either Black or Hispanic mothers. There were some other minor differences; however, it was concluded that the interpretation of the score of a particular child is not greatly influenced by ethnic differences. The inventories are considered to be relatively independent measures, and the child's score on one cannot be generalized to another.

Children who score in the lowest 16 percent in the medical model of the SOMPA are considered to be at risk of organic anomaly; hence, the errors or negative events fit a deficit model that measures pathological signs.

All of the children in the social-system sample were grouped into 21 age categories at four-month intervals, and the mean and standard deviation for each group on each of the six ABIC scales (subscales) were calculated. *Reliability* coefficients for the scaled scores on the ABIC were calculated for each age level, 5–11 years. The reliability coefficients for the ABIC subscales are somewhat lower than for the Average Scaled Scores. For the subscales, the range of split-half reliability coefficients was from .71 to .98. All of the average scaled-score coefficients were .95 and above.

Mercer cites that *construct validity, face validity,* and *content validity* are not directly relevant to this test. The validity of an indirect measure, such as a test, that is being used to predict performance in a social role is determined by its predictive power. In this context, the values and expectations of the members of the social system are taken as "given" and the technical task is to predict those who will succeed and fail in that system. To determine this prediction, correlation between 1967 WISC IQs and Teacher's Grades and Ratings in 1967–68 and 69 for Elementary School children were run. Although she found that such correlations indicate better than chance predictions, it is her opinion that they are no substitute for having the child's teacher participate in the assessment process by contributing additional information on the child's adaptive fit in the classroom.

The final decision was to retain the WISC-R as a measure of School Functioning Level in the social-system model and utilize it as a basis for calculating Estimated Learning Potential in the pluralistic model. She cites seven reasons: (1) The WISC-R used in the social-system model to predict produces statistically significant validity coefficients; (2) the WISC-R is among the most reliable tools available for assessment; (3) the internal validity of the WISC-R is sound; (4) the WISC-R is individually administered and does not depend upon a child's ability to read; (5) both the WISC-R and the WPPSI can be administered to young children who are just beginning their educational careers; (6) the Pluralistic Model uses multiple regression equations to estimate the sociocultural norms for groups for the purpose of making inferences about learning potential. Any test used for this purpose must be highly reliable.

Mercer has been very thorough in explaining every step and procedure of her approach to standardization. According to the reliability coefficients, the social-system model shows greater reliability than the medical model. This system is one of the newest and most innovative approaches to aid in determining whether a child is mentally retarded.

Itemized Points.

1. The SOMPA includes two other tests that have their own standardization—the WISC-R and Bender Visual Motor Gestalt.
2. The ABIC is the adaptive Behavior Scale within the system.
3. The standard deviation for the scales appropriate for such statistics is 15 and the mean is 100.
4. In addition to IQ, the SOMPA shows learning potential involving the student's culture and background.
5. The SOMPA is a good test for placement of the mentally retarded.
6. The SOMPA was standardized on children from the State of California.

Summary

The formal tests discussed in this chapter are introduced by a short review of the history of intelligence testing. This early concern among educators for understanding the individual differences regarding intellectual capacity set the stage for further differentiation of assessment, through the measurement of achievement of the basic skills and through the diagnostic approach to each basic skill.

This chapter describes the two most commonly used individual intelligence tests, the Wechsler Scales and the Stanford Binet. The cognitive processes measured in these tests are identified and the standardization procedures provided by the test authors are briefly reviewed. Since the Stanford Binet has no profile as do the Wechsler Scales, the Sattler model is presented. To help in the analysis, worksheets are provided. These worksheets show how the levels of the individual capacities according to the factors involved may be graphed. Additional information is provided by the identification of the learning components measured by each subtest. The Wechsler subtest measures are identified and standardization data are presented.

Other intelligence tests reviewed are the McCarthy, Slosson, Pictorial Test of Intelligence, Columbia Mental Maturity, Leiter International Performance Scale, and the Peabody Picture Vocabulary Tests.

Three adaptive Scales are discussed in this chapter, the Vineland Social Maturity Scale, the AAMD Adaptive Behavior Scale, and the ABIC. The latter is a part of System of Multicultural Pluralistic Assessment (SOMPA), which is one of the latest scales to be used in the diagnosis of mental retardation. The AAMD is particularly useful in curriculum planning for the mentally retarded.

Student Assignments

1. *For each age level on the Stanford Binet beginning at Year III, examine the abilities (learning components) measured at that level and at two age levels below and two age levels above. Compare the number and kind of abilities measured within this span with the abilities measured on the Wechsler Scales, specifically the WPPSI. Do the abilities of the Stanford Binet III year level measure the same abilities as measured on the Wechsler Scales?*

2. *Using the Sattler Model, devise a graph using hypothetical scores and suggest functions wherein a diagnostician/teacher may further pursue observation or testing to determine whether there are weaknesses or strengths in a child's abilities.*

3. *Examine the Stanford Binet Scale to determine whether it is more verbal or more performance oriented.*

4. *A child, age 9½ years, has WISC-R scaled scores of*

Information	*9*	*Picture Completion*	*9*
Similarities	*10*	*Picture Arrangement*	*5*
Arithmetic	*7*	*Block Design*	*6*
Vocabulary	*8*	*Object Assembly*	*7*
Comprehension	*7*	*Coding*	*5*
Digit Span	*6*	*Mazes*	*5*

Use the analysis sheet and find the categories that indicate weaknesses.

5. *Compare the subtests on the WISC-R and the MSCA and determine whether the two tests measure the same abilities.*

6. *Each student should secure a copy of a manual for any one test described in this chapter and find evidence of the standardization procedure. Share this information with the entire class and compare with information on the same test provided in this chapter.*

7. *Compare the information on the Adaptive Scales with information in the Buros Mental Measurement Yearbook on these adoptive scales. Do reviewers have the same opinions concerning these tests? Discuss this information with other members in the class.*

8. *Examine the descriptions of the AAMD and the SOMPA and defend your choice of either for the purpose of planning a curriculum for a mentally retarded child.*

REFERENCES

Anastasi, A. *Psychological testing,* 3rd ed. New York: Macmillan, 1968.

Arnold, G. F. Review of the Leiter international performance scale. In Buros (ed.) *The fourth mental measurements year book.* Highland Park, N.J.: Gryphon Press, 1953, pp. 448–449.

Bannatyne, A. Diagnosing learning disabilities and writing remedial prescriptions. *Journal of Learning Disabilities,* 1968, *1,* no. 4: 242–249.

Bannatyne, A. Diagnosis: a note on recategorization of the WISC scaled scores. *Journal of Learning Disabilities,* 1974; 7: 272–274.

Bligh, H. F. Concurrent validity on two intelligence measures for young children. In Huddleston, E. M. (Ed.) *The 16th Yearbook of the National Council on Measurements Used in Education.* New York: National Council on Measurements Used in Education, 1959, pp. 56–66.

Bush, W. J., & Mattson, B. D. WISC test patterns and underachievers. *Journal of Learning Disabilities,* 1973, *6,* no. 4: 251–256.

Bush, W. J., & Waugh, K. *Diagnosing Learning Disabilities,* 2nd ed. Columbus, Ohio: Charles E. Merrill Publishing Company, 1976.

Clements, S. C. *Minimal brain dysfunction in children.* Washington, D.C.: Department of Health, Education and Welfare, 1966.

Davis, E. E. Concurrent validity of the McCarthy scales of children's abilities. *Measurement and Evaluation in Guidance,* July 1975, *8:* 101–104.

Doll, E. *The Vineland social maturity scale.* Minneapolis: Educational Test Bureau, 1947.

Dunn, L. M. *Peabody picture vocabulary test manual.* Minneapolis: American Guidance Service, 1965.

Dyer, H. An interview with Dr. Henry S. Dyer. Jeanne Shea, interviewer. New York: J. Walter Thompson, 1962 (record).

Fischman, R., Proger, B. B., & Duffey, J. B. The Stanford Binet revisited: A comparison of the 1960 and 1972 revision of the Stanford Binet intelligence scale. *Journal of Special Education,* Spring 1976, *10,* no. 1: 83–90.

Freeman, F. S. *Theory and practice of psychological testing,* 3rd ed. New York: Holt, Rinehart and Winston, 1962.

French, J. L. *Manual: Pictorial test of intelligence.* Boston: Houghton Mifflin, 1963.

Glasser, A. J., & Zimmerman, I. L. *Clinical interpretation of the Weschler intelligence scale for children.* New York: Grune and Stratton, 1967.

Graham, E. E. Weschler Bellevue and WISC scattergrams of unsuccessful readers. *Journal of Consulting Psychology,* 1972, *16,* no. 4: 268–271.

Guilford, J. P. *The nature of human intelligence.* New York: McGraw-Hill Book Company, 1967.

Guilford, J. P. Three faces of intellect. *The American Psychologist,* 1959, *14:* 469–479.

Himelstein, P. Review of the PTI. *Seventh mental measurement yearbook.* Highland Park, N. J.: Gryphon Press, 1972, pp. 748–749.

Hirschfang, S. Jaramillo, S., & Benton, J. B. Comparisons of scores on the revised Stanford Binet, Columbia mental maturity scale (CMMS), and the Goodenough draw-a-man test of children with neurological disorders. *Psychological Reports,* 1966, *19:* 15–16.

Kaufman, A. Factor structure of the McCarthy scales at five age levels between 2½ and 8½. *Educational and Psychological Measurement,* Autumn 1975, *35:* 641–656.

Kaufman, A. Do normal children have flat profiles? *Psychology in the Schools,* July 1976, *XIII,* no. 3: 284–285.

Kaufman, A. *Intelligence testing with the WISC-R.* New York: John Wiley and Sons, 1979.

Kaufman, A. S., & DiCuio, R. F. Separate factor analyses of the McCarthy scales for groups of black and white children. *Journal of School Psychology,* Spring 1975, *13:* 10–18.

Koppitz, E. *The Bender Gestalt test for young children.* New York: Grune and Stratton, 1975.

Lambert, N., Windmiller, M., Cole, L., & Figueroa, R. *AAMD behavior scale: Public school version.* Berkeley, Calif.: University of California, 1974.

Leiter, R. G. *General instructions for the Leiter international performance scale.* Los Angeles: Western Psychological Services, 1969.

Leiter, R. G. Part II of the manual for the 1948 revision of the Leiter international performance scale, Evidence of the reliability and validity of the Leiter tests. *Psychological Service Center Journal,* 1959, *11:* 1–72.

McCarthy, D. *Manual: McCarthy scale of children's abilities.* New York: Psychological Corporation, 1972.

McCarthy, J. M., & Elkins, J. Psychometric characteristics of children enrolled in the child service demonstration centers: The search for homogenous clusters. Tucson, Ariz.: Leadership Training Institute in Learning, Department of Special Education, University of Arizona (unpublished paper).

McGlannan, F. K. Familial characteristics of genetic dyslexia; Preliminary report from a pilot study. *Journal of Learning Disabilities,* 1968, *1,* no. 3: 185–191.

Meeker, M. N. El Segundo, Calif.: Institute for Applied S.O.I. Studies, 1963, 1973, 1974 (unpublished research).

Meeker, M. N. *Structure of intellect.* Columbus, Ohio: Charles E. Merrill Publishing Company, 1969.

Mercer, J., & Lewis, J. *System of multicultural pluralistic assessment.* New York: Psychological Corporation, 1979.

Milgram, N. A. A note on the Peabody picture vocabulary test in mental retardates. *American Journal of Mental Deficiency,* 1967, *72:* 496–97.

Money, J. (Ed.) *Reading disability: Progress and research needs in dyslexia.* Baltimore: Johns Hopkins Press, 1962.

Newland, T. E. Psychological assessment of exceptional children and youth. In Cruickshank, W. (Ed.) *Psychology of exceptional children.* Englewood Cliffs, N.J.: Prentice-Hall, 1971.

Nihira, K., Foster, R., Shellhaas, M., & Leland, H., *AAMD adaptive behavior scale.* Washington. D.C.: American Association on Mental Deficiency 1969, 1974.

Piers, E. V. Review of the Quick Test. In Buros, O. K. (Ed.), *The sixth mental measurement yearbook*. Highland Park, N.J.: Gryphon Press, 1965, pp. 826–827.

Rappaport, D., Gill, M., & Schaefer, *Diagnostic psychological testing*, Vo. I. Chicago: Yearbook Publishers, 1945.

Rosenbert, L. A., & Stroud, M. Limitations of brief intelligence testing with young children. *Psychological Reports*, 1966, *19*: 721–722.

Salvia, J., & Ysseldyke, J. E., *Assessment in Special and Remedial Education*. Boston: Houghton Mifflin, 1978.

Sattler, J. M. Analysis of functions of the 1960 Stanford Binet intelligence scale, form L-M. *Journal of Clinical Psychology*, 1965, *21*: 173–179.

Sattler, J. *Assessment of children's intelligence*, rev. ed. Philadelphia: W. B. Saunders, 1974.

Slosson, R. L. *Slosson intelligence test (SIT) for children and adults*. New York: Slosson Educational Publications, 1963.

Terman, L. M., & Merrill, M. A. *Measuring intelligence*. Boston: Houghton Mifflin, 1937.

Terman, L. M., & Merrill, M. A. *Stanford-Binet intelligence scale, Form L-M*. Boston: Houghton Mifflin, 1960.

Tucker, J. *The structure of intellect analysis*. Austin, Texas: Foxx Printing Company, 1972.

Valett, R. W. A clinical profile for the Stanford Binet. *Journal of School Psychology*, 1964, *2*: 49–54.

Wechsler, D. *Measure of adult intelligence*. Baltimore: Williams and Wilkins, 1939.

Wechsler, D. *Manual for the Wechsler intelligence scale for children*. New York: Psychological Corporation, 1949.

Wechsler, D. *The measure and appraisal of adult intelligence*, 4th ed. Baltimore: Williams and Wilkins, 1958.

Wechsler, D. *Manual for the Wechsler adult intelligence scale*. New York: Psychological Corporation, 1959.

Wechsler, D. *Manual for the Wechsler preprimary scale of intelligence*. New York: Psychological Corporation, 1967.

Wechsler, D. *Manual for the Wechsler intelligence scale for children, revised*. New York: Psychological Corporation, 1974.

Wiebe, R. Unpublished work sheet on the WISC-R, Denton, Texas: Texas Woman's University, 1979.

Wiebe, R. Unpublished work sheet analysis on the McCarthy scales of children's abilities. Denton, Texas: Texas Woman's University, 1980.

Wiebe, R. & Watkins, E. Factor analysis of the McCarthy scales of children's abilities on preschool children. *Journal of School Psychology*, 1980, *18*, no. 2.

Chapter 7

Achievement, Language, and Learning-Ability Tests

When the study of this chapter has been completed, one should have the following:
1. *Knowledge of commonly used achievement tests*
2. *Knowledge of the reliability and validity of the achievement tests described*
3. *Knowledge concerning the difference between achievement and diagnostic instruments*
4. *Knowledge of the commonly used language and learning ability tests*
5. *Knowledge of the reliability and validity of the language and learning ability tests described*
6. *Knowledge of the functions to assess when diagnosing basic skills*

Introduction

Achievement and language and learning-ability tests, in addition to intelligence tests, are used in assessing the performance of individuals. An assessment battery generally includes several categories of tests, of which intelligence and achievement comprise the basic instruments used; additional measurements employed, particularly in public schools, are language and/or learning-ability tests. Whereas intelligence tests measure potential for learning, achievement tests measure *what has been learned.* Language tests measure various functions of language development; in contrast, learning-ability tests are more like aptitude and/or intelligence tests, in that they measure the specifics of an individual's learning potential. This chapter is concerned with commonly used achievement, diagnostic, language, and learning-ability instruments.

Achievement Tests

Achievement tests may be either norm-referenced or criterion-referenced and designed for individual or group administration. Individually administered tests are generally preferred for children/youth who are having difficulty in learning. Group achievement tests are preferred when large numbers of students are to be assessed for purposes of determining gains made in a classroom during a specific period of time. Achievement tests may measure more than one basic skill. As a general rule, the skills measured are reading, spelling, and arithmetic. An achievement test, when used as a diagnostic tool, will usually measure only one basic skill and its related components. For example, a reading test may measure reading recognition, reading comprehension, reading fluency, and sound discrimination. In each skill measured, there may be subclassifications that influence the development of that basic skill.

For initial screening, a short individually administered Achievement Test such as the Wide Range Achievement Test (WRAT) or the Peabody Individual Achievement Test (PIAT) is usually employed. Such tests evaluate the general level of achievement in reading, arithmetic, and spelling and the results may suggest additional steps in the evaluation of the person.

The test design requires a particular approach to measuring the achievement level in each of these skill areas. Since a skill such as reading involves many components, not all will be measured by a single test. Also, the format may be more oral than written, and, if a person has a problem in demonstrating knowledge in a particular way, may signify a lower competency than is actually the case. For example, spelling is generally measured by writing words from memory, as is the case with the WRAT. However, the PIAT uses a multiple-choice format. The visual stimulus is made up of four choices, three of which are incorrect. The student is required to choose the word presented as correct. For many youngsters, either of these test designs will provide valid results. However, among some learning-disabled children and youth, learning problems exist that could cause an individual to fail to integrate the motor skills of recall without visual cues; thus, the person might not remember how to write a known word. An individual might be able to spell the word orally, also, and would be penalized if the only response allowed were a written one.

The prevailing practice has been to use only one achievement test, but intelligent use of achievement measures suggests the necessity of providing more than one method of presentation and/or response. In recognition of this, many diagnosticians often administer both the WRAT and the PIAT spelling and math tests. Harmer and Williams in their 1978 research attest to the wisdom of such dual use in the assessment of math. They found that the two math portions of the WRAT and PIAT at grade 4 up to grade 12 show discrepant grade levels on the same individuals. Whereas the arithmetic section of the WRAT presents most problems in a form calling for little or no reading ability, the PIAT makes extensive use of work problems.

Examples of the arithmetic format of the WRAT include problems similar to

$$
\begin{array}{cccc}
85 & 6.52 & 33 & 12\% \text{ of } 125 = \\
-25 & \times\ .12 & 125 & \\
& & +\ 64 & \sqrt{53361}
\end{array}
$$

Examples of the PIAT include problems similar to the following:

What would be the effect on the
product of dropping the zero from
the multiplier in this statement?

$$
\begin{array}{r}
16371 \\
\times\ \ 760 \\
\hline
\end{array}
$$

1. The product would be one-tenth as great.
2. The product would be one one-hundredth as great.
3. The product would be ten times as great.
4. The product would be the same.

Six boys earned $96.00 altogether. They divided the money equally among themselves. How much was each boy's share?

1. $11.00
2. $9.60
3. $16.00
4. $12.00

The difference in test format, testing procedures, method of scoring, and test content for various age groups may pose problems for children/youth who have specific perceptual or other learning problems.

Another related problem is seen in the work of Jenkins and Pany (1978), who found that there may be curriculum bias in standardized reading-achievement tests; i.e., some achievement tests may not measure the reading content that was taught in some schools. Examiners must be aware of this possibility, and when extreme scores exist in their assessment of achievement, they must look into the specific curriculum programs to determine prior experiences of the child involved. It may be that local school systems will have to develop some form of criterion-referenced or curriculum-based assessment tools to use as substantiating evidence when there are reasonable doubts.

It should also be recognized that no one test is infallible in providing exact levels. Many variables may be influencing the success or failure of student responses to reading and/or other basic subjects. The examiner must examine the content and design of the test and should consider means of presentation and responses when in the process of making educational decisions. Screening for diagnostic purposes and frustration levels should be the purpose, along with determining present level of achievement. Most earned-achievement grade levels are not mastery levels, since the norms are determined by the mean score of the students at that grade level. Therefore, for many students the grade level indicated by the test may represent a frustration level instead of a mastery level. Remediation must not be limited to the grade level indicated by the test and above because (1) learning skills such as reading, arithmetic, and spelling involve many components; (2) tests have an error of measurement; and (3) some prerequisites to mastery at that level may not have been learned. The skilled clinician will recognize that the individual will need assistance at the grade level and also below indicated grade level with some components of the skill.

A norm-referenced achievement test may not provide the information needed to plan remediation. It may show weakness but not identify the skill or cognitive deficiency. For example, failure to solve a problem in division correctly may not be from a failure to understand the division process. If the problem had a zero in the dividend, the failure to solve the problem correctly may have resulted from a deficiency in certain subtraction skills. Likewise, failure to spell a word correctly may result from a number of difficulties, ranging from some auditory problems to failure to know and/or apply certain spelling rules. In order to plan for instruction, one must have information regarding skill and knowledge deficiencies. Diagnostic tests are designed to provide this information. There is a need for both norm-referenced achievement tests and specifically designed diagnostic tests. One gives us achievement level information, the other, when correctly used, helps us to know more specifically what to do in our reteaching.

Specific Achievement Tests

Peabody Individual Achievement Test (1970)

Description and Administration Procedure
The Peabody Individual Achievement Test (PIAT) by Lloyd M. Dunn and Frederick C. Markwardt is an individually administered test designed for individuals from kindergarten through grade 12, ages 5-3 through 18-3. The test provides six scores: mathematics, reading recognition, reading comprehension, spelling, general information, and total. It is an untimed test, although it is suggested that generally after about 30 seconds on a mathematics item and 15 seconds on the other subtest items, the client should be encouraged to make a choice or give an answer (Dunn and Markwardt, 1970, p. 1). Using these directions, the time for administration is 30–40 minutes.

The Mathematics, Reading Comprehension, and Spelling subtests have four-option multiple-choice pictorial format. The Reading Recognition subtest requires oral-reading responses and the General Information subtest has an open-ended format. The PIAT utilizes a basal and ceiling format. Five consecutive correct items establish the basal level; the ceiling is established when a subject misses five out of seven consecutive items.

Standardization Information
The PIAT included 2,889 subjects in the norming. There were more than 200 included at each grade level except kindergarten, which included 159. The distribution at each grade level was essentially equally divided by sex. Females represented 51.5 percent of the sample. The population matches the 1969 U.S. Census population very adequately and the students involved would be considered to be enrolled in the mainstream of education, namely, attending regular classrooms of the public school.

The reliability of the PIAT was originally determined by readministering the test to samples of 50–75 students at each of the following grade levels: kindergarten, first, third, fifth, eighth, and twelfth grades. The retesting was done approximately one month after the first administration for each subject. The split-half reliability technique was rejected, to avoid the possibility of spuriously high estimates of reliability. This is likely when items have been carefully ordered in difficulty and utilized for basal and ceiling procedures, as is the case with the PIAT.

Pearson product-moment correlations were calculated for each subtest and for the total score. The greatest confidence can be placed in the stability of the reading recognition and total scores. The median coefficient for each of these was found to be .89. Lesser confidence can be placed in mathematics (.74), general information (.76), spelling (.65) and reading comprehension (.64). Since these are the median coefficients, one-half will be higher at some grade levels. They range from a low of .42 in spelling at the kindergarten level, to a high of .94 for reading recognition at the third-grade level. The median reliability at grade levels 1–12 was very consistent, varying from .77 at third grade to .80 at first-, fifth-, and eighth-grade levels.

The authors emphasize the use of the standard-error-of-measurement scores for the subtests and total. These prevent the test user from putting an undue level of confidence in the differences among the various subtests for students. The standard errors of measurement have a range of 2–7 on the various subtests at the various grade levels to a range of 7–16 for the total score. Of significance to users of the test with younger children is the fact that the standard error is smaller at the younger age levels.

The authors attempted to establish content validity by reviewing an extensive test of curriculum materials and then minimizing bias toward any one curriculum. The final items for each subtest, 84 for each subtest except reading comprehension which has 64, were drawn from about 300 items originally developed for the subtest. They report they used item-discrimination and difficulty indices in this selection process. Internal consistency was built in by selecting items that correlated most highly with the total score on that subtest. The subtests were designed to provide a wide-range, quick-screening test rather than to sample critical skills and knowledge at each level.

To determine concurrent validity, the PIAT was correlated with the Peabody Picture Vocabulary Test (PPVT), form A. The overall median correlation was .57 (p. 50). They varied by grade level from a .42 at kindergarten to .69 at the third-grade level, and by subtest from a median of .40 for spelling to .68 for general information.

Several studies report on correlations with the Wide Range Achievement Test as well as other tests. Sitlington's (1970) subjects were 46 educable mentally retarded adolescents achieving at the third-grade level. In general, the PIAT subtests correlated more highly with their WRAT counterparts than with any of the other measures: PIAT mathematics vs. WRAT arithmetic .58; PIAT reading recognition vs. WRAT reading .95; PIAT spelling vs. WRAT spelling .85; (Dunn and Markwardt, 1970, p. 51)

Soethe studied the concurrent validity of PIAT with WRAT and WISC for a small sample of normal, reading-disabled, and mentally retarded children ranging in age from 7-9 to 16-1, with a mean age of 11 years, 3 months. The correlation of PIAT reading subtests and WRAT reading yielded high correlation, even though the tasks on the tests are dissimilar. These were highest for normal individuals and lowest for MR students, with totals being .89 for the PIAT reading recognition, and .84 PIAT reading comprehension and WRAT reading. Moderate correlations were found between PIAT and WRAT math and spelling subtests. As with reading, the highest correlations were with normal children. The correlation between WISC information and PIAT general information was almost nonexistent (.02).

The above studies, as well as others (Wetter and French, 1973; Baum, 1975), show that regardless of the type of population studied (mentally retarded children or adolescents, normal, reading-disabled, learning-disabled), the lowest relationships between the PIAT and the WRAT were in arithmetic and spelling and the highest in reading.

Interpretation and Use

The PIAT was normed primarily on an Anglo population with only 4.3 percent of the standardization sample comprising minority children. There is always a question regarding the validity of test norms applied to a population not representative of the test group. It has been found that the PIAT is as applicable to Mexican-American children as to their Anglo counterparts (Dean, 1977). Comparable verification has not been reported for Blacks as of this time.

The first 18 items of the Reading Recognition subtest count as the first 18 items of the Reading Comprehension Test. This necessitates some caution in interpreting the

Reading Comprehension scores with subjects functioning at the lower grade levels. Their Reading Comprehension score may be measuring more word recognition than comprehension. As further evidence of this, one must note that the PIAT Reading Comprehension has a rather high correlation with the WRAT Reading subtest (.77) (Baum, 1975). The WRAT Reading subtest is a measure of word recognition.

There is a significant common factor responsible for the PIAT Reading Recognition and Reading Comprehension scores and the WRAT Spelling subtest score, since the correlations between these are .81 and .77, respectively. The common factor represented by the achievement in these two areas is 66 percent and 59 percent, respectively. It is imperative, therefore, that the tests be limited to screening and not be used for diagnostic purposes.

The standard error of measurement should be used with all tests to make a more valid interpretation. Dunn and Markwardt (1970) offer the following advice on selection of the appropriate standard error of measurement when the subject is achieving well above grade placement or age mates. They advise that one pick those that correspond most clearly to the actual achievement level of the subject rather than his grade placement or age. For a 12-year-old subject placed in the sixth grade but achieving at the third-grade level, use the grade-3 standard error of measurement. One must remember that the standard-error-of-measurement values are based on raw scores, and not on the derived scores. One must apply the standard error to the raw score and then read the equivalent derived score.

The authors have provided a rough guide for determining quickly whether there is a significant difference between subtests. They indicate that if there is a difference between subtest scores at the K-1 level of 8 or more points; grades 2 and 3 of 13 or more points; and grades 4–12 of 15 or more points, one can be certain 95 times out of 100 that there is a true difference. This is intended to be a rough guide; and should be used as such. Since the raw-score means and the standard deviations are not the same from subtest to subtest, this approach is subject to some error. A more valid interpretation of significant differences can be made between subtests and the total test score. Using "t" test with median standard errors of measurement across grade levels, Silverstein (1981) suggests the following differences are required for significance at the .05 level when comparing each PIAT subtest score with the mean of all subtest scores.

Math	13.44
Reading Recognition	10.13
Reading Comprehension	15.25
Spelling	15.05
General Information	13.05

For .01 level of confidence, the differences in the subtest score and the total score increase approximately 4.5 points, except for Reading Recognition, which is 3.19.

One must not lose sight of the fact that the PIAT is most appropriately used as a screening instrument. The use of the significance of the difference between scores applies to the subtest scores and tells one if there is a real difference in the abilities of the student, as measured by the various subtests. It is not to be used to determine conclusively the true grade level of the student.

The high correlation between the WRAT and PIAT suggests that they are measuring much the same thing and, therefore, either one can be used. In certain cases, one may find the use of the General Information score at all levels and the breakdown of the reading scores at the upper levels found on the PIAT to be of some advantage over the WRAT. There is probably little value in administering both the reading comprehension and reading recognition at the lower levels, since both subtests tend to be measuring recognition. Burns (1975) emphasizes that the reading comprehension test is not appropriate to indicate reading comprehension for primary level EMRs, and, further, that in many instances percentile and normalized standard scores did not extend low enough for appropriate measurement.

Itemized Facts.

1. The PIAT is an individually administered test that measures mathematics, reading, spelling, and general information for students in grades kindergarten through 12.
2. The standard error of measurement, varying from 2 to 7 points, is smaller for younger age levels.
3. The highest correlations of PIAT and WRAT scores are with normal children and in Reading and Spelling.
4. The PIAT norms can be used with confidence with Mexican-American children.
5. The PIAT Reading Comprehension score for the lower grade levels is heavily loaded with Word Recognition.
6. The PIAT is a screening test and not a diagnostic test.
7. To find a significant difference between scores, one must first apply the standard error of measurement to the raw score, and then apply it to the derived scores.

Wide Range Achievement Test (1936, 1946, 1965, 1976, 1978)

Discussion and Administration Procedure
The Wide Range Achievement Test (WRAT) developed by Jastak (1937, 1946) and Jastak and Jastak (1965,1976,1978) is a widely used screening test for spelling, arithmetic, and reading. The reading test is a word-recognition test and the arithmetic test is one of computation. It is individually administered and as a norm-referenced test has been used for screening pupils for special-class placements and for academic assessment.

The WRAT consists of two levels. Level I is designed for students 5–11 years of age and Level II for those 12 years and older. The three subtests take 20–30 minutes to administer. The test blank contains both Levels I and II.

Three kinds of scores are available: grade ratings, percentiles, and standard scores (comparable to the IQ of standard IQ tests). The grade equivalents for the raw scores are printed on the test form for each subtest.

The spelling test includes copying marks, writing one's name, and writing words pronounced by the examiner. In cases of severe impairment, the time limit of 15 seconds per word may be extended and the subject may spell the words orally. The spelling section can be administered to a group of not more than five individuals.

The Reading test is administered individually. This is a word-recognition test in which the student pronounces the words aloud to the examiner. There is a 10-second time limit and the ceiling is 12 consecutive failures.

The Arithmetic test is composed of an oral part and a written part. The oral part is always administered individually, but the written part may be administered in groups of up to five individuals.

Standardization Information

The 1978 WRAT was normed on children and adults in seven states. No attempt was made to obtain a representative national sample. However, all ethnic groups were included and in the proportion in which they were represented in the population at large. All cases used in the norms were administered ability tests and selected so as to represent appropriate proportions of average, superior, and inferior abilities.

The norm groups for each age level for each subtest are composed of 50 percent males and 50 percent females. The number for each of these groups ranges from 400 to 600, with only two age groups in each of the subtests in Levels I and II having 400. All age-level norms for the subtests above 7 years of age included 600 subjects in the norming population.

Split-half coefficients of correlation range between .94 and .98 for both Level I and Level II. The coefficients of correlation between Level I and II, when administered to children 9–14 years at the same sitting, range from .88 to .94 for reading and spelling and from .79 to .89 for arithmetic (Jastak and Jastak, 1978, p. 46)

Since the WRAT does not have alternate forms, a clinician must know what to expect if the test is repeated within a short interval of time. The WRAT was administered to 106 children who were attending special-education classes for emotionally disturbed or slow-learning children in a large metropolitan school system. Sixty-three of these were administered the WRAT Level I 2 weeks apart, and 43 were administered the test in the spring and again 22 weeks later, with the summer months intervening. The test-retest reliability coefficients for all subtests were highly significant at both the 2-week and the 22-week interval. (Woodward, Santa-Barbara, and Roberts, 1975). They ranged from .87 for arithmetic with the 22-week interval, to .98 for reading with the 2-week interval. The scores from the reading test rose after the 22-week interval, when little formal education had taken place, but was negligible after the two-week interval. This supported Delong's study reported by Jastak and Jastak (1978), in which 73 of 77 subjects were found to vary less than 10 percent from one WRAT administration to another.

Other data suggest that the test can be administered to students within a relatively short period of time and still maintain consistency. If both are given on the same day, one can expect the second administration to produce results 4–6 standard score points higher than on the first administration. After a 3-month interval, the differences in results are minimal or nonexistent, except as the age factor affects the results.

Internal consistency is one measure used to validate tests. The intercorrelations of the WRAT subtests Level I range from .691 to .938; for Level II the range was .646 to .928. The highest intercorrelations were between Reading and Spelling, lowest between Reading and Arithmetic.

The WRAT shows a high correlation with other achievement tests. McCoy found a coefficient of .74 with the Woody-Sangren Silent Reading Test and .80 with the New Stanford Reading Test (Wagner and McCoy, 1962). The Stanford Achievement Test (1973) was used as a criterion of achievement in comparing the WRAT with neurologically impaired and emotionally handicapped children. The correlations were highly significant as they reached a correlation level of .80. These ranged from .66 for 13-year-olds to .90 for 8-year-olds (Williamson, 1979).

In other studies, the WRAT was compared to the Stanford Achievement Test and the Metropolitan Test. The correlations of WRAT Reading to Stanford Reading and WRAT Arithmetic to Stanford Arithmetic were consistently in the .70s and .80s through grade

9. They were slightly less on the Metropolitan for grades 10–12 (Jastak and Jastak, 1978).

Content validity of the test can be questioned, since, for example, the generic term *reading* is more than word recognition and the generic term *arithmetic* is more than computation; yet, these are the specific behaviors measured in these two subtests. In the same vein, spelling on the WRAT measures only the written ability to spell. If the clinician makes note of what the tests really measure, there should be no problem involved in using the test to make decisions concerning these specific behaviors of the basic skill.

Interpretation and Use

The WRAT was initially designed to satisfy the clinical requirement of a test to differentiate between mastery of codes and mastery of thought (Jastak and Jastak, 1978). Their rationale was that tests that measure cognitive functions are unsatisfactory tools for diagnosing specific learning or coding disabilities. They believe learning disabilities exist mainly in the area of coding skills. To the extent that this is true, one can use the WRAT to compare the level of coding skills to intelligence, and see if the possibility of a learning disability exists. However, some people question the assumption of Jastak and Jastak and emphasize that this assumption is based on limited research.

Some research has shown that the WRAT overestimates grade-level equivalents (Williamson, 1979). The mean-score difference overestimation for boys was 6.4 months and 9.4 for girls, when compared to the Stanford Achievement Test. The range was 4.0 months for 8-year-olds, to 9.0 months for 13-year-olds. Since the WRAT was administered by teachers, it suggests that the test administrator was placed in a supportive role that may have affected the scores. One must be alert to overestimation when a teacher administers the test. One must remember that a test may have a high correlation with a validity criterion and yet agree poorly in some aspects. Such is the case with a validation study of the WRAT and instructional placement in two basal reading series. The WRAT Reading correlated at .86 and .90 with Harper and Row and Macmillan reading series (Bradley, 1976). Yet the WRAT yielded inflated scores, according to these measures. The WRAT Reading would have resulted in overplacement of 94 percent of the students in the Harper and Row Basal Reading Series. The WRAT Reading yielded scores that overplaced 96 percent of the students by from one to seven reading levels in the Macmillan Reading Program. Forty-five percent of these were by three or more reading levels (Bradley, 1976). This suggests that one must be careful of any test when used for placement in a basal program. Moreover, the WRAT cannot be used to place students in the Harper and Row and Macmillan Reading Series, and in all likelihood in other series. Also, grade placement norms represent the mean scores of students in the normative sample. The test maker does not provide data that say any of the students at a grade level can read a particular reading book. For placement in a reading series, the WRAT should be supplemented by other tests and classroom observation.

It appears that although the WRAT and PIAT are both used for screening, their scores are not necessarily interchangeable, and this is particularly true of arithmetic. One study (Harmer and Williams, 1978) found that of 62 children given the spelling tests, the mean scores for the first four grades varied a maximum of one month, and grades 5–11 varied from 2 to 6 months. In reading they varied a maximum of 3 months through grade 7 and 1–8 months in grades 8–11. The arithmetic scores were consistent through grade 3 with no more than one month's difference. Beginning with grade

4, they varied from 1 year, 2 months to 4 years, 4 months. PIAT yielded the higher scores from grades 4 up. One must note that the sample in each grade level was small, but, whereas the scores were very similar in reading and spelling, there were significant differences for these same students in arithmetic, beginning with grade 4 (Harmer and Williams, 1978). The same data are reflected whether the samples represent mildly or severely learning-disabled children (Scull and Brand, 1980), (Stoneburner and Brown, 1979). The WRAT tests computational skills, whereas the PIAT emphasizes problem solving and general conceptual development. It has been hypothesized that the WRAT with emphasis on computation may not only be testing an area where students are weakest, but, since the format is similar to the drill-type work that students have had, their past experiences of failure with this format elicit inappropriate behavior. (Scull and Brand, 1980).

If it is necessary to administer the WRAT a second time to a subject, one can expect a slight increase in scores. The estimated pure test-retest variability for a 2-week period is as follows: Reading 2.01, Spelling 1.68, and Arithmetic 1.42 raw-score units. (Woodward, Santa-Barbara, and Roberts, 1975).

Although generally it is not necessary or desirable to give both the WRAT and PIAT, it may be desirable to give the arithmetic subtests, since they are measuring something different. The WRAT is tapping skills that are more subject to learning disabilities; the PIAT measures quantitative concepts rather than coding skills.

Itemized Facts.

1. The WRAT is an individually administered test that measures word recognition, arithmetic computation, and written spelling.
2. The test can be administered within 30 minutes.
3. The norms for each subtest at each age level are composed of an equal number of males and females.
4. The WRAT subtests can be safely readministered at 3-month intervals.
5. The WRAT shows a high correlation with other achievement tests, yet overestimates grade-level equivalents.
6. The WRAT is not a satisfactory instrument to use in placing students in a basal reading series.
7. The WRAT and PIAT subtest scores are similar in spelling, reading, and (through third grade) in arithmetic. After that, PIAT scores are 1.2–4.4 years higher than WRAT scores.

The Stanford Achievement Test (1973 edition)

Description and Administration Procedures
The 1973 edition of the Stanford Achievement Test (SAT) by Madden, Gardner, Ruddman, Karlson, and Merwin measures school achievement from grade level 1.5 to 9.5. The complete battery contains six levels, with a total testing time ranging from 190 minutes for Primary I to 320 minutes for both Intermediate Levels I and II. The content of the tests is indicated below.

Primary I. Grades 1.5–2.4; 12 or 13 scores: vocabulary, reading (3 scores), word-study skills, mathematics computation and applications, listening comprehension, spelling (optional), total auditory, total reading, total mathematics, total; 190 minutes in eight sessions.

Primary II. Grades 2.5–3.4; 16 scores: vocabulary, reading (3 scores), word-study skills, mathematics concepts, mathematics computation, mathematics applications, spelling, social science, science, listening comprehension, total auditory, total reading, total mathematics, total; 260 minutes in eight sessions.

Primary III. Grades 3.5–4.4. 15 scores: vocabulary, reading comprehension, word-study skills, mathematics concepts, mathematics computations, mathematics applications, spelling, language, social science, science, listening comprehension, total auditory, total reading, total mathematics, total; 295 minutes in eleven sessions.

Intermediate I. Grades 4.5–5.4. 15 scores: vocabulary, reading comprehension, word-study skills, mathematics concepts, mathematics computation, mathematics applications, spelling, language, social science, science, listening comprehension, total auditory, total reading, total mathematics, total; 320 minutes in eleven sessions.

Intermediate II. Grades 5.5–6.9. 15 scores: vocabulary, reading comprehension, word-study skills, mathematics concepts, mathematics computation, mathematics applications, spelling, language, social science, science, listening comprehension, total auditory, total reading, total; 320 minutes in eleven sessions.

Advanced. Grades 7.0–9.5., 12 scores: vocabulary, reading comprehension, word-study skills, mathematics concepts, mathematics computation, mathematics applications, spelling, language, social science, science, total reading, total mathematics, total; 260 minutes in nine sessions.

The Test of Academic Skills (TASK 1972) is the upper end of the SAT. It includes tests in Reading, English, and Mathematics and is designed for grades 8–13. Also, the Stanford Early School Achievement Test (SESAT 1969–70) is for grades K–1.8. With these two tests, one is provided an articulated series of tests from kindergarten through the 13th grade level.

The Stanford is a norm-referenced test and, also, a criterion-referenced test. The individual items test achievement of various specific objectives of learning. A correct response indicates some minimum level of the ability, with reference to what that item measures.

The SAT provides the students with practice tests to familiarize them with the procedures they will use in each test. Pictorial materials are used extensively at Primary I and II levels to minimize reading. Also, where reading ability may be measured rather than the content desired, the examiner reads the materials to the students.

Standardization Information

For the Primary through Advanced Levels, over 275,000 pupils, stratified on a variety of variables, were selected from 109 school systems in 43 states for the three standardization programs used. The TASK battery norms were based on an October testing of 46,961 students in grades 8–13 drawn from 29 states.

The SAT standardization provides norms from the May testing to reflect end-of-year performance, and the October testing to reflect the beginning-of-year performance. For Primary Levels I and II, there was a February testing so the norms could reflect mid-year performance. Since there is more rapid growth in achievement in grades 1 and 2, this standardization procedure for valid mid-year norms was decided upon instead of extrapolating from the October-May norms.

To provide opportunities for expectancy levels, the Otis-Lennon Mental Ability Test (OLMAT) was administered to the standardization sample. This provided a standard norm group for each grade level, with a normal IQ distribution and a mean OLMAT deviation IQ, in which the mean is 100 and the standard deviation is 16.

The reliability coefficients are expressed as split-half estimates, based on odd-even scores corrected by the Spearman-Brown formula and Kuder-Richardson Formula 20 estimates. The standard error of measurement scores are also presented in the manual.

The coefficients using the Spearman-Brown formula ranged between .85 and .96. For SESAT, the reliability coefficients ranged from .76 to .85. All of the reliability coefficients reported for TASK are above .92.

The coefficients based on the Kuder-Richardson Formula 20 for the SAT range between .85 and .95. Of 668 coefficients reported, only 30 fell below .80 and all of these were in Primary I and II Level tests. These are found in the Mathematics Concepts and Listening Comprehension test of Primary I and the Social Science, Science, Vocabulary, and Mathematics Application tests of Primary II. The standard error of measurement for all tests ranges from 2.6 to 4.0.

To make certain that the test content would be valid in the sense of being in harmony with the present-day instructional objectives of what is being taught in the schools, a thorough analysis of the most widely used series of textbooks in the subject areas was made. All items recommended for inclusion in the book were prepared by curriculum specialists. Following this procedure, the items were edited by five groups of individuals, including a minority group who reviewed the items to determine the appropriateness of the content for special cultural backgrounds. Construct validity was established through examining characteristics such as (1) decreasing difficulty of items with school-grade progress, (2) correlation with prior editions of the Stanford Achievement Test and other achievement tests, (3) lack of, or low correlation with, variables known to have little or no relationship to achievement in particular areas, and (4) internal-consistency indices of items.

The SAT authors made a special effort not to produce a biased instrument. The normed group approximates the proportion of Blacks and Hispanics in the national population. Minority persons were employed as item writers, artists, content advisors, and reviewers. Therefore, no item was included that had not been reviewed by a minority group, nor was any art work included that showed cultural, racial, or sex bias. Of particular interest to those working with the deaf and blind is that the SAT had been adapted and/or normed for each of these handicapping conditions.

Interpretation and Use

An achievement battery is an important yardstick by which instructional efforts are measured. The SAT does this very well and is one of the most respected of achievement batteries. To understand a test and how to use it adequately, one must rely on an understanding of the various subtests, information provided by the publishers of that battery, and research and empirical evidence from its use. The publishers of the SAT have published a number of guides and technical reports. Users are given concrete suggestions, not only on how to interpret a particular score, but also information on the type of remedial instruction that appears to be warranted.

The tests yield four types of scores: grade equivalents (except for TASK), percentile ranks, stanine, and scaled scores. The scale scores permit one to convert all raw scores to a common scale so that measures of student growth can be made across the battery. Scores are comparable from grade to grade, battery to battery, and form to form. The stanine analysis of pupils in class allows for analyzing and interpreting pupil perform- ance. One can (1) compare pupils with others at the same grade level; (2) identify class strengths and weaknesses; (3) identify pupils who might need additional instruction; and (4) use it for grouping individuals (Lehman, 1975).

The following points regarding the subtests are relevant to interpretation and use of the battery.

1. The vocabulary items, except in SAT Advanced Level and in the TASK, are dictated by the examiner; the student selects the word that best completes a sentence. This measures verbal development independent of reading ability.
2. The vocabulary words are 50 percent subject-content words (found in school subjects) and 50 percent general-vocabulary words. An analysis of the vocabulary can help determine if subject-content-vocabulary deficiency may be contributing to subject difficulties.
3. Phonics is deemphasized in the SAT Reading, but the Word Study Skills Test in Primary II and above has a section to study phonics.
4. The Social Science and Science Tests emphasize process of learning and investiga- tion rather than facts. At Primary I and II Levels, pictures rather than words are used to minimize the effect of reading ability. When reading is involved, the material is read to the examinees.
5. The Mathematics Tests stress meaning and understanding rather than skill with numerical operations.
6. Listening Comprehension was added to this edition. It attempts to measure the ability to comprehend spoken communication. The examiner reads a selection and then the student answers questions about it. There may be some question about whether too much reliance is placed on memory, especially at the lower levels (Lehman, 1975). The total auditory score is an important score to use in ascertaining difficulties in school and lack of school success.

Itemized Facts.

1. The Stanford Achievement Test is both a norm-referenced and a criterion- referenced test.
2. The SAT measures achievement in grade levels 1.5–9.5.
3. The SESAT, SAT, and TASK provide an articulated series of tests from kindergarten through 13th-grade level.
4. The SAT is a very reliable test, with coefficients ranging between .85 and .95.
5. The SAT is as nonbiased an achievement test as can logically be expected to be produced.
6. The testing time for the complete battery ranges from 109 minutes for Primary I level to 320 minutes for the Intermediate levels.

California Achievement Tests, Form C and D (1978)

Description and Administrative Procedures

The California Achievement Test (CAT), forms C and D is a series of tests designed to measure the achievement of students from the beginning of kindergarten through the twelfth grade. There are ten overlapping levels in Form C and seven in Form D. The levels and recommended grade ranges of Form C are as follows.

Test Levels	Grade Levels
10	K.0–K.9
11	K.6–1.9
12	1.6–2.9
13	2.6–3.9
14	3.6–4.9
15	4.6–5.9
16	5.6–6.9
17	6.6–7.9
18	7.6–9.9
19	9.6–12.9

The various levels make it easier to use the tests in functional-level testing; it also permits increased coverage of curricular materials at a particular grade level. The names of the CAT tests and their test levels are found in Table 20.

Table 20. Tests and Levels Found in CAT C and D

Content Area	Test	10	11	12	13	14	15	16	17	18	19
Prereading	Listening for Information	X									
	Letter Forms	X									
	Letter Names	X									
	Letter Sounds	X									
	Visual Discrimination	X									
	Sound Matching	X									
Reading	Phonic Analysis		X	X	X						
	Structural Analysis			X	X						
	Reading Vocabulary		X	X	X	X	X	X	X	X	X
	Reading Comprehension		X	X	X	X	X	X	X	X	X
Spelling	Spelling			X	X	X	X	X	X	X	X
Language	Language Mechanics			X	X	X	X	X	X	X	X
	Language Expression		X	X	X	X	X	X	X	X	X
Mathematics	Mathematics Computation		X	X	X	X	X	X	X	X	X
	Mathematics Concepts and Applications	X	X	X	X	X	X	X	X	X	X
Reference Skills						X	X	X	X	X	X

The C and D forms both provide optional locator tests to facilitate functional-level testing. The first Locator Test is designed to be used in grades 1–6, and Locator Test 2 is designed to be used in grades 6–12. The Locator Tests consist of short vocabulary and mathematics sections, which the publisher indicates are reliable in matching students who are in the same grade with different levels of C and D.

The CAT, 1970 edition, is a well-known test battery, which has been extensively used in school assessment since its publication, as was the previous edition. The 1978 edition is not a revision of the 1970 test. All items are new except in Level 10. The authors first determined the objectives to be measured and then wrote items specifically designed to measure these predetermined objectives. The test is both a norm-referenced test and a criterion-objective-referenced test. The test measures achievement in prereading, reading, spelling, language, mathematics, and reference skill.

Standardization Information

There were 114,620 students in the tryout for the CAT. The target population for which the norms are intended included all public-school districts with total enrollment of 11 or more students that are listed in the 1970 Census School District Data Tapes and all Catholic schools listed in the official 1975 Catholic Directory.

The 1978 CAT was standardized at two periods in the school year on the same students. This makes it possible to report more realistic normative data throughout the year.

All of the items in the tryout were reviewed for racial, ethnic, and sex bias by men and women belonging to various ethnic groups. Data were examined separately for Black students. Point biserial correlation was also employed in efforts to eliminate racial and ethnic bias.

To determine test-retest reliability, the CAT C and D Forms were administered over short interval periods and over 6-month intervals. For both the short interval (2–3 weeks) and the 6-month-interval period of testing, the coefficients for the total battery were .90 and above, except in a very few cases. At Level II, Grade 1 on the short-interval testing, the coefficient of correlation was .83 for Reading and Mathematics. At Grade K, the Total Battery coefficient for prereading was .76, and at Grade 1 the total battery coefficient for math was .76; at Grade 2 the Total Battery coefficient for Mathematics was .88.

Individual subtest test-retest correlations show a greater score variance over the 6-month interval testing. Some of the correlations involving Level II are quite low. The authors report that this reflects the fact that Level II is very difficult for students in the early months of Grade 1. Also, over the short-interval test-retest period, the coefficient for language expression was found to be very low (.35). One would need to be very cautious about making educational decisions concerning these subtests at Level II, Grade 1.

To establish content validity, the development of the test began by securing current curriculum guides and other instructional materials from all state departments of education and most major cities in the United States. After review of the objectives stated in these materials, and the basic skills identified as common to most curricula, a comparison was made of these objectives and basic skills with those of two CTB/McGraw-Hill criterion-referenced instruments, the Prescriptive Reading Inventory (PRI), and the Diagnostic Mathematics Inventory (DMI). The DMI and the PRI objectives had been developed through analysis of the most widely used basal texts. The resulting pool of objectives became the primary basis for the CAT C and D category objectives.

Once a set of category objectives was chosen, guidelines were developed concerning the number of items needed to measure such category objectives and the kinds of items necessary to cover the specific skills.

Interpretation and Use

The CAT 1978—as do all new tests and in particular test batteries—has to await research and analysis to establish some specific uses of the test data. Although there is much information on the 1970 edition, this edition cannot use those data. As a new test, it will have to await further research and evidence to determine the most critical use of the data. However CTB/McGraw-Hill has consistently provided test users with appropriate technical data and guides for use of the tests. This is also true of this edition of the CAT.

Although all the objectives determined for this battery cannot be listed here, anyone using the CAT C and D can easily become familiar with exactly what the test is measuring. Technical Bulletin No. 1 provides information on all of the objectives. For example, the Language Expression objectives are organized under three major subcategories: Usage, Sentence Structure, and Paragraph Organization. Under usage are included nouns, irregular nouns/verbs, pronouns, verbs, and adjectives. The content under Sentence Structure includes subject/verbs, modifying words, modifying/transitional words, complete/incomplete/run-on, verbosity/repetition, and misplaced modifiers/and nonparallel structure. Paragraph organization includes sequence, sequence/topic sentence, sequence/topic, and concluding sentence.

Itemized Facts.

1. The CAT Forms C and D are not a revision of the 1970 edition of the California Achievements Tests, but a newly designed and formulated test battery.
2. There is an overlapping of grade levels in the test levels that provides for more accurate measurement within a grade level.
3. The CAT is as free of bias as one can logically expect an achievement test to be.
4. Nearly 115,000 students were used in the standardization of the CAT.
5. The Battery is less reliable at the kindergarten and grade-1 levels. For other levels, the coefficients of correlation are mostly .90 and above.

Reading Tests

When achievement tests are identified with a specific skill area, e.g. reading, they may be called *diagnostic* tests if they provide for an analysis of the components involved in the particular skill. A diagnostic test not only will provide information concerning deficiencies in a particular skill, but will also show the areas such as word comprehension, listening, word analysis, or other possible areas where the individual is weak. Some of these tests are individually administered and some are group administered. The Reading tests in achievement-test batteries such as the SAT and CAT can be diagnostic when an analysis is made of the components of the reading process. A description of several reading tests is as follows.*

---

*A book by Eldon K. Ekwall, *Locating and Correcting Reading Difficulties* (Columbus, Ohio: Charles E. Merrill, 1970) provides a criterion diagnostic assessment of reading difficulties and remediation procedures for 28 reading difficulties. The checklist used to identify these 28 difficulties is available from your instructor.

Durrell Analysis of Reading Difficulty (1980)

Description and Administration Procedures

The Durrell Analysis of Reading Difficulty (Durrell, 1980) consists of a series of tests and situations in which the examiner may observe in detail various aspects of a child's reading. The range of the test covers reading difficulty from the nonreader to the level of sixth-grade ability. Its primary purpose is to discover weaknesses and faulty habits in reading that may be corrected in a remedial program. The test provides a check list for recording observations of difficulties the child displays. This is considered to be more important than the level of achievement. The check list contains items of greatest significance in remedial work. The check lists and test situations are provided for three levels of reading: (1) nonreader or preprimer level, (2) primary-grade reading level, and (3) intermediate-grade reading level. The content of the tests consists of the following parts:

Oral Reading Tests
  Eight paragraphs with comprehensive questions; check lists for observation of phrase reading, word skills, voice, enunciation, and expression; general reading habits; norms for oral-reading level

Silent Reading Tests
  Eight paragraphs, equal in difficulty to the oral-reading paragraphs; norms for silent reading and check lists for mechanics of silent reading

Listening Comprehension
  Seven paragraphs, one for each grade level, with comprehension questions

Supplementary Paragraphs
  Eight paragraphs, equal in difficulty to the oral- and silent-reading paragraphs; may be used for supplementary testing or written recall

Word Recognition and Word Analysis
  Word cards and a tachistoscope; one list for grade 1 and another for grades 2–6; norms for recognition and analysis, and a phonics inventory

Visual Memory of Word Forms
  Identification tests for primary grades, writing from memory for intermediate grades; norms for both tests

Auditory Analysis of Word Elements
  Identification tests for primary grades, writing from oral presentation for intermediate grades; norms for both tests

Spelling and Handwriting
  Two spelling lists, one for primary and one for intermediate grades; check lists and norms; norms for speed of handwriting from copy; check lists of faults

Suggestions for Supplementary Tests and Observations
  Suggestions for evaluating study abilities; methods of detailed analysis of word abilities and spelling; observing reading interest and effort

Special Tests for the Nonreader or the Preprimer Reader
  Visual Memory of Word Forms: Primary test is used
  Auditory Analysis of Word Elements: Primary test is used
  If child does not know letters, the test for learning to hear sounds in words is provided.

Letter Recognition: Letter naming, identifying letters named, matching letters, copying letters

Phonics: Tests are provided for ability to give sounds of letters and blends

Learning Rate: Test to check ability to remember words taught

Listening Comprehension

Standardization Information

The Durrell Analysis of Reading Difficulty Test is planned primarily for observing faulty habits and weaknesses in reading pertinent to a remedial program. The check list is more important in diagnostic analysis than norms (Bond, Tinker and Wasson, 1979). The norms presented are based on no fewer than 1,000 children for each test, and they have been found to check satisfactorily against other measures of reading (Durrell, 1980). No other standardization information is presented to the clinician in the Manual.

Interpretation and Use

Since the grade norms for the oral- and silent-reading tests are based on time required for reading, it is particularly important that the timing be accurate. Also, since any remediation resulting from the Durrell is based on the observation of difficulties, it is extremely important that the examiner know the items in the check list for each test and watch for pertinent difficulties or faulty habits. If the examiner fails to notice weaknesses for any reason, it is permissible to ask the child to repeat the test for a sufficient time to note the item or items omitted.

The check list for spelling includes the following: (1) omits sounds, syllables; (2) adds sounds, syllables; (3) incorrect sounds; (4) slow handwriting. These are the four common causes of spelling difficulties, as identified by Durrell (1980). Remediation is based on the observations that relate to the difficulties in spelling (Durrell, 1980).

1. Inability to spell phonetically is evidenced by omission of essential sounds, addition of sounds, or incorrect letters for the sounds of the words.
2. Inability to recall correct visual form of the word, which is usually indicated by spelling phonetic words correctly and nonphonetic words incorrectly
3. Slow handwriting, causing the child to forget the rest of the word
4. Not understanding the meaning of the word and spelling a word different than the one required.

The purpose of the check list of difficulties on the record form accompanying each test is to relate the difficulties to remediation. The Check List of Instructional Needs (Figure 36), which is a part of the Individual Record Booklet and is reproduced on page 229, is completed based on the observation of the examiner.

If the Durrell Analysis of Reading Difficulty is used to examine the strengths and weaknesses according to the check lists provided, that is, the kind of reading errors made, the test can be very useful, especially in the hands of an experienced teacher. Use of the instrument for grade placement or for other uses without further evidence of reliability and validity is not warranted.

Itemized Facts.

1. The Durrell Analysis of Reading Difficulties provides a check list for recording observations of reading difficulties encountered by the child.
2. No reliability or validity studies are reported in the Manual.
3. The Durrell provides for three levels of reading: preprimer, primary, and intermediate grades.
4. Timing of the tests and observation of reading weaknesses are the key to obtaining data for diagnosis.
5. A check list for identifying instructional needs is provided for the diagnostic study.
6. The test should not be used for grade placement.

Gates-MacGinitie Reading Tests (1972)

Description and Administrative Procedures

The Gates-MacGinitie Reading Tests (Gates and MacGinitie) are a group of screening tests designed to assess both group- and individual reading skills from kindergarten through the twelfth grade. Basically, the skills measured in the total series are vocabulary, comprehension, and speed and accuracy (the latter is not measured in the Primary forms). Each test, with the exception of the Readiness Skills, is available in a minimum of two equivalent forms and in both hand- and machine-scored editions.

In the vocabulary test at grades 1, 2, and 3, the child views four printed words and a picture representing one of the words. A choice is made by circling each word that is appropriate. In grades 4–12, the student must identify the appropriate word that has the same meaning as a stimulus word.

For a measure in comprehension, the child must read a paragraph and then choose a picture that represents the theme in the paragraph (for grades 1 and 2, the selection may be only a sentence). For grade 3, a paragraph is presented and choices to answers are made; for grades 4–12, the student is required to fill in blank spaces within a paragraph.

The speed-and-accuracy subtest is presented in separate booklet form for grades 1 and 2. For grades 4–12, it is presented as a part of the survey form. This subtest involves short paragraphs, followed by questions or sentences to be completed. The time limit is 5 minutes and the test measures the speed of reading in which a child can perform and understand the content of what has been read.

Standardization Information

Norms for the hand-scored edition of Primary A, B, C, and CS and the hand-scored and machine-scored editions of Survey D and E were established by a nationwide standardization in 1964 and 1965. The machine-scored edition of Primary A, B, C and CS was developed in 1970 and 1971. The 1964–1965 norms for the Gates-MacGinitie Reading Tests were established by administering the tests to a nationwide sample of approximately 40,000 students in 37 communities. The communities selected were representative on the basis of size, geographical location, educational level, and family income.

The alternate-form reliability coefficients were obtained by administering one form of the test on one day and a second form on another day. Split-half reliability coefficients were also computed, in order that comparison could be made with tests that

Figure 36.*

Check List of Instructional Needs

NON–READER OR PREPRIMER LEVEL	PRIMARY GRADE READING LEVEL	INTERMEDIATE GRADE READING LEVEL
Needs help in:	*Needs help in:*	*Needs help in:*

NON–READER OR PREPRIMER LEVEL

Needs help in:

1. Listening comprehension and speech
___ Understanding of material heard
___ Speech and spoken vocabulary

2. Visual perception of word elements
___ Visual memory of words
___ Giving names of letters
___ Identifying letters named
___ Matching letters
___ Copying letters

3. Auditory perception of word elements
___ Initial or final blends
___ Initial or final single sounds
___ Learning sounds taught

4. Phonic abilities
___ Solving words
___ Sounding words
___ Sounds of blends — phonograms
___ Sounds of individual letters

5. Learning rate
___ Remembering words taught
___ Use of context clues

6. Reading interest and effort
___ Attention and persistence
___ Self-directed work

7. Other
___ _____
___ _____
___ _____
___ _____

PRIMARY GRADE READING LEVEL

Needs help in:

1. Listening comprehension and speech
___ Understanding of material heard
___ Speech and spoken vocabulary

2. Word analysis abilities
___ Visual memory of words
___ Auditory analysis of words
___ Solving words by sounding
___ Sounds of blends, phonograms
___ Use of context clues
___ Remembering new words taught

3. Oral reading abilities
___ Oral reading practice
___ Comprehension in oral reading
___ Phrasing (Eye-voice span)
___ Errors on easy words
___ Addition or omission of words
___ Repetition of words or phrases
___ Ignoring punctuation
___ Ignoring word errors
___ Attack on unfamiliar words
___ Expression in reading
___ Speech, voice, enunciation
___ Security in oral reading
___ _____
___ _____
___ _____

4. Silent reading and recall
___ Level of silent reading
___ Comprehension in silent reading
___ Attention and persistence
___ Unaided oral recall
___ Recall on questions
___ Speed of silent reading
___ Phrasing (Eye movements)
___ Lip movements and whispering
___ Head movements Frowning
___ Imagery in silent reading
___ Position of book Posture
___ _____
___ _____

5. Reading interest and effort
___ Attention and persistence
___ Voluntary reading
___ Self-directed work Workbooks

INTERMEDIATE GRADE READING LEVEL

Needs help in:

1. Listening comprehension and speech
___ Understanding of material heard
___ Speech and oral expression

2. Word analysis abilities and spelling
___ Visual analysis of words
___ Auditory analysis of words
___ Solving words by sounding syllables
___ Sounding syllables, word parts
___ Meaning from context
___ Attack on unfamiliar words
___ Spelling ability
___ Accuracy of copy Speed of writing
___ Dictionary skills: Location, pronunciation, meaning
___ _____
___ _____

3. Oral reading abilities
___ Oral reading practice
___ Comprehension in oral reading
___ Phrasing (Eye-voice span)
___ Expression in reading Speech skills
___ Speed of oral reading
___ Security in oral reading
___ Word and phrase meaning
___ _____

4. Silent reading and recall
___ Level of silent reading
___ Comprehension in silent reading
___ Unaided oral recall
___ Unaided written recall
___ Recall on questions
___ Attention and persistence
___ Word and phrase meaning difficulties
___ Sentence complexity difficulties
___ Imagery in silent reading

5. Speeded reading abilities
___ Speed of reading (Eye movements)
___ Speed of work in content subjects
___ Skimming and locating information

6. Study abilities
___ Reading details, directions, arithmetic
___ Organization and subordination of ideas
___ Elaborative thinking in reading
___ Critical reading
___ Use of table of contents References

7. Reading interest and effort
___ Voluntary reading
___ Variety of reading
___ Self-directed work

report only split-half reliabilities. These coefficients were obtained with the Vocabulary items and Comprehension passages, but not for the Speed and Accuracy tests. Table 4 in the Technical Manual shows the 1964–65 reliability testing (Split-Half) to range between .88 and .96, and the Alternate-Form reliability to range between .67 and .89. The reliability established by the 1971–72 testing was established in 1971 for all grades except first grade, which was established in May, 1972. Standard score means and standard deviations for each test form and alternate-form reliability coefficients of the standard scores were obtained for each grade level within each school. The average standard score means ranged between 49.1 and 56.5. Average standard-score standard deviations ranged between 8.0 and 8.7. The average alternate-form reliability range was .73–.88 and the split-half reliability coefficients ranged between .90 and .94.

Gates and MacGinitie (1972) report a concurrent validity study by Davis to show median coefficients of .84 for Primary C Vocabulary, .79 for Primary C Comprehension, .78 for Survey D Vocabulary, and .80 for Survey D Comprehension. There is little information concerning validity to assist one in determining appropriate use for this test.

Interpretation and Use

Although this is an easy test to administer and the usual scores are provided—grade, percentile, and standard scores—one must use this test with some caution. The authors report the validity to rely on face values and they suggest that a user analyze the test for face validity. Perhaps it is measuring what it is purported to measure but more information on validity is needed. Its use should be limited to screening, even though the Technical Manual has a section for interpreting differences between test scores.

Itemized Facts.

1. The norms on the Gates-MacGinitie are based on a population of 40,000 students representing kindergarten through twelfth grade.
2. The split-half coefficients of correlations showed a range in the reliability of the test from .88 to .96.
3. Few validity studies are reported on this test.
4. The Gates-MacGinitie should be limited for use as a screening instrument.
5. The skills of reading measured are vocabulary, comprehension, and speed and accuracy.

Gray Oral Reading Tests (1967)

Description and Administration Procedures

The Gray Oral Reading Tests by Gray and Robinson were designed to measure growth in oral reading from early first grade to college and to aid in the diagnosis of oral-reading difficulties. Types of errors are recorded, so that insights can be gained into the kinds of instruction needed.

The tests are available in four forms that are similar in organization, length, and difficulty. The first passage of each form is introduced by a picture that provides the setting for the reading. Each passage thereafter is self-contained, so that the examinee may begin with any passage without being penalized because of the omission of previous ones. The size and quality of type and the format of each passage generally conforms to the level for which it was designed. The difficulty of each passage is increased by several means: difficulty of vocabulary, range and density of vocabulary, syllabic length of words, length and complexity of the structure of sentences, and maturity of concepts.

Three objective measures are recorded for each passage. The errors made are recorded as the passage is read. The time (in seconds) for reading each passage is carefully recorded. Both time and the total number of errors are used in the tentative norms to determine the grade equivalent in oral reading. In addition, four comprehension questions calling for the literal meaning of each passage are included. The questions are limited to the literal meaning because they can be scored objectively, and because the test is not designed to measure comprehension. These scores are used to secure information about the child's approach to reading.

Standardization Information

The four forms of the Gray Oral Reading Tests were standardized on 502 individuals from two school districts in Florida and in both the suburban and metropolitan areas of Chicago.

For reliability information, Robinson (1967) reports coefficients of intercorrelation among grade scores on each of the four forms at each grade level. For all subjects, the range was from .973 to .982; for girls from .977 to .981; and for boys from .969 to .983. The standard error of measurement offers a second estimate of the reliability of the tests. Errors of less than 4.00 points may be expected in the total passage score for any pupil 68 percent of the time.

Information on the validity of the test is quoted as being established because of the procedures used in constructing the test and the fact that pupils randomly selected from "representative groups," as judged by the cooperating schools, obtained scores that distinguished one grade from another.

Interpretation and Use

An oral-reading test provides a clinician with information about reading that is not available with other tests. The Gray Oral Reading Test provides an opportunity to observe the student in the process of reading and, therefore, to identify difficulties in the reading process.

There are limited data on reliability and validity on this test and its use must take into consideration this fact. This limits the usefulness of the test in many cases; yet, any instrument that can provide the clinician with clues regarding reading style, difficulties, and the literal comprehension abilities of a student has some uses.

A further caution is necessary when using the norms of this instrument. In the standardization sample, the mean IQ at each grade level and, of course, for the total was at the upper end of the normal range of intelligence. This was an apparently more selective group than the normal population and this must be taken into consideration in using the norms.

Itemized Facts.

1. The Gray Oral Reading Tests are available in four forms similar in organization, length and difficulty.
2. The standard error of measurement is less than 4.
3. The validity is not well established and reported in the Manual.
4. Intercorrelation among grade scores is reported to be above .97.
5. The norms may reflect a higher reading level than is represented by the general population.
6. The test provides an opportunity to study reading style, difficulties experienced, and literal comprehension of material read.

Reading Miscue Inventory (1972)

Description and Administration Procedures
The Reading Miscue Inventory (RMI) by Goodman and Burke is a test to aid in the analysis of a student's oral reading. *Miscue* is the term used to designate any deviation from the printed material noted while the child is reading. A series of questions is provided in the RMI to help the teacher determine the quality and variety of the reader's miscues. These questions focus on the effect each miscue has on the meaning of what is being read, and they also help the teacher to analyze the available language used and the background information. From this information, a Reader Profile is constructed. Reading strategies and a pattern of strengths and weaknesses are shown on the graph from which a reading program may be planned.

There are five discrete steps to follow in gathering the reading data:

1. Oral Reading and Taping
    A recording is made of the student reading an unfamiliar passage. The teacher sits beside the student with a specially prepared copy of the text, marking the reader's miscues, but not offering any help. The student is asked to retell the story. Without asking leading questions, the teacher probes until the student offers as many details of plot, character, and description as can be recalled.
2. Marking Miscues
    The teacher replays the tape at a later time to confirm and reevaluate the miscues made during the oral reading and to make calculations for a retelling score.
3. Using the RMI Questions and the Coding Sheet
    The teacher lists each miscue on the RMI Coding Sheet. This process affords the teacher the opportunity to determine the relevant comprehension relationships and grammar-meaning relationships. A few arithmetic computations are made and the results are ready to place on the RMI Reader Profile.
4. Preparing the RMI Reader Profile
    Information is transferred from the RMI Coding Sheet to the Reader Profile. This profile charts in graph form the pattern of the student's strengths and weaknesses in reading. A yearly evaluation of a student's progress in reading may be made from comparison with Profiles made the year before.
5. Planning the Reading Program
    The patterns of strengths and weaknesses taken from the Profile provide the basis for planning a reading program for the child. Programs may be planned on an individual basis or for groups of children who show similar profiles.

The manual provides information for the teacher to figure percentages of miscues made by the student. Patterns that designate strengths, partial strengths, weaknesses, and overcorrection are provided for the area on grammatical relationship.

Standardization Information
No references are made in the manual about the reliability or validity of the evaluation. The authors do cite four important assumptions that underlie the RMI and the research from which it originated. They are:

1. All readers bring an oral-language system to the reading process.
2. All readers bring the sum total of their past experiences to the reading process.

3. Reading materials represent the language patterns and past experiences of the author.

4. Reading is an active language process that involves constant interaction between the reader and the text.

If the teacher can accept these assumptions, an implication is that this inventory is a valid approach to the reading procedure.

What is apparent after one reviews the total inventory is that Goodman and Burke have made a good task analysis of the reading process as they see it.

Interpretation and Use

Users of this inventory will very likely agree that it covers nine very common areas in reading where children often make errors. These are: dialect, intonation, graphic similarity, sound similarity, grammatical function, correction, grammatical acceptability, semantic acceptability, and meaning change. Good remediation procedures are based on a task analysis of the process and of the errors a student makes. The RMI provides an opportunity to analyze the reading difficulties of a child, based on an analysis of the errors in these areas.

For the skilled reading teacher, this inventory should have high appeal; however, it is not a quickie test and will demand time, both in learning how to use it and in preparing for, administering, and scoring a single test for an individual. We would be in agreement with the authors when they say that it reflects the convictions that teachers will be more quick to make changes in reading curriculum and methods when they are provided with an effective procedure (RMI) that allows them to gain insight into the reading process at the same time that it helps them to evaluate the reading of their students.

Itemized Facts.

1. The RMI is an inventory to assess errors in nine areas of reading where children are likely to make errors.
2. Validity is limited to face validity.
3. A recording of the student's reading and retelling of the story aids in the evaluation of miscues.
4. A reading profile is constructed to show strengths and weaknesses in reading.
5. No reference is made regarding the reliability of the evaluation.
6. The analysis of miscues focuses on more than just types of errors, but on effects of the miscue on meaning and on language used.

The Woodcock Reading Mastery Tests (1973)

Description and Administrative Procedures

The Woodcock Reading Mastery Tests are a diagnostic battery of five individually administered tests designed to assess a student's reading placement and to diagnose strengths and weaknesses of reading skills. It is designed to evaluate students from kindergarten through grade 12.

The five tests measure diverse reading skills. A brief description of each test is given below.

1. The Letter Identification Test is given to students in the first six grades only, and it is anticipated that most students will achieve a perfect score by the end of the fourth grade. The letters include manuscript, cursive, and some unusual styles of print.
2. The Word Identification Test: the words range in difficulty from beginning reading to twelfth grade.
3. The Word Attack Test: nonsense words are utilized and the student uses phonic- and structural-analysis skills.
4. The Word Comprehension Test: an analogy format is used to measure knowledge of words.
5. The Passage Comprehension Test: a modified cloze format is used. One word is deleted from each of 85 passages. At the lower level, picture clues are provided.

The Manual is very clear regarding directions for administering the various tests and very detailed regarding standardization procedures and the types of derived scores and what they mean. The administration time is 30–40 minutes. Although one point is scored for each correct answer, the examiner may desire to put incorrect responses verbatim for diagnostic purposes. The responses are open-ended, with no multiple-choice items.

There are a number of scores that can be derived from the tests. Age and grade scores are available, as are mastery scores, an achievement index, percentiles, stanine and standard scores, and a method to adjust norms to reflect the socioeconomic level of the community in which the child lives. There may be little use for age-equivalent scores, except as one may desire to compare reading performance with chronological age or mental age. Standard scores are normalized and assume a mean of 50 and a standard deviation of 10. Reference scales provide the basis for a criterion-referenced interpretation of performance. These scales illustrate reading tasks on which a person with a given mastery score has a 50-percent likelihood of success. Additionally, it indicates the grade level at which average students demonstrate 50-percent mastery and 90-percent mastery with that task. Mastery scores identify the easy-reading level, grade level, and failure reading level for a student.

The Woodcock provides separate boy and girl norms, and this is a commendable feature. In order to modify norms to reflect the socioeconomic status of the local community, various factors reflecting the community must be identified and utilized in calculating the adjustment values to be applied at each grade level. These adjusted scores may be a substitute for local norms (Woodcock, 1973).

The scoring takes approximately 15 minutes for the minimal amount of information usually desired. Additional time required depends on the extent to which a person desires to use the tables provided to obtain more extensive information.

Standardization Information
The sample for standardization was made up of 5,252 students, kindergarten level through the twelfth grade in 141 schools from 50 school districts. Schools selected ranged from New Hampshire to Florida, to California and Washington on the West Coast. The stratified random sampling was similar to the U.S. Census report, 1970. However, the sample drawn from communities of 1,000–2,500 and from cities 10,000–50,000 were far from represented in the proportion shown in the 1970 census report.

Split-half reliabilities corrected by the Spearman-Brown formula were in the .90s for both forms of all subjects and for the Total for grade levels 1.2–10.9, except Letter Identification and Word Comprehension. Reliability ranged from .83 to .96 for lower grades for Letter Identification. Split-half reliability for Letter Identification at grade level 7.9 was .02 and .20 for both forms. Lengthening the test by combining the two forms produced correlations in the high .90s for all except Letter Identification (Woodcock, 1973). Alternate-form reliabilities with tests taken a week apart ranged from .16 to .94. At the 2.9 grade level, the coefficients of correlation ranged from .84 for Letter Identification to .97 for Total Reading. At the 7.9 level, they ranged from .16 for Letter Identification to .93 for Word Identification, with a Total Reading of .83.

Content validity was established on the basis that the test items were drawn from the domain of reading—namely letter and word identification—tasks of word attack, and tasks of comprehension. The other approaches to establish validity are not strong and, in some cases, represent questionable approaches. Other studies have been made on certain subtests and Total Reading (Memory, Powell, and Callaway, 1980; Powell, Moore, and Callaway, 1981). The Total Reading, Word Identification, and Passage Comprehension Tests were compared to an Informal Reading Inventory (IRI) developed at the University of Georgia and used in their Reading Clinic; Spache Diagnostic Reading Scales; and the Slosson Oral Reading Test. Using the Pearson Product Moment correlation, it was found that all tests of significance of the reported correlations showed two-tailed probabilities below the .001 level, and that the differences between the means of the following were significant at the .05 level: Comprehension and Total Reading, Word Identification, and a derived competency score; the IRI Instructional Level and Passage Comprehension; and the average of Word Identification and Passage Comprehension. The differences on both the Spache Instructional level and the Comprehension Level were significant for the Woodcock Total Reading, Word Identification, Competency score and the average of Word Identification and Passage Comprehension. The Passage Comprehension was also significantly different from the Spache Comprehension level (Memory, Powell, and Callaway, 1980).

The Woodcock Reading Mastery Tests and the University of Georgia Informal Reading Inventory, which is a valid instrument in that Reading Clinic, correlate highly and measure similar abilities. Likewise, when the Word Identification and Passage Comprehension Test scores are compared and the lower of the two used to identify instructional level, this score, on the average, was essentially the same as the instructional level determined by the IRI. It underestimated the IRI by less than a month (Memory, Powell, Callaway, 1980). As measured by these three instruments, the Woodcock is a valid Reading Test and is an accurate alternative to an Informal Reading Inventory for assessing reading abilities.

The Word Comprehension Test has been criticized because of its verbal-analogies format. Analogies are generally associated with vocabulary and reasoning, not comprehension. Laffey and Kelly (1979) believe that one cannot determine what is really being measured, since several deficiencies could cause a poor performance. Others say it is a measure of a general verbal ability and is misplaced when used in a reading test. Powell, Moore, and Callaway (1981) studied the relationship of the Woodcock reading and three intelligence tests. The WISC-R Vocabulary, Similarities and Information subtests and Verbal IQ, Peabody Picture Vocabulary Test, and the Slosson Intelligence Test were the intelligence tests used in the study. The correlations found between the

Woodcock Word Comprehension Test and the measures of sight vocabulary ranged from .437 to .733, the correlations between the WWC and measures of Passage Comprehension ranged from .654 to .895. Five of the six measures presented orally were nonsignificant. The PPVT showed a slight statistically significant correlation ($r = .145$ $p<.05$) (Powell, Moore, and Callaway, 1981).

The Woodcock Word Comprehension Test is more a function of reading than of a general verbal factor. It is much more closely allied with word-identification tasks in reading than in assessment of verbal intelligence.

Interpretation and Use

The Woodcock Reading Mastery Test has been found to be a valid test to use in reading. The authors have provided numerous scales to aid in understanding the levels of reading of a subject. Part of the diagnostic value of the test comes from understanding the subtests and what they measure, observation of the client during testing, and an analysis of errors made on the test. The Letter Identification Test has the lowest reliability of any of the subtests. Also, a single error may change the grade-level equivalency from 6.2 to 12.9. A score of 44 indicates a grade equivalency of 6.2; a perfect score of 45 places one at the top of the scale at 12.9. The fact is that the letters in this test take different forms, which may cause a lower score than the actual one, since the subject may know the letter but not in the form presented. It has been suggested that one not use the Letter Identification test with older, more able students if the recommended procedure of assigning 173 mastery points of the resulting grade-level score fell outside the range of the other four scales. In this case, the Total Reading score would be the average of the four other tests.

The Word Attack Test can be diagnostically beneficial if the examiner identifies deficiences in word-attack skills used by the subject. There is not much to differentiate the sixth-grade level from the twelfth-grade level. Pronouncing 80 percent of the words correctly yields a sixth-grade placement, 90 percent correct places one at the twelfth-grade level.

The Word Comprehension Test is not measuring general intelligence, as has been suggested, but is related to comprehension. The examiner needs to be alert to be sure the young subjects are able to remember the analogy format at all times so they will not be penalized. This may be difficult for some.

The Passage Comprehension Test has been criticized as measuring closure rather than comprehension (Laffey and Kelly, 1979). Comprehension involves a number of skills and abilities, of which using clues is one. It measures closure, forcing the child to use a skill that is not usually tapped in a comprehension test.

The Woodcock is a joint norm-referenced, criterion-referenced test. It describes a person's competency with a given task, compared to others on the same task. It is not completely criterion-referenced, in that objectives are not listed for the tests and all the test items cannot be converted into statements of clear instructional objectives. It does, however, allow one to predict the relative mastery of a student in reading situations at various difficulty levels along a grade scale.

The mastery scale provides information on the reading performance of a child. The mastery scale identifies an easy-reading grade level, a failure reading level, and a grade level, which is the level at which average students demonstrate 90-percent mastery with that level. The failure reading level is the grade level at which the student would show only 75-percent mastery of the tasks on which the average students at that grade level would perform at 90-percent mastery. These provide a teacher with an instructional range within which to direct instruction. A very significant statistical feature of the mastery scale is that it has been designed to have equal units. A clinician can study changes within an individual at any level and with any of the five tests.

It is helpful to chart a mastery profile to show the easy-reading level (96-percent mastery of material the average student masters at 90 percent), the failure level, and the student's grade level. The student's actual grade placement at each of the levels for each test plus total reading is then observable.

The authors of the test have made it possible to show a student's standing from many perspectives graphically. For example, the Achievement Index can be used to give an index of reading retardation or acceleration. The Reference Scales are useful for providing a basis for criterion-referenced interpretation of a child's performance, even though the specific objective is not provided. These scales allow one to show for each mastery score on what items a person with that score has a 50-percent likelihood of success, the grade level at which average students have 50-percent mastery, and the grade level at which average students demonstrate a 90-percent mastery with that same task.

The Woodcock Reading Mastery Test is a popular test among school psychologists and educators. Recent validity studies have enhanced this test in the minds of many diagnosticians. It is a very useful test.

Itemized Facts.

1. Standard scores are normalized with a mean of 50 and a standard deviation of 10.
2. The test identifies for each student an easy-reading level, average of grade levels, and failure reading level.
3. There are separate norms for boys and girls.
4. Split-half reliabilities were in the .90s for all subtests except Letter Identification.
5. It is a norm-referenced test with a modified criterion-referenced capability.
6. The Word Identification Test can be used as a quick, rough indicator of a student's reading-achievement level.
7. The analogy format of the Word Comprehension Test does, in fact, measure a reading function, rather than a verbal intelligence.
8. The test format calls for open-ended responses.

Arithmetic Tests

Keymath Diagnostic Arithmetic Test (1971)

Description and Administration Procedures

The only individualized test of arithmetic skills to be discussed in this section is the KeyMath Diagnostic Arithmetic Test by Connolly, Nathman, and Pritchett. Other arithmetic tests are included in the achievement Batteries. The test is both a criterion-referenced and a norm-referenced test. The 14 subtests, designed to cover content from preschool level through sixth grade, are divided into three major areas: Content, Operations, and Applications. Specifically, these are organized as follows:

Content	Operations	Applications
A. Numeration	D. Addition	J. Word Problems
B. Fractions	E. Subtraction	K. Missing Elements
C. Geometry and symbols	F. Multiplication	L. Money
	G. Division	M. Measurement
	H. Mental Computation	N. Time
	I. Numerical Reasoning	

A metric supplement was added in 1976. It includes questions on metric measures of linearity, mass, capacity, area, and temperature.

The administration time is approximately 30 minutes. The authors utilize basal and ceiling levels to reduce the time it would otherwise take. The starting point for each new test is suggested from the average of the basals of all the previous tests. With the exception of written computation items in the four operations, each test item is presented orally and the subject responds orally. Items are presented in an open-ended format, with colored pictures used where necessary to minimize the impact of the written word. In addition, the subject is not required to read because the math achievement is affected by reading skill.

KeyMath yields four types of diagnostic information: (1) grade-equivalent scores, (2) scores related to the three major areas of Content, Operations, and Application, (3) subtest performance on the 14 subtests, and (4) an analysis of performance on the individual items. Analysis of item content is facilitated by providing a behavioral objective to be used for items answered incorrectly. This enhances remedial instruction.

Standardization Information

The KeyMath norming sample consisted of 1,222 subjects representing grades K through 7. These were drawn from nine states: two from the west coast, two from the east coast, and five from midwestern states. The sample had a larger proportion of white subjects from communities under 50,000 population and a smaller proportion of whites from communities over 50,000. The proportion of Black subjects in communities of 50,000 or more was about three times as great in the norming sample as in the U.S. population. Also, in the U.S. population as a total, there was a somewhat larger proportion of other races represented in the sample.

The authors of the test point out the possibility of guessing on a test, and in this case an open-ended format was adopted to reduce this influence and enhance reliability. The reliability was established from a split-half analysis of the calibration population's performance on the items. Between the individual subtests, the median coefficients ranged between .64 and .84. When all 209 items are given, the median coefficient was .96. The reliability of individual subtests at several levels is low.

The items on the subtest are arranged in order of increasing difficulty. To determine item difficulty, each subject in the sample was administered a set of 51 items selected for measurement at that grade level. The easiest item was one that 90–95 percent of the subjects at that grade level were expected to complete correctly. The second item was one in which 75 percent were successful. The third item had a 50-percent chance of being worked correctly, the fourth item, a 25-percent chance, and the fifth item only 5–10 percent chance of being correct.

Three kinds of validity are discussed in the manual: content, face, and concurrent. Regarding content validity, about 3,000 youngsters were tested individually with portions of the KeyMath during its development and before its norming. The data from these studies were used for item revision and assessment of the effectiveness of directions, mode of presentation, and related factors that influence validity. Face validity was enhanced by the inclusion of colorful material, a variety of tasks, and carefully controlled basal and ceiling position. This was done to maximize the student's interest and cooperation. Concurrent validity was obtained by the comparison of the test performance to other criteria, some of which were the predecessors to KeyMath. Connolly (1968) reported a .59 correlation between the performance on a predecessor of KeyMath and the measured intelligence of 45 educable mentally retarded adolescents. He also correlated the performance of 28 normal fifth graders on this same instrument with their performance on the arithmetic portion of the Iowa Test of Basic Skills, and obtained a .69 correlation with the reasoning measure and a .38 with the full scale Iowa arithmetic scores. These correlations are reported to be significant at the .05 level.

Kratochwill and Demuth (1976) compared the KeyMath and the WRAT to the Metropolitan Achievement Test, Primary I Form F, using 37 Title I rural youth with a mean age of 6 years, 6 months. The KeyMath had a correlation of .63 with the Metropolitan Total Score, which was obtained 1 year after the KeyMath and WRAT Arithmetic subject were administered. Word Problems, Numerical Reasoning, and Money demonstrated the highest correlations, ranging from .53, .45, and .44, respectively. In this case, the KeyMath was found to have moderate predictive ability. In the same study the WRAT correlation was .17.

There is a significant relationship between KeyMath and the California Arithmetic Test (CAT) for learning-disabled children. The relationship was significant at the .05 level on the Total scores, the Reasoning area of the CAT, the Content and Application area of KeyMath, the Fundamentals area of the CAT, and Operations area of KeyMath (Tinney, 1975).

Interpretation and Use

One aid in the diagnostic use of KeyMath is that for each item in the test, a behavorial objective for teaching is presented in the Manual. This criterion-referenced approach assists in both diagnosis and remediation.

Although a child is not penalized for lack of reading ability with KM, since reading is not required, one should be alert to the fact that children with auditory-receptive or verbal-expressive deficits may be penalized. Tests with other formats may need to be utilized with these children.

The reliability of the subtests at several levels is low. It is important to plot the standard error of measurement on the Diagnostic Record, so that a difference is not presumed where it may not be. Of course, knowledge and use of the SE are desirable when using any test.

Goolstein, Kahn, and Cowley (1976) point out some problems with using the KM with the EMR population. They found the EMRs tended to reach their ceiling level quite rapidly because of a lack of items at the midrange of the subtests. This suggests a pattern of slight underachievement on a majority of the tests, with marked underachievement on the Missing Element Test.

There is a relatively small number of items in the Basic Operations subtest. The examiner should note any unusual situations that could result in an inflated or deflated score.

The following work sheets (Figures 37 and 38) are provided to aid in analyzing data from the KeyMath Diagnostic Arithmetic Test (Wiebe, 1979).

Directions for Use–KeyMath Worksheet (Wiebe, 1979)

1. Record the raw score for each subtest of the KeyMath to the left of the subtest listing.
2. Using the raw score for each subtest, find the corresponding grade equivalent from the table. Should the raw score be less than or greater than the table grades, use the closest grade equivalent and indicate direction with a ＞(greater than) or ＜(less than) sign.
3. Enter the grade equivalent in the spaces provided for each subtest on the worksheet.
4. For each "Area" add the grade scores of the subtests in that area. Record the sum in the space marked "Area Total."

Figure 37. KeyMath Worksheet

Raw
Score

Est.
Grade
Score

_____ Numeration   _____
_____ Fractions   _____
_____ Geometry & Symbols   _____
                AREA TOTAL _____ ÷3 = _____ CONTENT
                                                Grade Est.

_____ Addition   _____
_____ Subtraction   _____
_____ Multiplication   _____
_____ Division   _____
_____ Mental Computation   _____
_____ Numerical Reasoning   _____
                AREA TOTAL _____ ÷6 = _____ OPERATIONS
                                                Grade Est.

_____ Word Problems   _____
_____ Missing Elements   _____
_____ Money   _____
_____ Measurement   _____
_____ Time   _____
                AREA TOTAL _____ ÷5 = _____ APPLICATIONS
                                                Grade Est.
                                  _____ TOTAL TEST
                                                Grade Score

Comments:

Figure 38. KeyMath Estimated Grade Equivalents

Raw Score	Word Problems	Missing Elements	Money	Measurement	Time
27	—	—	—	*	—
26	—	—	—	*	—
25	—	—	—	9.2	—
24	—	—	—	8.0	—
23	—	—	—	7.2	—
22	—	—	—	6.5	—
21	—	—	—	6.1	—
20	—	—	—	5.5	—
19	—	—	—	5.2	*
18	—	—	—	4.8	8.4
17	—	—	—	4.3	6.9
16	—	—	—	4.1	6.1
15	—	—	—	3.9	5.3
14	*	—	—	3.7	4.8
13	*	—	9.2	3.5	4.2
12	8.2	—	7.7	3.2	3.7
11	6.7	—	6.6	3.0	3.3
10	5.3	—	5.7	2.8	2.9
9	4.2	—	4.8	2.6	2.7
8	3.7	—	4.1	2.5	2.5
7	3.2	*	3.4	2.3	2.2
6	2.8	5.2	2.9	2.0	2.0
5	2.4	4.3	2.5	1.6	1.7
4	1.9	3.9	2.1	1.3	1.4
3	1.3	3.6	1.6	0.8	1.0
2	0.6	3.1	1.2	*	0.5
1	*	2.6	0.5	*	*

Raw Score	Addition	Subtraction	Multiplication	Division	Mental Computation	Numerical Reasoning
27	—	—	—	—	—	—
26	—	—	—	—	—	—
25	—	—	—	—	—	—
24	—	—	—	—	—	—
23	—	—	—	—	—	—
22	—	—	—	—	—	—
21	—	—	—	—	—	—
20	—	—	—	—	—	—
19	—	—	—	—	—	—
18	—	—	—	—	—	—
17	—	—	—	—	—	—
16	—	—	—	—	—	—
15	*	—	—	—	—	—
14	8.2	*	—	—	—	—
13	6.4	9.5	—	—	—	—
12	5.5	7.8	—	—	—	*
11	4.6	6.6	*	—	—	8.7
10	4.0	5.6	8.7	*	*	6.5
9	3.5	4.7	7.0	9.5	7.3	5.4
8	2.9	3.9	6.2	7.7	6.1	4.4
7	2.5	3.2	5.3	6.6	5.2	3.9
6	2.1	2.7	4.5	5.9	4.4	3.3
5	1.8	2.1	3.9	5.0	4.0	2.7
4	1.4	1.6	3.4	4.1	3.5	2.2
3	0.8	0.9	3.0	3.5	2.9	1.8
2	*	*	2.5	2.4	2.0	1.4
1	*	*	2.1	1.1	0.7	0.8

Raw Score	Numeration	Fractions	Geometry & Symbols
27	—	—	—
26	—	—	—
25	—	—	—
24	*	—	—
23	*	—	—
22	9.5	—	—
21	8.0	—	—
20	6.8	—	*
19	6.0	—	9.0
18	5.4	—	6.8
17	4.9	—	5.3
16	4.3	—	4.3
15	3.8	—	3.8
14	3.4	—	3.5
13	2.9	—	3.1
12	2.5	—	2.7
11	2.1	—	2.5
10	1.8	9.5	2.1
9	1.4	8.0	1.8
8	1.2	7.0	1.4
7	0.8	6.2	1.2
6	0.5	5.4	0.8
5	*	4.7	0.5
4	*	4.0	*
3	*	3.4	*
2	*	2.3	*
1	*	1.2	*

*Not calibrated

5. Divide each "Area Total" as indicated on the worksheet to determine the area grade estimates.
6. To determine the total test estimate, add the 3 area grade estimates and divide that sum by 3.

You now have four estimates of grade-level achievement upon which to compare a child's current grade placement and/or achievement based upon other measures of academic ability.

Itemized Facts:

1. Reading is minimized in the KeyMath Diagnostic Arithmetic Test, so math achievement is not affected by reading skills.
2. KeyMath tests children from preschool level through sixth grade.
3. The 14 subtests measure math in three major areas: content, operations, and applications.
4. The text can be administered in approximately 30 minutes.
5. An open-ended format is used to reduce the influence of guessing inherent in a multiple-choice format.
6. Some studies report the correlations of KeyMath to standardized achievement tests as significant at the .05 level. This was not true with the WRAT.
7. This is both a norm- and criterion-referenced test.
8. The KeyMath tends to show an underachievement level for EMRs.

Language and Learning-Ability Tests

Language and/or learning-ability tests have been, and continue to be, used to assess processing skills of children and youth who have not made satisfactory progress in school in relation to their peers. Since they have not made normal progress, there must be a reason or reasons. When intelligence is ruled out as a reason for lack of learning, one must look elsewhere. These tests have been used as a part of a battery, with the assumption that they will help identify causes for the difficulty in learning. The expectation is that identified weaknesses and strengths will provide target areas for remediation. The ultimate goal of the testing and the remediation is to help the subjects to learn the basic skills of reading, written communication, spelling, and calculating. Oral- and written-language skills are necessary for a person to function fully in a democratic society.

Research is controversial concerning use of language- and learning-ability tests as the basis for remediation. While the controversy regarding "from thence shall remediation procedures flow" is being debated, no one appears to refute the necessity for a child/youth to have the skills to understand words, follow directions, write from dictation, express thoughts through speaking and writing, make association between events, objects, situations, and to perceive data correctly and remember information. Language- and learning-ability tests are designed to measure these operations.

It is difficult to design a test that measures a single function without some other function's affecting the score. This is so well known, for example, with an arithmetic test with word problems. To what extent does the reading involved affect the score in arithmetic that the subject receives? Language- and learning-ability tests are designed to assist in understanding what problems and strengths a person has in learning. Since they may load to some degree on another factor and because learning is a complicated process, one will not expect one subtest alone to measure a single specific function. Likewise, one would hesitate to single out one aspect of a learning process as the cause of the learning problem. It may be central, but likely not the single cause. Language- and learning-ability tests can give a more global picture of how a person is functioning than can often be found by other evaluation approaches. They provide various means of making language and learning assessments that aid in making educational decisions. They provide background information, for example, in visual and/or auditory-processing strengths and weaknesses, which influences the choice of materials and the physical arrangements of the teaching environment for purposes of optimal learning. When these tests are used by competent examiners and teachers who understand needs of children and what the tests are really measuring, the results have been productive in individual cases. They have also had an impact on the content of special-education training.

Clinical Evaluation of Language Functions (1980)

Description and Administration Procedures
The Clinical Evaluation of Language Functions (CELF) by Semel and Wiig is designed to assist psychologists, special educators, speech and language pathologists, and other educators and clinicians in identifying the nature and degree of language disabilities in school-age children. It provides differentiated measures of selected language functions in the areas of phonology, syntax, semantics, memory, word finding, and retrieval for students in kindergarten through twelfth grade. In-depth assessment or pragmatics of phonology is not a part of the design.

The CELF is an individually administered test. Subtests may be administered in their totality and in the sequence presented, or they may be administered individually as selective language probes and in a different sequence than presented. Suggestions for extension of additional testing are provided for many of the subtests. Semel and Wiig recommend that the test be complemented by administration of standardized measures of receptive-vocabulary development and by the analysis of a spontaneous-speech sample. The time involved in giving the entire test is estimated to be approximately 75 minutes.

The CELF is composed of 11 subtests separated into processing and production functions of language and 2 supplementary subtests designed to probe aspects of processing and production at the level of speech sounds.

Processing Subtests

1. *Processing Word and Sentence Structure*: This subtest was designed to assess the child's ability to process and interpret word and sentence structure. There are 26 items. Each of the items is associated with an assembly of four pictures, one of which provides an accurate pictorial representation of the meaning of the stimulus sentence and three of which serve as foils.

2. *Processing Word Classes*: This subtest is designed to evaluate the child's ability to perceive relationships between verbal concepts and to identify word pairs that are associated by semantic class, verbal opposite, spatial, temporal, agent-action, and superordinate—subordinate.

3. *Processing Linguistic Concepts*: This subtest was designed to evaluate the child's ability to process and interpret oral directions that contain linguistic concepts requiring logical operations such as *and*, *either*, and *if . . . then*. The accurate interpretation of these concepts depends upon (1) knowledge of the logical operations required and (2) perception and interpretation of the logical relationships expressed among the remaining concepts in the sentence.

4. *Processing Relationships and Ambiguities*: This subtest was designed to evaluate the child's ability to process and interpret logico-grammatical and ambiguous sentences containing: (1) comparative, (2) passive, (3) temporal-sequential, (4) familial, (5) analogous relationships, (6) idioms and metaphors, and (7) proverbs. The items probe aspects of language processing that reflect (a) simultaneous analysis and synthesis ability, (b) logical-processing ability, and (c) ability to go beyond the concrete numinative function of words and grasp their abstract meanings in figurative language.

5. *Processing Oral Directions*: This subtest was designed to evaluate the child's ability to interpret, recall, and execute oral commands of increasing length and complexity. The items tap aspects of language processing related to (1) the retention and recall of verbal directions of increasing level, (2) the analysis, synthesis, and recall of adjective sequences of increasing length, (3) the interpretation and recall of serial position, and (4) the interpretation and recall of left-right spatial orientation.

6. *Processing Spoken Paragraphs*: This subtest was designed to evaluate the ability to process and interpret spoken paragraphs and recall salient information presented. The accurate interpretation and recall of the contents of the paragraphs depends upon, among others, (1) knowledge of the vocabulary presented, (2) ability to process the syntactic structure of the sentence, (3) ability to abstract salient information contained in the paragraphs, and (4) retention and recall of the details upon questioning.

Production Subtests

7. *Producing Word Series*: This subtest was designed to assess (1) the child's accuracy, fluency, and speed in recalling and producing selected word series in long-term memory, (2) the accuracy in the recall and retrieval of automatic serial language, and (3) the speed of retrieval and production of selected word series.

8. *Producing Names on Confrontation*: This subtest was designed to evaluate the accuracy, fluency, and speed in naming colors, forms, and color-form combinations in a sustained confrontation-naming task. The subtest probes the following processes: (1) accuracy in the rapid retrieval of common words, (2) fluency and agility in formulating words in rapid naming, and (3) speed of word identification and retrieval.

9. *Producing Word Associations*: This subtest was designed to evaluate the quantity and quality of the retrieval of semantically related word series from long-term memory. The subtest probes the following aspects: (1) fluency and flexibility in identifying and retrieving members of a semantic class, (2) speed of identification and retrieval of semantically related words, and (3) use of associative grouping strategies (associative clustering) in word identification and retrieval.

10. *Producing Model Sentences*: This subtest was designed to assess the child's productive control of sentence structure in a sentence-repetition task. The subtest probes aspects of language production related to (1) knowledge of sentence-formation rules (linguistic competence), (2) retention and recall of sentence structure, (3) dependency on semantic content and consistency for retention and recall, and (4) resistance to deviations in meaning and structure in the immediate recall of word sequences.

11. *Producing Formulated Sentences*: This subtest was designed to evaluate the child's ability to formulate and produce sentences when words and sentences from choices are limited and when semantic and syntactic constraints are introduced by a word that must be included. There are 12 stimulus words. The student is asked to make a sentence with each of these words. A scoring guide for sentence types is provided.

Supplementary Tests:

12. *Processing Speech Sounds*: This subtest was designed to evaluate the child's ability to discriminate between speech sounds (phonemes) in minimally different word pairs.

13. *Producing Speech Sounds*: This subtest was designed to survey the child's accuracy in articulating selected elicited speech sounds (phonemes). The test probes aspects of language production related to (1) the motor encoding of speech sounds and (2) the habitual patterns of speech-sound articulation. The format approximates conditions in spontaneous speech production.

Standardization Information

The standardization sample was reported to be stratified to reflect the 1970 U.S. Census as closely as was possible, but the authors report that there was limited success in identifying children in the four major geographic regions defined by the U.S. Bureau of the Census. They had a larger percentage Elementary group from the Northeast and the West geographic regions (33.3 and 40.4), and a smaller percentage from the North Central and South East regions (10.9 and 15.3). The Advanced group sample included 21.7 percent from the Northeast, 43.1 percent from the North Central, 14.5 percent from the Southeast, and 17.0 percent from the West. There were 634 in the Elementary sample and 771 in the Advanced sample. The distribution of the samples regarding occupation of parents generally reflects the 1970 Census, except for white-collar workers, in which both Elementary and Advanced samples had lower percentages than in the total population. Eighty-eight percent of the sample came from the White racial group; eleven percent constituted the Nonwhite. For this reason, the authors caution examiners in interpreting the scores of nonwhite children when using this test.

The stability of the CELF Screening Tests, as measured by test-retest correlations, was examined in three separate studies and ranged from total test coefficients of .77–.85 (p = .01). Internal-consistency measures, using Cronbach's alpha, ranged from .60 to .78 (p = .01) on the Advanced Level Screening. Lower coefficients were observed between processing and production items, however, indicating the desirability of examining processing and production through separate sets of items.

The test-retest correlation of the processing subtests was .93 and of the production subtest .89.

Concurrent validity was established by comparing the scores of children's performances on the CELF with children's performance on the Illinois Test of Psycholinguistic Abilities, Verbal subtests of the Detroit Test of Learning Aptitude, and the Northwestern Syntax Screening Test. With both Elementary and Advanced groups, the coefficients of correlation ranged between .46 and .62. Other concurrent-validity studies of the CELF Diagnostic Battery subtests with seven related measures yielded numerous significant positive correlations, ranging from .42 to .94 (p = .01).

Interpretation and Use

Error-analysis grids are provided for the majority of the subtests, to help isolate specific language stimuli that present difficulties, and to help discern error patterns in children's responses.

There are no age norms, so a student is compared to his grade level. If a student falls below the norm for the grade level on the production tests and has normal intelligence, placement in learning-disability classes on the basis of the child's oral expression should be considered. The production subtests measure various aspects of oral-expression tasks.

Semel and Wiig (1980) suggest that any child who falls below his/her grade-level criteria be given extensive testing. The criteria for extensive testing are provided in the manual, which aids in this decision.

Dialect is always a problem in assessing language. The authors of the test have provided the user with information concerning dialectal differences to be used in making a diagnosis. Any time one is evaluating language functions of culturally and ethnically different children, the testing and the interpretation must proceed with caution and with a clear understanding of different styles of language production.

For use in determining significant differences between the subtests on the diagnostic battery, a table (Table 21) showing the means, standard deviations, standard errors of measurement, and probable errors of measurement for Processing Items, Production Items, and Total Score for Elementary and Advanced levels is provided. The authors present this as a useful index of the reliability of the test and cite the following example. Consider several third-grade-level students who have the total score of 25 on the CELF. The *probable error of measurement* (P.E.M.) associated with this score is approximately 1.8 score points (see Table 21). The chances are even (fifty-fifty) that a student from this group has a "true score" that lies within 1.8 score points of 25. Thus, his "true ability" can be considered to be between 23 and 27.

Semel and Wiig explain further in their examples that an interval obtained by adding and subtracting one *standard error of measurement* (S.E.M.) to and from the student's score has a greater probability of defining his "true level". For a first grader who scores 25 on the test, the S.E.M. is 2.9 and an approximate interval of 22–28 is established. It can be said, then, that the chances are approximately two-out-of-three that the "true" score lies between 22 and 28. Then to make a more definite statement about the level of the pupil's score, one could add and subtract an amount equal to twice the S.E.M. This wide interval shows the odds to be almost twenty-to-one that the interval contains his true score. One can, thus, be relatively certain that the pupil who scores 25 had a true score between 19 and 31. It is expected that, in a class of 35 pupils, one or two students will have true scores that lie outside the intervals of two standard errors of measurement, and there is no precise way to determine which, if any, have been mismeasured by this amount (Semel & Wiig, 1980, p. 30).

Itemized Facts.

1. The CELF identifies the nature and degree of language disabilities in school-age children.
2. Eleven percent of the norm sample was nonwhite.
3. The reliability of the CELF is significant at the .01 level of significance. The test-retest correlations are approximately .90.
4. There are no age norms.
5. The test provides guides concerning dialectal differences as an aid in making a diagnosis.
6. The standard error of measurement for the total test varies from 2.2 to 2.9, with a median of 2.6.

Table 21. Means, Standard Deviations, Standard Errors of Measurement, and Probable Errors of Measurement for Processing Items, Production Items, and Total Score: Elementary and Advanced. (Semel and Wiig, 1980, p. 30)

	Processing Items				Production Items				Total Score			
	Mean	S.D.	S.E.M.	P.E.M.	Mean	S.D.	S.E.M.	P.E.M.	Mean	S.D.	S.E.M.	P.E.M.
Elementary												
K	17.3	4.5	2.3	1.6	6.9	2.2	1.5	1.0	24.2	6.1	2.8	1.9
1	20.0	5.1	2.3	1.6	9.2	3.4	1.6	1.1	29.2	7.4	2.9	2.0
2	23.7	4.4	2.1	1.4	10.9	3.8	1.4	.9	34.6	7.1	2.6	1.8
3	23.3	3.7	2.1	1.4	11.4	4.4	1.3	.9	34.7	6.5	2.6	1.8
4	24.8	3.2	1.9	1.3	13.6	2.3	1.1	.7	38.4	4.4	2.2	1.5
5	22.1	2.8	1.9	1.3	10.9	1.5	1.1	.7	32.9	3.4	2.2	1.5
Advanced												
5	24.9	3.5	2.0	1.3	10.3	3.1	1.7	1.1	35.2	5.7	2.7	1.8
6	24.9	4.0	2.1	1.4	10.6	2.5	1.7	1.1	35.6	5.2	2.7	1.8
7	26.8	3.9	2.0	1.3	11.8	2.5	1.7	1.1	38.6	5.4	2.6	1.8
8	26.7	4.1	2.0	1.3	12.0	2.3	1.7	1.1	38.6	5.0	2.6	1.8
9	25.5	2.9	1.8	1.2	12.7	2.3	1.6	1.1	38.2	4.3	2.4	1.6
10	22.2	2.9	1.7	1.1	13.1	2.3	1.5	1.0	35.1	4.6	2.3	1.6
11–12	26.3	3.0	1.7	1.1	13.3	2.5	1.6	1.1	39.6	4.6	2.3	1.6

↑ probable errors of measurement

Illinois Test of Psycholinguistic Abilities ITPA (Kirk, McCarthy, and Kirk, 1968)

Description and Administrative Procedure

The acquisition and use of language has been studied for many years. Until recently, remedial work on linguistic deficiencies was limited to speech correction; testing for educational and remedial programs was done on a trial basis only. The ITPA was originally conceived as a diagnostic intraindividual test of psychological and linguistic functions, with its principal use to diagnose a child's psycholinguistic abilities and disabilities, so that remediation could follow (Kirk, 1968). Its design originated from Hull's formulations and Osgood's psycholinguistic model. The model is three dimensional and includes (1) channels of communication, or the routes through which the content of communication flows, (2) the psycholinguistic processes involved in the acquisition and use of language, and (3) levels of organization that refer to whether a habit of communication is automatic or requires a mediating process of using symbols to carry the meaning of an object.

A psycholinguistic ability can be defined as a specific process at a specific level via a specific channel. Each of these diminsions can be further delineated and must be understood to use the ITPA effectively for diagnosis and remediation.

Psycholinguistic process refers to the acquisition and use of all the habits required for normal language usage. There are three main sets of habits: reception, association, and expression. The process of reception consists of the sum of those habits necessary for the attainment of meaning through either visual or auditory linguistic symbols or stimuli. The process of association consists of the sum of those habits necessary for manipulating linguistic symbols internally. Tests that demonstrate the presence of associative ability include word-association tests, analogies tests, and similarities and differences tests. The process of expression consists of the sum of those habits necessary for expression in words or gestures.

Levels of organization refers to the functional complexity of an organism. Some psycholinguistic activities exhibited by humans appear to demand much higher levels of organization than others. Two levels are important for language acquisition—representational and automatic-sequential. The representational level includes activities that require the meaning or significance of linguistic symbols. The automatic-sequential level includes activities that require the retention of linguistic-symbol sequences and the execution of the automatic action that follows different linguistic structures. The redundancies within a language make certain responses automatic.

Channels of communication are the sensory-motor paths by which linguistic symbols are transmitted, received, and responded to. The ITPA is divided into two parts—reception and response. Pure receptive ability requires only a mode of reception—hearing or sight. How the subject responds has no relevance to a test of receptive ability. Similarly, expressive ability requires only a mode of response—speech or gesture. Associative ability or any combination of abilities, however, requires the interaction of all the channels of communication.

Kirk elected to include 12 tests in the battery as most educationally relevant. Following is a definition of each test:

The representational level: These tests assess the subject's ability to receive and interpret meaningful symbols (reception); relate symbols on a meaningful basis (association); or express meaningful ideas in symbols (expression).

Reception
1. Auditory Reception examines the ability to comprehend the spoken word.
2. Visual Reception examines the ability to comprehend pictures and written words.
Association
1. Auditory Association examines the ability to relate auditory symbols in a meaningful way.
2. Visual Association examines the ability to relate visual symbols in a meaningful way.
Expression
1. Verbal Expression examines the ability to express ideas through spoken words.
2. Manual Expression examines the ability to express ideas through gestures.

The automatic-sequential level: These tests assess nonmeaningful uses of symbols, i.e., long-term retention and short-term memory of symbol sequences. Automatic tests make frequent use of language's numerous redundancies, which lead to highly over-learned or automatic habits for directing syntax and inflection without conscious effort.

Automatic tests
1. Grammatic Closure helps in predicting future language abilities from past achievements. It is specifically related to the correct use of grammar.
2. Visual Closure measures the perception interpretation of any visual object when only a part of it is shown.
Sequential tests
1. Auditory Sequential Memory examines the ability to repeat a sequence of auditory symbols correctly. A modified digit-repetition test measures this linguistic skill.
2. Visual Sequential Memory examines the ability to reproduce a sequence of visual symbols correctly. The subject duplicates the order of a sequence of pictures or geometrical designs that are shown and then removed.
Supplementary tests
1. Auditory Closure measures the perceptual interpretation of any sound when only some of it is heard.
2. Sound Blending measures the communication of sound blends by determining how well the person is able to blend together the sounds heard.

The Examiner's Manual emphasizes that persons who administer the ITPA have adequate background in test administration and that they not be considered valid examiners until they have administered a minimum of 10 practice tests (Kirk, 1968, p. 15). Furthermore, the standardized procedures must be followed rigidly.

Since the test is appropriate for children 2–10 years of age, different starting points are specified for children of differing ability levels. Unless a person is suspected of being retarded or gifted, the starting point will be the item for the person's chronological age.

The ITPA is designed to establish a basal level and a ceiling, so that all items do not need to be administered to all children. The manual is explicit regarding the order in which the tests are to be administered and such things as when an item may be repeated.

Although there are 12 tests, the two supplementary subtests, auditory closure and sound blending, are not administered to all children. Their chief clinical use is with children who show potential or actual problems in reading and/or spelling (Kirk, 1968, p. 20).

The manual provides tables for determining composite psycholinguistic age (PLA) norms using the 10 basic subtests only and the PLA for each of the 12 subtests. Scaled-score norms reflect the mean performance of the norm groups of approximately 1,000 children between the ages of 2 and 10 years. The mean of the scale scores is 36 and the standard deviation is 6.

Standardization Information

The Illinois Test of Psycholinguistics was normed on an average group of children of ages two to ten years. *Average* is defined as average (1) intellectual functioning, (2) school achievement, (3) sensory-motor integrity, and (4) characteristics of personal-social adjustment and English-speaking family background. Grade levels represented were kindergarten and preschool and first through fourth grades. Children from five communities in Illinois and Wisconsin were administered the abbreviated 1960 Stanford-Binet Intelligence Scale, Form L-M. If a child's score fell within ± 1 standard deviation of the mean (IQ 84–116), the child was included in the normative group. There were 962 children chosen from 2,413 in the final sample population. Four percent of these were Black.

Means and standard deviations (in months) are presented in table form in a separately published account of the characteristics of the test (Paraskevopoulos and Kirk, 1969). These means and standard deviations are shown for each age (PLA) level and for the psycholinguistic quotient (PLQ). The PLQs are ratio scores obtained by dividing the Psycholinguistic Age by the Chronological Age. Since the sample was made up of average children, deviation PLQs could not be completed without questionable extrapolations. The PLQ means and standard deviations differ at each level, with a range of 95.8–101.1 months. Paraskevopoulos and Kirk (1969) warn the administrators of the tests about using mental ages to show differences between subtest scores. Instead they recommend the use of scaled scores.

Using the data of the 962 children in the standardization sample, internal-consistency coefficients were computed by the Kuder-Richardson (1937) #20 formula. *Internal consistency* refers to the homogeneity of items within a test. This assists in determining the extent to which items in the test measure the same functions. The correlations are shown in Table 22.

Table 22. Range of Internal-Consistency Coefficients for Each Age Level for the 12 Subtests

Age	Range of Coefficients	
	Restricted Intelligence Range	Corrected for Restricted Intelligence Range
2-7/3-1	.53–.96	.68–.96
3-7/4-1	.49–.90	.67–.96
4-7/5-1	.59–.89	.73–.95
5-7/6-1	.51–.91	.72–.95
6-7/7-1	.51–.91	.60–.95
7-7/8-1	.64–.91	.76–.95
8-7/9-1	.45–.90	.45–.93
9-7/10-1	.48–.90	.69–.95

The range for the ITPA Composite coefficients for all ages (Restricted Intelligence) was .89–.93. The range for the ITPA Composite coefficients for all ages (Corrected for Restricted Intelligence) was .92–.96. When the coefficients were corrected for restricted intelligence, in most instances the coefficients were higher. From age 3-7 to age 9-1, Auditory Reception had the highest coefficients. Between ages 2-7 and 5-1, Visual Closure was shown to have the lowest coefficients; and between ages 7-7 and 10-1, Auditory Closure was shown to have the lowest coefficients.

For stability reliability, a 5- to 6-month test-retest interval was selected on the assumption that a remedial program is usually of at least 4–6 months' duration. Three age levels were selected: 3-7/4-1, 5-7/6-1, 7-7/8-1. The range of these reliability coefficients is shown in Table 23.

For the restricted range, the coefficients for the composite scores were .70–83 for all three age groups, when corrected for restricted intelligence range, the coefficients for the composite scores were .87–.93 for all three age groups.

From the information in Tables 22 and 23, it can be seen that internal-consistency reliability is much higher than the stability reliability (test-retest). Paraskevopoulos and Kirk (1969) cite several factors that influence the stability of the test. They are: (1) the precision of the test itself as a measuring instrument, (2) day-to-day stability of examinee's performance, and (3) stability of the trait measured. They add that the educational intervention between test and retest can change the rate of development of psycholinguistic abilities. Regarding these variables and the lowered reliability of the test-retest findings, they caution the user to interpret stability coefficients in conjunction with data that show the portion of variation due to each of the factors. The technical manual provides standard errors of measurements for raw scores, for scaled scores, and for psycholinguistic ages in months. The user of this test should refer to this statistical information before making educational decisions from the differences in the subtest scores.

The studies of the ITPA show much disagreement regarding the diagnostic validity of the ITPA. Many studies, such as Golden and Steiner (1969) and Elkins (1972), point to the discriminatory power of some subtests. Elkins, in his study, for example, showed significant differences on verbal expression, grammatic closure, auditory sequential memory, and sound blending between good and poor readers. There was not always a consistency in the subtest patterns, as Macione (1969) found poor readers had scores significantly below normal readers on visual closure, visual sequential memory, sound blending, and grammatic closure. Other studies of concurrent validity have been done—by McCarthy and Olson (1964), Horner (1967), Milgram (1967) and Washington and Teska (1970)—and, in general, their findings have been supportive of

Table 23. Range of Five-Month Stability Coefficients for the ITPA Scores for 4-, 6-, and 8-year-Old Children for All Subtests

Age	Range of Coefficients	
	Restricted Range	Corrected for Restricted Intelligence
4-year-olds	.35–.61	.67–.90
6-year-olds	.21–.82	.38–.86
8-year-olds	.12–.86	.28–.89

the validity of the ITPA. Hammill and Larsen (1974) and Newcomer and Hammill (1975), and Newcomer (1975) in receiving a number of studies using the ITPA, did not find the subtests discriminated well enough to establish a remedial program or were significant measures of academic achievement. Furthermore, they concluded that the effectiveness of psycholinguistic training was not conclusively demonstrated. Their analysis of the research caused them to conclude that the research did not show the ITPA to have construct validity. In two studies involving Hammill, construct-validity designs were used (Newcomer, Hare, Hammill, and McGettigan, 1975; Hare, Hammill, and Bartel, 1973). In the Hare et al. (1973) study, six subtests were involved and were reported to be essentially confirmed as being valid. The Newcomer et al. (1975) study was "clearly supportive of the assumption of Kirk, McCarthy, and Kirk that the ITPA measures discrete psycholinguistic variables, at least when administered to normal fourth grade children" (Newcomer and Hammill, 1976, p. 37). Except for the Visual Closure subtest, they cite the visual channel to be completely without substantiation as a valid dimension. Regarding construct validity, their final statement is that, with the exception of the channel dimension, the ITPA can be regarded as a valid representation of the test-model and to some extent of the Osgood model as well; for the most part, the subtests do not tap the same constructs.

Arter and Jenkins (1979), under a contract supported by the National Institute of Education, did a comprehensive review of the research related to assumptions regarding the differential diagnosis–prescriptive teaching instructional model. This involves the assessment of psycholinguistic and perceptual motor abilities. Their assumptions and summary of studies regarding the ITPA are as follows.

Assumption: Existing tests used in Differential Diagnosis are reliable. An analysis of the studies showed that the ITPA total score reliability is acceptable, but the subtest reliabilities are not on the test-retest procedure. All ITPA used are acceptable on split-half reliabilities, except the visual closure.

Assumption: Existing tests used for Differential Diagnosis are valid. Arter and Jenkins reported on the following types of validity.

Concurrent Criterion Validity—

While some individual investigation reported validity coefficients that were satisfactory, most findings as reported by Newcomer and Hammill (1975) indicated Grammatic Closure, Sound Blending, Auditory Association, and Total Score had concurrent validity to achievement when intelligence was not controlled, and only Grammatic Closure and Total Score when IQ was controlled.

Predictive Criterion Validity—

The ITPA Total score is a useful prediction of general achievement. Some studies showed that the ITPA was a useful predictor; others showed no significant predictive ability. The subtests of Visual Discrimination, Auditory Discrimination, and Auditory Blending showed a consistent pattern of correlating with various academic skills at an acceptable level.

Diagnostic Validity—

The review of the studies did not show the ITPA to be able to distinguish between good and poor readers.

Construct Validity—

The factor-analytic studies indicated the ITPA to be highly related to IQ, and provided much support for the levels and dimensions hypothesized in the model.

Assumption: Prescriptions can be generalized from differential diagnosis to remediate weak abilities. A summary of the studies failed to support the trainability of underlying psychological abilities. Less than half of the studies showed that the training efforts yielded dividends in ability growth.

Assumption: Remediation of weak abilities improves academic achievement.

The ITPA was not singled out in this part of the study.

Assumption: Prescriptions can be generalized from ability profiles to improve academic achievement, with no direct training of weak abilities. The studies reviewed showed that matching instruction to a student's modality strength failed to produce differential improvement in reading. They do not report on whether other academic areas may be more amenable to teaching modality strength.

Arter and Jenkins (1977) concluded, after reviewing all the studies, that a more substantial research base is necessary to determine the validity of the differential diagnosis–prescriptive teaching model of assessment and instruction.

Recently proponents of the ITPA have questioned some of the previous studies and, with some change in research design, support the ITPA as a valid discriminating test. A study by Elkins (1981), who did a discriminant analysis, found that Visual Association, Grammatic Closure, and Auditory Sequential Memory discriminated at the .01 level between learning disabled and the control group. Auditory Sequential Memory is the most important subtest in discriminating between the two groups. However, Elkins (1981) emphasized that the power of the test is not in the individual subtest, but in its significance when combined with the other subtests. He further states that training on individual discriminating subtests is not recommended; rather, a diagnostic analysis of each case is suggested in terms of process, channel, and level of communication.

Kavole (1981) did an interesting study. He took 36 studies assessing the effectiveness of psycholinguistic training done since 1974 and used a meta-analysis approach. The primary sources of these studies were those included in Hammill and Larsen's (1974) review. He questioned the narrative description of selected studies and the so-called "box score" report, which does not shed light on the magnitude-of-treatment effect. The meta-analysis (Glass, 1976, 1977) approach provides a procedure for integrating primary data across an entire domain of studies, so that the overall magnitude of effect produced by the treatment process is provided (Kavole, 1981). It quantifies the magnitude of effect into a summary analysis called *Effect Size (ES)*. This statistic is the mean difference between experimental and control groups, divided by the standard deviation of the control group. The results of the individual studies are transferred into standard units that can be combined and studied simultaneously. Interpretation is comparable to a z score if we assume there is a normal distribution of responses to psycholinguistic training. The ES can be classified as small (.20), moderate (.50), and large (.80).

Kavole reported the following ITPA subtest Effect Sizes: small—Auditory Reception, Visual Reception, Grammatic Closure, Auditory Sequential Memory, and Visual Sequential Memory; those classified as moderate were Auditory Association, Visual Association, Verbal Expression, and Manual Expression. The small number of controlled evaluations precluded conclusions on the effectiveness of psycholinguistic training for Visual Closure, Auditory Closure, and Sound Blending. He found psycholinguistic training to be of value for Auditory Reception, Visual Reception, Grammatic Closure, Auditory Sequential Memory, and Visual Sequential Memory, as well as Visual Expression.

Kavole's study supported psycholinguistic training programs and indicated that previous reviews generally underestimated the positive effect of psycholinguistic training. "The average child receiving training directed at outcomes measured by the ITPA performed better than 65% of untrained children" (Kavole, 1981, p. 507). For the Expressive subtests (VE and ME), average subjects who had psycholinguistic training stood at the eighty-fourth percentile of a comparison group. This is not, of course, to suggest that all facets of the psycholinguistic approach are equally amenable to remediation. The expressive constructs are more remedial than the others.

Interpretation and Use

There has been much controversy regarding exactly what the 12 subtests measure. Some factor-analysis studies have identified five factors, and not twelve. That is, some of the subtests load very heavily on the same factor. These studies have special significance to users of the ITPA and their use of it as a diagnostic instrument. Two studies factor-analyzed the ITPA alone (Chronkhite and Penner 1975, Burns and Watson 1973) and one the ITPA and the WISC combined (West and Wilborn, 1975–76). The names of the subtests were somewhat misleading in some of the cases, and the following description identifies the factors and the tests that load on them. The first term for each factor is how Chronkhite and Penner identified the factor and the descriptive term in parenthesis is how Burns and Watson labeled the factors.

1. Integration-Perception (Visual Language): Skills that involve reception and patterning of nonverbal stimuli or nonverbal pattern recognition
   a. Visual Closure
   b. Visual Association
2. Representation-Perception (General Language/Closure): Skills that involve verbal pattern recognition
   a. Auditory Closure
   b. Sound Blending
3. Integration-Organizing Process (Memory/expressive language): Skills that involve the retention of a perceived pattern to link pattern recognition and coordinated response
   a. Visual Sequential Memory
   b. Auditory Sequential Memory
4. Representation-Organizing Process (General Auditory language): Skills that use language as a means to organize information
   a. Auditory Reception
   b. Grammatic Closure
   c. Auditory Reception
5. Integration-Expression (Expressive Language): Skills requiring coordinated responses of a nonlanguage nature
   a. Manual Expression
   b. Verbal Expression (It does not measure higher level Language Skills— Chronkhite and Penner, 1975, p. 510)

Since the ITPA falls into five categories, it is desirable to plot the subtests to reflect these. This can be done by taking the Profile Abilities Graph of the ITPA and plotting all related scores the same color, or designing a profile chart, with the subtests that

Figure 39. WISC-ITPA Abilities Profile Chart

Area Tested	Mean Score

Visual Organization and Comprehension of Symbols
   WISC Comprehension
   WISC Picture Completion
   WISC Picture Arrangement
	————

Visual Analysis
   WISC Coding
   WISC Block Design
   WISC Object Assembly
	————

Visual-Auditory Memory
   ITPA Visual-Motor Sequencing (Visual Sequential Memory)
   ITPA Auditory Decoding (Auditory Reception)
   ITPA Auditory-Vocal Automaticity (Grammatic Closure)
   ITPA Auditory-Vocal Association (Auditory Association)
	————

Verbal-Symbolic Retention
   WISC Information
   WISC Arithmetic
   WISC Similarities
   WISC Vocabulary
	————

Note: Reprinted by permission of the authors from Dorris E. West and Bobbie L. Wilborn, "WISC-ITPA Abilities Profile," *Academic Therapy*, Winter 1975–76, *11*: 214.

measure the same factor listed together. This would help a person to see overall disabilities and not try to remedy a specific skill as identified by the name of a specific subtest.

The WISC-R remains one of the most used tests in assessment of learning disabilities. It and the IPTA measure somewhat the same dimensions of ability and intellectual processes (West and Wilborn 1975–76, Newcomer, 1975). West and Wilborn, factoring the two tests together, found four factors common to the two tests. Three of these can be measured by the WISC alone and one by the ITPA alone. Figure 39 identifies the four factors with the subtests that measure them. The mean score would be a summary of the subtests for each of the four abilities. Due to the difference in mean standard scores of WISC and ITPA, they cannot be directly compared. However, one can observe whether there is a strength or deficit in each area by comparison to mean standard scores for each test.

In addition to using the factors identified in the ITPA (and WISC) for diagnosis and as a guide for remediation, there are certain characteristics of some of the subtests that one must observe. The Grammatic Closure test has rather consistently been found to have predictive validity. However, it is not a valid test to use with speakers of nonstandard English. It has been found that 23 of the 33 subtest items are potentially high risk for dialect speakers, and that in 11 of the high risk items, responses that were acceptable in nonstandard English were responsible for 52–100 percent of all errors made by nonstandard-English-speaking students. Do not make an educational decision regarding nonstandard-English-speaking students from this subtest alone (Grill and Bartel, 1977).

Three of the subtests seem to have predictive validity for reading. Auditory Association, Grammatic Closure, and Sound Blending provide minimal validity for reading when intelligence is not controlled. When intelligence is controlled, Newcomer (1975) found that only Grammatic Closure retained a significant relationship to reading to use for prediction.

A subtest that has loading on several factors but no high one is Visual Reception. This indicates that it is rather ambiguous and, therefore, should not be interpreted alone. It can be interpreted only as one looks at the total profile.

The Visual Closure subtest has been found to be more a measure of figure-ground than it is of visual closure. There is no doubt, as shown in the factoral studies, that it is a measure of what is perceived. However, because the problem of figure-ground is so important with learning-disabled children, one should check on this before one knows if closure is really what is being measured (Harth and Justen, III, 1977).

Two formulas have been developed to obtain a psycholinguistic age from selected ITPA subtests with a high degree of validity. Using the Grammatic Closure test in the following formula shows a coefficient correlation of .934 with Chronological Age.

Estimated PLA (expressed in months) = 31.22 + 2.67 G.C. raw score. If one adds Auditory Association and Visual Closure to the formula, the correlation is increased to .954.

Est. PLA = 26.48 + 1.27 (GC) + .70 (AA) + .73 (VC)

(Cronkhite and Penner, 1975)

There is little doubt that the subtests are not pure tests measuring exactly what the name implies and that some load rather heavily on other factors. However, this is true of all tests in varying degrees. The factor-analytic studies have identified what the subtests load on, so it is important to group the subtests on the appropriate factors and use these factors in the diagnostic procedure. These studies have made the ITPA a more useful instrument, since this information can be used with the information available from validity studies of the subtests to arrive at a better understanding of the child.

Itemized Facts.

1. The ITPA model is three dimensional and includes: channels of communication, psycholinguistic processes, and levels of organization.
2. Kavole and Hammill et al., analyzing essentially the same research, came to different conclusions regarding the validity of ITPA training.
3. There are 10 regular subtests and two supplementary tests, which factor analysis has reduced to five abilities.
4. Grammatic Closure has predictive ability for reading, but is an invalid test for users of nonstandard English.
5. The Visual Reception subtest measures more than visual reception and cannot be used alone to measure this ability.
6. Stability coefficient for 4-, 6-, and 8-year-olds over a 4–6-month period for the Composite Scores was .87–.93.
7. A relatively valid psycholinguistic age can be found by inserting the raw score from Grammatic Closure in the formula—PLA = 31.22 + 2.67 (Grammatic Closure).

The Picture Story Language Test (1965)

Description

The Picture Story Language Test by Myklebust measures skill with the written word. The intent is to furnish a developmental scale for children, and it is also useful in the study of adults. The test consists of a picture about which a story is to be written.

The test is comprised of three scales. One measures length (productivity scale), another measures correctness (syntax scale), and the third measures content or meaning (abstract-concrete scale).

The productivity scale measures total number of words, total number of sentences, and the number of words per sentence. The syntax scale measures accuracy of word usage, use of word endings, and punctuation. The abstract-concrete scale is concerned with the nature of the thoughts expressed. It is divided into five levels, each representing an increment in the extent to which the content of the story manifests use of abstract ideas.

A person of any age can be compared with the norms, which indicate the extent to which an average child 7–17 years of age is successful in communicating ideas. Average testing time is 20 minutes; however, there are no time limits and rarely does a child require more than 30 minutes. The norms are reported as percentiles.

Standardization Information

The test was standardized on 747 children selected from three types of public school populations: metropolitan, rural, and suburban. The children were from all socioeconomic levels, with a wide variety of cultural backgrounds. No other specifics are reported in the text regarding the sampling.

Myklebust (1965) describes the problem of test-retest approach for his test as difficult because of the developmental aspects of behavior in children; for this reason a second testing in the reliability studies followed the first testing by only a few days. (No reliability coefficients are shown for this short interval testing.) The split-half procedure was used to study the reliability of the Syntax and Words Per Sentence scores. Odd-even procedure was not applicable to Total Word, Total Sentence, and Abstract-Concrete scores. The sample consisted of 208 stories selected randomly for the age range of 7–15 years. The scores for Words Per Sentence and Syntax for the even-numbered sentences were compared with the odd numbered. These data are shown in Table 24.

Although only two correlations reached .90 or above, each of the coefficients was determined to be significant at the .01 level of confidence.

Myklebust inaugurated a longitudinal study in which the test was given to a large sample of school children once a year for three years. The data gained from this investigation were to establish the extent to which the PLST reliably measured growth of facility in the use of the written word. This, as well as other studies, showed growth in writing ability over a period of time. Myklebust cites six cases showing growth patterns in Total Words, Total Sentences, Words Per Sentence, Syntax, and Abstract-Concrete scores. This growth was shown on repeated administrations of the test to children with language disorders enrolled for remedial training.

Table 24. Odd-Even Reliability Coefficients for WPS and Syntax*

Age	Words Per Sentence		Syntax	
	N	Coefficient	N	Coefficient
7	33	.84	33	.90
9	37	.74	37	.92
11	47	.38	47	.56
13	47	.54	47	.52
15	44	.64	44	.74
Total	208	.82	208	.88

*Significance for each correlation was found to be at the .01 level.

Note: Reprinted by permission, from H. R. Myklebust, *The Development and Disorders of Written Language*, vol. 1 (New York: Grune and Stratton, 1965), p. 150.

The validity of the test entailed several considerations, since there were no other tests of exactly the same nature. In terms of Words Per Sentence, comparisons were made with the studies of Stormzand and O'Shea, Heider and Heider, and Hillocks (Myklebust, 1965). This comparison gave validity to this scale. Since Productivity, Abstract-Concrete, and Syntax all reflect a maturation pattern, as is typical of normal growth in development, face validity of these tests was assumed. Kleuver (1976) has extended a study of language development through the first and second grades with the Picture Story Language Test and has shown the progressive language development through these two grade years. His study gives further substantiation to the face validity of this test.

The data presented on interscorer reliability are very thoroughly covered and presented in detail in the book *Development and Disorders of Written Language* (Myklebust, 1965). Interscorer reliability was found to be unusually good; however, Myklebust points out that previous training in scoring the Syntax scale appears to be a critical factor. Since the scoring requires an inordinate amount of time, a study was made to determine means of scoring only a part of the story. The findings show that for most purposes only the first three sentences need be scored; however, in cases of handicapped children and of those with language disorders, it is advisable to score the entire story.

Interpretation and Use

The Picture Story Language Test provides qualitative information on writing tasks. It is a good screening instrument to identify the developmental writing level of children. It provides a task-analysis guide for writing and, regardless of what writing test a diagnostician/teacher may use, information from Myklebust will make the interpretation easier.

Myklebust (1965) identified the clinical and educational situations in which the test can be applied. They are as follows:

1. As a diagnostic instrument for the study of children with language disorders and other types of learning disabilities
2. As a research tool to investigate the relationships between written language and aspects of behavior, such as intelligence

3. To determine the achievement level of a given class or of a larger group in order to note the progress made from one year to another
4. To compare the advantages of various educational methods
5. To study the range and nature of written-language abilities geographically
6. To ascertain levels of written-language ability for purposes of grouping and teaching
7. To define errors of written language that characterize the performances of the deaf, aphasic, mentally retarded, speech defective, emotionally disturbed, dyslexic, and dysgraphic
8. To obtain data for comparatively analyzing facility with the spoken, read, and written word
9. As a tool for studying grammar and the syntactical development of sentence structure
10. As a measure of the geriatric deterioration of verbal behavior
11. As a means for comparing the languages used in various countries psycholinguistically
12. As an indication of literacy*

Itemized Facts.

1. The Picture Story Language Test is comprised of three scales with one measuring productivity, one measuring correctiveness, and the third measuring meaning.
2. The average testing time is 20 minutes but there are no time limits.
3. Odd-even reliability for two subtests for which this was an applicable procedure was .82 and .88.
4. For most purposes and to save time only the first three sentences need to be scored.
5. This is a screening instrument to identify the developmental writing level of children.
6. The test is applicable for a number of uses.

Test of Written Language (1978)

Description and Administrative Procedures
The Test of Written Language (TOWL) (Hammill and Larsen, 1978) is an instrument designed to measure five abilities that the authors identify as necessary if one is to write in a meaningful manner. These five basic abilities or components are

a. Productive Component, or the ability to generate enough meaningful sentences to express adequately one's thoughts and feelings
b. Mechanical Component, or handwriting ability
c. Conventional Component, or the ability to use accepted rules established for punctuation, capitalization, and spelling
d. Linguistic Component, or the ability to use serviceable syntax and semantic structures
e. Cognitive Component, or the ability to write in a logical, coherent, and sequenced manner, so that the material is readily understandable to another person

---

*By permission, from H.R. Myklebust, *The Development of Disorders of Written Language*, Vol. 1 (New York: Grune and Stratton, 1965), pp. 70–71.

The Test of Written Language (TOWL) is composed of seven tests to measure the five basic abilities. The test includes a spontaneous writing format that sets it apart from most written-language tests. The child is shown three pictures and is asked to make up a good story to go with the pictures. The mechanical, productive, and cognitive components are measured entirely from this spontaneous format. The conventional component is measured by a spelling test and by having the subject rewrite sentences that are shown without capitalization and punctuation.

Four of the seven subtests call for a detailed scoring procedure that involves some subjective evaluation. The authors checked the inter-scorer reliability by checking the scoring of 15 experienced teachers. The percentage of agreement among the scorers was .93 for Thematic Maturity, .97 for Thought-Units, .76 for Handwriting, and .98 for Vocabulary (Hammill and Larsen, 1978).

Standardization Information

The test was standardized on 1,712 children, ages 8–14, residing in nine states extending from Texas to Massachusetts. The sex and residence of the sample approximated very closely the national population, as shown by the 1970 U.S. Census.

Both scaled scores and grade equivalents are provided. The scaled scores are based on children from 8-6 to 14-5 years of age. The grade equivalents extend from grades 2 through 8. The total score is called a Written Language Quotient and has been set with a mean of 100 and a standard deviation of 15. The scaled scores of the subtests have a mean of 10 and a standard deviation of 3. Setting the means and standard deviations in this manner, so they are comparable to the accepted IQ mean and S.D., aids consultants in using such tests for diagnosis and comparison.

The internal consistency of the three subtests, where homogeneity of the items was an objective of the authors, was reported for six age intervals ranging from 9-0 to 14-5 years of age. The tests were Spelling, Word Usage, and Style. The coefficients ranged from .75 to .92, with three of the 18 reporting less than .80. All were statistically significant beyond the .01 level of significance (Hammill and Larsen, 1978).

The test-retest method yielded reliability coefficients of the subtests from .62 for vocabulary to .96 for spelling. The median correlation was .86.

The validity of the TOWL for grades 3 and 4 was measured against the Picture Story Language Test (Myklebust, 1965). Each TOWL subtest was correlated with the three aspects of writing measured by the PSLT. Of the 24 separate correlations produced, four were not statistically significant at the .05 level; two correlated at the .05 level; and the other 18 were significant at the .01 level of confidence. Hammill and Larsen (1978) validated the TOWL with ratings of the written story by experienced teachers. The Written Language Quotient had a validity coefficient of .58.

Interpretation and Use

The Test of Written Language is unique, in that it uses a spontaneous story written by the subject with a standardized scoring procedure to measure writing ability. It makes it possible to determine a student's particular strengths and weaknesses and, also, to determine how a student compares to a standardized norm population. The TOWL subtests were much less valid for the mentally retarded and adolescents with learning disabilities. It appears to be a useful test for evaluating written-language ability. However, as with every new test, one must await additional research to determine its true worth. The reader is urged to be alert to additional documentation on its applicability and validity as a test to evaluate written-language ability.

Itemized Facts.

1. The TOWL measures five basic abilities necessary in order to write in a meaningful manner.
2. Three of the five basic abilities are measured by a spontaneous-writing format.
3. The inter-scorer correlation of 15 experienced teachers, scoring the spontaneous writing section of the TOWL, ranged from .76 for handwriting to .98 for vocabulary.
4. Scaled scores and grade equivalents are provided the user.
5. The Total Score, identified as Written Language Quotient, has a mean of 100 and a standard deviation of 15.
6. The internal consistency of Word Usage, Spelling, and Style was statistically significant beyond the .01 level of significance.
7. The TOWL subtests are less valid for the mentally retarded and adolescents with learning disabilities than for normal students.

Test of Adolescent Language (1980)

Description and Administration Procedures

The Test of Adolescent Language (TOAL) (Hammill, D. et al., 1980) is one of the few tests designed to measure the language abilities of adolescents. It can be used to identify those students who are significantly below their peers in language proficiency and, also, to identify particular kinds of language strengths and weaknesses that individual adolescent students may possess.

The model from which the test was developed included six language abilities. These are spoken language, written language, semantics (labeled vocabulary in the test structure), syntax (labeled grammar in the test structure), receptive language, and expressive language. The combinations possible among these six abilities produce eight components, and tests were developed to represent each of the resulting components. By combining the results of the subtests, four additional components of language ability may be obtained. These are listening, speaking, reading, and writing. The TOAL, therefore, provides the clinician with scores for ten language factors and an overall Adolescent Language Quotient.

Standardization Procedure

The TOAL was standardized on a sample of 2,723 students between the ages of 11 and 18 years of age. They were drawn from 17 states and 3 Canadian provinces. The sample did not include any students who were identified as handicapped. The sample was representative of the sex and residence of the U.S. population.

The test-retest reliability of the TOAL was reported for both the subtests and for the composite quotient. The coefficients of the subtests ranged from .74 to .90, with a median of .82. The 10 composite scores had a range of coefficients from .82 to .98. The Adolescent Language Quotient was reported as .97 (Hammill et al., 1980).

To establish the validity of the TOAL, the authors correlated it with five criterion tests. The tests were the Peabody Picture Vocabulary Test and the Memory for Related Symbols of the Detroit Test of Learning Aptitude for spoken language (listening and speaking); and the Reading and Language Totals from the Comprehensive Test of Basic Skills and the total score of the Test of Written Language for written language (reading and writing). The validity coefficients of the Total TOAL and the PPVT was .62, the DTLA subtest .59, the Reading Total from the CTBS .83, and the Language Total from the CTBS .66. The correlation of the Total TOAL and the TWL was .67 (Hammill et al., 1980).

Interpretation and Use

To aid the clinician in interpretation and use of the results, the norms for the subtests were set with a mean of 10 and a standard deviation of 3; the ten component variables, which are made up of combinations of the subtests, have a mean of 100 and a standard deviation of 15. The component scores, which are identified as quotients, can be compared to the results of other tests of mental abilities because of the similarity of the means and standard deviations.

purpose The TOAL may be used as a screening instrument to determine if additional study needs to be undertaken to determine more about the student's performance and abilities. An analysis of the subtests assists in analyzing the student's abilities. The subtests are Listening/Vocabulary, Listening/Grammar, Speaking/Vocabulary, Speaking/Grammar, Reading/Vocabulary, Reading/Grammar, Writing/Vocabulary, and Writing/Grammar. The TOAL should not be used for placement of students.

The user is counseled to investigate further research on this test as it appears in the literature. Although the test authors applied very professional procedures in developing the test, further studies may provide supportive data, or they may suggest certain cautions and restrictions in its use. This admonition is true for any new test appearing on the market.

Itemized Facts.

1. The TOAL is one of the few tests designed to measure the language abilities of adolescents.
2. Scores are provided for ten language factors and an overall Adolescent Language Quotient.
3. Over 2,700 youths between the ages of 11 and 18 were used in the standardization sample. None of the sample was identified as handicapped.
4. The test-retest reliability coefficients of correlation for the subtests ranged from .74 to .90. The Adolescent Language Quotient was .97.
5. The ten language factors are set with a mean of 100 and a standard deviation of 15.
6. The TOAL is a screening instrument and should not be used for placement of students.

Learning Aptitude Tests

Detroit Tests of Learning Aptitude (1967)

Description and Administrative Procedures

The Detroit Tests of Learning Aptitude, by Harry J. Baker and Bernice Leland (1967), comprise a comprehensive individual psychological examination with a practical design for a diagnostic instrument. There are 19 subtests, each a scale by itself, and from these a variety of batteries may be selected for specific cases. These include the blind and visually handicapped, the deaf and the acoustically handicapped, the orthopedically handicapped, the cerebral palsied, the speech handicapped, the neurologically handicapped and brain injured, and the emotionally disturbed/maladjusted. The batteries of tests may also measure the special disabilities of both normal and mentally retarded people and the outstanding talents of the mentally gifted. Baker and Leland identify eight mental faculties in their 19 subtests. These are listed in Table 25. The flexibility a clinician has in designing a diagnostic battery from the subtests, ease of handling, and the fact that students tend to enjoy the tasks has enhanced the popularity of the DTLA.

Age norms have been developed for the nineteen subtests. A general mental age is derived from the median ages of whatever series of tests have been administered. Subjects are usually administered from 9–13 subtests, with the decision based on the insight of the clinician as to which are the most appropriate. Some are recommended to be omitted for various mental age levels. See Table 25. This test is undergoing a new standardization at this printing.

Standardization Procedures

The standardization on the DTLA was made on pupils from the Detroit Public Schools. Initially, fifty pupils at every age level, with IQs between 90 to 110, were used; on subsequent testing 150 pupils at each level were tested. Reliability was first established on 48 cases ($r = .959$, with interval of 5 months between testing). A second correlation of .67 was found for a group of 792 pupils seven to twelve years with intervals of 2–3 years between testing.

Sixteen subtests were correlated with each other on the performance of 100 children (ages 8–12 years) and the "great majority of correlations fell from .2 to .4 indicating a fairly low yet positive correlation" (Baker, 1967). The reported information on the DTLA can be seen to be very inadequate. Mention is made in the manual of comparisons between the score performances on the DTLA and other well-known tests, but the tests are not named. The author claims that the test is a suitable test for both the mentally retarded and the average student.

A correlation study usinig the DTLA, Stanford-Binet, and WISC IQ scores was conducted by Chiappone (1968). Product moment correlations were computed, using 24 persons with the DTLA and the Stanford-Binet and 27 with the DTLA and WISC. The correlations were reported as significant between the DTLA and the S-B and WISC Full Scale, Verbal and Performance. The Index of Forecasting Efficiency was reported at .50 for the Detroit and S-B. This would allow for satisfactory substitution between them (Chiappone, 1968).

Table 25. Subtests on the Detroit Test of Learning Aptitude

*	Subtests	Mental Faculties	Subtest Numbers
b. c.	1. Pictorial Absurdities	(a) Reasoning and Comprehension	1,2,8,10,15,17
a.	2. Verbal Absurdities	(b) Practical Judgment	5,7,10,18
b. c.	3. Pictorial Opposites	(c) Verbal Ability	2,4,11,19
a.	4. Verbal Opposites	(d) Time and Space Relationships	10,12,17
	5. Motor Speed	(e) Number Ability	7,14
	6. Auditory Attention Span for Unrelated Words	(f) Auditory Attentive Ability	6,7,13,18
b. c.	7. Oral Commissions	(g) Visual Attentive Ability	1,3,9,12,16,17,18
c.	8. Social Adjustment A		
	9. Visual Attention Span for Related Syllables	(h) Motor Ability	5,7,12,18
c.	10. Orientation		
	11. Free Association		
	12. Designs		
	13. Auditory Attention Span for Related Syllables		
b. c.	14. Number Ability		
	15. Social Adjustment B		
a.	16. Visual Attention Span for Letters		
a.	17. Disarranged Pictures		
a.	18. Oral Directions		
a.	19. Likenesses and Differences		

*a. Should be omitted at M.A. levels 3–6 years
b. Should be omitted at M.A. levels 9–12 years
c. Should be omitted at M.A. levels 14 years and older

Interpretation and Use

The Detroit Test of Learning Aptitude has been used extensively since 1935, even though the reports on standardization procedures have been meager and no validity studies are reported in the Manual. Diagnosticians should be aware of these limitations and, until such time as the validity of the test has been determined, it should be supported by other data when major educational decisions are to be made. However, selected subtests of the DTLA have been found useful by specialists who work with L.D. children (Faas, 1976), (Wiebe and Harrison, 1978). Braggio (1980) found some of the subtests to be useful to identify learning styles of youngsters that facilitate learning of LDs. He was able to take the subtests Motor Speed, Visual Object Attention, Memory for Designs, Visual Attention Span for Letters, and Disarranged Pictures and take the errors made by a subject and then give those items again and find out what was a preferred kind of an approach in trying to answer them. He identified three task approaches: Vocal Response, where the child had to tell what was required to make a correct response, Visual-manual Response, and a Covert Response, in which he could not vocalize or make a visual manual response. Identifying the preferred learning approach and then encouraging the teacher to utilize this information in the instructional program resulted in increased learning. He believes that what keeps the nondisabled learner from being disabled is that he has many task approaches to learning; whereas, the learning disabled has limited approaches to performing any task of learning.

Banas and Wills (1978,79,80) see the DTLA as being of great value in analyzing the errors for information about immediate intake and recall. They have taken each subtest and identified what tasks it requires, things to check that may influence the score, and what to use to cross check the score. Users of the DTLA will find this series of articles useful in diagnosis and remediation. They emphasize that the DTLA is to be used as supplemental information to other tests such as the WISC-R.

An aid to analyzing data from the DTLA is a profile graph (Figure 40) to be used with elementary- and middle-school children, ages 7 through 14 (Bohning, 1979). A bar graph can be constructed by shading each subtest to match the mental-age value. This graphic form aids in explaining scores to parents and teachers.

Although many uses of subtest data of the DTLA are evident, one must be evermindful that the DTLA does not provide the user with the technically adequate information expected of any test publisher. This lack of information limits the confidence one can place in the instrument and restricts the user in making a valid analysis of the tests. Although a test may be used under these conditions, it places a heavy responsibility on the user. Until such time as technically adequate information is provided, the user will need supporting data for major educational decisions.

Itemized Facts.

1. Standardization reports on the DTLA published in the manual are meager.
2. The clinician can choose subtests to study different mental facilities.
3. The DTLA can be used to identify a preferred learning style.
4. Age norms are provided for the 19 subtests, plus a general mental age.
5. No validity studies are reported in the manual.

Name:__________________ **CA:**_____

Date:____________________________

Examiner:____________________________

PROFILE GRAPH FOR SELECTED SUBTESTS OF DETROIT TESTS OF LEARNING APTITUDE

Directions:

1. Record the raw score and mental age value in the box under each subtest; use the weighted raw score for Subtests 6 and 9.
2. Shade the graph bar under each subtest to match the mental age value; the shaded graph indicates the level of functioning when tested.
3. A pattern of intraindividual strengths and weaknesses is revealed on the graph. If the child's expectancy age is known it can be drawn as a horizontal line and labeled EA. A comparison can then be made between individual functioning on each subtest and expectancy age.

	Selected Detroit Subtests								
	Subtest 4	Subtest 5	Subtest 6	Subtest 13	Subtest 9	Subtest 16	Subtest 8	Subtest 18	Subtest 19
Raw Score									
Mental Age									
	VERBAL OPPOSITES Abilities Tested: Vocabulary Concepts and Auditory Association	MOTOR SPEED AND PRECISION Abilities Tested: Eye-hand Coordination and Psychomotor Speed	AUDITORY ATTENTION SPAN FOR UNRELATED WORDS Abilities Tested: Auditory Attention and Auditory Memory	AUDITORY ATTENTION SPAN FOR RELATED SYLLABLES Abilities Tested: Auditory Attention and Auditory Sequential Memory	VISUAL ATTENTION SPAN FOR OBJECTS Abilities Tested: Visual Attention and Visual Memory	VISUAL ATTENTION SPAN FOR LETTERS Abilities Tested: Visual Attention and Visual Sequential Memory	SOCIAL ADJUSTMENT A Abilities Tested: Social Judgment and Reasoning and Social Adjustment	ORAL DIRECTIONS Abilities Tested: Comprehension, Auditory Sequential Memory, and Auditory-Visual-Motor Association	LIKENESSES AND DIFFERENCES Abilities Tested: Verbal Expression and Conceptual Maturity

Mental Age Increments: 18-0, 17-6, 17-0, 16-6, 16-0, 15-6, 15-0, 14-6, 14-0, 13-6, 13-0, 12-6, 12-0, 11-6, 11-0, 10-6, 10-0, 9-6, 9-0, 8-6, 8-0, 7-6, 7-0, 6-6, 6-0, 5-6, 5-0, 4-6, 4-0

Profile sheet it is expressive lang.

FIGURE Profile graph for selected subtests of Detroit Tests of Learning Aptitude.

Figure 40. Profile Graph for Selected Subtests of Detroit Tests of Learning Aptitude.

Woodcock-Johnson Psycho-Educational Battery (1977)

Description and Administrative Procedures

The Woodcock-Johnson Psycho-Educational Battery (Woodcock and Johnson) is a set of wide-age-range, individually administered, standardized tests that measure cognitive abilities, scholastic aptitudes, achievement, and interests. The complete battery contains 27 subtests, organized into three parts. The three parts of the Battery and the numbers and names of the subtests included in them are shown in Table 26.

Part One consists of 12 cognitive-ability subtests, ranging in complexity from tasks of visual matching and auditory blending to tasks of concept formation and reasoning with analogies. Scores based upon performances from specified combinations of these subtests provide information about a subject's broad cognitive ability, four cognitive factors, and four scholastic aptitudes. A special combination of two subtests from Part One (Quantitative Concepts and Antonyms-Synonyms) provides a preschool scale of broad cognitive ability.

Part Two of the Battery contains 10 subtests that measure several aspects of scholastic achievement. Scores from seven of these subtests provide information regarding skill in reading, mathematics, and written language. The remaining three subtests measure knowledge of science, social studies, and humanities.

Part Three of the Battery contains five subtests that measure a subject's level of preference for participating in scholastic or nonscholastic activities.

Table 26. Woodcock-Johnson Psycho-Educational Battery

Part One: Tests of Cognitive Ability

1. Picture Vocabulary	7. Visual Matching
2. Spatial Relations	8. Antonyms-Synonyms
3. Memory for Sentences	9. Analysis-Synthesis
4. Visual-Auditory Learning	10. Numbers Reversed
5. Blending	11. Concept Formation
6. Quantitative Concepts	12. Analogies

Part Two: Tests of Achievement

13. Letter-Word Identification	18. Dictation
14. Word Attack	19. Proofing
15. Passage Comprehension	20. Science
16. Calculations	21. Social Studies
17. Applied Problems	22. Humanities

Part Three: Tests of Interest Level

23. Reading Interest	26. Physical Interest
24. Mathematics Interest	27. Social Interest
25. Language Interest	

The Battery may be administered in its entirety, or single subtests or clusters of subtests may be administered to meet specific appraisal needs. If information from the entire Battery is not needed, the examiner is encouraged to apply the principle of selective testing and administer only those portions of the Battery necessary to obtain the information upon which decisions are to be based. A table is provided on the second page of each response booklet to indicate which subtests must be administered to obtain certain measures. The authors advise that conscientious application of the principle of selective testing will save considerable testing time. For example, they state that if detailed information regarding a subject's cognitive abilities is not needed, the examiner may administer a brief scale of cognitive ability, consisting of only two subtests and requiring only 15 minutes.

Scoring of the subtests requires very little time, since it involves simply counting the correct responses in each subtest. If desired, the test can be scored by the publisher. The summary and interpretation of test results requires a little over 30 minutes for Part One and less than 30 minutes for Parts Two and Three combined. The average time for administration of Part One is approximately one hour. Parts Two and Three combined also require about one hour.

A prerecorded cassette tape is provided with the test book containing Part One. This tape is to facilitate standardized administration of the Blending, Memory for Sentences, and Numbers Reversed subtests. The tape also includes a pronunciation guide for reference by the examiner while learning to administer and score the tests. A 12-page response booklet is used with each of the test books for recording responses, summarizing results, and interpreting test performance.

Standardization Information

Normative data for the Battery were gathered from 4,732 subjects in 49 communities widely distributed throughout the United States. About 3,900 of these subjects constituted the school sample (subjects attending kindergarten through grade 12). Data for the school sample were drawn from 42 communities during the period April 1976–March 1977. Table 27 shows the distribution of the norming sample by age. The stratifying variables were considered as follows: sex, both male and female, were chosen from white, Black, Indian, Spanish, and other races; occupational status was of the white-collar, blue-collar, service workers, farm workers, and the unemployed; the geographic region involved the Northeast, North Central, South, and West; and the type of community involved was both urbanized and nonurbanized. The approximate percentage of subjects falling in each level of each variable was determined in 1975 using the available 1970 U.S. Census data. The entire standardization procedure is covered

Table 27. Distribution of the Norming Sample by Age

Age	Number
3–5	555
6–17	3,577
18–19	152
20–39	158
40–64	193
65 and above	97
Total	4,732

very thoroughly in the technical manual (Woodcock, 1978), which should be ordered separately from the Test Battery.

Reliability.   Reliability statistics were calculated for all subtests across their range of intended use. All subtests except 2, 4, 7, 9, and 11 had reliabilities calculated using the split-half procedure and corrected by the Spearman-Brown formula. Subtests 2 and 7 are speeded tests such that estimation of their reliability by split-half procedure was considered inappropriate. Test-retest correlations were reported for these two tests. Subtests 4, 9, and 11 are tests that may be discontinued at specified cutoff points if the subject is doing poorly. The reliability of these three tests was determined by various procedures that involved Rasch calibration for each length of test where a discontinuance was allowed (Woodcock, 1978), and a formula that considered the number of test lengths, the number of subjects taking the test, and the standard deviation of ability scores. The formula is identified and explained fully in the Technical Manual for the Battery.

Cluster reliabilities were also established using different methods for the unweighted and weighted cluster scores. The reliability of the unweighted clusters was calculated by a simplification of the formula used in determining the weighted cluster scores, a formula by Guilford (1954). Both of these formulas are also explained fully in the Technical Manual.

Subtest reliability ranges are shown in Table 28 and cluster reliabilities are shown in Table 29.

Validity Data.   The types of validity established on the Woodcock-Johnson Battery are criterion-related validity, content-validity, and construct-validity studies.

The criterion-related-validity studies (concurrent and predictive) included correlations between the test and other tests with both normal and clinical groups. Many tests were used and in each case a different sampling number was included. Only a few coefficients are reported here. The correlation between Broad Cognitive Ability (Pre-School Scale) and the Stanford-Binet is .83; between the reading test of the battery and

Table 28. Subtest Reliability Range According to Age and Grade

Age and Grade		Reliability Range
Age	3	.72–.95
	4	.57–.95
Grade K		.81–.97
	1	.60–.97
	3	.70–.92
	5	.61–.92
	8	.63–.95
	12	.65–.93
Age	20–39	.76–.97
	40–64	.77–.99
	65+	.82–.96
Median Range for all subtests and age/grade groups = .65 to .95		

The lowest reliability coefficients were found on the Visual Matching Subtest, a timed test where test-retest reliability was obtained. The Cluster Score Reliabilities are found in Table 29.

Table 29. Cluster Score Reliabilities

Cluster	Age 3	Age 4	K	Grade 1	Grade 3	Level Grade 5	Grade 8	Grade 12	Age 20–39	Age 40–64	Age 65+
Part One:											
Broad Cognitive Ability											
Full Scale	—	—	—	.97	.97	.96	.97	.97	.98	.98	.98
Brief Scale	—	—	—	.91	.92	.91	.94	.93	.95	.96	.98
Preschool Scale	.93	.92	.94	.94	—	—	—	—	—	—	—
Scholastic Aptitudes											
Reading Aptitude	—	—	—	.94	.93	.93	.95	.95	.96	.97	.99
Mathematics Aptitude	—	—	—	.94	.92	.86	.88	.86	.87	.90	.91
Written Language Aptitude	—	—	—	.92	.92	.90	.93	.93	.96	.96	.97
Knowledge Aptitude	—	—	—	.93	.94	.93	.95	.95	.96	.97	.98
Part Two:											
Reading	—	—	—	.98	.96	.95	.96	.94	.97	.97	.96
Mathematics	—	—	—	.92	.92	.91	.90	.93	.94	.96	.95
Written Language	—	—	—	.92	.93	.94	.94	.93	.95	.97	.98
Knowledge	.90	.92	.93	.92	.91	.92	.95	.94	.94	.96	.96
Skills (Preschool)	.84	.86	.93	.97	—	—	—	—	—	—	—
Part Three:											
Scholastic Interest	—	—	—	—	—	.92	.91	.93	.93	.96	.96
Nonscholastic Interest	—	—	—	—	—	.81	.84	.87	.92	.89	.90

the Iowa total reading test scores, the range is .76 to .81. The range of correlations reported between the Battery's Mathematics Cluster and the Iowa Total Mathematics is .62 to .77; and the Written Language Cluster from the Battery has a correlation range of .74 to .84 with the Iowa Language score.

Two studies that provide evidence regarding the validity of the Battery for predicting end-of first-grade achievement are reported. Cognitive-ability scores were obtained at the end of kindergarten for 42 subjects and at the beginning of grade one for 73 subjects. Scores for the two samples were correlated with achievement scores obtained at the end of first grade. The correlations between the cognitive ability scores for each of these groups and their end-of-the-first-grade achievement scores were found to range between .52 and .67 for Reading, .44 and .60 for Mathematics, .55 and .68 for Written Language, .60 and .76 for Knowledge, and .58 and .70 for Skills.

For content validity, the items for the Battery were developed with contributions from outside experts, including experienced teachers and curriculum consultants. In each subtest, the items were selected and designed to be comprehensive and representative of a wide range of difficulty.

Construct validity, the extent to which scores on a test relate to some theoretical construct, is established for this Battery through intercorrelations among the subtests and the results of a "cluster-analysis" procedure that provides a visual portrayal of the pattern and degree of relationships among a set of measures. A table showing these interrelationships is shown in the Manual and the author reports that the information shown suggests that each subtest in the Battery is measuring a different ability.

The standardization procedure used in the development of this test and the coverage of the procedure appear to meet the highest standards of standardization. The result is that the Battery compares in a superior way with many of the testing instruments presently used in psycho-educational evaluation.*

Interpretation and Use

The Woodcock-Johnson Battery is one of the most thoroughly standardized and researched individual-assessment instruments ever released. The manual and Technical Manuals cover extensive material and are well written.

An important feature of the W-J is that the norms for all parts of the battery are based on data from the same sample of subjects. It is, therefore, possible to make direct comparisons among the cognitive ability, scholastic aptitude, achievement, and interest scores for a student.

Many factors influence school learning: intelligence, environment, motivation, teaching methods, interest, emotional state, physical handicaps, and a host of other major and minor factors. These keep correlations between an instrument and school learning from being very high. The W-J correlates with school learning better than the Wechsler scales. The typical correlation of the W-J to school learning is .78 and the Wechsler .66 (Woodcock, 1980).

Some studies have questioned the deviation IQ based on the W-J broad cognitive ability scale (Reeve, Hall, and Zakraske 1979; Ysseldyke, Shinn, and Epps 1980). Reeve reported the W-J mean score was 13 points lower than the WISC-R. Yesseldyke found

---

*The Woodcock-Johnson Psycho-Educational Battery is being standardized in Spain at this time.

the W-J mean score to be about 8 points lower than the WISC-R. Woodcock countered these reports by pointing out flaws in the research design, plus other factors that would account for these discrepancies in the scores (Woodcock, 1980). Until such time as studies have been made which correct certain research design flaws as alleged by Woodcock, we will have to wait for verification of the reported information. Until that time, we cannot accept the reported score differences of Reeve (1979) and Yesseldyke (1980) (Woodcock, 1980).

The Woodcock-Johnson Psycho-Educational Battery is one of the best broad-based diagnostic instruments presently available for use. It is recommended for use in the assessment of school children.

A final word is in order. Special caution is needed to see that errors do not manifest themselves in the final results used in decisions affecting the child. Any test involving a number of parts and having many subtests is more likely to result in errors in administration, scoring, and profiling than a more simplified test. The administrator of the Woodcock-Johnson should be familiar with the administration and scoring procedures before attempting to use it. Although scoring is relatively simple, a high degree of error may creep in by the time the results are profiled. It is imperative, therefore, that special cautions be exercised in the administration, scoring, and profiling of the Woodcock-Johnson.

Itemized Facts.

1. The Woodcock-Johnson Psycho-Educational Battery consists of 27 subtests that measure cognitive abilities, scholastic achievement, and interests in scholastic and nonscholastic activities.
2. A pre-recorded cassette tape facilitates standardized administration of parts of the battery.
3. The W-J was standardized on over 4,700 subjects, ranging in age from 3 to 65 years.
4. Subtest reliability coefficients ranged from .57 to .99 across the total age range.
5. Extensive validity studies have been made on the W-J. These show it to be a valid test.
6. The norms for each of the three parts are comparable, so that direct comparisons can be made across all parts of the Battery for each student.

Structure of Intellect Learning Abilities Test (1975)

Description and Administrative Procedures

The SOI Learning Abilities test (SOI-LA) by Meeker and Meeker (1975) is a unique test, in that it is based on a specific theory of intelligence (formulated by Guilford, 1959). It, however, is not an intelligence test. Its purpose is not to find out how intelligent a student is; it is a test of specific learning abilities, which has clusters designed for the purpose of determining a student's learning aptitude for reading and arithmetic (SOI-LA, 1975).

In determining content design for subtests, the authors first made an examination for the SOI abilities related to math and reading and to Piaget's construct of how intelligence is developed. Following this procedure, 24 tasks were chosen to identify readiness abilities. Twenty two of these are visual and two, Memory for Symbolic Units and Memory for Symbolic Systems, can be both visual and auditory.

The authors report that the SOI-LA Test departs in a significant way from the traditional use of norms as a criterion against which a child is rated. As an approach to testing, it does not ask "how much;" it asks, instead, "what kind." It measures many separate intellectual abilities, not just general intelligence. It is diagnostic in nature, in that it measures those abilities fundamental to reading, arithmetic, and basic creativity. The test results are shown in a profile for each student, referenced to his or her own overall performance on the test. If a student is achieving at grade level, its purpose is to show whether the prerequisite intellectual abilities will support higher achievement. If a student is achieving beyond expected grade levels, its purpose is to show what abilities make him or her superior, so that these abilities can be further emphasized. The profile shows an individual pattern of strengths and weaknessess, which can allow for appropriate curriculum planning. This feature of the SOI-LA approach, which relates the individual's profile of learning abilities to techniques to be used for teaching, is a highly significant feature of the SOI-LA. Vice and Gonzales (1979) report very impressive results in a study carried on from 1976 to 1979 in the Fountain Elementary School in Pueblo, Colorado, using the SOI-LA approach to instruction. Their data support the conclusion that SOI evaluation with training and instruction based on the results makes a difference in arithmetic-related basic abilities. In comparison with a control group, the experimental groups made significant gains that are being sustained (Vice and Gonzales, 1980).

Standardization Information

The first norming procedure for the SOI-LA Test is not reported in the manual of directions. Rather, it is reported in fly sheets printed by the SOI Institute. The initial set of data reported covers 17 of the 24 subtests in the test. The data represent research with the kindergarten, first-, second-, and third-grade children. The number and race of children involved were 1,652 Anglos, Blacks, and Mexican-Americans, the percentages of which are not reported. The split-half reliability procedure was used on the 17 subtests, and the coefficients ranged between .64 and .96. The subtests not reported in this study are DMU*, CFU, CSU, MSU, CFC, EFC, MFU, and NFU. The technical data manual (1980) followed this fly sheet. It reports normal score equivalents, standard deviations and means, and sample sizes to compute correlations among the subtests. The Alternate Form of the SOI was completed in 1980.

Interpretation and Use

The Structure of Intellect Learning Abilities Test (SOI-LA) is a unique test, which helps teachers and parents to understand some of the abilities required to master reading and arithmetic, and to see the strengths and deficits a subject has in each of these. Abilities are not static or unchanging, but subject to development. As these skills are developed through training and changes in instructions, achievement improves (Meeker and Meeker). Meeker and Meeker have developed materials to aid in this development.

The profile form (Table 30) and Readiness Abilities Form (Figure 41) show how the raw scores may be plotted to show gifted, superior, grade level, limiting, or disability levels for each individual. The teacher and parent can see the strengths and weaknesses of the learning abilities of the child, as identified by the Structure-of-Intellect model.

---

*See Figure 41 for abilities identified by three-letter codes.

TABLES OF EVALUATION FOR THE SOI-LA BASIC TEST

	CFU	CPC	CFS	CFT	CSR	CSS	CMU	CMR	CMS	MFU	MSU	MSS	MSI	EFU	EFC	ESC	ESS	NFU	NSS	NST	NSI	DFU	DMU	DSR
Ceiling	16	10	26	26	8	8	30	25	21	28	18	18	18	26	17	27	8	33	8	201	21	56	140	186
Intermediate	12	8	24	14	5	7	20	22	19	14	15	14	9	19	11	21	7	25	6	142	20	28	73	80
Grade 6	12	7	16	11	5	7	16	20	18	14	14	12	9	18	11	18	6	24	6	128	16	24	65	67
Grade 5	11	7	12	10	4	6	14	18	16	13	13	10	7	17	10	14	5	22	5	106	14	23	59	65
Grade 4	10	6	8	9	3	6	12	16	13	13	11	7	6	15	9	12	4	21	4	97	12	22	51	62
Grade 3	9	6	7	8	2	5	11	15	12	12	10	4	5	13	8	10	3	20	3	86	9	21	35	50
Grade 2	8	5	5	7	1	3	7	12	9	11	8	3	4	11	7	7	2	19	1	67	8	18	29	35
Grade 1	5	3	1	4	–	2	2	5	3	6	5	2	2	5	4	1	–	7	–	4	3	9	20	21
	CFU	CPC	CPS	CFT	CSR	CSS	CMU	CMR	CMS	MFU	MSU	MSS	MSI	EFU	EFC	ESC	ESS	NFU	NSS	NST	NSI	DFU	DMU	DSR

How to use: Draw a line above at present grade level. Plot the student's scores on the table to obtain the grade-level performance. Within-grade comparisons can be obtained by using the appropriate grade-level section from the table below.

Relating scores to school learning: See reverse side for parent report form that relates scores to reading, arithmetic, writing and creativity readiness

	CFU	CPC	CFS	CFT	CSR	CSS	CMU	CMR	CMS	MFU	MSU	MSS	MSI	EFU	EFC	ESC	ESS	NFU	NSS	NST	NSI	DFU	DMU	DSR
Gifted Level	14	9	26	19	8	8	23	24	21	21	18	18	15	23	14	26	8	33	8	172	21	38	102	99
Superior Level	14	9	26	18	6	8	22	24	21	19	17	17	12	21	13	25	8	33	8	165	21	35	90	90
INTERMEDIATE	12	8	24	14	5	7	20	22	19	14	15	14	9	19	11	21	7	25	6	142	20	28	73	80
Limiting Level	10	6	15	11	3	6	17	20	15	10	15	14	7	16	9	16	6	19	4	115	15	18	52	44
Disabling Level	9	5	7	9	2	6	14	17	13	7	15	8	5	14	9	13	5	14	2	96	11	15	40	35
Gifted Level	14	9	26	16	8	8	19	24	21	21	18	16	15	23	14	25	8	33	8	163	21	38	100	99
Superior Level	13	8	25	15	6	8	17	23	20	18	16	14	12	21	13	23	7	33	8	150	21	32	87	88
GRADE 6	12	7	16	11	5	7	16	20	18	14	14	12	9	18	11	18	6	24	6	128	16	24	65	67
Limiting Level	10	5	10	8	2	6	13	18	14	9	10	4	7	15	8	14	4	18	3	108	12	14	42	33
Disabling Level	8	3	5	6	2	5	11	15	11	5	5	0	5	13	7	11	2	11	1	87	11	10	29	24
Gifted Level	14	8	23	15	7	8	19	24	21	21	17	15	11	22	12	19	8	33	8	139	21	35	89	99
Superior Level	13	8	18	14	6	8	16	23	20	18	15	12	9	21	11	18	7	32	8	117	20	28	78	88
GRADE 5	11	7	12	10	4	6	14	18	16	13	13	10	7	17	10	14	5	22	5	106	14	23	59	65
Limiting Level	9	5	4	7	2	5	10	17	10	9	7	3	4	14	8	11	4	17	3	92	10	14	38	31
Disabling Level	7	3	3	6	1	4	8	14	9	5	4	0	4	12	7	10	2	11	1	74	8	10	26	22
Gifted Level	14	8	20	14	6	8	17	19	16	20	16	12	9	20	12	18	7	33	8	134	18	35	72	98
Superior Level	12	8	15	11	5	7	14	18	15	17	15	12	7	18	11	15	6	30	6	120	16	30	63	86
GRADE 4	10	6	8	9	3	6	12	16	13	13	11	7	6	15	9	12	4	21	4	97	12	22	51	62
Limiting Level	7	4	2	6	2	4	8	14	10	7	6	3	4	12	8	7	2	14	2	77	8	14	24	30
Disabling Level	6	3	1	5	1	4	5	12	8	4	4	0	4	10	7	6	1	11	0	60	5	10	15	20
Gifted Level	14	8	14	12	5	8	14	19	16	19	16	7	6	16	12	13	7	32	7	120	16	33	57	69
Superior Level	12	8	11	10	4	7	13	17	15	16	14	7	6	15	11	12	6	27	5	110	13	28	48	58
GRADE 3	9	6	7	8	2	5	11	15	12	12	10	4	5	13	8	10	3	20	3	86	9	21	35	50
Limiting Level	7	4	2	6	1	5	8	12	8	7	5	0	2	10	5	7	1	11	1	66	6	14	19	25
Disabling Level	5	3	1	5	1	0	3	10	7	4	2	0	2	9	4	5	1	11	0	48	4	9	13	18
Gifted Level	13	8	11	10	5	7	10	16	14	17	12	6	6	16	10	11	5	32	6	90	14	30	53	66
Superior Level	11	7	9	9	4	7	9	14	12	15	11	5	5	14	9	9	4	27	4	77	12	26	38	58
GRADE 2	8	5	5	7	1	3	7	12	9	11	8	3	4	11	7	7	2	19	1	67	8	18	29	35
Limiting Level	5	3	1	5	0	1	4	9	6	6	4	0	2	9	5	4	1	13	0	20	5	10	19	20
Disabling Level	4	2	1	4	0	0	3	7	5	1	2	0	1	7	4	3	0	9	0	11	4	8	12	15
Gifted Level	10	6	9	9	–	6	7	13	9	11	11	4	6	10	8	5	–	21	–	26	8	24		
Superior Level	8	5	7	7	–	5	5	10	7	10	10	3	5	8	7	3	–	14	–	9	7		53	35
GRADE 1	5	3	1	4	–	2	2	5	3	6	5	2	2	5	4	1	–	7	–	4	3	9	20	21
Limiting Level	2	1	0	1	–	1	0	1	1	0	0	0	1	2	0	–		3	–	0	0	0	6	12
Disabling Level	1	0	0	0	–	0	0	0	0	0	0	0	0	0	0	0	–	0	–	0	0	0	4	7
	CFU	CPC	CFS	CFT	CSR	CSS	CMU	CMR	CMS	MFU	MSU	MSS	MSI	EFU	EFC	ESC	ESS	NFU	NSS	NST	NSI	DFU	DMU	DSR

Performance	Percentile	Performance Interpretation
Gifted level	94	Very strong ability—can be compensating for weaknesses, if any
Superior level	84	Strong ability—can be compensating for weaknesses, if any
Grade level	50	Expected level—no problems indicated
Limiting level	16	Weak ability—potential problems indicated, unless remediated
Disabling level	6	Very weak ability—severly inhibiting fo skills development, unless remediated

Table 30. Tables of Evaluation for the SOI-LA Basic Test

Itemized Facts.

1. The SOI-LA is based on a specific theory of intelligence.
2. It identifies abilities necessary to learn reading and arithmetic.
3. There are two forms of the SOI-LA.
4. Split-half reliability was reported on 17 of the subtests, with coefficients reported ranging from .64 to .96.

Name _____ Grade _____ Date _____

READINESS ABILITIES

READING (Foundational abilities)

____ **CFU** – Visual closure
____ **CFC** – Visual conceptualization
____ **EFU** – Visual discrimination
____ **EFC** – Judging similarities and matching of concepts
____ **MSU (visual)** – Visual attending
____ **MSS (visual)** – Visual concentration for sequencing

READING (Enabling skills)

____ **CMU** – Vocabulary of math and verbal concepts
____ **CMR** – Comprehension of verbal relations
____ **CMS** – Ability to comprehend extended verbal information
____ **MFU** – Visual memory for details
____ **NST** – Speed of word recognition

ARITHMETIC

____ **CFS** – Constancy of objects in space (Piaget) *
____ **CFT** – Spatial conservation (Piaget) *
____ **CSR** – Comprehension of abstract relations *
____ **CSS** – Comprehension of numerical progressions
____ **MSU (auditory)** – Auditory attending
____ **MSS (auditory)** – Auditory sequencing
____ **MSI** – Inferential memory *
____ **ESC** – Judgment of arithmetic similarities
____ **ESS** – Judgment of correctness of numerical facts
____ **NSS** – Application of math facts
____ **NSI** – Form reasoning (logic) *
    * Indicates mathematics-related ability

WRITING

____ **NFU** – Psycho-motor readiness

CREATIVITY

____ **DFU** – Creativity with things (figural – spatial)
____ **DSR** – Creativity with math facts (symbolic)
____ **DMU** – Creativity with words and ideas (semantic – verbal)

How to use: Select the present grade level placement for the student, plot the student's scores from the test on the five-level table for that grade (on the reverse side), then, using the following system of symbols:
    ' + + ' for gifted, ' + ' for superior, 'o' for average, ' – ' for limiting, ' – – ' for disabling
transfer the appropriate symbols to the form above; this will relate the performance level of the student to reading, arithmetic, writing, and creativity areas of school learning.

Figure 41. Readiness Abilities Form

Kaufman Assessment Battery for Children (1981)

Description

The Kaufman Assessment Battery for Children (K-ABC) by Kaufman and Kaufman is a battery of individually administered tests designed to measure the intellectual (problem-solving) abilities and academic achievement of children ages 2-6 through

12-11. The battery consists of 10 to 12 tests, depending on the age of the child, and has an administration time of about one hour.

The achievement scale of the battery consists of five tests: Famous Faces and Places, Arithmetic, Picture Vocabulary, Riddles, and Reading. These tests are designed to measure a child's verbal knowledge and level of language development (Picture Vocabulary and Riddles), understanding of numbers and numerical concepts (Arithmetic), ability to read and comprehend letters and words (Reading), and general information (Famous Faces and Places).

Of particular significance in this battery are the intellectual (problem-solving) measures included and their application to learning. The intellectual tests are designed to assess (1) simultaneous processing and (2) successive processing. *Simultaneous integration* refers to the synthesis of separate elements into groups, these groups often taking on spatial overtones. The essential nature of this sort of processing is that any portion of the result is at once surveyable without dependence upon its position in the whole (Das, Kirby, and Jarman, 1979). Tests within the K-ABC that are designed to measure simultaneous processing are Magic Window, Memory for Places, Triangles, Gestalt Closure, Overlapping Pictures, Matrices, Visual Analogies, Concept Formation, and Memory for Faces.

Successive integration, on the other hand, refers to the processing of information in serial order. The important distinction between this type of processing and simultaneous processing is that in successive processing the system is not totally surveyable at any one time. Rather, a system of cues consecutively activates the components (Das, Kirby, and Jarman, 1979). The K-ABC tests designed to measure successive processing are Photo Series, Hand Movements, Bells, Jungle River, Memory for Numbers, Memory for Words, and Paired Associates (Kaufman and Kaufman, 1980).

The processing scales are not only related to the factor-analytic studies of Das, but also to cognitive psychology (Neisser, 1967) and cerebral specialization (Orstein, 1977). Neisser (1967) identifies two modes of mental organization. One is serial processing, primarily concerned with the analytical and sequential ordering of linguistic stimuli; the parallel process, on the other hand, is holistic and carries out many actions independently. Orstein (1977) believes there is cerebral specialization: that analytical thinking is carried out in the left hemisphere of the brain and that holistic processing is done in the right hemisphere. The K-ABC provides a diagnostic picture of intellectual processing of the individual that can be incorporated into the total diagnostic profile.

Standardization

The standardization is being completed in 1981. It will be based on a national sample stratified on the basis of sex, race, community size, geographic region, parental occupation, and special-education category. The last stratification variable refers to the inclusion of speech impaired, learning disabled, mentally retarded, emotionally disturbed, and other special-education groups in the sample in proportion to the number of these children in the school age population (Kamphaus, 1980).

Reliability is to be determined by test-retest procedures and studies of internal consistency. It is reported that construct validity of the processing scales has been established through factor analysis for the national tryout on 782 subjects (Kamphaus, 1980).

Interpretation and Use

Little information is presently available on this test. No validity studies have been reported on the achievement scale. Since the intellectual processing and achievement testing was done on a common sample, some very interesting research is contemplated. Although the authors of this book have not had a chance to use this battery, it is one that all clinicians should know about and investigate for use in diagnosis.

Itemized Facts.

1. No standardization information is presently available.
2. The K-ABC is designed to provide a diagnostic picture of intellectual processing of the individual.
3. The K-ABC is designed to measure problem-solving ability and achievement.
4. The intellectual processing and the achievement testing were done on a common sample.

Summary

An assessment battery dealing with school-age students will include achievement, language-, and learning-ability tests. This chapter discusses some of the commonly used tests in these areas.

The achievement tests may be norm-referenced or criterion-referenced and designed for individual and/or group administration. The tests discussed are the Peabody Individual Achievement Test, Wide Range Achievement Test, Stanford Achievement Tests, and California Achievement Tests. Both the PIAT and WRAT are individually administered achievement tests. Each measures achievement in reading, mathematics, and spelling, with the PIAT's also measuring general information. Although the tests are measuring the same areas, they differ somewhat in what they are measuring and how they measure it. Each of these tests is designed for screening rather than for placement.

The two group-administered test batteries discussed in this chapter, the SAT and CAT, are both well designed from a standpoint of validity and standardization procedures. They were not only adequately normed for use as norm-referenced tests, but designed for use in the criterion-referenced mode. The publishers of each battery made a special effort to remove sex and race bias from their tests.

The Reading Tests included are primarily diagnostic in nature. The standardized diagnostic tests described are Durrell Analysis of Reading Difficulty, Gates-MacGinitie Reading Tests, Gray Oral Reading Tests, and Woodcock Reading Mastery Tests. The Woodcock Reading Mastery Tests are norm referenced and partly criterion referenced. This series of tests provides many different types of scores for the clinician to use in determining the reading ability of the individual and for norm-reference use. An instrument similar to the diagnostic reading tests is the Reading Miscue Inventory. This Inventory provides a format for observing the child's reading and identifying specific reading errors that are made.

The KeyMath Test is a criterion-referenced test as well as a norm-referenced test. Reading ability is not a factor in this test, so the achievement level is more likely to reflect a true math achievement than one in which the results may be reflecting a reading as well as a math factor.

Language- and/or learning-ability tests are used to assist a clinician in detecting why a person has not learned as well as expected. The tests discussed include Clinical Evaluation of Language Function, Illinois Test of Psycholinguistic Abilities, Picture Story Language Test, Detroit Test of Learning Aptitude, Test of Written Language, Test of Adolescent Language, Woodcock-Johnson Psycho-Educational Battery, Structure of Intellect Learning Abilities Test, and the Kaufman Assessment Battery for Children. The SOI-LA and Kaufman-ABC tests differ somewhat from the other tests in this area. The SOI-LA is established on a theory of intelligence and, as such, identifies components of learning as they apply to reading and arithmetic. The K-ABC assesses simultaneous processing and successive processing of materials as intellectual measures that apply to learning. This information becomes a part of the diagnostic data bank. The theoretical bases from which the other tests were developed are discussed.

The tests described herein comprise only a small sampling of the tests available for use in assessment of achievement, language, and learning abilities.

Student Assignments:

1. *Compare reliability evidence on the language tests described in this chapter.*
2. *Research possible reasons that the reliability coefficient of .42 for spelling at the kindergarten level on the Peabody Individual Achievement Test would be so much lower than a .94 for spelling at the third-grade level.*
3. *Examine the ways a diagnostician/teacher could make diagnostic use of information on a subtest of reading recognition, written spelling, and math computation (visually presented) on, e.g., the WRAT. Relate this procedure to Task Analysis.*
4. *Compare the diagnostic functions measured on the Stanford Achievement Test with those found on the California Achievement Test.*
5. *Identify the errors (miscues) on the RMI and supply examples of each kind of error.*
6. *Support reasons for the adoption of any reading test described in this chapter.*
7. *Since there are insufficient reliability and validity data reported on the Detroit Test of Learning Abilities, research articles to find evidence to document its use.*
8. *Review the* Buros Mental Measurement Yearbook *to find other information on the tests reviewed in this chapter.*

REFERENCES

Arter, J. A., & Jenkins, J. R. Differential diagnosis—prescriptive teaching: A critical appraisal. *Review of Educational Research*, Fall 1979, *49*, no. 4: 517–555.

Baker, J. J., & Leland, B. *The Detroit tests of learning aptitude; Examiner's handbook.* Indianapolis: Bobbs-Merrill Co., Inc., 1967.

Banas, N., & Wills, I. H. The vulnerable child: Prescriptive teaching from the DTLA. *Academic Therapy,* September 1978, *14*, no. 1: 107–112.

Banas, N., & Wills, I. H. The vulnerable child: Prescriptive teaching from the DTLA. *Academic Therapy,* January 1979, *14*, no. 3: 363–368.

Banas, N., & Wills, I. H. The vulnerable child: Prescriptive teaching from the DTLA. *Academic Therapy,* March 1979, *14*, no. 4: 493–496.

Banas, N., & Wills, I. H. The vulnerable child: Prescriptive teaching from the DTLA. *Academic Therapy,* May 1979, *14*, no. 5: 617–620.

Banas, N., & Wills, I. H. The vulnerable child: Prescriptive teaching from the DTLA. *Academic Therapy,* September 1979, *15*, no. 1: 103–106.

Banas, N., & Wills, I. H. The vulnerable child: Prescriptive teaching from the DTLA. *Academic Therapy,* November 1979, *15*, no. 2: 237–240.

Banas, N., & Wills, I. H., The vulnerable child: Prescriptive teaching from the DTLA. *Academic Therapy,* January 1980, *15*, no. 3: 363–369.

Baum, D. D. A comparison of the WRAT and the PIAT with learning disability children. *Educational and Psychological Measurement*, Summer 1975, *35*: 487–493.

Bohning, G. A profile graph for interpreting the Detroit tests of learning aptitude. *Psychology in the Schools*, July 1979, *16*, no. 3: 338–341.

Bond, G. L., Tinker, M. A., Wasson, B. B. *Reading difficulties* 4th ed. Englewood Cliffs, N.J.: Prentice-Hall, 1979.

Bradley, J. M. Evaluating reading achievement for placement in special education. *The Journal of Special Education*, February 1976, *10*, no. 3: 237–244.

Braggio, J., Braggio, S., Varner, R., Smothers, E., & Lanier, J. Predicting success and failure of learning disabled children on academic tasks. *Journal of Educational Research*, November/December 1980, *74*, no. 2: 88–95.

Burns, E. An evaluation of the Peabody individual achievement test with primary age retarded children. *Psychology in the Schools*, January 1975, *12*, no. 1: 11–14.

Burns, G. W., & Watson, B. L. Factor analysis of the revised ITPA with underachieving children. *Journal of Learning Disabilities*, June/July 1973, *6*, no. 6: 371–376.

Chiappone, A. D. Use of the Detroit tests of learning aptitude with EMR. *Exceptional Children*, November 1968, *35*: 240–241.

Chronkhite, G., & Penner, K. A reconceptualization and revised scoring procedure for the ITPA based on multivariate analysis of the original normative data. *Journal of Speech and Hearing Research*, Spring 1975, *18*: 505–520.

Connolly, A. J., Nachtman, W., & Pritchett, E. M. *KeyMath diagnostic arithmetic test manual.* Circle Pines, Minn.: American Guidance Service, Inc., 1976.

Das, J. P., Kirby, J. R., & Jarman, R. F. *Simultaneous and successive cognitive processes.* New York: Academic Press, 1979.

Dean, R. S. Analysis of the PIAT with Anglo and Mexican-American children. *Journal of School Psychology,* Winter 1977, *15,* no. 4: 329–333.

Delong, A. R. The limits of accuracy of the test scores of educable mentally retarded individuals. *Journal of the Association for Research in Growth Relationships,* 1962, *3*: 26–44 (from Jastak and Jastak, 1978).

Dunn, L. M., & Markwardt, F. C. *The Peabody individual achievement test: examiner's manual.* Circle Pines, Minn.: American Guidance Service, Inc., 1976.

Durrell, D. D. *Durrell analysis of reading difficulty: manual of directions.* New York: Harcourt, Brace and World, 1955.

Elkins, J. Some psycholinguistic aspects of the differential diagnosis of reading disability in grades 1 and 2. Queensland, Australia: University of Queensland, 1972 (unpublished doctoral dissertation).

Elkins, J., and Sultmann, W. F. ITPA and learning disability: a discriminant analysis. *Journal of Learning Disabilities,* February 1981, *14,* no. 2: 88–92.

Evertts, E., Van Roekel, B. H. *Harper and Row basic reading series.* Scranton, Pa.: Harper and Row, 1966.

Faas, L. Unit 8 the Detroit tests of learning aptitude. In *Learning disabilities: a competency based approach.* Boston: Houghton Mifflin, 1976.

Gates, S. I., & MacGinitie, W. I. *The Gates-MacGinitie reading tests.* New York: Teachers College Press, Columbia University, 1972.

Glass, G. V. Primary, secondary, and meta-analysis of research. *Educational Researcher,* 1976, *5*: 3–8.

Glass, G. V. Integrating findings: The meta-analysis of research. In Shulman, L. S. (Ed.), *Review of research in education.,* 1977, *5*: 351–379.

Golden, N. E., & Steiner, S. R. Auditory and visual functions in good and poor readers. *Journal of Learning Disabilities,* September 1969, *2*: 476–481.

Goodman, Y. M., & Burke, C. L. *Reading miscue inventory manual.* New York: Macmillan, 1972.

Goodstein, H. A., Kahn, H., & Cawley, J. F. The achievement of educable mentally retarded children on the KeyMath diagnostic arithmetic test. *Journal of Special Education,* Spring 1976, *10,* no. 1: 61–70.

Gray, W. S. Gray oral reading test. (H. Robinson, ed.) Indianapolis: Bobbs-Merrill Company, 1967.

Grill, J. J., & Bartel, N. Language bias in tests: ITPA grammatic closure. *Journal of Learning Disabilities,* April 1977, *10,* no. 4: 229–235.

Guilford, J. P. Three faces of intellect. *The American Psychologist,* 1959, *14*: 469–479.

Hammill, D. D., & Larsen, S. C. Effectiveness of psycholinguistic training. *Exceptional Children,* September 1974, *41*: 5–14.

Hammill, D. D., & Larsen, S. C. *Test of written language.* Austin, Texas: PRO-ED, 1978.

Hare, B., Hammill, D., & Barten, N. Construct validity of selected Illinois tests of psycholinguistic subtests. *Exceptional Children,* 1973, *40*: 13–20.

Harmer, W. R., & Williams, F. The wide range achievement test and the Peabody individual achievement test: A comparative study. *Journal of Learning Disabilities,* December 1978, *11,* no. 10: 667–670.

Harris, A. J., & Clark, M. K. *Macmillan reading program.* New York: Macmillan, 1965.

Harth, R., & Justen, J. E. The validity of the ITPA visual closure subtest. *Academic Therapy*, Spring 1977, *XII*, no. 3: 261–265.

Horner, R. D. A factor analysis comparison of the Illinois test of psycholinguistic abilities and picture language story test with mentally retarded children. *Exceptional Children*, 1967, *34*: 183–189.

Jastak, J. K. & Jastak, S. R. *The wide range achievement test.* Wilmington, Del.: Guidance Associates of Delaware, 1976.

Jenkins, J. R., & Pany, D. Standardized achievement tests: How useful for special education? *Exceptional Children*, March 1978: 448–453.

Kamphaus, R. W. Personal correspondence with senior author, August 14, 1980.

Kavale, K. Functions of the Illinois test of psycholinguistic abilities (ITPA): Are they trainable? *Exceptional Children*, April 1981, *47*, no. 4: 496–510.

Kirk, S., McCarthy, J., & Kirk, W. D. *Examiner's manual: Illinois test of psycholinguistic abilities*, rev. ed. Urbana, Ill.: University of Illinois Press, 1968.

Kleuver, R. Denver, Colo.: Denver University, 1976 (unpublished research).

Kratochwill, T. R., & Demuth, D. M. An examination of the predictive validity of the KeyMath diagnostic arithmetic test and the wide range achievement test in exceptional children. *Psychology in the Schools*, October 1976, *13*, no. 4: 404–406.

Laffey, J. L., & Kelly, D. Woodcock reading mastery tests. *The Reading Teacher*, December 1979, *33*: 335–339.

Lehman, I. J. A review of the Stanford achievement series 1973. *Journal of Educational Measurement*, Winter 1975, *12*, no. 4: 297–306.

Macione, J. Psycholinguistic correlates of reading disabilities as defined on the Illinois test of psycholinguistic abilities. Vermillion, S.D.: University of South Dakota, 1969 (unpublished doctoral dissertation).

Madden, R., Gardner, E. F., Rudman, H. C., Karlsen, B., & Merwin, J. C. *The Stanford achievement test.* New York: Harcourt Brace Jovanovich, Inc., 1973.

McCarthy, J. J., & Olson, J. L. *Validity studies on the Illinois test of psycholinguistic abilities.* Urbana, Ill.: University of Illinois Press, 1964.

Meeker, M. *Structure of intellect.* Columbus, Ohio: Charles E. Merrill, 1969.

Meeker, M. N. El Segundo, Calif.: Institute for Applied SOI Studies, 1963, 1973, 1974 (unpublished research).

Memory, D., Powell, G., & Callaway, B. A study of the assessment characteristics of the Woodcock reading mastery tests. *Reading Improvement*, Spring 1980, *17*: 48–52.

Milgram, N. A. A note on the Peabody picture vocabulary test in mental retardates. *American Journal of Mental Deficiency*, 1967, *72*: 496–97.

Myklebust, H. *The development of disorders of written language*, vol. 1. New York: Grune and Stratton, 1965.

Neisser, U. *Cognitive psychology.* New York: Appleton-Century-Crofts, 1967.

Newcomer, P. The ITPA and academic achievement. *Academic Therapy*, Summer 1975, *X*, no. 4: 401–406.

Newcomer, P., & Hammill, D. *Psycholinguistics in the schools.* Columbus, Ohio: Charles E. Merrill Publishing Company, 1976.

Newcomer, P., Hare, B., Hammill, D., & McGettigan, J. Construct validity of the Illinois test of psycholinguistic abilities. *Journal of Learning Disabilities*, 1975, *8*, 220–231.

Orstein, R. E. *The psychology of conscience.* New York: Harcourt Brace Jovanovich, Inc., 1977.

Paraskevopoulas, J. N., and Kirk, S. A. *The development and psychometric characteristics of the revised Illinois test of psycholinguistic abilities.* Urbana, Ill.: University of Illinois Press, 1969.

Piaget, J. *The child's conception of number.* New York: W. W. Norton and Co., 1965.

Piotrowski, R., and Grubbs, R. D. Significant subtest score differences on the WISC-R. *Journal of School Psychology,* Fall 1976, *14,* no. 3: 202–206.

Piotrowski, R. Abnormality of subtest score differences on the WISC-R. *Journal of Consulting and Clinical Psychology,* June 1978, *46,* no. 3: 569–570.

Powell, G., Moore, D., and Callaway, B. A concurrent validity study of the Woodcock word comprehension test. *Psychology in the Schools,* January 1981, *18*: 24–27.

Reeve, R. E., Hall, R. J., & Zareski, R. S. The Woodcock-Johnson tests of cognitive ability: Concurrent validity with the WISC-R. *Learning Disability Quarterly,* 1979, *2*: 63–69.

Robinson, H. (Ed.) *Gray oral reading test.* Indianapolis: Bobbs-Merrill Co., Inc., 1967.

Scull, J. W., and Brand, L. H. The WRAT and the PIAT with learning disabled children. *Journal of Learning Disabilities,* June/July 1980, *13,* no. 6: 350–352.

Semel, E. M., and Wiig, E. H. *Clinical evaluation of language functions* Columbus, Ohio: Charles E. Merrill Publishing Co., 1980.

Silverstein, A. B. Pattern analysis on the PIAT. *Psychology in the Schools,* January 1981, *18,* 13–14.

Sitlington, P. L. Validity of the Peabody individual achievement test with educable mentally retarded adolescents. Honolulu: University of Hawaii, 1970, (unpublished masters thesis).

Soethe, J. W. Concurrent validity of the Peabody individual achievement test. *Journal of Learning Disabilities,* November 1972, *V,* no. 10: 47–49.

Stoneburner, R. L., & Brown, B. A. A comparison of the PIAT and WRAT performances of learning disabled adolescents. *Journal of Learning Disabilities,* November 1979, *12,* no. 9: 631–634.

Tiegs, E. W., & Clark, W. W. *California achievement tests. Technical bulletin, no. 1.* Monterey, Cal.: CTB/McGraw-Hill, 1979.

Tinney, F. A. A comparison of the KeyMath diagnostic arithmetic test and the California arithmetic test used with learning disabled students. *Journal of Learning Disabilities,* May 1975, *8,* no. 5: 57–59.

Tuinman, J. J., Kinzer, C., & Muhtadi, J. A short cut to testing passage comprehension. *Reading Horizons,* 1980, *20*: 103–105.

Vice, N., & Gonzales, R. El Segundo, Calif.: Presentation at Advanced SOI Conference, July 1980.

Wagner, R. F., & McCoy, F. Two validity studies of the wide range achievement test. Richmond, Va: Virginia Academy of Science, 1962 (Reported Jastak and Jastak, 1978).

Washington, E. D., & Teska, J. A. Correlations between the wide range achievement test, the California achievement test, the Stanford Binet and the Illinois test of psycholinguistic abilities: *Psychological Reports,* 1970, *26*: 291–294.

West, D., & Wilborn, B. A WISC-ITPA abilities profile. *Academic Therapy,* Winter 1975–76, *11*: 209–215.

Wetter, J., & French, R. W. Comparison of the Peabody individual achievement test and the wide range achievement test in a learning disability clinic. *Psychology in the Schools*, July 1973, *10*, no. 3: 285–286.

Wiebe, M. A. Unpublished KeyMath work analysis sheet. Denton, Texas: Texas Woman's University, 1979.

Wiebe, J., and Harrison, K. Relationship of the McCarthy scales of children's abilities and the Detroit tests of learning aptitude. *Perceptual and Motor Skills*, 1978, *46*, 355–359.

Williamson, W. E. The concurrent validity of the 1965 wide range achievement test with neurologically impaired and emotionally handicapped pupils. *Journal of Learning Disabilities*, March 1979, *12*, no. 3: 68–70.

Woodcock, R. W. A response to some concerns raised about the Woodcock-Johnson psycho-educational battery. *A paper presented at the tenth annual invitational conference on leadership in special education.* Minneapolis, Minn.: November 24,25, 1980. Revised 2-6-81.

Woodcock, R. W. *Woodcock reading mastery tests: manual.* Circle Pines, Minn.: American Guidance Service, 1973.

Woodcock, R. W., & Johnson, M. B. *Woodcock-Johnson psycho-educational battery.* Boston: Teaching Resources Corporation, 1977.

Woodward, C. A., Santa-Barbara, J., and Roberts, R. Test-retest reliability of the wide range achievement test. *Journal of Clinical Psychology*, January 1975, *31*: 81–84.

Ysseldyke, J. E., Shinn, M. R. & Epps, S. *A comparison of the WISC-R and the Woodcock-Johnson tests of cognitive ability.* Research Report No. 36. Minneapolis: Institute for Research on Learning Disabilities, University of Minnesota, 1980.

Part III

Special Education Assessment

Parts I and II have covered informal and formal approaches to assessment and a detailed examination of materials and strategies to be used. Part III covers assessment of seven special-education categories and makes application of these materials and strategies to the specific handicapping conditions. The seven special-education categories are: the early-childhood handicapped, multiply handicapped, auditorily and visually handicapped, mentally retarded, learning disabled, and the emotionally disturbed. The three handicapping conditions discussed in Chapter 8 and the three discussed in Chapter 9 are arbitrarily grouped for convenience. Chapter 10 provides information concerning procedures in reporting data to parents and also legal aspects of assessment of the handicapped child. Two papers in Chapter 8 have been contributed by guest authors, Louise H. Murphy and Claud "R" Zevely, and Jane Norris.

Chapter 8

The Exceptional Child, Multiply Handicapped, and the Visually and Auditorially Impaired

The student who has studied this chapter should:

1. *Understand why young handicapped children should not be labeled*
2. *Be able to choose specific tests to be used for the early childhood- and multiply handicapped, and the visually and auditorially impaired*
3. *Have knowledge of establishing rapport with young handicapped children*
4. *Be able to choose tests for the measurement of skills that fall within the affective, psychomotor, or cognitive domains*
5. *Be able to describe check lists and rating scales*
6. *Choose tests that may be used for the multiply handicapped*
7. *Understand a systems approach to assessment of the multiply handicapped*
8. *Understand the Hauessermann approach to assess cognitive development in the multiply handicapped*
9. *Understand the issues involved in assessing the auditorially and visually impaired*
10. *Have knowledge of a procedure to follow in assessment of the auditorially and visually impaired*
11. *Understand the unique differences in the procedures for assessment of the auditorially and the visually impaired.*

Introduction

Each category of special education is unique, not only in terms of major characteristics of each group, but also in terms of how behaviors in each group are to be assessed. Though the standard tests, intelligence, achievement and aptitude, may be used with all special-education children, the means of presentation and content of each may have to be modified to measure various attributes of growth and development. Where there are inner-language problems with any individual, communication is very difficult and techniques in testing must be altered or modified according to the specific need. This is particularly true in evaluating the multiply handicapped. Also, when preschool children are to be assessed, there are normal developmental patterns that differ with each child and that may suggest learning disabilities, when in reality the children are undergoing only sequential growth changes, as in learning to handle a pencil correctly or in developing concepts of up and down. Only specific parts of tests may be given to the visually and auditorially impaired. For instance, for evaluation of the visually impaired, the performance part of the Wechsler Scales cannot be used because sight is required. For the auditorially impaired, part of the Stanford-Binet and the Verbal part of the Wechsler Scales cannot be used in evaluation because hearing is necessary.

The assessment of the very young, the auditorially and visually impaired, and the multiply handicapped are examined in this chapter. The choice of placing these three groups within one chapter is not made because of any significant relationship. There, of course, can be an overlapping of these categories, for example, there may be a very young child who is blind and deaf, resulting in a multiply handicapped condition in a preschool individual. However, special-education children have always been studied by categories, and it is the general rule for state education agencies to establish guidelines for assessment and placement. Each category is examined as a separate entity with its own inherent issues discussed. Tests appropriate for use with each group are listed, as well as strategies and techniques. Two of the papers herein are by guest authors, namely Louise Hollar Murphy and Claud "R" Zevely, and Jane Norris.

Assessment of Young Exceptional Children
(by Louise Hollar Murphy and Claud "R" Zevely)

The early formative years are considered by authorities to be the most important years for both physiological and intellectual development. For exceptional children, those requiring special education and related services (Hallahan and Kaufman, 1978), these early years may be more crucial than for the normal, and the sooner they are recognized, the greater the chances that prevention of academic failure may be possible. Kirk (1958) found that mentally retarded children would more likely make significant gains in their first public-school experiences if they had been provided early-childhood training, and it has long been known that training for the blind and deaf must begin as soon as possible after birth. It seems apparent that it must not be left to chance that young handicapped children will pick up the information and skills that their nonhandicapped peers do in their normal daily experiences. An accurate assessment of many of these young exceptional children, then, becomes of utmost importance if appropriate social, physical, psychological, and educational skills are to be developed. When deficits are known, intervention may change their lives from dependent citizens to productive, contributing, happy members of society.

It is not difficult to determine sensory deprivation in young children, as in blind and deaf conditions, but assessment for the purpose of making decisions concerning learning disabilities, mental retardation, and emotional problems is not so simple. Infant and early-childhood tests have been used for several decades for the purpose of making predictions about the behaviors of young children at later ages. However, as early as the 1930s, it was a well-established fact that the tests for measurement of predicting *intelligence* in the infant and very early childhood ages could not be considered as dependable (Bayley, 1933; Bayley and Jones, 1937, Honzik, 1938). This was not necessarily considered to be a fault solely of the tests, but also a fault of the erratic growth patterns of the very young child. Often, criticism is made that the immaturity of young children makes accurate measures impossible and that the influence of the environment on both intelligence and social behavior is such that predictions for intelligence can not be made unless predictions for the environment also can be made. In the process of standardizing The Measurement of Intelligence for Infants and Young Children, Cattell (1940) found that a child who had obtained an IQ of 73 at three months and an IQ of near 90 at both six and nine months, continued to make steady gains. At age three years, her assessed IQ was 150, and at 4 years this child remarked to the examiner that she was animate but her doll was inanimate. It thus appears evident that predictions regarding intelligence of the very young child are considered to be questionable. What may be said of intelligence may be said of some other behaviors. For example, how can a child who has not been exposed to academic training be labeled learning disabled?

It is imperative that the diagnostician, whether teacher, parent, psychologist or consultant, be made aware of the necessity of making adequate judgment concerning the behaviors of these young exceptional children. Errors in such judgment may lead to inappropriate educational and social experiences for them and may result in *labeling**, which can be ravaging at any age, but may be socially and psychologically devastating to a young exceptional child.

The errors made in the evaluation of young children can result from a number of conditions, including failure to select appropriate assessment instruments, misjudgments or misinterpretations of test results, and the failure to discriminate normal development from abnormal development. To prevent such error, persons involved in the early childhood assessment should (1) understand normal developmental patterns of the young child; (2) recognize the kinds of handicapping conditions; (3) know appropriate observation techniques (see Chapter 4); and (4) be adept in choosing the correct instruments, as well as making proper interpretations of the information obtained.

Major emphasis in this paper is placed on the assessment of children for the purpose of placement in special education and for obtaining information needed for individual education plans. Particularly, standardized instruments and check lists/rating scales to

---

*The label that appears to be appropriate for the very young and preschool child is a category known as *at risk*; i.e., if certain behaviors have indicated a problem. When teachers work with children who deviate somewhat from the norm in their behaviors, they have the opportunity to determine through training whether real problems exist. This lessens the possibility of incorrectly labeling a child at such a young age. Jansky and de Hirsch (1972), Tjossen (1976), and Mercer (1979) are among those who were instrumental in using the terms *at risk* or *high risk* for the children who appear to be low in intelligence or slow in some basic developmental skills.

be used with the very young are discussed.* Other critical sensory deficits such as visual/auditory impairment are found in another paper in this chapter. The use of standardized tests for young handicapped children is discussed as follows:

Use of Standardized Tests

There are standardized tests that may be used with the young handicapped child. These measures generally have two explicit advantages over informal measures, as in criterion-referenced tests and check lists: (1) they include information on test reliability and validity; and (2) they supply norms for interpreting the scores that allow the examiner to compare a child's score with the scores of similar children or with the child's own earlier score. These two advantages put certain constraints on standardized testing. Directions for the administration and scoring of standardized tests are usually specified in detail in the test manual. Often the exact words for the examiner to use in giving directions are indicated and any liberties taken by the examiner in either the administration or the scoring of the tests may invalidate the scores and make the norms useless for interpretation. Such liberties are difficult to circumvent when testing young children. In order to get valid responses from young children, the examiner must establish a warm, secure, nonthreatening relationship with them and must be sure the children's attention and interests are focused on the tasks. In addition, the examiner must be sure that young children understand what is expected of them. Thus, a psychometric dilemma may be precipitated: the maintenance of the examiner/examinee rapport that must accompany the testing of young children, the focusing of attention, and the clarifying of directions may require the examiner to take liberties with the test administration and perhaps with the test scoring—liberties that in themselves may invalidate the scores.

In spite of the constraints upon standardized testing of young children, a proliferation of new assessment instruments is seen in the bulletins sent out by publishing companies. These instruments reflect the current interest in early development and particularly in the early identification of handicapping conditions. Standardized tests for young children assess all major areas of development: the affective domain, the cognitive domain, and the psychomotor domain. Tests for young children are designed to be administered either to individuals or to groups. In addition, some tests are designed for particular populations such as the culturally disadvantaged, children with specific/multi-handicaps, particular age groups, Spanish-speaking children—all of whom may be high-risk children for learning the basic skills.

The quality of the vast array of standardized tests for young children varies tremendously. Oscar Buros, editor of the *Mental Measurements Yearbook*, warned:

> Test publishers continue to market tests which do not begin to meet the standards of the rank and file of *Mental Measurements Yearbook* and journal review-

---

*Multidisciplinary experimentation and discoveries are leading us toward the age of scientific assessment and diagnosis. Chall and Mirsky (1978) suggested a test battery for the twenty-first century, which includes, among other items, behavior and photographic analysis designed to identify motor patterns, cerebral dominance, and related psychological and psychomotor capacities. By both behavioral and electrophysiological means, attentional capacities would be assessed and brain size and maturity evaluated. Brain neurohumoral balance and maturity would be analyzed by means of biochemical assays performed on a few drops of urine and blood. This is for the future; however, from this innovative idea, we may look forward to a completely different approach and expect to improve the diagnostic procedure of children continually.

ers. At least half of the tests currently on the market should never have been published. Exaggerated, false, or unsubstantiated claims are the rule rather than the exception (1972, p. xxviii).

The warning to examiners is, of course, to be wary of tests and to evaluate tests carefully before selecting an assessment instrument.

The selection process is simplified by the use of critical reviews of tests for young children. One such earlier review, which is still of value because of its provision of information covering specific domains to be measured in young chidlren, is the CSE-ECRC Pre-School/Kindergarten Test Evaluations (Hoepfner, 1971), which analyze 120 tests containing 630 subtests for young children. Each subtest was described and assigned to one or more of the following categories:

The Affective Domain
   1. The development of personality
   2. The development of social skills
   3. The development of motivation
   4. The development of aesthetic appreciation
The Intellectual Domain
   5. Cognitive functioning
   6. Creativity
   7. Memory
The Psychomotor Domain
   8. Physical coordination
The Subject Achievement Domain
   9. Arts and crafts
  10. Foreign language
  11. Functions and structures of the human body
  12. Health
  13. Mathematics
  14. Music
  15. Oral language skills
  16. Readiness skills
  17. Reading and writing
  18. Religion
  19. Safety
  20. Science
  21. Social studies

The authors set criteria for the 120 tests examined under the different domains: (1) measured validity, (2) examinee appropriateness, (3) administrative usability, and (4) normal technical excellence. Only a few of these tests are cited in this paper. They were rated high on at least the first two criteria. They are:

Affective Domain
   Primary Academic Sentiment Scale
   California Test of Personality

Psychomotor Domain
  Ring and Peg Test of Behavior Development
  Metropolitan Readiness Test
  Valett Developmental Survey of Basic Learning Abilities

Cognitive Domain
  Wechsler Preschool and Primary Scale of Intelligence
  Wechsler Intelligence Scale for Children
  Ayres Space Test
  Boehm Test of Basic Concepts
  Pictorial Test of Intelligence
  Columbia Mental Measurement Scale

When the person involved in testing is choosing a testing instrument for a young child, the CSE-ECRE evaluation may be used as a guide to determine whether measures are covered for the purposes needed. For example, a kindergarten teacher may observe that a child (Tom) is not adjusting to the other children. The teacher may begin an observation procedure by keeping a daily log noting the child's different behaviors during the day. At the end of an arbitrarily designated period, the teacher may check these daily behaviors and decide that an evaluation is needed. Observation data may suggest that Tom is very shy and will not compete in any of the play activities. He answers questions and appears to be normally intelligent. The teacher may examine the domains from the CSE-ERCE list to seek the information as to which area to relate his behavior. This choice will likely be an assessment that includes the domains of social and personality measures, and the referral will reflect this need. Tests to be considered in this case could be the Primary Academic Sentinel Scale and the California Test of Personality. Other domains, of course, could be considered for assessment, if so desired, and the teacher may use check lists in the initial observation procedure. A discussion of check lists and rating scales is found in the following section.

Check Lists/Rating Scales

Check lists and rating scales are useful and comprehensive instruments to assess preschool children*. They are valuable because they are *criterion-referenced***, meaning that they are designed to match specific objectives, such as whether the child can shake his head *no*. Check list/rating scales can be developed around any observable aspect of child development or behavior. They are congruent with what is going on in the child's life.

Most check lists/rating scales are constructed around one or more of the following general areas of development: physical, social, intellectual, or attitudinal. Assessment in these areas can identify deviation in development among young exceptional children.

Three of the many rating scales and check lists available to educators are *Developmental Guidelines for Teachers and Evaluators of Multi-handicapped Children*

---

*See Chapter 4 for other observation and screening techniques.
**See Chapter 2 for other information on criterion-referenced tests.

(Langley, 1976) Inner Language Scale (Branston and Dubose, 1974) and *Developmental Indicators for Assessment of Learning* (Mardell and Goldenberg, 1972), known as *DIAL*. The Langley instrument is a comprehensive scale useful for both teachers and evaluators. Langley views *teacher* and *evaluator* as synonyms: ". . . to be able to teach is to be able to evaluate." She further writes, "Evaluation is an on-going process which seeks to developmentally delineate a child's functioning level in areas critical to his potential to functionally adapt to his environment." Major developmental areas covered in the Langley scale are (1) cognitive-adaptive, (2) communication, and (3) socialization. In each of the three developmental areas, the author has a comprehensive, sequential listing of skills. This developmental guideline is presented as follows:

Developmental Guidelines for Teachers and Evaluators of Handicapped Children (Compiled by Beth Langley)*

Introduction

Teacher and *evaluator* are synonymous labels; for to be able to teach, one must be able to evaluate not only the child's abilities, but also the abilities of an individual program to enhance and advance the educational development sequentially. Evaluation is an ongoing process that seeks to delineate developmentally a child's functioning level in areas critical to potential to adapt functionally to the environment.

Development is a continuous temporal progression from a simple to a complex organization of behavior. The sequence of development may exhibit gaps in specific stages; some children may spend more or less time than others in mastering each stage; and each child may vary within individual abilities to accomplish differential developmental tasks. All children progress through the same developmental sequence, but at different rates and through multivariant means. The child must build basic skills into the behavioral repertoire, so that previous learning experiences may be used to facilitate acquisition of higher-order skills. Ilg and Ames (1955) summarized, "To get to the top, the child has to climb all of the steps." Although much the same for everybody, the way in which an individual "climbs the steps" will depend upon a basic learning style., Goals must be analyzed into small steps, so that the child experiences success with each new adventure on the way to "the top."

These guidelines (Table 31) have been based on a developmental model to assist the teacher in defining a child's strengths and weaknesses and to suggest sequential-programming areas appropriate for children's needs within a specific developmental level and learning process. Through the use of these guidelines, a daily evaluation can determine how the child is doing and what will aid the teacher in making decisions regarding the child's individual plan.

---

*By permission of Beth Langley, Pinellas County Schools, St. Petersburg, FL 33705. Materials herein may be reprinted for personal use if reference is given to author and source.

Table 31. Developmental Guidelines

1 to 2 Months

COGNITIVE/ADAPTIVE

Sensory Schemas:
Accommodates visually to objects within 7-1/2" of eyes
Orients to sound and light
Blinks at the shadow of a hand
Horizontal, vertical, and circular coordinated eye movements
Startle response to sound
Responds to bell, rattle, or other sharp sound

Motor Schemas:
Turns head in reaction to paper on face
Lifts head when tilted and held at shoulder
Turns from side to back
Reflexive grasp of object placed in hand

COMMUNICATION

Receptive:
Activity ceases when child approached by sound
Activity increases at sound of noisemaker

Expressive:
Begins random vocalizing
Vowel-like sounds similar to *E* and *A*
Throaty noises and gurgles

SOCIALIZATION

Personal-Social:
Responds to voice
Quiets when picked up
Eyes follow moving person

Social-Self:
Thrusts arms and legs in play

2 to 3 Months

COGNITIVE-ADAPTIVE

Visual Pursuit:
Follows moving object with eyes
Glances from one object to another

Motor Schemas:
Engages in simple play with rattle
Hands remain predominantly open
Elevates self on arms in prone position

COMMUNICATION

Receptive:
Stops and changes activity in responses to voice
Searches with eyes for sound

Expressive:
Repeats some syllable while babbling
Develops vocal signs of pleasure
Single vowel sounds: *ah, oh, uh*

SOCIALIZATION

Personal-Social:
Visually recognizes mother
Reacts to disappearance of face
Looks at speaker and responds by smiling

3 to 4 Months

COGNITIVE-ADAPTIVE

Visual Pursuit & Permanence of Objects:
Head follows dropped toy

Means-Ends Relationships:
Reaches for dangling toy
Brings toy to mouth
Ulnar-palmar grasp

Causality:
Plays with hands
Sight of toy excites child

Motor Schemas:
Rolls from back to side, returns

COMMUNICATION

Receptive:
Localizes speaker by turning head
Responds to speech or other sounds by vocalizing

Expressive:
Coos and chuckles
Laughs, vocally expresses pleasure when played with
Vocalizes two or more syllables

Nonverbal:
Imitates imitation of own ongoing behavior

Table 31 (continued)

Social-Self:
Anticipates feeding at sight of bottle
Visually regards spoon

Causality:
Visually orients to side
tickled

4 to 5 Months

SOCIALIZATION

Personal-Social:
Aware of strange situation

COGNITIVE-ADAPTIVE

Means-Ends Relationships:
Radial-palmar grasp on cube
Exploitive paper play
Actively plays with toys
Manipulates table edge
Reaches for cube
Holds objects placed in hand

Permanence of Objects:
Notices when objects are gone
Visually regards a pellet

Construction of Objects in Space:
Recovers dropped toy
Approaches mirror image

COMMUNICATION

Expressive:
Laughs during play with objects
Babbles same sounds
Vocalizes B, P, M

Receptive:
Definitely looks for speaker
Ceases crying when someone talks to
  him

SOCIALIZATION

Social-Self:
Loves sitting position
Watches his hands
Pulls at clothing

Personal-Social
Vocalizes a social response
Spontaneous social smile

5 to 6 Months

COGNITIVE-ADAPTIVE

Permanence of Objects:
Looks for dropped toy

Construction of Objects in Space:
Picks up inverted cup

Means-Ends Relationships:
Obtains object by pulling string (nonin-
tentional)
Transfers objects from hand to hand
Reaches for 2nd cube
Rotates wrist
Pulls tissue from face

Motor Schemas:
Bilateral reaching
Pulls to sitting position
Rolls from back to stomach

COMMUNICATION

Receptive:
Smiles in response to voices and music
Recognizes and responds to name

Nonverbal:
Engages in simple motor acts, pauses, resumes

Expressive:
Deliberate imitation of known sounds
Babbles to faces and mirrors
Babbles *sh, goo,* razzing sounds
Vocalizes sounds similar to *O* and *U*
Expresses anger, displeasure with sounds other than crying

SOCIALIZATION

Social-Self:
Smiles at image in mirror
Accepts solid foods such as mashed bananas
Picks up spoon
Three nap periods in 24 hours

Table 31 (continued)
6 to 7 Months

COGNITIVE-ADAPTIVE

Permanence of Objects:
Looks for fallen spoon

Means-Ends Relationships:
Persists in reaching
Shakes or manipulates bell, other sound toy
Retains 2 of 3 cubes offered

Causality:
Manually locates site tickled
Manipulates mirror
Attends to scribbling

COMMUNICATION

Receptive:
Stops in response to *NO* half of the time
Distinguishes friendly, warning, angry voice patterns
Responds to words or gestures to *COME UP, BYE-BYE*

Nonverbal:
Searches with single modality for removed object
Imitates visually perceptible movements already known

Expressive:
Vocalizes 4 or more different syllables
Repeats combination of 2 or more different syllables
Imitates growl and cough

SOCIALIZATION

Personal-Social:
Discriminates strangers
Anticipates being picked up, stretches out arms
Smiles and vocalizes to people
Responds to *BYE-BYE*

Social-Self:
Pats bottle
Drinks assisted from cup or glass
Prepares for biting off bits of cracker, cookie by "munching"

7 to 8 Months

COGNITIVE-ADAPTIVE

Construction of Objects in Space:
Pulls out large pegs

Causality:
Rings bell on purpose
Bangs objects on tray
Localizes sound on either side on a
   plane with his ears

Means-Ends Relationships:
Reaches with one hand
Turns over object, puts in mouth
Secures 3 cubes
Radial-digital grasp on cube
Adaptively secures toy by string

Motor Schemas:
Crawls on tummy
Bounces in standing position

COMMUNICATION

Receptive:
Expects action or object in response to a repetition of a stimu-
   lus
Attends to familiar words when accompanied with tone, ges-
   ture, or situation: "Where's Daddy? No-No"
Appears to recognize names of common objects

Nonverbal:
Attempts to reproduce activity of objects previously watched

Expressive:
Appears to name things in own language
Plays speech gesture games, pat-a-cake, peek-a-boo

SOCIALIZATION

Personal-Social:
Enjoys pat-a-cake games
Demands to be fed from cup, takes only couple of swallows

Social-Self:
Brings feet to mouth
Pats mirror image
Concentrates on single toy, following it if put in motion
Chews and swallows strained foods
Intervals of dryness 1–2 hours in length
Long morning nap, short afternoon; vice-versa

Table 31 (continued)

8 to 9 Months

COGNITIVE-ADAPTIVE

Permanence of Objects:
Uncovers toy hidden under cloth

Construction of Objects in Space:
Searches persistently for dropped object
Fingers holes in pegboard
Uprights objects handed to him reversed

Means-Ends Relationships:
Combines two toys in midline
Neat pincer grasp on cube

Causality:
Bangs toy in imitation

COMMUNICATION

Receptive:
Appears to understand some simple verbal requests
Sustains interest in picture 1 minute if named

Nonverbal:
Uses some gestures: shakes head for NO
Pushes away adult's hand in attempt to retain an object or as
reaction to unpleasant thing

Expressive:
Shouts for attention to self
Considerable intonation in vocalizations

SOCIALIZATION

Personal-Social:
Offers toys to others
Shows awareness of other children
Demands personal attention

Social-Self:
Bites and chews toys
Reaches persistently for toys out of reach
Grows impatient as watches meal prepared

9 to 10 Months

COGNITIVE-ADAPTIVE

Permanence of Objects:
Picks up cup to secure cube
Finds toys hidden under barriers
Looks for contents removed from container

Means-Ends Relationships:
Puts cube in cup
Leans forward to recover toy
Crumples piece of paper
Tries to grasp toy through transparent container

Causality:
Stirs spoon in cup

Motor Schemas:
Moves from lying to hands and knees

COMMUNICATION

Receptive:
Gives toy or other objects to others on verbal request
Interested in faces and expressions

Expressive:
Speaks first words: mams, daddy, name of pet
Short exclamations: Oh-Oh!
Jargon like utterances of 4 or more syllables

Nonverbal:
Actions cause him to notice new results and he then repeats action intentionally

SOCIALIZATION

Personal-Social:
Waves Bye-Bye

Social-Self:
Content in self absorbed play
Holds own bottle
Feeds self cracker

Table 31 (continued)

10 to 12 Months

COGNITIVE-ADAPTIVE

Permanence of Objects:
Unwraps toy placed in cloth
Looks for toy first place observed it being hidden

Construction of Objects in Space:
Bangs crayon, accidental marks
Pushes adult's hand with crayon
Looks at pictures in books
Reaches for toy image in mirror

Means-Ends Relationships:
Crude release of toys
Releases pellet into bottle
Precise pincer grasp on pellet
Places 3 to 8 cubes in cup

Causality:
Squeeks toy in imitation
Pushes toy car

COMMUNICATION

Receptive:
Follows simple commands: LOOK AT ME, GIVE ME, WHERE'S THE BALL?
Stops actions in response to NO
Demonstrates understanding by responding with appropriate gestures to several verbal requests

Nonverbal:
Vague tugging when he wants something
Places adult's hand on object and pushes
Imitates actions known but not visually observed
If an object routinely hidden and found under A is then hidden under B, child searches under A
Exhibits call sounds

Expressive:
Begins to imitate new sounds and words
Usually vocalizes in varied jargon patterns while playing alone
Uses 3 or more words with some consistency
Talks to toys and people through the day using long vocal patterns

SOCIALIZATION

Personal-Social:
Friends and strangers received with smiles
Likes to give and take in simple games
Likes to be chased

Social-Self:
Responds to rhythmic music by body or hand movements in approximate time to music
Long midmorning nap, unstable afternoon nap
May be dry after nap: Mother has temporary success in placing child on toilet
Lifts bottom when diapered
Enjoys manipulating spoon
Chews and swallows chopped food
Drinks from cup with minimal assistance
Cooperates in dressing by offering appropriate limb

1 to 1½ Years

COGNITIVE-ADAPTIVE

Permanence of Objects:
Looks in second place toy hidden

Construction of Objects in Space:
Attempts to imitate strokes: scribbles back and forth
Waits for toy in place it should appear
Requires experimentation to place one block on top of another without their toppling

Construction of Objects in Space:
Places one or two pegs in board
Stacks shapes on three-holed formboard
Places circle in formboard
Fills container with blocks

Means-Ends Relationships:
Turns several pages at a time
Tries to reach on toes to get objects above him
Removes lids from boxes
Closes round box
Flings or rolls ball forward
Dumps pellet from bottle
Attains toy with stick

Discrimination:
Looks at pictures selectively
Picks up a few color chips of the same color

Causality & Imitation:
Attempts to imitate stroke
Pats a squeak toy in imitation
Pushes three-cube train in imitation

Motor Schemas:
Walks alone

Table 31 (continued)

COMMUNICATION

Receptive:

Selects and brings something from another room upon verbal request

Identifies 2 or more familiar objects from a group of 4 or more common objects

Recognizes names of various parts of body; hair, mouth, eyes, ears, hands

Comprehends simple questions

Carries out two consecutive directions with a ball or other object

Expressive:

Uses five or more true words [12 months]

Uses seven or more true words [16 months]

Frequent use of consonants; *T, D, W, N, H*

Begins using words rather than gestures to express wants and needs

Names many things and actions

Nonverbal:

Attempts to obtain desired objects by using voice in conjunction with pointing and gesturing

Describes actions with hands

Points to call attention to things

Systematic imitation of new models including those invisible to the child

Has a "GIVE ME THAT" gesture

Hands objects to adult and waits expectantly

SOCIALIZATION

Personal-Social:

Seldom obeys commands: enjoys oppositional behavior

NO is favorite word

Treats people as objects

Social-Self:

Capable of sense of humor, fear, anxiety, love, anger and jealousy

Takes favorite toys to bed

Naps of 1-2 hours after noon meal

Discards bottle: independently drinks from cup

Replaces cup on table when finished

Feeds self sandwich

Feeds self with overhand grasp on spoon

Scoops food with bowl of spoon
Pulls off socks from toes
Indicates wet pants by patting or crying

1½ to 2 Years

COGNITIVE-ADAPTIVE

Construction of Objects in Space:
Scribble is more circular
Vertical and horizontal line imitated 2 of
   3 times
Forces tops on boxes without regard for
   shape of box
Builds tower of 3 to 4 cubes
Places square and triangle
Completes three-hold formboard
   through trial and error
Completes pegboard with square
   holes
Retrieves toy from regular places

Means-Ends Relationships:
Solves pellet in bottle problem without
   demonstration
Turns pages of book one at a time
Puts rings on pole in any order

Discrimination & Memory:
Points to three parts on doll
Points to 3 pictures in book
Plays with several objects and misses
   one if taken

COMMUNICATION

Receptive:
Upon verbal request, points to several parts of the body and
   various items of clothing shown in large pictures
Demonstrates understanding of distinctions in personal pro-
   nouns: you, me.
Follows series of 2 or 3 simple but related commands
Recognizes and identifies almost all common objects and pic-
   tures of common objects when named
Understands approximately 200 words

Expressive:
Imitates 2 and 3 word sentences
Imitates environmental sounds
Vocabulary of 10 to 20 words
Refers to self by own name
Begins combining words into phrases: go bye-bye, daddy
   come
Uses pronouns, making errors in syntax

Table 31 (continued)

Nonverbal:
Responds to familiar situations
Watches face for cues
Leads adult to what he wants in next room
Makes gestures learned in repeated sensori-motor activity and brought to mind from present situation
Understands pointed commands: Be quiet, give me a kiss, I don't want that, Where, Who, What?
Looks for object he has not observed being hidden

SOCIALIZATION

Personal-Social:
Resistant to changes and sudden transition
Imitates actions of adults: reading paper, sweeping, dusting, washing car
Participates in rough and tumble play
Responds often with NO when asked if ready for bed, need to toilet, put away toys.
Plays beside or sits with other children but doesn't engage into play with them
Separate from Mother to go to day-time center with other children of own age
Enjoys visiting in familiar persons' homes

Social-Self:
Carries doll around
Enjoys pulling toys
Puts own possessions where belong
Discriminates own clothing from others: sweater
Holds and eats with fork but doesn't yet pierce
Goes to refrigerator and points to juice
Enjoys opening drawers and playing with contents
Pulls off socks over heels
Pulls off shoes, minimal assistance with pulling laces
Zips and unzips own clothing
Pulls on mitten, cap, socks with minimal help
Pushes arms into shirt when placed over head
Indicates readiness for toileting by removing self from presence of mother when eliminating
Helps in pulling down pants
Accepts soap, towel, washcloth but doesn't apply
Passes brush over hair: not a true stroke
Places toothbrush in mouth but doesn't brush

2 to 2½ Years

COGNITIVE-ADAPTIVE

Spatial Relationships:
Imitates construction of train by aligning two blocks
Builds a tower of 5–7 cubes
Forces a block into occupied space
Covers a square box
Tries to fold paper
Places halves of a circle together
Plays with fitting nesting cups together but no spatial comparison
Adapts readily to reversed formboard
Imitates a circle with marker
Makes two lines to form a cross but they don't intersect

Visual-Motor Integration:
Unscrews lids from jars
Strings three large beads with long tipped lace

Quantitative Reasoning:
Gives two blocks in response to two fingers
Discriminates big and little objects

Association:
Identifies objects when described in terms of function: drink from, wear on foot, eat cereal with

Discrimination:
Matches objects to objects
Matches picture to picture
Matches simple forms:
    circle, square, triangle
Inconsistently matches a few colors

Memory:
Repeats two or more numbers correctly

COMMUNICATION

Receptive:
300–400 words in vocabulary
Listens to simple songs and stories
Enjoys being read to and brings books to have read
Identifies smaller parts of body: eye-brow, elbow, knee
Identifies objects when described in terms of use
Points to action pictures when verbally described

Expressive:
Repeats words over and over
Uses common phrases
Responds to: what's your name, what does a doggie say?
Uses some prepositions and pronouns: in, on, me, you
Talks about actions
Labels common objects: pencil, key, ball, book
Asks for help with personal needs

Table 31 (continued)

Nonverbal:
Anticipates toy from gesture
Exhibits natural gestures
Demonstrates deferred imitation in situation

SOCIALIZATION

Personal-Social:
Able to wait a few minutes to delay gratification
Doesn't share but finds substitute toys
Engages in parallel play
Adjusts play behavior to partner's ability
Mimics actions of others
Warmly responsive to adults
Imagination entering into play

Social-Self:
Demands to take toys to bed
Asks to go to toilet: verbal distinction—bladder
Pulls pants up after toileting
Can remove underpants
Removes shirt or coat when unfastened
Unties laces
Puts on button shirt with minimal help when offered in correct position
Pulls on pullover shirt given in correct position
Initiates hand washing by turning on water
Helps in bathing: pulls washcloth over body part
Initiates brushing motion with toothbrush: requires help to complete
Eats with fork and can pierce carrots, soft meats, etc.
Enjoys drinking from fountain

2½ to 3 Years

COGNITIVE-ADAPTIVE

Spatial Relationships:
Imitates circular stroke
Builds a 10-cube tower
Inserts a square in shape box
Nests four sequential cups through trial and error
Copies a short line of pegs
Definitely folds 8" square in half
Builds a 3 cube chair in an attempt to imitate a 3 cube pyramid

Conceptual Grouping:
Given a cup and a dish, selects from toy dog, orange, and spoon object completing the group

Visual-Motor Integration:
Holds regular crayon with finger tips
Snips with scissors
Strings small beads
Turns the handle on a jack-in-the-box three revolutions without letting go
Hammers a peg toy
Clips clothespins on a can

Quantitative Reasoning:
Counts serially to three
Understands concept of 1

Discrimination:
Matches two colors
Lines blocks up by color groups
Matches four colors of blocks to matching colored bowls

Association:
Matches several common objects to bright simplified pictures of each

COMMUNICATION

Receptive:
Demonstrates understanding of all common verbs
Demonstrates understanding of prepositions: *In, on,* and *under*
Demonstrates understanding of most common adjectives
Carries out three simple verbal commands given in one long utterance
Demonstrates understanding of very long and complex syntactical structures

Expressive:
Can tell both first and last name
Can name gender when asked if boy or girl
Usually can be understood outside family
Sentences usually have 10–11 words
Uses some plural forms correctly in speech
Uses several verb forms correctly in relating what is going on in action picture
Names and talks about what he has drawn
Relates experiences from recent past

Table 31 (continued)

SOCIALIZATION

Personal-Social:
Doesn't easily adapt to any situation
Sets up rigid sequence of events that must follow each other
Beginning to separate easily from Mother
Likes to play alone but engages in cooperative play
Enjoys performing for others
Beginning to take turns
Helps put things away
Likes to help with simple tasks in house
Demonstrates violent emotions
Afraid of thunder, squeals of police cars, fire engines

Social-Self:
Boys attempt to stand to urinate
Few toileting accidents
Removes pullover shirt
Removes button shirt if unbuttoned
Washes hands with minimal assistance
Attempts to dry hands
Helps in drying after bath: pulls towel over body instead of rubbing
Uses fork with an overhand grasp
Spills minimal amount when eating

3 to 3½ Years

COGNITIVE-ADAPTIVE

Spatial Relationships:
Copies a circle
Imitates straight cross
Copies four-block train with chimney
Imitates 3-cube pyramid
Nests four cups through visual comparison
Matches several nesting barrels that screw together
Completes Seguin formboard through trial and error

Visual-Motor Integration:
Cuts across a strip of paper
Screws together nesting kegs
Builds tower of 10-12 cubes

Quantitative Reasoning:
Begins to understand 1-1 correspondence
Counts serially to 5
Gives two blocks out of ten

Association:
Sorts four colors without matching colored bowls
Matches objects to pictures that are not identical matches of the objects
Matches two-variable forms [color and shape]
Categorizes pictures of common objects

Puts together picture of man cut into 2
    pieces at waist
Performs with Montessori cylinders

COMMUNICATION

Receptive:
Identifies five primary colors
Vocabulary consists of more than 1000 words
Comprehends -wh questions
Comprehends *no* used to indicate non-existence in syntactical
    forms.
Comprehends verbs + ing ending

SOCIALIZATION

Personal-Social:
Likes to conform
Likes to give, share experiences and toys
Loves new words
Likes to make new friends
Cooperative play takes place of parallel
Afraid of dark, animals, policeman
Helps set the table and help with other household tasks

Memory:
Remembers one color of six presented
Recognizes missing picture of three
Repeats two to three digits
Sorts two colors into opaque containers
    without matching

Expressive:
Labels five primary colors
90% of verbal responses intelligible
Repeats six to seven syllable sentences
Sentence length from four to five words
Deals with non present situations verbally
Begins to use complex sentences
Uses plurals, past tense, personal pronouns, and prepositions *in,*
    on, under in syntactical structures

Social-Self:
May wake self up and ask to toilet
Flushes toilet
Pushes feet into shoes: not right feet
Pulls on long pants independently
Undresses rapidly and well: unbuttons
Dresses independently except for fastenings and heavy outer
    clothing
Laces holes but not in the correct sequence
Buttons by pulling button from opposite side when pushed by
    adult
Eats independently with only occasional help
Pours efficiently from a pitcher into a stable glass

Table 31 (continued)

3½ to 4 Years

COGNITIVE-ADAPTIVE

Spatial Relationships:
Imitates a 3 cube oblique bridge
Completes a 10 hole formboard
Assembles 10 nesting cups through trial and error
Puts together two halves of simple picture
Draws a man by forming a circle with appendages
Matches cut-out geometrical forms
Imitates a square: corners rounded
Copies a straight cross
Understands long and short

Quantitative Reasoning:
Matches quantity of blocks or small objects: 3, 4, 5
Counts serially to 10
Sorts three sizes of objects

Inductive Reasoning:
Selects cubes matching a pattern
Alternates two colors when given a pattern to complete

Memory:
Remembers 1 picture from 15
Remembers two colored blocks from six [three pairs]
Remembers at least one nursery rhyme

Discrimination:
Matches cut-out geometrical forms
Sorts some Decroly pictures
Completes simple Lotto games

Association:
Finds from a group another animal the same as a model depicted on another page
Groups miniature objects by general characteristics
Comprehends same-different concept

COMMUNICATION

Receptive:
Follows 2-stage commands
Points out animals, objects, foods from a large group of other pictures

Expressive:
Complex sentence structures used more frequently; wh questions and interrogative reversals dominate syntactical structures
Answers simple questions with three or more words

Receptive:
Recognizes time [day opposed to night] in pictures
Recognizes all major colors
Comprehends demonstrative nouns: *this, that, these*
Comprehends verb + er suffix [hitter]
Comprehends adjectives + est suffix [fattest]
Comprehends negative *not* [not jumping]

SOCIALIZATION

Personal-Social:
Tensional outlets exaggerated
Demanding of adults
Jealous of attention paid to others
Enjoys playing with other children
Sings songs learned from listening to other children
Engages in dramatic play

Social-Self:
Wipes self with assistance
Manipulates medium sized buttons
Fastens snaps
Washes and dries hands independently
Bathes self with supervision: assistance required to clean thoroughly
Applies toothpaste to brush
Brushes hair independently
Spreads soft foods on bread with knife
Serves self from container
Wipes mouth with napkin when reminded

4 to 5 Years

COGNITIVE-ADAPTIVE

Spatial Relationships:
Copies a square
Imitates 6 cube pyramid
Completes puzzles cut into several pieces
Makes two reversals with Pintner-Paterson Manikin

Quantitative Reasoning:
Identifies number concept two and three [3 blocks from 10]
Comprehends 1-1 correspondence with differing variables: [blocks on top of dots]

Discrimination:
Matches domino patterns
Tries to cut simple shapes
Matches letter and number cards
Sorts all Decroly patterns
Completes several Lotto cards simultaneously

Table 31 (continued)

Solves Seguin formboard by visual comparison
Matches simple parquetry patterns
Sequentially orders ten lengths of paper varying in size from large to small

COMMUNICATION

Receptive:
Identifies opposite concepts: Brother is a boy, sister is a _____; Father is a man, mother is a _____
Comprehends senses: What do we do with our eyes, ears?
Discriminates appropriate picture in response to "Show me which one has the longest ears, gives us milk." Identifies which of two pictures is prettier or uglier
Comprehends prepositions: *at side of, in front of, between.*
Comprehends noun + er suffix [painter]
Comprehends adjective + er suffix [smaller]
Comprehends simple imperative sentences
Comprehends noun phrase with two adjective modifiers [big red house]
Tends to re-enact in body posture and gestures what is told in story

Sequential Memory:
Remembers 2-step paper fold
Reproduces simple sequential tapping patterns
Repeats four digits
Recites a poem from memory

Expressive:
Manually demonstrates functional sequence of objects
Answers questions requiring analogy and comparison: ["Why do we have houses, why do we have books?"]
Retells fairy tale in logical sequence

Association:
Shifts categories when sorting shapes of different colors when cued [by shape first, then by color]

SOCIALIZATION

Personal-Social:
Enjoys being defiant of parental demands
Enjoys bathroom and elimination words
Initiates action and stays with it without adult control
Goes around neighborhood independently
Prefers children of own sex but no hesitation about playing with the opposite sex
Enjoys playing in a group
Shares possessions
Accepts responsibility

Social-Self:
Knows name, address, and telephone number
Toilets self independently
Distinguishes front from back of clothing
Independently puts on button shirt
Turns shirt right side out
Buttons small buttons
Laces shoes but doesn't yet tie them
Engages zipper
Buckles
Washes face independently
Puts toys away; cleans up room
Hangs up coat

5 to 6 Years

COGNITIVE-ADAPTIVE

Spatial Relationships:
Copies a triangle
Prints capital letters
Colors a circle, staying within lines
Copies 6 cube stairs
Copies a checked block pattern from its one-dimensional model
Completes puzzle of man divided into six parts
Puts together 2 halves of a rectangle cut diagonally

Quantitative Reasoning:
States five pennies worth more than nickel
Counts ten objects
Matches one to one to a line of 6 blocks

Sequential Memory:
Imitates two step triangular fold
Accomplishes a four step fold
Rote counts to 30

Discrimination:
Creates words with letters to match a model word

Association:
Matches and sorts with paper and pencil, marking the one that does not belong

Table 31 (continued)

Copies a model of a square made with pegs

Completes Seguin formboard rapidly without errors

Projects size of object regardless of its physical appearance

Knows right or left on self but not on others

Memory:
Remembers domino patterns in order to select the same one after removal of a model

Inductive Reasoning:
Alternates two blocks of one color with a block of another color to complete a sequential pattern.

Expressive:
Language essentially complete in structure and form
Correct usage of all parts of speech
100% production and use of all consonants
Corrects own errors in learning to pronounce new words
Reads by way of pictures
Relates fanciful tales in own words
Names penny, nickel, dime
Answers questions directly
Defines words in terms of use
Lacks the power of explicit reasoning

COMMUNICATION

Receptive:
Follows 3-stage command
Comprehends quantitative adjectives: pair, few, many
Comprehends verb number agreement: [is vs. are]

SOCIALIZATION

Personal-Social:
Tries only things which he feels he can accomplish

Self-centered: own action and pleasure take precedence over everything else

Differentiates self concept by putting himself in opposition to mother: other times showers her with notes and presents he has made

Social-Self:
Selects own clothing
Ties laces independently
Draws own bath water
Bathes self with supervision
Uses table knife for cutting
Makes simple sandwiches

Enjoys going places with father
Content to stay near home
Afraid of bodily harm: dogs, the dark, that mother will not return
Play involves make believe
Dresses up in adult clothing
Shows an interest in sports requiring participation of several children
Prefers children of own age and best friends are of the same sex
Plays simple table games

Gets own cereal
Handles self well at table
Assists in making bed
Empties trashcans and ashtrays
Sweeps with supervision
Wipes silverware and dishes
Folds simple articles: T-shirts, socks, towels
Makes simple purchases: (gum, candy, bread)
Waters plants
Brushes teeth independently; handles toothpaste and applies on brush

6 to 7 Years

COGNITIVE-ADAPTIVE

Spatial Relationships:
Reproduces complex designs with paper and pencil, blocks, and pegs
Synthesizes parts into organized integrated wholes
Copies color patterns drawn on paper with blocks or parquetry pieces in which more than one block is required to make up a color section in which lines do not indicate separate blocks
Perfect performance on Pintner-Paterson Manikin
Copies horizontal diamond
Begins to draw two-dimensional man

Quantitative Reasoning:
Adds and subtracts within 10

Inductive and Deductive Reasoning:
Identifies what is missing from picture
Discriminates simple likenesses and differences
Begins to understand the meaning of comic pictures

Memory:
Remembers five digits
Reproduces simple designs from memory
Remembers sight words

Discrimination:
Reads on a 1st to 2nd grade level
Matches objects to words
Prints simple words, alphabet, numbers: reversals not resolved

Table 31 (continued)

COMMUNICATION

Receptive and Expressive:

Comprehends and expresses the meaning of "half"

Comprehends and expresses most quantity adjectives such as: *first, second, third,* and *last*

Comprehends and expresses most quality adjectives

Comprehends and expresses personal gender pronouns: *he, she, it*

Comprehends passive voice: "He is carried by the horse."

Comprehends and expresses future tense

Differentiates A.M. and P.M.

Takes simple messages over the telephone

Efficiently uses the telephone, remembers several phone numbers: home, friend, parent's work number

Gestures appropriately to nine verbal commands

SOCIALIZATION

Personal-Social:

Continually seeking new experiences

Finds it difficult not to win every time

Cannot accept criticism or blame

Finds it difficult to choose between things

Worries about being liked

Seeks approval for his actions

Sensitive to other's behavior

Enjoys playing games with rules

Afraid of supernatural: ghosts and witches

Fears sleeping alone in a room or of being the only one on the floor of a house

Crying is easily brought on

Social-Self

Uses money purposefully and efficiently

Does simple jobs for allowance

Cleans mirrors and windows

Dusts

Engages in simple baking activities: toast, soups, slice and bake cookies, stirs batter

Cuts, slices, and peels

Polishes shoes

Sews simple embroidery stitch

References for Developmental Guidelines:

Bayley, N. *Bayley scales of infant development*. New York: Psychological Corporation, 1969.

Blum, L. H., Burgemeister, B., & Lorge, I. *Columbia mental maturity scale*. New York: Harcourt, Brace Jovanovich, Inc., 1954.

Bzoch, K., & League, R. *The receptive expressive emergent language scale*. Gainesville, Fla.: The Tree of Life Press, 1970.

Carrow, E. *Test for auditory comprehension of language*. Austin, Tx: Urban Research Group, 1967.

Doll, E. *The Vineland scale of social maturity*. Circle Pines, Mn.: American Guidance Service, 1965.

Elloseff, J. *Screening test for use with the visually oriented deaf-blind*. Unpublished duplicated paper by Perkins School for the Blind.

Haeussermann, E. *Developmental potential of preschool children: an evaluation of intellectual, sensory, and emotional functioning*. New York: Grune and Stratton, 1958.

Ilg, F., & Ames, L. D. *Child behavior from birth to ten*. New York: Harper and Row, 1955.

Johnson, C. *Developmental levels with the environment*. In Robbins, N., *On the education of deaf-blind children*. Watertown, Ma.: Perkins School for the Blind, 1972.

Knobloch, H., & Pasamanick, B. (Eds.) *Gesell and Armatruda's developmental diagnosis: The evaluation and management of normal and abnormal neuropsychologic development in infancy and early development*, 3rd ed. Hagerstoron, Md.: Harper and Row, 1974.

LeLand, B., & Baker, H. *Detroit tests of learning aptitude*. Indianapolis: Bobbs-Merrill Co., Inc., 1959.

Phillips, J. L. *The origins of intellect: Piaget's theory*. San Francisco: W. H. Freeman and Company, 1969.

Taylor, E. *Psychological appraisal of children with cerebral defects*. Cambridge, Mass.: Harvard University Press, 1961.

Terman, L. M., & Merrill, M. A. *Measuring intelligence, revised Stanford/Binet Tests*. Boston: Houghton Mifflin Co., 1937.

Zimmerman, I. L., Stainer, V., & Evatt, R. *The preschool language scale*. Columbus: Charles E. Merrill, 1969.

Table 32. Inner Language Scale*

	Object Concept	Object Permanence	Causality	Imitation
1–4 Months	Child follows an object or light with eyes through 180° arc. Eyes linger at spot object or light is last seen. 1	Child follows an object or light with eyes through 180° arc. Eyes linger at spot object or light is last seen. 2	Child engages in hand-watching behavior. 3	If adult mimics child's arm or hand movements, child imitates adult in turn. 4
4–8 Months	Child engages in simple motor acts with an object, pauses, then resumes same actions. 5	When an object is removed, child searches briefly for it. Search is confined to one modality. 6	When an object is in the visual presence of the child, the child engages in simple motor acts previously experienced in contiguity with the object in an apparent effort to maintain or reproduce the activity of the object. 7	Using actions in his repertoire, child imitates adult's hand or arm movements. (Note: Here the adult initiates the action whereas in #4, the child initiated the action.) 8

8–12 Months			
Child intentionally manipulates objects in an exploratory manner, turning them, feeling surfaces, etc. (Notes: Here the child is interested in the object itself; in #5 child's interest is mainly in the motor acts he performs with the object.)	When an object is taken from a child, he searches persistently at the place from which the object was removed, even though he saw an adult place it elsewhere. (Note: Search will be multi-sensory.)	Child waits for adult to do things for him; attacks a barrier to a toy as if it caused him frustration. (Note: Here the child is able to perceive others as causes of activity; in #7 he was aware mainly of himself in connection with activity.)	Child imitates adult's actions using actions in his repertoire. He can now imitate actions that he cannot see his body perform.
9	10	11	12
12–18 Months			
Child drops an object repeatedly and follows the fall of the object through space; this is performed with several different objects.	When an object is hidden, child will search for it in the last place he observes it being hidden. (Note: In #10 the child can not follow the object to a new locale; in #14 he can follow the object to a new locale provided he observes it being hidden.	Child signifies desire for adult to repeat an action by returning object to adult and waiting.	Child can imitate actions new to his repertoire through gradual approximations; child imitates action in a more precise manner.
13	14	15	16

*Reprinted by permission of Rebecca Dubose, University of Washington, Seattle, WA 98105. The material herein shall not be reproduced or quoted in any form without express reference to authors and source.

References to Table 32.

Chatelanat, G., Bricker, W., Robertson, M., & Spritzer, S. *Sensorimotor curriculum, stage 1, 2,* and *3, for young developmentally delayed children.* Nashville, Tenn.: Infant, Toddler, and Pre-school Research and Intervention Project, John F. Kennedy Center, George Peabody College for Teachers, 1973.

Gesell, A., & Amatruda, D. S. *Developmental diagnosis.* New York: Paul D. Hoeber, Inc., 1974.

Guldager, V. *Body image and the severely handicapped Rubella child.* Watertown, Mass.: Perkins School for the Blind, 1970.

Phillips, J. L. *The origins of intellect: Piaget's theory.* San Francisco: W. H. Freeman Co., 1969.

Robbins, N. Development and assessment of non-verbal communication and language. In *On the education of young deaf-blind children.* Watertown, Mass.: Perkins School for the Blind, 1974.

Uzgiris, I. C., & Hunt, J. McV. *An instrument for assessing infant psychological development.* Urbana, IL: Psychological Development Laboratory, University of Illinois, 1966.

Table 32 *(inner language scale),* compiled by Branston and Dubose, covers language skills for children between the ages of 1 month and 18 months. The scale is beneficial to early-childhood assessment because many handicapped children may not have developed inner language, even though they are much older than the age range covered. By using this quick check-list scale, a teacher may determine where the child is in developing basic inner-language skills. The scale, which is based on object concept, object permanence, causality, and imitation, is presented in its entirety. The Inner Language Scale training activities developed by Branston and Dubose are available through your instructor.

Developmental Indicators for Assessment of Learning (DIAL)
(by C. Mardell and D. Goldenberg)

The third check list/rating scale to be described in this paper is The Developmental Indicators for Assessment of Learning (DIAL), which is used to assess children in four major areas (1) Gross-motor, (2) Fine-motor, (3) Concepts and (4) Language Skills. Two other areas may be included as supplementary. They are Affective and Social measures. Sensory screening for vision and hearing is also recommended, to be used in conjunction with the other areas; the profile sheet provides a place for recording such data.

The Gross-motor assessment involves throwing, catching, skipping, hopping, galloping, and standing still for 30 seconds. The Fine-motor assessment involves cutting, building towers with blocks, rhythm claps, and finger movements. Information obtained from the concepts area includes knowing, naming and sorting colors, following oral commands, naming body parts, and knowing opposites. The language measure deals with communication skills such as understanding speech sounds, parts of speech, and oral conversation, which involves the use of complete sentences. The speech therapist should administer this portion of the test.

The advantage of the DIAL is that it may be administered to large groups of preschool children in one day. Usually, a large room, such as a school gymnasium, is set up with stations at places in the room. One station involves gross-motor assessment; another station is for fine-motor, etc. A different teacher/assessor is trained for each station and the small children are brought to each station by volunteer helpers, who see that each child visits each station. Normally, the nurse or other trained personnel administers the visual and sensory tests in a nearby room that is quieter and more private, specifically for the hearing assessment. The age norms for both boys and girls range between 2 years, 8 months and 5 years, 5 months.

The DIAL instrument was field tested with 4,423 preschool children in eight regional sites. The instrument proved to aid in the identification of high-risk preschoolers. It was used in the following case study, which format is adapted to address skill areas named in P.L. 94-142.

EARLY-CHILDHOOD ASSESSMENT

Name: John K   *Date Examined:*
Birthdate: *Examiner:*
C.A.: 4-9

I. *Language Factors*
A. English is the language spoken in the home.
B. See the discussion of other language factors, listed under Related Intellectual Skills.

II. *Physiological Factors*
A. *Appearance:* John K. is extremely small of stature for his age. His walking gait appears abnormal until one realizes he has only peripheral vision. His hands are very small and give the appearance of being deformed. At birth he had bilateral syndactylism (double thumbs on both hands), which was surgically corrected.
B. *Hearing:* Unable to test upon entrance to school because of his failure to respond or because of the nature of the test.
C. *Vision:* Unable to test left eye. Only peripheral vision in the right eye.
D. *Gross-motor:* When John came to the school, he was unable to get a drink by himself because he could not push down the lever at the drinking fountain, a function with which most three-year-olds have very little difficulty.

On the DIAL test using a scaled score 0-3, he scored the following:

1.	Throwing	0
2.	Catching	0
3.	Jumping	2
4.	Hopping	0
5.	Skipping	1
6.	Standing still	0
7.	Balancing	0
		3

Expected minimum for age—14

E. *Fine Motor Skills*
    1. Matching   3
    2. Building   3
    3. Copying shapes   1
    4. Cutting   0
    5. Copying letters   0
    6. Touching fingers   0
    7. Clapping hands   0
                   Total   7
Expected minimum for age—14

III. *Related Intellectual Skills*
  A. *Conceptual*
    1. Sorting blocks   2
    2. Naming colors   3
    3. Counting   2
    4. Positioning   2
    5. Following directions   3
    6. Identifying concepts   2
    7. Identifying body parts 3
                     Total   17
Expected minimum for age—14

  B. *Communication*
    1. Articulation   0
    2. Remembering   0
    3. Naming nouns, verbs   1
    4. Coping   0
    5. Naming self, age, sex   0
    6. Classifying   0
    7. Telling a story   0
                     Total   1
Expected minimum for age—14

IV. *Social and Psychological*

John K. comes from a family of moderate financial means. They express what appears to be a sincere interest in him and his development. They recognize many of his weaknesses and have expressed the belief that John uses non-language means of manipulating the adults in his life. This could, in part, be the reason for his low score in communication.

Summary: John K. is a small child four years and nine months of age. He shows deficits in gross-motor, fine-motor, and communication skills. His visual anomaly is probably a factor in his slow development in motor skills.

Conceptual skills were by far his greatest strengths. For a boy of John K.'s age, one would expect a minimum of 14, but he scored 17 which is more than one year above expectancy. This indicates that he does have the intellectual power to process, store, and retrieve certain kinds of information.

Communication skills manifest a scaled score of 1, which is below expectancy. On the test he answered only with grunts; but in other circumstances when language surfaced, it was near that expected of a four-year-old.

Recommendations: Even though he will be old enough to attend kindergarten next year, it is recommended that he stay in the Early Childhood Education class because of the gains that he made toward the end of the year. Other tests indicate that he is not ready for the work in kindergarten. It is also recommended that remediation continue to be based on the results of the test data obtained.

_____

Reporting Diagnostician

The DIAL is representative of a good screening instrument procedure that may have many years of usefulness. Whereas the first two check lists, *Developmental Guidelines* and *Inner Language Scale*, may be used as criterion-referenced scales to aid in curriculum decisions, the DIAL is often instrumental in helping make decisions as to whether a child should enter first grade or stay in kindergarten a second year. However, it may also be used as a criterion-referenced test to aid in educational plans. One of the DIAL's greatest advantages is its facility in being used with a large group of children.

No check lists, including these three, should be used to designate a handicapped category. The dangers of mislabeling children have already been discussed. Whether standardized tests or check lists are to be used with early-childhood-handicapped children, it is reemphasized that any child with certain deviant behaviors be only considered as *at risk*. If the child is slow in one of the areas of development, it may be only a developmental difference in timing and, as such, should be used only as a criterion reference for close observation. In some cases, opportunity for learning may be provided or time for development should be allowed, without pressure to make a premature change. If a child, for example, is unduly shy, group planning that involves cooperative children could be in order. Also, if a child is slow in handling a pencil correctly, perhaps some gross-motor activities such as grasping junglegym bars or tricycle handles may be in order first, followed by more fine-motor tasks, such as placing clothes pins on boards. Using early-childhood testing instruments for purposes such as those identified above will help prevent the improper categorization that could in many cases adversely affect not only the school performance of the child, but also his entire life.

References

Brandston, M.D., & Dubose, R. Inner language scale. Nashville, Tenn.: George Peabody College for Teachers, 1974 (unpublished paper).

Buros, O. K. (Ed.), *The seventh mental measurements yearbook*, 2 vols. Highland Park, N.J.: The Gryphon Press, 1972.

Caldwell, B. M. The importance of beginning early. In Jordon, J. B., & Daily, R. F. (Eds.), *Not all little red wagons are red.* Arlington, Va.: The Council for Exceptional Children, 1973.

Cattell, P. *The measurement of intelligence of infants and young children.* New York: Psychological Corporation, 1940.

Chall, J. S., & Mirsky, A. F. The implications for education. In Chall, J. S., & Mirsky, A. F. (Eds.), *Education and the brain* (Seventy-seventh Yearbook of the National Society for the Study of Education), part II. Chicago: The University of Chicago Press, 1978.

Decker, C. A., & Decker, J. R. *Planning and administering early childhood programs,* 2nd ed. Columbus, Ohio: Charles E. Merrill Publishing Company, 1980.

Educational Testing Service. *An annotated bibliography of references to tests and assessment devices.* Princeton, N.J.: Test Collection, Author, undated mimeograph.

Hallahan, D. P., & Kauffman, J. M. *Exceptional children: Introduction to special education.* Englewood Cliffs, N.J.: Prentice-Hall, 1978.

Hendrick, J. *The whole child: New trends in early education,* 2nd ed. St. Louis: C. V. Mosby Company, 1980.

Heopfner C. S., & Nummendal, S. G. (Eds.). *CSE-ERCRC preschool/ kindergarten test evaluations.* Los Angeles: Center for the Study of Education, University of California, 1971.

Jansky, J., & de Hirsch, K. *Preventing reading failure.* New York: Harper & Row, 1972.

Johnson, O. G., & Bommarito, J. W. *Tests and measurements in child development: A handbook.* San Francisco: Jossey-Bass, 1971.

Kirk, S. *Early education of the mentally retarded.* Urbana, Ill.: University of Illinois Press, 1958.

Langley, B. Developmental guidelines for teachers and evaluators of multi-handicapped children. Nashville, Tenn.: George Peabody College for Teachers, 1976 (unpublished paper).

Mardell, C., & Goldenberg, D. *DIAL: Development indicators for the assessment of learning: Manual.* Edison, N.J.: Childcraft Educational Corp., 1972.

Mercer, J., & Lewis, J. *System of multicultural pluralistic assessment.* New York: Psychological Corporation, 1979.

Stott, L. H., & Ball, R. S. Infant and preschool mental tests: Review and evaluation. Monography of Social Research in Child Development 30, 1965, Serial No. 101.

Tjossen, T. D. (Ed.) *Intervention strategies for high risk infants and young children.* Baltimore: University Park Press, 1976.

Assessment of the Multiply/Severely Handicapped
(by Jane Norris, Ed.D.)

An individual who is multiply handicapped is one who has a combination of handicaps, as defined by criteria for any specific handicapping condition that results in multisensory or motor deficiencies and developmental lag in cognitive, affective, or psychomotor domains. A severely handicapped individual is one who, first, meets the eligibility of one or more of the legally defined handicapping conditions and who, second, is so disabled that the impairment interferes with normal development in the self-help skills, communication process, social/emotional behaviors, and intellectual functioning. This impairment is interfering to the degree that the individual is almost completely dependent.

Identification of the severely and multiply handicapped has never been a difficult task. To determine that a severe handicap exists, one need spend only a short time with a child who is blind and/or deaf, with no speech, and/or with orthopedic problems. When evaluation is involved, the process is much more complex. If we choose to assess, for example, the cognitive and motor skills, we are confronted with a task that is not so simple.

Until 1975, the major force prompting the evaluation and training of the severely handicapped had come from the concerned and empathic citizens who believed that it was a moral responsibility to provide better education opportunities for this group. And prior to this time most of the organized and structured programs were in operation only in institutions. The passage of public law 94-142, a right to education act, forced the public schools to accept the responsibility of providing assessment and education for those who were not physically or mentally able to compete in the normal education structure. Throughout the nation, where training was in force, the emphasis for this group was based on self-help, elementary language, motor, and social skills. There were no specific intelligence, aptitude, or achievement tests that could be used for evaluation, and there were no specific programs that had been heralded as the best guidelines for training those who, in many cases, had no language, no sight, and no hearing.

The changes brought about since 1975 have involved (1) finding these severely handicapped children; (2) determining their existing skills and their undeveloped skills; and (3) making appropriate plans for individualized training sessions. This paper is concerned with the second point mentioned above, determining existing skills and underdeveloped skills, i.e., *assessment*.

The purpose of an assessment of the multiply and the severely handicapped is the same as that of the other special-education categories—to determine the presence or absence of disabilities that may or may not be contributing to the educational needs of the student/individual. All assessment in the public schools, of course, should be for the purpose of guiding and directing curriculum planning. It is meaningless unless it relates to the development of the skills needed in the act of living and surviving beyond the level of mere existence.

The assessment must include much prior data gathering. Questions to be answered should deal with such information as mobility, physical-health status, emotional stability, and speech and language development. Once these questions have been answered, the diagnostician/psychologist may plan for the evaluation by making decisions concerning (1) instruments to use, (2) location of the testing, and (3) the physical equipment needed during the assessment period.

The domains to be covered in the testing should include information concerning cognitive-, affective-, and psychomotor-skill development. Severity of the expected duration of the handicapping condition also should be included.

Assessment Instruments and Procedures

The testing instruments to be used in assessment of the multiply handicapped are generally confined to adaptive-behavior scales; however, for the multiply handicapped, adaptations of other types of tests can be used, for instance, adaptations of various intelligence and achievement tests. Anastasi (1976) lists and describes three major categories of tests for special populations as being ". . . tests for the infant and preschool level, tests suitable for persons with diverse sensory and motor handicaps, and tests designed for use across cultures or subcultures." The first two categories are relevant to this discussion. For infant and preschool level, she suggests the Gesell Development Schedules, Bruininks-Oseretsky Test of Motor Proficiency (1978), the American Association of Mental Deficiency Adaptive Behavior Scale (1974), the Vineland Social Maturity Scale (1982), the Bayley Scales of Infant Development (1942), the McCarthy Scales of Children's Abilities, and the Piagetian Scales.

For various types of sensory impairment, Anastasi suggests the Hiskey-Nebraska Test of Learning Aptitudes for the deaf (1966); adaptations of the Wechsler (1975) and Binet (1972) Intelligence tests for the blind; and adaptations of the Leiter International Performance Scale (1969) of the Porteus Mazes (1965), the Raven's Progressive Matrices (1960), and the Peabody Picture Vocabulary Test (1981), and the Columbia Mental Maturity Scale (1972) for children with motor handicaps.

Whereas Anastasi suggests tests to use for special populations, Hammer (1974) suggests an approach to assessment that would precede the choice of tests to use. He organizes this approach around systems drawn from the field of developmental psychology. These are identified as Systems of Behavior that include Physical, Social, Emotional, and Mental. Hammer explains that these systems should be only a part of the guide—that the process of organization of Language, Thoughts, Ideas, Concepts, Imitation, Perception, Motor Output, and Sensory Input should be related to each of the Systems of Behavior. As a guide for the diagnostician, he suggests a graph (Figure 42), as follows:

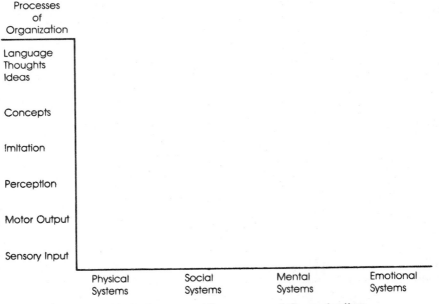

Figure 42. Systems and Processes of Organization

Hammer states that the process of organization provides a framework in which the systems of behavior may be observed, either in the classroom or in an assessment procedure. Sensory input is cited as the basic level of assessment of the organization process and is difficult to measure. From the motor output, it is possible to infer sensory function. For example, if a child were touched on the arm, followed immediately by the therapist's lifting up the arm, and this were repeated several times, the child should fairly soon lift the arm independently at the touch. This would indicate that there is a sensory input, which is inferred by his motor response output, and this would involve the physical system. Perception is another process that must be inferred from the output side through imitative behavior. To measure this (and involving the social system) the question to ask is, "Can the child imitate what is to be done in a social system?" Using Hammer's framework provides a means of collecting information and determining where the child is in the different systems of behavior.

Another approach to the assessment of the severely handicapped is that of Sailor and Horner and described by Sailor and Haring (1977). As a foundation to this approach, Sailor and Haring aver that the end product of assessment is the formulation of goals and precise objectives for basic-skill development. These instructional objectives must develop components of complex skills in a meaningful, functional sequence. In order to do this, the assessment should show precisely where the student is in terms of skills and which skills need to be taught immediately to advance the child's development. They present a detailed analysis of several assessment systems. The analysis involves three positions on a continuum of comprehensiveness.

1. Screening: Position 1 Systems
Time element involved—about two weeks
Example tests are:
TARC Assessment System (Sailor and Mix, 1975)
Portage Project Guide to Early Education: Instructions Checklist (Shearer et al., 1970)
Purpose: to provide a thumbnail sketch of the child's current skill level across various domains
2. The Pennsylvania Model: Position II System
Sailor and Haring present the Pennsylvania Model as the best system that falls between thumbnail screening and full-scale comprehensive assessment. This Pennsylvania Model (Somerton and Turner, 1975) assesses the student's current competency in sensory, motor, self-care, communication, perceptual-cognitive, and social interaction development. Subdomains sampled include auditory, visual, and tactual discrimination, gross- and fine-motor competencies, feeding, drinking, toileting, dressing, washing, and bathing.
An example from the Competency Checklist on Auditory discrimination is as follows
_____ 1. Child searches for sound with eyes.
_____ 2. Child turns head toward source of loud sound.
_____ 6. Child responds to "no."
_____14. Child demonstrates ability to identify mechanical sounds: i.e., cars, trucks, trains, airplanes etc.
Sailor and Haring report that this system, while representing a start in the right direction, may not in each case communicate to the teaching staff the child's current baseline-skill level on a wide number and range of basic service need skill areas. They suggest that the third level of assessment systems is more fully comprehensive.
3. Position III Systems
The Position III Systems are considered to be more complex and time consuming. The example tests they site are:
The Balthazar Scales of Adaptive Behavior (Balthazar, 1971a, 1971b, 1971c, 1971d)
The AAMD Adaptive Behavior Scales (Nihira, et al, 1974)
Behavior Progression Checklist (BCP, 1973)
(The AAMD is described in Chapter 6 and the BCP is described in Chapter 2.)

Regarding the three position levels, Sailor and Haring suggest the following procedures as a rule of thumb:

1. Use Position I, Screening to get started with a child when time is short.
2. Use Position II to conduct educational assessment and formulate an educational plan.
3. Use Position III as guides to formulate instructional objectives following assessment (Sailor & Haring, 1977, p. 15).

Van Etten, Arkell, and Van Etten (1980), in their list of various developmental check lists, include several of the tests recommended by Sailor and Haring. They are listed as follows:

1. Developmental Activities Screening Inventory (Dubose and Langley, 1977)
2. Neonatal Behavioral Assessment Scale (Brazelton, 1973)
3. Behavioral Characteristics Progression (VORT Corp, 1973)
4. Callier-Azusa Scale (Stillman, 1974)
5. Developmental Profile (Alpern and Boll, 1972)
6. Pennsylvania Training Model: Individual Assessment Guide (Somerton and Turner, 1975)
7. Uniform Performance Assessment System (University of Washington, 1977)
8. Camelot Behavioral Checklist (Foster, 1974)
9. TARC Assessment Inventory for Retarded Children (Sailor and Mix, 1975)
10. Teaching Research Motor-Development Scale (Fredericks, Baldwin, Doughty, and Walter, 1972)
11. Environmental Prelanguage Battery (Horstmeier and MacDonald, 1978)

In reviewing some of the tests in the prior lists, it should be noted that less than a day is required for collecting the information covered therein; however, it is the opinion of some (Haeussermann, 1968; Sailor and Haring, 1977) that comprehensive assessment of the severely and multiply handicapped will need to extend over a two-to-three-week period. Because of the complexity of determining the needs of these children, an approach such as Hammer suggests is a good beginning position. This is to insure that all systems are considered whether position level I, II, or III is used. For example, at the *screening level*, (I), ideas from the Physical, Social, Emotional and Mental may be used, but a smaller number of behaviors will be checked in each area. And if one uses this level, the time element will not be as great as at levels II and III. Most comprehensive scales, as the BCP, will include all of the systems mentioned by Hammer, but if they are not found in the tests used at levels II and III, it would be wise to search elsewhere for tests that cover all aspects of growth and development.

Sailor and Horner (1976), Haring (1977), Dubose (1978), and chapters 2, 6, and 7 in this text include discussions of the instruments listed. The use of any of these should provide a group of tests from which choices could be made to determine social and motor skills. Cognitive functioning can be measured on some of these but cognitive skills remain the most difficult to measure in the severely handicapped and in some multiply handicapped. With such "hard-to-reach" children, the diagnostician is faced with a challenge of finding varied means of presenting the stimulus items found within the tests. One of the very good resources to provide help in modifying questions and commands is found in the work of Hauessermann (1968). Though her scale is older than some of the other scales, her approach is very basic and helpful in establishing communication with the severely handicapped. Her instrument, the Developmental Potential of Preschool Children (Hauesserman, 1968), has norms that cover wide spans of ages. It could be more aptly identified as criterion-referenced, rather than norm-referenced; even more than this, it can be said to be a test that attempts to *find detours to determine cognitive functioning* and this is what is helpful to a diagnostician. An introduction to Hauessermann's philosophy and an example of her test is presented in the following discussion.

The Work of Hauessermann

Hauessermann structured her assessment interview around 40 basic items that include the following major areas: physical functioning, sensory intactness and sensory behavior, self-awareness, self-concept and body image, intellectual functioning, and emotional-social behavior. She bases her education evaluation on her 25 years of clinical experience with atypical children, and her belief is that the objective of the examination is to provide information concerning the positive qualities of a child's functioning, the difficulties the child faces in mastering problems when they are presented in the standard fashion, and the information about special circumstances that is needed to create appropriate conditions for learning in the handicapped individual. Hauessermann insists that standardized tests were never designed to answer questions that arise in a rehabilitation situation. Further, she says that the object of standardized testing is the determination of the relative performance status of an individual in comparison with a standardized population, and not the analysis of any single person's unique functioning. She stresses the fact that to plan an effective educational program for an individual child, it is as important to understand the pattern of his learning as it is to know the intelligence level, or the mental age he has achieved. This point of Hauessermann's should, of course, be considered for all children needing help in learning, and not just the severely handicapped.

In Hauessermann's (1968) interview the beginning evaluation is designed to start with items that should be accomplished at a two-year level and continues up to six years, six months. In the first item, the examiner places a shoe, spoon, comb and brush, and a cup on an empty table. The child is asked to indicate the item named by the examiner by following directions such as, "Look. . . .," "Give me . . .," or "Show me . . .". At each step directions are given as to what to do next if the child has succeeded. If the child has still failed, the examiner is to use the next lower modification and continue to retreat gradually, step by step, to lower levels of demand, until the child begins to function. The level on which the child is finally able to function must be evaluated as the developmental level achieved in this particular area.

Item number one, Recognition of Concrete Familiar Lifesize Objects, when named has ten modifications that take into consideration such steps as, e.g., (1) reducing the choices from four to two; (2) using pantomime to see if there is a lack of understanding of the verbal commands; and (3) the introduction of a doll, to see if the child can show proper use of the items with it. The choices may be continually reduced by removing the doll. Then determine if the child will open his or her mouth if a spoon is placed near the face, or if the child will refuse or push away a shoe that is placed near the face—the purpose of which is *object recognition*.

Hauessermann devotes a complete chapter to modifications of each item on the evaluation. These modifications consider sensory deprivations such as blindness and deafness. She stresses in her descriptions of some evaluation situations that (1) the examiner's careful observation of how the child prepares herself to approach the task presented and (2) whether the examiner perseveres or adapts to the physical limitations is sometimes more important than whether or not the child passes the items presented.

This brief review provides an overview of a philosophy concerning assessment of the multiply/severely handicapped. This philosophy stresses such points as the necessity of "trying another way", using the vernacular of Marc Gold (1971), to ascertain cognitive-functioning abilities. Intellectually, the trained diagnostician realizes the necessity of taking a number of developmental scale items and presenting them to individual children in unique ways; but it is Hauessermann's clinical experience and observation that have brought the challenge and difficulties in this process of evaluation into a clear perspective. Her evaluation techniques make the development of an individualized educational plan for the multiply/severely handicapped individual truly individual, and it is recommended that diagnosticians/psychologists employ her ideas in assessment of children with whom it is difficult to communicate. The following example covers an evaluation at the position I level. It has suggestions for beginning training. The teacher should follow such an evaluation with a more comprehensive scale.

SCREENING ASSESSMENT FOR THE MULTIHANDICAPPED

Name: Toby   *Examined:*
Birthdate: *Examiner:*
                                                         C. A.: 6-1

Physical and Behavioral Factors

Toby is a thin child of six-years and two-months of age. He is blind and deaf and he does not walk. His legs and arms are underdeveloped and he stays in a wheelchair much of the day with his head bent forward. He makes sounds frequently which are unintelligible. The medical reports list sensory hearing of loud sounds and some sight—possible flashes. Toby often has tantrums, but they do not last long; the parents leave him alone during these times and this seems to lessen the length of the spells. Through his years he has been cared for as a baby—being fed, bathed and dressed without efforts to have him help himself.

Cognitive and Performance Factors

The first step in this evaluation was to determine whether Toby could learn to respond to different signs presented kinesthetically. The forefinger of the diagnostician was placed in the palm of his right hand. Immediately Toby was lifted under both arms to help him stand up. This was repeated over a period of five times, each time allowing him to stand with help. The sixth presentation after the signal, Toby began to raise his own arms in response—ready to stand up.

The second step was to put a spoon in his hand and move it to a bowl with cooked cereal. After about five dips, he was given the spoon. He started a movement toward the bowl and hesitated. With a slight touch in the right

---

Note: The techniques used were modified from Elsa Hauessermann (1958).

direction, it was found that he could follow the procedure of learning to help himself.

The third step was to place two balloons in a pillow case and move his right hand over both balloons—touching each one; then moving his hand away. This was repeated twice and then he was led to explore the pillow case to become aware of the Gestalt of the presentation. One of the balloons was then removed and his hand placed back over the one left. He moved his hand as if searching for the second balloon. This procedure was followed by adding a third balloon. It was discovered that Toby had a concept of three.

To determine Toby's knowledge of what to do with clothes, Toby's shoes and socks were taken off. He was allowed to feel the shoe and then the shoe was handed to him. He moved the shoe back toward the foot but dropped it. The shoe was then pressed to his face and he pushed it away and lifted the foot. He was then handed both sock and shoe. Toby handed the sock back first and lifted the foot. The mother reported that he had often given signs similar to these actions. It became evident that Toby makes associations like a two and one-half year old.

Information from parents reveals that Toby has not had any formal help and the mother realizes that he had given signs that he was ready to be trained to help himself under controlled conditions. These criterion-referenced data show that Toby is trainable but that no reference made as to intellectual level is necessary at this time. It is apparent that structured training should begin.

Recommendations for his program are to begin with:

1. Self-feeding and self-help training
2. Playing games of kinesthetic hide and seek with objects to help develop quantitative concepts
3. Training for understanding of clothing items as to use
4. Training of signals (kinesthetic) to obtain specific responses, as indicating whether he wants food, mother, father, water and other meaningful needs.

Reporting Diagnostician

References

Alpern, G. E., & Boll, T. J. *Developmental profile.* Aspen, Colo.: Psychological Development Publications, 1972.

Anastasi, A. *Psychological testing.* New York: Macmillan Publishing Co., Inc., 1976.

Balthazar, E. E. *Balthazar scales of adaptive behavior, part one: Handbook for the professional supervisor.* Palo Alto, Calif.: Consulting Psychologist Press, Inc., 1971a.

Balthazar, E. E. *Balthazar scales of adaptive behavior, part two: Handbook for the rater technician.* Palo Alto, Calif.: Consulting Psychologist Press, Inc., 1971b.

Balthazar, E. E. *Balthazar scales of adaptive behavior, part three: The scales of functional independence.* Palo Alto, Calif.: Consulting Psychologist Press, Inc., 1971c.

Balthazar, E. E. *Balthazar scales of adaptive behavior, part four: Workshop and training manual.* Palto Alto, Calif.: Consulting Psychologist Press, Inc., 1971d.

Bayley, N. *Bayley scales of infant development.* New York: Psychological Corporation, 1942.

Behavioral characteristics progression (BCP). Palo Alto, Calif.: VORT Corp., 1973.

Brazelton, B. T. *Neonatal behavioral assessment scale.* Philadelphia: J. B. Lippincott, 1973.

Bruininks, R. H. *Bruininks-Oseretsky test of motor proficiency.* Circle Pines, Minn.: American Guidance Service, 1978.

Burgemeister, B., Blum, L. H., & Lorge, I. *Columbia mental maturity scale.* New York: Psychological Corporation, 1972.

Burke, D. *Piagetian attainment kit.* Monterey, Calif.: Publishers Test Service, 1973.

Dubose, R. F. Development of communication in nonverbal children. *Education and Training of the Mentally Retarded,* 1978, *13,* 37–41.

Dubose, R. F., & Langley, M. B. *The developmental activities screening inventory.* Boston: Teaching Resources, 1977.

Doll, E. *Vineland social maturity scale,* rev. ed. Minneapolis: Education Test Bureau, 1982.

Dunn, L. M., & Dunn, L. M. *Peabody picture vocabulary test,* revised ed. Minneapolis: American Guidance Service, 1981.

Foster, R. W. *Camelot behavioral checklist.* Lawrence, Kansas: Camelot Behavioral Systems, 1974.

Fredericks, H. D., Baldwin, V. L., Doughty, P., & Walter, L. F. *The teaching research motor-development scale for moderately and severely retarded children.* Springfield, Ill.: Charles C Thomas, 1972.

Gesell, A. *Gesell development schedules.* Cheshire, Conn.: Nigel Fox, 1940.

Gold, M. Try another way. Indianapolis: Film Productions of Indianapolis, 1975 (film).

Hammer, E. K. Psychological assessment of the deaf-blind child: The synthesis of assessment and educational services. Paper presented to the International Seminar on Deaf-Blind. Condover, Shrewsbury, England: Royal National Institute for the Blind, July 29, 1974.

Haring, N. G. From promise to reality. *AAESPH Review,* 1977, *2*: 307.

Hauessermann, E. *Developmental potential of preschool children.* New York: Grune and Stratton, 1958.

Hiskey, M. *Hiskey-Nebraska test of learning aptitude.* Lincoln, Neb.: Union College Press, 1966.

Horstmeier, D. S., & MacDonald, J. D. *Environmental prelanguage battery.* Columbus, Ohio: Charles E. Merrill Publishing Company, 1978.

Leiter, R. G. *Leiter international performance scale.* Los Angeles: Western Psychological Services, 1969.

McCarthy, D. *McCarthy scales of children's abilities.* New York: Psychological Corporation, 1972.

Nihira, K., Foster, R., Shellhass, M., & Leland, H. *AAMD adaptive behavior scale manual.* Washington, D.C.: American Association on Mental Deficiency, 1974.

Porteous, S. D. *Porteous mazes.* New York: Psychological Corporation, 1965.

Ravens, J. C. *The coloured progressive matrices.* London: H. K. Lewis and Company. New York: Psychological Corporation, 1962.

Sailor, W. & Haring, N. G. *Some current directions, in education of the severely/multiply handicapped. AAESPH Review,* June 1977, 3–22.

Sailor, W., & Horner, R. Educational assessment strategies for the severely handicapped. In Haring, N. & Brown, L. *Teaching the severely handicapped.* New York: Grune and Stratton, 1976.

Sailor, W., & Mix, B. J. *The TARC assessment system.* Lawrence, Kans.: H. and H. Enterprises, 1975.

Shearer, D., Billingsley, J., Frohman, A., et al. *The Portage guide to early education: instructions and checklist,* experimental ed. Portage, Wisc.: Cooperative Educational Service Agency, N. 12, 1970.

Somerton, M. E., & Turner, K. D. *Pennsylvania training model: Individual assessment guide.* Harrisburg, Pa.: Pennsylvania Department of Education, 1975.

Stillman, R. D. *Assessment of deaf-blind children: The Callier-Azusa scale.* Reston, Va.: The Council for Exceptional Children, 1974.

Terman, L., & Merrill, M. *Stanford Binet intelligence scale.* Boston: Houghton Mifflin, 1972

Uniform performance assessment system (UPAS). Seattle: University of Washington, 1977.

Van Etten, G., Arkell, C., & Van Etten, C. *The severely and profoundly handicapped.* St. Louis: C. V. Mosby Co., 1980.

Wechsler, D. *Wechsler intelligence scale for children—revised.* New York: Psychological Corporation, 1975.

Auditorially Impaired and
Visually Impaired

The assessment of the auditorially impaired and the visually impaired poses a number of problems to psychologists and educational diagnosticians. First, there have been relatively few instruments designed for the specific handicapped population. This has forced the examiners to use tests that must be adapted for use with the specific handicapped. Some of the content or the mode of presentation of the original test may be inappropriate for the auditorially impaired or the partially sighted. This means, of course, that the material and the mode of presentation of many desirable tests must be adapted for the specific handicapping condition before they can be used. This affects the standardized procedure for the administration and there is no guarantee that the changed version is equal to the original.

Second, even when material is adapted for use with the disabled by agencies who utilize specialists to do this—as the American Printing House for the Blind did for the visually impaired—there may not be appropriate norms for use with the test. Diagnosticians know that the norms need to be modified for use with the individual, but do not know in what way and how much.

Third, when standardized tests standardized on a normal population are used with the sensorially handicapped, there is almost always a lowering of the test reliability (Jensema, 1978). A test that may have had acceptable reliability for the nonhandicapped may not with the handicapped population.

Fourth, there is a shortage of research that may be generally applicable to the use of the test data. There is a more limited population from which to draw, and many in the research population may have other handicapping conditions or treatment programs that make it difficult to generalize results.

Communication in the test administration may also be a problem with the sensorially handicapped, and this is especially true with the deaf. A recent study (Levine, 1974) reported that 96 percent of the school psychologists surveyed reported major difficulties in testing the deaf. Thirty-seven percent reported difficulties in communication and 46 percent indicated difficulties with the tests, such as lack of adequate tests, absence of norms for the deaf, and problems of interpretation.

Faced with these dilemmas, some psychologists have hesitated to attempt assessment, believing that the use of any instrument in which the results could be influenced by the handicap should be avoided, while others have operated on the premise that the handicapped child will be competing with normal individuals and, therefore, the disabled child must be evaluated on the same basis as the nondisabled person. Neither of these approaches is satisfactory.

The problems of lack of appropriate test norms and/or tests specifically designed or adapted for use with the specific handicapped and lack of extensive research are far from being solved, but strides to overcome these problems have been made. For the most effective evaluation of the partially sighted and auditorially impaired, it takes more than a brief sampling of a person's behavior. It must proceed from the living-learning environment and back again to that environment. This necessitates extensive communication with the teacher and observation of the child in his environment. The evaluator can combine appropriate test data with extended observation of the sensorially handicapped child to make a more valid assessment. A visually limited child tends to be cautious in approaching a task. The score on the test may be affected by the cautious approach. What may be more educationally significant is the extent that caution affects learning tasks in the classroom. Observation of behavior in the classroom and in the testing environment becomes very significant in the psychoeducational assessment of the sensorially disabled.

The uniqueness of assessment of the blind and deaf and, in particular, the multiply handicapped; the problems of the assessment tools available; and the need for specificity in the instructional modes suggest that the educational diagnosticians/psychologists and the teacher must work closely together. Porter (1978–79) suggests a four-component process in the assessment procedure that should include:

1. A preassessment conference with the referring person/s to gather educationally relevant information concerning the referred student.
2. A preassessment observation of the referred student within the classroom or a natural learning setting.
3. A psychoeducational assessment guided by the background information gathered in steps 1 and 2.
4. A postassessment conference with the referring person to generate specific instructional and curricular implications from the assessment finding.

Hearing Impaired

It is necessary for the diagnostician to understand the hearing characteristics of the hearing-impaired child. It is not simply a case of recognizing that there is a hearing loss, but also what are the specific conditions under which the hearing loss affects the child. Wharton (1966) summarized some of the variations to be expected in the hearing-impaired when she indicated that a child may hear well when she is within a few feet of the speaker, but may not hear beyond that distance. Some speech elements may be heard, some imperfectly, and some not at all. A child may hear speech in a quiet room, but fail to hear it when there is a noisy background. Familiar words may be understood well in conversation; but new words may not be heard, unless there is special help.

Some voices may be heard better than others, and carefully articulated words may be understood, though slovenly spoken words may not be. Amplification of sounds may be needed and a child may hear when he is in good physical condition, but may not hear normally when he is experiencing some illness. Last, Wharton says that a child may supplement hearing with speech reading to simulate a state of hearing greater than that which really exists.

Mental-Ability Tests

The performance section of the WISC and WISC-R is used extensively in testing the hearing impaired. Other intelligence tests often used with the deaf and hard-of-hearing include the Leiter International Performance Scale (1959), The Arthur Adaptation of The Leiter International Performance Scale (1962), the Hiskey-Nebraska Test of Learning Aptitude (1966), Columbia Mental Maturity Scale (1972), and Goodenough-Harris (Levine, 1974). She also reports that the more common personality tests used are the Bender-Gestalt (1938), Draw-a-Person (1963), and House-Tree-Person (1966), with the Wide Range Achievement Test (1976), Stanford Achievement Tests (1964), and Metropolitan Achievement Tests (1978) the most often used tests to measure achievement levels of the hearing impaired.

The Hiskey-Nebraska Test of Learning Aptitude (1966) was first published in 1941 and was the first individual test of mental ability specifically designed for young deaf children and standardized upon such children in this country (Hiskey, 1966).

It is a performance test that can be administered in pantomime and requires no verbal response from the subject. In 1957, norms were published for hearing children, and with those norms verbal instructions may be used.

Age norms were established, but are referred to as *learning age* rather than *mental age, learning quotient* rather than *intelligence quotient.* Hiskey wanted to distinguish scores for the deaf from the mental age used with the hearing population, since there could be unfair comparisons between the two. Since IQ tests tend to measure or be influenced by the previous learning experiences in the home, school, and culture in which a person resides and the hearing impaired are limited in the processing of all these experiences, a deaf person will generally have a somewhat depressed score when compared to nonimpaired subjects.

The split-half reliability reported on the Hiskey-Nebraska is very satisfactory. For ages 3–10, it is .95 for the deaf subjects, and .93 for hearing subjects; for those aged 11–17, it is .92 and .90, respectively. The author reports validity correlations of .86 with the Stanford-Binet for ages 3–10 and .78 for those aged 11–17. A WISC correlation was reported of .82 for children in the age range of 5–11.

Although the Performance Scale of the WISC and now the WISC-R has been used extensively in testing the hearing impaired, diagnosticians have been impeded by the lack of norms for the deaf population. Sisco and Anderson (1978) have recently completed a standardization of the WISC-R on deaf children in which they report deaf norms, specific subtest findings, and a complete description of the standardization process of deaf forms for the WISC-R.

The sample used in the standardization included 1,228 deaf children from throughout the United States. They were balanced against the background variables in the WISC-R population and were also found to be fairly consistent with the 1970 census report. It was concluded that the deaf standardization sample was representative of deaf children in general throughout the United States.

The mean WISC-R Performance IQ for the deaf sample was 95.7 with a standard deviation of 17.55. The lower mean IQ and greater variability, as compared to the WISC-R IQ of 100 and a standard deviation of 15, supports much previous research and hypothesis of workers with the deaf regarding depressed IQ and greater variability of the scores of the deaf, when compared to the hearing population. The differences between the mean IQ and the standard deviation for the deaf and hearing populations sampled were reported to be significant beyond the .01 level (Sisco and Anderson, 1978).

Table 33 gives the scaled-score subtest pattern for the deaf standardization sample. The deaf sample scored at or slightly higher than the hearing sample on mazes and object assembly and did poorest on picture arrangement and coding.

The variability within the deaf sample was not evenly distributed across all ability or age levels. Most of the variability was concentrated in the Picture Arrangement and Coding tests. Figure 43 graphically portrays the variability of the deaf sample to the norms for hearing children for the various subtests (Sisco and Anderson, 1978).

Diagnosticians and psychologists need to be aware that the bright, high-scoring deaf tended to perform similarly to their hearing peers. Also, at all age levels, the deaf children had maze scores similar to or slightly better than hearing children. After age 12, the performance of average-to-above-average deaf children was similar to that of hearing children on the Picture Arrangement subtest; but on the Coding subtest, deaf children performed considerably below hearing children at all ages. This was particularly true of those of below-average ability (Sisco and Anderson, 1978). The deaf children who scored in the mild-to-moderate range of retardation did not follow the pattern of the average-to-above-average of catching up with their hearing peers as age increased. They continued to perform considerably below their hearing peers on all subtests at all age levels. The studies of Hirshoren et al. (1979), Graham and Shapiro (1953), and Goetzinger and Rousey (1957) also found that deaf children did best on Object Assembly.

Table 33. Scaled-Score Subtest Pattern for Deaf Standardization Sample

	Scaled Score Mean	S.D.	t*
Picture Completion	9.51	3.23	−5.72**
Picture Arrangement	8.71	3.74	−15.07**
Block Design	9.48	3.37	−6.07**
Object Assembly	10.32	3.24	+3.74**
Coding	8.03	3.32	−23.01**
Mazes	10.03	3.49	+.35N.S.***

*t calculated for significance of difference between subtest scaled-score mean for deaf sample and WISC-R scaled score mean of 10

**Significant beyond .01 level

***Incorrectly printed as a minus (−) in Office of Demographic Studies Publication (Series T, No. 1, November, 1977).

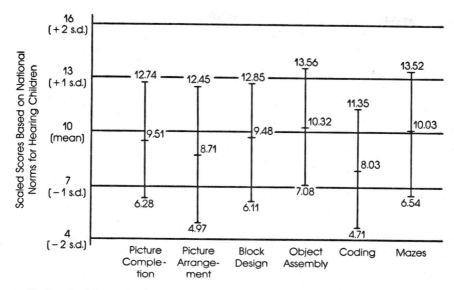

Figure 43. Scaled-Score Distribution for Deaf Sample, by Reference to National Norms for Hearing Children: Mean Scaled Score ± One Standard Deviation

In the absence of deaf norms for the WISC-R, Hirshoren (1979) attempted to validate the use of the regular norms with the deaf, by comparing WISC-R results with those obtained on the Hiskey-Nebraska deaf norms. He used 59 deaf students who were tested on the WISC-R and the Hiskey-Nebraska and concluded that even without deaf norms, the WISC-R Performance scale was satisfactory for testing the IQ of deaf children. He found the difference in the IQs of the two tests not to be significant. Table 34 shows the test characteristics reported by Hirshoren et al. (1979).

It is recommended that norms on the WISC-R established for the deaf (Sisco and Anderson, 1977) be used with deaf children, rather than hearing norms, even though Hirshoren found a close relationship in the IQ scores of the Hiskey-Nebraska Test of Learning Aptitude and the hearing norms of the WISC-R Performance scale.

Hirshoren agrees with Gianereco (1967) that the Wechsler scales are not clinically useful predictors of school achievement for deaf children between the ages of 8 and 13 years of age. Gianereco prefers the Hiskey-Nebraska as a predictor of academic achievement because of the higher-than-average correlations between the Hiskey-Nebraska scores and the Stanford and Metropolitan Achievement Tests. Neyhus (1969) found the Wechsler Scales to be less selective in identifying academic failures than the Hiskey-Nebraska. He was able to demonstrate that the memory items of the Hiskey-Nebraska

Table 34. Test Characteristics of the WISC-R
Performance Scale and Hiskey-Nebraska

Test	Variable	X Scores	Range	S.D.
Hiskey-Nebraska Test of Learning Aptitude	Learning Age— Months	116.70	77–152	21.57
	Learning Quotient	89.86	57–131	16.53
WISC-R	Performance IQ	88.07	52–129	17.83

identified the lower-functioning, hearing-impaired student and, therefore, could discriminate better between deaf adolescents who are good and poor learners than the WISC Performance.

The necessity for most examiners to use performance rather than verbal scales to test the deaf poses a problem in adequately predicting school success. Anastasi (1976, p. 253) has pointed out that verbal measures of intelligence are better predictors of academic functioning than performance items. Perhaps with this idea Brill's (1962) suggestion that a 10 percent reduction in the Wechsler Performance IQ gives a more accurate estimate of the academic potential of deaf adolescents than the actual score obtained on the Performance scale.

The Leiter International Performance and the Arthur Adaptation of the Leiter are used quite regularly with the deaf population, although they have not been normed on the hearing impaired. Anderson and Stevens (1970) reported in their sampling of School Superintendents for the Retarded Deaf that 45 percent indicated the Leiter Scales were the preferred measure of intelligence used in their schools.

The Leiter scales (LIPS) (1969) were developed to provide a culture-free nonverbal method of assessing intelligence, based primarily on abstract concepts. The basal ages are 2 years for the Leiter and 3 years for the Arthur Adaptation (AALIPS) and are, therefore, useful for preschoolers. Most children seem to enjoy the materials on the Scales and they merit consideration where rapport seems inadequate.

Many studies show that the LIPS and AALIPS scores tend to be lower than the Stanford-Binet and the Wechsler Performance Scale. Orgel and Dreger (1955) in a study of normal school children found 40 out of 48 higher Stanford-Binet scores than Leiter scores. When the Stanford-Binet scores were above 120, the Leiter Scale scores were at least 12 points lower in every case, and in three instances were 35–46 points lower. Sharp (1957) and Birch and Birch (1951) found Wechsler Performance scores to be higher in every case than the LIPS scores. These included slow learners, as well as those in the low-average-to-high-average range. Although other studies have shown a slight elevation of Leiter (Sisco and Anderson, 1978) and the Arthur Adaptation of the Leiter (Ritter, 1976) to the WISC or WISC-R, the numbers of subjects are too small to generalize. Therefore, caution must be exercised in using the Leiter Scales in placement without recognizing this tendency toward lower scores when compared to the Stanford-Binet and the Wechsler performance scale. This is especially true for the average-to-above-average students (Ratcliffe and Ratcliffe, 1979).

A general conclusion can be drawn that any one of the most popular IQ tests with hearing norms may be about as good as another, so long as one is aware of certain tendencies of each test under various conditions. Those tests that minimize communication problems in administration and have deaf norms available will be most useful to the school psychologist or educational diagnostician.

Readiness Testing

Hearing-impaired children have been described as being retarded academically from 1.0 to 2.24 years (Kodman, 1963). Age is not a valid criterion to determine readiness for school for deaf children because of their inability to process experiences adequately. Being able to ascertain when students are likely to perform satisfactorily in school is important for all children, but especially for the physically handicapped. The Boehm Test of Basic Concept is an instrument that measures 50 basic concepts considered necessary for satisfactory academic achievement during kindergarten and first and second grades. This test is most useful for the disadvantaged and handicapped. Although research validity for this test is scarce, it does appear to have good face validity. Davis (1974) compared hearing and hearing-disabled children on the Boehm Test of Basic Concepts (1971). She found the hearing impaired to have great difficulty with the concepts of space, quality, and time.

Table 35 illustrates the deficiency of certain concepts of hearing-impaired children as compared with non–hearing impaired.

The Boehm Test of Basic Concepts is easily administered and interpreted. It has value for use with the deaf and hard-of-hearing as a readiness test, since they are so handicapped in developing many concepts that hearing children easily develop through adequate processing of their experiences.

Hearing Screening

Although hearing loss is checked by health personnel or speech and hearing specialists, and not by psychologists or diagnosticians, inadequate screening can affect the diagnosis. Pure tone screening, which is used extensively, does not effectively detect middle-ear problems, where the hearing loss is less than 20–25 decibel (Cass & Kaplan, 1979). Winchester (1974) reports that at least 90 percent of the hearing problems encountered in schools are related to minor, nonpainful cases of otitis media, causing a 15–20 decibel hearing loss. Serous otitis media (SOM) has its highest incidence in children up to 9 years of age. It has not been considered significant, since it does not necessarily lead to permanent hearing loss and most children outgrow it by age 9. However, it will affect the learning of many youngsters during the first 3 years of schooling and pure tone screening will miss it.

Cass and Kaplan (1979) recommend acoustical-impedance measurement plus pure tone screening to identify those with hearing loss, whether permanent or temporary. Katz (1978) believes that conductive hearing loss that results from SOM is a form of auditory deprivation. He states: "The practical importance of this information is that conductive hearing loss: (1) can interfere with the acquisition of good auditory perceptual skills; (2) can adversely influence language development; (3) can increase the likelihood of having a significant learning disability; and (4) in children and adults, can

Table 35. Comparison of Percentage of Normal-Hearing and Hearing-Impaired Children Answering Correctly the Ten Concepts Most Often Missed by the Experimental Subjects (Davis, 1974)

Concept	Hearing Impaired	Normally Hearing
Between	37	100
Always	45	87
Medium Sized	29	96
Separated	33	100
Left	45	87
Pair	20	79
Skip	41	87
Equal	41	87
Third	50	92
Least	25	100

lead to aberrant results on auditory tests that might be mistaken for signs of gross retrocochlear or brain lesions".

It is important for the psychologist or educational diagnostician to have information regarding the screening done for hearing loss. If only pure-tone screening is performed, one may be assessing a child who has a hearing impairment that has not been identified.

Auditory-Skills Testing

Although the general assessment of auditory skills may be thought of as outside the area of testing of the deaf, the hearing-impaired child may have various auditory deficiencies. The Goldman-Fristoe-Woodcock Auditory Skills Test Battery (1976) offers a wide range of diagnostic instruments. Normative data have been obtained on subjects from 3 to 80 years of age. The battery consists of 12 tests grouped into four clusters: Auditory Selective Attention, Auditory Discrimination, Auditory Memory, and Sound-Symbol tests.

The reliability coefficients for combined ages for all tests range from .86 to .98. Test reliability was also reported for three age ranges: 3–8, 9–18, and 19 and over. For the age range of 3–8, the coefficient of reliability was .78 to .97 for the 12 tests, with a median of .87. For the 9–18 age range, they were from .46 to .96, with a median of .77. The norming sample ranged from 405 to 4,790, with a mean of approximately 500 across the three age groups for most tests. The manual provides both norm-referenced data and criterion-referenced information. Clinical data are provided for those with mild speech and learning difficulties and those with severe learning difficulties.

The intercorrelations among the tests are sufficiently low to infer that the tests measure different abilities rather than a general auditory-perception ability. Also, the correlations support the hypothesis of age-related development.

This test may prove to be the most useful test in auditory perception available to diagnosticians. It is designed for both diagnostic and remedial purposes and should be an aid in educational planning.

Visually Impaired

Psychologists and diagnosticians have received little training to test either the visually impaired or multiply handicapped. In addition they find very few tests* available that have been designed specifically for the visually impaired. This lack of appropriately designed tests has necessitated making adaptations in the tests designed for the nonblind. Langley (1978–79) suggests some general guidelines for adapting tests for use with the blind that should be heeded. "Only through judicial selection and combination of subtests and test items from various scales can one obtain an estimate of the child's maximum potential. Adaptations of items must be done cautiously and the effects of the adaptation on standardization should be regarded. Common adaptations of materials and procedures include adding a sound element to materials, substituting two- or three-dimensional objects for pictures, creating raised-line figures, supplying supplemental oral directions, and physically guiding the child to explore stimulus items or manipulating him/her through task demands."

---

*An extensive list of tests useful in the assessment of visually impaired children are available from your instructor. Information on publishers with address, age of child for whom designed, type of test, and comments on use and administration is provided.

She further states that tests administered to multiply handicapped should have, among several other characteristics, the following:

1. Items should be easily adaptable to an auditory or tactual mode.
2. Items should be variable, should be accurate, and simple representations of the real item and the materials should be multi-sensory in nature. Both verbal and performance items should be available in order to maintain the child's maximum attention and to assess global abilities. Often visually impaired children have a wealth of stored rote facts but exhibit no problem-solving strategies.
3. Scoring of items should be minimally dependent upon the speed of performance.

The visually deficient child, by necessity, will rely heavily on auditory input. It is imperative that the hearing be checked and corrected to the extent possible. Expressive and receptive language may suggest hearing problems. If there is a communication problem and it is not caused by a hearing deficit, the reason or reasons must be found.

There may be other handicapping conditions that the visually impaired child is experiencing. These may include mental retardation, emotional disturbances, residuals from cerebral palsy, and orthopedic problems. The multiple problems complicate the assessment and planning for individualized learning opportunities. Klineman (1975) has indicated that standardized tests are not adequate for determining baseline information to design educational programs for the multiply handicapped. There must be a study of the child's developmental processes. She has formulated a four-step process to diagnose and implement an educational program. It is necessary to start with a comprehensive medical and psycho-social evaluation to locate and treat any physiological deterrents to learning. The second step is the assessment of the child's functioning levels. These would include orientation and mobility, communication, self-care, and socialization. The next step involves observing the child to see what provides reinforcement and, last, an evaluation of the child's response to specific instructional approaches over an extended period of time to discover capabilities. The four-step procedure is also applicable to the assessment of the visually impaired without multiple handicapping conditions.

Tests alone will not provide a total picture of the child from which to develop an educational plan. One must recognize the multiple causes for a behavior and try to understand the reason for it. The lack of locomotion in a visually impaired child may result from any one or more of several reasons. For example, it may be inability resulting from some neuro-physical condition, but it also may be from fear or passivity. A child who has a lot of bumps and bruises may be a person who (1) just does not learn from mistakes or (2) a person with a neuro-sensory deficit. A child who lacks manipulative skills and does not explore his environment may be fearful or inhibited due to a number of causes, including being overdisciplined. Teachers of the visually impaired and the multiply handicapped blind can provide valuable information regarding what a child can do and does accomplish under various conditions and within specific environments. Observation by the psychologist or diagnostician, as well as observational reports by others, is extremely important to the total assessment of the visually impaired child.

The visually impaired child will experience a lag in development in some areas, compared to his or her sighted peer. An important element of the assessment of the young impaired child is to determine his or her developmental level.

Developmental Screening

The Denver Developmental Screening Test (1969) is an individually administered screening inventory that helps to identify children with developmental lags, from birth to 6 years of age. It covers the areas of language, fine and gross motor, adaptive, and personal-social development. It is a quick and easy instrument to administer. It was standardized on 1,036 normal children between the ages of 2 weeks and 6-4 years. Rather than providing a developmental age, the results are categorized as normal, abnormal, and questionable. It correlated at .97 with the Yale Developmental Examination and published reliability results range from .66 to .93 at the various years. Although norms extend from birth to 6 years of age, it is much more acceptable as a screening instrument beginning with age 3 or 4 years.

Two other instruments to assist in screening are the Social Maturity Scale for Blind Preschool Children by Maxfield and Buchholz (1957) and the Preschool Attainment Record (PAR, 1966). The PAR (1966) was developed by Doll and is often used to supplement the Vineland Social Maturity Scale for preschool children with various handicapping conditions. The results are translated into an attainment age, as compared to mental age, and an attainment quotient, as compared to a social quotient. The Preschool Attainment Record provides for the physical, social, mental, and language attainment of children from 6 months to 7 years. It is intended to be used to determine the developmental level of children for whom verbal intelligence tests are not appropriate. The Preschool Attainment Record is well adapted for use with the visually and auditorially impaired.

Mental Ability

Generally, the Performance Scale of the WISC or WISC-R is not administered to the visually impaired, but if a child has sufficient vision to perform the required tasks, it can and probably should be used. The value may be in studying the task approaches used by the child. The examiner may better understand how the child adapts to the visual handicap. Other things one may check on include such things as what visual strategies the child employs, whether the child can sequence, and what is the status of eye-hand coordination. The experienced examiner will study many more of the child's approaches to the task to aid in determining appropriate approaches to educational instruction.

The three verbal subtests on which the visually impaired score the lowest are Comprehension, Similarities, and Vocabulary (Gilbert and Rubin, 1965; Hopkins and McGuire, 1966; and Tillman, 1967). Of the three subtests, Comprehension ranked the lowest, and on the three studies identified, Similarities ranked next lowest, with Vocabulary third. Tillman (1967b) indicated the reason that the visually impaired lag behind the sighted on Comprehension and Similarities is that the visually impaired tend to approach abstract conceptualization problems from a concrete and functional level. He further explains that visually impaired children tend to lag behind sighted children developmentally, with reference to abstract conceptualization and, therefore, do less well on the Similarities subtest. Visually impaired children do lack adequate social experience, partly from social isolation and partly from an inability to experience their social environment fully. This tends to depress the Comprehension scores on the WISC, which assesses common-sense judgment and judgment based on broad social experience. The Vocabulary score tends to be depressed because of a poverty of experience resulting from the handicap. Consequently, they are less likely to elaborate on the meaning of the Vocabulary words, which could result in higher credit.

Tillman (1967a) ranked the verbal subtests on the WISC in the following order, based on test reliability for the blind: Arithmetic, Information and Vocabulary (tie), Similarities, and Comprehension. The WISC-R has provided new items to the Comprehension subtest, which makes it a better subtest for the blind.

Achievement and Diagnostic Tests

Achievement testing of the visually handicapped is beset with numerous problems. The establishment of acceptable norms is difficult. First, there is the limited population of visually handicapped upon which to draw. Second, except for the totally blind, the amount of vision available for processing cognitive information is infinitely varied. Third, to adapt tests designed for the sighted to the visually handicapped will likely result in either elevated or depressed scores, as compared to the sighted norms. It has been hypothesized that such things as the modification of time to compensate for the slower reading rate of the visually handicapped may result in elevated scores (Nolan, 1962). The omission of certain visually oriented items such as graphs may also result in elevated scores for the blind when using sighted norms (Trismen, 1967). There is little evidence to support the thesis that the tactual experiences of the blind are conceptually equivalent to the visual experiences of the sighted child, and this may tend to depress the scores. The sighted norms must be used cautiously and as a rough guide. A study of the adaptation made in the test and longitudinal data regarding the student is necessary for a more valid assessment. Diagnosticians should be aware of the instructional problems associated with the development of concepts and computations of the visually impaired. It has been found that the mathematical-achievement level of the visually impaired is considerably below that of their normally sighted peers. Some investigations found the blind child to be 15–27 percent below sighted peers (Hayes, 1941) (Nolan and Ashcroft, 1959) (Brothers, 1972).

The most popular achievement-test battery used with visually handicapped students is the Stanford Achievement Test. Three years after it was first published in 1923, it had been adapted for the blind in braille. In 1970, the American Printing House for the Blind produced a large-type version of the Stanford Achievement tests; in 1973, the Stanford Test of Academic Skills extended this battery upward, so that now educators of the visually handicapped have a relatively complete normed series of standardized achievement tests for school-age youngsters. Administration of the battery is very time consuming and may take several days to complete, a characteristic that limits its use.

Other achievement batteries have been partially adapted for the visually impaired. For example, the Iowa Test of Basic Skills is available in both braille and large print, but nonsighted norms are provided for grades 3–9 only. The omission of nonsighted norms at the lower-grade level for many of the achievement batteries reduces the utility of the tests for educational planning.

The Wide Range Achievement Test (1976) has been used extensively as a means of obtaining achievement levels for educational planning quickly. Although the test is available in both braille and large-point editions, there are no norms for visually handicapped students. Alfred, Moore, and Simon (1979–80) felt a need to see if the WRAT sighted norms could be used with the visually impaired. They tested 21 blind and partially blind students at the Western Pennsylvania School for Blind Children. Time limits in reading and arithmetic were ignored. Highly significant (p>. 001) correlations were obtained between teacher ratings and all WRAT subscores for the large-print readers. Significant correlations (p>.01) were obtained in reading and spelling, but not in arithmetic, for braille readers. Further correlations were obtained between WISC-R verbal IQs and WRAT subtests. A significant correlation (p>.01) was obtained between verbal IQ and spelling, a correlation at the .05 level between verbal IQ and arithmetic, and no significant correlation between reading and WISC-R verbal IQ. The conclusion was that the WRAT appeared to be a valid instrument for use with the visually handicapped.

In 1977, the Durrell Listening-Reading Series was published in both large-print and braille editions by the American Printing House for the Blind. It is designed to provide a comparison of children's reading and listening abilities. According to Durrell, the purposes of the DLSR "... are to identify children with reading disabilities and to measure the degree of retardation in reading as compared to listening. Knowledge of discrepancies between a child's understanding of spoken language and of printed words is basic to analysis of reading disabilities and diagnosis of remedial needs" (Durrell, 1977).

Although there was adequate reliability reported on the DLRS for sighted children, there was none for the visually impaired. Since the test was published there has been a limited study (71 visually handicapped subjects) done by Wood (1979) to determine the reliability of this instrument with the blind and visually handicapped. The reliability reported by Wood (1979) on the visually handicapped students, Intermediate grade level, and using split half technique corrected for full length by the Spearman-Brown formula, was listening .91; reading, .93, and total, .96. Each was significant at the .01 level of significance.

The results were compared to the Stanford Achievement Test scores available on each student and the correlation on reading was .89 and listening .69. These were significant at the .01 level.

Although this is a limited study, it does suggest the Durrell Reading Series has value for use with intermediate students with visual handicaps to determine any retardation of reading, as compared to listening, when there are no auditory problems.

Ozias (1975) has summarized the situation with achievement tests and achievement testing. "Given the present 'state of the art' the tests now available are useful but limited by procedural, conceptual and methodological problems". There are no precise guidelines for the diagnostician to follow in making interpretations of achievement-test scores. A judgment must be made using all the available data from tests, personal observations, and information from teachers and other personnel.

Case Studies

The following evaluations on Romana, a visually impaired child, and Janie, an auditorially impaired child, are examples of assessment procedures. They do not employ all of the tests discussed in this paper. They, however, do include a battery of parts of tests that help designate levels of functions from which curriculum planning may proceed.

PSYCHO-EDUCATIONAL EVALUATION

Name: Romana

Birthdate:

Examiner:

School:

C.A.: 5-8   *Sex:* F

Date:

I. Assessment of Physical, Mental, Sociological and Emotional Conditions

Language

English is the language spoken in the home.

Physical

A. Appearance: Romana is a black-haired, blue-eyed blind child of five years and eight months. She is slightly small for her age, but within normal limits. She was dressed neatly in good clothes and was clean and neat.

B. Health: No problems in health were reported, except her blindness.

C. Gross-motor skills: She walks and has good balance.

D. Fine-motor skills: She holds her fork and spoon comfortably, but does not try to handle a pencil.

Emotional/Behavioral

Romana is a very shy child. She often puts her thumb in her mouth. Her mother was concerned that she might not respond well to a stranger. She answered the questions very quietly in the beginning then became a little bolder and answered in a more normal manner.

Sociological

Romana's parents are both working, but they keep a woman in the home to care for Romana. The father works for an oil company and her mother works in the library. They are stable people and very interested in their child's welfare. They take her to church and other community assemblies when appropriate. Romana has the social skills of saying "thank you" and she appears to be very polite.

On the Vineland Social Maturity Scale she was found to be developing socially as a normal blind child her age. She helps her mother set the table after the plates have been stacked conveniently for her (she is an only child). She cares for herself at the toilet and bathes herself with some assistance.

Intellectual

Romana was examined on the verbal part of the Wechsler Intelligence Scale for Children-Revised, and was found to be functioning in the normal range of intelligence. Her verbal scale IQ was found to be 95. All scores were directly around the mean of the tests except memory for digits on which she dropped into the dull-normal range.

II. Assessment of Educational Performance Levels

No achievement test could be administered according to standard procedure. Romana has not started the study of braille yet but she has listened to cassette tapes designed for teaching readiness skills for math, general information and concept training. She can count 15 items with no problems and she was able to answer the simple math problems on the WRAT to show an achievement level at kindergarten .7.

III. Assessment of Learning Competency

Two auditory tests on the Detroit Test of Learning Aptitude were administered and Romana was able to remember a group of unrelated words as a child of six years and three months. She was able to remember related syllables as a six-year-old. The three tests on the Illinois test of psycholinguistic abilities showed a function between ages 5-5 and 6-0. These levels are consistent with expectancy for Romana and it is believed that she is ready to enter first grade training.

Summary

Romana is a small, shy but very nice and pleasant blind child who shows a functional level within the normal range. She should be capable of learning braille; also, she should continue to be provided learning experiences through tapes for the blind.

PSYCHOMETRIC DATA

Name: Romana   *Examined:*
Birthdate: *Age:* 5-8   *Examiner:*
State I: Physical, Mental, Sociological, and Emotional Conditions

Wechsler Scales		Verbal		Performance	
Verbal IQ:	95	*Information:*	9	*Picture Completion:*	—
Perfor. IQ:	—	*Similarities:*	10	*Picture Arrange.:*	—
Full Sc.:	—	*Arithmetic:*	9	*Block Design:*	—
		Vocabulary:	9	*Object Assembly:*	—
		Comprehension:	9	*Coding:*	—
		Digit Sp.:	(6)	*Mazes:*	—

Other Intelligence Tests:

	Basal Age:	*Mental Age:*
	Ceiling:	
	Chrono. Age:	*IQ:*

Other Data:

Vineland Social Maturity Scale—was able to perform social tasks between ages 5 and 6 years

State II: Educational Performance Levels

Achievement Levels	Grade	%	SS	Level	IQ	IQ-SS Discrepancy
Reading Recog.						
Reading Comp.						
Spelling						
Arithmetic WRAT	Kg .7	39	96	Ave.	95	1
General Inf.						
Total						
Reading Cluster						
Math Cluster						
Written Lang. Cl.						
Knowledge Clus.						

Stage III: Learning Competencies

Language and Learning Test Data:*   Test/s used: Detroit Test of
Learning Aptitude & Illinois Test of
Psycholinguistic Abilities

Auditory Attention for Words:	MA = 7-4
Auditory Attention for Related Syllables:	MA = 7-6

Visual and/or Motor Tests: Auditory Tests: ITPA

Mental Age: —   Mental Age: 5-5 to 6-0
Comments: —   Comments: Auditory Perception: MA = 5-6
      —   Auditory Sequencing Memory: MA = 5-5
      Auditory Association: MA = 6-0

PSYCHO-EDUCATIONAL EVALUATION

Name: Janie   *School:*
Birthdate: *C.A.:* 8-5   *Sex:* F
Examiner: *Date:*

I. Assessment of Physical, Mental, Sociological and Emotional Conditions

Language

English is the language spoken in the home. Janie does not speak except for a few inarticulate sounds. She has minimal use of sign language as also does the mother.

Adapted by Wilma Jo Bush, Ed. D., West Texas State University

Physical

A. Appearance: Janie is a nice looking child with blond hair and blue eyes. She was clean and neat and was within normal limits in growth and development for a child her age.

B. Health: There is an earlier history of minor childhood illnesses, but for four years she has been relatively free of any problems except her hearing loss. She has a perceptive hearing loss—90 decibels in the right ear and 80 decibel loss in the left ear with help of a hearing aid, which, as can be seen, is not very helpful.

C. Gross-motor skills: Within normal limits

D. Fine-motor skills: Janie is slow in fine-motor tasks which require pencil manipulation.

Emotional/Behavioral

It was not difficult to establish rapport with Janie and she appeared willing to have her teachers leave the testing room. She responded in a very friendly and outgoing manner, very polite and mannerly. She motioned in questioning gestures if she could remove her jacket. She was aware of things about her, for when I got up to turn on the fan, she laughed as the wind hit her and turned to show me where it was blowing the papers. She did show some mild hyperactivity by getting out of her chair several times, and it was difficult to keep her eyes focused on a stimulus pattern in several tasks. She maintained her friendly behavior, however, during the two to three hour period.

Sociological

Janie's family moved from a small town where there were not facilities for training the deaf. Her father has a new position as a car salesman. Her mother does not work outside of the home; she takes care of their two children, Janie and a brother of six years.

The mother has tried to do what she could in terms of helping Janie. The only help she has received from others is that of advice from doctors and teachers. It is because of Janie that the family made their move to a city where the public school has a room for the deaf.

Intellectual and Learning Competencies

Janie was examined on three tests to determine ability. The IQ of 82 on the Hiskey-Nebraska, the Performance IQ of 78 on the WISC-R and the DAP IQ of 80 indicate that Janie is capable of functioning in the dull-normal range of intelligence. An earlier California Mental Maturity IQ of 80, obtained elsewhere, substantiates this level of performance.

II. Assessment of Educational Performance Levels

Educational

Since Janie has limited signing ability it was possible to find some achievement levels for her. On the Peabody Individual Achievement Test it was possible to measure a grade level of 1.1 in math, grade .03 in spelling and .05 in reading. She knew that there is an alphabet but could not make sounds to indicate that she knew the separate letters.

III. Assessment of Learning Competencies

There are some weaknesses which, naturally, are within the language area and are more specifically related to memory for colors, memory for sequencing items, and ability to fill in detail in drawings. These were determined from the Hiskey-Nebraska test and on these subtests she functioned between the age levels of five and six years. At this same level on the WISC-R Performance scale her score on the Coding subtest suggests a severe difficulty in relating small designs with numbers. She kept trying to place a number under a like number instead of placing the design identified with that number. Her problem, thus, appears to be, not in ability to copy designs, but in ability to associate the designs quickly, i.e., she is slow to assimilate some visual stimuli with motor performance.

It was easier for Janie to work with three dimensional items. Where pencil-manipulation is required she is not as adept as when working with blocks and puzzles. In dealing with three-dimensional items she works within the low-normal range. There was one normal ability—the discrimination of likenesses and differences.

Summary

Janie is a child who has the support and love of her parents, but she has been deprived of a proper education for the deaf. She functions in the dull range of intellectual development, but it is believed that with proper training her functioning level can be appreciably increased.

It is evident that she needs structured help in the development of language skills through both signing and oral means.

_____

Reporting Diagnostician

PSYCHOMETRIC DATA

Name: Janie   *Examined:*
Birthdate: *Age:* 8-5   *Examiner:*
State I: Physical, Mental, Sociological, and Emotional Conditions

Wechsler Scales		Verbal		Performance	
Verbal IQ:	—	*Information:*	—	*Picture Completion:*	6
Perfor. IQ:	78	*Similarities:*	—	*Picture Arrange:*	6
Full Sc.:	—	*Arithmetic:*	—	*Block Design:*	8
		Vocabulary:	—	*Object Assembly:*	8
		Comprehension:	—	*Coding:*	4
		Digit Sp.:		*Mazes:*	(4)

Other Intelligence Tests:

Hiskey-Nebraska	Basal Age:	5-0	Mental Age:	7-0
	Ceiling:	9-0		
	Chrono. Age:	8-5	IQ:	82

Other Data:

Bead Pattern:	MA = 5-0	Block Patterns:	MA = 6-0
Memory for Colors:	MA = 5-0	Compl. of Drawings:	MA = 5-6
Picture Identification:	9-0		
Picture Association:	MA = 7-6		
Paper Folding:	MA = 6-6		
Visual Attn. Span:	MA = 5-6		

State II: Educational Performance Levels

Achievement Levels	Grade	%	SS	Level	IQ	IQ-SS Discrepancy
PIAT						
Reading Recog.	.05	− 1%	Below 65	Below Average	82	(17)
Reading Comp.						
Spelling	0.3	− 1	Below 65	Below Average	82	(17)
Arithmetic	1.1	4	74	Below Average		8
General Inf.						
Total						
Reading Cluster						
Math Cluster						
Written Lang. Cl.						
Knowledge Clus.						

Stage III: Learning Competencies

Language and Learning Test Data:* Test/s used:

Visual and/or Motor Tests*: Bender   Auditory Tests: _____

Mental Age: about 5-6   Mental Age:
Comments: Very slow in making   Comments:
    drawings. Angles were
    difficult for her.

Adapted by Wilma Jo Bush, Ed.D., West Texas State University

References

Anderson, D. W., Moore, M. W., & Simon, J. L. A preliminary assessment of the validity and usefulness of the WRAT with visually handicapped residential school students. *Education of the Visually Handicapped*, Winter 1979-80, *XI*, no. 4: 101–108.

Anastasi, A. *Psychological testing.* New York: Macmillan, 1976.

Anderson, R. M., & Stevens, G. D. Policies and procedures for admission of mentally retarded deaf children to residential schools for deaf. *American Annals for the Deaf*, January 1970, *115*: 30–36.

Arthur, G. *Arthur adaptation of the Lieter international performance scale.* Los Angeles: Western Psychological Services, 1962.

Balow, I. H., Farr, R., Hogan, T. P., & Prescott, G. A. *Metropolitan achievement tests.* New York: Psychological Corporation, 1978.

Barrett, S. S. Assessment of vision in the program for the deaf. *American Annals of the Deaf*, May 1978, *123*, no. 3: 745–752.

Bell, V. H. An educator's approach to assessing preschool visually handicapped children. *Education of the Visually Handicapped*, October 1975, 7: 84–89.

Bender, L. *Bender visual motor Gestalt test.* New York: Psychological Corporation, 1938 and 1946.

Bennett, F., Hughes, A., & Hughes, H. Assessment techniques for deaf-blind children. *Exceptional Children*, January 1979, *45*, no. 4: 287–288.

Birch, J. W., Tisdall, W., Peabody, R. L., & Sterrett, R. School achievement and effect of type size on reading in visually handicapped children. Pittsburgh: University of Pittsburgh, 1966 (Cooperative Research Project No. 1766, Contract No. OEC-4-028).

Boehm, A. E. *Boehm test of basic concepts.* New York: Psychological Corporation, 1971.

Brill, R. G. The relationship of Wechsler IQ's to academic achievement among deaf students. *Exceptional Children*, 1962, *28*: 315–321.

Brothers, R. J. Arithmetic computation by the blind: A look at current achievement. *Education of the Visually Handicapped*, March 1972, *4*: 1–8.

Buck, J. N. *House-tree-person technique: Revised manual.* Los Angeles: Western Psychological Services, 1966.

Burgemeister, B., Blum, L. H., & Lorge, I. *Columbia mental maturity scale.* New York: Psychological Corporation, 1972.

Carlson, J. S., & Dillon, R. Measuring intellectual capabilities of hearing impaired children: Effects of testing-the-limits procedures. *The Volta Review*, May 1978, *80*: 216–224.

Cass, R., & Kaplan, P. Middle ear disease and learning problems: A school system's approach to early detection. *Journal of School Health*, December 1979, *49*, no. 10: 557–560.

Davis, J. M. Performance of young hearing impaired children on a test of basic concepts. *Journal of Speech and Hearing Research*, September 1974, *17*, no. 3: 242–251.

Davis, J. M. Reliability of hearing impaired children's responses to oral and total presentations of the test of auditory comprehension of language. *Journal of Speech and Hearing Disorders*, November 1977, *XLII*: 520–527.

Doll, E. *Preschool attainment record (PAR).* Circle Pines, Minn.: American Guidance Service, 1966.

Durrell, D. D., Hayes, M. T., & Brassard, M. B. *Durrell listening-reading series.* New York: Psychological Corporation, 1970.

Frankenburg, W. K. & Dodds, J. B. *Denver developmental scale.* Denver: Ladoca Project and Publisher Foundation, 1969.

Gerwick, S., & Ysseldyke, J. E. Limitations of current psychological practices for the intellectual assessment of the hearing impaired: A response to the Levine study. *The Volta Review*, April 1975, 77, no. 4: 243–248.

Gianereco, C. The Hiskey-Nebraska test of learning aptitude (revised) compared to several achievement tests. *American Annals of the Deaf*, 1967, *112*: 566–577.

Gilbert, J., & Rubin, E. Evaluating the intellect of blind children. *The New Outlook for the Blind*, 1965: 238–240.

Goetzinger, C. P., & Rousey, C. L. Study of Wechsler performance scale (form II) and the Knox cube test with deaf adolescents. *American Annals for the Deaf*, 1957, *102*: 388–398.

Goldman, R., Fristoe, & Woodcock, R. *Goldman-Fristoe-Woodcock test of auditory discrimination.* Circle Pines, Minn.: American Guidance Service, 1976.

Graham, E. E., & Shapiro, E. Use of performance scale of Wechsler intelligence scale for children with the deaf child. *Journal of Consulting Psychology*, 1953, *17*: 296–298.

Hayes, S. P. *Contributions to a psychology of blindness.* New York: American Foundation for the Blind, 1941.

Henry, V., & Lyall, J. H. Ability screening and program placement for deaf-blind children and adults. *The Volta Review*, April 1973, 75, no. 4: 227–231.

Hirschoren, A., Hurley, O. L., & Kavale, K. Psychometric characteristics of the WISC-R performance scale with deaf children. *Journal of Speech and Hearing Disorders*, February 1979, *44*, no. 1: 73–79.

Hiskey, M. S. *Hiskey-Nebraska test of learning aptitude manual.* Lincoln, Neb.: Union College Press, 1966.

Hopkins, K. D., & McGuire, L. Mental measurement of the blind: The validity of the Wechsler intelligence scale for children. *International Journal for the Education of the Blind*, 1966, *15*, no. c: 65–73.

Jastak, J., Bijou, S., & Jastak, S. *Wide range achievement test.* New York: Psychological Corporation, 1976.

Jensema, C. A comment on measurement error in achievement tests for the hearing impaired. *American Annals for the Deaf*, June 1978, *123*, no. 4: 496–499.

Katz, J. The effects of conductive hearing loss on auditory function. *Journal of the American Speech and Hearing Association*, October 1978, *20*: 879–886.

Klineman, J. Hidden abilities discovered among multiply-handicapped blind children. *Education of the Visually Handicapped*, October 1975, 7: 90–96.

Kodman, Jr., F., Educational status of hard of hearing children in the classroom. *Journal of Speech and Hearing Disorders*, August 1963, *28*: 297–299.

Langley, B. M. Psychoeducational assessment of the multiply-handicapped blind child: Issues and methods. *Education of the Visually Handicapped*, Winter 1978–79, *X*, no. 4: 97–115.

Leiter, R. G. *Leiter international performance scale.* Los Angeles: Western Psychological Services, 1959.

Levine, E. S. Psychological tests and practices with the deaf: A survey of the art. *The Volta Review*, May 1974, 74, no. 5: 298–219.

Levine, E. S. Psychological contributions. *The Volta Review*, 1976, 78, no. 4: 23–33.

Ling, D., Ling, A. H., & Pflaster, G. P. Individualized educational programming for hearing-impaired children. *The Volta Review*, May 1977, *79*, no. 4: 204–230.

Madden, R., Gardner, E. F., Rudman, H. C., Karlsen, B., & Merwin, J. C. *Stanford achievement test: 1973 edition*. New York: Psychological Corporation, 1973.

Margolis, H. The kindergarten auditory screening test as a predictor of reading disability. *Psychology in the Schools*, October 1976, *13*, no. 4: 399–403.

Maxfield, K., & Buchholz, S. *A social maturity scale for preschool blind children*. New York: American Foundation for the Blind, 1957.

Mira, M. The use of the Arthur adaptation of the Leiter international performance scale and the Nebraska test of learning aptitude. *American Annals of the Deaf*, 1962, *107*: 224–228.

Neyhus, A. I. Assessment for individualized education programming. *The Volta Review*, September 1978, *80*: 286–295.

Nolan, C. Y. Evaluating the scholastic achievements of visually handicapped children. *Exceptional Children*, 1962, *28*: 493–496.

Nolan, C. Y., & Ashcroft, S. C. The Stanford achievement computation tests: A study of an experimental adaptation for Braille administration. *International Journal for the Education of the Blind*, 1959, *8*: 89–92.

Orgel, A. R., & Dreger, R. M. Comparative study of the Arthur Leiter and Stanford Binet intelligence scale. *Journal of Genetic Psychology*, June 1955, *86*: 359–365.

Ozias, D. K. Achievement assessment of the visually handicapped. *Education of the Visually Handicapped*, October 1975, *VII*, no. 3: 76–84.

Porter, J., & Holzberg, B. C. The changing role of the school psychologist in the age of PL 94-142: From conducting testing to enhancing instruction. *Education of the Visually Handicapped*, Fall 1978–79, *X*, no. 3: 71–74.

Ratcliffe, K. J., & Ratcliffe, M. W. The Leiter scales: A review of validity findings. *American Annals of the Deaf*, February 1979, *13*, no. 4: 38–45.

Ritter, D. R. Intellectual estimate of hearing impaired children: A comparison of three measures. *Psychology in the Schools*, October 1976, *13*, no. 4: 397–399.

Rudner, L. M. Using standardized tests with the hearing impaired: The problem of item bias. *The Volta Review*, January 1978, *80*, no. 1: 31–39.

Sharp, H. C. Comparison of slow learners' scores on three individual intelligence scales. *Journal of Clinical Psychology*, October 1957, *13*: 372–374.

Sisco, F. H., & Anderson, R. J. Current findings regarding the performance of deaf children on the WISC-R. *American Annals of the Deaf*, April 1978, *123*, no. 2: 115–121.

Social maturity scale. New York: American Foundation for the Blind, 1957.

Spungin, S. J., & Swallow, R.-M. Psychoeducational assessment: Role of psychologist to teacher of the visually handicapped. *Education of the Visually Handicapped*, October 1975, *VII*, no. 3: 67–76.

Tillman, M. H. The performance of blind and sighted children on the Wechsler intelligence scale for children: Study. II *International Journal for the Education of the Blind*, 1967a, *16*, no. 3: 65–74.

Tillman, M. H. The performance of blind and sighted children on the Wechsler intelligence scale for children: Study II. *International Journal for the Education of the Blind*, 1967b, *16*, no. 4: 106–112.

Trismen, D. A. Equating Braille forms of sequential tests of educative progress. *Exceptional Children*, 1967, *33*: 419–424.

Wharton, G. P. Hard of hearing child: A challenge to education. *The Volta Review*, May 1966, *68*; 351–353.

Winchester, R. New advances in screening for auditory disorders in children with emphasis on impedance audiometry. Philadelphia: Philadelphia Public Schools, Division of Special Education, Itinerant Hearing Service and Hearing Instruments (Report on Symposium, April 17, 1974).

Wood, T. A. The usability of the adapted Durrell listening-reading series with students in the intermediate grades. *Education of the Visually Handicapped*, Summer 1979, *XI*, no. 2: 33–38.

Summary

This chapter covers assessment data for four specific-category conditions—the early-childhood handicapped, the multiply handicapped, the auditorially handicapped, and the visually handicapped. One paper prepared by Murphy and Zevely deals with assessment of the young child in special education. They cite warnings about the danger of labeling young handicapped children and they present a case study that includes data from the DIAL, an early-childhood assessment instrument. The second paper by Norris covers information on multiply handicapped individuals. Adaptive scales are recommended for use with this group, the group that is possibly the most different to assess for cognitive skills. The paper on the auditorially and visually impaired also cites the difficulty in finding the kinds of instruments to be used. Except for a few tests, such as the Hiskey-Nebraska for the deaf and the braille adaptation of the Stanford Binet, most assessment batteries include only *parts of instruments* that have been normed on the nonhandicapped individual. Case studies as examples are presented with each paper.

Student Activities

1. *Student will study three assessment instruments for the young handicapped and compare differences among the three. Determine what skills are measured.*
2. *Student will identify the differences between the assessments of the four categories covered in this chapter.*
3. *Research abstracts that cite the use of tests for the four categories mentioned in this chapter.*

Chapter 9

The Learning Disabled, the Mentally Retarded, and the Emotionally Disturbed

The student who has studied this chapter should:
1. *Have knowledge about the assessment procedure of the learning disabled, the mentally retarded, and the emotionally disturbed*
2. *Be able to identify the learning disabled, the mentally retarded, and the emotionally disturbed*
3. *Know the general requirements for placing the learning disabled, mentally retarded, and emotionally disturbed in special education*
4. *Know the procedure to follow in converting raw scores to standard scores*
5. *Be able to describe procedural differences, including specific kinds of tests*

Introduction

The largest number of handicapped children in the public schools (excluding the speech handicapped) are the learning disabled, the mentally retarded, and the emotionally disturbed. These three categories comprise the group considered to be moderately handicapped. The learning-disabled group constitutes about 2.3 percent of the school population, the mentally retarded about 1.83 percent, and the emotionally disturbed about .6 percent (Mandell and Fiscus, 1981). These figures are somewhat lower than those of earlier years, which ranged around 9 percent for the composite group. Differences in the size of the specific populations arise from the different interpretations of what features make up each classification and from the degree of impairment in each case. The three papers in this chapter, whose purpose is to examine means of assessment, provide identification of each category and the evaluation procedures to follow.

Traditionally, procedures for evaluation of the handicapped do not remain consistently the same throughout the years. However, the changes made are not major and the information needed to make plans for their education remains somewhat the same, though it may be couched under different outline organizations. This needed information consists largely of scores representing capacity and achievement. Sometimes, scores that represent certain degrees of motivation are recorded; however, motivation is generally determined/inferred by observation by teachers and parents.

Children in all three categories should be observed by qualified personnel to justify need for specialized training in a less competitive environment. For placement in special-education classes, the learning-disabled children must (by law) be shown to have a discrepancy between mental ability and achievement; the mentally retarded must show severe deficits in both mental and social abilities, and the emotionally disturbed must be shown to be unable to cope with peers and teachers in the class-rooms, i.e., exhibit inappropriate behavior that interferes with academic achievement.

In this chapter, an attempt is made to explain possible courses of action to pursue in this process of special-education placement and planning in the public schools. Each category is covered separately with example case studies that have been made on the various handicapped children.

Assessment of the Learning Disabled

There have always been nonachieving children who cannot be placed in discrete categories such as "blind", "deaf", "intellectually retarded", "emotionally disturbed", or "physically handicapped". They are children who are sighted, yet do not "correctly" interpret visual stimuli. They may be children who hear, yet fail to discriminate specific sounds, sound blends, or even words. They may have normal intelligence, yet be retarded in the achievement of basic skills. This specific population of children now identified as *learning disabled* constitutes one of the last legal categories listed among the special-education group. Professionals concerned with this handicapping condition have differed somewhat in their definitions and in their choice of identifying terms. *Dyslexia, perceptual/perceptual-motor*, and *language disabilities* have headed the list of commonly used terms. For such information, read from Myklebust (1968, 1971), Johnson and Myklebust (1967), McCarthy and McCarthy (1969), Kirk and McCarthy (1975), Bush and Waugh (1976), Lerner (1976), Kaufman and Hallahan (1976), Myers and Hammill (1976), Johnson and Morasky (1977), Wallace and McLoughlin (1979), and Gearhart (1973).

The very nature of a concept of learning disabilities is based on the premise that there are abilities that operate normally in the growth and development process. When these abilities are not functioning adequately, a child may not be able to perform successfully in the school. It is these inadequate functioning abilities toward which evaluations have been directed in the past, and toward which they will be directed in the future. While the direction has remained consistently the same, a fluid condition has existed regarding the means to reach the target. The criterion for identification of the learning-disabled child for placement purposes has made a chameleon change. No longer is the diagnostician/psychologist required to determine differences in psychological-processing abilities, learning styles, and/or failure. For placement purposes, it must be determined that underachievement is identified by discrepancies between intellectual capacity and achievement in any of the following categories: reading, writing, spelling, math, expression, and listening skills. Though identification of learning disabilities in Public Law 94–142 states that a learning disability means a disorder in one or more of the psychological processes involved in understanding or in using language, spoken or written, which may manifest itself in an imperfect ability to listen, think, speak, read, write, spell or to do mathematical calculations, the criteria for *placement* in a learning-disability class do not now, as in the past, require that these psychological processes be identified. The *Federal Register*, Volume 42, Number 250, Thursday, December 29, 1977, specifically cites the criteria to be as follows:

121a.541 Criteria for determining the existence of specific learning disability.
(a) A team may determine that a child has a specific learning disability if:
(1) The child does not achieve commensurate with his or her age and ability levels in one or more of the areas listed in paragraph (a)(2) of this section, when provided with learning experiences appropriate for the child's age and ability levels; and
(2) The team finds that a child has a severe discrepancy between achievement and intellectual ability in one or more of the following areas:
(i) Oral expression;
(ii) Listening comprehension;
(iii) Written expression;
(iv) Basic reading skill;
(v) Reading comprehension;
(vi) Mathematics calculations; or
(vii) Mathematics reasoning.
(b) The team may not identify a child as having a specific learning disability if the severe discrepancy between ability and achievement is primarily the result of:
(1) A visual, hearing, or motor handicap;
(2) Mental retardation;
(3) Emotional disturbance; or
(4) Environmental, cultural or economic disadvantage.

The rationale for such an approach was that those with specific learning disabilities may demonstrate their handicap through a variety of symptoms such as hyperactivity, distractibility, attention problems, concept association problems, etc. The end result of these symptoms is a severe discrepancy between achievement and ability. If there is no severe discrepancy between how much should have been learned and what has been learned, there would not be a disability in learning.
Immediately following the criteria statement are other requirements for the assessment procedure. These requirements are as follows:

121a.542 Observation
(a) At least one team member other than the child's regular teacher shall observe the child's academic performance in the regular classroom setting.
(b) In the case of a child of less than school age or out of school, a team member shall observe the child in an environment appropriate for a child of that age.
121a.543 Written report.
(a) The team shall prepare a written report of the results of the evaluation.
(b) The report must include a statement of:
(1) Whether the child has a specific learning disability;
(2) The basis for making the determination;
(3) The relevant behavior noted during the observation of the child;
(4) The relationship of that behavior to the child's academic functioning;

(5) The educationally relevant medical findings, if any;

(6) Whether there is a severe discrepancy between achievement and ability which is not correctable without special education and related services; and

(7) The determination of the team concerning the effects of environmental, cultural, or economic disadvantage.

(c) Each team member shall certify in writing whether the report reflects his or her conclusion. If it does not reflect his or her conclusion, the team member must submit a separate statement presenting his or her conclusions.

It can be seen that legal assessment of learning disabilities not only requires intelligence and achievement testing, it also requires that an observer trained in the characteristics of learning-disability problems observe and report (1) behaviors that are typical of learning disability children and, (2) the relationship of these behaviors to the child's academic functioning.

The major responsibility of the Local Independent School District is to determine its own procedure concerning (1) how children are to be referred, (2) obtaining parental consent for testing, (3) personnel responsible for assessment, (4) scheduling for observation and testing, and (5) scheduling for Admission, Review and Dismissal (ARD) Committee meeting. The first concern of the diagnostician/psychologist is to determine the dominant language spoken in the home and the proper procedure to follow in three stages of assessment:

Stage I   Assessment of Physical, Mental, and Sociological and Emotional Conditions
Stage II Assessment of Educational Performance Levels
Stage III Analysis of the Competency Skills and Determination of Procedures and
           Techniques to be used in Individualized Programs.

Before any assessment begins, it should be documented through either a home-language survey or formal assessment of the dominant language in both expressive and receptive domains. The diagnostician/psychologist then must know which tests to use within the three stages and then must know how to determine discrepant differences. A list of commonly used tests for language documentation that may be given before the formal assessment are available from your instructor.

Determining Discrepant Differences Between Tests

Stage I involves intelligence measures. Stage II involves educational performance. Thus, we must look for differences that exist between behaviors within these two stages. In Stage I, evidence must be determined to show that any difference in learning is not attributable to mental retardation, cultural/language/environmental, or emotional problems. When these conditions are excluded as variables influencing the learning process, the procedure to determine differences between mental ability and educational performance may follow. This difference should be determined between (1) the child's achievement and the mean achievement of the district and (2) the child's achievement and the child's ability to perform. Most districts have school norms and it is a simple procedure to compare the child's scores on the same achievement test used to develop the district's norms. To determine *any differences* between the child's ability and the child's achievement is not as simple. Ideally the two tests, intelligence and achievement, should have been standardized on the same population, but this is not the case among standardized tests. Several procedures are available to make this determination, but first the diagnostician must have evidence that the tests in both areas are valid and reliable. This information should be given in the technical manuals of each test. Reliability, for purposes of making major education decisions on an individual, should be as much as .90. Reliability for screening purposes on individuals should be as much as .80.

Assuming that tests used to determine discrepancies are reliable and valid, one may then begin the procedure to examine ways and means of finding whether the discrepancies are significant. Coulter, Johnson, and Walton (1979) recommend the following five methods:

(1) Comparison of scores from instruments with identical means and standard deviations
(2) Comparison of scores using a standard-score formula (conversion of one test's scores to the same metric as the other test)
(3) Comparison of scores using z-score formula (conversion of both tests' scores to z-scores)
(4) A simplified conversion formula
(5) Percentile conversion table

Procedure Number I

Step 1
List Scores for Intellectual Functioning:
    Name of test(s)_____
    Mean_____ Standard Deviation_____
    Verbal IQ (if applicable)_____
    Performance IQ (if applicable)_____
    Full Scale IQ (if applicable)_____
Scores for Achievement*
    Name of test(s)_____
    Area assessed_____
    Mean_____ Standard Deviation_____
    Score(s)_____
Step 2
Select scores for comparison
    (1) intellectual functioning_____
    (2) academic achievement in specific area_____
    (3) subtract (1) from (2)_____
Step 3
Compare the subtrahend of (3) with the standard deviation of the tests, which are the same in this procedure. If the result shows that the score of (3) is more than the standard deviation of the tests, there is evidence to support the professional judgment that there is a severe discrepancy between academic achievement and intellectual functioning in one (or more) specific ability.

---

*There may be more than one achievement test used, and more than one area may be assessed, such as reading and arithmetic, etc.

intelligence test (handwritten margin note)

Procedure Number II

Comparison of scores using a standard score formula.

When the two tests have different metrics, e.g., where the mean of one test is 100 and the standard deviation 15, and the mean of the other test is 50 and the standard deviation is 10, one may use the following formula to convert the scores of one test to be the same as those of another.

$$x = \left(\frac{\text{s.d. for IT}}{\text{s.d. for AT}} \right) SS - \left[\left(\frac{\text{s.d. for IT}}{\text{s.d. for AT}} \right) \overline{X} \text{ of AT} - \overline{X} \text{ of IT} \right]$$

achievement test (handwritten note)

x = the student's score expressed in the metric of the intelligence test
X = Mean
IT = Intelligence Test
AT = Achievement test
SS = Student's score on the Achievement Test

Example:
Mean of Intelligence Test = 100
s.d. of Intelligence Test = 15
Mean of Achievement Test = 50
s.d. of Achievement Test = 10
Student's score on achievement Test = 25
Student's IQ = 98

$$x = \left(\frac{15}{10} \right) 25 - \left[\left(\frac{15}{10} \right) \left(50 \right) - 100 \right]$$

$(1.5 - 50)$ (handwritten)

$-75 - 100$ (handwritten)

x = 37.5 - [75 - 100]
x = 37.5 - [-25]

x = 62.5

In this case, let us say that the student's IQ on the WISC-R is 98. (The WISC-R has a mean of 100 and a standard deviation of 15.) The student's score of 25 on the Math achievement test (which test has a mean of 50 and a standard deviation of 10) has been converted to a standard score of 62.5 by the above formula. The standard score is now in the metric of the intelligence test (WISC-R) and the 62.5 standard score can be subtracted from the IQ of 98. The difference is 35.5, a figure much more than the standard deviation of 15 needed to show a significant discrepancy. This student can be considered to be achieving at a significant degree below his/her ability.

Procedure Number III

Comparison of scores using z-score formula.

Another method to compare any two scores from instruments with different means and standard deviations is to convert both scores into z scores and compare their relative distances from the means of their respective instruments. The formula is:

$$z = \frac{X - M}{S}$$

The standard score (z) is equal to the obtained score (X), minus the mean of the instrument (M), divided by the standard deviation of the instrument (S). For example, let us say that the student made an IQ of 81 on the WISC-R, on which the mean is 100 and the standard deviation is 15. The following calculations are: $z = \dfrac{81-100}{15} = -1.27$

scored more than one s.d. below:

The student scored more than one standard deviation below the mean on the IQ test. The example for the achievement-test conversion is as follows:
The student's score on a reading achievement test is 36. Using the formula above the following is shown: $z - \dfrac{36-50}{10} = -1.4$

tells us how many S.D. below the mean.

The student is 1.4 standard deviations below the mean on the achievement test. Comparison of the scores on both tests involves subtracting the achievement z score from the intelligence z score. $(-1.27) + (-1.4) = 13$

The student is not one standard deviation below his/her ability and therefore, does not meet the criterion of being significantly slow in reading. This student would not qualify for special-education placement in an LD room, based on examination of reading ability.

Procedure Number IV
Simplified Conversion Formula.

This formula, which is comparable to the other conversion formulas, may be used if desired. The standard score derived may be subtracted from the IQ standard score to determine whether a severe discrepancy exists.

$$SS - 100 + 15 \dfrac{(x - \bar{X})}{s.d.}$$

where SS = standard score
x = student's achievement score
$\bar{X}$ = mean of achievement test
s.d. = standard deviation of achievement test
Example: If a student had a score of 25 on a spelling-achievement test and an IQ score of 87 on the WISC-R, and if the Achievement test mean were 50 and the S.D. were 10, we would find the following calculation:

$$SS = 100 + 15 \dfrac{25-50}{10}$$
$$= 100 + 15 \dfrac{(-25)}{10}$$
$$= 100 + 15(-2.5)$$
$$= 100 + (-37.5)$$
$$= 62.5$$

If we subtract this standard score of 62.5 from the student's IQ of 87, we have a difference of 24.5, which is more than one standard deviation below. The student, thus, has a severe discrepancy between her intelligence and her achievement.

Procedure Number V

Percentile Conversion Table.

Often scores are not reported in terms of means and standard deviations. In such cases, the Percentile Conversion Table (Table 36) may be used to convert any percentile to a standard score with a mean of 100 and a standard deviation of 15. This function converts the achievement-test data to the same metric as most intelligence tests, thereby allowing for direct comparison. Coulter et al. (1979) warn that certain problems are inherent in using percentile data. The increments between scores cannot be assumed to be equal and there is a certain sensitivity of data lost, in that different raw scores may yield the same percentile rank. Distortion between scores is particularly evident at the extremes of the distribution. Also, when converting percentiles to standard scores, a normal distribution of the sample is assumed, a condition not always met with the actual data.

The following evaluations are examples of possible procedures to follow in making assessments for learning-disabled children. It can be seen from the psychometric data on Monty (Column, IQ-SS) that he functions in achievement more than one standard deviation below his capacity, as shown by his highest IQ. This lack of achievement is seen in all the basic skills, except in knowledge. The evaluation on Brent provides a different picture. He is achieving well within the limits of his ability, except in math. His is a marginal case of learning disability, but there is no question about the need for special training to help him compete.

PSYCHOLOGICAL EVALUATION

Name: Monty   *Examined*:
Birthdate: *Examiner*:
                                                     C.A.: 10 = 0

I. Language Factor

English is the language spoken in the home.

II. Physiological Factors

Appearance: Very blond hair and blue eyes. Nice-looking.
Health: Normal.
Fine-motor skills: Slow psychomotor speed. Visual-motor coordination is not adequate for his years. He has difficulty in pencil manipulation in terms of steady control.
Gross-motor skills: Normal.

III. Emotional/Behavioral Factors

Monty was very outgoing and friendly. He injected many relevant remarks during the testing and he appeared to enjoy all the tasks. There was no evidence of any emotional problems.

IV. Intellectual Factors

Monty was examined on the WISC-R and was found to be functioning in the normal range of intelligence in both the verbal and performance areas. There was a significant scatter of scores which showed that he had superior ability in vocabulary and in discrimination of essential detail. The Peabody Picture Vocabulary IQ substantiates the very high vocabulary ability. He also has bright average ability in comprehension. Some lower scores are indicative of weaknesses in visual-motor coordination and in memory and/or concentration.

V. Educational Factors

The achievement scores show that Monty is achieving at the second grade in reading (word attack, passage comprehension and letter word identification). In Math he is achieving at the third grade level and in written language at the middle second grade level. Only in his knowledge skills is he average in achievement, at grade 5.4. Severe and mild deficits are indicated by his second and third grade achievements.

VI. Learning Competencies

Monty's learning problems appear to be in the area of visual-motor coordination and in memory and concentration skills. He is underachieving in reading, math, and written language to the degree that he can qualify for learning-disability resource rooms. He needs much remediation in kinesthetic techniques; tracing on a daily basis should be a major part of his training. In math, remediation should involve techniques that use concrete objects and much repetition until he can understand the process. The tracing in the kinesthetic activities should aid his written language skills.

VII. Summary

Monty is a very cheerful blond-headed boy who is functioning in the normal range of intellectual ability. He is underachieving significantly in math, reading and written language. Remediation on a daily basis for approximately forty-five minutes a day is recommended. The remediation should involve academic content that he is facing daily, but the technique should be approached through kinesthetic and concrete procedures.

Reporting Psychologist

PSYCHOMETRIC DATA

Name: Monty   *Examined:*
Birthdate: *Age:* 10-0 *Examiner:*
State I: Physical, Mental, Sociological, and Emotional Conditions

Wechsler Scales		Verbal		Performance	
Verbal IQ:	106	*Information:*	11	*Picture Completion:*	14
Perfor. IQ:	104	*Similarities:*	11	*Picture Arrange.:*	11
Full Sc.:	105	*Arithmetic:*	7	*Block Design:*	11
		Vocabulary:	14	*Object Assembly:*	10
		Comprehen.:	12	*Coding:*	7
		Digit Sp.:	(7)	*Mazes:*	(8)

Other Intelligence Tests:

Peabody Picture	*Basal Age:*	—		*Mental Age:*	14-6
Vocabulary Test	*Ceiling:*	—			
	Chrono. Age:	10-1		*IQ:*	130

Table 36. Percentile Conversion Table*

Percentile Rank	Standard Score (Mean = 100 SD = 15)	Percentile Rank	Standard Score (Mean = 100 SD = 15)	Percentile Rank	Standard Score (Mean = 100 SD = 15)
99	135	59	103	19	87
98	131	58	103	18	86
97	128	57	103	17	86
96	126	56	102	16	85
95	125	55	102	15	84
94	123	54	102	14	84
93	122	53	101	13	83
92	121	52	101	12	82
91	120	51	100	11	82
90	119	50	100	10	81
89	118	49	100	9	80
88	118	48	99	8	79
87	117	47	99	7	78
86	116	46	98	6	77
85	116	45	98	5	75
84	115	44	98	4	74
83	114	43	97	3	72
82	114	42	97	2	69
81	113	41	97	1	65
80	113	40	96		
79	112	39	96		
78	112	38	95		
77	111	37	95		
76	111	36	95		
75	110	35	94		

74	110	34	94
73	109	33	93
72	109	32	93
71	108	31	92
70	108	30	92
69	108	29	92
68	107	28	91
67	107	27	91
66	106	26	90
65	106	25	90
64	105	24	89
63	105	23	89
62	105	22	88
61	104	21	88
60	104	20	87

*A resource guide.

Other Data:

State II: Educational Performance Levels

Achievement Levels	Grade	%	SS	Level	(Highest) IQ	IQ-SS Discrepancy
Reading Recog.	WRAT: 3.5	21	Below 88	Average	106	(18)
Reading Comp.						
Spelling	WRAT: 3.0	16	Below 85	Average	106	(21)
Arithmetic	WRAT: 3.2	18	Below 86	Average	106	(20)
General Inf.	—	—	—	—	—	
Total	—	—	—	—	—	
Woodcock-Johnson Reading Cluster	(W-J B) 2.3	8	Severe 79	Deficit	106	(27)
Math Cluster	W-J B: 3.2	11	Mild 82	Deficit	106	(24)
Written Lang. Cl.	W-J B: 2.6	8	Severe 79	Deficit	106	(27)
Knowledge Clus.	W-J B: 5.4	62	105	Average	106	(1)

Stage III: Learning Competencies
Language and Learning Test Data   Test/s used: —

Visual and/or Motor Tests: Bender   Auditory Tests: —
  Mental Age: Normal   Mental Age: —
Comments: Shaky hand control but   Comments:
  design drawn within normal
  limits.

Adapted by Wilma Jo Bush, Ed.D., West Texas State University

PSYCHOLOGICAL EVALUATION

Name: Brent   *Examined:*
Birthdate: *Examiner:*
                                                           C. A.: 13-10

I. Language Factors

English is the language spoken in the home.

II. Physical Factors

A. Appearance: Brent is a nice-looking light-brown-haired boy with hazel-green eyes. He was dressed in sport shirt and jeans and was clean and neat.

B. Health: There were apparently no critical health problems; however, he is on Retalin for the purpose of calming his hyperactivity tendencies (not noticed on this day) and he did become sick at his stomach after about 2 hours of the session. His mother reported that the Ritalin, while keeping him calm, did make him nauseated.

C. Fine-motor Skills: There was impairment in his fine-motor skills: his reproductions on the Bender were irregular. He made small circles for dots and some of his figures were crowded together. On the Graham-Kendall MFD test his designs were more accurate and better organized. This indicated that he has *more difficulty* in eye-hand coordination when he copies from a visual stimulus than from *memory* of a visual stimulus.

D. Gross-motor Skills: Normal

III. Emotional/Behavioral Factors

On this date Brent was placid and calm showing no evidence of the hyperactivity as reported in his past experiences. Toward the very end of the session he did mention that he had a stomachache. I asked if he could continue for about ten more minutes. He responded in the affirmative and appeared willing to continue.

The testing moved along smoothly for he was polite and cooperative. His spontaneous remarks were relevant and appropriate and it seemed difficult to believe that this socially outgoing boy could have experienced the traumas of extreme hyperactivity and school failures.

IV. Intellectual Factors

Brent was examined on the WISC-R and found to have a verbal IQ of 87, performance IQ of 93 and Full-Scale IQ of 89. These IQ's indicate a slight increase over the 1979 scores as did the 1979 show an increase over a 1978 evaluation. The medication and the special education program appear to be having a positive influence affecting greater maturity and motivation.

His PPVI IQ was found to be 81, a level which is congruent with his vocabulary scaled scored on the WISC-R and which fact substantiates a mild vocabulary weakness.

V. Educational Factors

The WRAT achievement scores were found to be grade 8.5 for reading recognition, grade 6.7 for spelling and grade 5.3 for math. Reading comprehension on the PIAT was found to be grade 5.0. The standard scores from these levels were found to range between 78 and 103. Only the standard score of 78 on math is found to be as much as one standard deviation below his highest IQ of 93 (WISC-R Performance). The other levels of achievement are commensurate with his intellectual capacity, a fact which attests to a school program which has been helpful.

VI. Learning Competencies

What appears to be apparent from this battery of tests and from past reports is that Brent does have a visual-coordination problem. His memory for information, abstract reasoning and vocabulary ability appear to be his weakest verbal abilities, however, only his memory for information shows a significant difference from his highest scaled scores.* His psychomotor speed and his visual-motor coordination are shown to be mildly slow in comparison with his other performance abilities.

His memory for information weakness does not signify a pure memory weakness, since his memory for digits and his memory for designs were found to be normal. On both the WISC-R and the DTLA his memory for facts and for the sequencing of related information show significant drops in performance.

Brent's strengths are shown to be in visual discrimination and in visual planning/organization abilities. Where math problems are concerned, this strength does not appear to help him, for working math problems presented in visual forms was found to be his weakest achievement and below his capacity as shown by his problem solving skills in math on the WISC-R.

Summary

Brent is functioning as a slow learner with IQ's ranging between 87 and 93. His reading skills are above expectancy, his spelling skills at expectancy, and his arithmetic achievement below expectancy. The fifteen point difference between performance IQ of 93 and WRAT arithmetic standard score of 78 shows that he is achieving one standard deviation below his ability level which qualifies him for learning disability placement. The State requirements do state more than one standard deviation is necessary, but one point difference is generally accepted as a valid qualification. Since Brent was moved out of special education (ED) and placed in the seventh grade, which he failed, it is hoped that he might be moved into a learning disability room this time to allow him to receive special help which his test profile indicates is needed. He is not strong enough to compete satisfactorily with his peers unless he has special education, and he is marginally weak enough in arithmetic achievement to qualify for L/LD. His emotional problems of the past appear to be non-existent at this time. Special education is very effective for this young adolescent.

———————————————

Consulting Psychologist

*Piotrowski (1976) difference scores

PSYCHOMETRIC DATA

Name: Brent   *Examined:*
Birthdate: *Age:* 13-10   *Examiner:*
State I: Physical, Mental, Sociological, and Emotional Conditions

Wechsler Scales		*Verbal*		*Performance*	
Verbal IQ:	87	*Information:*	6	*Picture Completion:*	11
Perfor. IQ:	93	*Similarities:*	7	*Picture Arrange.:*	10
Full Sc.:	87	*Arithmetic:*	10	*Block Design:*	9
		Vocabulary:	8	*Object Assembly:*	8
		Comprehen.:	9	*Coding:*	8
		Digit Sp.:	(10)	*Mazes:*	(10)

Other Intelligence Tests:

Peabody Picture	*Basal Age:*	—	*Mental Age:*	10-5
Vocabulary Test	*Ceiling:*	—		
	Chrono. Age:	13-10	*IQ:*	81

Other Data:

State II: Educational Performance Levels

Achievement Levels	*Grade*	*%*	*SS*	*Level*	*Highest IQ*	*IQ-SS Discrepancy*
Reading Recog.	WRAT: 8.5	58	103	Average	93	10
Reading Comp.	PIAT: 5.0	14	84	Below Ave.	93	(9)
Spelling	WRAT: 6.7	27	91	Below Ave.	93	(2)
Arithmetic	WRAT: 5.3	7	78	Below Ave.	93	(15)
General Inf.						
Total						
Reading Cluster						
Math Cluster						
Written Lang. Cl.						
Knowledge Clus.						

Stage III: Learning Competencies

Language and Learning Test Data*   *Test/s used:* Detroit Test of
                                                         Learning Aptitude
Auditory Attention for Syllables: MA = 8–0
Visual Attention for Letters   MA = 11–9

Visual and/or Motor Tests* Bender   Auditory Tests: _____

   Mental Age: Not established but   *Mental Age:* 8–0
          below average   (memory in sentences)
   Comments: *Comments:* Same as Auditory Attention
                                                    test on DTLA
                                                    MFD test scores in normal range.

Summary

This paper identifies the learning-disabled child according to PL 94-142. The emphasis is on the responsibility of the diagnostician and the local school agency. Suggestions for the diagnostician are provided to aid in the process of determining differences between the achievement performance and the mental ability of the client involved. The case studies are representative of the information to be covered prior to the conference between the multi-disciplinary evaluation team and the parent.

References

Bush, W. J. & Waugh, K. W. *Diagnosing learning disabilities.* Columbus, Ohio: Charles E. Merrill Publishing Company, 1976.

Coulter, A., Johnson, M., & Walton, J. *A resource guide for the identification of learning disabilities.* Austin, Texas: Department of Special Education Developmental Programs, March, 1979.

Géarhart, B. R. *Learning disabilities: Educational strategies.* St. Louis, Mo.: C. V. Mosby Co., 1973.

Johnson, D. J., & Myklebust, H. R. *Learning diabilities: educational principles and practices.* New York: Grune and Stratton, 1967.

Johnson, S. W., & Morasky, R. L. *Learning disabilities.* Boston: Allyn and Bacon, 1977.

Kaufman, J. M., & Hallahan, D. P. *Teaching children with learning disabilities.* Columbus, Ohio: Charles E. Merrill Publishing Company, 1976.

Kirk, S. A., & McCarthy, J. M. *Learning disabilities: ACLD papers.* Boston: Houghton Mifflin Co., 1975.

Lerner, J. W. *Children with learning disabilities.* Boston: Houghton Mifflin Co., 1976.

Mandell, C. J., & Fiscus, E. *Understanding exceptional people.* St. Paul, Minn.: West Publishing Company, 1981.

McCarthy, J. J., & McCarthy, J. F. *Learning disabilities.* Boston: Allyn and Bacon, 1969.

Myers, P. I., & Hammill, D. D. *Methods for learning disorders,* New York: John Wiley and Sons, Inc., 1976.

---

*Adapted by Wilma Jo Bush, Ed.D., West Texas State University.

Myklebust, H. R. (Ed). *Progress in learning disabilities: Vol. II.* New York: Grune and Stratton, 1971.

Myklebust, H. R. (Ed) *Progress in learning disabilities: Vol. I.* New York: Grune and Stratton, 1968.

Wallace, G. W., & McLoughlin, J. A. *Learning disabilities: concepts and characteristics.* Columbus, Ohio: Charles E. Merrill Publishing Company, 1979.

Assessment of the Mentally Retarded

The concept of subaverage intellectual functioning has always been associated with the term *mental deficiency.* The concept, also, has included recognition of the social skills or adaptive behaviors of individuals. As early as 1937, Tredgold's definition of mental deficiency gave consideration to both mental and social points of view: ". . . a state of incomplete mental development of such kind and degree that the individual is incapable of adapting himself to the normal environment of his fellows in such a way as to maintain existence independently of supervision, control, or external support" (Tredgold, 1937, p. 3). Doll (1941), only a few years later, voiced his views with even more stringent points. He asserted that if an individual were to be defined as mentally deficient this person must be socially incompetent, that is, socially inadequate, and that this incompetence must be obtained at maturity. His all-encompassing definition was stated as follows: "Mental deficiency is a state of social incompetence obtaining at maturity, or likely to obtain at maturity, resulting from developmental arrest of intelligence because of constitutional (hereditary or acquired) origin: the condition is essentially incurable through treatment and unremediable through training except as treatment and training instill habits which superficially compensate for the limitation of the person so affected while under favorable circumstances and for more or less limited periods of time" (Louttit, 1957, p. 86). Inherent within these two early definitions can be seen the functions to be assessed in order to determine mental deficiency. Yet, and in spite of these clearly descriptive qualities that designate this state of mental deficiency in an individual, investigators have been known to label any individual as mentally defective who scores less than an IQ of 70 on an intelligence test. Sarason (1953) pointed to the unquestioning faith that some put on the diagnostic meaningfulness of the IQ, by using the example of the not-infrequent case in which a child with an IQ of 68 or 69 is committed to an institution, though the one with an IQ of 71 or 72 is not. In such a case, the assumption is that any slight difference in test score between two individuals is a reflection of some kind of significant difference in their past, present, or future status. Doll (1947) pointed out specific inadequacies of the IQ approach by explaining that the use of any single IQ discounts the important multiple aspects of mental measurements, the disparity of results from different systems of psychometric measurement, the probable error of any single measure of intelligence, the distinction between brightness and level, and the overlap in intelligence between high-grade feeble-mindedness and low-grade normality. He pointed out further that this single approach stops short at any arbitrary "statistical gate post" and does not concern itself with the many ramifications of the conditions that, if adequately explored, would reveal the absurdity of its point of view.

Dependence on the single intelligence score as the sole criterion of mental deficiency seems to have been largely an American phenomenon. The Mental Deficiency Act of 1913 in England emphasized the criterion of social adequacy rather than intellectual competency (Sarason, 1953), but in the United States the emphasis (in the past) has been more on intellectual aspects, i.e., for identification purposes. This emphasis on the intelligence of the individual could have come from the fact that Doll's definition really differentiated feeble-mindedness (mental deficiency) from intellectual retardation. In the latter, there is intellectual inadequacy with the likelihood of ultimate social competence, in the former, essential incurability is the hallmark. In this context, the term *mental retardation* actually carries the concept that the child is retarded in the intellectual function only (implying academic difficulty) and the trend to use only intelligence measures as a criterion for placement in special-education classes evolved as the general practice. The use of the term *mental retardation* (educable and trainable) rather than *mental deficiency* became preferred among educators, and *mildly/moderately retarded* became the preferred term within the medical profession. Though the Vineland Social Maturity Scale as a measure of social skills was available by 1947, it was used more in clinics and institutions than in the public schools, except in some cases. One of the authors of this text, Bush, has had personal experience over a period of 25 years in schools and clinics where social maturity scales were always used with minority children and with any children who performed with wide intertest variability within and between tests. Because of a lack of qualified school personnel, unallocated funds for evaluation, and the general understanding that the term *mental retardation* did not designate an incurable condition, the use of an intelligence test became the major criterion for qualifying children for placement in classes for the mentally retarded in public schools. The main emphasis was expectation of academic difficulty, not *social difficulty*.

In most states, the rule of thumb was that the child in question must have IQ scores two standard deviations below the mean on either the Stanford Binet or one of the Wechsler Scales. When time allowed, many school clinicians used achievement tests, also, assuming that if achievement were commensurate with the intellectual level, as much as the two standard deviations below the mean, the child was assuredly a candidate for special-education placement in the program for the mentally retarded.

The stigma of mental retardation under any name has continued to be a threat to many parents. Law suits occurring in recent years against schools for misplacement of some children in special-education classes attest to the accusation of the misclassification and the labeling of children as being mentally incapable of experiencing success in life. Among the issues were: (1) culturally different children were being discriminated against; (2) some parents could not accept the fact that their children were mentally slow to a significant degree; (3) the normalization principle became prominent (Kolstoe, 1976); and (4) demands were made for proof of retardation through lack of social adaptation, as well as lack of mental ability.

The American Association on Mental Deficiency Adaptive Behavior Scale (AAMD Adaptive Scale) by Nihira, Foster, Shellhaus, and Leland (1969) became one of the most prominent adaptive scales since Doll's Vineland Social Maturity Scale in 1947. It was more comprehensive than the Vineland and was very useful in curriculum planning for the mentally retarded, as well as being a decisive factor in measuring social skills. As the pressure on public schools became more forceful regarding social-skill measures, Lambert, Windmiller, Cole and Figueroa (1974) standardized a public-school version of the AAMD Adaptive Behavior Scale. On this scale, the teachers could answer most of the questions about the child under consideration. Both of the editions of the Adaptive

Behavior Scale were helpful in devising developmental programs for children at all three levels of mental retardation.

It was after Public Law 94-142 that many State authorities in special education sought more specific means for placement, and Mercer's System of Multicultural Pluralistic Assessment (1978) became one of the prominent scales for decision making, since it was standardized with the WISC-R. Not only does this scale have a social measure and an intelligence measure, but it also accounts for the variabilities of cultures—Blacks, Hispanics, and Whites.

It appears that a full turn has been made to return to the original definitions of mental deficiency for guidance in identifying mental retardation in children. The child must be shown to be both mentally and socially retarded in order to qualify for special-education classes. While these two areas constitute the basis for decision making, some states do not allow the administration of tests of intelligence. They use only achievement and/or adaptive scales.

The writers recommend that all information possible be used in making decisions about retardation. This information should include (1) opinions of both parents and teachers, (2) intelligence-test scores and intertest variability, (3) social maturity data, and (4) achievement-test scores from both criterion-referenced and grade-level data.

The following case studies are offered as representative of a data collection for the purpose of placement and curriculum planning for the retarded.

PSYCHO-EDUCATIONAL EVALUATION

Name: Sandy   School:
Birthdate: C.A.: 11-3   Sex: F   Grade:
Examiner: Examined:

I. Assessment of Physical, Mental, Sociological, and Emotional Conditions.
Language
─────────

English is the language spoken in the home, but there was little evidence of speech except for a few words.
Physical
─────────

a. Sandy is a brown-haired girl who appeared to be normal in height and weight for her eleven years and three months.

b. Health: Medical records show that Sandy is a Down's Syndrome child. No current illnesses were reported.

c. Fine-motor Skills: Sandy is developmentally slow. Her mental age for fine-motor skills is about four years.

d. Gross-motor Skills: Except for being awkward in running and skipping, her gross-motor skills appear to be rather normal. She can stand on tiptoes for ten seconds and can throw overhand, but is not skilled in doing either.

Emotional/Behavioral

Part II of the AAMD Scale was not administered, but an interview was held with the mother concerning Sandy's behavior. Sandy is apparently socially adjusted when with other children. In the classroom for the mentally retarded she is relatively well behaved. She does run away from home periodically.

Sociological

The father is a farmer with a high school education and the mother is a school teacher with a bachelor's degree. Both parents are stable people and are well respected in the community. They readily accept the fact that Sandy is a retarded child. This is a second evaluation after a four-year period and was requested by the parents to determine any changes.

Intellectual

The Stanford Binet was administered and she was found to be functioning as a retarded individual at the borderline of severe retardation. Sandy failed to base completely at the two-year level on the Stanford Binet, Form L-M, for she did not identify all of the body parts required at that level. At the 2-6 level she failed all tasks except identifying articles by use, but at the 3-0 level she passed all of the tests except the vocabulary. All of the perceptual-motor activities were passed at this age. At the 3-6 level, there were three perceptual tasks passed and one passed at the 4-0 level. No tasks were passed at the 5-0 year level. The Stanford Binet IQ was found to be 28 and the PPVT IQ was found to be 21.

II. Assessment of Educational Performance Levels

It was not possible to obtain any scores from educational measures (achievement tests) with Sandy.

The AAMD Adaptive Behavior Scale was administered and the enclosed profile reveals that Sandy is well below the regular norms in all functions. Physical development and vocational activities in comparison with normal eleven-year-olds are found at the 25th and 19th percentile respectively. Other skills are at a lower percentile. In comparison with trainable children the norms show that she competes fairly well.

III. Assessment of Learning Competency

Sandy's strengths are within the performance area where she functions as a trainable retarded child, but in the verbal area she functions as a severely retarded individual. She does not understand directions except those given in very simple statements.

The major curriculum should be built on skills for independent functioning and for vocational activities. Discrimination training should involve sorting and classification with minimal verbal instruction. These sorting skills with finger dexterity skills are necessary for future job positions in sheltered workshops.

Summary

Sandy is a relatively quiet child but one who enjoys being with her peers. She functions in the trainable range in the performance area and in the severe range in the verbal area. Skills necessary for sheltered workshop positions should be given priority in her public school curriculum.

Reporting Diagnostician/Psychologist

Figure 44. Profile Summary

Name: _Sandy_   C.A. _11 - 3_   Examined: _8 - 7 - 1980_

Birthdate: _5 - 14 - 69_   Examiner: _____

AAMD Adaptive Behavior Scale   Part One

Deciles	I Independent Functioning	II Physical Development	III Economic Activity	IV Language Development	V Numbers and Time	VI Domestic Activity	VII Vocational Activity	VIII Self-Direction	IX Responsibility	X Socialization
D9 (90)										
D8 (80)										
D7 (70)										
D6 (60)										
D5 (50)	[48]	[47]	[44]							
D4 (40)				[38]					[41]	
D3 (30)		(25)			[24]		[25]			
D2 (20)							(19)	[14] (11)	(16)	[12]
D1 (10)	(11)			(1)	(3)	(0)				(7)

Attained Scores	54	21	0	18	1		2	8	2	12

TMR norms ☐---☐   Norm age group: 11^3–12^2
Regular norms ◯——◯

PSYCHO-EDUCATIONAL EVALUATION

Name: Trina   School:
Birthdate: C.A.: 6-6   Sex: F   Grade:
Examiner: Examined:

I. Assessment of Physical, Mental, Sociological, and Emotional Conditions

Language
English is the language spoken in the home.

Physical
    a. Trina is small in stature for her years. She is in the fourteenth percentile when compared with other children her age. (SOMPA-Medical Model)
    b. All of her physical dexterity tasks show percentile ranks of ten and below. She is considered to be much slower in physical skills than her age-peers.
    c. Fine-motor skills are also found to be below average. The results of her Bender Visual-Motor Gestalt Test placed her in the fourth percentile.
    d. Visual and auditory acuity are both within normal limits.
    e. No unusual health problems were reported by mother.

Emotional/Behavioral
    Trina is a shy child who sits quietly at her desk and waits to be instructed. She appears to enjoy looking at picture books and hearing nursery rhyme records. The teacher reports that she never disturbs other children and her very pleasant, docile nature makes her a favorite of many of the other students, particularly the slower students in the room.

Sociological
    Trina's father is the manager of a small store in a small town of about ten thousand population. The father had one year of college and the mother finished the 12th grade in high school. They are both very stable citizens and accept the fact that Trina is very slow. The mother does not work outside of the home and spends much time with both her daughters. The older sister is nine years of age and is very protective of Trina.

Intellectual
    Trina was examined on the WISC-R test and was found to be functioning in the mildly retarded range. Her Verbal IQ was found to be 60, her Performance IQ 64, and her Full Scale IQ 59.

II. Assessment of Educational Performance Levels
    a. Achievement test scores are reported on the Psychometric Summary Sheet and are summarized as follows: Trina could not perform well enough to score on the PIAT. She does not seem to comprehend likenesses and differences. When asked to point to another, she pointed to all the items.
    b. Her problems with school subjects and skills are that she does not appear to understand what the teacher instructs her to do.
    c. Trina is below the 1st percentile and it was not possible to obtain a standard score from her achievement performance.

III. Assessment of Learning Competency
    Information from the SOMPA ABIC shows that Trina is in the high risk area in terms of adaptive behavior. She shows difficulty in assuming self-maintenance and earner/consumer responsibility. She adapts as a slow learner in her family and community role, but all other adaptive behaviors are well within the retarded range. At this time Trina should have a kindergarten program which involves readiness and perceptual-motor tasks. No significant strengths and weaknesses were found to suggest emphasis in any single area.

Summary

Trina is a small child who not only has earned scores on the WISC-R to support intellectual functioning within the educable mentally retarded range, her estimated learning potential also suggests that she is adapting like an educable mentally retarded individual. Developmental skill in every perform-ance area is found to be very slow.

It is recommended that she be placed in a room for the educable mentally retarded and that her program include training in both verbal and perceptual-motor activities.

_____

Reporting Diagnostician/Psychologist

PSYCHOMETRIC DATA

Name: Trina   *Examined:*
Birthdate: *Age:* 6-6   *Examiner:*
State I: Physical, Mental, Sociological, and Emotional Conditions

Wechsler Scales	*Verbal*		*Performance*	
Verbal IQ: 60	*Information:*	3	*Picture Completion:*	5
Perfor. IQ: 64	*Similarities:*	5	*Picture Arrange.:*	5
Full Sc.: 59	*Arithmetic:*	3	*Block Design:*	3
	Vocabulary:	3	*Object Assembly:*	4
	Comprehen.:	4	*Coding:*	5
	Digit Sp.:	(5)	*Mazes:*	(5)

Other Intelligence Tests:

	Basal Age:	—	*Mental Age:*	
	Ceiling:	—		
	Chrono. Age:	—	*IQ:*	

Other Data:

SOMPA:
Weight by height: 14th%
Physical dexterity: 10th % and below
Health history inventory: Prenatal/Postnatal—At Risk

State II: Educational Performance Levels

Achievement Levels	Test	Test	Test	IQ-SS =	Grade	% SS
Reading Recog.	PIAT				Below K.	
Reading Comp.	PIAT				Below K.	
Spelling	PIAT				Below K.	
Arithmetic	PIAT				Below K.	
General Inf.	PIAT				Below K.	
Total	PIAT				Below K.	

Reading Cluster   _____

Math Cluster   _____

Written Lang. Cl.   _____

Knowledge Clus.   _____

Stage III: Learning Competencies

Language and Learning Test Data: *Test/s used:*

Visual and/or Motor Tests: SOMPA   Auditory Tests: SOMPA

   Mental Age: Mental Age:
Comments: Visual Acute—Not at risk   Comments: Auditory Acuity
   Bender Visual-Motor Gestalt—14th%   not at risk.

SOMPA SOCIAL SYSTEM MODEL

Adaptive Behavior Inventory for Children (ABIC)

	Scaled Score	Percentile
Family	25	4
Community	29	8
Peer Relations	10	Below 1
Non-Academic School Roles	21	3
Earner/ Consumer	19	2
Self-Main- tenance	10	Below 1
ABIC Ave. Scaled Score	19	2

School Functioning Level (SFL)

WISC-R   Verbal IQ: 60   *Performance IQ:* 64   *Full Scale IQ:* 59

Pluralistic Model

Estimated Learning Potential (ELP)
Scaled Score: Verbal: 60   *Performance:* 64   *Full Scale:* 59

   Sociocultural Scales
Own Ethnic Group: White

*Adapted by Wilma Jo Bush, Ed.D., West Texas State University.

	Scaled Score	Percentile
Family Size	54	58
Family Structure	57	70
Socioeconomic Status	45	35
Urban Acculturation	47	48
School Culture		
Family Size	54	58
Family Structure	59	70
Socioeconomic Status	45	35
Urban Acculturation	47	48

References

Doll, E. A. The essentials of an inclusive concept of deficiency. *American Journal of Mental Deficiency,* 1941, *46:* 214–219.

Doll, E. A. Is mental deficiency curable? *American Journal of Mental Deficiency,* 1947a, *51:* 420–428.

Doll, E. A. *Vineland social maturity scale,* Minneapolis: Educational Test Bureau, 1947.

Kolstoe, O. P. *Teaching educable mentally retarded children.* New York: Holt, Rinehart and Winston, 1976.

Lamberth, N., Windmiller, M., Cole, L., & Figueroa, R. *AAMD adaptive behavior scale, public school version.* Washington, D.C.: American Association on Mental Deficiency, 1975.

Louttit, C. M. *Clinical psychology of exceptional children,* 3rd ed. New York: Harper and Brothers, 1957.

Mercer, J. R., & Lewis, J. F. *SOMPA.* New York: The Psychological Corporation, 1977.

Mercer, J. R. *Labeling the mentally retarded.* Berkeley, Calif.: University of California Press, 1973.

Nihira, K., Foster, R., Shellhaus, M., & Leland, H. *Adaptive behavior scales.* Washington, D.C.: American Association on Mental Deficiency, 1969.

Nihira, K., Foster, R., Shellhaus, M., & Leland, H. *AAMD adaptive behavior scale.* Monterey, Calif.: New School Edition Publishers, Test Service, 1981.

Sarason, S. B. *Psychological problems in mental deficiency.* New York: Harper and Brothers, 1953.

Assessment of the Emotionally Disturbed

In many public school districts, the identification of most handicapping conditions falls within the domain of the school diagnostician. This is generally not true, however, in the case of the emotionally disturbed. To perform such duties, a diagnostician must have the added credential of psychologist in most states. When diagnosticians are not also certified psychologists, psychiatrists and other psychologists in private practice are employed for such purposes of determining whether a student is emotionally disturbed.

Because of the complexity of differentiating "true" emotional disturbance from other handicapping conditions that may also show overshadings of abnormal behavior, a paper was included in Chapter 4 of this text. Its purpose is to make the readers aware of the dangers of labeling children who may only appear to be disturbed. In that paper, Fairchild provides a look at the discrepancies that complicate the procedure of identification of normal vs. abnormal behavior. The reader is referred to that article for clarification of the symptoms and signs of emotional disturbance.

The brief discussion presented here serves to provide (1) a practical definition for emotionally disturbed students in the public schools, and (2) evaluations that should make it easier to discriminate this particular problem from other handicapping conditions.

Identification

A student who is considered to be emotionally disturbed is one who has been evaluated by a qualified diagnostician, who determines that the following conditions exist:

(1) an inability to learn that cannot be explained by other defined handicapping conditions
(2) an inability to build or maintain satisfactory interpersonal relationships with peers and teachers
(3) inappropriate types of behavior or feelings under normal conditions
(4) a general, pervasive mood of unhappiness under normal circumstances
(5) a tendency to develop physical symptoms or fears associated with personal or school problems*

Point number one regarding inability to learn should be assessed through criterion-referenced, intelligence, and achievement tests. Points two, three, four, and five should be assessed by trained personnel through observation and interview techniques. The following procedure is recommended:

Step I. Data Collecting for Referrals

Referrals from the teacher should be preceded by careful observation. Check lists could be made to be used as guidelines to determine which behaviors are occurring and whether they occur under the same or different conditions each day. When the first deviant behavior is observed, the teacher should secure her check list and make a tally regarding it or any other deviant behavior for a period of a week or two. The referral should follow with the documented evidence from the tally.

An example of a check list is illustrated in Figure 45.

Step II. Evaluations

The evaluations from the professional should specify (1) the severity of the emotional disturbance, (2) the functional implications of the disability for schoolroom instruction, (3) the consistency of in-school and out-of-school behavior patterns and (4) recommendations for management in the educational setting.

Case Study #1 is an example of a situation in which a student is recommended by a teacher as emotionally disturbed, but after evaluation is instead found to be learning-disabled. Case #2 is a case of youth who shows valid signs of emotional problems.

---

*Public Law 94-142 Regulations, Section 121a5(8)

Figure 45. Check List for Inappropriate Behaviors*

	Monday	Tuesday	Wednesday	Thursday	Friday
Specific Fears					
Nervous Habits					
Cruelty, Aggression					
Lying and Stealing					
Speech Difficulties					
Timidity, Shyness, Withdrawn					
Daydreaming, Laziness, Lack of Concentration					
Excitability and Restlessness					
Lack of Appetite					
Junk Food Addict					
Disobedience					
Tantrums					
Babyish Behavior and Frequent Crying					
Bladder Control Problem					
Tendency to Headaches, Stomachaches, or other					
Easily and Frequently Tired					
Undesirable Sex Habits					
Obsessive-Compulsive					
Confused-Disorganized					
Nonconforming Attitudes					
Inadequate Schoolwork					
Other Behaviors not listed					

*Check class or time of behavior on each day.

PSYCHOLOGICAL EVALUATION

Name: Martin   *Examined:*
Birthdate: *Examiner:*
                                                        C. A.: 13-4

Language Factor
  English is the language spoken in the home.

Behavior and Appearance
  Martin is a light-brown-haired, blue-eyed boy of thirteen years and four months. He appears to be normal in height and weight for his years. He was dressed in sport shirt and jeans and was moderately clean and neat. He was referred by his teacher for possible emotional problems because of misbehavior and learning difficulties in the school. Learning problems were reported to be in language and math, the two subjects for which the reporting teacher is responsible.
  During this session this youth was pleasant and responded as if he were quite sure of himself. When he did not know an answer, he quickly responded that he had not had that in school, a behavior which indicated a shifting of blame. Indications of some mild insecurity began to show later in the testing by a question as to what would happen if he did not pass this test. He was reassured and the testing moved along smoothly.

Implications for School Functioning
  Martin held his pencil in his right hand in a very tight grip and he was slow in the manipulation of writing. It was if he had to deliberately draw each letter or symbol. He rotated several of his Bender designs and could not remember some of the designs on the Graham-Kendall test. He printed all of his spelling words which is not typical of youth his age.
  His major deficits in learning appear to deal with written tasks. He also tends to remember visual facts better than auditory facts. Martin should be allowed much time to complete his written responses and when it is ascertained that he understands the principles in math, his assignments should not be lengthy in terms of repetition of the same type problems. He uses a phonetic approach in spelling, but needs help in remembering the sequence of the letters.

Intellectual Factors
  The results from the WISC-R show that this is a young man of average intelligence with a tendency to function erratically. His verbal IQ was 87, performance score 105, and his Full Scale IQ was 95. Tasks dealing with pencil manipulation tend to be more difficult than other performance tasks.

Achievement Factors
  The Wide Range Achievement Test places this eighth grader as reading at grade 7.1, spelling at grade 5.2 and working math at grade 5.8. In math Martin

is having more difficulty with fractions than with other functions. Also he did not complete many problems in the ten minute period allowed.

Personality Factors

Martin is reported by his teacher to be disobedient in class—often refusing to complete his assignments. She says he sits and stares and will not respond to her demands. On the schoolground he appears to relate fairly well with his schoolmates. He does tend to brag sometimes about where he has been and what he has done. This grandiose behavior is not exaggerated but appears to be a front for his fears regarding failures in school. His misbehavior has only been reported by his teacher in English and math. Other teachers report that he is slow but not disruptive. Martin portrays a dislike for school and says that he wishes he didn't have to attend school. He shows a need for acceptance, but other than bragging and refusal to respond regularly in English and math, he shows no behavioral differences.

Summary

The impression is that this young man has a learning disability which is manifested primarily by inability to express his thoughts in writing. He has difficulty with spelling and with math. In oral conversation he does not seem to have the same problem. It appears that he has a conflict with one teacher because he cannot perform the tasks which are required of him. It is recommended that he be placed in a resource room for special help in language and math. The emotional problems reported appear to be minor and identified to exist in only isolated situations in the school.

_____

Reporting Psychologist

Psychometric Data for Martin
_____

Intelligence: WISC-R Verbal Scaled Scores		Verbal IQ 87 Performance IQ 105 Performance Sc. Scores		Full Sc. 95
Inf.	7	Pic. Comp.	15	
Sim.	10	Pic. Arrang.	9	
Ar.	8	Bl. Des.	9	
Voc.	8	Obj. Assem.	15	
Comp.	7	Coding	6	
D.S.	(7)	Mazes	(8)	

Achievement: Wide Range Achievement

	Grade	Standard Score	Percentile
Reading	7.1	95	37
Spelling	5.2	83	13
Arithmetic	5.8	87	19

Projective Tests:
Rorschach, Thematic Apperception Test, Sentence Completion

PSYCHOLOGICAL EVALUATION

Name: Steven   *Examined:*
Birthdate: *Examiner:*
C.A.: 11-5

Language Factor
English is the language spoken in the home.

Behavior and Appearance
Steven is an eleven year, five month old boy who will be in the fifth grade in
the fall. He is brown-haired, blue-eyed, medium height (he did not know his own
height), slight build (64 pounds), fair complexioned youngster. He has poor
grooming habits and dirty fingernails and he was carelessly dressed. When left
to his own resources, it is likely that he has marginal hygiene habits.

When he entered the examination setting, Steven was nervous and
apprehensive. Earlier in the afternoon in a play session, he had been
accidentally knocked by another youngster into a wall and had banged his
head, receiving a small cut. He came into the room holding an ice bag on his
head. He displayed a lack of enthusiasm about being tested, worked with very
little effort and for only short periods of time. His speech was quick and naive.
Bragging was common and it was evident that his "come-on" was such that he
would alienate his peers. He answered simple questions; balked or dismissed
any questions of depth.

Implications for School Functioning
Steven has poor fine-muscle motor coordination, but his gross-motor coordination is slightly better. He organizes and monitors his work marginally and
immaturely and is easily distracted by any activity going on around him. He is
quite restless and seems to have the need to be up and active as much as
possible. He tends to want to put his hand on things and he is the type of
youngster that would be pushing and shoving other youngsters in the classroom.

Intellectual Factors
On the WISC-R Steven was found to be functioning in the dull normal range
of intellectual ability. His WISC-R Full Scale IQ was found to be 85 and there
was not a significant difference between his verbal and performance abilities.

He has a limited interest range and his awareness centers around himself. It
is hard for him to deal with new situations and he generalizes very poorly on
any lesson that he learns to another situation somewhat similar. He has poor
judgment and uses little common sense in problem solving. He tends to rely on
a rote memorized mode of response. His memory is erratic and spotty and he is

poorly motivated to attend to most activities that go on in him unless an active, play-like type of situation.

Achievement Factors

When the Wide Range Achievement Test was administered, Steven leaned back in the chair and very shortly began to cry, protesting that his head hurt. Even though he had started this part of the session by saying that he liked math the best in school and found geography to be hard, he could not follow through with any effort. As soon as the test was removed and he was given activities to draw or which required simple responses (non-school type), he relaxed and began to participate again. It was not possible to obtain an accurate measure of his achievement in this session.

Personality Factors

Steven is an expansive and grandiose youngster and many of his responses to situations around him are inappropriate. He tends to behave in an exaggerated fashion and is inclined to tell falsehoods to attempt to gain attention and to avoid unpleasantness. He is eager to be accepted by adults and has almost given up on trying to make children accept him and include him in their activities. He finds it very difficult to delay gratification and gives little thought to the consequences of his behavior. He is impatient and tolerates frustration very poorly. He tries to manipulate people but lacks the patience and the skill to do so with success and, after he has started the manipulation, will tend to give it up and use a more frontal approach, alienating those around him. He has limited ability to understand what are the positions of other people or what the viewpoint of other people might be, and as a result, has very poor success in making any friendships at all. His contact with reality is naive and restricted and, while he has some fantasy life, it is of a non-productive nature and periodically it possesses a mild bizarre quality. He gives and receives affection in a shallow way and is puzzled by the requirements placed upon him by any · social situation. He regards the world as a confusing, buzzing, difficult place in which to survive and to gain attention or approval. He tends to use direct, aggressive attacks in trying to solve problems and, if that fails to work, tends to want to resort to repression or denial and to walk away from the problem as much as possible.

Summary

Steven is a youth who portrays critical emotional problems. He needs much structure to help him develop new patterns of behavior. His training should be milieu therapy, i.e., planned for both in-school and out-of-school.

Since achievement levels could not be obtained in this session the teacher who has Steven in class daily should obtain criterion-referenced data for purposes of planning his curriculum. With an 85 IQ he is expected to be behind his peers, but with the confusion that he apparently experiences, he is expected to be achieving even below his capacity/mental age. Cheney and Morse* suggest

---

*From *Conflicts in Classroom* by Long, Morse and Newman.

excellent techniques to use with the emotionally disturbed. These are recommended as well as the following principles:
1. Activities which present challenges but which are within the realm of success must be employed.
2. Present new learning situations and experiences aimed at correcting and gradually replacing inadequate habits and patterns of behavior with more appropriate and effective ones, e.g., role playing.
3. Provide purposed structure for each activity. ·
4. Stop activities before they become ineffective by lack of attention/interest.
5. Academics should be presented through activities which are valued by Steven.
6. Present responsibilities which can be carried out—ones that give a child a sense of pleasure.
7. Use the terms *rights* and *responsibility* frequently in reference to all involved in Steven's environment.
8. Learning should be active and involve sensory input through all channels.
9. Present materials that move from *easy* to a *slight challenge*, then move to new materials.

Reporting Psychologist

PSYCHOMETRIC DATA FOR STEVEN

Intelligence: WISC-R	*Verbal* IQ: 81	*Performance* IQ: 91	*Full* Scale: 85

Verbal Scaled Scores		Performance Scaled Scores	
Inf.	7	Pic. Completion	10
Sim.	9	Pic. Arrange.	7
Arith.	8	Block Design	8
Voc.	8	Obj. Assem.	10
Comp.	5	Coding	10
Di. Sp.	(6)	Mazes	(7)

Projective Tests:
    Rorschach
    Thematic Apperception
    Sentence Completion

Achievement Tests:
    Wide Range Achievement
    Incomplete Information.

Summary
This paper has identified the emotionally disturbed child according to Public Law 94-142. The procedure to follow in the evaluation process is described and a check list of inappropriate behaviors is provided. The case studies are representative of the information needed for the multidisciplinary team in making placement decisions.

Summary

This chapter covers assessment procedures and general information on the learning disabled, the mentally retarded, and the emotionally disturbed. The paper on the learning-disabled identifies the definition of this group according to P.L. 94-142 and describes five different methods to aid in determining whether discrepancies between achievement and intelligence scores are significant.

The paper on mental retardation emphasizes the need to show both social and intellectual deficits before decisions are made for placement in the program for the retarded. The major social adaptive scales are identified and suggestions made for the information needed for the total evaluation.

Assessment of the emotionally disturbed is described as being complex because of the differences of opinion among authorities. The definition provided for this group involves four different behaviors that must exist before a final identification of emotional disturbance may be made. A check list is provided to aid in the observation procedure.

Case studies of each handicapping condition are included.

Chapter 10

Reporting Assessment Data

The student who has studied this chapter should be able to do the following:
1. *Determine the content to include in a report*
2. *Evaluate a report according to a critical question check list*
3. *Understand the uses and misuses of qualifying words in report writing*
4. *Organize the data into a report form*
5. *Understand the reason for clarity in the report*
6. *Understand the ethical aspects of reporting scores to parents*
7. *Understand the legal aspects of reporting to parents and teachers*
8. *Report levels of function by use of check lists*

Introduction

A major part of any evaluation process is the report of the findings, whether oral or written. The goal is to communicate clearly. The emphasis in this chapter is on the written report; however, oral discussion may greatly facilitate communication of the findings and recommendations. Although the report is made in response to a referral and for the use of that person, one must not lose sight of the fact that it is for the benefit ultimately of the client.

Psychological reports have been criticized for lack of specificity, use of special jargon, failure to use behavioral description, and writing to impress rather than to communicate. These are valid criticisms and one must guard against allowing them to creep into a report.

Format is not a critical issue. Reports should be devised to meet the needs of particular situations. There are some commonly accepted guidelines regarding the content of the report, beginning with the identification of the subject and ending with a summary of the test or observation findings and recommendations.

Other factors to be considered when writing a report include the ethical aspects of reporting and the legal aspects of decisive commitments. One who is in possession of test data must understand both ethical and legal implications of reporting such information.

Terminology, Length, and Design for Target Populations

A report should be written to be understood by everyone involved—from lawyers, doctors, and teachers to parents of all professions and levels of education. The teacher should be able to understand the terms used and relate them to teaching materials and to the learning of the child. Parents should also be able to understand the terms and relate them to practical experiences in the home. Zimmerman and Woo-Sam (1973) suggest that technical jargon should be minimized and that the writer should be able to communicate even the most difficult concept in simple language. Huber (1961) states that the most difficult skill to acquire in report writing is the knack of writing in a straightforward way. Identifying simple terms that will be interpreted in the same manner by people from different disciplines is not as easy as it would appear. For example, the simple term *rote memory* can be defined several different ways. To a teacher, it can mean memory for numbers, as in counting, or memory for letters, as in repeating the alphabet; to a psychologist, rote memory could be interpreted as memory for a list of nonsense syllables. In order to facilitate communication, the writer should provide specific definitions, so that any target population will understand the terms used. An example would be

John's rote memory for numbers, *as in counting to 15*, was found to be inconsistent and thus unreliable.

The length of the report will, of course, vary among cases. However, a safe guideline is that it should not cover more than two typewritten pages, single spaced, and with double spacing between paragraphs. The length of any report may influence whether the busy reader will read all of it or only portions of it. If the design does not have topics clearly separated, the reader may do no more than scan the report for scores or read the last few lines. Headings should separate observation of overt behavior from the discussion of test results.

Although reports may be organized in various ways, they tend to include the following sections:

1. Identification
Name
Sex
Birthdate
Chronological age
Examiner's name
Date of examination
2. Reason for referral
Purpose
Source
Circumstances

3. History of case

School behavior

    (Home influences and behavior are usually obtained by a social worker and more often found in psychological rather than educational evaluations.)

4. Psychometric information

Tests used

Scores (when appropriate) or levels of function

5. Behavior and appearance of subject

Attitudes

Dress

Method of approach to tasks

6. Summarization of test results

Level of intellectual functioning and impressions of reliability or validity

7. Recommendations

8. Evaluator's signature and identifying role as psychologist, consultant, or educational diagnostician

    Of course, reports may have many more separate sections, but the above will generally provide enough subheadings to allow for an easy flow of the information to the user.

    Qualifiers tend to weaken a report, particularly if used in any excess. Huber (1961) states that terms like *appears to be, might be,* and *seems to be* make the results indecisive, especially if you are giving your professional opinion. He suggests that one qualify when there is slim evidence to make a professional judgment. People opposed to use of standard tests in schools unwittingly present a reason for the use of qualifiers when they argue that tests are unfair to various socioeconomic and cultural groups. Their premise is that data are inaccurate if they come from standardized tests. To avoid the pitfall of inaccurate reporting, the use of *appears to be, seems to be,* and *might be* becomes appropriate in many instances. The use of these terms in clinical reporting in the past has been an arbitrary choice, and this use often has added to the fluency of the report. In the final analysis, in order to evaluate for accuracy, all qualifiers may be omitted in the initial writing, and then those that would make the statements more accurate in terms of what is actually known could be added to the report. The trend toward accountability and increased awareness of the law demand a careful look at what can and cannot be proved. Martin (1972) is emphatic in his concern about absolutism in report writing. He differs from Huber and indicates that words such as *seems, appears,* and *probably* may be as close to absolutism as one can or should come. Of course, the report will contain specifics on test data, reports on behavior, and verbatim statements of the client to provide support for interpretation. Legal and ethical implications suggest that if they cannot be supported, do not make absolute statements.

    Use of the names of tests or subtests in reports is also important. To diagnose is to examine all the test data and "rule out" all evidence that would contradict such findings (Weed, 1969). In medicine, a doctor may observe fever and sore throat in a child but will rule out measles in favor of mumps if the jaws are swollen. Using this as a guideline, it should be logical to weigh one possibility against the other when one is trying to determine weaknesses or strengths in the modalities of learning. In educational diagnosis, the various modalities of learning are measured by the variety of tests used. Thus, it is logical and reasonable that one may report by cross-checking and by calling tests by name. When reporting to parents, the reporter may need to consider whether this much information will be of interest and understood. Some parents would appreciate the opportunity to learn about normative data on their children.

The following questions can serve as a check list and a guide in writing a report:

1. Did I answer the question implied in the referral?
2. Have I stated the information as simply and concisely as possible?
3. Is it written in a style and language that the user can understand?
4. Have I made any sweeping generalizations that I have difficulty in documenting?
5. Have I used behavioral descriptions in place of technical jargon?
6. Can decisions be made on the basis of information I provided?
7. Did I write to inform or to impress?
8. Did my report have a focus or major theme, so that it would be easy for the user to follow?
9. Did I include relevant background data and identifying material?
10. Did I distinguish between clinical interpretation and facts?
11. Have all ambiguous terms been defined and clarified?
12. Did I use abbreviations and initials that may confuse my reader?
13. Did I include any negative statements—such as "The client has no apparent physical problems"—that could be stated better in a positive manner?
14. Did I observe the physical, emotional, social, and intellectual levels of the student and use this information in the report?
15. Have I used labels where an explanation would be more appropriate?

Ethical Aspects of Reporting Symbols

Reporting of actual test scores to parents and teachers has not been accepted by many authorities. This has been particularly true of IQ scores. Wilson (Bonder and Wilson) lists the following reasons for not telling parents their children's IQs: (1) limited test results may not be reliable; (2) interpretation of test results is too complex; and (3) parents may put pressure on children or give up hope if they know the scores. Lagerman (1961) in his argument against IQ tests points out that knowledge of such scores may discriminate against some youth in terms of choice of studies.

Bonder (Bonder and Wilson) counters this by saying that if parents know the scores, they can be shown how to work with their children who have high IQs and can avoid the habit of making odious comparisons between siblings who differ significantly in intellectual functioning. Cannon (1973) reports that many psychologists are now providing parents with copies of their reports on students and are receiving favorable feedback from them. Since passage of Section 438 of the General Education Provisions Act dealing with privacy rights of parents and students, commonly known as the Buckley Amendment, this philosophical argument may have been rendered irrelevant.

Teachers should know their student's IQs. Since they have access to many standardized group tests, which may or may not provide valid IQs, scores provided by trained diagnosticians or psychologists dispel invalid information obtained from less reliable sources. Knowledge of IQ scores also aids in prescriptive planning. It helps teachers choose materials that will challenge but not inundate the slow learner and motivate the gifted child. Of course, IQ scores should be reported with an explanation of their standard errors.

Whether scores should be reported in specific symbols (numerical) or as levels (above average, average) should be a matter of school policy and should reflect community demands. Once this has been established, the consultant should follow the accepted standards.

Legal Aspects of Reporting

In many states, the legal rights of parents and their children have long been clearly defined. The courts have ruled that parents have the right to any data that dictate grade placement, special services, or categories for their children. In addition, parents have been given the right to the control of and release of the data. Murdock (1971) questions any practice that withholds written reports from parents on professional or ethical grounds. He says that the purpose of any evaluation is to facilitate the learning process, which requires the joint effort of parents, teacher, and diagnosticians. Machowsky (1973), Robbins and Carrigan (1971), and Hyman (1972) stress the liability involved, should diagnosticians withhold information from parents or release it to others without proper consent. Martin (1971) has excellent coverage of the specifics of privileged information.

Whereas many states have had rulings regarding open school records, the mandate from the national level dispels any question as to whether closed records may continue to exist. The Buckley Amendment to the Educational Provisions Act of 1974 gave parents access to their child's records. A person 18 and older not only has access to these records, but also with certain exceptions is the only one who can authorize their release.

It is now common for school systems to seek the advice of the legal profession to eliminate misuse of student records and to set standards for future use of information in these records (correspondence with Karen Johnson, 1974). While no hard and fast rules can be set, there are a few guidelines that will help eliminate possible harm to students. One important rule is that when parents or students view records, a professional person should be present to explain the information. Isolated bits of numerical data, such as achievement scores and IQs, are of little value unless they are correctly interpreted. A second rule is that observation should be carefully and factually reported, and interpretations of the incident being recorded should be avoided. Consultants and teachers should avoid drawing conclusions about a child's behavior that they are not academically qualified to make. Labeling, which may inadvertently cause a receiving teacher to react inappropriately to students without giving them a chance, should be avoided. Not only is this a professional and ethical act, but it may prevent litigation procedures if heeded. Where inaccurate classifications are made, very often lawsuits follow. Categorical labels, in many cases, are said to create a stigma that becomes a greater handicap to the child's success than his or her original condition (Mandell and Fiscus, 1981, p. 30).

The concern for the human rights of the handicapped has had far-reaching affects. It has now been legislatively mandated (P.L. 94-142) that the handicapped individual has a right to be given a nondiscriminatory evaluation before educational decisions are made. The renowned cases that have had a very forceful impact for the nonlabeling of children are the Diana v. State Board of Education in 1970 and the Larry P. v. Riley in

1972, both of which were in the state of California. The Diana v. State Board case concerned nine Hispanic students who had been placed in classes for the mentally retarded on the basis of intelligence tests that had been standardized largely on Anglo middle-class children. When retesting was done, using the same tests but translated into Spanish, all children made scores that were higher and disqualified them from the classroom for the mentally retarded. This case was settled out of court and the resulting feature was the stipulation that future intelligence tests be given in the child's own language. The Larry P. case involved six Black students who were alleged to have been misclassified as educable mentally retarded. The charge was that the intelligence tests used did not consider the differences between the cultural background of the black students and the white students. In this suit the court concluded that IQ-test results could negatively affect expectations of black students and that this could lower their academic performance. In 1974, a California court ruled that no tests be used that did not account for cultural background and that Black children not be placed in classes for the mentally retarded on the basis of such tests (Gearhart, 1981, p. 20). The case of Larry P. was officially upheld (1979), so that the diagnostician cannot legally use tests inappropriate because of ethnic or cultural bias for placement purposes. For other information concerning litigation procedures and the handicapped, read from Mandell and Fiscus (1981), Gearhart (1980), and Cartwright, Cartwright, and Ward (1981).

The following *portion* of a psychological evaluation is an example of final reporting that emphasizes what should be done. It omits all numerical-data explanation of the rationale behind its conclusions and recommendations. An example of how to report the recommendations is presented. It is this part of an evaluation that a parent and teacher will be more interested in reading.

PSYCHOLOGICAL EVALUATION

Name: WD   *Examined:*
Birthdate: *Examiner:*

Appearance and Behavior:

WD was a nice-looking five-and-a-half-year-old child, who appeared normal in all physiological aspects of growth and development. He was dressed in good clothes and was clean and neat.

There was no problem with separation from his mother and he appeared willing to remain in the testing room. It was, however, a demanding chore to keep him occupied with the tasks. Though he was quiet and obedient, he was distracted by the external stimuli of the room, such as the articles on the desk, the typewriter, and books stacked on the shelves. When his task was not a writing task, he often marked on any paper nearby.

By presenting a new test to him immediately after having finished one, it was possible to keep him working for one and one-half hours. After this period of time, he began to tire. The testing was completed on the second day.

In both sessions, WD spoke much too softly to be heard distinctly. There seemed to be no articulation problem, but it was necessary to have him repeat his words and sentences often.

Summary and Recommendations

WD was examined and found to be functioning between the retarded range and the low range of intellectual ability. His quotient score placed him in the retarded range, but his range of functions showed that he could not be classified as a true retardate, since he showed some capacity to function at the (low) normal level.

He was shown to have a perceptual problem, which has, no doubt, influenced his communication and motor skills to the degree that he is immature in fine-motor skills, as he is in pencil manipulation.

It is recommended that he be given the following remedial help. The asterisks at various numbers designate the activities that should be performed on a daily basis five days a week.

*1. WD should trace geometric designs such as circles, squares, crosses, and diamonds on template, if available. If not, the remediation teacher (RT) should take WD's hand and trace over the designs until WD can consistently follow the patterns with his forefinger, independent of help. (It is a good practice to have the third finger lap over the forefinger in training.)

2. WD should have a triangle pencil guard to aid his grasp. Following the tracing, the RT should hold his hand, helping him to draw these designs until he has mastered the tasks. (Diamonds are not generally mastered independently until a mental age of seven years is reached.)

3. The entire perceptual program in the Nunn-Jones book (1972), *The Learning Pyramid: Potential Through Perception*, should be gradually built into his daily training. The program is easy to follow and the equipment shown can be modified to make the training tasks available.

4. Every request made of WD should be made in short, simple statements. It should be determined that WD has understood the request by showing or repeating.

*5. WD should be provided opportunities to see and discriminate two colors at a time. Select different colors for discrimination and practice until he can call them correctly 10 days consecutively. Use a variety of colored objects, as well as colored shapes and designs.

6. WD's routine should be structured in such a way that he can learn what to count on next.

*7. Train for auditory skills by presenting opportunity to discriminate sounds of horns, whistles, barking, and other such common noises.

8. Do not begin any formal reading program until WD has mastered well the visual discrimination of large geometric designs and auditory discrimination of gross sounds (as in #7 above). His formal training should be put off for a year; then introduce some late-kindergarten and first-grade tasks such as recognition of letters, numbers, and letter sounds.

9. If WD behaves in inappropriate ways, he should not be made to feel guilty, but should understand that he cannot engage in such behavior.

Consistency and firmness are essential. Be certain before making rules that the one in authority can see that the rules are carried out. Otherwise, WD can learn that he can "get away" with his inappropriate behavior.

.   Consultant

The summary graphs, Figures 46 and 47, may be used as a supplement to the report. They provide a convenient way to report data in levels and can be checked according to the levels of function. They do not provide discrete normative data regarding

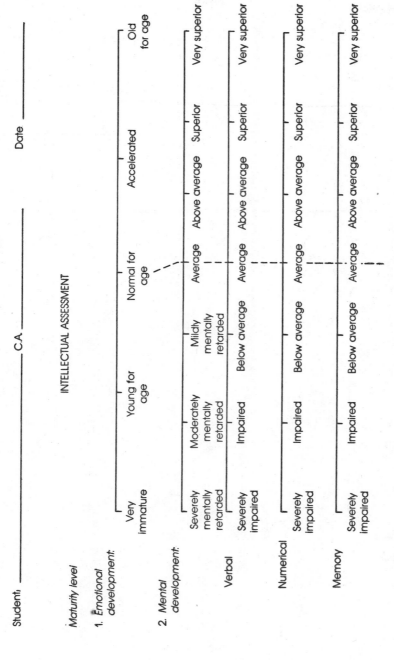

Figure 46. Summary of Evaluation*

*Adapted from Jamie Quintanilla, M.D., FAPA Former Medical Director, Killgore Childrens Psychiatric Center and Hospital, Inc., Amarillo, Texas

Figure 46 (Continued)

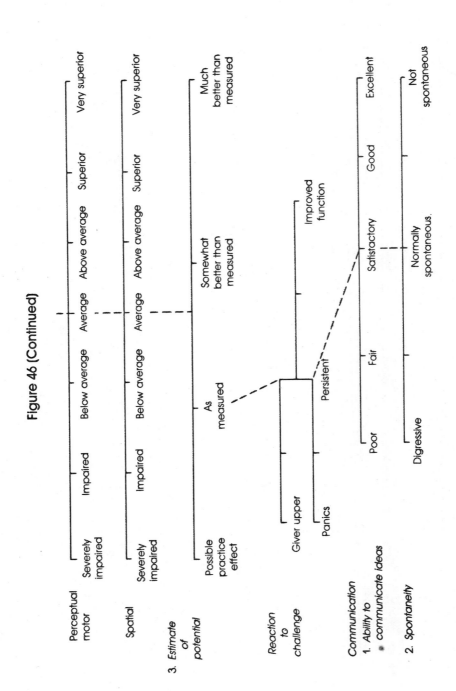

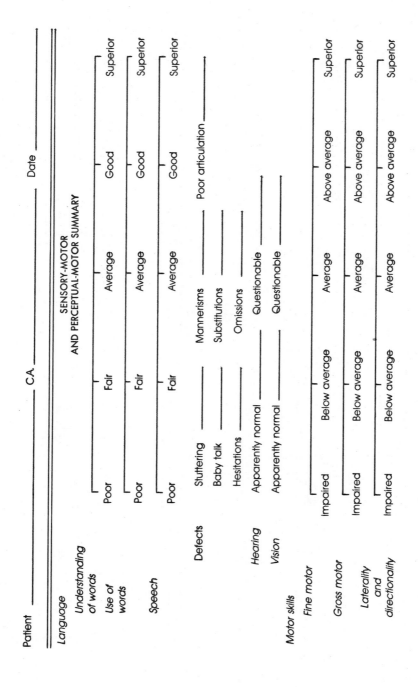

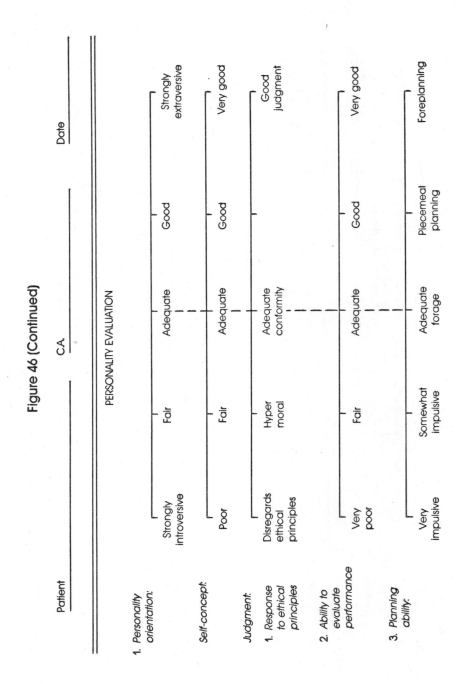

Figure 46 (Continued)

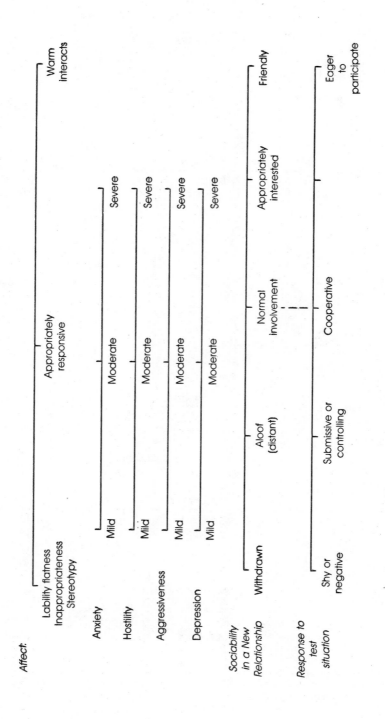

Figure 47. Behavior Summary

Activity				
Hyperactive constantly moving— movement varies with task	Fidgeting	Average	Quiet unless requested to move	Relaxed

Effort				
Refuses to make effort	Effort varies with task	Average	Applies self effectively	Works to best of ability

Cooperation				
Refuses	Reluctant	Average	Cooperates compliantly	Works with eagerness

Attention				
Very impulsive— acts without instruction	Does not attend	Average	Attends	Very alert

Concentration				
Quits task after few minutes	Easily distracted from task	Average persever- ance of task	Distracted only by extreme circum- stances	Concen- trates on one task for long time

Motor Skills				
Defective coordination	Clumsy	Average motor coor- dination	Above average control	Unusual motor coordination control

Conversational Skill				
Refuses to speak	No spontaneity— not relevant	Average skills appropriate	Talkative— relevant	Talkative— highly skilled

Self-Image				
Extremely critical of work	Satisfied with inadequate work or apologetic	Average recognition of poor work	Accepts mistakes with regret	Good self- esteem

Figure 47 (Continued)

		Comprehension		
Rarely understands instructions	Needs much elaboration	Average— may require elaboration	Above average— does not need elabo- ration	Quickly grasps problem— anticipates

achievement, but they portray graphically information concerning the severity of the functions evaluated. Since communication is absolutely necessary for a report to have value, this graphic picture can provide a helpful supplement to the formal report.

In some cases, summary graphs such as Figures 46 and 47 may be used as the final reporting instrument without a formal psychological report. If they are used in this way the clinician should add a final summary in essay form. This essay should be free of jargon and be easily understood by both teachers and parents (Erwin and Cannon, 1974).

Summary

Examination of the issues involved in reporting test data brings into focus the problem of educational jargon. A report must be understood by parents, teachers, and people in other professions. Also, the content of reports should be examined in terms of the legality of withholding or releasing test findings. Many states are explicit in their rulings regarding confidentiality and individual rights. It is clearly apparent that diagnosticians must first acquaint themselves with the laws and regulations of their state and then make their reporting plans accordingly.

Summary forms for report writing are provided to aid the reporter in designating levels of function and/or activity after making a careful analysis of the test results. In addition a design for a report format is provided.

Student Assignments

1. *Student will secure psychometric data on a child from a local diagnostician and will choose the terms that will have to be explained to a parent.*
2. *Student will research information on reporting to parents and will discuss the following problems. How would you prepare for the visits?*
   (a) Mrs. Martelli calls the school and requests the opportunity to see her son's records. She wishes to have the counselor talk with her.
   (b) Mr. and Mrs. Thompson are called to the school to be informed of the results of their daughter's school evaluation. The evaluation shows that the child is retarded. The parents are reluctant to accept the idea that she may be handicapped.
3. *Student will make up a protocol of strengths and weaknesses, using the evaluation forms from Figure 46 and Figure 47.*

REFERENCES

Bonder, J. B., & Wilson, J. A. R. *Should you be told your child's IQ?*, Washington, D.C.: NEA Publication #38–232, National Education Association.

Cannon, T. M. Change and the school psychologist. *The School Psychologist,* 1973, *XXVII,* no. 4: 10.

Cartwright, G. P., Cartwright, C. A., & Ward, M. E. *Educating special learners.* Belmont, Calif.: Wadsworth Publishing Co., 1981.

Erwin, W. M., & Cannon, T. M. Ethical consideration in the role of the school counselor. *TPGA Journal,* 1974, *3,* no. 1: 12.

Gearhart, B. R. *Special education for the '80s.* St. Louis: C. V. Mosby Co., 1980.

Huber, J. T. *Report writing in psychology and psychiatry.* New York: Harper and Row, 1961.

Hyman, I. Editorial in *The School Psychologist, XXVI,* no. 4: 1972.

Lagermann, J. D. Let's abolish I.Q. tests. *The P.T.A. Magazine,* 1966, *56,* no. 4: 7–11.

Machowsky, H. The school psychologist and the parent's right to know. *The School Psychologist,* 1973, *XXVII,* no. 4.

Mandell, C. J., & Fiscus, E. *Understanding exceptional people.* St. Paul, Minn.: West Publishing Company, 1981.

Martin, W. T. *Writing psychological reports.* Jacksonville, Ill.: Psychologist and Educators, Inc., 1971.

Murdock, J. B. Who is the client? *The School Psychologist,* 1971, *XXVI,* no. 2.

Nunn, N., & Jones, C. *The learning pyramid: Potential through perception.* Columbus, Ohio: Charles E. Merrill Publishing Company, 1972.

Robbins, M. J., & Carrigan, W. C. Professional liability and school psychology. *The School Psychologist,* 1971, *XXV,* no. 2.

Weed, L. L. *Medical records, medical education and patient care.* Cleveland: The Press of Case Western Reserve University, 1969.

Zimmerman, I. L., & Woo-Sam, J. M. *Clinical interpretation of the Wechsler adult intelligence scale.* New York: Grune and Stratton, 1973.

Appendix A

WISC-R Profile

Name _____

Age _____ Birthdate _____ School _____ Date of Test _____ Examiner _____

Raw Score Equivalents for Test Ages

Tests	Age Equivalents and Raw Scores*											Abilities Measured
	6½	7½	8½	9½	10½	11½	12½	13½	14½	15½	16½	
VERBAL												
Inform.	6	8	11	12.5	14	16	17.5	18.5	19.5	21	22.5	Information from experience and education
Simil.	7	8.5	10	11.5	13.5	15	16.5	18	19.2	20	21	Logical and abstract thinking ability
Arith.	6	8	9.5	11	12	13	13.5	14	—	15	15.5	Concentration and arithmetic reasoning
Vocab.	15–16	19–20	24	27	30–31	34	37	39.4	42	45	48	Word knowledge from experience and education
Comp.	8–9	11	13	15	17	20	22	23.5	25	26	27	Practical knowledge and social judgment
Dl. Span.	7	9	10	10.8	11.5	12	13	13.6	14.2	14.9	15.5	Attention and rote memory
PERFORMANCE												
P. Compl.	12	14	16	17	18	19	20	20.9	21.5	21.9	22.5	Visual alertness and visual memory
P. Arrang.	11–13	17	20	23	26	28	29.5	30.9	31.9	32.9	34	Interpretation of social situations
B. Design	8–9	12–13	16–17	22	26–27	31	35	38	41	43	46	Analysis in formation of abstracts
O. Assem.	12	15	17.5	19.5	21.5	22.5	22.9	24.5	25.2	26	27	Putting together of concrete forms
Code A	31–34	39–40										
Code B		32	36–37	41	46	50–51	54–55	58–59	62	66–67		Speed of learning and writing symbols
Mazes	13	16	18.5	20	21	22.3	23.3	23.9	24.4	24.9	26	Planning and following a visual pattern

*The numbers (raw scores) with decimals are approximations.

Appendix B

Wechsler Intelligence Scale for Children: Scaled Score Profile

NAME _____

I.Q. _____ VERBAL _____ PERFORMANCE _____ FULL SCALE _____

SEX _____ DATE _____

VERBAL SCALED SCORES

	0	1	2	3	4	5	6	7	8	9	10	11	12	13	14	15	16	17	18	19	20
Information General Knowledge—Long Term Memory From Experience—Education	0	1	2	3	4	5	6	7	8	9	10	11	12	13	14	15	16	17	18	19	20
Comprehension Practical Knowledge and Social Judgment—Reasoning—Logical Solutions	0	1	2	3	4	5	6	7	8	9	10	11	12	13	14	15	16	17	18	19	20
Arithmetic Concentration, Enumerating—Arithmetic Reasoning—Sequencing	0	1	2	3	4	5	6	7	8	9	10	11	12	13	14	15	16	17	18	19	20
Similarities Relationship & Abstract Thinking—Association of Abstract Ideas	0	1	2	3	4	5	6	7	8	9	10	11	12	13	14	15	16	17	18	19	20
Vocabulary Word Knowledge—Verbal Fluency—Expressive Vocabulary	0	1	2	3	4	5	6	7	8	9	10	11	12	13	14	15	16	17	18	19	20
Digit Span Attention, Concentration, Rote & Immediate Memory—Sequencing	0	1	2	3	4	5	6	7	8	9	10	11	12	13	14	15	16	17	18	19	20
Verbal I.Q.	44	50	56	62	69	75	81	87	94	100	106	113	119	123	131	138	144	150	156		

Note: Table is continued on following page.

406

PERFORMANCE SCALED SCORES

Picture Completion — Visual Memory & Alertness to Details	0 1 2 3 4 5 | 6 7 8 | 9 10 11 12 | 13 14 15 16 17 18 19 20
Picture Arrangement — Interpretation of Social Situation—Sequencing—Visual Alertness	0 1 2 3 4 5 | 6 7 8 | 9 10 11 12 | 13 14 15 16 17 18 19 20
Block Design — Reproduce Abstract Design from Pattern—Visual Perception	0 1 2 3 4 5 | 6 7 8 | 9 10 11 12 | 13 14 15 16 17 18 19 20
Object Assembly — Reproduce Familiar Forms from Memory—Visual Retention—Visual Organization	0 1 2 3 4 5 | 6 7 8 | 9. 10 11 12 | 13 14 15 16 17 18 19 20
Coding — Speed and Accuracy of Learning Meaningless Symbols—Immediate Visual Memory—Motor Control	0 1 2 3 4 5 | (6) 7 8 | 9 10 11 12 | 13 14 15 16 17 18 19 20
Mazes — Planning & Following Visual Pattern—Motor Control	0 1 2 3 4 5 | 6 7 8 | 9 10 11 12 | 13 14 15 16 17 18 19 20
Performance I.Q.	-44 51 58 65 | (72) 79 86 | 93 100 107 114 | 121 128 135 142 149 156
Full Scale I.Q.	-46 49 56 64 | 71 78 85 | 93 100 107 115 | 122 129 138 144 151 154
Percentile Rank	-1 3 8 13 | 33 50 67 81 | 92 97 99+

RETARDED   AVERAGE   SUPERIOR

407

Appendix C

Selected Behavior Traits and/or Life History Characteristics Associated with Patterns of Deviant Behaviors in Children

BEHAVIOR TRAITS

Conduct Disorder	*Personality Disorder*	*Immaturity*	*Socialized Delinquency*
Disobedience	Feelings of inferiority	Preoccupation	
Disruptiveness	Self-consciousness	Short attention span	
Fighting	Social withdrawal	Clumsiness	
Destructiveness	Shyness	Passivity	
Temper tantrums	Anxiety	Daydreaming	
Irresponsibility	Crying	Sluggishness	
Impertinence	Hypersensitivity	Drowsiness	
Jealousy	Seldom smiles	Prefering younger playmates	
Shows signs of anger	Fingernail chewing	Masturbation	
Acts bossy	Depression, chronic sadness	Giggling	

LIFE HISTORY CHARACTERISTICS

Conduct Disorder	Personality Disorder	Immaturity	Socialized Delinquency
Profanity	Object chewing		
Attention seeking	Easily flustered		
Boisterousness	Picked on by others		
	Playing with toys in class		
Assaultive	Seclusive	Habitually truant from home	Has bad companions
Defying authority	Shy	Unable to cope with a complex world	Engaging in gang activities
Inadequate guilt feelings	Sensitive	Incompetent, immature	Engaging in cooperative stealing
Irritable	Worried	Not accepted by delinquent subgroup	Habitually truant from school
Quarrelsome	Timid	Engaging in furtive stealing	Accepted by delinquent subgroups
	Has anxiety over own behavior		Staying out late at night
			Strong allegiance to selected peers

Note: This table is adapted from Herbert Quay and John Werry, *Psychopathological Disorders of Children* (New York: John Wiley & Sons, Inc., 1972). Reprinted by permission.

Appendix D

Identification of Earlier Learning Disability Categories

The earlier attempts at classification of learning disabilities show that terms have grown out of medical reports and special education. These classifications are broad in nature, each having unique characteristics. However, there are similar symptoms and characteristics found within 12 groups.

Though these broad categories offer little measurable help in determining a style of learning or a specific deficiency in learning, they do in some cases identify global classifications that can ultimately be used in securing legislative action for the provision of funds.

The purpose of adding these 12 categories is to provide the reader a brief resource to examine an important historical approach to identifying learning problems.

1. Minimal brain injury (MBI), or minimal brain dysfunction (MBD)
2. Aphasia or dysphasia
3. Dyslexia (not to be confused with alexia)
4. Perceptual impairment or perceptual-motor impairment
5. Specific language disability
6. Neurological impairment
7. Word blindness
8. Strephosymbolia
9. Hyperkinesia
10. Hypokinesia
11. Dyspraxia
12. Educational retardation

Minimal Brain Dysfunction

Minimal brain dysfunction is used to designate a condition in children in which the neurological impairment is "minimal"; behavior and learning are affected, without lowering the general intellectual capacity. This dysfunction may manifest itself in various combinations of impairment of perception, conceptualization, language, memory, and the control of attention, impulse, or motor function. This term also has been widely used as a result of the work of Alfred A. Strauss and has been adopted by several states to designate what special education facilities are needed for hyperactive children who have learning problems. In addition to Strauss's work (1955, 1947), Kephart (1960) Cruickshank (1958), Clements and Lehtinen (1964), Birch (1964), Penfield (1939) and Johnson and Myklebust (1967) have offered effective curricula for these children.

Although symptoms are present during the preschool years, the typical child does not show severe characteristics until beginning school. Here such a child first experiences the pressure of being required to perform according to specification. Hampered by deficiencies, the minimally brain-damaged child gradually falls behind because underlying problems have not been detected.

Minimally brain-damaged children may exhibit any number of the symptoms. They may find it difficult to keep up with class in reading, spelling, and arithmetic. Their penmanship may be illegible. They may have trouble grasping concrete and abstract concepts. Their performance may be erratic: high in some areas, low in others. They may appear to be in perpetual motion, spending more time under the seat than in it. They may be easily distracted, shifting their attention for no apparent reason and being able to concentrate for only short periods of time. Usually they are emotionally unstable. Moods change rapidly from one extreme to another, and any frustration or disappointment may cause tantrums, crying spells, or hostility.

Clements (1966) offers some very specific symptoms of minimal brain dysfunction:

Test-Performance Indicators

1. Spotty or patchy intellectual deficiencies; achievement low in some areas, high in others
2. Below mental-age level on drawing tests (man, house, etc.)
3. Geometric figure drawings poor for age and measured intelligence
4. Poor performance on block design and marble board tests
5. Poor showing on group tests (intelligence and achievement) and on daily classroom examinations that require reading
6. Characteristic subtest patterns on the Wechsler Intelligence Scale for Children, including "scatter" with both verbal and performance scales: high verbal—low performance; low verbal—high performance

Impairments of perception and concept formation

1. Impaired discrimination of size
2. Impaired discrimination of right-left and up-down
3. Impaired tactile discriminations
4. Poor spatial orientation
5. Impaired orientation in time
6. Distorted concept of body image
7. Impaired judgment of distance
8. Impaired discrimination of figure-ground
9. Impaired discrimination of part-whole
10. Frequent perceptual reversals in reading and in writing letters and numbers

11. Poor perceptual integration; unable to fuse sensory impressions into meaningful entities

Specific neurologic indicators

1. Few, if any, apparent gross abnormalities
2. Many "soft" equivocal or borderline findings
3. Reflex asymmetry frequent
4. Frequency of mild visual or hearing impairments
5. Strabismus
6. Nystagmus
7. High incidence of left and mixed laterality, and confused perception of laterality
8. Hyperkinesis
9. Hypokinesis
10. General awkwardness
11. Poor fine visual-motor coordination

Disorders of speech and communication

1. Impaired discrimination of auditory stimuli
2. Various categories of aphasia
3. Slow language development
4. Frequent mild hearing loss
5. Frequent mild speech irregularities

Disorders of motor function

1. Frequent athetoid, choreiform, tremulous or rigid movements of hands
2. Frequent delayed motor milestones
3. Frequent tics and grimaces
4. Hyperactivity
5. Hypoactivity

Academic achievement and adjustment (chief complaints about the child by his parents and teachers)

1. Reading disabilities
2. Arithmetic disabilities
3. Spelling disabilities
4. Poor writing, printing, or drawing ability
5. Variability in performance from day to day or even hour to hour
6. Poor ability to organize work
7. Slowness in finishing work
8. Frequent confusion about instructions, yet success with verbal tasks

Disorders of thinking processes

1. Poor ability for abstract reasoning
2. Thinking generally concrete
3. Difficulties in concept formation

4. Thinking frequently disorganized
5. Poor short-term and long-term memory
6. Thinking sometimes autistic
7. Frequent thought perseveration

Physical characteristics

1. Excessive drooling in the young child
2. Thumb-sucking, nail-biting, head-banging, and teeth-grinding in the young child
3. Food habits often peculiar
4. Slow to toilet train
5. Easy fatigability
6. High frequency of enuresis
7. Encopresis

Emotional characteristics

1. Impulsive
2. Explosive
3. Poor emotional and impulse control
4. Low tolerance for frustration
5. Reckless and uninhibited; impulsive, then remorseful

Sleep Characteristics

1. Body or head rocking before falling into sleep
2. Irregular sleep patterns in the young child
3. Excessive movement during sleep
4. Sleep abnormally light or deep
5. Resistance to naps and early bedtime, i.e., seems to require less sleep than the average child

Relationship capacities

1. Peer group relationships generally poor
2. Overexcitable in normal play with other children
3. Better adjustment when playmates are limited to one or two
4. Frequently poor judgment in social and interpersonal situations
5. Socially bold and aggressive
6. Inappropriate, unselective, and often excessive displays of affection
7. Easy acceptance of others alternating with withdrawal and shyness
8. Excessive need to touch, cling, and hold on to others

Variations of physical development

1. Frequent lags in developmental milestones; e.g., motor, language, etc.
2. Generalized maturational lag during early school years
3. Physically immature; or
4. Physical development normal or advanced for age

Characteristics of social behavior

1. Social competence frequently below average for age and measured intelligence
2. Behavior often inappropriate for situation and consequence apparently not foreseen
3. Possibly negative and aggressive to authority
4. Possibly antisocial behavior

Variations of personality

1. Overly gullible and easily led by peers and older youngsters
2. Frequent rage reactions and tantrums when crossed
3. Very sensitive to others
4. Excessive variation in mood and responsiveness from day to day and even hour to hour
5. Poor adjustment to environmental changes
6. Sweet and even-tempered, cooperative and friendly (most commonly the so-called hypokinetic child)

Disorders of attention and concentration

1. Short attention span for age
2. Overly distractible for age
3. Impaired concentration ability
4. Motor or verbal perseveration
5. Impaired ability to make decisions, particularly from many choices

Such an array of symptoms leaves little for other learning-disorder categories. Though they are symptoms that accompany the minimally brain-injured child, they cannot be confined to this singular kind of disorder. They do overlap with the symptoms in all other learning-disorder categories, and they can be found at any level of development from the severely retarded to the intellectually superior.

It is with this last point that some authorities disagree in regard to learning disorders. The brain-damaged syndrome, which was really the prototype for the learning-disorder syndrome, is now considered to be at the normal intelligence level. However, the consultant must understand the wide fluctuation of abilities typical of the MBI child, even though their condition seems to limit them to the average range of intellectual ability. The IQ of the MBI can show: (1) a retarded level of mental development, (2) a normal level of mental development, (3) a superior level of mental development, (4) a high performance intelligence over verbal intelligence, and (5) a high verbal intelligence over performance intelligence. In addition, there is likely to be a wide scattering of abilities that fall erratically into all levels of development. Furthermore, the problem can easily be compounded by an emotional disturbance that may cause the MBI syndrome to overlap into another category. Figure A-1 shows the involvement that can be expected of the minimally brain-injured child.

Aphasia

Aphasia refers to a condition in which a child fails to acquire meaningful spoken language by the age of 3 or 3½ years. This inability to speak cannot be explained by deafness, mental retardation, speech-organ defects, or environmental factors. Inconsis-

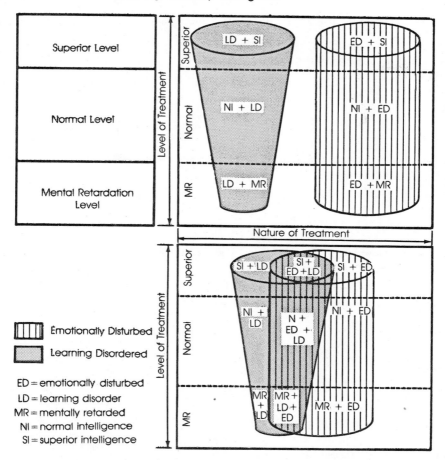

Figure A-1. Intellectual Level and Problem Areas of the MBI

tent audiograms and observations that the child sometimes hears more than others or that he ignores very loud sounds are all suggestive of aphasia. (The consultant or school psychologist probably will not be confronted with severe cases, and the cases mild enough for public-school placement are likely to be placed in rooms for the minimally brain injured.)

Aphasia exists in many forms, with symptoms as multiple as the many kinds of atypical behavior it affects. A short, representative list of symptoms for three of the major categories of this condition follows:

Receptive aphasia

1. Cannot identify what is heard
2. Cannot carry out directions
3. Poor vocabulary
4. Does not understand what is happening in pictures
5. Does not understand what is read

Expressive aphasia

1. Seldom talks in class
2. Has trouble imitating children
3. May talk but not express coherent ideas
4. Seldom uses gestures
5. Drawing and writing are poor

Inner aphasia

1. Does not make associations; therefore, abstract reasoning is difficult
2. Will respond inappropriately when called upon
3. Slow to respond

Dyslexia

Dyslexia, a reading disability, is another type of learning disorder. The term has been used in the field of medicine for about eight decades, but because of the lack of understanding and the lack of academic pressure on the masses of children, it was not generally accepted by educators until recently. It is now becoming more widely used to identify children with normal intelligence who are having difficulty competing with other students in the public schools.

Dyslexia, as compared with other reading difficulties, concerns primarily word perception. *Dorland's Medical Dictionary* (1965) defines it as: (1) an inability to read understandingly due to a central lesion, and (2) a condition in which reading is possible but is attended with fatigue and disagreeable sensations. Some authorities refer to *specific dyslexia*, while others refer to *developmental dyslexia*. The former makes reference to some organic pathology; the latter refers to the possibility of a lag in growth and development. Most authorities use the term *specific dyslexia* to mean a specific reading disability in children who have some neurological involvement. McGlannan differentiates *genetic dyslexia* from other types and defines it as ". . . one demonstrable effect of a basic genetic anomaly manifested essentially by inconstancy of spatial and temporal relations. This inconsistency results in inadequate association and integration of symbols with attendant language disabilities. Concurrent and customary presenting symptoms are ambilaterality, directional confusion, and maturational lags" (McGlannan, 1968, p. 185).

Although authorities suggest that the physical factor has some connection with dyslexia, they propose different factors for the origin of the disorder. In spite of this disagreement, all of them concur that dyslexia is nothing more than a specific reading problem. Therefore, it describes only one part of the comprehensive field of learning disorders.

Symptoms

1. Impairment in right-left orientation
2. Tendency to read words backwards, such as "was" for "saw"
3. Lack of finger dexterity
4. Difficulty with mental arithmetic, *dyscalculia*, sometimes known to accompany dyslexia

5. Memory (immediate recall) may be impaired
6. Auditory difficulties may occur—may not be able to sound back words and sounds that are heard
7. Visual memory—may not be able to revisualize objects, words, or letters
8. In reading aloud, the child may not be able to convert visual symbols into their auditory equivalents to pronounce words correctly

Perceptual Impairment or Perceptual-Motor Impairment

The terms *perceptual impairment* and *perceptual-motor impairment,* which are particularly emphasized by Kephart, Barsch, Money, and Cratty to describe learning disabilities, are really not one and the same, yet they do identify similar problems. The consultant should be aware that perception can be identified without the motor counterpart. Perception per se assumes discrimination, or the function of distinguishing between sensory stimuli. These stimuli, in turn, must be organized into a meaningful pattern. The child discriminates and interprets an object as a whole. But when perceptual-motor impairment occurs, the integration between perception and the motor-movement patterns is disrupted. The child who does not perceive adequately cannot translate through the motor pathway. Conversely, the child who has an initial lack of motor control cannot adequately perceive. It follows, therefore, that the perceptual-motor match is not completed, and for that reason the child is not able to see or to hear normally. Obviously, a child with this problem would have difficulty in understanding and expressing ideas. Studies on the growth and development of the child (Sherrington, 1951; Gesell, 1940; and Piaget, 1967) give the motor data priority, since motor-movement patterns precede awareness. This sequence of motor movement before perception describes the problems underlying learning disabilities and suggests operative methods of remediation that can be used by both the parent and the teacher.

Symptoms

1. Poor visual-motor coordination
2. Poor body balance while walking forward, backward, or sidewise
3. Lack of skill in jumping and skipping
4. Difficulty in perceiving self in time and space
    (a) Will not be able to tell time at the appropriate growth period (Chancey and Kephart, 1968; Bateman, 1968)
    (b) Will not know readily the parts of the body
    (c) Will be clumsy in relation to other children
    (d) Will not readily respond to directions of right and left—a laterality problem
5. Difficulty in making normal rhythmical movements in writing and may tend to increase or decrease the size, shape, color, or brightness
6. An uneven or jerky ocular movement
7. Trouble with object constancy—with size, shape, color, or brightness
    (a) Letters may become reversed—a *d* becomes a *b,* for example
    (b) Difficulty in establishing consistent responses; that is, may know how to spell or read a word on one day but not on the next

Specific Language Disability

Specific language disability is commonly used by speech- and language-disorder specialists in the United States. In particular, it can be seen in the writing of Myklebust. In addition, Johnson (1967), Kirk (1962), McCarthy, J. J. and Kirk (1968), and Jeanne McCarthy (1967), authors from various fields of special education, use this term to designate learning disorders.

In order to speak intelligently of specific language disabilities, one must first consider the specifics of language development. Johnson and Myklebust (1967) indicate three kinds of language—inner, receptive, and expressive. McCarthy and Kirk (1968) use psycholinguistic terms to describe language behavior that is either representational or automatic-sequential. Strauss and Kephart (1955) follow the development of the child from a perceptually undifferentiated world to a world in which form and shape are discernible and the foundations for speech, motor skills, and cognitive functions are established.

Many neo-Myklebust students group all learning disorders under the term *language disability.* Although this is a good generic term, some differentiation may be necessary in order to see it in relation to perceptual disability and perceptual-motor disability. Perception, although related to the way one interprets through the senses, covers neither conceptual thinking nor expressive language in its more specific meaning. Neither does it include automatic-sequential response. Language, on the other hand, includes all three of them; yet, because of them it is still dependent upon perception. Although the term *language disability* identifies a broad spectrum of learning methods, it does not involve motor patterns which, in addition to perception, are a significant aspect of learning. The relationship of motor, language, and perception activities to one another can be recognized from birth and has been explained by Piaget (1967), Sherrington (1951), Kephart (1960), and others. It appears, then, that the integration of the term *language disability* with the term *perceptual-motor disability* offers a complete approach to the malfunctioning learning process. The Roach-Kephart Theoretical Constructs, reproduced in Figure A-2, show how these two are related (Roach, 1966, p. 3).

Of all 12 categories discussed in this book, language disability and perceptual-motor disability are the two that should be most carefully considered in every case study. Even though any of the other ten categories may identify some portion of the problem, they offer little or no remedial planning. To diagnose a problem is not sufficient. One must also determine its source in order to plan remediation through the correct channels of learning. If, however, we choose to use perceptual-motor disability and/or language disability as a frame of reference, we have by our approach already established a direction for remediation. In other words, the choice of tests for diagnosis determined by the frame of reference can subsequently aid in identifying the weakness.

Symptoms

1. Child may be slow to express himself and may stumble over words in doing so
2. May be a very talkative youngster, yet find it difficult to express ideas about an object or situation
3. May score below 10 on some WISC verbal subtests, and yet function normally on others

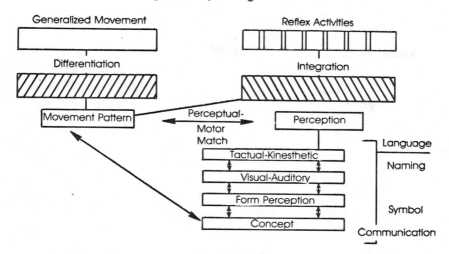

Figure A-2. The Roach-Kephart Theoretical Constructs

4. Instead of saying, "Both of these pianos play," child may say, "These pianos play both"
5. Will often have difficulty in acquiring meaning and, therefore, may not follow directions adequately
6. May find it difficult to relate experiences in normal sequence of verbal expression
7. May have difficulty in telling time or in determining direction
8. May read well but not grasp meaning
9. May have difficulty in comprehending the spoken word
10. May also have a visual problem with the written word
11. Will likely have difficulty remembering words, spelling, and discriminating words that sound or look similar

Neurological Impairment

One of the most general of all these terms is *neurological impairment,* and among those who have approached learning disorders from this view are Denhoff (1968), Birch (1964), and Boshes and Myklebust (1964). Though the term *neurological dysfunction* has had fairly widespread use in the United States, its generic aspects include a myriad of characteristics that do not necessarily apply to the child with learning disabilities. By definition, neurological impairment is any malfunction that affects the nervous system in any way. It includes orthopedic impairment, cerebral palsy, and certain types of mental retardation, although the former two may or may not accompany a learning problem. The consultant has to be certain that when this kind of disorder is under consideration, the doctor or the educator identifies it specifically as neurological impairment, and not as minimal brain injury or perceptual-motor impairment.

The fields of medicine, neurology, pediatric neurology, neuropsychology, neuropsychiatry, and encephalography supply a great deal of information on this kind of malfunction. The Doman-Delacato team (1965) in Philadelphia has given special emphasis to this disorder; however, professionals in medicine, psychology, and education are not all in agreement with their theory.

Word Blindness

Word blindness has so often been used synonymously with *dyslexia* that it needs very little additional explanation. Kussmaul, one of the great figures in German medicine, introduced the terms *word-blindness* and *word-deafness* in 1877 as distinct from *aphasia.*

> In medical literature we find cases recorded as aphasia which should not properly be designated by this name, since the patients were still able to express their thoughts by speech and writing. They had not lost the power either of speaking or of writing; they were no longer able, however, although the hearing was perfect, to understand the words which they heard, or, although the sight was perfect, to read the written words which they saw. The morbid inability we will style, in order to have the shortest possible names at our disposition word-deafness and word-blindness (caecita et surditas verbalis). Kussmaul, 1877, p. 770)

Although the consultant will not find many sources who use the term *word blindness,* Bannatyne (1968) and Critchley (1964) are two prominent authorities who do include it in their writings.

Symptoms

The consultant should refer to the symptoms listed under dyslexia, for it is difficult to differentiate between those of dyslexia and those of word blindness.

Strephosymbolia

In 1925, Dr. Samuel Orton from Iowa introduced the term *strephosymbolia,* which means "twisted symbols." The disorder is one of perception, in which objects may appear reversed, as in a mirror. It is a reading difficulty inconsistent, however, with a child's general intelligence. Although Dr. Orton related this problem to laterality and to possible genetic factors, Victor Rosen (1955) wrote a paper that identified the term with psychological factors. For purposes of identifying and labeling this disorder, the consultant should restrict the definition to Orton's original concept.

Symptoms

1. Confusion between similar but oppositely oriental letters (*b—d, q—p*)
2. A tendency to reverse direction in reading

Hyperkinesia

Specifically, *hyperkinesia* means an abnormally increased mobility, motor function, or activity. It is related somewhat to Denhoff's concept of the Hyperkinetic Impulse Syndrome and has been discussed by Strauss in relation to the Strauss Syndrome. The hyperkinetic child usually finds it difficult to remain in one position at a desk for more than a few minutes. Learning problems often accompany this disorder; however, studies show that children without learning problems move around about the same amount of time. The time of day and the conditions under which the child is hyperactive can determine whether or not the child is suffering from hyperkinesia. If the increased activity occurs at inappropriate times and if there is a learning disorder, the child is probably hyperkinetic, implying normal intelligence hindered by some specific learning disability.

Symptoms

1. Short attention span for age
2. Wants to move from one activity to another without due preparation time
3. Often leaves seat without permission
4. Butts into conversations and activities without being asked

The language symptoms and the perceptual-motor symptoms of a child with minimal brain injury may also be present in the hyperkinetic child.

Hypokinesia

Hypokinesia means abnormally decreased mobility, motor function, or activity. Often the hypokinetic child is mistakenly called lazy or uninterested because of lack of participation and inability to finish work.

The terms *hyperkinetic* and *hypokinetic* are not comprehensive enough to describe the child with a learning disability. Rather, they describe characteristics that merely accompany, or in some instances cause, a learning problem. Therefore, the consultant should use them only for distinguishing behavior patterns, and not for identifying a type of learning disorder. For example, "This child exhibits the traits of a specific language disability with hypokinetic or hyperkinetic tendencies."

Symptoms

1. Child may work diligently, but never seems to be able to complete the work
2. Child may stop and dawdle, lose interest—this may be accompanied by other problems, such as distractibility
3. Low scores may occur on tests requiring motor output
4. May be a slow reader and sometimes a poor articulator

Dyspraxia

The partial loss of ability to perform coordinated movements is known as *dyspraxia*. This loss of movement, as it relates to the learning problem, is particularly evident in the child's inability to write properly. This form of dyspraxia is known as *dysgraphia*. The prefix *dys*, meaning difficult, implies difficulty in movement (dyspraxia), difficulty in writing (dysgraphia), and difficulty in reading (dyslexia). Johnson and Myklebust (1967) and Strong (1965) are among the writers who use the terms *dyspraxia* and *dysgraphia* in regard to children with learning disorders. *Apraxia, agraphia,* and *alexia* are also used in such literature. However, since those terms prefixed by *a* are more specifically identified with cortical lesions, and since they connote an absence or an inability, educators should always use the terms prefixed by *dys*, in order to avoid implications of medical diagnosis.

Symptoms

1. Child has poor eye-hand coordination
2. Has difficulty in carrying out purposeful movements
3. Unable to make proper use of objects
4. May also have difficulty expressing a definite idea because of a rush of other ideas into the consciousness

Educational Retardation

The term *educational retardation* has been used throughout the United States in the past to distinguish those children who have been held back, culturally deprived, or retarded because of unchallenging educational experiences from those who suffer from irremedial retardation. Today, although it still encompasses problems of lack of opportunity, educational retardation covers a wide range of disabilities. It has been used synonymously most often with cultural deprivation. However, the two terms are not identical, even though they overlap in meaning. Educational retardation specifically identifies a state of underachievement caused by *lack of or inadequate* opportunity; whereas cultural deprivation specifically identifies a culturally induced condition of any recognized deficiency, whether educational, physiological, or psychological. These deficiencies can be found at any socioeconomic level.

A glimpse into the complexity of this problem shows that educationally retarded children may be deprived because they lack: (1) gross-motor development, (2) language development, (3) psychoneurological efficiency, (4) a variety of environmental experiences, (5) good teaching practices, (6) individual attention, or (7) emotional support for the sake of security and confidence in learning. Figure A-3 reveals why the terms *educational retardation* and *cultural deprivation* need to be clearly defined.

It should be emphasized that a child may be deprived in any of the above areas and still not have a learning disorder. A child may even be educationally retarded, in terms of underachieving in reading, spelling, writing, or some other academic area, yet still not have a learning disorder. At this point, one can see the difference between a learning disorder and cultural deprivation or educational retardation; yet many culturally deprived children have learning disorders (Denhoff, 1968). The consultant should know that if a student is underachieving because of lack of educational stimulation, and not because of lack of gross motor and neurological development, the child will probably respond very readily to a program of training. If, on the other hand, the child has a lack of gross-motor and neurological development in addition to the lack of educational stimulation, there is, in all probability, a learning disorder that requires an individually structured program. In this case, remediation would be somewhat less effective. The consultant who can detect the subtle differences between these deficiencies will then be in a position to evaluate the child's need and to advise the teacher on the amount and kinds of demands made on the child.

Symptoms

Educationally retarded children may exhibit some of the same kinds of problems as those of children with physical learning disabilities. For example, they may have failed to develop the technique of moving from left to right when reading, or they may show

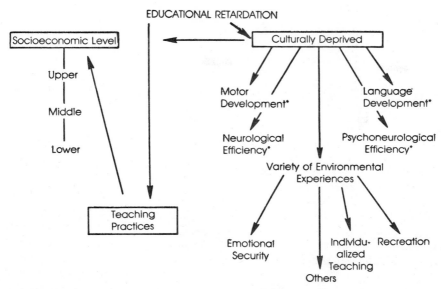

Figure A-3. Distinctions Between Educational Retardation and Cultural Deprivation

*May result in learning disorders

some signs of immaturity in reversals of letters and numbers. When educational retardation is caused by lack of opportunity and is not compounded by other learning disorders, remediation can generally be achieved rather quickly.

Summary

Brief coverage of the 12 most common terms used to describe learning disorders indicates the complexity of this broad area. The consultant should be willing to accept terms convenient and useful to those in other fields, such as education, law, medicine, and communication media. It is imperative, however, that consultants learn the specific semantics intended, so that any consultation will result in meaningful communication.

Little can be gained by insisting on the use of terminology with restricted meaning. Who can say what is the most descriptive term when the causes for poor academic work are myriad and the manifestations are erratic, alike, and different, all within the same classification?

REFERENCES

Barsch, R. H. *Achieving perceptual motor efficiency.* Seattle, Wash.: Special Child Publications, 1967.

Birch, H. G. *Brain damage in children: the biological and social aspects.* Williams and
Wilkins, 1964.

Boshes, B., & Myklebust, H. R. A neurological and behavioral study of children with
learning disorders. *Neurology,* 1964, *14,* no. 1: 7–12.

Clements, S. D. *Minimal brain dysfunction in children.* Washington, D.C.: U.S. Department of Health, Education and Welfare, 1966.

Clements, S. D., Lehtinen, L. E., & Lukens, J. E. *Children with minimal brain injury.*
Chicago: National Society for Crippled Children and Adults, 1964.

Cruickshank, W. M., & Johnson, G. O. (Eds.). *Education of exceptional children and
youth.* Englewood Cliffs, N.J.: Prentice-Hall, 1958.

Delacato, C. H. *The diagnosis and treatment of speech and reading disorders.* Springfield, Ill.: Charles C Thomas, 1965.

Denhoff, E. The measurement of psychoneurological factors contributing to learning
efficiency. *Journal of Learning Disabilities,* 1968, *1,* no. 11: 635–644.

Dorland's medical dictionary, 24th ed. Philadelphia: W. B. Saunders Co., 1965.

Gesell, A. *The first five years of life.* New York: Harper and Bros., 1940

Johnson, D. J., & Myklebust, H. R. *Learning disabilities: educational principles and
practices.* New York: Grune and Stratton, 1967.

Kephart, N. C. *The slow learner in the classroom.* Columbus, Ohio: Charles E. Merrill
Publishing Company, 1960, 2d edition, 1971.

Kirk, S. A. *Educating exceptional children.* Boston: Houghton Mifflin, 1962; 2nd edition, 1972.

Kussmaul, A. Disturbances of speech. In von Ziemssen, H. (Ed.), *Cyclopaedia of the
practice of medicine,* vol. 15. New York: William Wood, 1877.

McCarthy, J. J., & Kirk, S. *The Illinois test of psycholinguistic abilities,* rev. ed. Urbana,
Ill.: University of Illinois Press, 1968.

McCarthy, J. M. How to teach the hard to reach. *Grade Teacher,* May–June 1967:
97–101.

Orton, S. T. Word blindness in school children. *Archives of Neurology and Psychiatry,*
1925, *14:* 581–615.

Penfield, W. *Speech and brain mechanisms.* Princeton, N.J.: Princeton University Press,
1959.

Piaget, J., & Inhelder, B. *The child's conception of space.* New York: W. W. Norton and
Co., 1967.

Roach, E. C., & Kephart, N. C. *The Purdue perceptual-motor survey.* Columbus, Ohio:
Charles E. Merrill Publishing Company, 1966.

Sherrington, C. *Man on his nature.* Cambridge, England: Cambridge University Press,
1951.

Strauss, A. A., & Kephart, N. C. *Psychopathology and education of the brain-injured child,* vol. 2. New York: Grune and Stratton, 1955.

Straus, A. A., & Lehtinen, L. E. *Psychopathology and education of the brain-injured child,* vol. 1. New York: Grune and Stratton, 1947.

Strong, R. Identification of primary school age children with learning handicaps associated with minimal brain disorder. University of Utah, 1965 (doctoral dissertation).

Glossary I.

Definitions of Categories in the Structure of Intellect*

Operations

Major kinds of intellectual activities or processes; things that the organism does with the raw materials of information, information being defined as "that which the organism discriminates"

C *Cognition:* immediate discovery, awareness, rediscovery, or recognition of information in various forms; comprehension or understanding

M *Memory:* retention or storage, with some degree of availability, of information in the same form it was committed to storage and in response to the same cues in connection with which it was learned

D *Divergent Production:* generation of information from given information, where the emphasis is on variety and quantity of output from the same source; likely to involve what has been called *transfer;* this operation is most clearly involved in aptitudes of creative potential.

N *coNvergent Production:* generation of information from given information, where the emphasis is on achieving unique or conventionally accepted best outcomes. It is likely the given (cue) information fully determines the response

E *Evaluation:* reaching decisions or making judgments concerning criterion satisfaction (correctness, suitability, adequacy, desirability, etc.) of information

Contents

Broad classes or types of information discriminable by the organism.

F *Figural:* information in concrete form, as perceived or as recalled possibly in the form of images, the term *figural* minimally implies figure-ground perceptual organization, visual spatial information is figural. Different sense modalities may be involved; e.g., visual kinesthetic.

---

*From Mary Meeker, *The Structure of Intellect* (Columbus: Charles E. Merrill Publishing Co., 1969), 195–96.

426

S *Symbolic:* information in the form of denotative signs, having no significance in and of themselves, such as letters, numbers, musical notations, codes, and words, when meanings and form are not considered

M *seMantic:* information in the form of meanings to which words commonly become attached, hence, most notable in verbal communication but not identical with words; meaningful pictures also often convey semantic information.

B *Behavioral:* information, essentially nonverbal, involved in human interactions where the attitudes, needs, desires, moods, intentions, perceptions, thoughts, etc., of other people and of ourselves are involved

Products

The organization that information takes in the organism's processing of it

U *Units:* relatively segregated or circumscribed items of information having "thing" character; may be close to Gestalt psychology's "figure on a ground"

C *Classes:* conceptions underlying sets of items of information grouped by virtue of their common properties

R *Relations:* connections between items of information based on variables or points of contact that apply to them; relational connections are more meaningful and definable than implications.

S *Systems:* organized or structured aggregates of items of information; complexes of interrelated or interacting parts

T *Transformations:* changes of various kinds (redefinition, shifts, or modification) of existing information or in its function

I *Implications:* extrapolations of information, in the form of expectancies, predictions, known or suspected antecedents, concomitants, or consequences, the connection between the given information and that extrapolated is more general and less definable than a relational connection.

Glossary II.*

General

Acalculia—the loss of ability to perform mathematical functions.

Accommodation—the ocular-focusing adjustment for clear vision at varying distances.

Agnosia—the inability to identify familiar objects through a particular sense organ.

Agraphia—the inability to recall kinesthetic writing patterns; i.e., cannot relate the mental images of words to the motor movements necessary for writing them.

Alexia—the loss of ability to receive, associate, and understand visual language symbols as referents to real objects and experiences; a severe reading disability is usually considered the byproduct of brain dysfunction; not to be used synonymously with dyslexia, which may have multiple causes.

Aphasia—the loss of ability to comprehend, manipulate, or express words in speech, writing, or gesture; usually associated with injury or disease in brain centers that control these processes.

   Auditory aphasia—inability to comprehend spoken words; the same as word deafness and receptive aphasia.

   Expressive aphasia—inability to remember the pattern of movements required to speak, even though one knows what he wants to say.

Apraxia—the loss of ability to perform purposeful motor patterns.

Astigmatism—a condition of unequal curvatures along the various meridians in one or more of the refractive surfaces (cornea, anterior or posterior surface of the lens) of the eye, in consequence of which the rays from a luminous point are not focused at a single point on the retina but are diffused or spread out.

Auding—listening, recognizing, and interpreting spoken language; more than just hearing and responding to sounds.

Auditory association (auditory-vocal association, ITPA)—the ability to relate spoken words in a meaningful way; the ITPA uses a version of the familiar analogies tests to

---

*Some terms are not explained beyond one single-concept definition. These appear to be the ones accepted and understood as having a common meaning. Other terms are elaborated upon in the hope that the coverage will more fully explain the many ideas associated with the term or concept.

assess this ability. The subject must complete the test statement by supplying an analogous word. Example: Soup is hot; ice cream is _____ .

Auditory closure—the act or ability to conceptualize accurately in a complete and meaningful form words and/or sounds that are perceived in incomplete form.

Auditory discrimination—the ability to identify and accurately choose between sounds of different pitch, volume, and pattern; includes the ability to distinguish one speech sound from another.

Auditory imperception—failure to understand oral communication and the significance of familiar sounds.

Auditory memory (auditory-vocal sequencing, ITPA)—the ability to repeat a sequence of symbols correctly; to test this, immediate auditory recall is requested. The ITPA subtest resembles the standard digit-repetition test except that (1) digits are uttered at a rate of two per second, which is double the usual rate; (2) the examiner drops his voice at the end of the digit sequence; (3) sequences are repeated if the subject fails to repeat the original presentation correctly; and (4) some digit sequences contain the same digit twice.

Auditory perception—the ability to receive and understand sounds.

Auditory reception (auditory decoding, ITPA)—the ability to understand the spoken word; the ITPA subtest used to measure this function includes questions that require only "yes" and "no" responses, in order to eliminate the necessity of a child's explaining what is understood. Example: Do females slumber?

Bilateral—pertaining to the use of both sides of the body in a simultaneous and parallel fashion.

Binocular fusion—the ability to integrate simultaneously into a single percept the data received through both eyes when they are aimed at the same position in space.

Body image—awareness of one's own body (including the precise location of its parts in time and space); it includes the impressions one receives from internal signals, as well as feedback received from others.

Brain damage—any structural injury or insult to the brain, whether by surgery, accident, or disease.

Closure—the process of achieving completion in behavior or mental act; the tendency to stabilize or to complete a situation; closure may occur in any sensory modality.

Cognitive structure—the mental process by which an individual becomes aware of and maintains contact with his internal and external environments.

It includes the processes of discrimination, association, integration, and categorization. Since language involves a proper selection of meaningful symbols, it is representative of the processes and levels of cognition. The linguistic symbol becomes a meaningful answer when the person is able to use a word or words to name, associate, or identify specific entities of a category.

It includes such things as selectivity of attention, the deployment of attention, the categorizing of behavior, memory formation, and attitudes toward confirmable versus unconfirmable experiences.

If we locate a candy store from one starting point, we can find it from another because we "know" where it is. A smooth-running skill illustrates a learned habit; knowing alternate routes illustrates cognitive structure. It has the dimension of clarity, and its synonyms are insight and understanding.

Cognitive style—a person's characteristic approach to problem solving and cognitive tasks; for example, some persons tend to be analytical, seeing parts, while others tend to be wholistic, seeing things in their entirety with little awareness of components.

Compulsiveness—insistence on performing or doing things in habitual ways.

Concretism—an approach to thinking and behavior in which a person tends to regard each situation as essentially new and unique. Such a person fails to see essential similarities between situations that others accept as similar or even identical.

Constancy phenomenon—the tendency for brightness, color, size, or shape to remain relatively constant despite marked changes in stimulation; a phenomenon in which the color of an ordinary object is relatively independent of changes in illumination or in other viewing conditions.

Convergence—the ocular pointing mechanism by which the eyes are "aimed" at a target; it enables one to see a single object at varying distances.

Crossing the midline—the movement of the eyes, a hand and forearm, or a foot and leg across the midsection of the body without involving any other part of the body; i.e., without turning the head, twisting or swaying the trunk, or innervating the opposite limb.

Depth perception—that aspect of visual perception that deals with the direct awareness of the distance between an object and its observer; the awareness of distance between the front and the back of an object, so that it is seen as three-dimensional; the ability to perceive the third dimension in a flat picture that is actually two-dimensional.

Differentiation—the ability to sort out and use independent parts of the body in a specific and controlled manner; example, the ability to innervate the muscles of one arm without innervating in a similar fashion the muscles of the other arm or any of the parts of the body not required by the task

Directionality—the projecting of all directions from the body into space; the child must develop laterality within his own organism and be aware of the right and left sides of his own body before he is ready to or able to project these directional concepts into external space.

Discrimination—the process of detecting differences as (1) auditory discrimination, or the ability to identify sounds with respect to likenesses and differences and (2) visual discrimination, or the ability to discriminate between different objects, forms, and/or letter symbols.

The ability to differentiate or distinguish quality, intensity, frequency, judgments, abilities, and other characteristics: these differences may be between numbers, letters, sounds of letters, persons, objects, etc. It may refer to one's ability to differentiate essential from nonessential details. The ability to discriminate depends in large measure upon one's relative familiarity with the object.

Discrimination learning—the process by which stimuli come to acquire selective control over behavior; *discrimination* is the term used to describe the control so achieved. An organism can discriminate between two stimuli if induced, under suitable circumstances, to respond differently in the presence of the two stimuli and to do so reliably.

Dissociation—the inability to see things as a whole or as a Gestalt; there is a tendency to respond to a stimulus in terms of parts or segments and difficulty combining the parts to form a whole.

Distractibility—the ready and rapid shifting of attention through a series of unimportant stimuli; a morbid or abnormal variation of attention; inability to fix attention on any subject; a symptom of mental functioning of a person with brain damage.

Distraction may be caused by anxiety invading the thinking process. The tendency for a person's attention to be easily drawn to extraneous stimuli or to focus on minor details, with a lack of attention to major aspects.

Similar to short attention span; however, the latter more appropriately suggests an inability to concentrate on one thing for very long, even without distractions. The term is often used to replace *hyperactivity* in psychological literature. The child is constantly distracted from one situation to another by stimuli that may involve any sense and can be either external or internal to a child.

Dysgraphia—the inability to write or to copy letters, words, and numbers; the child can see accurately what to write but cannot manage correct writing movements; usually associated with brain dysfunction.

Dyskinesia—partial impairment of voluntary-movement abilities resulting in incomplete movements, poor coordination, and apparently clumsy behavior.

Dyslexia—partial inability to read or to understand what one reads either silently or aloud; condition is usually, but not always, associated with brain impairment.

Visual dyslexias rarely learn from a global word approach, but they can learn individual sounds and put them together into words. Auditory dyslexias can learn words as a whole but do not learn through phonics.

Dysnomia—the inability to recall a word at will, even though one knows the word and recognizes it when said to him.

Elaboration—embellishment by the addition of variations of associated ideas or movements.

Emotional lability—the tendency toward recurrent emotional behavior characterized by sudden unexplainable shifts from one emotion to another.

Experimentation—the ability, desire, and willingness of a child to test a newly learned movement, task, or idea to see how many different ways it can be used by itself or in correlation with other movements, tasks, or ideas; elaboration is the result of experimentation.

Eye-hand coordination—the ability to organize perceptually, by joining together in the mind's eye, and to reproduce manually; poor development of motor skills and left-right confusion could be a result of poor eye-hand coordination.

Eye-hand coordination skill—this skill consists of the eyes' steering the hand(s) accurately and skillfully through the three coordinates of space—right and left, up and down, fore and aft—which are matched with the coordinates of the body and vision, for the purpose of manipulating tools or forming the symbols of language. It enables one to make visual discriminations of size, shape, texture, and object location. It is dependent upon use, practice, and integration of the eyes and hands as paired learning tools.

Eye-movement skill (ocular motilities)—This skill consists of the ability to align both eyes on an object quickly and accurately, to release and move in a controlled manner to another object, or to maintain alignment on a moving object. This skill provides a consistent visual input to be matched to other sensory inputs and the experiences of the organism.

Inadequate ability in eye-movement skills is revealed in head turning instead of eye movement, short attention span, frequent loss of place on the page, omission of words and phrases, confusion of left and right directions, poor orientation, writing or drawings on the page, or stumbling and clumsiness in playground activities.

Eye teaming (binocularity)—The purpose of this skill is to provide speed and effectiveness in visual identification and interpretation of printed details. The accuracy and speed of "focusing" is dependent upon the degree of eye teaming achieved.

There are two aspects to be observed by the teacher: (1) horizontal teaming—alignment of both eyes so that they are in position to inspect the same symbol at the same instant (to provide singleness and clearness of all materials), and (2) near-to-far, far-to-near teaming—immediate clarity and accuracy of recognition of objects or symbols at all points in space.

Indications of inadequate abilities in eye teaming are complaints of seeing double; repetition of letters within words or words in the same sentence; omission of words or numbers; closing of one eye; extreme head tilt or working on one side of desk; poor orientation of writing or drawing on paper; total postural deviation that continues at all desk activities; excessive blinking; comprehension lower than apparent abilities; or extreme fatigue when working with any visual materials.

Figure-ground relationship—"Geometrical patterns are always seen against a background and thus appear object-like, with contours and boundaries. We may think of such figure-ground organization as basic to stimulus patterning. Patterns do not have to contain identifiable objects to be structured as figure and ground. Patterns of black and white and many wallpaper designs are perceived as figure-ground relationships and very often figure and ground are reversible" (Hilgard, 1962, p. 193). The part seen as *figure* tends to appear slightly in front of the background, even though you know it is printed on the surface of the page. You seem to look through the spaces in and around the figure to a uniform background behind, whether the background is white or black.

"Gestalt psychologists have been particularly interested in figure-ground relationships and other patterned aspects of stimulation and have suggested a number of principles" to explain the results of patterning and perceptual structuring (Hilgard, 1962, p. 194). There are four principles: (1) proximity; (2) similarity; (3) continuity; and (4) closure.

Proximity. Look at the dots in Figure A-4. They appear to be arranged in horizontal rows in A and in vertical columns in B. Why? Merely because in A they are closer together in rows, and in B they are closer together in columns. It takes effort to counteract proximity to see the dots in columns and rows in the other directions.

Similarity. In Figure A-5 all the dots are equally spaced, so that proximity is not an important factor in determining whether we emphasize horizontal or vertical lines. Now, the influence of similarity is compelling. We see rows of dots and rows of small circles, so we group like items together.

Continuity. In Figure A-6 what does A appear to be? It is easy to break it down into the two parts shown in B—a wavy line over a rectangular motif. Again if we expend some effort, we can break it into the two parts shown in C. But there is little doubt about the greater naturalness of B because the parts are more continuous this way. The wavy line continues as a wavy line and the right-angled figures continue at right angles.

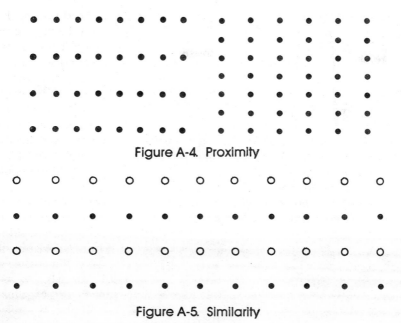

Figure A-4. Proximity

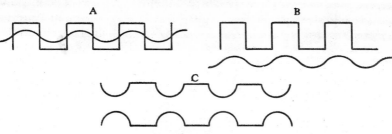

Figure A-5. Similarity

Figure A-6. Continuity

Figure A-7. Closure

Closure. "The tendency for incomplete figures to become complete in perception is called *closure*" (Hilgard, 1962, p. 195). The picture in Figure A-7 illustrates this tendency.

Fine-motor development—the maturation and refinement of the small muscles in the extremities of the body such as finger and wrist movements and eye-hand coordination.

Form Perception—the ability to perceive an arrangement or pattern of elements or parts constituting a unitary whole, wherein the elements are in specific relationships with one another.

Frustration level—a degree of task difficulty that a child is incapable of performing at a given time.

Generalization—the process of deriving or inducing (a general concept or principle) from particulars; for example, by recognizing many types of chairs as chairs, a child is categorizing objects that are similar and yet different.

Generalized movement—a wave of movement that sweeps through the whole body; parts of the body such as arms and legs move, not in relation to their function, but only as adjuncts of the total movement.

Gerstmann's syndrome—a combination of disabilities including finger agnosia, right-left disorientation, acalculia, and agraphia.

Gestalt—a term used to express any unified whole whose properties cannot be derived just by adding the parts and their relationships; more than the sum of its parts.

Grammar closure (auditory-vocal automatic, ITPA)—the ability that permits one to predict future linguistic events from past experience; the ITPA assesses this ability by requiring the subject to complete a statement with an inflected word; for example: "Here is an apple. Here are two _____." The nature of the inflection supplied indicates the ability of the subject to predict what will be said. Linguistically, normal children learn these inflections in a rather systematic way. A certain number of errors are expected from children right up to the end of the test in much the same way that normal children continue to make articulation errors up to and beyond ages 7–10. Only when excessive errors are made do we infer disability.

Gross motor activity—an activity or output in which groups of large muscles are used and the factors of rhythm and balance are primary.

Haptic—the term used to denote both the kinesthetic and the tactile senses as one sense.

Hemispherical dominance—refers to the fact that one hemisphere of the brain generally leads the other in control of body movement, resulting in the preferred use of left or right.

Hyperactivity—excessive activity; the person seems to have a surplus of energy and is unable to control movements for even a short length of time.

Hyperkinesis—excessive mobility or motor function or activity.

Hyperlexia—the skill of reading developed to a very high level, above other academic skills.

Hyperopia—hypermetropia; a condition in which parallel rays are focused behind the retina due to an error in refraction.

Hypoactivity—pronounced absence of physical activity.

Hypokinesis—reduced motor function or activity, often giving the appearance of listlessness.

Imperception—the inability to interpret sensory information correctly; a cognitive impairment rather than impairment of a sensory organ.

Impulsiveness—the tendency to act on impulse; responding without thinking, which is often explosive behavior where learning disorders exist.

Inferential reasoning—the act of obtaining a judgment or logical conclusion from given data or premises; more precisely, a psychological or temporal process by which the mind passes from a proposition or propositions accepted as true to other propositions believed to be so connected to the first as to make the latter true.

Inference implies forming judgments on the basis of cognition or belief not explicitly recognized. There is transposition of previous learned knowledge to new analogous situations or cognitive restructuring and integration of prior and current experience to fit the demands of an objective.

Integration—the pulling together and organizing of all stimuli impinging on an organism at a given moment; also involved is the tying together of the present stimulation with experience variables retained from past activities; the organizing of many individual movements into a complex response.

Kinesthetic—the sense that yields knowledge of the movements of the muscles of the body and the positions of the joints.

Kinesthetic method—a method of treating reading disability by having pupils trace the outline of words and numbers or in other ways incorporating muscle movement to supplement visual and auditory stimuli.

Laterality—complete motor awareness of both sides of the body.

Learning disability—Children with learning disabilities are those (1) who have educationally significant discrepancies among their sensory-motor perceptual, cognitive, academic, or related developmental levels that interfere with the performance of educational tasks; (2) who may or may not show demonstrable deviation in central-nervous-system functioning; and (3) whose disabilities are not secondary to general mental retardation, sensory deprivation, or serious emotional disturbance.

Learning expectancy level—Kaluger and Kolson (1969) have suggested a formula to determine learning expectancy. It is predicated on the assumption that there is a difference of 5 years between grade placement and the age of an average child with no anomalies. For example, there is a difference of 5 years between grade 1 and age 6 and a difference of 5 years between grade 12 and age 17.

"When using the L.E.L. formula to find a child's potential level, use the chronological age (C.A.) in years and months (ex.: 8 yrs., 3 mos.) as if it were the time that a reading achievement test was given. If an IQ is known but not the M.A., use the following procedure:

$$I.Q. \times C.A. = M.A. - 5 = learning\ expectancy\ level$$

1. Multiply IQ (with a decimal before last two numbers) times the chronological age, also given with a decimal value (example: 8 yrs., 3 mos. = 8.25). (See table below.)
2. Then subtract 5 (always 5).
3. Answer is Learning Expecting Level, which is the grade level at which the child should be accomplishing.
4. Always list reading achievement test scores with L.E.L., so they can be compared.
5. Recognize that the greater the difference between the L.E.L. and the C.A., the more likely that extenuating circumstances could affect the reading level—for example:

$$I.Q. \times\ C.A.\ (yrs.) =\ M.A.\ (yrs.)\ -5 = L.E.L.$$
$$0.93 \times\quad 8.25\quad =\quad 7.7\quad -5 = grade\ 2.7$$

Use this table to convert months into percentages of a year.

11 months = 0.91	5 months = 0.42
10 months = 0.83	4 months = 0.33
9 months = 0.75	3 months = 0.25
8 months = 0.67	2 months = 0.17
7 months = 0.58	1 month = 0.08
6 months = 0.50	

Learning quotient—Myklebust and his associates have suggested a quantitative classification of learning disabilities. The extent of the learning disability is calculated as
a ratio between potential and achievement.

$$EA \text{ (expectancy age)} = \frac{MA + CA + GA \text{ (grade age)}}{3}$$

The learning quotient is a measure of discrepancy between expected (potential) and
actual achievement in various areas of learning.

$$LQ \text{ (learning quotient)} = \frac{AA \text{ (achievement age)}}{EA \text{ (expectancy age)}}$$

A learning quotient of 89 or below determines that a child has a learning disability.
(Myklebust, 1967, pp. 5–6).*

Left-to-right progression—recognizing letter or word sequences correctly; can be disturbed if laterality has not been established.

Manual expression (motor encoding, ITPA)—the ability to express ideas in meaningful gestures; in a testing situation, the subject responds to a picture of an object by
showing the examiner what should be done with the object.

Maturational lag—the concept of differential development of areas of the brain and of
personality, which mature according to recognized patterns; a lag signifies a slow
differentiation or irregularity in this pattern without a structural defect, deficiency,
or loss.

Memory span—the number of related or unrelated items that can be recalled immediately after presentation.

Mixed cerebral dominance—the theory that hemispheric dominance has not been
adequately established and that learning problems may be due wholly or partly to
the fact that one cerebral hemisphere does not consistently lead the other in the
control of bodily movement.

Neurological examination—an examination of sensory or motor responses, especially
the reflexes, to determine whether or not there are localized impairments of the
nervous system.

Nonreader—the child who is unable to profit from the best instruction in any of the
skill areas; therefore, is unable to learn to read from conventional methods; commonly referred to as *dyslexia, neurological deficiency, minimum brain damage,* or
specific reading disability; the nonreader's disabilities are often complicated by his
emotional involvement in his gross failure and physical defects.

 The nonreader is generally identified as one who has made scant progress in
learning after two or more years of instruction in reading. The number of words he
recognizes at sight is negligible, perhaps twenty-five or fewer. He confuses words and
has difficulty in spelling.

Organicity—refers to central-nervous-system impairment.

Perception—a cognitive process that involves understanding, comprehension, and
organization; the interpretation of sensory influences; the mechanism by which intellect recognizes and makes sense out of sensory stimulation; the accurate mental
association of present stimuli with memories of past experiences.

---

*Helmer R. Myklebust, *Progress in Learning Disabilities,* Vol. 1 (New York: Grune & Stratton, 1967) pp.
5–6. Paraphrased by permission of the author and the publisher.

Perception of self—perceptions of the self may have varying degrees of agreement with reality. What apparently occurs, as a result of emotional blocking, is deficiency of perception of self, a deficiency not understood by the person involved and that cannot be prevented or overcome without help. Therefore, when a person is said to be suffering from a deficiency of perception, either insights are inconsistent with one another or the deductions made from them do not concur with the data of observation.

Perceptual-motor—the perceptual-motor process includes input (sensory or perceptual activities) and output (motor or muscular activities). A division of the two is impossible, for anything that happens to one area automatically affects the other. Any total activity includes input, integration, output, and feedback.

Perceptual organization—a more or less systematic arrangement of relatively separate parts into a whole in order to fulfill a function; it involves voluntary attention and the ability to organize and join together in the mind's eye. Perceptual organization includes spatial orientation.

Perseveration—the inability to develop a new response to a new or altered stimulus; continuing to behave or respond in a certain way when it is no longer appropriate.

Psychoneurology—the area of study concerned with the behavioral disorders associated with brain dysfunctions in human beings.

Redundancy—the art of presenting the same information to as many of the senses as simultaneously as possible in a given task; for example, when tracing a square on sandpaper with the finger, a child sees the square, hears the movement of the finger across the rough surface, feels the tactual contact of the finger with the paper, and also feels the kinesthetic or muscular movements in the hand and arm.

Remediation—that function which redirects or circumvents an impaired procedure in learning; it implies compensatory methods that facilitate learning rather than cure learning disorders.

Rigidity—resistance to undertaking a new kind of response.

Rotation of design—the revolving of a visual pattern on its axis, clockwise or counterclockwise; in the *Bender Visual-Motor Gestalt Test,* if the rotation of a design is spontaneous, it may be indicative of an emotional disturbance and/or neurological disorder.

Sensorimotor skill—a skill in which muscular movement is prominent but under sensory control; for example, riding a bicycle is not simply a pattern of skilled movements. The bicycle rider has to watch the traffic and the bumps in the road and guide by them. These considerations in calling attention to the sensory control of skill explain the somewhat awkward term *sensorimotor skill.*

Sensory-motor ability—the ability to act and perform as directed by the senses; the ability to hear and do things in response to a given stimulus; it is associated with how well a person is coordinated when dealing with the senses of hearing, seeing, tasting, smelling, feeling, and motor ability.

A person becomes aware of the external world by applying all sense modalities and movements simultaneously. One develops self-awareness and a sense of being separate from the outside world. One learns to control the skeletal movements, to control the movement of specific parts of the body, and to manipulate objects.

Size constancy—the tendency for the perceived size of an object to remain constant irrespective of the size of the retinal image caused by that object.

Sociopath—a person characterized by asocial or antisocial behavior; one who cannot adjust to the culture; a personality disorder in which behavior expresses rebellion against, or at least an unwillingness to conform to the demands of, society; individuals classified as such are not neurotic, psychotic, or mentally defective but manifest a marked lack of ethical or moral development and an inability to follow the socially approved codes of behavior. Sociopaths often accompany their acts with regrets and expressions of proposed future behavior that is socially acceptable. They are quite vain and lack guilt feelings, and they seem unable to form lasting relationships or to reform even under threat of punishment.

Space perception—the direct awareness of the spatial properties of an object, especially in relation to the observer; the perception of position, direction, size, form, and/or distance by any of the senses.

Spatial relationship—the ability to perceive the position of two or more objects in relation to one's self and in relationship to one another; the ability to see similarities in shape, size, etc., of two or more objects.

Children's perception of spatial relationships has a direct bearing on their performance in reading and computations. They must be able to perceive positional relationships between various objects or points of reference. Spatially, a person is the center of his/her own world and perceives objects in relation to self. Body image acts as a zero focus or point of reference in terms of the knowledge of the person's space world. Any fault in body image will be reflected in the perception of outside objects.

Piaget and Inhelder state that there are five basic steps in the process of the perception of space. They are not necessarily unique or distinct but may very well overlap (Piaget and Inhelder, 1967, pp. 5–8).

1. The most elementary spatial relationship that can be perceived is that of "proximity" or "nearby-ness".
2. The second spatial relationship is that of separation; that is, the blending of two nearby elements may be segregated as analytic perception develops.
3. The third relationship is order or succession—the positioning of one element before the other. One fundamental part of order is symmetry, represented by double-order or reverse-order perception.
4. The fourth relationship is that of enclosure or surrounding, which develops as a concept of "betweenness" and undergoes a complex evolution as the first three steps develop. This evolution brings about three-dimensional perception.
5. The last relationship is that of continuity. This is the development of continuous perception in relation to lines, surfaces, etc.

Spatial-temporal translation—the ability to translate a simultaneous relationship in space into a serial relationship in time, or vice versa; for example, the child must recognize the square as a whole when seen in space and reproduce it in time as an organized series of lines and angles. To achieve in many of the tasks we set, the child must be able to organize impressions in both of these areas and to shift fluently from one to the other as the situation demands.

Specific language disability—Usually the term is applied to those who find learning to read and spell very difficult but who are otherwise intelligent. More recently, any language deficiency—oral, visual, or auditory—is identified by this term.

Splinter skill—a restricted approach to a specific problem that exists in isolation, "splintered off" from the remainder of the child's activity; its usefulness is limited, adequate for only one type of activity. This isolated response also confuses the child, who is required to live with two basic learning sets between which there is little or no connection, and with educational skills that have been memorized because they were learned out of context, that is, outside and above the child's performance level. They, too, are isolated facts that the child can neither elaborate nor integrate.

Stimulation level—the level of activity that demands just enough effort on the child's part to keep interest and to encourage further experimentation.

Strabismus—that condition wherein the extraocular muscles are not in a state of balance and a dysfunction of fusion is present; as a result, the eyes are out of alignment; lack of coordination of the eye muscles so that the two eyes do not focus on the same point.

Strephosymbolia—twisted symbols; a reversal of symbols observed in the reading and writing performance of children with learning disabilities (e.g., *was* for *saw*).

Structuring—the act of arranging an activity in a way that is understandable to children and conducive to performance, or in other words, arranging the task so that children are aware of what is expected of them; once the task is structured, the children should be left to perform without additional cueing.

Tactile or tactual—refers to the sense of touch; the term expresses both the child's sense of touch, as applied to a given object or task and the instructor's tactual clues that the child receives.

Tactual-kinesthetic—a combination of the sense of touch and the sense of muscle movement.

Temporal—pertaining to time or time relationships; the ability to recognize the limits of time with understanding; in early childhood, time is not "an ever-rolling stream" but simply concrete events embedded in activity. Time and space are not differentiated from each other. Movement must occur in time, and the child must project awareness of time into object relationships.

Tolerance level—the level at which the child can perform without any effort and soon become bored or uninterested.

Unilateral—one-sided; the child who is unilateral uses one side of the body and ignores the other.

Verbal expression—the ability to express ideas in spoken words; the ITPA tests this ability by asking the subject to describe a simple object such as a block or ball. The score depends on the number of unique and meaningful ways in which a given test object is characterized.

Visual association (visual-motor association, ITPA)—the ability to relate visual symbols in a meaningful way; to measure this, the ITPA requires the subject to select from among four pictures the one that "goes with" a given stimulus picture.

Visual classification and grouping—a cognitive process that gives meaning, organization, and structure to the visual field or a subdivision of it, depending upon the concentration of the viewers' gaze; it is related to the physiological and psychological maturation of the viewer; the identification of objects or elements within the visual field or subdivision thereof and the establishment of a pattern of relationships dependent upon the identification.

Visual closure—measures the perceptual interpretation of any visual object or thing when only a part of it is shown.

Visual memory (visual-motor sequencing, ITPA)—the ability to reproduce a sequence of visual stimuli from memory; the IPTA uses chips, each having a picture of a geometric form; the examiner arranges the chips in a certain order, allows the subject to observe this order for five seconds, mixes the chips, and requires the subject to reproduce the sequence.

Visual-motor ability—the ability to visualize and to assemble material from life into meaningful wholes; the ability to see and to perform with dexterity and coordination; the ability to recognize part-whole relationships in working toward a goal that may be unknown at first; the ability to control body or hand movements in coordination with visual perception.

Visual reception (visual decoding, ITPA)—the ability to comprehend pictures and written words; the ITPA uses a picture test, and the child responds by pointing to pictures indicating that he/she comprehends them.

Index

Now, More Than Textbooks